ECONOMIC GROWTH AND DEVELOPMENT

FRONTIERS OF ECONOMICS AND GLOBALIZATION

11

Series Editors:

HAMID BELADI
University of Texas at San Antonio, USA

E. KWAN CHOI
Iowa State University, USA

FRONTIERS OF ECONOMICS AND GLOBALIZATION VOLUME 11

ECONOMIC GROWTH AND DEVELOPMENT

Edited by

Olivier de La Grandville

*Department of Management Science and Engineering,
Stanford University, Stanford CA*

United Kingdom – North America – Japan
India – Malaysia – China

Emerald Group Publishing Limited
Howard House, Wagon Lane, Bingley BD16 1WA, UK

First edition 2011

Copyright © 2011 Emerald Group Publishing Limited

Reprints and permission service
Contact: booksandseries@emeraldinsight.com

British Library Cataloguing in Publication Data
A catalogue record for this book is available from the British Library

ISBN: 978-1-78052-396-5
ISSN: 1574-8715 (Series)

ABOUT THE SERIES: FRONTIERS OF ECONOMICS AND GLOBALIZATION

This series is aimed at economist and financial economists worldwide and will provide an in-depth look at current global topics. Each volume in the series will focus on specialized topics for greater understanding of the chosen subject and provide a detailed discussion of emerging issues. The target audiences are professional researchers, graduate students, and policy makers. It will offer cutting-edge views on new horizons and deepen the understanding in these emerging topics.

With contributions from leading researchers, each volume presents a fresh look at today's current topics. This series will present primarily original works, and employ references appropriate to the topic being explored.

Each volume will bring a set of highly concentrated chapters that will provide in-depth knowledge to a target audience, while the entire series will appeal to a wide audience by providing them with deeper knowledge on a broad set of emerging topics in the global economy.

The *Frontiers of Economics and Globalization* series will publish on topics such as:

– Frontiers of Trade Negotiations
– Frontiers of Derivative Pricing
– Frontiers of International Lending and Debt Problems
– Frontiers of Economics Integration
– Frontiers of Trade and Environment
– Frontiers of Foreign Exchange
– Frontiers of International Finance
– Frontiers of Growth of Open Economies
– Frontiers of Futures Pricing
– Frontiers of International Financial Markets
– Frontiers of Investment Banking
– Frontiers of Mergers and Acquisitions
– Frontiers of Government Policy and Regulations
– Frontiers of Multi-Sector Growth Models
– Frontiers of Intellectual Property Rights
– Frontiers of Fragmentations and Outsourcing

Hamid Beladi
E. Kwan Choi
Series Editors

ABOUT THE EDITOR

Olivier de La Grandville is visiting professor in the Department of Management Science and Engineering at Stanford University, a position he has held since 1988. A professor of economics at the University of Geneva between 1978 and 2007, he has also held visiting positions at the Massachusetts Institute of Technology, Ecole Polytechnique of Lausanne, University of Neuchâtel, University of Western Australia, and more recently at Frankfurt University.

He is the author of seven books on a wide range of topics in microeconomics, macroeconomics, finance, economic growth and development. His last two books are *Bond Pricing and Portfolio Analysis – Protecting Investors in the Long Run*, MIT Press, 2002, and *Economic Growth – A Unified Approach*, Cambridge University Press, 2009.

His research work has been published in international journals such as the *American Economic Review, Econometrica, Journal of Economic Behaviour and Organization, Journal of Macroeconomics, Journal of Economics, Financial Analysts Journal, Oxford Review of Economic Policy, Studies in Nonlinear Dynamics and Econometrics, Australian Journal of Mathematical Analysis and Applications, Journal of Inequalities in Pure and Applied Mathematics*, and many other scholarly journals.

ABOUT THE VOLUME

Economics as a descriptive and normative science was born when a fundamental question was raised: How can a society improve its well-being? In other words, how can an economy grow? In Western societies, this concern started being addressed very slowly only lately, at the end of the Renaissance. Why not earlier? Torn by civil wars, decimated by plagues, the Middle Ages had never experienced anything close to even a moderate increase in welfare, and in those dark days it would have taken a bold thinker to even envisage the concept of growth or development. As the French historian Pierre Gaxotte strikingly wrote: "the man of the Middle Ages does not know of time and numbers."

It is not surprising, therefore, that we owe to Arab civilization the first comprehensive description of the causes of economic growth. In his *Introduction to History* (1377), Ibn Khaldun gives us the main keys that may lead a society to grow, as well as those that will entail its downfall, and it may be not only a good place but also an opportune time to recall what Ibn Khaldun stressed: excess consumption can be the starting point of an undoing of civilization.

Growth can be viewed as a natural fractal process; but precisely as a fractal, it is subjected to sudden, unexpected falls, that we sometimes call "accidents of history." Those disruptions of a natural process may be revolutions, civil wars, general conflicts. But they are also self-inflicted upon societies by the faulty organization of their economic and social life, exemplified by the absence of the rule of law, the inordinate distribution of political power, inequalities in social status, or the abuse of monopolistic positions, among which prominently stands the extraordinary privilege to create money. In 1817 already, David Ricardo famously wrote in his *Principles of Political Economy*: "Experience shows that neither a State nor a bank ever had the unrestricted power of issuing paper money without abusing that power," a lesson barely learned today, two centuries later.

Since the very beginnings of economics as a science, the challenge of making societies escape from poverty and attain some degree of prosperity has always been, and will remain, a fundamental issue. It was and it is still recognized today that this central venture is multifaceted. Inasmuch as investment and technical progress are central in the growth and development process, many other dimensions must be taken into consideration, such as institutions, the openness of the economy, and the protection of the environment. This book will present cutting-edge research on each of these issues.

Olivier de La Grandville
November 2011

LIST OF CONTRIBUTORS

Rabah Arezki	International Monetary Fund, IMF Institute, NW, Washington DC, USA
Kenneth J. Arrow	Department of Economics, Stanford University, Stanford CA, USA
Graziella Bertocchi	University of Modena and Reggio Emilia, Dipartimento di Economia Politica, Modena, Italy
Michael Binder	Goethe University Frankfurt, Faculty of Economics and Business Administration, Frankfurt am Main, Germany
Raouf Boucekkine	Aix-Marseille School of Economics, GREQAM, Marseille, France; Economics School of Louvain, Université catholique de Louvain, IRES and CORE, Montesquieu, Louvain-la-Neuve, Belgium
Susanne Bröck	Union Investment, Frankfurt am Main, Germany
David Cuberes	Department of Economics, University of Sheffield, Sheffield, UK
Richard H. Day	Emeritus Professor of Economics, University of Southern California (USC), University Park, Los Angeles, CA, USA
David de La Croix	Economics School of Louvain, Université catholique de Louvain, IRES and CORE, Montesquieu, Louvain-la-Neuve, Belgium
Robert Feicht	Chair of Economic Theory, University of Erlangen–Nürnberg, Germany

Davide Fiaschi	University of Pisa, Dipartimento di Scienze Economiche, Italy
Donald A. R. George	School of Economics, University of Edinburgh, UK; Department of Economics, University of Canterbury, New Zealand
Jean-Marie Grether	Institute of Economic Research, University of Neuchatel, Switzerland
Thorvaldur Gylfason	Department of Economics, University of Iceland, Iceland
Bjarne S. Jensen	Department of Environmental and Business Economics, University of Southern Denmark, Denmark
Michał Jerzmanowski	Department of Economics, Clemson University, SC, USA
Andros Kourtellos	Department of Economics, University of Cyprus, Nicosia, Cyprus
Olivier de La Grandville	Department of Management Science and Engineering, Stanford University, Stanford, California, CA, USA
Andrea Mario Lavezzi	Dipartimento di Studi su Politica, Diritto e Società, University of Palermo, Palermo, Italy
Ulla Lehmijoki	Department of Political and Economic Studies, University of Helsinki, Finland
Miguel A. León-Ledesma	School of Economics, Keynes College, University of Kent, Canterbury, Kent, UK
Omar Licandro	Barcelona Graduate School, IAE-CSIC, Barcelona, Spain
Nicole Andréa Mathys	Swiss Federal Office of Energy and University of Neuchatel, Institute of Economic Research, Neuchatel, Switzerland

Peter McAdam   Research Department, European
Central Bank, Kaiserstrasse 29,
Frankfurt am Main, Germany;
Department of Economics, University
of Surrey, Guildford, UK

Theodore Palivos   Department of Economics,
University of Macedonia, Thessaloniki,
Greece

John Pawley   Business School, University of
Western Australia, Crawley, WA,
Australia

Pietro F. Peretto   Department of Economics, Duke
University, Durham, NC, USA

Enrico Saltari   Dipartimento di Economia e Diritto,
Facoltà di Economia, Università
"La Sapienza", Rome, Italy

Mathan Satchi   School of Economics, Keynes
College, University of Kent,
Canterbury, Kent, UK

Robert M. Solow   Department of Economics,
Massachusetts Institute of Technology,
Cambridge MA, USA

Erling Steigum   Department of Economics, BI
Norwegian School of Management,
Oslo, Norway

Wolfgang Stummer   Department of Mathematics and
School of Business and Economics,
University of Erlangen–Nürnberg,
Germany

Giuseppe Travaglini   Dipartimento di Economia, Società e
Politica, University of Urbino,
Urbino, Italy

Ernst Juerg Weber   Business School, University of
Western Australia, Crawley, WA,
Australia

Alpo Willman   Research Department, European
Central Bank, Frankfurt am Main,
Germany

Jianpo Xue

China Financial Policy Research Center, School of Finance, Renmin University of China, Beijing, China

Chong K. Yip

Department of Economics, The Chinese University of Hong Kong, Shatin, N.T., Hong Kong

Milad Zarin-Nejadan

Institute of Economic Research, University of Neuchâtel, Neuchâtel, Switzerland

CONTENTS

FOREWORD

A prominent headline in today's *New York Times* (January 29, 2011, p. B1) announces that "U.S. Economic Growth Bounces Back to Rate Seen Before Recession." We know exactly what this means. Nevertheless the phrase irritates me, and I am not sure whether I am defending clarity and precision or merely being pedantic. The accompanying news story says that real GDP "grew at an annual rate of 3.2 percent in the fourth quarter" of 2010. So the recession gap between potential output and actual output narrowed a little. Most of that 3.2 percent increase in real aggregate output has in my (precise? pedantic?) mind little or nothing to do with economic growth. It represents an increase in aggregate demand, easily accommodated within existing capacity. The 3.2 percent might have been 6.2 percent, as in some other cyclical recoveries, and that would clearly have been an implausible "growth" rate. To be more specific, this increase in natural output was not the result of any favorable change in the determinants of long-run growth. Instead, it was the consequence of the Federal Reserve's unprecedented policy of asset purchaser and credit expansion for anti-cyclical reasons, along with some help from the last effects of earlier fiscal stimulus.

There is a reason why my reaction may not be mere semantic pedantry. Political factions and parties regularly propose policies that they claim will promote "economic growth." More often than not, if these policies will do anything to increase aggregate output, they are aimed at closing a gap between potential and actual output, at eliminating a current deficiency of effective demand. This may be good or bad, depending on current circumstances and the particular policy proposed. But they are often not policies that will do anything for what I mean, and what theory means, by economic growth, that is, growth of potential output itself, trend growth. Policy debate needs to be clear about this.

Having started down this path, I will mention another error that is sometimes made, occasionally even by economists: a failure to distinguish carefully between level effects and (steady state) growth-rate effects. For example, improvements in economic efficiency, such as might follow from abolition of a distorting tax or a reduction of monopoly power, are sometimes described as growth enhancing. What theory suggests, however, is that such events increase the output produced from given resources. So they may lead to increased output at every point of time, but not to a faster long-run rate of growth. When such an improvement occurs, there may be a temporary acceleration of growth as the economy approaches its higher potential; but that will exhaust itself, and the long-run growth rate remains what it was. I think such improvements should be counted as a form of "growth policy." Their effects last for a long time. But they should not be confused with events that actually do change the long-run growth rate, a much more powerful and difficult thing to do.

Just because its focus is, or should be, on the factors that govern the long-term trend, once growth economics gets beyond basic model building it tends to spread over many topics and aim for fundamentals. The modern version of the theory of economic growth has deep and far-ranging roots, searching for understanding the way a tree searches for water. Theory suggests that investment in routine physical capital, in innovation-connected physical capital, in human skills and capabilities, and in the human and institutional infrastructure of technological and organizational innovation itself all play fundamental roles in determining the trajectory of an economy's potential output. None of these basic processes is simple in its underlying causal pattern or in its observed manifestations. Inevitably, then, current research on economic growth covers a broad variety of topics, well exemplified in this book.

Thus research on economic growth involves the analysis of household behavior (saving, skill acquisition), business and entrepreneurial behavior, and even makes use of whatever is known or thinkable about the enterprise of scientific research. So growth economics is inevitably both microeconomic and macroeconomic. That is not to say that one does the microeconomics first, and then adds up the results over all the relevant agents to draw the implied macroeconomic conclusions. It is hard (for me, anyway) to imagine that attempt actually succeeding. More likely, aggregative growth theory, pure and applied, creates macro-models using the insights obtained from microeconomic analysis of the relevant kinds of decisions and behavior.

The twenty two diverse chapters in this book look like normal science, in Kuhn's sense. That is probably because they are in fact normal science. They are working within roughly the same paradigm, and either exploring on of the fundamental determinants of the growth trajectory or thinking through its implications for the growth path itself. In this context an interesting question arises: what are the main research directions in which progress in growth economics has been sought, and presumably found?

The most prominent such project has consisted of attempts to endogenize what had previously been treated as exogenous determinants of growth, the notable examples being technological innovation and the accumulation of human capital. If I can simply offer a judgment without seriously defending it, my view is that, yes, it has been shown that interesting things can be said about these topics, but no, not much tangible progress has been made.

In the case of technological innovation, formal progress in endogenization has so far required resorting to rather special models of production and rather mechanical accounts of the chancy process of invention and application. One indication of the obstacles encountered in this quest is the difficulty in mapping the idiosyncratic and colorful history of innovation – transistor, interactive websites, satellite radio, the MRI – into the bland, colorless language of labor, capital, factor augmentation, and the rest. I think this has to do with the intrinsic intractability of the problem, not with lack of imagination or effort.

In the case of human capital, I suspect that a major obstacle has been that data limitations have focused attention primarily on formal schooling (which is itself measured without serious attention to quality). Researchers in this field, like everyone else, understand that much human capital is acquired informally, in families, workplaces, military units, and so on; but merely grasping the fact is not much help in modeling. So there is a real obstacle to progress.

Endogenizing the role of organizations and social institutions is no doubt more difficult still, partly for similar reasons and partly because there are conceptual gaps. So this direction for normal science will be with us for a long time.

Another direction for normal science consists of extending and clarifying existing models. Examples include allowance for several produced goods and primary factors (including nonrenewable natural resources), demographic events, environmental effects, international trade, and so on. Some of the following chapters fall into this category.

Finally, I will mention the utility of more theoretical work that studies the properties of growth trajectories, some of it with roots in much earlier theory: response patterns after exogenous shocks, effects of alternative lag structures, optimality properties of alternative parametric choices, factor biases in technological change. Here too there are notable examples in this book.

I do not know if one should worry about the difficulty of incorporating all or most of the diverse stands of research represented here in a canonical model of economic growth. That would be a nice culmination of all this normal science. But it is too much to hope for now. What might be possible and useful, however, is to distinguish which of the many micro–macro trails is likely to make a big difference in quantitative understanding of growth trajectories. The chapters that follow are contributions to that goal.

Robert M. Solow
January 2011

CHAPTER 1

How Growth Can Undermine Growth: Three Examples

Kenneth J. Arrow

Department of Economics, Stanford University, Stanford, CA 94305-6072, USA
E-mail address: arrow@stanford.edu

I intend here to present, not a model, but some speculations on the factors that will influence the course of economic growth over the long run. By "long," I mean over the following century or more. Beyond that, speculation is useless, though a few specific consequences of our present actions can be estimated.

More specifically, I want to examine three areas in which technological progress will tend to create factors that will work to limit further gains in economic productivity.

The models of economic growth developed by econometricians and studied by economic theorists recognize the role of conventionally defined factors of production, labor, capital goods, and natural resources, and, a little less traditionally, human capital. But these do not suffice to explain actual economic growth, and so an additional variable is introduced, total factor productivity (or some related concept). This is supposed to be a recognition of an improvement in our technological knowledge, a large part (but by no means all) of which is in turn a reflection of the growth in scientific knowledge of the world.

What I want to emphasize should not be surprising to an economist. We usually note that any gain is never pure; it involves a cost somewhere. All we ask of an economic system is that each gain is greater than the costs needed to achieve it. Here I concentrate on exhibiting situations in which technological progress raises problems that tend to undermine further technological progress.

I organize the following set of remarks as follows. In Section 1, I consider technological progress in the production of health and argue that it has in turn created new problems for further economic development. Section 2 deals with the consequences of technological progress in the conduct of war and the possible negative feedbacks on growth. Section 3 remarks on the interaction among productivity growth, population, and the mutual impacts of natural capital and growth.

Frontiers of Economics and Globalization
Volume 11   ISSN: 1574-8715
DOI: 10.1108/S1574-8715(2011)0000011006

1. The Impact of Medical Progress

Among the good things that economic progress provides us is access to better health and longevity. The average life span in the advanced countries was of the order of 40 years in 1900; it is well over 70 a little more than a century later. It has also grown in less developed countries; as poor a country as Bangladesh has a life expectancy about 65. In fact it has been argued that inequality among countries in life expectancy is less than that in per capita income.

Clearly longevity has increased through a variety of the elements of technological progress. Some of these have operated through the market. Increased productivity in agriculture and improved living conditions in general have historically been important contributors to reduced mortality at all ages. Other aspects of technological improvement have operated through government channels. The emergence of medical knowledge about the role of the water supply in carrying some diseases combined with the technical ability to develop purification methods permitted a great reduction in mortality, especially among children. New medical knowledge led to immunization and vaccination procedures, which have greatly reduced some diseases.

An increasing role in the improvement of health and longevity is played by that hybrid allocation mechanism known as the medical profession. Of course, this is a very ancient institution, which has originated independently in different cultures. Its historical value is somewhat dubious, but there can be no doubt of the great contributions of medical treatment to health in the last century. There has been an enormous multiplication of knowledge embedded in pharmaceuticals and in diagnostic and therapeutic devices as well as in the knowledge embedded in physicians' minds and reference books which enables them to use it.

The improvements in the past especially worked to the reduction of infant and child mortality. That process has come close to reaching its limit, and current increases in longevity and health are mostly to be found among the elderly. I will briefly explore some consequences below.

I have referred to the medical system as a hybrid allocation system. It certainly has some characteristics of a market system. Physicians, hospitals, and other medical personnel and institutions are paid and have to pay others. They have to pay for materials, pharmaceuticals and others.

But it is also to be noticed that the economic behavior of the medical industry has always been constrained by ethical considerations of several kinds, more so than most industries. A physician is under an obligation not to charge for treatments that will be useless or harmful. (Historically, there was also a moral obligation to provide some medical care to the needy free of charge.)

Why medicine and its related technical arts are marked by such departures from ordinary market behavior has its roots in the nature of illness. In the first place, it is strongly individual; each medical service is different from any others, so that the usual economist's picture of a large number of interchangeable items is strongly inapplicable. In the second place, and related to the first, medical treatment requires a large amount of knowledge. One specializing in medicine will use the same information over and over again. A layman might, in principle, acquire the relevant information as needed, but he or she will use it only once. Hence, there are economies of scale in the use of medical information, so that any allocation system will move to having a particular set of individuals specialized in medicine.

This in turn means that patients will inevitably know less than the physicians who deal with them. This is one example of a widespread phenomenon that economists have begun to study only in the last fifty years, what has been termed, "asymmetric information." This refers to a situation where two or more individuals are contemplating a trade and where the individuals have differing knowledge about the commodities to be traded (and they are aware of the difference). For example, a physician will know more about the consequences of a treatment than the patient; hence, the latter cannot check to see if the physician has done well or given enough effort. Clearly, the usual picture of an arm's-length transaction where the buyer chooses on the basis of a given price is inapplicable here.

Practitioners and analysts in the insurance industry have of course long noted this problem. One seeking insurance generally (not necessarily) knows more about the risks than does the insurance company; hence, the population insured will be riskier than the population as a whole (this is known among actuaries as, "adverse selection"). Also, an insured will do less to avoid losses than one uninsured ("moral hazard"). These concepts have now received widespread application in the analysis of the medical system and elsewhere in the economy, most notably in the study of finance.

Since illness is very much a random occurrence from the point of view of the individual, a system of insurance will certainly serve an important economic function. The combination of insurance with the supply of medical services has become standard, but its operation is subject to all the issue I have just sketched. As a result, there has emerged a combination of government intervention and ethical constraints to avoid the adverse incentives created by asymmetric information.

There is one more complication. For whatever reason, the claim to some level of equality among individuals in the provision of medical care has been internationally recognized. One could imagine a world in which medicine and medical insurance are supplied by market forces, subject no doubt to some regulations, but in which no effort is made to equalize medical care. Individuals can buy protection but only in accordance with their means. Note that the costs of medical care in the United States come today to about $7,000 per person per year. Even with ideal insurance, it is clear that many will be priced out of the market. This outcome is usually judged unacceptable or at least undesirable.

It is widely accepted that, at least to an important extent, some government intervention is needed to produce the desired equity. Even in the United States, which has moved in this direction less than any other advanced country, about 50% of the total medical bill is paid by the government though several programs.

The costs of medical care are rising rapidly everywhere. In this case, this is the rather paradoxical result of increased medical productivity. Medical disorders that could not be treated at all (and therefore incurred low or zero costs) are now treatable, if only at considerable expense.

The combination of the these factors means that a major and increasing share of the economy will be run with active government participation and will be paid for by taxes, not ordinary prices. One does not have to be an unreserved admirer of market-based economies to hold that the capitalist system is an engine for improving the allocation of resources. Taxes do have excess burdens.

It is the growth of medical expenses that is basic to the current concern about the growth of the public debt, exaggerated as that fear is. Other important public concerns, such as state universities, are being cut back on to meet increasing medical expenditures.

This, then, is one area where technological progress and its attendant benefits are creating problems which will have some negative effects on future growth.

It may be remarked that there is a collateral issue raised by medical progress. Today, as remarked earlier, most of the health improvements result in increasing life expectancy at older ages. This imposes costs on another generally accepted social obligation, the provision of income after retirement. It is implied that the ratio of workers to total population will be decreasing, so that an increasing fraction of national income will not be compensated by production. Quantitatively, this is probably a less serious issue than medical expenditures themselves, but it points also to an increased proportion of taxes to national income with similar effects.

A reasonable policy to meet the increased need for retirement income is to raise the retirement age (the age at which the income begins). Not only do people live longer but they are more functional at any given age, so this policy is not unreasonable. However, raising the retirement age introduces a potential new problem for technical progress. Are older workers as capable of performing well with new techniques? I don't know the answer to this question, but it is one that has to be studied.

2. Technological Progress in Weapons

Technological progress has been as rapid in the equipment for fighting wars as anywhere else. Indeed, technological innovations originating in military purposes have frequently found civilian applications (and, of course, vice versa). The question is, will the destruction made possible by improved weaponry outweigh other gains?

So far, despite the enormous growth in destructivity, war has had little effect on growth over any extended periods. There have been two world wars of unprecedented destructive force. Yet graphs of world population or national income or national income per capita show only temporary fluctuations.

There has, however, been a dramatic turning point, the development of nuclear weapons. Their destructive power is orders of magnitude greater than that of any predecessor, and the technology for delivering them by missiles has also emerged. Further, as with virtually any technology, the costs of using nuclear weapons and missiles has come down to the point where even poor nations can acquire them.

When the United States and the Soviet Union were essentially the sole possessors of these technologies, they had sufficient understanding of the consequences to avoid their use, though the Cuban missile crisis was a close call. Mutual assured deterrence (bearing the very suitable acronym, MAD) depended on both mutual recognition of the facts and a preference to avoid self-destruction. It is not at all clear that the increasing membership of the nuclear club will necessarily have the same understanding and motivation.

The issue is made still more serious by the presence of an externality. A massive nuclear attack will produce radiation that will drift with the winds. A nuclear war between two countries (e.g., India and Pakistan) will create adverse consequences for many other countries. It has been argued with a good deal of evidence that a nuclear attack of sufficient (and by no means unrealistic) magnitude could affect the climate of the entire Earth, making it colder, and leading to a shortage of food and widespread death ("nuclear winter").

3. The Anthropocene Age

The provision of goods and services has always required drawing on the resources supplied by the biological and geological worlds. Food, the most elementary need for survival, was derived, first, by direct exploitation of nature (hunting, fishing, gathering nuts, berries, and other plant products) and, later, by agriculture and domestication of animals, that is, direct control of biota. The latter still requires nature, in the forms of land, climate, water, and the various constituents of soil. An increasingly important part of economic progress was the exploitation of the geosphere, in the use of minerals. Both wood, a botanical product, and stone, a mineral, have been used for making shelter. The tools used in agriculture and in other products, such as clothing and shelter, came mostly from minerals, first stone, then metals in increasing sophistication. All of these are also used in that ancient human activity, war, so widespread that it appears as almost a necessity.

The need for fuel became apparent. Fire for warming is one of the most characteristic and earliest innovations of humanity. But as the handling of metals and of pottery increased, there was also an industrial demand. Fuel needs were supplied basically by wood or its derivative, charcoal.

So long as the demands of the human community were small compared with the extent of nature, this demand for the services of natural resources did not create obstacles. The very success of human technology led to an increase in population as mortality declined and to an increase in per capita consumption and therewith the demands on animate and inanimate nature. So long as the human demands were limited, they could be met, partly by increasing productivity and partly by migration. Plato already spoke of the deforestation of Greece (from the breeding of goats), but there were still great areas of low population density in Europe. Population was also held down by occasional devastating epidemics, such as the Black Death in medieval Europe and the spread of smallpox and other diseases which decimated native Americans when Europeans arrived.

But gradually western Europe became a highly cultivated area; the forests of England, so much the content of medieval folklore such as the Robin Hood tales, disappeared. Hunting was no longer a significant source of food and, perhaps more seriously, wood became increasingly scarce as a fuel. The next and critical step was the exploitation of a mineral, coal, as a fuel for industry and warmth. Other fuels became exploited, whale oil for lighting, and petroleum and natural gas.

With the nineteenth and twentieth centuries, there has been a rapid growth in both demand factors (population and per capita consumption). Also, technological progress permitted the use of new natural resources, such as aluminum. Certain species of animals were driven close to extinction (e.g., whales and bison) and no longer available for use. There were predictions, not in the end verified, of the impending scarcity of mineral resources, such as coal, liquid oil, and some mineral ores. Deforestation, motivated primarily by the need for more land for agriculture but also by the demand for lumber for furniture, building, and, in some cases, firewood, has continued apace. Some fish species, formerly in great abundance, have rather suddenly become scarce (the collapse of the cod fisheries in the Grand Banks is an especially striking case).

On top of that, increased per capita income has led to a shift in demand to an increased use of meat, and this in turn requires a greater amount of arable land than a corresponding grain diet.

These additional pressures have been met in part by increased productivity in food and other resource-processing industries. Nevertheless, there must be a physiological limit to these gains. Those resources that are available in limited supply (such as minerals, both fuels and metals) must necessarily be used up in some period of time. Admittedly, the total supplies of exhaustible resources are unknown, and new discoveries are continually made. But clearly there must be a limit to this process, and it will gradually appear, if only over the next few centuries.

A thorough-going price system will not prevent a negative effect, but it will handle it efficiently and slow down its effects. But some of the worst obstacles to human welfare arise from failures of the market system, what the economists have called *externalities*. That is, some economic activities impose costs (monetary or functional) on others but are not required to compensate the losers. A typical situation is that of wastes from house heating or industrial activity which are dumped into water or air and then cause discomfort, adverse smells, medical problems, and even death. A medieval ordinance forbade the burning of coal in London because it made others uncomfortable. The "pea-soup" fogs of nineteenth-century London, so frequent in Sherlock Holmes stories, were due to the admixture of smoke from furnaces. By the twentieth century, it became clear that many deaths could be attributed to the pollution of the air. Similarly, wastes in water killed fish and even humans.

These disutilities frequently do not enter standard measures of national income but are nevertheless objects of policy. In most of the advanced world, there has been a considerable cleanup and reduction in air and water pollution.

But another form of air pollution has been increasingly recognized, the implications of emissions of carbon dioxide (and other similar gases) contained in any combustion of the usual fuels. For physical reasons, carbon dioxide is relatively transparent to solar radiation but blocks some outgoing radiation due to solar warming of the Earth. As a result, the Earth will tend to warm (usually referred to as the "greenhouse effect"), and it will warm more the higher the level of carbon dioxide. This effect was recognized by the great Swedish chemist, Svante Arrhenius in the 1890s but has received increasing emphasis recently, along with considerable evidence that the warming effects can be seen.

It should be noted that climate warming differs in one way important for policy from other forms of air pollution. Carbon dioxide, once in the atmosphere, leaves it very slowly. The residence time is measured in centuries, not in the months or less for the usual forms of air pollution.

Climate warming amounts to saying that the atmosphere is a receptacle for carbon dioxide (and some other gases), but it has a limited capacity. This phenomenon is an illustration of the general principle that human activity is growing to the point where it is on the same scale as the activity of the entire Earth.

Global warming is not only an important threat in itself but illustrates a general phenomenon. Technological progress has made mankind into a major factor in the organization of the Earth's biological system and even its physical and chemical structures, to the point that it can threaten their integrity. But technological progress has been based on using these materials. Hence, it may well have created a barrier to its further development.

CHAPTER 2

Commodity Price Volatility, Democracy, and Economic Growth

Rabah Arezki[a] and Thorvaldur Gylfason[b]

[a]International Monetary Fund, IMF Institute, 700 19th Street, NW, Washington, DC 20431, USA
E-mail address: rarezki@imf.org
[b]University of Iceland, Department of Economics, 101 Reykjavik, Iceland
E-mail address: gylfason@hi.is

Abstract
We use a new dataset on nonresource GDP to examine the impact of commodity price volatility on economic growth in a panel of up to 158 countries during the period 1970–2007. Our main finding is that commodity price volatility leads to a significant increase in nonresource GDP growth in democracies, but to no significant increase in autocracies. To explain this result, we show that increased commodity price volatility leads to a statistically significant and quantitatively large increase in net national saving in democracies. In autocracies, on the contrary, net national saving decreased significantly. Our results hold true when using indicators capturing the quality of economic institutions in lieu of indicators of political institutions.

Keywords: Commodity prices, volatility, democracy, economic growth

JEL classifications: D74, D63, F32, Q33

1. Introduction

Volatile terms of trade pose serious macroeconomic challenges to developing countries. In this chapter, we focus on the effects that commodity price volatility may have on economic growth in commodity-exporting countries. Figure 1 shows that over the past decades the volatility associated with various international commodity price indices is far greater than the volatility associated with manufactured product price indices.[1] This evidence suggests that countries that specialize in raw commodity exports face much greater macroeconomic volatility than

---

[1] This holds true when considering manufactured price indices for US imports and exports.

Frontiers of Economics and Globalization
Volume 11   ISSN: 1574-8715
DOI: 10.1108/S1574-8715(2011)0000011007

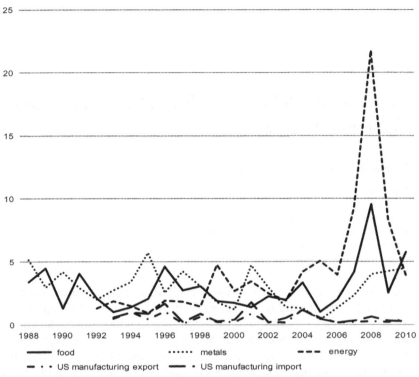

Fig. 1.   Volatility of commodity and manufactured product indices.
Source: *US Bureau of Labor Statistics (2011), IMF (2011), and the authors' own calculations. The volatility is measured by the annual standard deviation of monthly price indices deflated by the US CPI index.*

countries specializing in the export of manufactured products. The presence of volatility may complicate saving/investment decisions by governments, firms, and households and, in turn, affect long-run economic performance in commodity-exporting countries. For instance, increased volatility in government revenue may call for higher levels of precautionary saving.[2] Because revenues derived from natural resources transit directly to the government coffers (e.g., through state ownership, taxation, or export tariffs), they may be prone to rent-seeking behavior and thus end up not being saved or invested appropriately. In that context, institutions which may prevent misappropriation of natural resources and promote good policies may also play a crucial role in moderating the impact of

---

[2] This is especially the case in the presence of incomplete markets that may incapacitate governments in commodity-exporting countries trying to hedge against volatility using financial instruments.

volatility on economic growth in commodity exporting countries. In this chapter, we examine the impact of commodity price volatility on economic growth and net national saving using a new dataset on nonresource GDP in a panel of up to 158 countries during the period 1970–2007.[3]

This chapter aims to make two main contributions. First, unlike previous studies, the paper specifically focuses on volatility stemming from commodity price fluctuations at an infra-annual frequency. Indeed, when considering annual averages, one finds that the crude oil price increased by 36 percent between 2007 and 2008.[4] However, when considering monthly averages, one finds that the crude oil price decreased by 69 percent between July and December 2008. This suggests that the frequency at which the fluctuations in commodity prices are observed reflects very different realities worth pondering when investigating the economic impact of those fluctuations. From a policy perspective, it is, for instance, crucial for the government to consider the monthly changes in government revenues for liquidity management purposes rather than the average yearly changes in revenues (which are certainly more relevant for annual budget planning). Also, monetary authorities in commodity-exporting countries need to consider fluctuations in commodity prices at an infra-annual frequency to be able to conduct appropriate monetary and exchange rate policies. Second, the chapter focuses on the effect of commodity price volatility on the nonresource sector. To do so, we use a new dataset on nonresource GDP allowing us to avoid the "noise" introduced by the resource sector's contribution to overall GDP.[5] Indeed, separating the resource sector's contribution from overall GDP allows us to examine the externality that the resource sector activity exercises on the nonresource sector's long-run productivity. From a policy perspective, nonresource-sector GDP should be the relevant measure to be used when assessing the long-run economic viability of an economy whose natural resources have been depleted.

Our main finding is that increased commodity price volatility leads to a significant increase in nonresource GDP growth in democracies, but to no significant increase in growth in autocracies. To explain this result, we show that increased commodity price volatility leads to a statistically

---

[3] Our goal here is to assess the impact of volatility on saving broadly understood and not necessarily from a perspective of evaluating sustainability. We thus use overall saving rather than genuine saving (saving net of resource depletion). In addition, the Hartwick rule (setting genuine saving equal to zero, see Hartwick, 1977) is a commonly used benchmark but could be seen as too restrictive. Indeed, it fails to take into account the potential yield on the investments made out of "rent savings." If these are high, there can be considerable consumption out of rents on a sustainable basis.

[4] The crude oil (petroleum) price used is a simple average of three spot prices: Dated Brent, West Texas Intermediate and the Dubai Fateh, US$ per barrel, available from IMF (2011).

[5] Section 2 describes the estimation of nonresource GDP which takes into account the depletion of the stock of natural resources.

significant and quantitatively large increase in net national saving in democracies. In autocracies, on the contrary, net national saving decreased significantly. Our results hold true when using indicators capturing the quality of economic institutions in lieu of indicators of political institutions.

This chapter is related to the literature on macroeconomic volatility. Drawing on several of their earlier papers, Aghion and Banerjee (2005) explore the various causal connections between the trend growth of output and the volatility of output around the trend, concluding from empirical cross-country evidence that volatility hurts growth. Along similar lines, Ramey and Ramey (1995) provide evidence that volatility in economic growth diminishes average growth in a sample of 92 countries as well as in a sample of OECD countries. Even so, Gylfason, Holmström, Korkman, Söderström, and Vihriälä (2010, Ch. 4) demonstrate that significantly reduced output volatility from earlier times to the post–World War II period in several industrial countries including the United States, Canada, France, Germany, and the Nordic countries was accompanied by virtually unchanged average long-run growth everywhere. Building on Ramey and Ramey (1995), Mobarak (2005) finds that more democracy leads to lower volatility and more volatility reduces growth using simultaneous equation estimation method. He concludes that the volatility channel is crucial to understanding how democracy affects growth. Similarly, our chapter provides empirical evidence that democracy moderates the effect of volatility originating from (plausibly exogenous) fluctuations in international commodity prices on economic growth.

This chapter also relates to the literature stressing the importance of political institutions for improving policy outcomes (see, e.g., Persson, 2002). In their seminal contribution to the growth and institutions literature, Acemoglu, Johnson, and Robinson (2001, 2002) show that political institutions are key determinants of long-run economic development.

Further, this chapter relates more directly to the literature on the so-called resource curse, focusing specifically on the effects of natural resource endowments on the economic performance of commodity-exporting countries. This literature emphasizes several channels through which resource windfalls may affect economic performance, including the "Dutch disease" and deteriorating institutions, to name a few (for a survey, see Frankel, 2011). This chapter departs from the traditional Dutch-disease literature's distinction between tradable and nontradable sectors by focusing instead on the distinction between the resource and nonresource sectors. Overall, there is some evidence, albeit somewhat controversial, that commodity-exporting countries tend to grow less rapidly than noncommodity-exporting countries. Sachs and Warner (1995, 2001), Auty (2001), and Gylfason (2001) provided early evidence of a significant negative correlation between natural resource abundance and economic growth. In contrast, Alexeev and Conrad (2009) take a more skeptical view of the resource curse. Using traditional cross-sectional growth regressions, Alexeev and Conrad (2009) find that the empirical association between resource dependence and economic performance is not robust to using samples with different starting years or to the inclusion of additional controls, but they leave initial income out of their regressions, thus omitting conditional convergence, a crucial growth mechanism, from consideration. Our paper contributes to this literature by focusing on the volatility channel of the resource curse using data on nonresource-sector GDP growth.

The remainder of this chapter is organized as follows. Section 2 describes the data. Section 3 presents the estimation strategy and main results. Section 4 discusses a number of robustness checks. Section 5 summarizes our main findings.

2. Data

2.1. Nonresource GDP (NRGDP)

Nonresource GDP is approximated by subtracting the real value of natural resource rents from total GDP in 2005 PPP-adjusted USD (see Hamilton & Ruta, 2008, for details on the computation of resource rents).[6] Natural resources give rise to rents because they are not produced; in contrast, for produced goods and services competitive forces will expand supply until economic profits are driven to zero. An economic rent represents an excess return to a given factor of production. For each type of resource and each country, unit resource rents are thereby derived by taking the difference between world prices (to reflect the social opportunity cost of resource extraction) and the average unit extraction or harvest costs (including a "normal" return on capital). Unit rents are then multiplied by the physical quantity extracted or harvested to arrive at total rent.[7]

2.2. Commodity price index and volatility

We use a country-specific and plausibly exogenous commodity price index. The index consists of a geometric average of international prices of various commodities using (time-invariant) weights based on the average value of exports of each commodity in the GDP for a given country. Annual

---

[6] The data on resource rents are taken from WDI (2011). The GDP data are from Heston, Summers, and Aten (2009).
[7] The energy resources include oil, natural gas, and coal, while metals and minerals include bauxite, copper, gold, iron ore, lead, nickel, phosphate, silver, tin, and zinc.

international commodity price data cover the years 1970–2007 and are taken from UNCTAD Commodity Statistics, while our data on the value of commodity exports come from the NBER-United Nations Trade Database. Because the time-series behavior of many international commodity prices is highly persistent, commodity price shocks are identified by the (log) change in the international commodity price.[8] Our measure of volatility is the annual standard deviation of monthly changes in our commodity price index. The correlation between the log change in our commodity price index and its standard deviation is rather low and negative (-0.14). This suggests that the information contained in these two statistics is quite different and both statistics are worthy of use separately in our empirical analysis.

2.3. Democracy

Democracy is measured by the revised combined Polity score (Polity2) of the Polity IV database (Marshall & Jaggers, 2010). The classification uses a 10-point scale that categorizes four attributes of political systems: the competitiveness of political participation, the competitiveness of executive recruitment, the openness of executive recruitment and the constraints on the chief executive. At one end of the scale, $+10$, are the most politically competitive and open democracies. At the other, -10, are the least open and competitive autocracies. Following Persson and Tabellini (2003, 2006) and the Polity IV project, we classify countries as democracies (autocracies) if their Polity2 score is strictly positive (negative).

3. Empirical results

3.1. Estimation strategy

To examine the effects of commodity price volatility on long-run per capita economic growth, we estimate the following dynamic econometric model:

$$\Delta \text{Log NRGDP}_{i,t} = \alpha \text{Volatility}_{i,t} + \beta \text{Commodity Price Index}_{i,t}$$
$$+ \gamma_i + \delta X_{i,t} + \varepsilon_{i,t}$$

where γ_i are country fixed effects that capture time-invariant country-specific unobservable characteristics and $X_{i,t}$ a set of controls including initial per capita NRGDP, financial development (credit), trade openness (trade), and

---

[8] The commodities included in the commodity export price index are aluminum, beef, coffee, cocoa, copper, cotton, gold, iron, maize, oil, rice, rubber, sugar, tea, tobacco, wheat, and wood. In case there were multiple prices listed for the same commodity a simple arithmetic price average was used.

Table 1. Summary statistics

Variable	Observations	Mean	Standard deviation	Minimum	Maximum
Δ log NRGDP per capita	1392	0.016	0.046	−0.427	0.353
Initial log NRGDP	1208	8.505	1.139	5.551	11.259
Δ log commodity price index	1504	0.000	0.003	−0.012	0.027
Volatility	1050	0.053	0.084	0.000	0.717
Diversification	1060	0.170	0.199	0.004	1.000
Credit	1156	37.967	35.758	0.000	276.120
Trade	1214	79.013	43.391	7.210	423.800
Saving	981	9.897	11.763	−38.492	167.130

export diversification (diversification).[9] $\varepsilon_{i,t}$ is an error term. Table 1 provides basic summary statistics for the variables used in the empirical analysis. Because we estimate a dynamic panel data model we report system-GMM estimates (Blundell & Bond, 1998) as the presence of country fixed effects causes the fixed effects estimator to produce inconsistent estimates.[10] As a baseline regression, we estimate the average marginal effect of commodity price volatility on per capita NRGDP growth. We average our data over successive five-year intervals to smooth out business-cycle effects.[11] We then successively restrict our baseline analysis to democracies and then autocracies to test whether commodity price volatility has a dichotomous effect on NRGDP growth. To explain the effect of volatility on NRGDP growth, we then estimate the average marginal effect of commodity price volatility on the saving rate.[12]

3.2. Economic growth

The statistical results are presented in Table 2.[13] Our results suggest that the average marginal effect of commodity price volatility on NRGDP growth is both statistically and economically significant. Indeed, we find that an increase in commodity price volatility by one standard deviation

---

[9] Credit is proxied by domestic credit to the private sector (in percent of GDP). Trade is proxied by the sum of exports and imports of goods and services (in percent of GDP). Both credit and trade are obtained from WDI (2011). Export diversification is measured by a Herfindahl index obtained from Lederman and Xu (2010).

[10] In the system-GMM estimation we use the first lags as instruments for the lagged dependent variable to address the concern that too many moment conditions are used (for further discussion of this issue see, e.g., Roodman, 2009).

[11] We note that the dynamic panel data bias associated with the OLS fixed-effects estimator is bounded of order $1/T$, where T is the time-series dimension of the panel (see Nickell, 1981).

[12] By saving we mean net national saving (in percent of GNI) obtained from WDI (2011).

[13] First- and second-order serial correlation tests and the Hansen test on over-identifying moment conditions (not reported in the tables) indicate that the estimated models are correctly specified.

Table 2. *Commodity price volatility and NRGDP growth*

	All countries			Autocracies			Democracies		
	(1)	(2)	(3)	(4)	(5)	(6)	(7)	(8)	(9)
Initial log NRGDP	-0.0643**	-0.110***	-0.0682**	0.00578	-0.0239	0.00004	-0.0822**	-0.0715*	-0.0375
	(0.0295)	(0.0406)	(0.0310)	(0.0257)	(0.0301)	(0.0263)	(0.0402)	(0.0410)	(0.0438)
Volatility	0.0782		0.153***	-0.0448		0.0188	0.162**		0.277***
	(0.0604)		(0.0554)	(0.0752)		(0.0704)	(0.0732)		(0.0846)
Δ log commodity price index		2.740*	3.891**		-2.349	-2.316		3.387*	6.435**
		(1.510)	(1.533)		(2.048)	(2.186)		(1.909)	(2.745)
Diversification	0.0101	-0.113	-0.0864	0.116	0.0397	0.0983	-0.0179	-0.0926	-0.0666
	(0.0529)	(0.0696)	(0.0660)	(0.0814)	(0.0952)	(0.111)	(0.0552)	(0.0583)	(0.0593)
Credit	0.000562	0.00142**	0.000661	-0.000198	-0.000209	-0.000460	0.000665	0.000769	0.000216
	(0.000388)	(0.000583)	(0.000406)	(0.000418)	(0.000556)	(0.000423)	(0.000470)	(0.000502)	(0.000496)
Trade	0.000698***	0.000474	0.000477**	0.000731**	0.00145***	0.00122***	0.000565***	0.000490*	0.000145
	(0.000189)	(0.000301)	(0.000218)	(0.000363)	(0.000366)	(0.000330)	(0.000186)	(0.000264)	(0.000259)
Number of observations	555	555	555	197	197	197	357	357	357
Number of countries	150	150	150	61	61	61	88	88	88

Notes: The dependent variable is Δ log NRGDP per capita. The method of estimation is system-GMM (Blundell & Bond, 1998). Standard errors are shown in parentheses below the point estimates. *Significantly different from 0 at 90% confidence, **95% confidence, and ***99% confidence. Fixed effects are included but not reported.

leads to an increase in NRGDP growth by slightly less than a third of a standard deviation, as shown in column (3). This result contradicts the view that volatility is harmful for economic growth in commodity-exporting countries. However, the coefficient on volatility is no longer significant when we do not control for the annual change in our commodity price index, as shown in column (1).

We find that changes in our commodity price index and trade openness have a positive and statistically significant impact on NRGDP growth. Export diversification and financial development have no statistically significant effect on NRGDP growth but are, nonetheless, useful control variables. The significance and sign of those latter results should, however, be taken with caution as they might be plagued by endogeneity. This is less so the case for our measure of volatility in commodity prices as it is based on a plausibly exogenous source of fluctuations, namely, international commodity prices. Indeed, it is reasonable to assume that changes in domestic conditions or, more specifically, changes in the nonresource sector in the countries included in our sample do not affect international commodity prices.

When restricting our sample to autocracies, we find that commodity price volatility does not have a statistically significant effect on NRGDP growth, as shown in columns (4) and (6). It should also be noted that a change in commodity prices has a negative though not statistically significant effect on NRGDP growth, as shown in columns (5) and (6). The negative sign associated with the change in commodity prices echoes the results pertaining to the resource curse hypothesis suggesting that ample resource endowments weaken economic performance. When restricting our sample to democracies, however, we find that volatility has a statistically and economically significant effect on NRGDP growth, as shown in columns (7) and (9).[14] Using estimates from column (9), we find that an increase by one standard deviation in volatility leads to an increase by more than half a standard deviation in NRGDP growth. This effect is much larger than in our overall sample. This result could suggest that democracies have overcome the challenges posed by increased volatility by adopting policies that promote growth. In the following subsection, we provide some evidence that the saving channel can help explain why more volatility may lead to more rapid economic growth in commodity-exporting countries. Indeed, higher saving could help shelter commodity-exporting countries from shortfalls in government revenue, help finance or guarantee domestic private investments and also guard those countries against hasty spending programs, including excessively large and wasteful public spending.

---

[14] We also find that increases in the commodity price index lead to a statistically significant increase in NRGDP growth. Those results are broadly in line with those of Mehlum, Moene, and Torvik (2006) who provide some evidence that good economic institutions can alleviate the resource curse.

By contrast, more volatility – resource booms, in particular – may impede economic growth in autocracies. When national wealth is stored largely in a natural resource, renewable or not, a more common occurrence in autocracies than in democracies, there is less need for financial intermediation to conduct day-to-day transactions. Dissaving at the macroeconomic level can take place through more rapid depletion of the resource and saving can take place through less rapid depletion, or of more rapid renewal in the case of renewable natural resources. In some countries, such as the oil-rich OPEC states, saving also takes the form of deposits in foreign banks. In this case, domestic financial intermediation becomes even less important. In contrast, when saving is piled up at home in the form of physical capital, or human capital, domestic banks and equity markets assume paramount importance. By linking up domestic savers and investors, the domestic financial system contributes to a more efficient allocation of capital across sectors and firms, a growth benefit more commonly absent from autocracies than from democracies.

Not only is it thus possible for recurrent commodity booms associated with abundant natural resources to hamper the development of the financial system and hence to distort the allocation of capital but economic growth may slow down due to the detrimental effect of financial backwardness on the quantity and quality of saving and investment. King and Levine (1993a, 1993b) find that indicators of financial development and their predetermined components predict subsequent growth, physical capital accumulation, and improvements in the efficiency of capital allocation.[15] Hence, our hypothesis that natural resource dependence tends to go along with an underdeveloped financial system means, if King and Levine are right, that resource dependence also tends to hinder future gains in efficient capital deepening and economic growth.

Those results are in line with Acemoglu et al. (2001, 2002) who show that political institutions are key determinants of long-run economic development. Our results are also consistent with those of Mobarak (2005) who reports that democracies lead to more rapid growth through the volatility channel. It is important to reiterate that our results hold when controlling for variables such as economic diversification and financial development, which are potentially important factors mitigating volatility.

3.3. Saving

The results reported earlier suggest that commodity price volatility may have improved economic performance in democracies but not in autocracies. To scrutinize and interpret our results, we now systematically

---

[15] Benhabib and Spiegel (2000) report similar findings.

investigate the impact of commodity price volatility on saving behavior in commodity-exporting countries.

Table 3 presents the results of our estimates of saving regressions. On average, we find that commodity price volatility has a positive and economically significant effect on the saving rate as shown in column (1). Using results from column (1), we find that an increase in volatility by one standard deviation leads to an increase of saving by about a third of a standard deviation. However, the coefficient associated with volatility is no longer statistically significant when we do not control for changes in our commodity price index.

We also find, throughout columns (2)–(9), that changes in commodity prices encourage saving. This result suggests that an increase in revenue originating from commodity exports leads to increased saving across the spectrum of political institutions. However, our quantification exercise indicates that the response of saving to an increase in commodity prices is twice as large in democracies as in autocracies.[16] This result suggests that more accountable governments save effectively more than autocracies that tend to squander revenues derived from the exploitation of natural resources. Indeed, Gelb (1988) provides anecdotal evidence that governments in commodity-exporting countries often embark on large investment projects following commodity price booms. He argues that those investment projects were plagued by inefficiencies and also contributed to resource misallocation.

Further, we find that in autocracies more volatility translates into a statistically significant decrease in saving, as shown in column (4). The coefficient associated with volatility becomes positive when controlling for changes in our commodity price index but is not statistically significant. In contrast, in democracies more volatility leads to a statistically and economically significant increase in saving as shown in columns (7) and (9). Using estimates from column (9) we find that an increase by one standard deviation in volatility in democracies increases the saving rate by two-fifths of a standard deviation. This result again suggests that only governments which are subject to the scrutiny of the public as is the case in democracies save more when faced by higher volatility. Indeed, more accountable governments choose to build a buffer stock to effectively hedge against the vagaries of international commodity markets.[17] Moreover, governments in democracies are less prone to and less tolerant of rent

---

[16] Although the coefficients on volatility in columns (6) and (9) and the standard deviation in commodity price index are quite close, the standard deviation associated with saving is twice as high in autocracies as in democracies. It follows that the effect of commodity price changes is twice as high in democracies as in autocracies.

[17] The market for hedging appears to remain relatively impracticable for many commodity-exporting countries. Mexico is one of the few countries to have implemented a full hedging program using financial instruments. In that context, commodity-exporting countries are left with the sole option of building strong institutions to insulate themselves from procyclical and wasteful spending programs.

Table 3. Commodity price volatility and the saving rate

	All countries			Autocracies			Democracies		
	(1)	(2)	(3)	(4)	(5)	(6)	(7)	(8)	(9)
Lagged saving	0.572***	0.382***	0.449***	0.300***	0.380***	0.390***	0.673***	0.440***	0.506***
	(0.0687)	(0.0642)	(0.0656)	(0.0874)	(0.0807)	(0.0906)	(0.0864)	(0.0985)	(0.104)
Volatility	19.60		48.48***	−52.51**		3.912	38.61**		47.15***
	(17.48)		(18.49)	(25.06)		(32.01)	(18.40)		(17.57)
Δ log commodity price index		2,270***	2,381***		2,312***	2,013***		1,438**	2,025***
		(299.4)	(387.5)		(289.5)	(439.7)		(727.2)	(708.3)
Credit	0.113**	−0.217***	−0.213***	0.0762	−0.373***	−0.317***	0.0151	−0.0802	−0.142**
	(0.0447)	(0.0526)	(0.0629)	(0.104)	(0.0903)	(0.106)	(0.0340)	(0.0688)	(0.0650)
Number of observations	623	623	623	238	238	238	384	384	384
Number of countries	157	157	157	67	67	67	89	89	89

Notes: The dependent variable is the saving rate. The method of estimation is system-GMM (Blundell & Bond, 1998). Standard errors are shown in parentheses below the point estimates. *Significantly different from 0 at 90% confidence, **95% confidence, and ***99% confidence. Fixed effects are included but not reported.

seeking and, therefore, are likely to spend their revenues more effectively, yielding higher saving rates and higher rates of long-run economic growth. These results are consistent with the political economy literature which has stressed the importance of political institutions for better policy outcomes (see, e.g., Persson, 2002).

4. Robustness checks

To test whether our results are robust to the removal of outliers, observations with excessively high leverage were excluded from the sample. Specifically, all observations with DFBETAi,j statistics, where i indicates the country and j the time period, with an absolute value above a cutoff point equal to $2/\sqrt{n}$, where n is the number of observations in the original sample, were excluded (Besley, Kuh, & Welsch, 1980; Davidson & MacKinnon, 1993, pp. 32–39). For instance, we ended up removing 57, 13, and 27 observations from the samples used in the regressions presented in columns (1), (2), and (3) in Table 2 (these results are not reported in the tables). The results presented in Tables 2 and 3 are virtually unchanged and are robust to the use of different values for the cutoff point above which observations are dropped.

A relevant question is whether our results are robust to using the quality of economic institutions rather than political institutions. Indeed, the quality of economic institutions could be seen as an outcome of political institutions. The indicators of the quality of political institutions display a relatively high correlation with economic institutions (0.46 for the rule of law; 0.57 for corruption). Also, Mehlum et al. (2006), using standard cross-sectional growth regression, provide some evidence that good economic institutions can alleviate the resource curse. To test whether economic institutions play a moderating role in shaping the effect of commodity price volatility on economic growth, we split our sample between countries with a low and high quality of economic institutions based on rule-of-law and corruption indices from Political Risk Services (2009). Because the indices reflecting economic institutions range from 0 to 6, we classify countries as featuring poor (good) institutions when the average quality of institution indicator (available from 1985 onward) is below (above) 3. We do find robust evidence that both economic institution indices moderate the effect of commodity price volatility on nonresource GDP growth (the results not reported in the tables). Also, we confirm that the saving rate increases in countries with high-quality economic institutions in the face of higher volatility. Interestingly, higher volatility leads to a statistically significant decrease in saving in countries with a high degree of corruption but not in countries with high standards of rule of law. Indeed, more volatility may, in fact, lead to lower saving as it may provide more room for discretionary policies in countries with a poor institutional framework. Those results seem to support the view that political institutions as well as economic institutions do reduce rent seeking through increased public scrutiny and, thus, lead to higher saving rates which, in turn, encourage NRGDP growth in commodity-exporting countries.

5. Summary and conclusion

We examined in this chapter the impact of commodity price volatility on economic growth using a panel of up to 158 countries during the period 1970–2007. To do so, we used a new data set on nonresource GDP which enabled us to avoid the "noise" introduced by the resource sector's contribution to overall GDP. Our main finding is that increased commodity price volatility leads to a significant increase in nonresource GDP growth in democracies, but has no significant effect on growth in autocracies. We offer an explanation for this finding by documenting that increased commodity price volatility leads to a statistically significant and quantitatively large increase in net national saving in democracies while net national saving decreased significantly in autocracies. Our results also apply when we use indicators capturing the quality of economic institutions in lieu of indicators of political institutions, highlighting the importance of institutions in shaping the volatility channel of the resource curse.

If we went beyond our positive analysis of the impact of commodity price volatility on saving and economic growth presented in this chapter and took a normative standpoint, one potentially important direction for further research might be to determine the optimal level of precautionary saving in the face of commodity price volatility. Carroll and Jeanne (2009) model the incentives for the residents of a country to hold foreign assets, including the precautionary motive. The model suggests a convenient formula for the economy's target value of assets. However, the authors do not model the decision to extract natural resources. A broader portfolio allocation strategy of a country should balance the level of natural resource reserves over time with the level of net financial assets in response to increased volatility. It, therefore, remains to integrate the resource extraction decision into a portfolio model with a precautionary motive.

Acknowledgments

We thank Alan Gelb and Kirk Hamilton for useful comments and discussion. The views expressed in the chapter are those of the authors alone and do not necessarily represent those of the IMF. All remaining errors are ours.

References

Acemoglu, D., Johnson, S., & Robinson, J. A. (2001). The colonial origins of comparative development: An empirical investigation. *American Economic Review, 91*, 1369–1401.

Acemoglu, D., Johnson, S., & Robinson, J. A. (2002). Reversal of fortune: Geography and institutions in the making of the modern world income distribution. *Quarterly Journal of Economics, 117*, 1231–1344.

Aghion, P., & Banerjee, A. (2005). *Volatility and growth*. Oxford: Oxford University Press.

Alexeev, M., & Conrad, R. (2009). The elusive curse of oil. *Review of Economics and Statistics, 91*, 586–598, 602.

Auty, R. M. (2001). The political economy of resource-driven growth. *European Economic Review, 45*, 839–846.

Benhabib, J., & Spiegel, M. M. (2000). The role of financial development in growth and investment. *Journal of Economic Growth, 5*, 341–360.

Besley, D., Kuh, E., & Welsch, R. (1980). *Regression diagnostics: Identifying influential data and sources of colinearity*. New York: Wiley.

Blundell, R., & Bond, S. (1998). Initial Conditions and Moment Restrictions in Dynamic. *Panel Data Models. Journal of Econometrics, 87*, 115–143.

Carroll, C., & Jeanne, O. (2009). *A tractable model of precautionary reserves, net foreign assets, or sovereign wealth funds*. NBER Working Paper 15228. National Bureau of Economic Research.

Frankel, J. A. (2011). The natural resource curse: A survey. In Shaffer, B. (Ed.), *Export Peril*. University of Pennsylvania Press, forthcoming.

Davidson, R., & MacKinnon, J. (1993). *Estimation and inference in economics*. New York: Oxford University Press.

Gelb, A. (1988). *Oil windfalls: Blessing or curse?* New York: Oxford University Press, for the World Bank.

Gylfason, T. (2001). Natural resources, education, and economic development. *European Economic Review, 45*, 847–859.

Gylfason, T., Holmström, B., Korkman, S., Söderström, H. T., & Vihriälä, V. (2010). *Nordics in global crisis: Vulnerability and resilience*. The Research Institute of the Finnish Economy (ETLA), Helsinki.

Hamilton, K., & Ruta, G. (2008). Wealth accounting, exhaustible resources and social welfare. *Environmental and Resource Economics, 42*, 53–64.

Hartwick, J. M. (1977). Intergenerational equity and the investing of rents from exhaustible resources. *American Economic Review, 66*, 972–974.

Heston, A., Summers, R., & Aten, B. (2009). Penn World Table Version 6.3. Center for International Comparisons of Production, Income and Prices at the University of Pennsylvania, August.

International Monetary Fund. (2011). *World Economic Outlook* (WEO), October.

King, R. G., & Levine, R. (1993a). Finance and growth: Schumpeter might be right. *Quarterly Journal of Economics, 108,* 717–737.

King, R. G., & Levine, R. (1993b). Finance, entrepreneurship and growth: Theory and evidence. *Journal of Monetary Economics, 32,* 513–542.

Lederman, D., & Xu, L. (2010). *Commodities and structural volatility.* World Bank, mimeo.

Marshall, M., & Jaggers, K. (2010). Polity IV Project: Dataset Users' Manual. *Center for Global Policy,* George Mason University (www.cidcm.umd.edu/polity). [Polity IV Data Computer File, Version 2010. College Park, MD: Center for International Development and Conflict Management, University of Maryland.]

Mehlum, H., Moene, K., & Torvik, R. (2006). Institutions and the resource curse. *Economic Journal, 116,* 1–20.

Mobarak, A. M. (2005). Democracy, volatility, and economic development. *Review of Economics and Statistics, 87,* 348–361.

Nickell, S. (1981). Biases in dynamic models with fixed effects. *Econometrica, 49,* 1417–1426.

Persson, T. (2002). Do political institutions shape economic policy. *Econometrica, 70,* 883–905.

Persson, T., & Tabellini, G. (2003). *The economic effects of constitutions.* Cambridge: MIT Press.

Persson, T., & Tabellini, G. (2006). Democracy and development. The devil in detail. *American Economic Review Papers and Proceedings, 96,* 319–324.

Political Risk Services. (2009). International Country Risk Guide.

Ramey, G., & Ramey, V. A. (1995). Cross-country evidence on the link between volatility and growth. *American Economic Review, American Economic Association, 85,* 1138–1151.

Roodman, D. (2009). A note on the theme of too many instruments. *Oxford Bulletin of Economics and Statistics, 71,* 135–158.

Sachs, J. D., & Warner, A. M. (1995). *Natural resource abundance and economic growth.* NBER Working Paper No. 5398. National Bureau of Economic Research, Cambridge, MA. Retrieved from http://papers.nber.org/papers/w5398

Sachs, J. D., & Warner, A. M. (2001). The curse of natural resources. *European Economic Review, 45,* 827–838.

US Bureau of Labor Statistics. (2011). *Economic News Release.* Online Database.

WDI. (2011). *World Development Indicators.* Online Database.

CHAPTER 3

Growth, Colonization, and Institutional Development: In and Out of Africa

Graziella Bertocchi

Dipartimento di Economia Politica, University of Modena and Reggio Emilia,
Viale Berengario 51, 41100 Modena, Italy
E-mail address: graziella.bertocchi@unimore.it

Abstract
This chapter investigates the determinants of the growth performance of
Africa. I start by illustrating a broader research agenda that accounts not
only for basic economic and demographic factors but also for the role of
history and institutional development. After reporting results from
standard growth regressions, I analyze the role of Africa's peculiar
history, which has been marked by its colonization experience. Next, I
discuss the potential growth impact of state fragility, a concept that reflects
multiple facets of the dysfunctions that plague the continent. The last topic
I address is the influence, in and out of Africa, of the slave trades. The
chapter ends with critical conclusions and suggestions for further research.

Keywords: Growth, Africa, history, colonization, institutions

JEL classifications: O43, N17, H11

1. Introduction

One of the most challenging questions for modern growth theory is why
Africa has been underperforming for the entire postwar period, and
probably even before, if compared with the rest of the world. This fact
remains true even though, following a long sequence of disastrous decades,
the economic conditions of some African countries have shown a rapid
improvement since the mid-1990s (Sala-i-Martin, Pinkovskiy, & Fargas,
2010; Young, 2010).

There is a growing literature that has tried to document and understand
the African experience. An initial research line has attempted to compare
Africa, as a whole, with the rest of the world. For a cross-section of

Frontiers of Economics and Globalization
Volume 11   ISSN: 1574-8715
DOI: 10.1108/S1574-8715(2011)0000011008

countries, Barro (1991) shows that a dummy for sub-Saharan Africa exerts a significant and negative effect on the average growth of per-capita GDP for the 1960–1985 period, after controlling for a broad set of growth correlates. In the same vein, some progress toward a deeper understanding of the area's specific problems is made by Easterly and Levine (1997), who highlight the potential role of ethnic diversity, by Schmidt-Hebbel (1996), who focuses on fiscal policies, and by Sachs and Warner (1997), who emphasize the impact of geography.

One limit of the continent dummy approach is that it can only assess how Africa as a whole, or its sub-Saharan portion, differs from the rest of the world, thus obscuring important heterogeneities within the continent itself. Thus, a parallel line has attempted instead to emphasize specific cross-country differences within African samples. The purpose of this chapter is to illustrate the main results so far reached within this stream of the literature. Rather than at a complete survey, my goal is to offer a reconstruction of the path followed by this largely empirical exploration and of its main turning points. Moreover, I explain how research on the empirics of growth in Africa is inspired by a broader agenda, which has focused on the links among growth, history, and institutions.

The chapter is organized as follows. Section 2 briefly describes the general research agenda on growth, history, and institutions. Section 3 investigates the role of standard determinants of Africa's specific growth performances. Section 4 focuses on those historical factors that are particularly important for Africa, being determined by the history of the continent's colonization. Section 5 introduces the latest addition to the never ending list of candidate growth correlates, the concept of state fragility, and reviews its potential impact. Section 6 addresses the long-term influence on development, in and out of Africa, of the slave trades. Section 7 derives critical conclusions and indicates directions for further research.

2. Growth, history, and institutions

The present investigation on the determinants of growth in Africa is an ideal application of a broader research agenda that has developed in recent years around the combination of three main ingredients: the economics of growth, the theory of institutions, and their interrelationship with history.

The revival of growth theory during the 1980s, building on Solow's (1956) seminal contribution, is where this research line finds its deepest roots. Romer (1986) and Lucas (1988) are the first to adapt the Solowian model by embedding endogenous technical progress and human capital, with the goal of comprehending the postwar persistence of cross-country differences in growth performances.

At the same time, the field of development economics, by then largely merged with macroeconomic dynamics, has come to recognize the crucial role of history in shaping a country's destiny. Extended data collection, as a joint effort of economists, economic historians, and historians (Maddison, 2007), has broadened the time horizon for empirical investigations over a longer and longer time span, thus allowing researchers to answer old questions and also to raise new ones. On the modeling front, an influential literature has investigated the determinants of growth over the long run, to find a unified explanation of very different phases of the history of human development, going back to the Malthusian era and even beyond (Galor, 2011).

At the same time, extending the relevant time horizon backward has allowed economists to recognize an increasing role for institutional factors, besides purely economic ones. Indeed, the historical and institutional dimensions complement each other, since the economic impact of institutions tends to manifest itself more clearly in the long run. Building on the earlier intuition by North (1981), a broad set of institutions has entered the research agenda. Just to name a few contributors, Engerman and Sokoloff (1997) highlight the links among factor endowments, institutions, and differential growth paths. La Porta, Lopez-de-Silanes, Shleifer, and Vishny (1998) start a research line on the effects of legal institutions on various outcomes. Barro (1999) extends the growth regressions approach to the study of the links between growth and democracy. Acemoglu, Johnson, and Robinson (2004) point to institutions as the fundamental cause of long-run growth.

As explained in Bertocchi (2006), the case of Africa is especially promising as an application of the research line that combines growth, history and institutions, since the colonial institutions established in Africa mainly during the nineteenth century are likely to have shaped, directly and indirectly, the development of the area. Fenske (2010) provides a review essay on the role of institutions in African history and development and argues that even crucial growth factors such as geography, ethnic fractionalization, and colonial history operate largely through institutions. Nunn (2009) also provides a survey of the line of research on history and development, with a special focus on colonial rule as a unifying theme.

3. Growth in Africa

As previously explained, my main focus is on the differential growth performances within Africa. Among growth determinants, I start by discussing standard economic factors. Rodrik (1999) is among the first to adopt the growth regressions approach for a sample of African countries. With the goal of understanding the specific impact of trade policy, he replicates the specification chosen by Sachs and Warner (1997) for a sample of sub-Saharan African countries over the 1965–1990 period. The dependent variable is per capita growth and the explanatory variables preliminarily considered are initial per capita income, dummies for tropical climate and landlocked countries, life expectancy, public savings, institutional quality, measures of openness, and population growth. A more parsimonious specification that accounts for limited data availability shows a significant effect of initial per capita income, life expectancy, public savings, population growth, and export taxation. Thus, he establishes that, even within sub-Saharan Africa, there is evidence of convergence, while growth differentials are explained by a combination of human resources and macroeconomic policy. These findings are broadly in line with standard predictions from growth theory, suggesting that the sources of underdevelopment in sub-Saharan Africa are not specific to this region. However, the same exercise repeated over three subperiods (1964–1974, 1975–1984, and 1985–1994) reveals a much worse fit of each regression and a loss of significance of trade policy and demographics. This suggests that, over shorter horizons, growth rates tend to be unstable and that their determinants may vary over time, more widely in Africa if compared with the rest of the world.

Another attempt to measure growth within Africa is presented by Bertocchi and Canova (2002), who adapt the benchmark growth regressions initially proposed by Barro (1991). Over the 1960–1988 period, they select a specification including the combination of economic and sociopolitical variables, which displays the best explanatory power for average growth of per capita income for a cross-section of African countries. Such a combination includes the initial condition (and its square), the investment-output ratio, the percentage of working-age population in secondary school, the index of political rights, the index of ethnic fractionalization, and a dummy for oil-producing countries. As in Rodrik (1999), in the full sample these variables tend to be associated with significant coefficients with the expected sign. However, over subperiods, once again the picture varies considerably: in the 1960–1973 sample, only investment matters, while only the index of ethnic fractionalization is significant in the 1974–1980 sample, and very little significance is left in the final 1981–1988 sample. This non-robustness denies the existence of a single cause for Africa's poor growth performance over the period under consideration and suggests that different factors may matter for subsequent stages of development. In the initial stage, investment in physical capital appears to be the most important driver, while later on human capital accumulation and political rights emerge as crucial for growth. Bertocchi and Guerzoni (2011) produce updated evidence on the growth performance of the area by running comparable growth regressions over a yearly 1999–2004 panel. They find a tendency to convergence and that economic development is facilitated by schooling and government expenditures, while it is retarded by inflation and ethnic fractionalization. Over this time frame, the relationship between civil liberties and growth is nonlinear, suggesting higher growth for inter-mediate regimes, even though with marginal statistical significance.

In all the investigations reported above, geographical variables such as latitude and a dummy for landlocked countries, which usually matter in a world context, turn out not to contribute to the understanding of the local growth experience, possibly because they exhibit limited regional variation.

To conclude, while the analysis of standard growth factors does confirm, for Africa, conditional convergence, at the same time the influence of regressors other than the initial condition tends to vary significantly across samples, leading to unsatisfactory results that suggest a potential role for omitted variables.

4. History and colonization

The conclusion from the previous section is that standard growth determinants, even those reflecting current institutional characteristics, cannot provide a complete and robust description of the African case. One of the most promising avenues undertaken by subsequent research has been to gauge the potential impact of the history of the continent, with special emphasis on its colonization experience. The basic conjecture behind this avenue is that colonization may be the reason both for low average growth rates in Africa and, at the same time, for the observed heterogeneities across African countries. Africa represents a particularly appropriate setting to analyze the impact of colonial rule on growth because, historically, nowhere else was colonization so far-reaching and time-homogeneous in nature as in the African experience that began at the end of the nineteenth century, despite significant differences across individual countries and colonization regimes. The prevailing wisdom from the previous, huge literature outside of economics was that colonization was bad for colonial economies. According to the drain of wealth thesis, most of the colonial surplus was extracted by the metropolitan countries. Exploitation also distorted the colonial economies in many ways, by reducing physical and human capital accumulation and by generating dysfunctional institutions. An alternative point of view emphasizes instead the positive modernization impulses that came from the metropolises and the advantages deriving from the integration of the colonies into the world economic system. Within the economic literature, Lucas (1990) and Grossman and Iyigun (1995) develop static models of colonial domination, while early empirical contributions are represented by: La Porta et al. (1998), who focus on the legal origins associated with colonial heritage; Alam (1994), who compares the growth rates of sovereign countries and colonies, but with the exclusion of Africa; and Grier (1999), who studies the relationship between the length of colonial rule and growth.

For the 1960–1988 period, Bertocchi and Canova (2002) explore the empirical relevance of colonial variables for a sample of African countries within a standard growth regressions framework. To overcome the obstacle of data availability for the colonial period proper, they employ postwar data and historical information to identify the consequences of colonial domination for current performances. To this end, they classify African countries according to a number of indicators: their political status (i.e., colony vs. dependency vs. independent country) during the colonial period; their metropolitan ruler during domination; and the degree of economic penetration they were exposed to, as captured by the ratio of GNP to GDP at the end of the colonial period. Controlling for standard determinants, they find that in Africa, the identity of the metropolitan ruler and economic penetration do add explanatory power in cross-sectional growth regressions. Namely, British colonies have superior growth performances if compared with the former colonies of France, Italy, and Portugal, while higher economic penetration is detrimental. Moreover, the colonial indicators are correlated with measures of human capital accumulation and political distortions. Hence, several decades after the end of colonization, its legacy still exerts a significant impact on growth in Africa, both directly and indirectly. These results support the conjecture that colonial rule may indeed represent the omitted factor behind the relationship between local average growth rates and economic and sociopolitical factors. While the above conclusions are based on cross-country data for the 1960–1988 period, Bertocchi and Guerzoni (2011) review the evidence over a yearly 1999–2004 panel, to find that colonial indicators no longer contain any explanatory power, which suggests that the lasting influence of the colonial era may finally have faded in more recent times.

An influential and related research line that has also developed around the issue of colonization is based on the original contribution by Acemoglu, Johnson, and Robinson (2001). With the more general goal of establishing the importance of institutions for current development, they identify in colonial history an instrument for institutions, which can address their potential endogeneity. Indeed, reverse causation becomes a crucial issue when taking into account institutional variables, since the direction of causality with respect to income and growth is by no means obvious. They focus on a specific variable, the mortality rate of the initial settlers, about which they collect and compile information based on detailed historic sources. Settler mortality is exploited as an instrument for current institutions, by arguing that colonizers adopted very different policies in places with different mortality rates. In places where they faced high mortality, they could not settle and were therefore more likely to set up extractive institutions, which in turn persist in present times. Their two-stage least-squares estimates establish that institutions, and in particular the degree of property rights protection, do affect economic development. In the previously mentioned papers based on growth regressions, the potential for endogeneity is addressed indirectly by Bertocchi and Canova

(2002), who employ predetermined explanatory variables dated at the beginning of the sample period, and directly by Bertocchi and Guerzoni (2011), who instrument with its lag the only variable for which they find evidence of endogeneity, that is, government expenditure over GDP. For the sake of comparison between the two parallel streams of the literature on colonization, it should be also noticed that Acemoglu et al. (2001), because of the way their instrumental variable is generated, can only include former colonies in their sample. Moreover, they do not focus exclusively on Africa. Finally, they do not distinguish, as Bertocchi and Canova (2002) do, between colonies and dependencies, even though to some extent it could be argued that at least within Africa dependencies were established in lower mortality places.

Another related stream of the literature has gone even beyond the colonial period to discover the roots of current performances. Indeed, one cannot exclude a role for long-term factors that predate colonial domination. Examples are the following. Herbst (2000) points to the underdevelopment of precolonial polities. Bockstette, Chanda, and Putterman (2002) establish a link between state antiquity, a measure of the depth of experience with state-level institutions, and institutional quality. Gennaioli and Rainer (2007) uncover for Africa a positive association between stronger precolonial political institutions and public goods provision. Michalopoulos and Papaioannou (2010) show that tribal precolonial political institutions and class stratification still exert an effect on local economic activity in Africa, which they measure using satellite data on light density at night following Henderson, Storeygard, and Weil (2010). Finally, Nunn (2008a) studies the impact of the slave trades, while Nunn and Puga (2010) focus on the historic interaction between terrain ruggedness and Africa's slave trades, that is, between geography and institutions. In Section 6, I return to the issue of the slave trades in more detail.

More recently, micro-level data have also been exploited, with an even more precise focus on single African countries or specific subregions. One example of this line of research is Huillery (2009), who employs household surveys data on French West Africa to produce evidence that early colonial investments had large and persistent effects on current outcomes.

While the literature described so far is empirical, a few efforts have been made to model the underlying causal relationships within a dynamic setting. Bertocchi (1994) explicitly introduces colonization into a standard growth model with overlapping generations, to determine the net effect of modernization and the drain of wealth on the colonial economy. Colonization is modeled in the form of restrictions on direct foreign investment and exploitative activities, which may induce permanent distortions to physical and human capital accumulation and thus lead to negative growth rates even after decolonization. Nunn (2007) develops a game-theoretic model with multiple equilibria, only one of which is associated with secure property rights and a high level of production. In this setting, external extraction may drive a society into a low production equilibrium. Since this equilibrium is stable, the society remains trapped into it even after external extraction ends. Both models thus provide an explanation for the lasting legacy of colonial rule.

Summing up, colonial history has been shown to matter for growth in Africa, in a number of dimensions, but its influence has not been captured by a single explanatory variable that can identify the impact of colonization. Moreover, its effect appears to have faded over time, while the region is still underperforming. This implies that even accounting for colonial history does not yet provide a complete and consistent answer to the question about the determinants of African growth.

5. State fragility

The concept of state fragility (from now on, fragility) is perhaps the most recent newcomer to the debate about growth in Africa. Rather than to specific economic, institutional, or historical characteristics, the condition of fragility has been associated with combinations of multiple dysfunctions, including a country's inability to provide vital services, unstable and weak governance, persistent and extreme poverty, lack of territorial control, and high propensity to conflict and civil war. It is clear, however, that these dysfunctions can in turn be determined by repeated interactions across a number of factors over the long run. While it may be difficult to isolate the influence of each of these factors singularly, using a composite measure may facilitate the analysis.

Once again, Africa has played a central role in the analysis of fragility, since it is in this continent that fragility is especially widespread. Indeed the European Report on Development (2009) is entirely devoted to the problem of fragility in Africa. The potential growth impact of fragility and the consequent relevance of fragility for policy are also confirmed by the increasing attention of other international organizations. The 2011 World Development Report (World Bank, 2011) focuses on conflict countries. Development practitioners, such as the Government and Social Development Resource Centre (2010), also warn policymakers about the need to understand and respond to fragile situations.

One of the most widely used definitions of fragility is based on the Country Policy and Institutional Assessment (CPIA) that has been conducted by the World Bank since 1999. The ratings are intended to capture the quality of a country's policies and institutional arrangements, with a focus on the key elements that are within the country's control, rather than on outcomes (such as growth rates) that are also influenced by elements outside the country's control. Since the CPIA ratings represent criteria for aid allocation, they carry huge practical implications for policy.

On the basis of the CPIA, the World Bank defines as fragile those low-income countries scoring 3.2 and below (over a 1–6 range). From 1999 to 2005, the individual ratings have been kept confidential. However, the general rankings of countries have been made public. On the basis of the rankings, it is therefore possible to infer the distribution of the countries by quintile. On the basis of the resulting quintile distribution, the OECD defines as fragile those countries in the bottom two quintiles as well as those that are not rated. There is a partial overlap between the CPIA-based definitions of fragility and other related indexes such as the Failed State Index (published by the Fund for Peace), the Index of State Weakness (published by the Brookings Institution), the indicator of Failed & Fragile States (published by the Country Indicators for Foreign Policy project), and the Fragility States Index (published by Polity IV). While all these indicators record similar components, the choice of variables and their weighting schemes remain largely arbitrary.

There is a small but expanding literature on the link between fragility and development in Africa. Bertocchi and Guerzoni (2011) employ the OECD definition of fragility within a yearly panel dataset covering sub-Saharan Africa in the 1999–2004 period. Following the benchmark specification of Barro (1991) and Bertocchi and Canova (2002), they include in their growth regressions an initial condition for per capita income and a wide range of economic, demographic, geographic, and institutional factors. Their results indicate that the conventional measure of fragility employed by the OECD exerts no effect on economic development, once standard regressors are accounted for. However, when they apply a more severe definition of fragility, which only includes the countries in the bottom quintile, they find a clear, negative impact of this condition, even after controlling for endogeneity through instrumental variables estimation. Using a comparable sample and the OECD conventional definition, Baliamoune-Lutz (2009) highlights how fragility exerts a nonlinear impact on per capita income and that it tends to interact with several other factors: in fragile countries, beyond a threshold level, trade openness may actually be harmful to income, while small improvements in political institutions can have adverse effects. Fosu (2009) explores the growth impact of policy syndromes, which include among other components state breakdown, a concept that is in turn close to fragility since it refers to a condition involving civil wars and acute political instability (see Fosu & O'Connell, 2006, for a definition of policy syndromes). His findings are that the absence of policy syndromes encourages growth in Africa.

The potential endogeneity of fragility is a serious concern, which has been addressed by Bertocchi and Guerzoni (2010) by gauging the links between fragility and other standard growth determinants. They find that indeed, within Africa, fragility tends to be shaped by institutional development, a conclusion which questions its exogeneity. In particular, the probability of a country having a fragile state appears to decrease with the level of civil liberties and to increase with the number of revolutions, while economic factors do not matter. These findings differ sharply from those presented by Carment, Samy, and Prest (2008) for a world sample, over which per capita income appears to be the main driver of fragility. This radically different conclusion can be explained, once again, by the specificity of the African region, but also by the fact that the former study employs the OECD definition of fragility, while the latter employs the index of Failed & Fragile States.

Beside these empirical investigations, Besley and Persson (2011) propose a theoretical framework to understand how fragility can hamper development and growth. Their theory highlights how a state may become fragile in situations of external or internal conflict, high political instability, and heavy economic distortions, and how fragility may in turn lead to poverty traps.

While the above contributions focus on the direct link between fragility and development, others have looked at its indirect influence through aid allocation. Since the condition of fragility is a crucial determinant of the amount of aid a country receives from international organizations, growth can be affected by fragility also through this channel. The interaction between aid and fragility is addressed in a number of studies, none of which is specifically focused on Africa. However, given the preponderant role played by African countries among fragile ones, their results are still useful to the present perspective. Burnside and Dollar (2000) provide evidence that aid is most effective in developing countries with sound institutions and policies. However, this conclusion is questioned on several grounds by Hansen and Tarp (2001), Dalgaard, Hansen, and Tarp (2004), and Rajan and Subramanian (2008). McGillivray and Feeny (2008) study the growth impact of aid in a world sample of fragile countries and find that it depends on the relative degree of fragility. Chauvet and Collier (2008) analyze the preconditions for sustained policy turnarounds in failing states and show that aid matters, but its effect depends on its kind (e.g., financial aid vs. technical assistance).

As emphasized by the theory proposed by Besley and Persson (2011), fragility is closely associated with conflict. Therefore, the literature that has evaluated the growth impact of conflict is also relevant. Examples within this stream include Collier and Hoeffler (1998, 2002), who search for the economic causes of conflict and then establish that Africa is indeed more vulnerable to it, because of its poverty; Blanton, Mason, and Athow (2001), who focus on the relationship between colonial domination and postcolonial ethnic conflict in Africa; and Bleaney and Dimico (2011), who distinguish between the correlates of the probability of onset of civil war and the probability of its continuation.

To conclude, the introduction of the broad concept of fragility, which reflects a complex combination of the dysfunctions that are typical of several African countries, has stimulated renewed interest for research on the deep roots of development in the region. At the same time, however, a clear impact of fragility on economic outcomes has proved hard to assess, partly because of the different definitions employed and probably also because of its potential endogeneity.

6. Slavery

Another recent research line that has extended the perspective in a promising direction has focused on the long-term impact of the African slave trades not only for Africa but also for the recipient countries. This line of research is closely related to the previous ones since it emphasizes the role of historical factors and evaluates how their influence on economic outcomes may run through institutions. Nunn (2008a) first looks at the long-term effects of Africa's slave trades on Africa itself. On the basis of shipping records and historical documents, he constructs measures of the number of slaves exported from each country in Africa in each century between 1400 and 1900 and finds a robust negative relationship between the number of slaves exported and current economic performance. Thus, the African countries that are the poorest today are the ones from which the most slaves were taken, even after accounting for the possibility of selection into the slave trades. Moreover, the paper indicates that the procurement of slaves results in subsequent state fragility and ethnic fractionalization.

The spillover of Africa's slave trades on the economic performances of the receiving countries is the theme developed by Engerman and Sokoloff (1997, 2002), on the basis of historical evidence they provide for the New World. Their influential hypothesis can be summarized as follows. They first argue that factor endowments (climate, soil, crops, etc.) determined the suitability and hence the adoption of plantation slavery. In turn, the use of slave labor caused extreme economic inequality, which shaped the evolution of local institutions (including voting rights, the taxation system, and educational policy) in a way that hampered long-term economic development. With the goal of testing Engerman and Sokoloff's hypothesis, Nunn (2008b) examines the relationship among slavery, inequality, and economic development for a sample of 29 American countries and finds that the fraction of slaves over population in 1750 is indeed negatively correlated with per capita income in 2000. A similar negative relationship emerges for slave use, in each decade between 1790 and 1860, across states and counties within the United States, although no evidence is found that this relationship is driven by large scale plantation slavery, that is, by factor endowments. For the U.S. case, Nunn (2008b) also tests whether inequality is the channel through which slavery manifests itself on underdevelopment. The findings are once again mixed since, while it is true that slavery in 1860 is positively associated with contemporaneous land inequality, land inequality in 1860 is not correlated with income in 2000. Overall, these results confirm that slavery was detrimental for economic development, even though they question both the link between slavery and factor endowments and the role of inequality as the channel of transmission between slavery and current development. A closer look at the United States is taken by Bertocchi and Dimico (2010), who find that the negative influence of the slave share on current income is actually not robust to the inclusion of geographic controls that capture structural differences among regions, and even turns positive when state fixed effects are included. On the other hand, they find a negative impact of a dummy for slave states that, rather than the intensity of slave use, should rather reflect institutional differences, possibly linked to the Black Codes and the Jim Crow Laws. Moreover, they find that slavery has a positive and robust effect on current income inequality, that is, those U.S. counties that displayed a higher share of slaves over population are not necessarily poorer, but more unequal, in the present day. They also show that the impact of slave use on current income inequality runs through racial inequality and that the channel of transmission from slavery to inequality is human capital accumulation. In other words, current inequality is primarily influenced by slavery through the unequal educational attainment of blacks and whites. Finally, for a sample of Mississippi counties, Bertocchi and Dimico (2011) analyze the link between slavery and political institutions and show that the former, rather than de jure provisions such as poll taxes and literacy tests, is the main driver of blacks' restricted suffrage at the end of the nineteenth century. Consistently, race and the legacy of slavery, rather than suffrage, emerge as the main determinants of a broad set of indicators capturing multiple aspects of current development.

A provisional conclusion I can draw from the above findings is that, despite the fact that the Engerman and Sokoloff's hypothesis is only partially supported, across different samples and specifications, still there is evidence that Africa's slave trades had a long-lasting influence not only on Africa but also on the countries that used Africa as a source of slave labor.

7. Conclusion

The scope of this chapter was to reconstruct the main steps along the path leading to the discovery of the determinants of growth in Africa, taking into account subsequent waves of a large literature, which initiated from standard Solowian factors and ended up enclosing a wide array of additional considerations. While this literature had a broader scope, to account for the case of Africa was one of its main challenges. With the words of Easterly (2002), I can conclude that, in and out of Africa, the quest for growth has indeed been quite an elusive one. The list of proposed determinants of growth, or lack of it, has included, in order of appearance, physical capital, demographics, human capital, macroeconomic policies, geography, ethnic division, disease, and a large variety of historical and institutional factors. Fragility, a complex mix of dysfunctions, has been the latest newcomer to this list. Accounting for Africa's slave trades has allowed to broaden the perspective to growth spillovers even outside Africa itself. While some progress has been achieved, many questions are still open. While the list of potential growth correlates may not be exhausted yet, at least part of the responsibility for the absence of definite answers may actually fall not on lack of imagination about additional hypotheses but on the underlying growth regressions approach. The latter certainly has its limits even after the advancements obtained through more sophisticated techniques including instrumental variables and panel estimation. Still, as acknowledged in a critical essay by Wacziarg (2002), despite their trouble in identifying causal links and the lack of robustness of their results, growth regressions have represented a first step toward a deeper understanding of what may underlie simple empirical correlations based on reduced forms. Durlauf, Johnson, and Temple (2005) also recognize that most of the growth literature has simply attempted to investigate whether or not particular hypotheses can find any support in the data and to highlight systematic patterns. This approach, however, fails to capture the underlying channels of transmission. To establish causation, the estimated parameters must correspond to precisely identified links within a coherent framework derived from economic theory. Consider, for instance, the relationship between slavery and development. Even if it exhibited a robust statistical correlation, which is actually not the case, to understand its economic significance we would need a theory justifying the underlying mechanisms at work. In other words, why should past slavery still matter today? Because it reflects geography and initial factor endowments, because it shaped human capital accumulation in an unequal fashion, or else because it promoted divisive political institutions? To conclude, structural models based on rigorous theoretical predictions are the next, harder step for future research on the empirics of growth.

Acknowledgments

I would like to thank Olivier de La Grandville and Arcangelo Dimico for helpful comments and suggestions. Generous financial support from Fondazione Cassa Risparmio di Modena is gratefully acknowledged.

References

Acemoglu, D., Johnson, S., & Robinson, J. A. (2001). The colonial origins of comparative development: An empirical investigation. *The American Economic Review, 91,* 1369–1401.

Acemoglu, D., Johnson, S., & Robinson, J. A. (2004). Institutions as the fundamental cause of long-run growth. In P. Aghion & S. Durlauf (Eds.), *Handbook of economic growth* (pp. 385–472). Amsterdam: (Chap 6). North-Holland

Alam, M. S. (1994). Colonialism, decolonization and growth rates: Theory and empirical evidence. *Cambridge Journal of Economics, 18,* 235–257.

Baliamoune-Lutz, M. (2009). Institutions, trade, and social cohesion in fragile states: Implications for policy conditionality and aid allocation. *Journal of Policy Modeling, 31,* 877–890.

Barro, R. J. (1991). Economic growth in a cross section of countries. *Quarterly Journal of Economics, 106,* 407–444.

Barro, R. J. (1999). Determinants of democracy. *Journal of Political Economy, 107,* S158–S183.

Bertocchi, G. (1994). *Colonialism in the theory of growth.* Brown University Working Paper no. 94-14.

Bertocchi, G. (2006). Growth, history and institutions. In N. Salvadori (Ed.), *Economic growth and distribution: On the nature and causes of the wealth of nations* (pp. 331–349). Cheltenham: Edward Elgar Publishing.

Bertocchi, G., & Canova, F. (2002). Did colonization matter for growth? An empirical exploration into the historical causes of Africa's under-development. *European Economic Review, 46,* 1851–1871.

Bertocchi, G., & Dimico A. (2010). *Slavery, education, and inequality.* CEPR Discussion Paper no. 8073.

Bertocchi, G., & Dimico, A. (2011). *Race v. suffrage: The determinants of development in Mississippi.* CEPR Discussion Paper no. 8589.

Bertocchi, G., & Guerzoni, A. (2010). *Growth, history, or institutions: What explains state fragility in sub-Saharan Africa?* CEPR Discussion Paper no. 7745.

Bertocchi, G., & Guerzoni, A. (2011). The fragile definition of state fragility. *Rivista Italiana degli Economisti, 16,* 337–354.

Besley, T. J., & Persson, T. (2011). Fragile states and development policy. *Journal of the European Economic Association, 9,* 371–398.

Blanton, R., Mason, T. D., & Athow, B. (2001). Colonial style and post-colonial ethnic conflict in Africa. *Journal of Peace Research, 38,* 473–491.

Bleaney, M., & Dimico, A. (2011). How different are the correlates of onset and continuation of civil wars? *Journal of Peace Research, 48,* 145–155.

Bockstette, V., Chanda, A., & Putterman, L. (2002). States and markets: The advantage of an early start. *Journal of Economic Growth, 7,* 347–369.

Burnside, C., & Dollar, D. (2000). Aid, policies and growth. *The American Economic Review*, *90*, 847–868.

Carment, D., Samy, Y., & Prest, S. (2008). Determinants of state fragility and implications for aid allocation: An assessment based on the country indicators for foreign policy project. *Conflict Management and Peace Science*, *25*, 349–373.

Chauvet, L., & Collier, P. (2008). What are the preconditions for turnarounds in failing states? *Conflict Management and Peace Science*, *25*, 332–348.

Collier, P., & Hoeffler, A. (1998). On economic causes of civil war. *Oxford Economic Papers*, *50*, 563–573.

Collier, P., & Hoeffler, A. (2002). On the incidence of civil war in Africa. *Journal of Conflict Resolution*, *46*, 13–28.

Dalgaard, C.-J., Hansen, H., & Tarp, F. (2004). On the empirics of foreign aid and growth. *Economic Journal*, *114*, F191–F216.

Durlauf, S. N., Johnson, P. A., & Temple, J. R. W. (2005). Growth econometrics. In P. Aghion & S. N. Durlauf (Eds.), *Handbook of economic growth* (Vol. 1A, pp. 555–677). Amsterdam: North-Holland

Easterly, W. (2002). *The elusive quest for growth: Economists' adventures and misadventures in the tropics*. Cambridge, MA: MIT Press.

Easterly, W., & Levine, R. (1997). Africa's growth tragedy: Policies and ethnic divisions. *Quarterly Journal of Economics*, *112*, 1203–1250.

Engerman, S. L., & Sokoloff, K. L. (1997). Factor endowments, institutions, and differential paths of growth among new world economies: A view from economic historians of the United States. In S. Harber (Ed.), *How Latin America fell behind* (pp. 260–304). Stanford, CA: Stanford University Press.

Engerman, S. L., & Sokoloff, K. L. (2002). Factor endowments, inequality, and paths of development among new world economies. *Economía*, *3*, 41–88.

European Report on Development. (2009). *Overcoming fragility in Africa*. Robert Schuman Centre for Advanced Studies. San Domenico di Fiesole: European University Institute.

Fenske, J. (2010). *Institutions in African history and development: A review essay*. MPRA Paper no. 23120.

Fosu, A. K. (2009). *Understanding the African growth record: The importance of policy syndromes and governance*. UNU-WIDER Discussion Paper no. 2009/02.

Fosu, A. K., & O'Connell, S. (2006). Explaining African economic growth: The role of anti-growth syndromes. In F. Bourguignon & B. Pleskovic (Eds.), *Annual bank conference on development economics (ABCDE)* (pp. 31–66). Washington, DC: World Bank.

Galor, O. (2011). *Unified growth theory*. Princeton, NJ: Princeton University Press.

40 *Graziella Bertocchi*

Gennaioli, N., & Rainer, I. (2007). The modern impact of precolonial centralization in Africa. *Journal of Economic Growth, 12*, 185–234.

Government and Social Development Resource Centre. (2010). *Topic guide on fragile states.* University of Birmingham, Birmingham.

Grier, R. M. (1999). Colonial legacies and economic growth. *Public Choice, 98*, 317–335.

Grossman, H. I., & Iyigun, M. (1995). The profitability of colonial investment. *Economics & Politics, 7*, 229–242.

Hansen, H., & Tarp, F. (2001). Aid and growth regressions. *Journal of Development Economics, 64*, 547–570.

Henderson, V., Storeygard, A., & Weil, D. N. (2010). Measuring economic growth from outer space. *The American Economic Review.* Forthcoming.

Herbst, J. (2000). *States and power in Africa: Comparative lessons in authority and control.* Princeton, NJ: Princeton University Press.

Huillery, E. (2009). History matters: The long-term impact of colonial public investments in French West Africa. *American Economic Journal: Applied Economics, 1*, 176–215.

La Porta, R., Lopez-de-Silanes, F., Shleifer, A., & Vishny, R. W. (1998). Law and finance. *Journal of Political Economy, 106*, 1113–1155.

Lucas, R. E., Jr. (1988). On the mechanics of economic development. *Journal of Monetary Economics, 22*, 3–32.

Lucas, R. E., Jr. (1990). Why doesn't capital flow from rich to poor countries? *American Economic Review Papers and Proceedings, 80*, 92–96.

Maddison, A. (2007). *Contours of the world economy, 1-2030 AD: Essays in macroeconomic history.* Oxford: Oxford University Press.

McGillivray, M., & Feeny, S. (2008). *Aid and growth in fragile states.* UNU-WIDER Research Paper no. 2008/3.

Michalopoulos, S., & Papaioannou, E. (2010). *Divide and rule or the rule of the divided? Evidence from Africa.* CEPR Discussion Paper no. 8088.

North, D. C. (1981). *Structure and change in economic history.* New York, NY: W.W. Norton & Co.

Nunn, N. (2007). Historical legacies: A model linking Africa's past to its current underdevelopment. *Journal of Development Economics, 83*, 157–175.

Nunn, N. (2008a). The long-term effects of Africa's slave trades. *Quarterly Journal of Economics, 123*, 139–176.

Nunn, N. (2008b). Slavery, inequality, and economic development in the Americas: An examination of the Engerman-Sokoloff hypothesis. In E. Helpman (Ed.), *Institutions and economic performance* (pp. 48–180). Cambridge, MA: Harvard University Press.

Nunn, N. (2009). The importance of history for economic development. *Annual Review of Economics, 1*, 65–92.

Nunn, N., & Puga, D. (2010). Ruggedness: The blessing of bad geography in Africa. *Review of Economics and Statistics.* Forthcoming.

Rajan, R. G., & Subramanian, A. (2008). Aid and growth: What does the cross-country evidence really show? *Review of Economics and Statistics, 90*, 643–665.

Rodrik, D. (1999). *Trade policy and economic performance in sub-Saharan Africa.* Expert Group on Development Issues. Stockholm: Almqvist and Wiksell International.

Romer, P. M. (1986). Increasing returns and long-run growth. *Journal of Political Economy, 94*, 1002–1037.

Sachs, J. D., & Warner, A. M. (1997). Sources of slow growth in African economies. *Journal of African Economies, 6*, 335–376.

Sala-i-Martin, X., Pinkovskiy, M., & Fargas, R. T. (2010). *African poverty is falling ... Much faster than you think!* NBER Working Paper no. 15775.

Schmidt-Hebbel, K. (1996). Fiscal adjustment and growth: In and out of Africa. *Journal of African Economies, 5*(Suppl. (Pt. I)), 7–59.

Solow, R. M. (1956). A contribution to the theory of economic growth. *Quarterly Journal of Economics, 70*, 65–94.

Wacziarg, R. (2002). Review of easterly's the elusive quest for growth. *Journal of Economic Literature, 40*, 907–918.

World Bank. (2011). *World development report 2011: Conflict, security, and development.* Washington, DC: World Bank.

Young, A. (2010). *The African growth miracle.* Working Paper. London School of Economics, UK.

CHAPTER 4

On the Relation Between Investment and Economic Growth: New Cross-Country Empirical Evidence

Michael Binder[a] and Susanne Bröck[b]

[a]Faculty of Economics and Business Administration, Goethe University Frankfurt, Grüneburgplatz 1, 60323 Frankfurt am Main, Germany
E-mail address: mbinder@wiwi.uni-frankfurt.de
[b]Union Investment, Wiesenhüttenplatz 25, 60329 Frankfurt am Main, Germany
E-mail address: susanne.broeck@union-investment.de

Abstract
This chapter advances a panel vector autoregressive/vector error correction model (PVAR/PVECM) framework for purposes of examining the sources and determinants of cross-country variations in macroeconomic performance using large cross-country data sets. Besides capturing the simultaneity of the potential determinants of cross-country variations in macroeconomic performance and carefully separating short- from long-run dynamics, the PVAR/PVECM framework advanced allows to capture a variety of other features typically present in cross-country macroeconomic data, including model heterogeneity and cross-sectional dependence. We use the PVAR/PVECM framework we advance to reexamine the dynamic interrelation between investment in physical capital and output growth. The empirical findings for an unbalanced panel of 90 countries over the time period from at most 1950 to 2000 suggest for most regions of the world surprisingly strong support for a long-run relationship between output and investment in physical capital that is in line with neoclassical growth theory. At the same time, the notion that there would be even a *long-run* (let alone short-run) causal relation between investment in physical capital and output (or vice versa) is strongly refuted. However, the size of the feedback from output growth to investment growth is estimated to strongly dominate the size of the feedback from investment growth to output growth.

Keywords: Economic growth, investment, dynamic panels, causality

JEL classifications: C33, E22, O40

Frontiers of Economics and Globalization
Volume 11   ISSN: 1574-8715
DOI: 10.1108/S1574-8715(2011)0000011009

1. Introduction

Research aimed at understanding countries' long-run economic development has been a cornerstone of theoretical and empirical economic investigations for many decades. In the recent empirical growth literature,[1] significant effort has been expanded towards identifying the major determinants of cross-country differences in long-run output levels and growth rates. The predominant investigative tool used in this literature is the "Barro cross-section regression," which involves regressing a country's rate of output growth over a certain time period on an initial condition for the level of output as well as potential determinants of output growth, the latter measured as averages over the time span for which output growth is being considered (see, e.g., Barro, 1991, 1997).

One of the shortcomings of the Barro cross-section regression is the underlying statistical assumption that the regressors, the potential determinants of output growth, are all (strictly) exogenous.[2] Regressions of, say, output growth on variables such as the rate of investment in physical or human capital that *a priori* postulate the latter variables to be (strictly) exogenous may be helpful to understand the strength of the association of output growth with these variables, but cannot provide evidence as to whether these variables are in fact determinants of a country's rate of output growth in the sense that higher rates of investment in physical or human capital would precede accelerated output growth. It may well be that higher rates of investment in physical or human capital merely are a result of higher output (income) levels and growth rates. For purposes of policy analysis, it is clearly desirable, however, to be able to distinguish between the correlates and the determinants of output growth. Some of the empirical work within the Barro cross-section regression framework has attempted to address this problem by instrumentation. See, however, Durlauf (2001) for forceful arguments as to how problematic the specification of instruments in the context of cross-country output growth regressions is bound to be.

The simultaneity issue has even led some to argue that an econometric analysis of the growth process should be abandoned in favor of the quantitative theory approach of conducting simulation analyses for calibrated dynamic stochastic general equilibrium models (see, e.g., McGrattan & Schmitz, 1999). Of course, if any attempt is made to thoroughly evaluate the latter class of models, they will need to be estimated. Within the context of a model with cross-parameter and cross-equation restrictions, the same simultaneity issues then arise in

---

[1] See, for example, Durlauf and Quah (1999), Temple (1999), Islam (2003), Durlauf, Johnson, and Temple (2005), and Eberhardt and Teal (2011) for stimulating surveys of this literature to date.

[2] Other shortcomings of the Barro regression are addressed, for example, in Binder and Georgiadis (2011).

estimation as for an empirical growth model not containing such restrictions.

In this chapter, we advance a reduced-form panel vector autoregressive/ vector error correction model (PVAR/PVECM) framework that can be fruitfully used to overcome simultaneity problems in empirical growth analysis, that is, distinguish between the correlates and the determinants of output growth. Our PVAR/PVECM framework also accounts for systematic cross-country heterogeneity, distinguishes between short- and long-run dynamics, takes account of (possibly common) long-run relations between output and its potential determinants, as well as takes account of the cross-sectional dependence of shocks to the output growth process across countries. Using our framework, one may assess whether and to what extent changes in a set of variables precede output growth or are themselves triggered by higher output growth rates. Our PVAR/PVECM framework should therefore prove useful for the investigation of the sources and determinants of cross-country variations in macroeconomic performance rather broadly, though for reasons of scope, the focus in this chapter will be on the long-run interrelation between output and investment in physical capital.

From an econometric perspective, the PVAR/PVECM framework advanced in this chapter extends the single equation panel estimation and inference procedures of Pesaran, Shin, and Smith (1999) and Pesaran (2006, 2007) to the PVAR/PVECM setting. While this involves some new conceptual issues, many of the difficulties arising in considering the system of equations setting are of a computational nature. To preserve space, we refer the interested reader to Bröck (2008) for a detailed discussion of how to resolve the type of computational complexities arising in the implementation of our PVAR/PVECM framework.

Beyond presentation of our PVAR/PVECM framework, the focus of this chapter is rather on providing fresh insights into the long-run levels and growth relationship between investment in physical capital and output.[3] The debate on the particular role of physical capital investment in the output growth process in the more recent empirical growth literature dates back to DeLong and Summers (1991). Several studies have since examined whether higher rates of investment in physical capital precede accelerated output growth (as was argued by DeLong & Summers, 1991), or whether higher rates of investment are merely a result of higher output levels and growth rates. Notable contributions to

---

[3] In line with our chapter, the causality problem in output growth has so far in the literature been primarily addressed in settings isolating *one* of the possible determinants of cross-country variations in growth rates. *Inter alia*, Bils and Klenow (2000) argue that output growth spurs schooling (human capital accumulation), but not vice versa, and King and Levine (1993) argue that financial development is indeed causal for output growth.

this literature include Carroll and Weil (1994), Blomström, Lipsey, and Zejan (1996), and Attanasio, Picci, and Scorcu (2000).[4] These studies consider panel regressions of output growth on its own lagged values and on lagged values of the rate of investment in physical capital, and *vice versa*, and then test for Granger causality between output growth and the rate of investment in physical capital. Carroll and Weil (1994) as well as Blomström et al. (1996) argue that output growth spurs investment in physical capital, but not vice versa. There are a number of reasons why the empirical evidence in this line of work may be questioned.[5] The model specifications considered in these studies ignore that there may be long-run relations between the levels of output and the physical capital investment and that these long-run relations may impose restrictions on the dynamic interaction between output growth and the rate of investment in physical capital. This is of particular relevance because even if there was a causal relation between output growth and investment, it appears unlikely that there would be no short-run feedback between these two variables. In other words, allowing for both short- and long-run dynamics and distinguishing between these two types of dynamics is important. For growth issues, the relevant notion of causality appears to be whether investment is a long-run forcing variable for output, or vice versa, not whether there is a Granger-causal relationship between output and investment. Further reasons why the empirical evidence provided in Carroll and Weil (1994), Blomström et al. (1996) and Attanasio et al. (2000) is likely to be problematic are that in the first two of these papers, cross-sectional heterogeneity is restricted to enter through country-specific intercepts only (not allowing for country-specific dynamics) and that the issue of cross-country dependence of output growth shocks is not addressed in any of these three papers.

The remainder of this chapter is organized as follows. In Section 2, we describe our PVAR/PVECM framework. Sections 3 and 4 describe the Mean Group (MG) and Pooled Mean Group (PMG) estimation of the model. Section 5 *inter alia* considers the problem of testing for a common number of long-run relations across countries and of testing for weak exogeneity of (some of) the variables within the modeling framework. In Section 6, we turn to the empirical analysis of the long-run levels and growth relationship between investment in physical capital and output. Section 7 summarizes the chapter.

---

[4] To be precise, the concern of Carroll and Weil (1994) and of Attanasio et al. (2000) was with the dynamic interaction of output growth and saving. Here, we follow the recent empirical growth literature that has measured the rate of saving as the share of investment in physical capital in output and do not make an explicit distinction between saving on the one hand and investment in physical capital on the other hand.

[5] See also Bond, Leblebicioglu, and Schiantarelli (2007).

2. The PVAR/PVECM framework

We consider the following PVAR model:

$$\Phi_i(L)(w_{it} - \mu_i - \gamma_i t) = u_{it}, \quad i = 1, 2, \ldots, N, \quad t = 1, 2, \ldots, T_i, \tag{1}$$

where

$$w_{it} = \begin{pmatrix} y_{it} \\ x_{it} \end{pmatrix},$$

$$\Phi_i(L) = I_m - \sum_{k=1}^{p_i} \Phi_{ik} L^k, \tag{2}$$

where I_m denotes the identity matrix of dimension $m \times m$, and

$$u_{it} = \xi_i f_t + \varepsilon_{it}. \tag{3}$$

The vector w_{it} contains both endogenous and exogenous variables (i.e., output per capita and all potential determinants of it), μ_i represents an intercept vector, γ_i a time trend vector, $\Phi_i(L)$ denotes a lag polynomial in the coefficient matrices $\Phi_{ik}, i = 1, 2, \ldots, N; k = 1, 2, \ldots, p_i; u_{it}$ is a vector of disturbances that is generated according to (3), with factor loadings ξ_i and with an idiosyncratic disturbance vector ε_{it}. The subscript i refers to the ith cross-sectional unit in the panel, and the subscript t denotes the time period. We make the following assumptions:

ASSUMPTION A1. The disturbance vectors ε_{it} are independently and identically distributed across i and over t with $E(\varepsilon_{it}) = 0_{m \times 1}$ and $V(\varepsilon_{it}) = \Omega_{\varepsilon i}$. $\Omega_{\varepsilon i}$ is a positive definite symmetric matrix. Also, ε_{it} has finite fourth-order moments. The common effect f_t is independently and identically distributed over t with $E(f_t) = 0$, $\text{Var}(f_t) = \sigma_f^2$, and finite fourth-order moment; f_t and ε_{it} are independently distributed for all t and t', $t \neq t'$.

ASSUMPTION A2. The PVAR(p_i) model is stable in the sense that the roots of the characteristic equation

$$|\Phi_i(z_i)| = 0$$

are either equal to unity or fall outside the unit circle.

ASSUMPTION A3. T_i must be large enough such that the model can be estimated for each i separately. While T_i does not have to be the same for each i, for notational convenience only we shall from now on use a common T.

The error correction representation of (1), that we will call the Panel Vector Error Correction Model (PVECM), is given by

$$\Delta w_{it} = a_{0i} + a_{1i}t + \Pi_i w_{i,t-1} + \sum_{k=1}^{p_i-1} \Gamma_{ik} \Delta w_{i,t-k} + \xi_i f_t + \varepsilon_{it}, \tag{4}$$

where

$$a_{0i} = -\Pi_i \mu_i + \sum_{k=1}^{p_i} k \Phi_{ik} \gamma_i,$$

$$a_{1i} = -\Pi_i \gamma_i,$$

$$\Pi_i = -\left(\mathbf{I}_m - \sum_{k=1}^{p_i} \Phi_{ik} \right), \tag{5}$$

and

$$\Gamma_{ik} = -\sum_{l=k+1}^{p_i} \Phi_{il}, \quad k = 1, 2, \dots, p_i - 1. \tag{6}$$

The restrictions on a_{1i} present in (5) when $\gamma_i \neq 0$ ensure that the nature of the deterministic trending behavior of the level process $\{w_{it}\}_{t=1}^{\infty}$ remains invariant to the rank r_i of the matrix Π_i. We add one assumption for the PVECM:

ASSUMPTION A4. If Π_i has rank r_i, $r_i = 1, 2, \dots, m-1$, then:

$$\Pi_i = \alpha_i \beta_i' \tag{7}$$

where α_i and β_i are $m \times r_i$ matrices of full column rank, and the $(m - r_i) \times (m - r_i)$ matrix $\alpha_{i\perp}' \Gamma_i \beta_{i\perp}$ is of full rank, where $\alpha_{i\perp}'$ and $\beta_{i\perp}$ are $m \times (m - r_i)$ matrices of full column rank such that $\alpha_i' \alpha_{i\perp} = 0_{r_i \times (m-r_i)}$ and $\beta_i' \beta_{i\perp} = 0_{r_i \times (m-r_i)}$, and $\Gamma_i = -\Pi_i + \sum_{k=1}^{p_i} k \Phi_{ik}$.

Assumption (A4) rules out the possibility that the process $(w_{it} - \mu_i - \gamma_i t)_{t=1}^{\infty}$ admits explosive or seasonal unit roots except at the zero frequency; the processes $\beta_{i\perp}'(w_{it} - \mu_i - \gamma_i t)_{t=1}^{\infty}$ and $\beta_i'(w_{it} - \mu_i - \gamma_i t)_{t=1}^{\infty}$ are integrated of orders one and zero, respectively (see Binder, Hsiao, & Pesaran, 2005; Johansen, 1995).

As noted in the time-series setting by Pesaran, Shin, and Smith (2000), if some of the model variables are exogenous, estimation of the PVECM will be more efficient if based on a conditional model for the endogenous variables, say y_{it}, only. That is, in this case, it may be advantageous not to model the complete PVECM, including the equations for the exogenous variables. Partitioning the disturbance vector ε_{it} and its variance-covariance matrix $\Omega_{\varepsilon i}$ conformably with the partition of Δw_{it} into Δy_{it} (endogenous variables) and Δx_{it} (exogenous variables) as

$$\varepsilon_{it} = \begin{pmatrix} \varepsilon_{yit} \\ \varepsilon_{xit} \end{pmatrix}, \quad \text{and} \quad \Omega_{\varepsilon i} = \begin{pmatrix} \Omega_{yyi} & \Omega_{yxi} \\ \Omega_{xyi} & \Omega_{xxi} \end{pmatrix},$$

one may write ε_{yit} conditionally in terms of ε_{xit} as $\varepsilon_{yit} = \Theta_i \varepsilon_{xit} + \upsilon_{it}$, where $\Theta_i = \Omega_{yxi}\Omega_{xxi}^{-1}$, and $\upsilon_{it} \stackrel{i.i.d.}{\sim} (0_{m_y \times 1}, \Omega_{\upsilon i})$, with $\Omega_{\upsilon i} = \Omega_{yyi} - \Theta_i \Omega_{xyi}$.

Then the equations in the PVECM corresponding to the endogenous variables in (4) can be written as follows:

$$\Delta y_{it} = c_{0i} + c_{1i}t + (\Pi_{yi} - \Theta_i \Pi_{xi})w_{i,t-1}$$
$$+ \Theta_i \Delta x_{it} + \sum_{k=1}^{p_i-1} \Psi_{ik}\Delta w_{i,t-k} + \tilde{\xi}_i f_t + \upsilon_{it}, \tag{8}$$

where $c_{0i} = a_{y0i} - \Theta_i a_{x0i}$, $c_{1i} = a_{y1i} - \Theta_i a_{x1i}$, $\Psi_{ik} = \Gamma_{yik}, k = 1, 2, \ldots, p_i - 1$, $\tilde{\xi}_i = \xi_{yi} - \Theta_i \xi_{xi}$, with the partitions $\Pi_i = (\Pi'_{yi}, \Pi'_{xi})'$, $\Gamma_{ik} = (\Gamma'_{yik}, \Gamma'_{xik})'$, $k = 1, 2, \ldots, p_i - 1$, $a_{0i} = (a_{y0i}, a_{x0i})'$, $a_{1i} = (a_{y1i}, a_{x1i})'$, and $\xi_i = (\xi_{yi}, \xi_{xi})'$ conformably with the partition of w_{it} into y_{it} and x_{it}. That is, in (8), we model Δy_{it} conditional on its own past, on current and past values of Δx_{it}, and on the r_i cointegrating relationships between y_{it} and x_{it}; we call (8) the Panel Vector Autoregressive Distributed Lag (PVARDL) representation of the equations for the endogenous variables in the PVECM. Under the panel long-run forcing restrictions

$$\Pi_{xi} = 0_{m_x \times m} \tag{9}$$

it can be established using the arguments in Pesaran et al. (2000) that the marginal distribution of Δx_{it} is redundant for inference concerning the parameters of interest in the PVARDL model (8). Note that the long-run forcing restriction (9) precludes feedback from y_{it} to x_{it} in the long run, but does not impose any such restriction in the short run. In partitioned/conditional representation, the full PVECM can thus be rewritten as follows:

$$\Delta y_{it} = c_{0i} + c_{1i}t + \Pi_{yi}w_{i,t-1} + \Theta_i \Delta x_{it}$$
$$+ \sum_{k=1}^{p_i-1} \Psi_{ik}\Delta w_{i,t-k} + \tilde{\xi}_i f_t + \upsilon_{it}, \tag{10}$$

and

$$\Delta x_{it} = a_{x0i} + \sum_{k=1}^{p_i-1} \Gamma_{xik}\Delta w_{i,t-k} + \xi_{xi} f_t + u_{x,it}, \tag{11}$$

with

$$c_{1i} = a_{y1i} = -\Pi_{yi}\gamma_i, \tag{12}$$

$$c_{0i} = -\Pi_{yi}\mu_i + (\Gamma_{yi} - \Theta_i\Gamma_{xi} + \Pi_{yi})\gamma_i, \tag{13}$$

and

$$(\Gamma_{yi}', \Gamma_{xi}') = \Gamma_i = -\Pi_i + \sum_{k=1}^{p_i} k\Phi_{ik}. \tag{14}$$

Under the long-run forcing restriction (9), the rank restriction (7) now renders as

$$\Pi_{yi} = \alpha_{yi}\beta_i', \tag{15}$$

and Assumption (A4) reduces to[6]

$$\text{rank}(\Pi_{yi}) = r_i, \quad r_i = 0, 1, \ldots, m_y. \tag{16}$$

The details of estimation and inference for the PVECM and PVARDL model, including determination of the cointegrating rank, depend on whether the models in (4) and (10) contain non-zero intercepts and/or time trend terms, and, if so, whether the intercept and trend coefficients are restricted. Quite different deterministic behavior may be observed for the levels of the variables under differing values of the cointegrating rank r_i unless the coefficients associated with the intercept and/or the time trend terms are restricted to lie in the column space of Π_{yi}. In line with Pesaran et al. (2000), one may differentiate between five cases of interest:[7] **Case I:** No intercepts, no trends: $a_{0i} = 0$, $a_{1i} = 0$; **Case II:** Restricted intercepts, no trends: $a_{0i} = -\Pi_i\mu_i, a_{1i} = 0$; **Case III:** Unrestricted intercepts, no trends: $a_{0i} \neq 0, a_{1i} = 0$; **Case IV:** Unrestricted intercepts, restricted trends: $a_{0i} \neq 0, a_{1i} = -\Pi_i\gamma_i$, and **Case V:** Unrestricted intercepts, unrestricted trends: $a_{0i} \neq 0, a_{1i} \neq 0$.

3. Estimation under cross-sectional independence

To address the conceptual difficulties in estimation of the PVECM sequentially, we first assume that $\xi_i = 0$ and hence that the error terms are cross-sectionally independent. We will relax this assumption in Section 4.

We consider two leading specifications as to how the dynamics across countries can structurally differ: (i) all model coefficients are allowed to differ (in unrestricted fashion) across countries and (ii) the long-run slope coefficients are the same across countries, but the short-run coefficients are allowed to differ (in unrestricted fashion). Following the terminology of Pesaran et al. (1999) for the single-equation setting, we call the resultant

---

[6] The maximal possible rank of Π_{yi} is m_y, maintaining that the elements of x_{it} are not mutually cointegrated. Note that if $rank\ (\Pi_{yi}) = m_y$, it is not necessarily the case that all m variables in the PVECM are stationary; it is conceivable that the elements of y_{it} are not mutually cointegrated, but that y_{it} and x_{it} are cointegrated.

[7] For notational ease and to conserve space, in distinguishing these cases as well as for the remainder of our discussion of estimation and inference, we focus on the unconditional PVECM in (4). The discussion is readily adapted to the conditional PVARDL model in (10).

estimators for these two specifications the (i) MG estimators and (ii) PMG estimators.

3.1. The mean group estimator

Under this specification, we may estimate the PVECM (4) for each cross-sectional unit using reduced rank methods as suggested in the time-series literature (see, in particular, Johansen, 1995). To this purpose, let us define the following sample moment matrices

$$S_{00} = R0_i R0_i' / (T - p_i), \quad S_{10,i} = S_{01,i}' = R1_i R0_i' / (T - p_i),$$

$$\text{and} \quad S_{11,i} = R1_i R1_i' / (T - p_i)$$

where $R0_i = \Delta W_i M_i$, $R1_i = W_{i,-1}^* M_i$, $W_{i,-1}^* = (W_{i,-1}', \tau_{T-p_i}')'$, $M_i = I_{T-p_i} - \Delta W_{i,1}' (\Delta W_{i,1} \Delta W_{i,1}')^{-1} \Delta W_{i,1}$, $\Delta W_{i,1} = (\iota_{T-p_i}', \Delta W_{i,-1}', \Delta W_{i,-2}', \ldots, \Delta W_{i,-p_i+1}')'$, $W_{i,-1} = (w_{ip_i}, w_{i,p_i+1}, \ldots, w_{i,T-1})$, $\Delta W_{i,-l} = (\Delta w_{i,p_i-l+1}, \Delta w_{i,p_i-l+2}, \ldots, \Delta w_{i,T-l})$, $l = 1, 2, \ldots, p_i - 1$, ι_{T-p_i} is a $T-p_i$ vector of ones, and $\tau_{T-p_i} = (p_i + 1, p_i + 2, \ldots, T)'$. The long-run coefficient matrices, β_i, can then be estimated as follows:

$$\hat{\beta}_i' = V_i' G_i,$$

where $G_i = [\text{chol}(S_{11,i})]'^{-1}$, chol denotes the Cholesky decomposition, and V_i is composed of the eigenvectors corresponding to the r_i largest eigenvalues of $G_i S_{10,i} S_{00,i}^{-1} S_{01,i} G_i'$ (see, e.g., Lütkepohl, 1993). Partitioning β_i as $\beta_i = (\beta_{i,r_i}', \beta_{i,m-r_i}')'$, a commonly used (exact) identification of β_i is given by

$$\beta_i = (I_{r_i}, \beta_{i,r_i}^{-1'} \beta_{i,m-r_i}')' = (I_{r_i}, \phi_i')',$$

where β_{i,r_i}' and $\beta_{i,m-r_i}'$ are of dimension $r_i \times r_i$ and $r_i \times (m - r_i)$, respectively.[8]

The adjustment coefficient matrices, α_i, may be estimated as

$$\hat{\alpha}_i = R0_i R1_i' \hat{\beta}_i (\hat{\beta}_i' R1_i R1_i' \hat{\beta}')^{-1}. \tag{17}$$

Even if the long-run parameters differ across countries, rendering the $\hat{\beta}_i$ country specific, the cointegration rank may be the same across countries:

ASSUMPTION A5. Π_i has rank r, $r = 0, 1, \ldots, m - 1$, common across all cross-sectional units.

Under Assumption (A5) the MG estimators of α_i and ϕ_i can be obtained by averaging $\hat{\alpha}_i$ and $\hat{\phi}_i$ across cross-sectional units:

---

[8] See, for example, Boswijk (1995).

$$\hat{\alpha}_{\text{MGjs}} = \frac{1}{N} \sum_{i=1}^{N} \alpha_{ijs} \quad \text{and} \quad \hat{\phi}_{\text{MGks}} = \frac{1}{N} \sum_{i=1}^{N} \hat{\phi}_{\text{iks}}, \tag{18}$$

$j = 1, 2, \ldots, m$, $k = 1, 2, \ldots, m - r$ (in case of exact identification), and $s = 1, 2, \ldots, r$.

3.2. The pooled mean group estimator

In addition to Assumptions (A1)–(A5), under our second specification as to how the dynamics across countries structurally differ, following Pesaran et al. (1999), we assume homogeneous long-run coefficients across all cross-sectional units, that is,

$$\Pi_i = \alpha_i \beta', \quad i = 1, 2, \ldots, N. \tag{19}$$

While in general it seems unlikely that short-run dynamics are the same across countries, long-run relationships such as those underlying balanced growth paths may be common across countries, motivating (19). While (19) thus can have strong theoretical appeal, under (19), the PVECM (4) cannot be estimated on a country-by-country basis anymore, as there are now cross-section restrictions present. Assuming that T time-series observations are available, the log-likelihood function for the panel is given by

$$\ln L_{\text{PMG}}(\alpha_i, \Omega_i, \beta; r) = \sum_{i=1}^{N} \ln L_i(\alpha_i, \Omega_i, \beta; r)$$

$$= -\frac{(T - p_i)Nm}{2} \ln(2\pi) - \frac{(T - p_i)}{2} \sum_{i=1}^{N} \ln |\Omega_i|$$

$$- \frac{1}{2} \sum_{i=1}^{N} \text{tr}\{\Omega_i^{-1} \mathbf{E}_i \mathbf{E}_i'\}, \tag{20}$$

where $\ln L_i(\alpha_i, \Omega_i, \beta; r)$, $i = 1, 2, \ldots, N$, denotes the log-likelihood function for cross-sectional unit i, $\Omega_i = V(u_{it})$, and $\mathbf{E}_i = (\mathbf{R0}_i - \alpha_i \beta' \mathbf{R1}_i)$. To reduce complexity, it is useful to work with a log-likelihood function that is concentrated with respect to α_i, Γ_i, and the elements of Ω_i. The resultant likelihood function is given by[9]

$$\ln L_{\text{PMG}}^*(\beta; r) = c - \frac{(T - p_i)}{2} \sum_{i=1}^{N} \ln |\mathbf{A}_i^*|,$$

---

[9] The corresponding restrictions are given by

$$\alpha_i = \mathbf{R0}_i \mathbf{R1}_i' \beta (\beta' \mathbf{R1}_i \mathbf{R1}_i' \beta)^{-1} \quad \text{and} \quad \Omega_i = (\mathbf{R0}_i - \alpha_i \beta' \mathbf{R1}_i)(\mathbf{R0}_i - \alpha_i \beta' \mathbf{R1}_i)'/(T - p_i).$$

where $c = [(T - p_i)Nm/2][1 + \ln(2\pi)]$ and $\mathbf{A}_i^* = (T - p_i)^{-1}\mathbf{R}0_i(\mathbf{I}_{T-p_i} - \mathbf{R}1_i'$
$\boldsymbol{\beta}(\boldsymbol{\beta}'\mathbf{R}1_i\mathbf{R}1_i'\boldsymbol{\beta})^{-1}\boldsymbol{\beta}'\mathbf{R}1_i)\mathbf{R}0_i'$. To compute the PMG estimates satisfying the
long-run pooling restrictions in (19), we obtain initial estimates of $\boldsymbol{\beta}$ from
MG estimation and then implement a (projected) trust region method to
obtain the final maximum likelihood estimates of the common long-run
coefficients. This optimization method in practice is considerably more
robust when the true gradient is used. The first differential of (21) is given by:

$$\Delta \ln L_{\text{PMG}}^*(\boldsymbol{\beta}; r) = \sum_{i=1}^{N} \text{vec}(\mathbf{B}_i^* \mathbf{R}1_i \mathbf{R}0_i' \mathbf{A}_i^{*-1} \mathbf{C}_i^*)' \text{dvec}(\boldsymbol{\beta}),$$

where d denotes the differential, $\mathbf{B}_i^* = \mathbf{I}_m - \mathbf{R}1_i\mathbf{R}1_i'\boldsymbol{\beta}(\boldsymbol{\beta}'\mathbf{R}1_i\mathbf{R}1_i'\boldsymbol{\beta})^{-1}\boldsymbol{\beta}'$, and
$\mathbf{C}_i^* = \mathbf{R}0_i\mathbf{R}1_i'\boldsymbol{\beta}(\boldsymbol{\beta}'\mathbf{R}1_i\mathbf{R}1_i'\boldsymbol{\beta})^{-1}$. The gradient of (21) is then given by

$$\nabla \ln L_{\text{PMG}}^*(\boldsymbol{\beta}; r) = \sum_{i=1}^{N} \text{vec}(\mathbf{B}_i^* \mathbf{R}1_i \mathbf{R}0_i' \mathbf{A}_i^{*-1} \mathbf{C}_i^*)'. \tag{21}$$

To obtain estimates of the cross-section-specific adjustment coefficients
α_i, we compute the long-run relationship(s), $\hat{\boldsymbol{\beta}}'\mathbf{R}1_i$ and then maximize

$$\ln L_{\text{PMG}}(\alpha_i, \Omega_i; r) = -\frac{(T - p_i)Nm}{2}\ln(2\pi) - \frac{(T - p_i)}{2}\sum_{i=1}^{N} \ln |\Omega_i|$$

$$-\frac{1}{2}\sum_{i=1}^{N} \text{tr}\{\Omega_i^{-1}[\mathbf{R}0_i - \alpha_i(\hat{\boldsymbol{\beta}}'\mathbf{R}1_i)]$$

$$[\mathbf{R}0_i - \alpha_i(\hat{\boldsymbol{\beta}}'\mathbf{R}1_i)]'\}. \tag{22}$$

4. Estimation under cross-sectional dependence

Thus far, we have assumed cross-sectionally independent error terms.
However, if the error terms are cross-sectionally dependent of the form of
(3), hypothesis tests tend to be seriously size-distorted if these dependencies are spuriously ignored (see, e.g., Bröck, 2008; Pesaran, 2007).

Following the lines of reasoning for the single-equation setting in
Pesaran (2006, 2007), the common factor, f_t, in (3) can be approximated
by the cross-sectional means of $w_{i,t-1}$, $\overline{w}_{t-1} = N^{-1}\sum_{i=1}^{N} w_{i,t-1}$, as well as of
Δw_{it}, $\Delta \overline{w}_t = N^{-1}\sum_{i=1}^{N} \Delta w_{it}$, and its lagged values, $\Delta \overline{w}_{t-1}, \Delta \overline{w}_{t-2}, \ldots$ for N
sufficiently large. Consider a PVECM(1) model, where for simplicity
$m = 2$, $a_{0i} = a_{1i} = 0$, $\Pi_i = \Pi$, $\Phi_i = \Phi$, $\xi_i = \xi$, and $\Omega_{\varepsilon i} = \Omega_\varepsilon$, for all i, with
the cross-sectionally heterogenous coefficients differing randomly across i.
Averaging each equation of the resultant special case of the PVECM (4)
across i then leads to

$$\Delta \overline{w}_{1t} = \pi_{11}\overline{w}_{1,t-1} + \pi_{12}\overline{w}_{2,t-1} + \xi_1 f_t + \overline{\varepsilon}_{1t}$$

$$\Delta \overline{w}_{2t} = \pi_{21}\overline{w}_{1,t-1} + \pi_{22}\overline{w}_{2,t-1} + \xi_2 f_t + \overline{\varepsilon}_{2t},$$

$t = 1, 2 \ldots$, which under the reduced rank restriction $r_i = r = 1$ is equal to

$$\Delta \bar{w}_{1t} = \alpha_1(\beta_1 \bar{w}_{1,t-1} + \beta_2 \bar{w}_{2,t-1}) + \xi_1 f_t + \bar{\varepsilon}_{1t}$$

$$\Delta \bar{w}_{2t} = \alpha_2(\beta_1 \bar{w}_{1,t-1} + \beta_2 \bar{w}_{2,t-1}) + \xi_2 f_t + \bar{\varepsilon}_{2t},$$

with $V(\bar{\varepsilon}_t) = \Omega_\varepsilon / N$ and $\bar{\varepsilon}_t = (\bar{\varepsilon}'_{1t}, \bar{\varepsilon}'_{2t})'$. Each element of $\bar{\varepsilon}_t$ converges to zero in root mean squared error. As long as $\xi_j \neq 0, j = 1, 2,$[10] and for N sufficiently large, f_t converges in probability (up to a scalar constant) to $\Delta \bar{w}_{jt} - \pi_{j1} \bar{w}_{1,t-1} - \pi_{j2} \bar{w}_{2,t-1}, j = 1, 2$. Hence, f_t can be approximated by

$$f_t = (\Delta \bar{w}_{1t} - \pi_{11} \bar{w}_{1,t-1} - \pi_{12} \bar{w}_{2,t-1}) \xi_1^{-1}$$

and

$$f_t = (\Delta \bar{w}_{2t} - \pi_{11} \bar{w}_{1,t-1} - \pi_{12} \bar{w}_{2,t-1}) \xi_2^{-1}.$$

Applying this idea of Pesaran (2006) to the PVECM setting without specific regard for model parsimony, the common effect augmented (CEA) estimation of the PVECM involves estimation of

$$\Delta w_{it} = a_{0i} + a_{1i}t + \Pi_i w_{i,t-1} + \sum_{k=1}^{p_i-1} \Gamma_{ik} \Delta w_{i,t-k}$$

$$+ \sum_{l=0}^{p_i-1} \mathbf{B}_{il} \Delta \bar{w}_{t-l} + C_i \bar{w}_{t-1} + \varepsilon_{it}, \tag{23}$$

where $\mathbf{B}_{il}$, $l = 0, 1, \ldots, p_i - 1$, and C_i are full $(m \times m)$ matrices. As $\bar{w}_{t-1}$ is mutually cointegrated, (23) is balanced. The matrix $\Delta \mathbf{W}_{i\_1}$ need now be defined as $\Delta \mathbf{W}_{i\_1} = (\iota'_T, \Delta \mathbf{W}'_{i,-1}, \Delta \mathbf{W}'_{i,-2}, \ldots, \Delta \mathbf{W}'_{i,-p_i+1}, \overline{\mathbf{W}}'_{-1}, \Delta \mathbf{W}_{i\_1},$
$\Delta \overline{\mathbf{W}}'_{-1}, \Delta \overline{\mathbf{W}}'_{-2}, \ldots, \Delta \overline{\mathbf{W}}'_{-p+1})'$, $\quad \Delta \overline{\mathbf{W}}_{-l} = (\Delta \bar{w}_{p_i-l+1}, \Delta \bar{w}_{p_i-l+2}, \ldots, \Delta \bar{w}_{T-l}),$
and $\overline{\mathbf{W}}_{-1} = (\bar{w}_{p_i}, \bar{w}_{p_i+1}, \ldots, \bar{w}_{T-1})$.

In empirical practice, the CEA procedure may be at odds with considerations of model parsimony or simply not be feasible when the number of time-series observations is not sufficiently large. We therefore propose a two-step common effect augmented (TS-CEA) approach that relative to the CEA approach can notably conserve degrees of freedom. To motivate this procedure, suppose

$$\Delta w_{it} = a_{0i} + a_{1i}t + \alpha_i \beta' w_{i,t-1} + \sum_{k=1}^{p_i-1} \Gamma_{ik} \Delta w_{i,t-k} + \mathbf{G}_i v_t + \varepsilon_{it}, \tag{24}$$

and

---

[10] This condition can be tested if N and T are sufficiently large. Under the condition $\xi_i = \mathbf{0}_{m \times 1}$, the regression of $\Delta \bar{w}_{1t}$ on $\bar{w}_{1,t-1}$ and $\bar{w}_{2,t-1}$ must yield a perfect fit. See Pesaran (2006).

$$\Delta \bar{w}_t = d_0 + d_1 t + \Upsilon \bar{w}_{t-1} + \sum_{k=1}^{\bar{p}-1} \Psi_k \Delta \bar{w}_{t-k} + v_t,$$

$$\Upsilon = \varrho \phi', \quad \text{if} \quad \text{rank}(\Upsilon) < m, \tag{25}$$

where $\quad \mathbf{G}_i = \text{diag}(\xi_{1i}/\bar{\zeta}_1, \xi_{2i}/\bar{\zeta}_2, \ldots, \xi_{mi}/\bar{\zeta}_m), \quad v_t \equiv \Xi f_t \quad$ and $\Xi = \text{diag}(\bar{\zeta}_1, \bar{\zeta}_2, \ldots, \bar{\zeta}_m) = \text{diag}(\frac{1}{N}\sum_{i=1}^{N}\xi_{1i}, \frac{1}{N}\sum_{i=1}^{N}\xi_{2i}, \ldots, \frac{1}{N}\sum_{i=1}^{N}\xi_{mi}).$ Proxies for the common unobserved effects, v_t, in (24) may be obtained by first estimating the pure time-series VECM in (25).[11] Our TS-CEA procedure proposes to proxy v_t in (24) by $\hat{v}_t$ (rather than with the cross-sectional means as under CEA), so that

$$\Delta w_{it} = a_{0i} + a_{1i} t + \alpha_i \beta' w_{i,t-1}$$

$$+ \sum_{k=1}^{p_i-1} \Gamma_{ik} \Delta w_{i,t-k} + \Xi_i \hat{v}_t + \tilde{\varepsilon}_{it}, \quad i = 1, 2, \ldots, N, \tag{26}$$

where $\quad \tilde{\varepsilon}_{it} = \Xi_i(v_t - \hat{v}_t) + \varepsilon_{it}, \quad i = 1, 2, \ldots, N, \quad$ and $\Xi_i = \text{diag}(\xi_{1i}, \xi_{2i}, \ldots, \xi_{im}).$ Note that the PVECM in (26), in $\hat{v}_t$, features a generated regressor. Thus, in a two-step estimation of (24) and (26), the standard errors of the (long-run) coefficients in (24) need to be adjusted, following the principles in Pagan (1984). The derivation of the adjusted standard errors is rather involved, and we refer the interested reader to Bröck (2008).

Note that the TS-CEA procedure assumes that $\mathbf{G}_i$ in (24) is a diagonal matrix:

$$\text{vec}(\mathbf{G}'_i) = \mathbf{S}\varphi_i, \tag{27}$$

where S is a $m^2 \times m$ matrix of full column rank with known elements and φ_i an $m \times 1$ vector of unknown parameters. We obtain a consistent estimator of φ_i using iterative Seemingly Unrelated Regression (SUR) estimation of (26) subject to (27), with Π_i initially unrestricted and $\Omega_{\varepsilon i}$ replaced by an initial estimator based on residuals that are computed from ordinary least squares (OLS) equation-by-equation estimation. This yields estimates of $\Gamma_{ik}, k = 1, 2, \ldots, p_i - 1$, and Ξ_i, and we can then apply MG/PMG estimation to

$$\Delta w_{it} - \hat{\Xi}_i \hat{v}_t - \sum_{k=1}^{p_i-1} \hat{\Gamma}_{ik} \Delta w_{i,t-k} = a_{0i} + a_{1i} t + \alpha_i \beta' w_{i,t-1} + \hat{\varepsilon}_{it}, \tag{28}$$

where $\text{vec}(\hat{\Xi}'_i) = \mathbf{S}\hat{\varphi}_i$ and $\hat{\varepsilon}_{it} = \varepsilon_{it} - (\hat{\Xi}_i - \Xi_i)v_t - \sum_{k=1}^{p_i-1}(\hat{\Gamma}_{ik} - \Gamma_{ik})\Delta w_{i,t-k}.$

---

[11] Note that we do not suggest imposing the restrictions $\bar{\Pi} = \frac{1}{N}\sum_{i=1}^{N}\Pi_i$ and $\bar{\zeta} = \frac{1}{N}\sum_{i=1}^{N}\xi_i$ in such estimation.

5. Hypothesis testing

The PVECM framework involves a number of testable hypotheses. As is standard in the time-series context, before the PVECM is estimated, the order of integration of the variables involved should be determined. We will thus begin this section on hypothesis testing in the PVECM framework by outlining the panel unit root tests we employ. We will then turn to testing for the main aspects of the PVECM as described in Sections 2 to 4: cross-sectional structure of the error terms, cointegration rank, long-run parameter homogeneity, and long-run causality. We conclude this section by discussing the computation of impulse response responses as a means to obtain further structural insights from the PVECM.

5.1. Unit root tests

5.1.1. Unit root tests under cross-sectional independence

In case of cross-sectional independence, we carry out panel unit root tests as suggested by Im, Pesaran, and Shin (2003). For each cross-sectional unit, we run $\mathrm{ADF}(p_i)$ regressions of the form

$$\Delta y_{it} = d_{i0} + d_{i1}t + d_{i2}y_{i,t-1} + \sum_{j=1}^{p_i-1} d_{ij3}\Delta y_{i,t-j} + e_{it}, \tag{29}$$

$i = 1,2,\ldots,N; \ t = p_i + 1, p_i + 2, \ldots, T$. Defining $t\text{-bar}_{NT}$ to be the average of the cross-sectional unit-specific t-statistics for d_{i2}, the test statistic is given by

$$\psi = \frac{\sqrt{N}\{t\text{-bar}_{NT} - \frac{1}{N}\sum_{i=1}^N E[t_{iT}(p_i - 1, 0)|d_{i2} = 0]\}}{\frac{1}{N}\sum_{i=1}^N V[t_{iT}(p_i - 1, 0)|d_{i2} = 0]},$$

where $E(t_{iT}(p_i - 1, 0)|d_{i2} = 0)$ and $V(t_{iT}(p_i - 1, 0)|d_{i2} = 0)$ are the mean and variance correction factors, respectively. Under the null hypothesis $(H_0 : d_{i2} = 0 \ \forall i)$, ψ follows a standard normal distribution

5.1.2. Unit root tests under cross-sectional dependence

In the presence of cross-sectional dependence, Pesaran (2007) suggests to augment the cross-sectional unit specific $\mathrm{ADF}(p_i)$ regressions (29) by the cross-sectional means of $y_{i,t-1}$ and Δy_{it} and lags of Δy_{it} if $p_i > 1$, $\bar{y}_{t-1}$ and $\Delta \bar{y}_{t-k+1}$, $k = 1, 2, \ldots, p_i$, respectively. The cross-sectionally augmented $\mathrm{ADF}(p_i)$ regressions are given by

$$\Delta y_{it} = \delta_{i0} + \delta_{i1}t + \delta_{i2}y_{i,t-1} + \delta_{i3}\overline{y}_{t-1} + \sum_{j=0}^{p_i-1}\delta_{ij4}\Delta\overline{y}_{t-j} + \sum_{j=1}^{p_i-1}\delta_{ij5}\Delta y_{i,t-j} + e_{it}.$$

(30)

Following Pesaran (2007), we consider the following truncated test statistic:

$$\text{CIPS}^*(N, T) = \tfrac{1}{N}\sum_{i=1}^{N} t_i^*(N, T),$$

(31)

where $t_i^*(N, T)$ is the truncated version of $t_i(N, T)$, the t-statistic of δ_{i2} in (30):

$t_i^*(N, T) = t_i(N, T)$, if $-K_1 < t_i(N, T) < K_2$,

$t_i^*(N, T) = -K_1$, if $t_i(N, T) \le -K_1$,

$t_i^*(N, T) = K_2$, if $t_i(N, T) \ge K_2$,

where K_1 and K_2 are such that $\text{Pr}[-K_1 < t_i(N, T) < K_2]$ is sufficiently large; under a normal approximation of $t_i(N, T)$ as a benchmark

$$K_1 = -E(\text{CADF}_{if}) - \Phi^{-1}(\varepsilon/2)\sqrt{V(\text{CADF}_{if})},$$

$$K_2 = E(\text{CADF}_{if}) + \Phi^{-1}(1 - \varepsilon/2)\sqrt{V(\text{CADF}_{if})},$$

where is a sufficiently small positive constant, and CADF_{if} is the limiting distribution of $t_i(N, T)$. Critical values for $\text{CIPS}^*(N, T)$ may be found in Pesaran (2007).

5.2. Tests for cross-sectional independence

Pesaran (2004) provides a simple diagnostic test for cross-sectional dependence that is based on a simple average of all pair-wise cross-correlation coefficients of the OLS residuals from the cross-section-specific regressions in the panel. We extend this testing procedure to the multivariate case, where we compute pair-wise cross-correlation coefficients of the residuals obtained under the estimation procedures described in Sections 3 and 4. We define the sample estimates of the pair-wise cross-correlations of the residuals, $\hat{\rho}_{ij,kl}$, $i, j = 1, 2, \dots, N$, $i \ne j$, $k, l = 1, 2, \dots, m$, as

$$\hat{\rho}_{ij,kl} = \frac{\sum_{t \in \mathscr{T}_i \cap \mathscr{T}_j} (e_{ikt} - \overline{e}_{ik})(e_{jlt} - \overline{e}_{jl})}{\left[\sum_{t \in \mathscr{T}_i \cap \mathscr{T}_j} (e_{ikt} - \overline{e}_{ik})^2\right]^{1/2} \left[\sum_{t \in \mathscr{T}_i \cap \mathscr{T}_j} (e_{jlt} - \overline{e}_{jl})^2\right]^{1/2}},$$

where $\mathscr{T}_i$ is the set of dates over which time-series observations on w_{it} are available for the ith cross-sectional unit. The number of the elements in this set is defined by $\#\mathcal{T}_i$. $\mathcal{T}_i \cap \mathcal{T}_j$ is the common set of data points for cross-sectional units i and j, e_{ikt} are the residuals of the estimation procedure, and

$$\bar{e}_{ik} = \frac{\sum\limits_{t \in \mathcal{T}_i \cap \mathcal{T}_j} e_{ikt}}{\#(\mathcal{T}_i \cap \mathcal{T}_j)}.$$

The test statistic, CD_{kl}^*, is then computed as

$$CD_{kl}^* = \sqrt{\frac{2}{N(N-1)}} \left(\sum_{i=1}^{N-1} \sum_{j=i+1}^{N} \sqrt{T_{ij}} \hat{\rho}_{ij,kl} \right), \tag{32}$$

where $T_{ij} = \#(\mathcal{T}_i \cap \mathcal{T}_j)$. Under the null hypothesis of no cross-sectional dependence the test statistic, CD_{kl}^*, follows a standard normal distribution for N sufficiently large.

5.3. Tests for cointegration

5.3.1. Tests for cointegration under cross-sectional independence

For the case of cross-sectionally independent error terms, Larsson, Lyhagen, and Löthgren (2001) develop a method for testing for cointegration in heterogeneous coefficient panel models based on the approach suggested in the time-series literature by Johansen (1988, 1991, 1995) and based on the assumption of a common cointegration rank across cross-sectional units. Their suggested test statistic is given by

$$\Upsilon_{\overline{LR}}\{H(r)|H(m)\} = \frac{\sqrt{N}[\overline{LR}\{H(r)|H(m)\} - E(Z_k)]}{\sqrt{V(Z_k)}}, \tag{33}$$

where $\overline{LR}\{H(r)|H(m)\} = \frac{1}{N}\lambda_{i,trace}$. $\lambda_{i,trace}$ tests $H_0 : r \leq k$, $k = 0, 1, \ldots, m-1$, and is computed as $\lambda_{i,trace} = -T\sum_{j=k+1}^{m} \log(1 - \hat{\lambda}_{ij})$, where λ_{ij}, $j = 1, 2, \ldots, m$, are the estimated eigenvalues of Π_i, with $\lambda_{im} > \lambda_{i,m-1} > \ldots > \lambda_{i1}$; also,

$$Z_k \equiv \text{tr}\left\{ \int_0^1 [dW(a)]W(a)' \left(\int_0^1 W(a)W(a)' \right)^{-1} \int_0^1 W(a)[dW(a)]' \right\},$$

and W is a $k = (m - r)$ dimensional Brownian motion. Larsson et al. (2001) show that $\Upsilon_{\overline{LR}}\{H(r)|H(m)\}$ is standard normal. Bröck (2008) argues that it is important to compute different mean and variance correction factors, $E(Z_k)$ and $V(Z_k)$, for different lag orders p_i, and additionally, to use the exact mean and variance correction factors instead of the asymptotic ones.

5.3.2. Tests for cointegration under cross-sectional dependence

To account for cross-sectional dependence when testing for cointegration in the PVECM framework, we follow Bröck (2008) and distinguish between panel cointegration testing under the CEA and under the TS-CEA estimation procedures.

Cointegration testing under the CEA estimation procedure: Bröck (2008) suggests computing the mean of the individual $\lambda_{i,\text{trace}}$ statistics, $\overline{\lambda}_{\text{CEA}}(T, N)$, and provides simulation-based critical values of the distribution of the resultant $\overline{\lambda}_{\text{CEA}}(T, N)$ statistic.[12]

Cointegration testing under the TS-CEA estimation procedure: The test statistic for cointegration rank suggested above under the CEA procedure is severely mis-sized under the TS-CEA estimation procedure. Bröck (2008), following the lines of reasoning of Seo (1998, 2004) in the time-series context, argues that one should explicitly take account of stationary covariates when testing for cointegration rank, noting that $\hat{v}_t$ in (28) is a stationary and exogenous variable. The test involves first determining the rank of Υ in (25) using existing tests for cointegration as suggested in the time-series literature (here the trace-statistic derived by Johansen, 1988, 1991, 1995). Then (25) is estimated under the implied rank of Υ and the resultant $\hat{v}_t$ is substituted into (24). Finally, the Johansen trace-statistic for Π_i is computed for each cross-sectional unit. Turning to the distribution of the panel test statistic that can now be obtained: Following Seo (1998, 2004), Bröck (2008) defines ρ_{il}, $l = 1, 2, \ldots, m - r$, to be the long-run canonical correlation coefficients between the equation error with and without the stationary covariates, $\Xi_i \hat{v}_t + \varepsilon_{it}$ and ε_{it}, respectively.[13] Let $B(u)$ be a standard vector-Brownian motion and $F(u) = \{[B(u) - \int_0^1 B du]',$ $[u - \frac{1}{2}]\}'$ (supposing we are in **Case IV**). $W(u)$ is a standard $(m-r)$-vector Brownian motion with $E(W(1)B(1)') = \mathbf{P} = \text{diag}(\rho_1, \rho_2, \ldots, \rho_{m-r})$. Additionally,

$$
Q = \text{tr}\left\{ \int_0^1 \mathrm{d}WF' \left(\int_0^1 FF' \mathrm{d}u \right)^{-1} \int_0^1 F \mathrm{d}W' \right\},
$$

$b = E(Q)^2 / V(Q)$ and $a = E(Q) / Var(Q)$ (see Boswijk & Doornik, 2005). If q denotes the dimension of F and $z = m - r$, then

$$
E(Q) = \frac{E(\tilde{T})}{z} \sum_{k=1}^{z} \rho_k^2 + \left(1 - \frac{1}{z} \sum_{k=1}^{z} \rho_k^2 \right) zq,
$$

and

---

[12] Although the asymptotic distribution should not depend on p_i, Bröck (2008) argues that the small sample properties of this test statistic improve when accounting for cross-sectional unit specific lag orders.

[13] The following lines review the derivations by Seo (1998, 2004) and thus i is equal to unity.

$$V(Q) = V(\tilde{T}_k) \sum_{k=1}^{z} \rho_k^4 + 2\mathrm{Cov}(\tilde{T}_k, \tilde{T}_l) \sum_{k=2}^{z} \sum_{l=1}^{k-1} \rho_k^2 \rho_l^2$$

$$+ \frac{4E(\tilde{T})}{z} \sum_{k=1}^{z} \rho_k^2 (1 - \rho_k^2) + 2q \sum_{k=1}^{z} (1 - \rho_k^2)^2,$$

where

$$\tilde{T} = \mathrm{tr}\left\{ \int_0^1 \mathrm{d}\boldsymbol{B}\boldsymbol{F}' \left(\int_0^1 \boldsymbol{F}\boldsymbol{F}'\mathrm{d}u \right)^{-1} \int_0^1 \boldsymbol{F}\mathrm{d}\boldsymbol{B}' \right\},$$

and

$$\tilde{T}_k = \int_0^1 \mathrm{d}\mathrm{B}_k \boldsymbol{F}' \left(\int_0^1 \boldsymbol{F}\boldsymbol{F}'\mathrm{d}u \right)^{-1} \int_0^1 \boldsymbol{F}\mathrm{B}_k'.$$

B_k is the kth component of $\boldsymbol{B}$ (and thus, $\tilde{T} = \sum_{k=1}^{z} T_k$) and $V(\tilde{T}_k) = V(\tilde{T})/q - (q - 1)\mathrm{cov}(\tilde{T}_k, \tilde{T}_l)$. Values for $\mathrm{Cov}(\tilde{T}_k, \tilde{T}_l)$, $k \neq l$ may be found in Doornik (1998). Boswijk and Doornik (2005) show that the limiting distribution of the test statistic, $2a\lambda_{\mathrm{trace}}$, can be approximated by a χ^2-distribution with $2b$ degrees of freedom: $2a\lambda_{\mathrm{trace}} \tilde{} \chi^2(2b)$. For the panel setting, Bröck (2008) computes a_i and $2a_i\lambda_{i,\mathrm{trace}}$ for each cross-sectional unit, $i = 1, 2, \ldots, N$, where a_i is obtained is analogy to a. Afterwards, the mean, $\overline{\lambda}_{\mathrm{TS\text{-}CEA}}$, of the individual test statistics is computed, with $\overline{\lambda}_{\mathrm{TS\text{-}CEA}} = 1/N \sum_{i=1}^{N} 2a_i\lambda_{i,\mathrm{trace}}$. To derive the critical values for the $\overline{\lambda}_{\mathrm{TS\text{-}CEA}}$ test, $2b_i$ is obtained for each cross-sectional unit using simulated values of $E(\tilde{T})$ and $V(\tilde{T})$. b_i is computed as b for each cross-sectional unit. Under the assumption that the cross-section specific test statistics are independently distributed, the $\overline{\lambda}_{\mathrm{TS\text{-}CEA}}$ test can be approximated by the Gamma distribution $\Gamma(\sum_{i=1}^{N} b_i, 2/N)$.

5.4. Tests for long-run parameter homogeneity

As discussed in Section 3, the PMG estimator relative to the MG estimator imposes the long-run pooling/homogeneity restriction given by (19), $\Pi_i = \alpha_i\beta'$, $i = 1, 2, , N$. The PMG estimator is thus a restricted version of the MG estimator. One possibility to test for homogeneity of the long-run slope coefficients in β therefore is to employ a likelihood-ratio (LR) test. The PMG estimator imposes Ng restrictions on the unrestricted model underlying the MG estimator, where g is the number of long-run coefficients to be estimated ($g = rm - r^2$, in case of exact identification).[14] In practice, the LR test can easily prove to impose too tight a set of

---

[14] The LR test obviously is conditioned on the assumption of a common rank r across all cross-sectional units.

restrictions and result in over-rejection of the null hypothesis. A preferable alternative may thus be a Hausman test examining whether the PMG estimator provides an acceptable estimate of the mean of the distribution of the long-run slope coefficients. Note that the MG estimator is consistent but inefficient if long-run slope homogeneity holds; the PMG estimator in contrast is consistent and efficient under this null hypothesis. The Hausman test statistic is then given by:

$$h = (\hat{\phi}_{MG} - \hat{\phi}_{PMG})'[\hat{V}(\hat{\phi}_{MG}) - \hat{V}(\hat{\phi}_{PMG})]^{-1}(\hat{\phi}_{MG} - \hat{\phi}_{PMG}), \qquad (34)$$

with $\hat{V}(\hat{\phi}_{MG})$ and $\hat{V}(\hat{\phi}_{PMG})$ denoting consistent estimates of the variance-covariance matrices of $\hat{\phi}_{MG}$ and $\hat{\phi}_{PMG}$. Details of the computation of $\hat{V}(\hat{\phi}_{MG})$ in the single-equation setting are discussed in Pesaran, Smith, and Im (1996) and are readily adapted to our PVECM setting. The matrix involving the difference between variances, $\hat{V}(\hat{\phi}_{MG}) - \hat{V}(\hat{\phi}_{PMG})$, is not necessarily positive definite. To overcome this problem, one may use a seemingly unrelated estimation approach as in Weesie (1999).

5.5. Tests for weak exogeneity/long-run causality

As noted in Section 2, weak exogeneity/long-run causality does not preclude short-run feedback between the variables in question. It is therefore a weaker restriction than Granger causality. To test the long-run forcing restriction (9), we check on whether the lagged cointegrated terms enter the equations describing the first differences of x_{it}. To do so, we consider the sub-system regressions (assuming here for expositional purpose cross-sectional independence and homogeneity of the long-run coefficients):

$$\Delta x_{it} = a_{x0i} + \sum_{k=1}^{p_i-1} \Gamma_{xik}\Delta w_{i,t-k} + \alpha_{xi}\hat{\beta}' w_{i,t-1} + \varepsilon_{xit} \qquad (35)$$

or

$$\Delta y_{it} = a_{y0i} + \sum_{k=1}^{p_i-1} \Gamma_{yik}\Delta w_{i,t-k} + \alpha_{yi}\beta' w_{i,t-1} + \varepsilon_{yit}, \qquad (36)$$

$i = 1,2\ldots, N$, $t = p_i + 1, p_i + 2, \ldots, T$. To test whether $\{x_{it}\}$ is long-run forcing of $\{y_{it}\}$ (or vice versa), we estimate the system consisting of (35) and (36) through OLS with and without imposing the restrictions $\alpha_{xi} = 0$ ($\alpha_{yi} = 0$) for all i. Considering H_0: $\alpha_{xi} = 0$ ($\alpha_{yi} = 0$), $\forall i$, the implied LR statistic has a limiting χ^2 distribution with $m_x rN$ ($m_y rN$) degrees of freedom. We also apply this testing procedure to the CEA and TS-CEA model specifications.

5.6. Impulse responses and persistence profiles

As for purposes of investigating the dynamic interrelation between output and physical capital it does not appear essential to identify structural sources of shocks, we confine ourselves in this chapter to considering generalized impulse responses.[15] We consider two types of effects of shocks: the PVEC model cumulative effect, that is, the effect to the log-level variables, and the noncumulative effect on the variable growth rates. A complication arises when computing impulse responses in PVEC models featuring correlated effects augmentation. To see this, consider the term $u_{it} = \xi_i f_t + \varepsilon_{it}$. How to define a shock in such a setting, with respect to u_{it} or ε_{it}? As by assumption, f_t and ε_{it} are uncorrelated and $f_t \sim N(0, \sigma_f^2)$, f_t is unaffected by a shock to an element of ε_{it} and we define the term "a shock to an equation" of the PVEC model to mean a shock to one element of ε_{it}. As we argued that f_t can be eliminated by the augmentation of the model under consideration with the cross-sectional means, these augmentations should not play a role in the computation of the impulse responses, if only elements of ε_{it} are subject to a shock.[16]

When reporting the mean growth rate effects of a one standard deviation shock, we compute the impulse responses, $\mathrm{IR}(h)_{it}$, for each cross-sectional unit for horizons $h = 0, 1, \ldots, H$, and then compute the average effect $\overline{\mathrm{IR}}(h)_t = \frac{1}{N}\sum_{i=1}^{N}\mathrm{IR}(h)_{it}$. We obtain the confidence bands from the non-parametric variance-covariance matrix, $V[\overline{\mathrm{IR}}(h)_t]$, which is defined as follows:

$$V[\overline{\mathrm{IR}}(h)_t] = \frac{\sum_{i=1}^{N}[\mathrm{IR}(h)_{it} - \overline{\mathrm{IR}}(h)_t][\mathrm{IR}(h)_{it} - \overline{\mathrm{IR}}(h)_t]'}{N(N-1)}.$$

In addition to the mean impulse responses, we also compute mean persistence profiles. The persistence profile measures the effect of a system-wide shock rather than a variable-specific shock on the cointegrating relationship(s). We compute the cross-sectional unit-specific (scaled) persistence profile for the rth cointegrating relationship by

$$P_i(\boldsymbol{\beta}_r' w_{i,t-1}, h) = \frac{\boldsymbol{\beta}_r' \mathbf{A}_{ih} \boldsymbol{\Omega}_{\varepsilon i} \mathbf{A}_{ih}' \boldsymbol{\beta}_r'}{\boldsymbol{\beta}_r' \boldsymbol{\Omega}_{\varepsilon i} \boldsymbol{\beta}_r},$$

where $\mathbf{A}_{ih} = \mathbf{A}_{i,h-1}\boldsymbol{\Phi}_{ih} + \ldots + \mathbf{A}_{i,h-p}\boldsymbol{\Phi}_{ip_i}$, $h = 1, 2, \ldots, H$ and $\mathbf{A}_0 = \mathbf{I}_{m_y}$ and $\mathbf{A}_h < 0$, for $h < 0$. Again, the confidence bands are computed using the nonparametric variance-covariance matrix.

---

[15] See Binder, Chen, and Zhang (2010) for a structural identification of impulse responses in a panel setting; the identification procedure described in that paper exploits restrictions implied by the presence of cointegrating relations in the PVECM setting.

[16] We leave it to future research to consider "deep" shocks affecting both f_t and elements of ε_{it} in a setting where f_t and ε_{it} are correlated.

6. The relationship between investment in physical capital and output: Empirical evidence

6.1. Data

In compiling the data set underlying our empirical analysis of the long-run levels and growth relationship between investment in physical capital and output based on our PVAR/PVECM framework of Sections 2 to 5, we start with all 174 countries contained in Version 6.1 of the Penn World Tables by Heston, Summers, and Aten (2002).[17] We thus employ an unbalanced panel data set with observations from (at most) 1950 to 2000. In constructing what we call in what follows our *full sample*, we exclude those countries from the Penn World Tables data set that feature only 20 or less time-series observations on either GDP or investment (in physical capital) per capita, feature for some sample periods negative values of investment per capita and/or feature missing observations not only at the beginning or end of the sample period.[18] Following standard country-selection procedures in the empirical growth literature (see, e.g., Mankiw, Romer, & Weil, 1992), we also exclude countries that (i) had an average population size of 350,000 or less in the time period from 1960 to 1964 and/or that (ii) were centrally planned economies for most of the available sample period (one exception to this is that we do not exclude China, to be compatible on this ground also with country-selection procedures in much of the recent empirical growth literature), and/or (iii) rely on oil production as the dominant source of income. These country-selection criteria leave us with 90 countries for our *full sample*. For robustness checks and region-specific analysis, we also split this *full sample* into mostly regional subsamples on the basis of the World Bank classification: OECD, Europe, Latin America and Caribbean, Sub-Saharan Africa, as well as East Asia and Pacific (see Table 1).

6.2. Replicating Blomström, Lipsey, and Zejan

In a first step, we replicate the analysis of Blomström et al. (1996) using our data set (*full sample*). We do so to ensure that differences in empirical conclusions are not driven by differences in the data but rather by differences in econometric modelling.[19] Blomström et al. (1996) address

---

[17] Our use of this version of the Penn World Tables *inter alia* facilitates comparison of our empirical results with those in the comprehensive survey paper of Durlauf et al. (2005).

[18] We thus ensure that we can take logarithms of all observations, and can estimate the dynamic PVAR/PVEC models involving (at least) country-specific short-run dynamics with a reasonable number of data points.

[19] Blomström et al. (1996) using a previous version of the Penn World Table data analyze 101 countries over the time period from 1960 to 1985.

Table 1.   Data availability and subsamples

OECD (18)	Europe (15)	Latin America and Caribbean (18)	Sub-Saharan Africa (31)	East Asia and Pacific (13)	Additional countries not in regional subsamples (13)
Australia: 1950–2000	Austria: 1950–2000	Argentina: 1950–2000	Benin: 1959–2000	Australia: 1950–2000	Bangladesh: 1959–2000
Austria: 1950–2000	Belgium: 1950–2000	Bolivia: 1950–2000	Botswana: 1960–1999	China: 1952–2000	Canada: 1950–2000
Belgium: 1950–2000	Denmark: 1950–2000	Brazil: 1950–2000	Burkina Faso: 1959–2000	Hong Kong: 1960–2000	Egypt: 1950–2000
Canada: 1950–2000	Finland: 1950–2000	Chile: 1951–2000	Burundi: 1960–2000	Indonesia: 1960–2000	India: 1950–2000
Denmark: 1950–2000	France: 1950–2000	Colombia: 1950–2000	Cameroon: 1960–2000	Japan: 1950–2000	Israel: 1950–2000
Finland: 1950–2000	Germany: 1970–2000	Costa Rica: 1950–2000	Central African Republic: 1960–1998	Korea (Republic): 1953–2000	Jordan: 1954–2000
France: 1950–2000	Greece: 1951–2000	Dominican Republic: 1951–2000	Congo, Democratic Republic: 1950–1997	Malaysia: 1955–2000	Morocco: 1950–2000
Germany: 1970–2000	Italy: 1950–2000	Ecuador: 1951–2000	Cote d'Ivoire: 1960–2000	New Zealand: 1950–2000	Nepal: 1960–2000
Italy: 1950–2000	Netherlands: 1950–2000	El Salvador: 1950–2000	Ethiopia: 1950–2000	Papua New Guinea: 1960–1999	Pakistan: 1950–2000
Japan: 1950–2000	Norway: 1950–2000	Guatemala: 1950–2000	Ghana: 1955–2000	Philippines: 1950–2000	Sri Lanka: 1950–2000
Netherlands: 1950–2000	Portugal: 1950–2000	Guyana: 1950–1999	Guinea: 1959–2000	Singapore: 1960–1996	Syria: 1960–2000
New Zealand: 1950–2000	Spain: 1950–2000	Honduras: 1950–2000	Guinea–Bissau: 1960–2000	Taiwan: 1951–1998	Tunisia: 1961–2000
Norway: 1950–2000	Sweden: 1951–2000	Jamaica: 1953–2000	Kenya: 1950–2000	Thailand: 1950–2000	USA: 1950–2000
Spain: 1950–2000	Switzerland: 1950–2000	Mexico: 1950–2000	Lesotho: 1960–2000		
Sweden: 1951–2000	United Kingdom: 1950–2000	Panama: 1950–2000	Madagascar: 1960–2000		
Switzerland: 1950–2000		Paraguay: 1951–2000	Malawi: 1954–2000		
United Kingdom: 1950–2000		Peru: 1950–2000	Mali: 1960–2000		
USA: 1950–2000		Uruguay: 1950–2000	Mauritania: 1960–1999		
			Mauritius: 1950–2000		
			Mozambique: 1960–2000		
			Namibia: 1960–1999		
			Niger: 1960–2000		
			Rwanda:		

Table 1. (*Continued*)

OECD (18)	Europe (15)	Latin America and Caribbean (18)	Sub-Saharan Africa (31)	East Asia and Pacific (13)	Additional countries not in regional subsamples (13)
			1960–2000 Senegal: 1960–2000 Sierra Leone: 1961–1996 South Africa: 1950–2000 Tanzania: 1960–2000 Togo: 1960–2000 Uganda: 1950–2000 Zambia: 1955–2000 Zimbabwe: 1954– 2000		

the issue of Granger causality between output and investment in physical capital by means of fixed effects regressions of (i) five-year output growth rates on their own lags and on five-year averages of the ratio of physical capital investment to GDP lagged by at least one period and (ii) of five-year averages of the ratio of physical capital investment to GDP on their own lags and on five-year output growth rates lagged by at least one period. Output growth then is Granger causal for the investment-output ratio if the coefficients on lagged output growth in the equation for the investment-output ratio are not jointly insignificant, but the coefficients on the lagged investment-output ratio in the output growth equation are jointly insignificant. Replicating this simple approach for our data set, we obtain the same main qualitative finding that Blomström et al. (1996) did: Output growth is Granger causal for the investment-output ratio, but not vice versa.[20] However, while this is a rather strong finding, it appears problematic to put much weight on it, as it (i) ignores (the possibility of) long-run relations between output and physical capital investment, (ii) involves incredible pooling restrictions by neglecting cross-country heterogeneity of output and investment *dynamics*, and (iii) neglects cross-country dependencies of shocks to the output growth and investment processes.

---

[20] As the results are qualitatively the same as in Blomström et al. (1996), we do not report them here in more detail. The regression tables are available upon request.

6.3. Estimation and hypothesis testing results

We thus turn to our PVAR/PVECM framework of Sections 2 to 5, that addresses the shortcomings of Blomström et al. (1996) and allows to test for an economically more plausible form of a causal relation between output and investment in physical capital than is implied by Granger causality: The notion of weak exogeneity does not require the absence of both a bidirectional short- and long-run feedback mechanism, but only involves restrictions on the long run. To be precise, investment in physical capital is weakly exogenous (long-run forcing) for output if changes in the long-run relation between output and investment do not affect the short-run dynamics of investment in physical capital. Importantly, if such long-run causality holds this would not rule out short-run changes in output implying short-run changes in investment in physical capital. Long-run forcing type causality is therefore a notably weaker restriction than Granger causality. One of the advantages of our PVAR/PVECM framework is that it readily allows to test for such long-run causality. Denoting by $\ln y_{it}$ the logarithm of GDP per capita and by $\ln iv_{it}$ the logarithm of per capita investment in physical capital, we estimate the following models with our PVAR/PVECM framework:

- a PVEC model for the case where neither output nor investment is long-run forcing for the other variable:

$$
\begin{pmatrix} \Delta \ln y_{it} \\ \Delta \ln iv_{it} \end{pmatrix} = a_i + \Pi_{ai} \begin{pmatrix} \ln y_{i,t-1} \\ \ln iv_{i,t-1} \\ t-1 \end{pmatrix} + \sum_{k=1}^{p_i-1} \Gamma_{ik} \begin{pmatrix} \Delta \ln y_{i,t-p_i+1} \\ \Delta \ln iv_{i,t-p_i+1} \end{pmatrix} + u_{it},
$$

(37)

- two restricted PVEC models for the case where output (investment) is long-run forcing for investment (output):[21]

$$
\Delta \ln y_{it} = b_i + \pi_{yi} \begin{pmatrix} \ln y_{i,t-1} \\ \ln iv_{i,t-1} \\ t-1 \end{pmatrix} + \theta_i \Delta \ln iv_{it} + \sum_{k=1}^{p_i-1} \gamma_{yik} \begin{pmatrix} \Delta \ln y_{i,t-k} \\ \Delta \ln iv_{i,t-k} \end{pmatrix} + u_{yit},
$$

and

$$
\Delta \ln iv_{it} = c_i + \pi_{xi} \begin{pmatrix} \ln y_{i,t-1} \\ \ln iv_{i,t-1} \\ t-1 \end{pmatrix} + \theta_i \Delta \ln y_{it} + \sum_{k=1}^{p_i-1} \gamma_{xik} \begin{pmatrix} \Delta \ln y_{i,t-k} \\ \Delta \ln iv_{i,t-k} \end{pmatrix} + u_{xit}.
$$

---

[21] As noted in Section 2, the resultant model may also be called a PVARDL model.

Note that all three models allow for a cross-section specific linear trend coefficient in the cointegrating vector(s). If this coefficient was significant, output and investment are not co-trended. The following results are all based on dynamic specifications where the lag order is chosen using the Schwarz Bayesian Information Criterion (SBC), with a maximum lag order of 3, which seems conservative with annual data, but is also suggested by parsimony considerations. While for space considerations we do not report results based on the Akaike Information Criterion (AIC) model selection criterion, we have checked that our results are qualitatively robust to AIC-based model selection.

As stressed in Sections 4 and 5.2, all estimation and inference in the PVAR/PVECM framework can be crucially affected if cross-sectional dependence of the error terms is not addressed. We therefore begin the empirical analysis by testing for cross-sectional dependence in the PVEC model (4) (under initially unrestricted rank) if the u_{it}'s in the estimation are treated as cross-sectionally independent. Table 2 contains the resultant values of the CD-statistic of Equation (32) for the *full sample* and various subsamples. The results may be summarized as follows. The errors of the output growth and investment growth equations show strong signs of being cross-sectionally dependent across all samples; in addition, cross-equational cross-section dependence cannot be refuted either for all samples reported in Table 2. The *p*-values (not reported in Table 2) are virtually zero for all cases reported in Table 2. The three test statistics for the *full sample*, as well as the OECD and European countries' samples are large compared to the other subsamples, suggesting that the OECD and European countries are more integrated than those in Latin America and the Caribbean and as well as those in East Asia and the Pacific, in particular.

Table 2. **Test for cross-sectional dependence (H_0: cross-sectional independence)**

	CD_{11}	CD_{22}	CD_{12}
Full sample (90 countries)	35.42	81.11	−35.79
18 OECD countries	24.14	27.60	25.59
15 European countries	24.65	22.30	23.64
18 Latin American and Caribbean countries	7.26	9.63	6.56
31 Sub-Saharan African countries	36.82	8.29	−15.83
13 East Asian and Pacific countries	6.81	10.25	5.98

Notes: CD_{11}, CD_{22}, and CD_{12} denote the test statistic for the output per capita equation, the test statistic for the investment per capita equation and the cross-output per capita–investment per capita test statistic, respectively. The test statistics follow a standard normal distribution; see Section 5.2.

Michael Binder and Susanne Bröck

It is imperative, therefore, to reflect cross-sectional dependence in the PVAR/PVEC models: we do so invoking the CEA and TS-CEA approaches detailed in Section 4. How well do these approaches capture the cross-sectional dependencies? While the CD test is not applicable anymore after estimation through CEA or TS-CEA, the average cross-correlations are still informative. We analyze this in terms of average cross-correlation coefficients reported in Table 3. Clearly, the average cross-sectional correlations of the model error terms tend to decrease pronouncedly under our TS-CEA procedure, which appears effective, and more so than the CEA procedure. While for the European countries subsample the evidence points toward sources of cross-sectional dependence that go beyond what correlated effects augmentation can capture, the average cross-sectional correlations seem surprisingly close to zero under the TS-CEA procedure for all other subsamples as well as the full sample. As we know from the Monte Carlo simulations in Bröck (2008) that hypothesis tests are considerably size-distorted and coefficient

Table 3. *Effectiveness of correlated effects augmentation: average cross-sectional correlations*

		Raw data (level)	Raw data (first difference)	Uncorrelated errors	Errors under CEA	Errors under TS-CEA
Full sample	ρ_y	0.43	0.06	0.09	−0.01	0.04
	ρ_{inv}	0.28	0.04	0.20	0.48	0.02
	$\rho_{y,inv}$	0.34	0.04	−0.09	0.01	0.03
OECD	ρ_y	0.95	0.31	0.29	0.06	0.08
	ρ_{inv}	0.86	0.27	0.33	0.23	0.06
	$\rho_{y,inv}$	0.88	0.27	0.31	0.10	0.08
Europe	ρ_y	0.95	0.37	0.35	0.10	0.18
	ρ_{inv}	0.87	0.31	0.32	0.05	0.15
	$\rho_{y,inv}$	0.86	0.32	0.34	0.08	0.18
Latin America	ρ_y	0.71	0.11	0.09	0.01	−0.01
and Caribbean	ρ_{inv}	0.33	0.12	0.11	0.12	−0.00
	$\rho_{y,inv}$	0.40	0.10	0.08	−0.11	0.01
Sub-Saharan	ρ_y	0.08	0.04	0.32	0.13	−0.00
Africa	ρ_{inv}	0.06	0.01	0.33	0.10	−0.01
	$\rho_{y,inv}$	0.06	0.01	0.32	−0.14	−0.00
East Asia and	ρ_y	0.87	0.11	0.12	−0.02	0.05
Pacific	ρ_{inv}	0.76	0.12	0.18	0.45	0.01
	$\rho_{y,inv}$	0.80	0.10	0.10	0.18	0.03

Notes: The average cross-correlation of the output (investment) equation is denoted by ρ_y (ρ_{inv}). The average cross-output–investment correlation is denoted by $\rho_{y,inv}$.

estimates are biased in the PVAR/PVECM framework if cross-sectional dependence is spuriously ignored, as there is strong evidence from the CD tests that cross-sectional dependence is present, and as the CEA and even more so the TS-CEA approaches appear remarkably effective at removing the cross-sectional dependence observed, in the remainder of this section we focus on reporting results under the CEA and TS-CEA specifications.

A PVECM is appropriate if the variables under consideration are integrated of order one. Table 4 summarizes the results for the unit root tests of Section 5.1: The presence of a unit root in the output process cannot be rejected for the full sample as well as all subsamples, at least at a significance level of 5%. The evidence in favor of a unit root in the investment series is weak: Under a 10% significance level, the unit root null finds support only for the Latin American and Caribbean as well as the East Asian and Pacific country groupings. This is rather surprising, and at the same time, it is beyond the scope of this chapter to reconcile this panel evidence with the wealth of evidence in the time-series literature that investment in physical capital for industrial country data exhibits a unit root. Given that at times model specification in a vector error correction model should balance immediate statistical evidence with priors from other forms of data analysis (see, e.g., the seminal paper by King, Plosser, Stock, & Watson, 1991), we proceed by modelling output and investment in physical capital within a PVECM (rather than a PVAR in levels of these variables).

Table 5 reports cointegration test results based on the $\lambda_{CEA}(T, N)$ and $\lambda_{TS-CEA}(T, N)$ statistics discussed in Section 5.3. The test statistics show strong, perhaps even surprisingly strong, support for a cointegration rank of one, that is, a balanced growth path relationship between output and investment in physical capital, that is, $\ln y_{it} / \ln iv_{it}$ being a mean-reverting process. All statistics provide evidence in favor of a common cointegrating rank of one with one exception, for the East Asian and Pacific countries

Table 4.   Panel unit root test (H$_0$: unit root present)

	Output per capita	Investment per capita
Full sample (90 countries)	−2.19 [0.84]	−2.73 [0.00]
18 OECD Countries	−2.70 [0.07]	−3.45 [0.00]
15 European countries	−2.69 [0.09]	−3.50 [0.00]
18 Latin American and Caribbean countries	−2.25 [0.63]	−2.75 [0.05]
31 Sub-Saharan African countries	−2.66 [0.05]	−2.76 [0.01]
13 East Asian and Pacific countries	−2.42 [0.37]	−2.86 [0.03]

Notes: *p*-values reported in square brackets. The test statistic is computed according to Equation (31).

Michael Binder and Susanne Bröck

Table 5.   Panel cointegration tests (trace-statistics for cointegration rank r)

	H_0: $r = 0$ vs. H_1: $r = 2$	
	CEA	TS-CEA
Full sample (90 countries)	26.65 [0.03]	30.39 [0.00]
18 OECD countries	30.02 [0.01]	32.89 [0.00]
15 European countries	30.39 [0.01]	32.99 [0.00]
18 Latin American and Caribbean countries	32.39 [0.00]	27.65 [0.00]
31 Sub-Saharan African countries	26.46 [0.04]	26.16 [0.00]
13 East Asian and Pacific countries	27.03 [0.11]	33.95 [0.00]

	H_0: $r \leq 1$ vs. H_1: $r = 2$	
	CEA	TS-CEA
Full sample (90 countries)	6.26 [0.98]	6.90 [0.72]
18 OECD countries	6.77 [0.72]	5.57 [0.68]
15 European countries	7.94 [0.37]	6.93 [0.28]
18 Latin American and Caribbean countries	8.82 [0.21]	4.72 [0.99]
31 Sub-Saharan African countries	7.67 [0.41]	6.21 [0.87]
13 East Asian and Pacific countries	6.24 [0.85]	8.91 [0.01]

Note: *p*-values reported in square brackets.

under the CEA procedure. On these grounds, significant support is obtained for neoclassical growth theory building on a stationary and ergodic long-run relationship between output and physical capital. This evidence also suggests that investment in physical capital is an important correlate of long-run output levels.

Table 6 further expands on this point by reporting our estimated long-run elasticity of output per capita with respect to changes in per capita physical capital investment. With one exception, the estimates all feature the expected sign: An increase in investment per capita leads to an increase in output per capita. Only the MG estimates for the Latin American and Caribbean countries exhibit a positive sign, in light of all other estimates reported in Table 6 surely a negligible finding. For the PMG TS-CEA case, the estimated elasticities vary between 49% and 85%, in the *full sample* amounting to 65%. A couple of additional aspects of the results in Table 6 are worth noting: The MG estimates, specifically under TS-CEA, are a good bit more volatile than the PMG estimates, reflecting sensitivity to country-specific outliers. The PMG estimates, in contrast, exhibit much more limited variation across subsamples, reflecting a low degree of sensitivity to outliers. Finally, for Table 6, the PMG estimates of the long-run coefficients, PMG_{CEA} and PMG_{TS-CEA}, are similar in magnitude, but the standard errors are larger for the TS-CEA than the CEA estimation

Table 6. Panel VECM long-run coefficient on investment per capita

	Mean group estimation	
	CEA	TS-CEA
Full sample (90 countries)	−0.49 (0.27)	−0.46 (0.12)
18 OECD countries	−0.40 (0.19)	−0.91 (0.27)
15 European countries	−0.31 (0.15)	−1.51 (0.62)
18 Latin American and Caribbean countries	0.29 (0.73)	0.69 (0.73)
31 Sub-Saharan African countries	−0.22 (0.17)	−0.42 (0.37)
13 east asian and pacific countries	−0.37 (0.21)	−0.67 (0.19)
	Pooled mean group estimation	
	CEA	TS-CEA
Full sample (90 countries)	−0.63 (0.01)	−0.65 (0.11)
18 OECD countries	−0.58 (0.04)	−0.63 (0.05)
15 European countries	−0.59 (0.07)	−0.85 (0.08)
18 Latin American and Caribbean countries	−0.74 (0.07)	−0.66 (0.12)
31 Sub-Saharan African countries	−0.40 (0.06)	−0.49 (0.13)
13 East Asian and Pacific countries	−0.74 (0.11)	−0.60 (0.05)

Note: Standard errors reported in round brackets.

procedure for the *full sample* and almost all reported subsamples. In general, it thus appears useful to consider both CEA and TS-CEA-based estimation results, and make assessments taking into account the whole resultant set of findings. None of the results in Table 6 shed evidence, though, on the key economic question addressed in this chapter, namely, as to whether investment in physical capital is an important causal determinant of long-run output, whether the causality may be reverse, or whether there is no unidirectional causality.

We thus move to Table 7 presenting our results for the long-run forcing/ weak exogeneity restriction detailed in Section 5.5. One glance at the *p*-values reported in Table 7 makes clear that there is no evidence whatsoever that investment in physical capital would be long-run forcing (causal) for output or, reversely, output would be long-run forcing (causal) for investment. Recalling that the long-run forcing restriction is a weaker restriction than Granger causality, our evidence thus strongly refutes any notion of a causal relationship between output and investment in physical capital. In contrast, we find overwhelming evidence for a feedback relation between output and investment in physical capital in both the short run and the long run. Our findings are thus in stark contrast to the widely cited findings of Blomström et al. (1996). This finding in our perspective illustrates how critical a difference it can make in empirical work with cross-country panel models to give careful consideration both to model

Table 7.   Likelihood-ratio test for long-run exogeneity

	Output	
	CEA	TS-CEA
Full sample (90 countries)	430.64 [0.00]	455.22 [0.00]
18 OECD countries	113.75 [0.00]	89.95 [0.00]
15 European countries	85.01 [0.00]	71.27 [0.00]
18 Latin American and Caribbean countries	57.79 [0.00]	91.45 [0.00]
31 Sub-Saharan African countries	178.90 [0.00]	194.54 [0.00]
13 East Asian and Pacific countries	37.83 [0.00]	39.98 [0.00]

	Investment	
	CEA	TS-CEA
Full sample (90 countries)	872.31 [0.00]	504.97 [0.00]
18 OECD Countries	250.70 [0.00]	109.85 [0.00]
15 European countries	211.05 [0.00]	88.98 [0.00]
18 Latin American and Caribbean countries	240.59 [0.00]	122.97 [0.00]
31 Sub-Saharan African countries	205.24 [0.00]	148.91 [0.00]
13 East Asian and Pacific countries	141.10 [0.00]	76.42 [0.00]

Note: p-values reported in square brackets.

specification and to estimation and inference procedures used. Our findings also suggest a reconciliation between a reduced-form-based econometric approach to the empirical study of economic growth and basic tenets of general equilibrium neoclassical growth models in which both output and investment in physical capital are endogenous.

The results for tests for long-run parameter homogeneity as discussed in Section 5.4 are inconclusive. Table 8 documents that the Hausman test statistics are in favor of the PMG estimator imposing long-run homogeneity, but that the LR test statistics reject such long-run parameter homogeneity. This finding is reminiscent of analogous findings in the single-equation panel ARDL literature, and suggests that more work is needed to develop hypothesis testing procedures for partial parameter homogeneity in the PVAR/PVECM framework.

We finally turn to analyzing the full dynamic interaction between output and investment in physical capital using impulse responses as discussed in Section 5.6.[22] Given our findings above regarding the absence of even

---

[22] For a model stability check, we compute persistence profiles of a system-wide shock in all regional groups: If β indeed describes long-run relationships, the persistence profiles need to converge to zero as the time horizon h increases. All considered regions passed this test as the system-wide shock dies out after a finite time horizon. We do not report the results here, but they are available from the authors on request.

Table 8.   *Likelihood-ratio and Hausman test for long-run coefficient homogeneity*

	Hausman test	
	CEA	TS-CEA
Full sample (90 countries)	0.26 [0.61]	2.48 [0.11]
18 OECD countries	0.97 [0.33]	1.06 [0.30]
15 European countries	4.79 [0.03]	1.23 [0.27]
18 Latin American and Caribbean countries	2.01 [0.16]	3.45 [0.06]
31 Sub-Saharan African countries	1.23 [0.27]	0.03 [0.86]
13 East Asian and Pacific countries	4.43 [0.04]	0.10 [0.75]
	LR test	
	CEA	TS-CEA
Full Sample (90 countries)	402.37 [0.00]	321.16 [0.00]
18 OECD countries	57.17 [0.00]	56.92 [0.00]
15 European countries	53.40 [0.00]	45.45 [0.00]
18 Latin American and Caribbean countries	69.17 [0.00]	42.57 [0.00]
31 Sub-Saharan African countries	131.89 [0.00]	103.80 [0.00]
13 East Asian and Pacific countries	68.08 [0.00]	42.24 [0.00]

Note: *p*-values reported in square brackets.

long-run causality between output and physical capital investment, any Cholesky decomposition-based impulse response analysis would clearly be deficient even in terms of within-country identification. Even if such Cholesky-based identification was feasible within countries, it would seem heroic to pursue across countries, for a panel featuring up to 90 countries, and the interest being in impulse responses to shocks in all of these countries. We therefore compare generalized impulse responses, computed as the averages of the individual country impulse responses. To preserve space, we do not report the results based on MG estimation, but these are available on request. Tables 9 to 14 and Figures 1 to 6 document that the size of feedback from output growth to investment growth under both CEA and TS-CEA tends to strongly dominate the size of feedback from investment growth to output growth: Cumulated (long-run) effects of innovations to output growth tend to be at least as large for investment growth as for output growth, whereas cumulated (long-run) effects of innovations to investment growth tend to be at least twice as large for investment growth as for output growth. In this sense, there is much more important feedback from output growth to the rate of investment in physical capital than vice versa. These results thus suggest that while neither the causality arguments of DeLong and Summers (1991) nor those of Carroll and Weil (1994) and Blomström et al. (1996) find support at the broad cross-country level, the quantitatively stronger relationship is the

Table 9.   Cumulative effects of one-standard deviation shocks: full sample (90 countries)

Cumulative effects of	on	Time horizon (years)				
		1	5	10	25	∞
		CEA				
A shock to						
Output	Output growth	4.5% (0.2%)	4.1% (0.2%)	4.1% (0.2%)	4.1% (0.2%)	4.1% (0.2%)
Equation	Investment growth	6.6% (0.5%)	6.4% (0.4%)	6.4% (0.4%)	6.4% (0.4%)	6.4% (0.4%)
	Relative effect[a]	0.69	0.64	0.64	0.63	0.63
Investment	Output growth	2.2% (0.2%)	2.7% (0.2%)	2.7% (0.3%)	2.8% (0.3%)	2.8% (0.3%)
Equation	Investment growth	12.1% (0.6%)	5.9% (0.5%)	4.9% (0.4%)	4.6% (0.4%)	4.5% (0.4%)
	Relative effect[a]	0.18	0.45	0.56	0.61	0.62
		TS-CEA				
A shock to						
Output	Output growth	4.9% (0.2%)	4.6% (0.2%)	4.6% (0.2%)	4.6% (0.2%)	5.4% (0.5%)
Equation	Investment growth	7.2% (0.6%)	7.2% (0.4%)	7.2% (0.4%)	7.2% (0.4%)	8.3% (0.7%)
	Relative effect[a]	0.68	0.63	0.64	0.64	0.65
Investment	Output growth	2.4% (0.2%)	3.4% (0.2%)	3.9% (0.3%)	4.3% (0.3%)	4.8% (1.1%)
Equation	Investment growth	15.3% (0.7%)	9.7% (0.7%)	8.2% (0.6%)	7.5% (0.6%)	7.8% (1.6%)
	Relative effect[†]	0.16	0.35	0.48	0.57	0.62

Notes: The model is estimated assuming long-run parameter homogeneity (PMG). Standard errors are reported in round brackets.
[a]Relative change of output growth to investment growth.

Table 10.   Cumulative effects of one-standard deviation shocks: 18 OECD countries

Cumulative effects of	on	Time horizon (years)				
		1	5	10	25	∞
		CEA				
A shock to						
Output	Output growth	1.8% (0.2%)	1.5% (0.2%)	1.5% (0.2%)	1.5% (0.2%)	1.5% (0.2%)
Equation	Investment growth	4.3% (0.3%)	2.8% (0.3%)	2.7% (0.3%)	2.7% (0.3%)	2.7% (0.3%)
	Relative effect	0.43	0.55	0.56	0.56	0.57
Investment	Output growth	1.3% (0.2%)	0.9% (0.2%)	0.9% (0.2%)	0.9% (0.2%)	0.9% (0.2%)
Equation	Investment growth	4.2% (0.4%)	1.7% (0.4%)	1.6% (0.4%)	1.6% (0.4%)	1.6% (0.4%)
	Relative effect	0.32	0.52	0.54	0.55	0.55
		TS-CEA				
A shock to						
Output	Output growth	2.4% (0.2%)	2.5% (0.3%)	2.7% (0.4%)	2.7% (0.4%)	3.2% (0.6%)
Equation	Investment growth	6.6% (0.4%)	5.3% (0.6%)	5.0% (0.7%)	5.0% (0.8%)	5.1% (0.9%)
	Relative effect	0.37	0.48	0.54	0.60	0.63
Investment	Output growth	2.1% (0.2%)	2.1% (0.4%)	2.1% (0.5%)	2.3% (0.5%)	3.1% (0.8%)
Equation	Investment growth	7.1% (0.4%)	5.2% (0.8%)	5.2% (0.9%)	4.6% (1.0%)	4.9% (1.2%)
	Relative effect	0.29	0.41	0.49	0.58	0.63

Note: See Notes to Table 8.

Table 11.   Cumulative effects of one-standard deviation shocks: 15 European countries

Cumulative effects of	on	Time horizon (years)				
		1	5	10	25	∞
		CEA				
A Shock to						
Output	Output growth	1.8% (0.2%)	1.5% (0.2%)	1.5% (0.2%)	1.5% (0.2%)	1.5% (0.2%)
Equation	Investment growth	4.2% (0.4%)	2.7% (0.4%)	2.6% (0.3%)	2.5% (0.4%)	2.5% (0.4%)
	Relative effect	0.43	0.57	0.59	0.59	0.59
Investment	Output growth	1.2% (0.2%)	0.8% (0.2%)	0.8% (0.2%)	0.8% (0.2%)	0.8% (0.2%)
Equation	Investment growth	4.2% (0.5%)	1.6% (0.4%)	1.4% (0.4%)	1.3% (0.4%)	1.3% (0.4%)
	Relative effect	0.30	0.51	0.58	0.59	0.59
		TS-CEA				
A shock to						
Output	Output growth	2.6% (0.2%)	2.5% (0.3%)	2.6% (0.4%)	2.8% (0.5%)	2.7% (1.2%)
Equation	Investment growth	7.0% (0.5%)	5.1% (0.6%)	4.4% (0.7%)	4.0% (0.8%)	3.2% (1.4%)
	Relative effect	0.37	0.49	0.59	0.70	0.84
Investment	Output growth	2.1% (0.2%)	2.1% (0.3%)	2.3% (0.3%)	2.5% (0.7%)	2.3% (1.6%)
Equation	Investment growth	7.8% (0.6%)	5.3% (0.8%)	4.4% (0.9%)	3.9% (1.0%)	2.7% (1.8%)
	Relative effect	0.27	0.40	0.51	0.65	0.84

Note: See Notes to Table 9.

Table 12.   Cumulative effects of one–standard deviation shocks: 18 Latin American and Caribbean countries

Cumulative effects of	on	Time horizon (years)				
		1	5	10	25	∞
		CEA				
A shock to						
Output	Output growth	4.1% (0.3%)	4.0% (0.3%)	4.0% (0.3%)	4.0% (0.3%)	4.0% (0.3%)
Equation	Investment growth	6.5% (0.8%)	5.3% (0.4%)	5.4% (0.4%)	5.5% (0.4%)	5.5% (0.4%)
	Relative effect	0.63	0.76	0.74	0.74	0.74
Investment	Output growth	2.1% (0.3%)	2.5% (0.4%)	2.5% (0.4%)	2.5% (0.4%)	2.5% (0.4%)
Equation	Investment growth	10.1% (1.2%)	4.1% (0.9%)	3.3% (0.5%)	3.4% (0.6%)	3.4% (0.6%)
	Relative effect	0.20	0.60	0.76	0.74	0.74
		TS-CEA				
A shock to						
Output	Output growth	4.3% (0.3%)	4.3% (0.3%)	4.3% (0.3%)	4.3% (0.3%)	4.3% (0.3%)
Equation	Investment growth	7.6% (1.1%)	6.5% (0.5%)	6.4% (0.5%)	6.4% (0.5%)	6.4% (0.5%)
	Relative effect	0.56	0.64	0.66	0.67	0.66
Investment	Output growth	2.4% (0.3%)	3.7% (0.4%)	3.9% (0.5%)	4.0% (0.5%)	4.0% (0.5%)
Equation	Investment growth	14.4% (1.2%)	6.8% (0.9%)	6.1% (0.8%)	6.1% (0.8%)	6.0% (0.7%)
	Relative effect	0.17	0.39	0.54	0.64	0.66

Note: See Notes to Table 9.

Table 13.   Cumulative effects of one-standard deviation shocks: 31 sub-Saharan countries

Cumulative effects of	on	Time horizon (years)				
		1	5	10	25	∞
		CEA				
A shock to						
Output	Output growth	5.5% (0.4%)	4.6% (0.4%)	4.5% (0.4%)	4.5% (0.4%)	4.5% (0.4%)
Equation	Investment growth	7.6% (1.3%)	10.6% (1.0%)	11.1% (1.0%)	11.2% (1.0%)	11.2% (1.0%)
	Relative effect	0.73	0.43	0.40	0.40	0.40
Investment	Output growth	2.6% (0.4%)	4.1% (0.4%)	4.3% (0.4%)	4.3% (0.4%)	4.3% (0.4%)
Equation	Investment growth	18.1% (1.1%)	12.0% (1.0%)	11.0% (1.0%)	10.8% (1.1%)	10.8% (1.1%)
	Relative effect	0.14	0.34	0.39	0.40	0.40
		TS-CEA				
A shock to						
Output	Output growth	5.9% (0.4%)	4.9% (0.4%)	4.6% (0.4%)	4.6% (0.4%)	4.6% (0.4%)
Equation	Investment growth	6.2% (1.3%)	8.8% (0.9%)	9.4% (0.9%)	9.6% (0.9%)	9.6% (0.9%)
	Relative effect	0.95	0.56	0.49	0.48	0.49
Investment	Output growth	2.3% (0.4%)	4.3% (0.4%)	4.8% (0.5%)	5.1% (0.5%)	5.2% (0.5%)
Equation	Investment growth	20.4% (1.2%)	13.2% (1.0%)	11.2% (1.0%)	10.5% (1.1%)	10.6% (1.1%)
	Relative effect	0.11	0.32	0.43	0.48	0.49

Note: See Notes to Table 9.

Table 14.   Cumulative effects of one-standard deviation shocks: 13 East Asian and Pacific countries

Cumulative effects of	on	Time horizon (years)				
		1	5	10	25	∞
		CEA				
A shock to						
Output	Output growth	3.8% (0.3%)	3.4% (0.3%)	3.4% (0.3%)	3.4% (0.3%)	3.4% (0.3%)
Equation	Investment growth	6.4% (0.9%)	4.8% (0.4%)	4.6% (0.4%)	4.6% (0.4%)	4.6% (0.4%)
	Relative effect	0.58	0.71	0.73	0.74	0.74
Investment	Output growth	2.0% (0.4%)	1.7% (0.5%)	1.6% (0.5%)	1.7% (0.5%)	1.7% (0.5%)
Equation	Investment growth	8.6% (0.6%)	2.8% (0.9%)	2.3% (0.7%)	2.2% (0.7%)	2.2% (0.7%)
	Relative effect	0.23	0.61	0.72	0.74	0.74
		TS-CEA				
A shock to						
Output	Output growth	4.6% (0.4%)	4.7% (0.4%)	5.0% (0.5%)	5.2% (0.6%)	5.3% (0.7%)
Equation	Investment growth	9.2% (1.7%)	9.6% (1.1%)	9.0% (1.1%)	8.8% (1.2%)	8.8% (1.1%)
	Relative effect	0.50	0.49	0.56	0.59	0.60
Investment	Output growth	2.7% (0.4%)	3.5% (0.7%)	3.9% (0.8%)	4.3% (0.9%)	4.5% (1.0%)
Equation	Investment growth	12.9% (1.2%)	7.9% (1.9%)	7.8% (1.6%)	7.4% (1.6%)	7.4% (1.6%)
	Relative effect	0.21	0.44	0.50	0.59	0.60

Note: See Notes to Table 9.

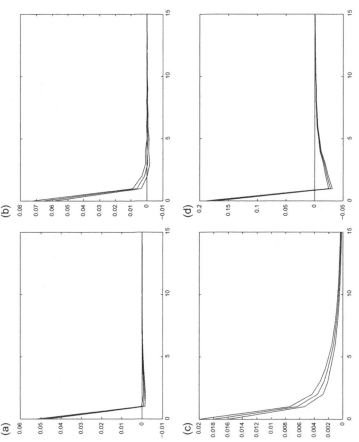

Fig. 1.   Impulse responses for the full sample: Effects of a one-standard deviation shock to (a) output equation on output growth, (b) investment equation on investment growth, (c) investment equation on output growth, and (d) investment equation on investment growth. Notes: The impulse responses and standard error bands plotted are based on the PMG TS-CEA estimation results. Impulse responses based on PMG CEA as well as the CEA and TS-CEA methodologies combined with MG are available from the authors upon request.

Michael Binder and Susanne Bröck

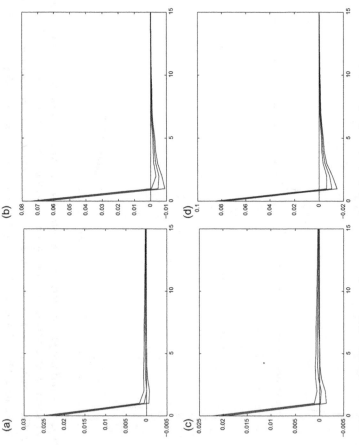

Fig. 2. Impulse responses for the OECD: Effects of a one-standard deviation shock to (a) output equation on output growth, (b) investment equation on investment growth (c), (c) investment equation on output growth, and (d) investment equation on investment growth. Notes: See Notes to Figure 1.

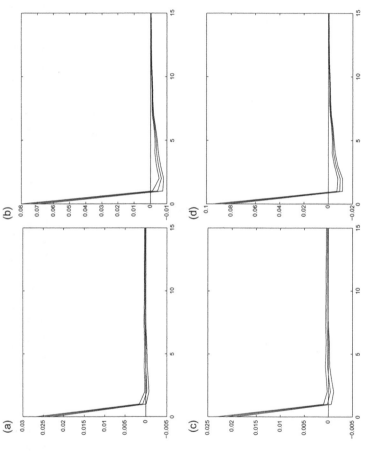

Fig. 3. Impulse responses for Europe: Effects of a one-standard deviation shock to (a) output equation on output growth, (b) investment equation on investment growth, (c) investment equation on output growth, and (d) investment equation on investment growth. Notes: See Notes to Figure 1.

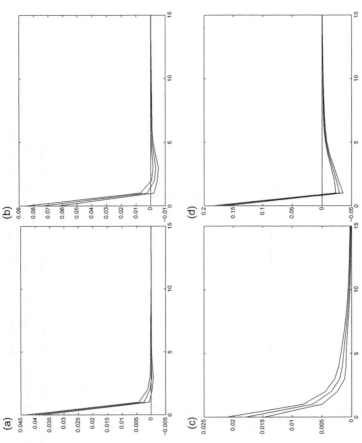

Fig. 4. Impulse responses for the Latin American and Caribbean countries: Effects of a one-standard deviation shock to (a) output equation on output growth, (b) investment equation on investment growth, (c) investment equation on output growth, and (d) investment equation on investment growth. Notes: See Notes to Figure 1.

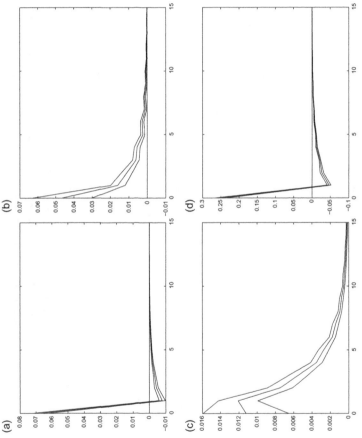

Fig. 5. Impulse responses for the Sub-Saharan African countries: Effects of a one-standard deviation shock to (a) output equation on output growth, (b) investment equation on investment growth, (c) investment equation on output growth, and (d) investment equation on investment growth. Notes: See Notes to Figure 1.

Michael Binder and Susanne Bröck

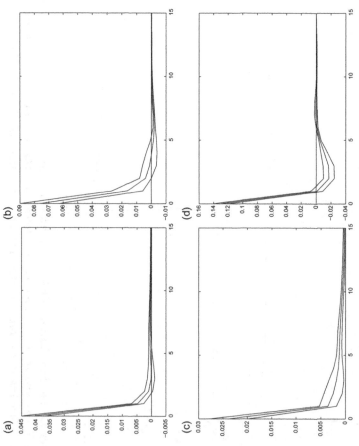

Fig. 6. Impulse responses for the East Asian and Pacific countries: Effects of a one-standard deviation shock to (a) output equation on output growth, (b) investment equation on investment growth, (c) investment equation on output growth, and (d) investment equation on investment growth. Notes: See Notes to Figure 1.

feedback from output to investment in physical capital. Our findings in this respect support the line of reasoning that the search for the determinants of long-run output levels and growth rates must look beyond the process of capital accumulation that traditionally has been the core of development growth modelling.

7. Conclusion

This chapter has advanced a PVAR/PVECM framework for purposes of reexamining the sources and determinants of cross-country variations in macroeconomic performance using large cross-country data sets. The widely cited findings of Blomström et al. (1996) focusing on the role of investment in physical capital for a country's macroeconomic performance and suggesting causality from output to investment in physical capital, but not vice versa, are problematic as they ignore possible long-run relationships between output and investment, do not explicitly separate between long- and short-run dynamics, neglect cross-country heterogeneity of (at least) the short-run dynamics, and disregard cross-sectional dependence. The PVAR/PVECM framework we have proposed captures the simultaneity of the potential determinants of cross-country variations in macroeconomic performance and carefully separates short- from long-run dynamics. Furthermore, our PVAR/PVECM framework captures cross-country dynamic heterogeneity and cross-sectional dependence.

We have used our PVAR/PVECM framework in this chapter to reexamine the dynamic interaction between investment in physical capital and output growth. Our empirical findings provide strong support for a long-run balanced growth relationship between output and investment in physical capital that is in line with neoclassical growth theory. At the same time, the notion that there would be even a *long-run* causal relation between investment in physical capital and output (or vice versa) is strongly refuted by our evidence. Finally, our evidence suggests that the size of the feedback from output growth to investment growth tends to strongly dominate the size of the feedback from investment growth to output growth.

Perhaps most importantly for future avenues for research on empirical work using the PVAR/PVECM framework is the development of methods to deal with more than bivariate settings when confronted with the (limited) number of time-series observations available in many cross-country development data sets. Such further research would help moving forward in identifying (causal) determinants of output growth among the large number of candidate variables that have by now been suggested in the empirical growth literature.

Acknowledgments

We are grateful to seminar and conference participants at Cambridge University, the European Commission, Goethe University Frankfurt, New School University, St. Gallen University, and Würzburg University for helpful comments on earlier versions of this chapter. We are also grateful to Georgios Georgiadis for his assistance in preparing this final version of the chapter.

References

Attanasio, O. P., Picci, L., & Scorcu, A. (2000). Saving, growth, and investment: A macroeconomic analysis using a panel of countries. *Review of Economics and Statistics, 82*, 182–211.

Barro, R. J. (1991). Economic growth in a cross section of countries. *Quarterly Journal of Economics, 106*, 407–443.

Barro, R. J. (1997). *Determinants of economic growth: A cross-country empirical study*. Cambridge, MA: MIT Press.

Bils, M., & Klenow, P. J. (2000). Does schooling cause growth or the other way around? *American Economic Review, 90*, 1160–1183.

Binder, M., Chen Q., & Zhang, X. (2010). *On the effects of monetary policy shocks on exchange rates*. CESifo Working Paper Series No. 3162.

Binder, M., Georgiadis, G. (2011). *Determinants of human development: Capturing the role of institutions*. CESifo Working Paper Series No. 3397.

Binder, M., Hsiao, C., & Pesaran, M. H. (2005). Estimation and inference in short panel vector autoregressions with unit roots and cointegration. *Econometric Theory, 21*, 795–837.

Blomström, M., Lipsey, R. E., & Zejan, M. (1996). Is fixed investment the key to economic growth? *Quarterly Journal of Economics, 111*, 269–276.

Bond, K. S., Leblebicioglu, A., Schiantarelli, F. (2007). *Capital accumulation and growth: A new look at the empirical evidence*. Mimeo, Nuffield College, Oxford.

Boswijk, H. P. (1995). *Identifiability of cointegrated systems*. Mimeo, Tinbergen Institute.

Boswijk, H. P., & Doornik, J. A. (2005). Distribution approximation for cointegration tests with stationary exogenous regressors. *Journal of Applied Econometrics, 20*, 797–810.

Bröck, S. (2008). *Estimation of and Hypothesis Testing in Heterogeneous PVAR Models under Cross-Sectional Dependence*. Doctoral Dissertation, Goethe University Frankfurt.

Carroll, C. D., & Weil, D. N. (1994). Saving and growth: A reinterpretation. *Carnegie-Rochester Conference Series on Public Policy, 40*, 133–192.

DeLong, J. B., & Summers, L. H. (1991). Equipment investment and economic growth. *Quarterly Journal of Economics*, *106*, 445–502.

Doornik, J. A. (1998). Approximations to the asymptotic distribution of cointegration tests. *Journal of Economic Surveys*, *12*, 573–593.

Durlauf, S. N. (2001). Manifesto for a growth econometrics. *Journal of Econometrics*, *100*, 65–69.

Durlauf, S. N., Johnson, P. A., & Temple, J. (2005). Growth econometrics. In P. Aghion & S. N. Durlauf (Eds.), *Handbook of Economic Growth* (pp. 555–677). Amsterdam: Elsevier.

Durlauf, S. N., & Quah, D. T. (1999). The new empirics of economic growth. In J. Taylor & M. Woodford (Eds.), *Handbook of macroeconomics* (Vol. 1, pp. 235–308). Amsterdam: Elsevier.

Eberhardt, M., & Teal, F. (2011). Econometrics for grumblers: A new look at the literature on cross-country growth empirics. *Journal of Economic Surveys*, *25*, 109–155.

Heston, A., Summers, R., Aten, B. (2002). Penn World Table Version 6.1, Center for International Comparisons at the University of Pennsylvania (CICUP).

Im, K. S., Pesaran, M. H., & Shin, Y. (2003). Testing for unit roots in heterogeneous panels. *Journal of Econometrics*, *115*, 53–74.

Islam, N. (2003). What have we learned from the convergence debate? *Journal of Economic Surveys*, *17*, 309–362.

Johansen, S. (1988). Statistical analysis of cointegrating vectors. *Journal of Economic Dynamics and Control*, *12*, 231–254.

Johansen, S. (1991). Estimation and hypothesis testing of cointegration vectors in Gaussian vector autoregressive models. *Econometrica*, *59*, 1551–1580.

Johansen, S. (1995). *Likelihood-based inferences in cointegrated vector autoregressive models*. Oxford: Oxford University Press.

King, R. G., & Levine, R. (1993). Finance and growth: Schumpeter might be right. *The Quarterly Journal of Economics*, *108*, 717–737.

King, R. G., Plosser, C. I., Stock, J. H., & Watson, M. W. (1991). Stochastic trends and economic fluctuations. *American Economic Review*, *81*, 819–840.

Larsson, R., Lyhagen, J., & Löthgren, M. (2001). Likelihood-based cointegration tests in heterogeneous panels. *Econometrics Journal*, *4*, 109–142.

Lütkepohl, H. (1993). *Introduction to multiple time series analysis* (2nd ed.). Berlin: Springer Verlag.

Mankiw, N. G., Romer, D., & Weil, D. N. (1992). A contribution to the empirics of economic growth. *The Quarterly Journal of Economics*, *107*, 407–437.

McGrattan, E. R., & Schmitz, J. A. (1999). Explaining cross-country income differences. In J. Taylor & M. Woodford (Eds.), *Handbook of Macroeconomics* (pp. 669–737). Amsterdam: North Holland.

Pagan, A. (1984). Econometric issues in the analysis of regressions with generated regressors. *International Economic Review, 25,* 221–247.

Pesaran, M. H. (2004). *General diagnostic tests for cross section dependence in panels.* CESifo Working Paper Series No. 1229.

Pesaran, M. H. (2006). Estimation and inference in large heterogeneous panels with a multifactor error structure. *Econometrica, 74,* 967–1012.

Pesaran, M. H. (2007). A simple panel unit root test in the presence of cross section dependence. *Journal of Applied Econometrics, 22,* 265–312.

Pesaran, M. H., Shin, Y., & R. Smith, J. (2000). Structural analysis of vector error correction models with Exogenous I(1) variables. *Journal of Econometrics, 97,* 293–343.

Pesaran, M. H., Shin, Y., & Smith, R. P. (1999). Pooled mean group estimation of dynamic heterogeneous panels. *Journal of the American Statistical Association, 94,* 621–634.

Pesaran, M. H., Smith, R. P., & Im, K. S. (1996). Dynamic linear models for heterogeneous panels. In L. Matyas & P. Sevestre (Eds.), *The econometrics of panel data* (pp. 145–195). Dordrecht: Kluwer Academic Publishers.

Seo, B. (1998). Statistical inference on cointegration rank in error correction models with stationary covariates. *Journal of Econometrics, 85,* 339–385.

Seo, B. (2004). *Efficient estimation and inference on cointegration in error correction models with stationary covariates.* Mimeo, Texas A&M University and Soongsil University.

Temple, J. (1999). The new growth evidence. *Journal of Economic Literature, 37,* 112–156.

Weesie, J. (1999). Seemingly unrelated estimation and the cluster-adjusted sandwich estimator. *Stata Technical Bulletin, 52,* 34–47.

CHAPTER 5

Vintage Capital Growth Theory: Three Breakthroughs

Raouf Boucekkine[a], David de la Croix[b] and Omar Licandro[c]

[a]Aix-Marseille School of Economics, GREQAM, 2 rue de la Charité, 13002 Marseille, France; Economics School of Louvain, Université catholique de Louvain, IRES and CORE, Montesquieu, 3, 1348 Louvain-la-Neuve, Belgium
E-mail address: Raouf.boucekkine@uclouvain.be
[b]Economics School of Louvain, Université catholique de Louvain, IRES and CORE, Montesquieu, 3, 1348 Louvain-la-Neuve, Belgium
E-mail address: David.delacroix@uclouvain.be
[c]Barcelona Graduate School, IAE-CSIC, Campus UAB, 08193 Bellaterra, Barcelona, Spain
E-mail address: omar.licandro@iae.csic.es

Abstract

Vintage capital growth models have been at the heart of growth theory in the 1960s. This research line collapsed in the late 1960s with the so-called embodiment controversy and the technical sophisitication of the vintage models. This chapter analyzes the astonishing revival of this literature in the 1990s. In particular, it outlines three methodological breakthroughs explaining this resurgence: a growth accounting revolution, taking advantage of the availability of new time series; an optimal control revolution, allowing to safely study vintage capital optimal growth models; and a vintage human capital revolution, along with the rise of economic demography, accounting for the vintage structure of human capital similarly to physical capital age structuring. The related literature is surveyed.

Keywords: Vintage capital, embodied technical progress, growth accounting, optimal control, endogenous growth, vintage human capital

JEL classifications: D63, D64, C61, 0 40

1. Introduction

Traditional aggregate production functions are built on the assumption of homogenous capital in the sense that all capital goods constituting the operating stock of capital have the same marginal contribution to output. In particular, new and old capital goods contribute equally in conveying

Frontiers of Economics and Globalization
Volume 11   ISSN: 1574-8715
DOI: 10.1108/S1574-8715(2011)0000011010

technical progress within the neoclassical paradigm (see Solow, 1956, 1957). Such a view of capital denies *de facto* any connection between the pace of investment and the rate of technological progress in the long run as it can be readily inferred from the Solow decomposition apparatus. However, the assumed *disembodied* nature of technical progress looks barely unrealistic, as acknowledged by Solow (1960) himself in a posterior contribution:

> *This conflicts with the casual observation that many if not most innovations need to be embodied in new kinds of durable equipment before they can be made effective. Improvements in technology affect output only to the extent that they are carried into practice either by net capital formation or by the replacement of old-fashioned equipment by the latest models ... (p. 91)*

Accounting for the age distribution of investment goods sounds as the natural way to cope with the latter criticism, and this actually suggested a central stream of the growth theory literature of the 1950s and 1960s, giving birth to what we shall refer to as vintage capital growth theory. Surprisingly, this stream almost collapsed in the late 1960s for different reasons. One is certainly because the embodiment debate, involving such pre-eminent economists as Denison, Jorgenson, Phelps or Solow, got stuck at that time. As clearly outlined by Hercowitz (1998), this blockage was partly due to limited statistical resources. Indeed, the construction of time series on the relative price of durable goods by Gordon (1990) plays a decisive role in th spectacular revival of the vintage capital literature in the 1990s. In the same vein, the recent conception of innovative tools for the mathematical treatment of delay-differential equations (in terms of both optimal control and numerical solution) to which a large class of vintage capital models lead has definitely helped in the development of a new vintage capital literature based on intertemporal optimization and departing from the constant saving rate assumption so widely adopted in the 1960s.

In this chapter, we analyze the evolution of the vintage capital growth literature over the past 50 years. We start by highlighting the salient characteristics and implications of the seminal vintage capital models built up in the late 1950s and 1960s (see also Boucekkine, de la Croix, & Licandro, 2008, for a summary). Then, we focus on the analysis of the recent impressive resurgence in the vintage capital literature. In particular, we identify three methodological breakthroughs:

1. *The growth accounting breakthrough.* The availability of times series on the relative price of equipment settles the old embodiment debate in the 1990s and opens the door to a new growth accounting methodology based on two-sector modeling and stressing the importance of investment-specific or embodied technological progress.
2. *The optimal control breakthrough.* Vintage capital frameworks allow to address the issue of replacement of obsolete capital goods and

technologies. Such a mechanism was thought to generate original short- and long-run dynamics compared to the traditional neoclassical growth model. All the analytical attempts to uncover such an original outcome in the 1960s did fail though. Recent advances in computational mathematics and optimal control of infinite dimensional dynamic systems allow to depart from the traditional fixed saving rate assumption and to move to vintage capital settings with intertemporal optimization and an explicit handling of transitional dynamics. Such a departure ultimately allows to identify new properties concerning transitional dynamics in vintage capital optimal growth models related to the replacement problem mentioned just above. An endogenous growth vintage capital theory also emerges with either technological and/or environemental concerns.

3. *The vintage human capital breakthrough.* The early vintage capital models only deal with age-structured physical capital though, as mentioned in the introduction of Section 5, extension to human capital seemed natural to many authors. Together with the rise of economic demography and the so-called unified growth theory (see Galor & Weil, 1999, for example), modeling vintage structures of human capital and analyzing their impact on the development process, technology diffusion and income distribution becomes an important line of research from the 1990s.

The structure of the chapter follows the presentation above. Section 2 is devoted to the description of the salient characteristics of the seminal vintage capital models constructed in the 1960s. Section 3 presents the embodiment debate and ends with a short exposition of the new two-sector accounting methodology. The new vintage capital optimal growth theory is presented in the next section with a somehow detailed (though nontechnical) analysis of the mathematical peculiarity of these models. Section 5 is a detailed description of models putting forward vintage human capital to tackle several key development issues.

2. Vintage capital models: seminal theory

2.1. The Johansen vintage capital model

Johansen's (1959) model is the first historical vintage capital model. It has two main features, a putty-clay assumption and a vintage capital structure. Capital is nonmalleable: while substitution between labor and capital is permitted *ex ante*, it is not allowed once capital is installed. Capital goods embody the best available technology at the date of their construction and the number of workers operating them is, as formulated by Sheshinski (1967), "fixed by design." The output produced by capital goods of vintage v at date $t \geq v$, say $Y(v,t)$, is given by:

$$Y(v, t) = F(K(v, t), e^{\gamma v} L(v, t)),$$

where $K(v,t)$ is the amount of capital of vintage v still operated at date t and $L(v,t)$ the amount of labor assigned, while $\gamma \geq 0$ designates the rate of embodied technical progress.[1] The production function $F(.)$ is assumed *neoclassical*: it has constant returns to scale and diminishing marginal rates of substitution. $K(v,t)$ is typically related to the amount of capital of vintage v constructed, say $I(v) = K(v,v)$, by a depreciation-based law of motion of the type:

$$K(v,t) = e^{-\delta(t-v)}I(v),$$

where $\delta \geq 0$ is the rate of instantaneous capital depreciation. Because proportions of production factors are fixed *ex post*, that is the amount of labor (measured in efficiency terms) associated with capital of vintage v is fixed for every $t \geq v$, the output per vintage can be written in the much simpler form:

$$Y(v,t) = F(1, \lambda(v))\, K(v,t) = g(\lambda(v))\, K(v,t),$$

where $\lambda(v) = e^{\gamma v}(L(v,t)/K(v,t))$. Notice that, by construction, function $g(.)$ is strictly increasing and strictly concave.

A fundamental mechanism at work in the Johansen model is the *obsolescence* scheme, determining the range of active vintages at any date. The quasi-rent of a vintage v at date t, $t \geq v$, is given by

$$\mu(v,t) = g(\lambda(v)) - \lambda(v)\, e^{-\gamma(t-v)}\, w(t),$$

where $w(t) = g'(\lambda(t))$ is the wage rate in terms of labor efficiency. An equipment of vintage v is operated as long as its quasi-rent remains positive. At any date t, the installation of a new vintage is always profitable, the associated quasi-rent being strictly positive, $\mu(t,t) = g(\lambda(t)) - \lambda(t)\, g'(\lambda(t)) > 0$, because function $g(.)$ is strictly increasing and concave. For t fixed, and for the associated wage rate, $w(t)$, the operation of the previously installed and less efficient vintages may not be profitable, and some are eventually scrapped. Therefore, Johansen's framework naturally leads to optimally finite-lived capital goods.

If we denote $\Omega(t,w)$ the set of vintages still utilized at date t for a given wage $w(t)$,[2] total demand for labor is equal to $\int_{\Omega(t,w)} L(v,t)\mathrm{d}v$. In a Solow growth set-up, namely under a constant investment rate s such that $K(t) = s \int_{\Omega(t,w)} Y(v,t)\mathrm{d}v$, and the labor market clearing (with exogenously given labor supply), Sheshinski (1967) proved that the Johansen model converges to a unique stable balanced growth path with finite capital lifetime. We shall come back to this important asymptotic result when

---

[1] Of course, disembodied technical progress could be trivially introduced.

[2] As pointed out by Sheshinski (1967), this set consists in one or more time intervals, provided $\lambda(v)$ is continuous (for $v < t$).

dealing with the Leontief vintage capital model studied by Solow, Tobin, Von Weizsacker, and Yaari (1966).

2.2. The Solow vintage capital model

The vintage capital model proposed by Solow (1960) builds on the seminal work of Johansen but differs in a fundamental aspect: factor proportions are not fixed *ex post*, they are freely variable over the lifetime of capital goods (putty-putty). The output per vintage follows a Cobb–Douglas technology

$$Y(v, t) = e^{\gamma v} \, K(v, t)^{1-\alpha} \, L(v, t)^{\alpha},$$

while total output is given by $Y(t) = \int_{-\infty}^{t} Y(v, t) \, dv$. In sharp contrast to Johansen's model, optimal capital lifetime need not be finite: due to the Cobb–Douglas production function, the marginal productivity of labor at $L(v,t) = 0$ is infinite, and the wage cost could be *ceteris paribus* covered by assigning arbitrary small amounts of labor to the oldest equipment, which is always possible in a putty-putty setting. Therefore, obsolescence does not show up through finite time scrapping but through a decreasing labor allocation to vintages over time, which in turn reflects a declining pattern for the value of vintages, as we shall see.

A striking outcome of Solow's (1960) model is its aggregation properties. Denote by $L(t)$ the total labor supply, that is, $L(t) = \int_{-\infty}^{t} L(v, t) \, dv$, and define $K(t)$ as

$$K(t) = \int_{-\infty}^{t} e^{\sigma v} I(v) e^{-\delta t} \, dv,$$

where $I(v)$ stands for, as in the Johansen's model, the amount of capital of vintage v installed in the economy, and $\sigma = \delta + (\gamma/(1-\alpha))$. If labor is homogenous, implying the marginal productivity of labor to be equal to the same wage rate regardless of the vintage operated, then the aggregate production function, $Y(t) = \int_{-\infty}^{t} Y(v, t) \, dv$, can be exactly written as

$$Y(t) = K(t)^{1-\alpha} L(t)^{\alpha}.$$

As mentioned by Solow (1960, p. 93), the putty-putty vintage capital model degenerates into the neoclassical model with the same aggregate production function and an exponential life-table assumption (at the rate δ), when $\gamma = 0$. Of course, the Cobb–Douglas specification is crucial to get such a result. As we show in Section 3, this aggregate model has been intensively used from the 1990s to analyze the viability of a growth regime driven by embodied (or investment-specific) technological progress, which is a characteristic of the technological regime conveyed by the information technologies. It is important to notice here that this aggregate model can be interpreted as a two-sector model. A first sector is the one described by the aggregate production above, which features a consumption good sector. In the formulation above, technological progress is fully embodied in capital. Of course we can introduce neutral technological progress as well, this will be done in Section 3. A second sector, more implicit, is the capital sector: production in this sector follows the law of motion

$$\dot{K}(t) = e^{\gamma_q t} I(t) - \delta K(t),$$

where $\gamma_q = \gamma/(1 - \alpha)$ is the rate of embodied technical progress. The term $e^{\gamma_q t}$ can be interpreted as productivity in the capital good sector, and as such, it also represents investment-specific technological progress because it only affects contemporaneous investment. This two-sector model, which is equivalent to the 1960 Solow vintage capital model, has become a key framework in the late 1990s, with important implications for growth accounting as we will see later.

A major contribution of Solow's work, clearly apparent in the 1960 model, is his thorough study of the implications of technical progress and changes in the quality of capital goods for the valuation of (durable) assets, which has ultimately led him to bring out a very sound theory of net output, depreciation and obsolescence. Without getting into too many details, one can get a flavor of this theory through the following simple point. Suppose output can be used only for consumption and investment, that is:

$$Y(t) = C(t) + I(t).$$

As we see in the next section, the accounting identity above is not innocuous since investment is reported without adjusting for productivity (or quality). Suppose now that one unit of consumption is forgone to invest in the capital sector at date t. Because the productivity in this sector is $e^{\gamma_q t}$, one can produce $e^{\gamma_q t}$ units of capital good. This implies a relative price of capital equal to $e^{-\gamma_q t}$. Therefore, while technological progress operates as a steady improvement in the quality of machines at a rate $\gamma/(1 - \alpha)$, it also induces an instantaneous obsolescence process (at the same rate) of the previously installed equipment. If the rate of embodied technical progress is significantly different from zero, such a process is likely to distort the typical growth aggregates, like net output, the growth rate of (net) output and productivity growth figures.

This important point has been at the heart of a recent rich literature around the productivity slowdown puzzle (see among many others, Greenwood & Yorokolgu, 1997; Whelan, 2002; Greenwood and Jovanovic, 2003). Actually, the discussion on the economic growth implications of embodied technical progress was tremendously controversial in the 1960s. It has witnessed an astonishing resurgence in the 1990s with the rise of the so-called *New Economy* and the availability of new economic statistical series (a move led by Robert Gordon, 1990), and has stimulated a quite important debate on growth accounting. We shall come back to this question in Section 3.

2.3. The vintage capital model with fixed factor proportions

In a famous joint contribution with Tobin, Yaari, and Von Weizsacker, Solow examined the polar case of a Leontief vintage capital production function. In this case, factor substitution is not allowed neither *ex ante* nor *ex post*. Not surprisingly, this model shares some key characteristics with the Johansen putty-clay model, notably concerning the obsolescence mechanism at work and the (qualitative) asymptotic behavior. A roughly general formulation of the Leontief production function per vintage is

$$Y(v, t) = a(v)K(v, t) = b(v)e^{\gamma v} \ L(v, t).$$

One unit of vintage capital v produces $a(v)$ units of output once combined with $(a(v)/b(v)) \ e^{-\gamma v}$ units of labor. In the simple case where $a(v) = b(v) = 1$, for all v, and no capital depreciation, so that $K(v, t) = I(v)$ for all v and t, the production function per vintage takes the elementary form

$$Y(v, t) = Y(v) = I(v) = e^{\gamma v} \ L(v),$$

for all $t \geq v$. We shall use this simple specification hereafter.

As in the Johansen model, and basically for the same reasons, capital goods should be scrapped at a finite time. Because of fixed factor proportions, capital goods become obsolete some time after their installation when their associated quasi-rents can no longer cover the labor cost. In the Leontief vintage capital model, the obsolescence conditions are straightforward. Under the usual competitive equilibrium conditions, the equilibrium (real) wage is equal to the marginal productivity of labor, which equals the inverse of the labor requirement of the oldest operating vintage in the Leontief case. If we denote by $T(t)$ the age of the oldest machines still in use (or scrapping time) at date t, the equilibrium wage is simply $e^{\gamma[t-T(t)]}$. The quasi-rent associated with an equipment of vintage v at date $t \geq v$ is therefore $1 - e^{-\gamma v} \ e^{\gamma[t-T(t)]}$, and it is exhaustible at finite time.

The main result established by Solow et al. (1966) concerns the asymptotic stability of the model under a constant saving rate and a clearing labor market (with an exogenously given labor supply). Under the condition that the saving rate is larger than the rate of embodied technological progress, and some more technical assumptions, Solow et al. show that the economy converges to a unique balanced growth path. As previously pointed out, Sheshinski came out with the same result on the Johansen model one year later. Therefore, it turned out that the vintage capital growth models, whatever their assumed technological structures, do deliver the same qualitative asymptotic behavior as the much simpler neoclassical growth model (with homogenous capital). This was a quite disappointing result because one would have expected that the obsolescence mechanisms at work in these models, specially when the equilibrium lifetime of equipment is finite, would distort the short-term dynamics and long-run outcomes. Indeed, when the equilibrium lifetime of equipment is finite, one would expect that replacement investment, here variable $I(t)$, would burst from time to time, giving rise to the so-called *replacement echoes*. Solow et al. and Sheshinski's results rule out such an occurrence in the long run. A recent stream of the vintage literature inspired by Malcomson (1975) has revisited this finding: relaxing the assumption of constant saving rate, common to the related literature of the 1960s, it is shown that whence intertemporal optimization is introduced (which involves the determination of an optimal scrapping time), investment cycles may show up as a a result of optimal replacement of obsolete machines (see notably Boucekkine, Germain, & Licandro, 1997). This recent "optimal growth" vintage capital literature is reviewed in Section 4.

3. The embodiment debate and implications for empirical growth: the accounting breakthrough

3.1. The embodiment controversy: Solow (with the help of Gordon) strikes back

In a famous statement, Denison (1964) claimed that "the embodied question" is unimportant. His argument was merely quantitative and starts with the assumption that embodiment should exclusively show up through the age distribution of the stock of capital. Using his own estimates of US growth in the period 1929–1957, he argued that if the average age can be changed by one year from 1960 to 1970, this cannot alter the annual growth rate (in the extreme cases) by more than 0.06 percentage points in the period 1960–1970.

Of course, Denison's reasoning is specific to a period of time, and it uses a quite conventional one-sector-based growth accounting exercise with a restrictive identification of the embodiment channels (exclusively, the average age of capital). In particular, it omits *de facto* the relative price of capital (in terms of the consumption good) channel: the latter variable must go down under an acceleration in the rate of embodied (or investment-specific) technical progress as explained in Section 2.2, and such an effect can be neatly represented and its growth implications studied in two-sector models, as recently emphasized, among others, by Greenwood, Hercowitz, and Krusell (1997). This idea was also strongly stressed by Solow (1960) but the lack of a compelling computation of the relative price of capital series was a clear limit to his claims. In this sense, Robert Gordon's relative price of equipment series for the United States have been very good news for the Solowian view, as brilliantly pointed out by Hercowitz (1998) in a recent essay on the embodiment controversy.

We shall give here a brief account of the central point of the discussion as started by Solow (1960) and Jorgenson (1966), and as it has evolved over time, especially after Gordon (1990).[3] The major difference between the accounting approach prescribed by Solow and the one defended by Jorgenson is in the resource constraint:

$$Y(t) = C(t) + I(t).$$

As already mentioned in Section 2.2, Solow does not adjust investment for quality while Jorgenson does. Precisely, Jorgenson would write the previous identity as:

$$Y(t) = C(t) + I^*(t) = C(t) + e^{\gamma_q t} I(t),$$

with the notations of Section 2 (γ_q denoting the rate of investment-specific technical progress). Let us also introduce neutral (or disembodied) technological progress in the production function of the consumption good as it is traditional in the neoclassical model: $Y(t) = A(t) K(t)^{1-\alpha} L(t)^{\alpha}$ where $A(t)$ designates neutral technological progress (in the sense that it affects all the stock of capital and not only contemporaneous investment). So the unique difference between the two frameworks is in the adjustement for quality of investment in the resource constraint. Incidentally, this difference is quite substantial: it means that investment-specific technological progress is costly in the Jorgenson setting: the larger γ_q, the larger the amount of final good diverted from consumption (or the larger the labor input required if one has in mind the aggregate production function in the final good sector). This does not occur in the Solow set-up. This said, the main point raised by Jorgenson to dismiss Solow's proposal is that it is impossible from the available data (at that time) to distinguish between investment-specific and neutral technological progress, that is between $A(t)$ and $e^{\gamma_q t}$. The point is rather straightforward: if the available data consist of time series on $C(t)$, $I(t)$, and $L(t)$, then the system of equations composed of the resource constraint (in both frameworks) and the law of motion of capital, together with the production function postulated, is trivially undetermined. Unless an ad-hoc identifying assumption is added, one cannot identify separately $A(t)$ and $e^{\gamma_q t}$. Traditional one-sector growth accounting builds on the restriction $\gamma_q = 0$. However such an assumption which may have looked reasonable in the 1960s sounds as roughly counter-factual since Gordon (1990), who clearly uncovered a downward trend in the series of the relative price of capital, which amounts to finding $\gamma_q > 0$. Ultimately it turns that Gordon's work has not only broken down the "indeterminacy" argument put forward by Jorgenson, it has also paved the way for a new accounting framework based on the two-sector model already described in Section 2.2. We shall say some words on this matter in the next section.

---

[3] A more theortical point is made by Phelps (1962) against what he called the "new investment" view inspired by Solow (1960). We shall restrict our discussion to the growth accounting debate.

3.2. Growth accounting under embodiment

Growth accouting under embodiment has been a fertile research line in the 90s with several important contirbutions. Key contributors are, among others, Hulten (1992), Greenwood et al. (1997), and Whelan (2002). Hulten's findings are discussed in Greenwood et al. (1997). To make the presentation as simple as possible, we rely on the latter (see also Greenwood & Jovanovic, 2003, for a broader perspective on this question). Let us consider the two-sector model in Section 2.2 enriched with a neutral technological progress component (as just above) and let us introduce a distinction between equipement and structures, as the former are the predominant channel of embodied technical progress. More specifically, we shall assume that investment-specific technological progress is exclusively conveyed through equipement.[4] The equations of the "accounting" two-sector model are:

$$Y(t) = A(t)K_e(t)^{\alpha_e}K_s(t)^{\alpha_s}L(t)^{1-\alpha_e-\alpha_s},$$

$$\dot{K}_e(t) = e^{\gamma_q t}I_e(t) - \delta_e K_e(t),$$

$$\dot{K}_s(t) = I_s(t) - \delta_s K_s(t),$$

$$Y(t) = C(t) + I_e(t) + I_s(t).$$

Standard computations yield the following decomposition of the growth rate of output (with the notation γ_x for the growth rate of x):

$$\gamma_Y = \frac{1}{1 - \alpha_e - \alpha_s}\gamma_A + \frac{\alpha_e}{1 - \alpha_e - \alpha_s}\gamma_q.$$

The formula gives the growth rate of the economy resulting from the two components of technological progress, neutral and investment-specific. One can exploit it to measure the contribution of each component to economic growth. This exercise is done by Greenwood et al. (1997) on US postwar data. Using Gordon's work, one is able to directly "observe" γ_q (around 4%). As in standard growth accounting, the rate of growth of neutral technical change, γ_A, is then computed residually, once the model conveniently calibrated.[5] Finally, one can evaluate the contribution to growth of each form of technological progress. Greenwood et al. found that more than 60% of output growth can be attributed to embodied technical progress, which is indeed a huge figure. Even though some aspects of the methodology can be discussed, this exercise is clean enough

---

[4] This is clearly an assumption. It is not obvious at all that the fraction of embodied technical progress in structures is negligible. Preliminary evidence tend to prove the contrary, see for example, Gort, Greenwood, and Rupert (1999).

[5] Greenwood et al. (1997) take the following numbers: $\alpha_e = 0.17$, $\alpha_s = 0.13$.

to suggest that embodied technical progress is an important source of US growth. This calls for a deep revisiting of growth accounting procedures (see Whelan, 2002, for a careful discussion). This finding also makes clear that not only vintage capital models are realistic technological representations, they are crucially important to understand how the growth process set in and how to control it. The next section provides a state of art in vintage modelling in the economic literature.

4. Optimal vintage capital growth models: The optimal control breakthrough

As outlined earlier, the seminal vintage capital models built up in the 1960s very often entail the assumption of a constant saving rate, and almost systematically concentrate on balanced growth paths characterization. The main reason behind is the complexity of vintage capital models, which involve a particular class of optimization problems and dynamic systems. This will be made clear along this section.

4.1. The mathematical peculiarity of vintage capital models

To fix ideas, let us shed light on the peculiar dynamic structure of the famous vintage capital model with fixed proportions (Solow et al., 1966) already described in Section 2.3. A key feature in the latter model is the determination of the scrapping time, $T(t)$. Suppose without loss in generality that labor supply is normalized to unity. Then, the labor market clears at date t if and only if

$$\int_{t-T(t)}^{t} I(v) e^{-\gamma v} \, dv = 1.$$

At $t = 0$, and for a given initial investment profile, $i(t)$ for $t < 0$, the equilibrium condition just above determines the initial scrapping time, $T(0)$. The latter statement already gives an idea of the peculiar dynamic systems one has to deal with when studying vintage capital models. In contrast to the more traditional growth models, there is no way to have a definite solution to the model if past investment profile is not given at least on a time interval $[-t_0 \ 0]$, $t_0 > 0$, while a single initial condition $K(0)$ is enough in traditional growth models. This features the infinite dimension nature of the dynamic systems induced by vintage capital models, a feature highlighted in Fabbri and Gozzi (2008). Differentiating the clearing-market condition above, one gets the following peculiar law of motion for the scrapping time:

$$\dot{T}(t) = 1 - \frac{I(t) e^{-\gamma T(t)}}{I(t - T(t))}.$$

The law of motion of scrapping is no longer an ordinary differential equation, it is a delay-differential equation: a delayed term $I(t - T(t))$ shows up. The latter reflects the replacement activity at finite scrapping time, $T(t)$, taking place in the economy. Moreover, the delay, $T(t)$, is an endogenous variable, which is a further complication.[6] So even abstracting away from dynamic optimization, the mathematical challenge one faces when dealing with transition dynamics in vintage capital models is at first glance a daunting task. Fortunately enough, recent advances in computational mathematics do allow to handle the class of dynamic systems discussed here. Indeed using up-to-date numerical methods, Boucekkine, Licandro, and Paul (1997) solved for the transition dynamics of the 1966 Solow et al.'s model. More precisely, they considered the three-dimensional differential system obtained by adding to the delay-differential identified above the Leontief vintage capital production function and the constant saving rule differentiated with respect to time. Because the system does include a delayed term representing replacement at finite time, as explained above, one would expect that some kind of replacement-induced oscillations will show up in the transition to an otherwise standard balanced growth path (previously characterized by Solow et al., 1966). Boucekkine et al. (1997) found that such short-term replacement echoes do not show up for a large class of past investment profiles.Transition dynamics do set in in the sense that all variables (including the scrapping time) vary over time and converge to their corresponding balanced growth values but the dynamics are mostly monotonic. Therefore, the work of Boucekkine et al. (1997) essentially extends the no-replacement echoes finding of Solow et al. (1966) to the short-term dynamics.

4.2. Vintage capital optimal growth models

The latter surprising (and disappointing) result has suggested further research. Among other lines of research, one direction taken builds on the following observation. Suppose that the scrapping time is constant, equal to T^o. Time differentiation of the labor market equilibrium condition above yields

$$\hat{I}(t) = \hat{I}(t - T^o),$$

where $\hat{I}(t) = i(t)\, e^{-\gamma t}$ is detrended investment. Therefore, if the scrapping time were to be constant, replacement echoes would govern investment dynamics, and thus, output dynamics too since technology is Leontief. Incidentally, the constancy of optimal scrapping rules is a salient property

---

[6] Delay-differential equations with endogenous delays are called state-dependent, see Boucekkine et al. (1997).

in a related operation research literature: such a rule is usually referred to as the Terborgh-Smith result as developed in Malcomson (1975).[7] Relying on this literature, Boucekkine et al. (1997) suggested to move to optimal growth set-ups for replacement echoes to show up. Accordingly, they replaced the constant saving rule by a Ramsey intertemporal optimal control problem with linear utility function while keeping all the other technological assumptions in the Solow et al. (1966) model. In such a case, the optimal scrapping time turns out to be effectively constant after a finite time adjustment period, which generates everlasting fluctuations in investment, output, and consumption, following the simple replacement echoes mechanism outlined just above. When utility of consumers is strictly concave, these fluctuations do arise in the short run but they get dampened in the long run by the induced consumption smoothing mechanism (see Boucekkine, Germain, Licandro, & Magnus, 1998). These results are in sharp contrast to the neoclassical growth model which typically gives rise to monotonic transition dynamics.[8]

Therefore, vintage capital optimal growth models do strikingly differ from the neoclassical growth model, at least in terms of short run dynamics, provided capital and labor are to some extent complementary. Admittedly, compared to the standard neoclassical model, the generated nonmonotonic investment paths are much more consistent with the observed dynamics either at the plant level (Doms & Dunne, 1998) or at the aggregate level (Cooper, Haltiwanger, & Power, 1999).

To end this section, some comments on the optimization techniques needed to handle vintage capital optimal growth models are in order. As explained in Section 3.1, the state equations involved in these models are infinite dimensional because they belong to the class of delay-differential or delay-integral equations. There is no obvious way to deal with the optimal control of such dynamic motions, which probably explains why the vintage capital literature has resumed so late. The natural preliminary question turns out to be whether it is safe to apply the typical optimal control apparatus (or slight variations of it), which is conceived to be applied for the optimal control of finite dimension ordinary differential equations, or to develop alternative techniques more adapted to the infinite dimensional models under scrutiny. The inherent methodological debate is addressed in Boucekkine, de la Croix, and Licandro (2004). These two approaches have been both taken in the recent vintage capital literature. On one hand, variational methods to derive the maxiumum

---

[7] See also the excellent book of Hritonenko and Yatsenko (1996) that brings out an extensive material on vintage capital modeling in this literature.
[8] A flavor of these results could be found in an early seminal contribution due to Benhabib and Rustichini (1991) who were the first to show that a departure from the typical exponential decay depreciation rule for physical capital in the neoclassical model is enough to give birth to nonmonotonic adjustment paths.

principle have been successfully applied by Malcomson (1975), Boucek-kine et al. (1997), and more systematically by Hritonenko and Yatsenko (1996, 2005, 2006). The techniques applied extend quite naturally and straightforwardly the classical variational method. On the other hand, Fabbri and Gozzi (2008) and Faggian and Gozzi (2010) have applied a novel dynamic programming method to solve vintage capital optimal growth models explicitly dealing with the infinite dimension of the problems tackled. A comparison between the two approaches is beyond the scope of this chapter. Nonetheless, and by construction, the dynamic programming method allows to obtain a finer characterization of optimal solutions, especially when the value function is explicitly obtainable as it is the case in some linear models (see again Fabbri & Gozzi, 2008; Boucekkine, Fabbri, & Gozzi, 2010). The variational methods requires more additional work, for example to figure out the sufficient optimality conditions or to study asymptotic stability issues.[9] In the absence of explicit solutions for the value function, the gap between the two groups of methods is certainly smaller: combining both seems a preferable strategy in such a case (as argued by Fabbri & Gozzi, 2008). To conclude, it is worth pointing out that the area of optimal control of age-structured human and nonhuman populations (to which vintage capital optimal growth models belong) has become quite active in the recent years.[10] It is highly important for economists aiming to incorporate age structures into the analysis to track these methodological developments; many questions are still open in this respect.

4.3. Vintage capital with endogenous growth

The models surveyed so far build on exogenous (embodied) technical progress. Indeed, until the late 1990s, there has been no work combining wintage capital and endogenous growth. The rise of the information technologies in the 1990s and the debate on the viability of what appeared as a new growth regime have stimulated a new stream of literature aiming at endogenizing embodied technical progress (see the excellent survey of Greenwood & Jovanovic, 2003). Before this new trend, vintage capital models have been mostly used to study the impact of obsolescence (that is the so-called replacement problem) and exogenous embodied technical progress. It is interesting to notice that even when technological progress is exogenous, purposive modernization strategies (namely, strategies

---

[9] It is easy to understand why: When the (linearized) dynamic systems are ordinary (linear) differential equations, stability involves the location of a finite number of roots of the corresponding characteristic polynomial. When the dynamic systems are delay-differential equations, the counterpart is the location of the infinite number of roots of a transcendental function.

[10] See a compilation of applications and methods in Boucekkine, Hritonenko, and Yatsenko (2010).

increasing the productivity of the operated capital stock) can be conducted using two different tools: investment (because technological progress is embodied) and scrapping. Scrapping may involve downsizing but in such a case downsizing entails modernization: old and obsolete capital goods are replaced by newer and more productive vintages. In the traditional neoclassical mode with homogenous capital, investment is not the vehicle of (exogenous) technological progress and such modernization strategies are not well-founded. As a consequence, vintage capital models are much more natural to frame these strategies and to evaluate the macroeconomic impact of modernization policies. Concrete modernization policies include investment subsidies, scrapping subsidies and tax treatment of capital income, which happen to be popular policy tools in several advanced economies, including the United States (See Cooley, Greenwood, & Yorokoglu, 1997). Endogenizing technological progress allows to reach an even more comprehensive set of modernization strategies and policies. Of course, this further refinement comes at a nonnegligible analytical marginal cost. Combining a vintage capital structure (with or without endogenous scrapping) and an R&D sector is a difficult task. Hereafter we shall briefly present a sample of contributions to this line of research.

Most of the papers endogenizing embodied technical progress have not encompassed the replacement problem, that is the possibility for the firms to shut down obsolete plants and to scrap obsolete capital goods. As correctly outlined by Greenwood and Jovanovic (2003), these contributions typically build on (or are formally equivalent to) the Solow putty-putty vintage capital model described in our Section 2.2. An important contribution to this line of research is due to Krusel (1998). To our knowledge, the latter paper is the first endogenizing embodied technical change through R&D activities. More precisely, research is conducted by the producers of capital goods who act as monopolists: the exclusive aim of these producers is to increase the productivity of capital goods, that is the level of investment-specific (or embodied) technical progress. Beside some weaknesses (like the presence of a scale effect), the model constructed by Krusell illustrates very well how purposive research activity in the capital sector can drive the growth of an economy, with some remarkable features like the decline of the relative price of equipment, which is admittedly a key stylized fact of modern economies after the 1960s. Boucekkine, del Rio, and Licandro (2003, 2005) have taken a similar approach: in the 2003 paper, embodied technical progress is modeled using Arrowian learning-by-doing; the 2005 paper is closer to Krusell's contribution in that it incorporates purposive R&D activities aiming to boost the productivity of capital goods. In both, the authors highlight the fact that a larger part of embodied technical progress in the overall growth rate of technological progress has a cost (obsolescence, which shows up in the decline of the relative price of capital) and an advantage (modernization, as new capital goods are more efficient). As a result, an R&D subsidy has an a priori ambiguous effect on growth. Nonetheless Boucekkine, Licandro, and del Rio (2005) establish that the modernization effect generally dominates the obsolecence costs inherent to embodied technical progress. A few papers have attempted to introduce an explicit vintage structure in an endogenous growth setting. One is due to Cooley et al. (1997) mentioned above. Another one is the vintage capital AK model with fixed capital lifetime studied by Boucekkine, Licandro, Puch and del Rio (2005). A large proportion of these papers are motivated by environmental and sustainability considerations. It is easy to guess how the vintage capital structure could be exploited in environmental frameworks. One could differentiate between successive vintages in terms of productivity, but differentiation can be operated on an environmental basis. Suppose that part of the R&D activities of an economy are devoted to decrease energy consumption in the production process (energy-saving technical progress) by conceiving cleaner machines over time. In such a case, successive vintages will be differentiated by their energy consumption, that is by their emissions. In this context, modernization would in first place aim to decrease energy consumption and emissions over time to cope with environmental sustainability criteria. Hart (2004) and Feichtinger, Hartl, Kort, and Veliov (2005) have taken this avenue. In the former, two types of R&D activities are possible: a first activity tends to develop more environment-friendly capital goods, and the other is the traditional productivity-enhancing research. Under some conditions, optimal combinations of the two types of R&D activities are shown to give rise to environmentally sustainable growth regimes.

In both papers,[11] the number of vintages is fixed, so that no endogenous scrapping is allowed. Yet, it seems obvious that scrapping of the least productive and the most polluting capital goods is a valid tool, and should be accounted for in any broad modernization strategy. Of course, adding endogenous scrapping to a general equilibrium model with vintage capital and R&D is analytically intractable in general, which explains why this task has not been undertaken so far. A shortcut has been recently taken by Boucekkine, Hritonenko, and Yatsenko (2011) who consider a firm problem with a vintage capital production function in line with Solow et al. (1966), endogenous scrapping and R&D activities to increase the rate of energy-saving technical progress. With this broad set of modernization action in hands, the firm has to design a strategy assuring long-run growth given scarcity of resources (through given exogenously rising resource price) and pollution quota constraints. General equilibrium extensions (with nonlinear utility functions for consumers) seem definitely not manageable analytically.

---

[11] And also in the Cooley et al. paper, which has the additional feature that growth is endogenized via a Lucas human capital accumulation mechanism in contrast to all the papers cited in this section.

5. Vintage human capital: the third breakthrough

Traditional vintage capital growth models typically consider an homogenous labor force. It is clear that just like physical capital is heterogenous, so is the labor force. This observation is commented in this way by Solow (1960, p. 91, footnote 2): "Of course, I could completely reverse the roles of L and K, and then it would be legitimate to speak of successive generations of workers as more efficient than their forbears ... ." It also goes without saying that introducing heterogenous labor force into one of the seminal vintage (physical) capital models seen before would dramatically complicate the analysis and surely break down some of the nicest equilibrium relationships established (as the Cobb–Douglas aggregate production function in the 1960 Solow model).

Yet the concept of vintage human capital has been more explicitly used in the literature since the early 1990s to treat some specific issues related to technology diffusion, inequality, and economic demography. A few models try to put in the same model physical and human vintage capital, among them Jovanovic (1998). We shall briefly outline here three lines of research taken with the human vintage capital approach.

5.1. Vintage human capital and technology diffusion

The basic idea conveyed by the recent contributions exploring this line of research is already in Zeckhauser's short note published in 1968. In a world with a continuous pace of innovations, a representative individual faces the typical question of whether to stick to an established technology or to move to a new and better one. The trade-off is the following: switching to the new technique would allow him to employ a more advanced technology, but he would loss the expertise, the *specific human capital*, accumulated on the old technique. Since it is costly to learn a new technique, there is an optimal switching timing problem here, which is solved in a very simple partial equilibrium set-up by Zeckhauser 40 years ago. More importantly, notice that in such frameworks the generated vintage human capital distributions pretty much mimic the vintage distribution of technologies, the time sequence of innovations being generally exogenously given. This is clearly the case in the recent papers by Chari and Hopenhayn (1991) and Parente (1994).

In the former (highly elegant) contribution, not only different technology vintages (and therefore vintage human capital) coexist, but in contrast to the early vintage capital models studied above, individuals keep on investing in old technologies for a while even though superior technologies are available. Here, the Zeckhauser mechanism plays a crucial role: human capital is technology-specific and immediate switching to a superior technology is not necessarily optimal: one may be better off skilled in an inferior technology than unskilled in an advanced one.[12] In Chari and Hopenhayn, the story is a bit more specific, and therefore more accurate. Each individual leaves two periods; every period, she can only work in one vintage. If she decides to work in a particular vintage, she becomes expert (or skilled) *in that vintage* at the end of the period, and then she can decide either to continue working with this technology or to switch to another vintage as unskilled. Therefore, at every period, any (surviving) vintage may be operated by skilled and unskilled individuals. In the spirit of the paper, the production function of any (operated) vintage may be written as

$$Y(v, t) = \gamma^v F(N(v, t), Z(v, t)),$$

where γ is the rate of technological progress, $\gamma > 1$, $N(v,t)$ the number of unskilled people operating vintage v at date t (part of them being old individuals who decide to switch technologies), and $Z(v,t)$ the number of skilled (and therefore old) individuals choosing this technology.

The fundamental contribution of Chari and Hopenhayn is to highlight the role of complementarity between skilled and unskilled, between old and new vintage human capital, a crucial aspect that was barely discarded, often by construction, in the early vintage literature. Chari and Hopenhayn show that this complementarity is key in shaping technology diffusion. In their framework, technology diffusion may be captured by the distribution of skilled (and old) individuals across vintages. The authors establish two main results for stationary distributions: first of all, the distributions are single-peaked, and second, the more old and new vintage human capital are complementary, the slower technological diffusion (or equivalently, the less people choosing to operate the newest technologies). Thus, beside replicating some of the crucial observed features of technology diffusion, the way different vintages interact is shown to be a decisive determinant of such a diffusion. The intuition behind this outcome is straightforward: for a young individual, the marginal return to choose an old technology is high if his (human capital) investment in such a technology is complementary enough with the pre-existing specific human capital. In such a case, few young workers will invest in the new technology, and technology diffusion is therefore likely to slowdown as the complementarity between old and new vintage human capital rises.

---

[12] A more recent exploitation of this mechanism in a vintage capital partial equilibrium set-up is due to Feichtinger, Hartl, Kort, and Veliov (2006).

5.2. Vintage human capital and inequality

An obvious implication of relaxing the hypothesis of labor force homogeneity is to generate labor income discrepancy (under the typically competitive conditions): *ceteris paribus* more skilled (and therefore productive) workers would receive higher wages. Of course, one has to be more specific about how capital and labor are actually combined in the workplace: a highly skilled worker on an outdated machine is not likely to be so productive. Yet one could legitimately think that considering vintage human capital is a good approach to income inequality. In a recent contribution, Jovanovic (1998) takes the argument a bit further and argues that vintage capital models are particularly well suited to explain income disparity across individuals and across countries. They are specially appropriate if one is primarily interested in getting beyond the typical exogenously generated inequalities: the latter would not arise as a consequence of given policy or initial endowments discrepancies but are the result of different investment strategies.

The complete argument relies on a natural nonconvexity in vintage capital models deriving from the indivisibility of machines. Though new machines are more productive, it is generally infeasible to replace all the old vintages (because of the resource constraint of the economy for example). Therefore, different vintages will coexist, and under the assumption that new technologies and skills are complementary, the best machines will be operated by the best skilled individuals, which in turn generates inequality. Moreover, "small differences in skills will translate into larger differences in productivities. This is due to nonconvexity. Had the economy been convex ... we would have improved all of the existing machines by a small increment ..." (p. 498). Notice that the argument is easily extensible to income inequality across countries.[13]

On the theoretical ground, Jovanovic's work is an important contribution to the vintage capital literature to the extent that it settles in a quite appealing way the hard problem of combining vintage physical capital and vintage human capital in a framework where the vintage distributions of both assets are endogenous. As argued above, this is a highly sensitive issue. Jovanovic proposes to resort to the assignment model *à la* Sattinger (1975) to go through it. In such a framework, firms combine machines and workers in fixed proportions, say one machine for one worker, at every instant. The typical assignment problem by a firm having acquired capital of a given vintage is to find the optimal vintage human capital or skill of the associated worker. This could be trivially formulated in standard vintage theory notations but we shall follow Jovanovic's elementary

---

[13] Hereafter, we shall omit the economic development reading of this contribution and focus on the vintage theory value-added.

formalism here, and speak about quality of machines (indexed by k) and quality of skills (indexed by s). The assignment problem faced by a firm owning a machine of quality k takes the form of the maximization with respect to the index s of the profit function:

$$\pi(k) = F(k, s) - w(s),$$

at every date t, with obvious notations. In particular, $w(.)$ is a given price function for labor skill. The production function $F(.)$ is linearly homogenous with $F_{12} > 0$. The first-order condition of the problem determines an optimal relationship $k = \Phi(s)$, which in turn fixes the profit of the firm which owns vintage capital of quality k as: $\pi(k) = F(k, \phi(k)) - w(\phi(k))$. If function $\phi(.)$ is increasing, then the best machines will be paired with the best skills, as needed. It is very important to note that the assignment problem is settled at any instant, and that reassignment is consequently assumed to be frictionless (think of workers free to move among firms or plants).

An interesting characteristic of Jovanovic's model is the obsolescence mechanism involved. Actually, it is very close to the one at work in the Johansen and Leontief vintage capital models, which is by no way surprising since firms combine workers and machines in fixed proportions in the underlying assignment model. Because labor resources are fixed and due to fixed factor proportions, old machines become unprofitable at a finite time and are eventually scrapped. By the envelope theorem, one actually gets $\pi'(k) = F_1(k, \phi(k)) > 0$, which simply reflects that the best machines are the most profitable. Under free entry, the condition $\pi(k) = 0$ will determine the minimal quality of machines still operated, and by the relationship, $k = (\phi)s$, one can also deduce the (minimal) skill paired with the worse machine still in use.

More importantly, and in contrast to Chari and Hopenhayn (1991), growth is endogenous in the Jovanovic paper: It comes from human capital accumulation à la Lucas (1988), and this has some very important implications compared to the set-ups based on the Zeckhauser mechanism. Growth of the stock of human capital determines the maximal quality of human capital available: if the worker has human capital, h, and works a fraction of time u (in production), then her skill is given by $s = u\,h$. If the best worker at date 0 has $h = 1$, then if all individuals choose the same u, the maximal skill is u, paired with best machine of quality $\phi(u)$ at the same date. Finally, the model is closed by an equipment sector: at any instant, a machine producer can produce one machine of any quality at a cost increasing in the quality of the machine, and including cost reducing external effects of the knowledge spillovers type. Not surprisingly, the shape of the involved cost function is a decisive determinant of the inequality obtained: the flatter is the marginal cost of improving machines, the larger the inequality. In case of large knowledge spillovers making the latter marginal cost steeper, the resulting inequality will be smaller.

In the balanced growth path, human capital will grow at a constant rate, and so will be shifted the distributions of vintage physical and human capital. When new vintages of physical capital come out, the best skilled workers will be immediately assigned to the latter vintages, the second best will go to the machines just abandoned by the best skilled workers, etc. This goes at odds with Chari and Hopenhayn's set-up where human capital vintage specificity induce a much slower switching of technologies. As correctly pointed out by Jovanovic, frictionless reassignment has its virtue: it implies persistent inequality in contrast to many competing vintage technology models like Parente's (1994) that bear leapfrogging and cannot serve to explain the persistent income discrepancies across countries. Nonetheless it is clear that a theory of economic development relying on technological decisions, and thus on technology diffusion, should certainly admit a certain degree of frictions in the reassignment process. This and other open issues are to be put to the credit of the highly stimulating 1998 vintage capital contribution of Jovanovic.

5.3. Demographic vintage human capital models

The relationship between demographic trends and economics is an area of research that is now expanding quickly. The importance of the economic growth process in fostering improvements in longevity has been stressed by the literature, but the feed-back effect of past demographic trends on growth, and in particular on the take-off of the Western World, remains largely unexplored. One likely channel through which demographics affect growth is the size and quality of the work force. In this view, generations of workers can be understood as being vintages of human capital, and studied with the same tools as vintages of physical capital.

An interesting point stressed by the empirical literature is that the relation between demographic variables, such as mortality, fertility and cohort sizes, and growth is anything but linear. Kelley and Schmidt (1995) highlight the ambiguous effect of crude death rates. Indeed, growth is slowed by the deaths of the workers but can be enhanced by the deaths of dependents. They provide several elements showing the importance of age-specific mortality rates. These nonlinear relationships stress the need to model the vintage structure of population. A key element is that different generations have different learning experiences and that the aggregate stock of human capital is built from the human capital of the different generations. This view is taken by de la Croix and Licandro (1999) and Boucekkine, de la Croix, and Licandro (2002) within an endogenous growth setup through human capital accumulation *à la* Lucas. In such frameworks, the vintage specificity of human capital does not rely on technological vintages as in Chari and Hopenhayn (1991) but on generation (or cohort) specific demographic characteristics.

Of course, the relevance of age-specific characteristics for economic analysis, including for human capital accumulation, is by no way new in the literature – see, for example, the life-cycle model with human capital investment of Ben-Porath (1967). The Ben-Porath mechanism has been recently subject to criticisms by Hazan and Zoabi (2006) and Hazan (2009). The latter paper shows that the lifetime labor input of American men born in 1840–1970 declined despite the dramatic gains in life expectancy. Hazan further argues that a rise in the lifetime labor supply is a necessary implication of the Ben-Porath-type model, which casts doubts on the possibility of such a model to explain the rise in schooling. Hazan's critique however only applies when survival curves are rectangular, see Cervellati and Sunde (2009).[14]

The novelty in the recent contributions is the general equilibrium and endogenous growth focus allowing to capture the nonlinear relationships of the type mentioned just above. Another new trend in the recent literature is the attempt to incorporate more realistic demographic ingredients, at least more realistic than the traditional Blanchard–Yaari-like models (see, e.g., Blanchard, 1985). A typical demographic vintage human capital model runs as follows (Boucekkine et al., 2002). The general structure is an overlapping generations in continuous time. The vintage structure primarily relies on the demographic ingredients. The set of individuals born in t, forming the cohort of vintage t, has a size say $\zeta\, e^{nt}$ where ζ is a scale parameter and n is the growth rate of population. The probability at birth of surviving at least until age a for any member of cohort t is given by :

$$m(a, t) = \frac{e^{-\beta_t(a)} - \alpha_t}{1 - \alpha_t}.$$

The survival law depends on two cohort-specific parameters, $\alpha_t > 1, \beta_t < 0$, and is a concave function of age. There is thus an upper bound on longevity obtained by solving $m(A_t, t) = 0$: $A_t = -\log(\alpha_t)/\beta_t$. Accordingly, α_t and β_t also determine life expectancy of the individuals of cohort t.

The vintage specificity of human capital comes from the schooling decision taken by the individuals of the same cohort. Precisely, the individuals have to decide how many years to spend in schooling, knowing that a better education will increase their labor income later. Optimal decisions are taken by maximization of expected intertemporal utility under the intertemporal budgetary constraint

---

[14] More precisely, the analysis in Hazan (2009) is developed under the assumption of a perfectly rectangular survival probability: Individuals are assumed to survive with probability one during all their life, and die with probability one when reaching their life expectancy.

$$\int_{t}^{t+A} c(t,z)R(t,z)\,\mathrm{d}z = \int_{t+T(t)}^{t+P(t)} h(t)w(z)R(t,z)\,\mathrm{d}z,$$

and to the rule of accumulation of human capital:

$$h(t) = \frac{\mu}{\eta}\overline{H}(t)T(t)^{\eta}.$$

The choice variables are consumption $c(t,z)$, schooling length $T(t)$, and retirement age $P(t)$. The retirement decision would makes sense in such a framework if for example the objective function includes a disutility of work. $R(t,z)$ is the contingent price of the consumption good, that is, the price at time t for buying one unit of good at time z conditional on being alive at time z. The parameter μ measures the efficiency in the production of human capital, and the parameter η is the elasticity of income with respect to an additional year of schooling. θ represents the time discounting rate. Finally, one can postulate a simple aggregate production function to close the model, $Y(t) = H(t)$, where $H(t)$ is aggregate human capital (across cohorts). Such a technology implies that the real wage par unit of human capital should be equal to 1 to ensure equilibrium in the labor market.

As it stands, the model has two important (and pro-factual) properties. First, schooling time is positively correlated with life expectancy. In the simplest case, that is, $\alpha = 0$, $\eta = 1$, and no disutility of work (as in de la Croix & Licandro, 1999), we can solve the model explicitly for optimal schooling, and obtain

$$T(t) = \frac{1}{\beta_t + \theta}.$$

We clearly see here that improvements in longevity of individuals in cohort t (drop in β_t) raise the optimal length of schooling, and thus they increase the level of human capital of this generation. Second, the model is able to generate nonlinear relationships between growth and demographic variables, consistent with Kelley and Schmidt findings. For example, Boucekkine et al. (2002) establish that the relationship between the growth rate per capita of the economy is a nonlinear function of the population growth rate n. In particular, there exists a value of demographic growth which maximizes economic growth par capita. The same nonlinearity arises in the relationship between the growth rate of the economy and life expectancy. This is not surprising in such models: a longer life has several conflicting effects. On one hand, it raises the incentives to educate and it reduces the depreciation rate of aggregate human capital. But on the other, it implies that the economy will be populated with more old people who did their schooling a long time ago, and such an effect is clearly harmful for economic growth.

The model of Boucekkine et al. (2002), although involved, paves the way for quantitative analyzes of the role of mortality in the industrial revolution. To exploit the full possibilities of the model, cohort life tables for the pre-industrial era are needed. Boucekkine, de la Croix, and Licandro (2003) use Perrenoud's data who constructed life tables from 1625 to 1825 on the basis of a wide nominative study in Geneva (Switzerland) and Beltrami's work based on parish registers to reconstitute age-group dynamics of the Venetian population over the period 1600–1790. The main finding of Boucekkine et al. (2003) is that the observed changes in adult mortality from the last quarter of the seventeenth century to the first quarter of the eighteenth century played a fundamental role in launching modern growth. This study thus promotes the view that the early decline in adult mortality is responsible for a large part of the acceleration of growth at the dawn of the modern age.

Various authors stressed that the rising density of population may have played a role in fostering the rise in literacy and education. Higher density can lower the cost of education through facilitating the creation of schools. Externalities can also be generated by denser population. High population density spurs technological change. Unified growth theory argues for â€œpopulation-induced" technological progress. Population needs to reach a threshold for productivity to accelerate. In de la Croix, Lindh, and Malmberg (2008), we extend the model to allow for an ad-hoc effect of density on total factor productivity:

$$\mu(t) = f(\text{density})$$

This allows to evaluate the respective importance of different mechanisms relating income growth to demographic change. The exercise is conducted by calibrating the model on Swedish long-term time series of mortality, education, age structure, and per capita income. The conclusion is that changes in longevity may account for as much as 20% of the observed rise in education over the period 1800–2000. Thus, longevity plays an important role, but by itself cannot explain more than a part of the rise in the education level in a model with no credit restrictions. The remaining 80% should be sought elsewhere, probably in the development of public subsidies to education and/or to the acceleration of skill-biased technical progress. The total effect of the demographic variables on growth is higher. Most income growth over this period would not have materialized if demographic variables had stayed constant since 1800.

To go beyond ad-hoc effects of density, Boucekkine, de la Croix, and Peeters (2007) build a theory connecting the creation of schools to population density thereby providing microfoundations to the relationship between density and productivity. We choose a simple geographical setting: a circle of unit circumference. We assume that, at every point of time, the cohort of the newborn generation is uniformly spread along the circle and has the same distribution of abilities at every location. We suppose that every point on the circle can accommodate a school and that schools are identical in their characteristics (same services, same quality, same reputation, etc.). The length of schooling is still chosen by individuals who maximize lifetime income, and depends on future wages, longevity, and the distance to the nearest school. The demand for schooling arising from each point on the circle as a function of the distance to the nearest school. Given the hypothesis on the dispersion of the population, it is obvious that schools will be optimally located if they are evenly spaced. Hence, for a given number of facilities, we can determine the literacy rate of the population, the total amount of fees paid by the pupils, and the total transportation costs. Accordingly, the school location problem is reduced to the single question: how many schools (or classrooms) will be founded at every date t to educate the newborn cohort? The number and location of educational facilities are determined, either chosen by the optimizing state or following a free entry process (market solution). Higher population density makes it optimal to increase school density, opening the possibility to attain higher educational levels.

Population size is a major determinant of school creation because the main source of a school revenues, tuition fees, depends on this demographic variable. This is true for both institutional arrangements (central planner and market). No school is viable below a certain threshold of population size. When the newborn population is low, the school creation or set-up costs are unlikely to be covered, hence no schools are created. Once the population reaches a threshold value, many schools may be created at once. The process by which illiteracy is eliminated is thus initiated by a jump. After this initial jump, the process takes place much more smoothly over time depending on the evolution of population density and of the attendance rate at schools of the successive cohorts, which in turn depends on the demographic, technological, and geographic factors outlined above.

Finally, let us briefly explain the dynamics in these models. The transition to the constant growth solutions usually follows second-order differential-difference equations, as time is continuous but the agents take discrete timing decisions (as schooling an retirement time). No theorem is available to assess directly the asymptotic behavior of the solutions of this kind of dynamic system. Such a theorem, called Hayes theorem, is only available for scalar and autonomous delay-differential equations with a single delay. No direct stability theorem is available for delay-differential systems with more than one delay since in this case the stability outcomes depend on the particular values of the delays. We can however study the stability of the dynamic system for different parameterizations of the model. Simulations can be ran usually with the assumption that the economy was initially on a balanced growth path. Dynamics turn out to be oscillatory. Indeed, generations of people are somehow like generations of machines, and we observe replacement echoes which are typical of models with delays. A simplified version of these echoes is found in discrete time overlapping generations models, where the eigenvalues are most of the times complex numbers which generate nonmonotonic dynamics (see Azariadis, Bullard, & Ohanian, 2004).

Such a line of research is quite recent and of course, many tasks remain to be addressed within the same framework. For example, endogenizing at least partially some of the demographic parameters like life expectancy (e.g., by including private and/or public health expenditures) is an interesting extension. More issues are still open, and the field of demographic vintage human capital models is by now quite promising.

6. Conclusion

The vintage capital literature has experienced a quite interesting evolution, with expansions, collapses and revivals, some spectacular in nature and magnitude. It is probably the case for many areas in many scientific disciplines. Yet we believe that this literature illustrates perfectly how technical constraints can limit the development of a research line, and how technical advances, some borrowed from other disciplines, can allow to relax these constraints and to spectacularly resuscitate a dying theory or paradigm. We have paid a special attention to clarify to which extent disciplines like computational mathematics and demography have helped resuming the vintage capital research program. Of course, many issues and extensions are still open. In particular, we believe that vintage capital models are a natural framework to study the environmental viability and, more broadly, the sustainability of a growth regime, as advocated in Section 4.3. Efforts in vintage capital research should be directed to study the latter questions. Last but not least, the dissemination of the vintage capital framework requires a much more intensive quantitative validation work in general equilibrium. So far only few researchers have undertaken this daunting task (notably, Cooley et al., 1997, and Gilchrist & Williams, 2000).

Acknowledgment

This chapter owes a lot to all those who have interacted with us along our 15-year-long research on vintage capital models. In first place, we would like to thank our co-authors: Fernando del Rio, Giorgio Fabbri, Marc Germain, Fausto Gozzi, Natali Hritonenko, Thomas Lindh, Alphonse Magnus, Bo Malmberg, Blanca Martinez, Christopher Paul, Dominique Peeters, Aude Pommeret, Luis Puch and Yuri Yatsenko. We also thank Antoine d'Autume, Jess Benhabib, Gustav Feichtinger, Oded Galor, Boyan Jovanovic, Peter Kort and Vladimir Veliov for their insightful and encouraging comments along the way. Boucekkine and Licandro acknowledge the financial support of the Spanish Ministry of Sciences and Technology (ECO2010-17943). Financial support from the French-speaking Community of Belgium through ARC grant 09/14-018 is also gratefully acknowledged.

References

Azariadis, C., Bullard, J., & Ohanian, L. (2004). Trend-reverting fluctuations in the life-cycle model. *Journal of Economic Theory, 119,* 334–356.

Benhabib, J., & Rustichini, A. (1991). Vintage capital, investment, and growth. *Journal of Economic Theory, 55,* 323–339.

Ben-Porath, Y. (1967). The production of human capital and the life cycle of earnings. *Journal of Political Economy, 75,* 352–365.

Blanchard, O. (1985). Debt, deficits, and finite horizons. *Journal of Political Economy, 93,* 223–247.

Boucekkine, R., del Rio, F., & Licandro, O. (2003). Embodied technological progress, learning and the productivity slowdown. *Scandinavian Journal of Economics, 105,* 87–98.

Boucekkine, R., del Rio, F., & Licandro, O. (2005). Obsolescence and modernization in the growth process. *Journal of Development Economics, 77,* 153–171.

Boucekkine, R., Fabbri, G., & Gozzi, F. (2010). Maintenance and investment: Complements or substitutes? A reappraisal. *Journal of Economic Dynamics and Control, 34,* 2420–2439.

Boucekkine, R., Germain, M., & Licandro, O. (1997). Replacement echoes in the vintage capital growth model. *Journal of Economic Theory, 74,* 333–348.

Boucekkine, R., Germain, M., Licandro, O., & Magnus, A. (1998). Creative destruction, investment volatility and the average age of capital. *Journal of Economic Growth, 3,* 361–384.

Boucekkine, R., Hritonenko, N., & Yatsenko, Y. (Eds.). (2010). *Optimal control of age-structured populations in economy, demography, and the environment.* Taylor & Francis, Oxon, UK; Routledge, New York, NY.

Boucekkine, R., Hritonenko, N., & Yatsenko, Y. (2011). Scarcity, regulation and endogenous technical progress. *Journal of Mathematical Economics, 47,* 186–199.

Boucekkine, R., de la Croix, D., & Licandro, O. (2002). Vintage human capital, demographic trends and growth. *Journal of Economic Theory, 104,* 340–375.

Boucekkine, R., de la Croix, D., & Licandro, O. (2003). Early mortality declines at the dawn of modern growth. *Scandinavian Journal of Economics, 105*(3), 401–418.

Boucekkine, R., de la Croix, D., & Licandro, O. (2004). Modelling vintage structures with DDEs: Principles and applications. *Mathematical Population Studies, 11,* 151–179.

Boucekkine, R., de la Croix, D., & Licandro, O. (2008). Vintage capital. In S. Durlauf & L. Blume (Eds.), *New Palgrave dictionary of economics* (2nd ed., pp. 628–631). Palgrave-McMillan.

Boucekkine, R., de la Croix, D., & Peeters, D. (2007). Early literacy achievements, population density, and the transition to modern growth. *Journal of the European Economic Association, 5*(1), 183–226.

Boucekkine, R., Licandro, O., & Paul, C. (1997). Differential-difference equations in economics: On the numerical solution of vintage capital growth models. *Journal of Economic Dynamics and Control, 21,* 347–362.

Boucekkine, R., Licandro, O., Puch, L., & del Rio, F. (2005). Vintage capital and the dynamic of the AK model. *Journal of Economic Theory, 120,* 39–72.

Cervellati, M., & Sunde, U. (2009). Longevity and lifetime labor supply: Evidence and implications revisited. IZA mimeo.

Chari, V. V., & Hopenhayn, H. (1991). Vintage human capital, growth, and the diffusion of new technology. *Journal of Political Economy, 99,* 1142–1165.

Cooley, T., Greenwood, J., & Yorokoglu, M. (1997). The replacement problem. *Journal of Monetary Economics, 40,* 457–499.

Cooper, R., Haltiwanger, J., & Power, L. (1999). Machine replacement and the business cycle: Lumps and bumps. *American Economic Review, 84,* 921–946.

de la Croix, D., & Licandro, O. (1999). Life expectancy and economic growth. *Economics Letters, 65,* 255–263.

de la Croix, D., Lindh, T., & Malmberg, B. (2008). Swedish economic growth and education since 1800. *Canadian Journal of Economics, 41,* 166–185.

Denison, E. (1964). The unimportance of the embodied question. *American Economic Review, 54,* 90–94.

Doms, M., & Dunne, T. (1998). Capital adjustment patterns in manufacturing plants. *Review of Economic Dynamics, 1,* 409–429.

Fabbri, G., & Gozzi, F. (2008). Solving optimal growth models with vintage capital: The dynamic programming approach. *Journal of Economic Theory, 143,* 331–373.

Faggian, S., & Gozzi, F. (2010). Optimal investment models with vintage capital: Dynamic programming approach. *Journal of Mathematical Economics, 46,* 416–437.

Feichtinger, G., Hartl, R., Kort, P., & Veliov, V. (2005). Environmental policy, the Porter hypothesis and the composition of capital: Effects of learning and technological progress. *Journal of Environmental Economics and Management, 50,* 434–446.

Feichtinger, G., Hartl, R., Kort, P., & Veliov, V. (2006). Anticipation effects of technological progress on capital accumulation: A vintage capital approach. *Journal of Economic Theory, 126,* 143–164.

Galor, O., & Weil, D. (1999). From Mathusian stagnation to economic growth. *American Economic Review, 89,* 150–154.

Gilchrist, S., & Williams, J. (2000). Putty-clay and investment: A business-cycle analysis. *Journal of Political Economy, 108,* 928–960.

Gordon, R. (1990). *The measurement of durable goods prices.* University of Chicago Press.

Gort, M., Greenwood, J., & Rupert, P. (1999). Measuring the rate of technological progress in structures. *Review of Economic Dynamics, 2,* 207–230.

Greenwood, J., Hercowitz, Z., & Krusell, P. (1997). Long-run implications of investment specific technological change. *American Economic Review, 87,* 342–362.

Greenwood, J., & Jovanovic, B. (2003). Accounting for growth. In E. Dean, M. Harper & C. Hulten (Eds.), *New directions in productivity analysis.* National Bureau of Economic Research.

Greenwood, J. & Yorokolgu, M. (1997). "1974," Carnegie-Rochester Series on Public Policy (Vol. 46, pp. 49–95).

Hart, R. (2004). Growth, environment and innovation – A model with production vintages and environmentally oriented research. *Journal of Environmental Economics and Management, 48,* 1078–1098.

Hazan, M. (2009). Longevity and lifetime labor input: Evidence and implications. *Econometrica, 77,* 1829–1863.

Hazan, M., & Zoabi, H. (2006). Does longevity cause growth? A theoretical critique. *Journal of Economic Growth, 11,* 363–376.

Hercowitz, Z. (1998). The embodiment controversy: A review essay. *Journal of Monetary Economics, 41,* 217–224.

Hritonenko, N., & Yatsenko, Y. (1996). *Modeling and optimization of the lifetime of technologies.* Dordrecht: Kluwer Academic Publishers.

Hritonenko, N., & Yatsenko, Y. (2005). Turnpike and optimal trajectories in integral dynamic models with endogenous delay. *Journal of Optimization Theory and Applications, 127,* 109–127.

Hritonenko, N., & Yatsenko, Y. (2006). Concavity in a vintage capital model with nonlinear utility. *Applied Mathematics Letters, 19,* 267–272.

Hulten, C. (1992). Growth accounting when technical change is embodied in capital. *American Economic Review, 82,* 964–980.

Johansen, L. (1959). Substitution versus fixed production coefficients in the theory of economic growth. *Econometrica, 29,* 157–176.

Jorgenson, D. (1966). The embodiment hypothesis. *Journal of Political Economy, 74,* 1–17.

Jovanovic, B. (1998). Vintage capital and inequality. *Review of Economic Dynamics, 1,* 497–530.

Kelley, A., & Schmidt, R. (1995). Aggregate population and economic growth correlations: The role of the components of demographic changes. *Demography, 32,* 543–555.

Krusel, P. (1998). Investment-specific R&D and the decline in the relative price of capital. *Journal of Economic Growth, 3,* 131–141.

Lucas, R. (1988). On the mechanics of economic development. *Journal of Monetary Economics, 22,* 3–42.

Malcomson, J. (1975). Replacement and the rental value of capital equipment subject to obsolescence. *Journal of Economic Theory, 10,* 24–41.

Parente, S. (1994). Technology adoption, learning-by-doing, and economic growth. *Journal of Economic Theory, 63,* 346–369.

Phelps, E. (1962). The new view of investment: A neoclassical analysis. *Quarterly Journal of Economics, 76,* 548–567.

Sattinger, M. (1975). Comparative advantage and the distribution of earnings and abilities. *Econometrica, 43,* 455–468.

Sheshinski, E. (1967). Balanced growth path and stability in the Johansen vintage model. *Review of Economic Studies, 34,* 239–248.

Solow, R. (1956). A contribution to the theory of economic growth. *Quarterly Journal of Economics, 70,* 65–94.

Solow, R. (1957). Technical change and the aggregate production function. *The Review of Economic Studies, 39,* 312–320.

Solow, R. (1960). Investment and technological progress. In K. Arrow, S. Karlin & P. Suppes (Eds.), *Mathematical Methods in Social Sciences 1959* (pp. 89–104). Stanford University Press.

Solow, R., Tobin, J., Von Weizsacker, C., & Yaari, M. (1966). Neoclassical growth with fixed factor proportions. *Review of Economic Studies, 33,* 79–115.

Whelan, K. (2002). Computers, obsolescence and productivity. *The Review of Economics and Statistics, 84,* 445–461.

Zeckhauser, R. (1968). Optimality in a world of progress and learning. *Review of Economic Studies, 35,* 363–365.

CHAPTER 6

Adaptive Economizing, Creativity, and Multiple-Phase Evolution

Richard H. Day

Emeritus Professor of Economics, University of Southern California (USC), University Park, Los Angeles, CA 90089, USA
E-mail address: rday@usc.edu

Abstract
Economic development is the outcome of an interaction between creative intelligence and adaptive economizing. Inventors and innovators continually perturb the possibilities for production, consumption, and social organization. Adaptive economizing enables individuals to cope with changing conditions and take advantage of new opportunities. Any seemingly stable situation that emerges is temporary. The process as a whole evolves out-of-equilibrium.

Keywords: Development, adaptation, technologies, growth, population, technological change

JEL classifications: O1, O3, O4, O330

> *We live, as it were, upon the front edge of an advancing wave crest and our senses of direction in falling forward is all we recover of the future's own path.*
>
> William James (quoted in Siemsen (2010)).

In the biological world, evolution proceeds through the emergence and interaction of various species of plant and animal life. With the arrival of humans, it proceeded within the species through the development of technology and the transformation of culture. This process was made possible by a remarkable leap in intelligence, inventiveness, and the capacity for elaborate social organization. Early humans fashioned tools and clothing that permitted them to populate one part of the world after another. Undoubtedly, the mental qualities that made this possible varied from person to person. That variation provided both the possibility of specialization and the desirability of cooperation. At the same time, it permitted experimentation outside prevailing norms. The result was an

Frontiers of Economics and Globalization
Volume 11   ISSN: 1574-8715
DOI: 10.1108/S1574-8715(2011)0000011011

elaboration of organizations and their development through successive stages of technology.

To understand this complex process, the concepts of infinite horizon optimality and equilibrium are of no use. Instead, economizing must be understood as an adaptive process based on bounded rationality. Then innovators and entrepreneurs who precipitate change must be introduced. Their activity requires mechanisms that maintain viability out-of-equilibrium. The resultant is a multiple-phase, evolutionary process that transforms human history through a sequence of advancing stages of technology and sociopolitical organization.

1. Adaptive economizing

The neoclassical theory of economic rationality and market equilibrium was already invested with adaptive content by Marshall who recognized that economic calculation was an incremental process that took place "at the margin" in response to utility and profit differentials. Walras described his tâtonnement process of price/quantity "groping" as a behavioral prerequisite for exchange, which would take place after equilibrium prices emerged. Cournot also recognized how competition among the few could lead to a sequence of adjustments out-of-equilibrium. In spite of those early developments, the adaptive out-of-equilibrium evolutionary nature of actual consumption, production, and exchange has not always been adequately accounted for in what passes for mainstream economic theory.

Indeed, one prominent theoretical school eschewed that task completely. Frank Knight, the prominent University of Chicago economist, was well aware of human frailty – especially its limited rationality. In spite of that, to discourage government officials from making conditions worse by tampering with what worked well enough in practice, he advocated thinking of the economy as a perfectly competitive, equilibrium system. Several of his followers describe the economy as if it were an unboundedly rational individual with a complete preference ordering over all possible time paths that could emanate from the current situation, just as it would be in an ideal socialist or fascist state.

Whatever one may think of this as an intellectual tour de force, it sheds no light whatsoever on how a market economy functions. A more relevant theory recognizes rational thinking as one among several means of determining action at any one time. When people do think rationally, they do so adaptively on the basis of limited, temporarily relevant information. Such behavior requires special arrangements for facilitating coordination of such independent behavior. Certainly, market economies of record are virtually always somewhat out-of-equilibrium. Let us consider then how producers and consumers really do solve the problems of inter-agent coordination while deciding how to proceed.

In reality, people economize by considering a relatively small number of alternatives among those that could or will eventually be thought about as time passes. They simplify the choice among them by arranging needs and wants in a priority order. The most important unsatisfied criterion at a given time guides choice. When it is satisfied (or "satisficed"), a second objective is considered, and so on until no more scope for further choice according to less important goals remains. This narrowing down includes the organization of plans into strategic and tactical components. After strategic objectives are determined, tactical actions can be planned to accomplish those objectives.

Prioritizing is typical of decision-making because it is often the best way to be effective in the exercise of choice. Those who cannot prioritize are often mired in quandaries, unable to "sort things out," unable to commit themselves to operational objectives. Economizing behavior does share something in common with optimizing algorithms that incorporate rules that limit the distance of succeeding steps in a sequence of trial choices. They embody the principle of local search, which forms a part of the core of behavioral economics, as, for example, described by Cyert, March, and Simon. Its mathematical representation consists of a sequence of relatively simple, constrained optimizations, each of whose constraints and objective function parameters depend on solutions of programs earlier in the sequence. These "recursive programs" include adaptive "zones of flexible response" that allow departures from the preceding choice to an extent that depends on experience.

By introducing a principle of increasing caution in response to failure, convergence to a stationary state or steady state could occur. But suppose all decision-makers did in fact behave in this way so behavior *did* converge. Such states might only be local optima with better candidates at some remove. Moreover, as conditions change from time to time due to external forces, a temporary equilibrium could be less effective than suboptimal behavior that failed to converge to a steady state but continued to search for better performance. Indeed, no one understands completely how the world works. No one can be sure that if their choices did converge, they would converge to the optimal solution of the *real* problem at hand.

This suggests that optimum-seeking behavior should not allow a succession of market punishments to discourage search altogether. Rather, *unmotivated search* should continue when local search temporarily gets "stuck." It can be driven by curiosity or eccentricity but not economic calculation of the usual kind. The abstract concept of infinite horizon optimality would seem to be fundamentally incompatible with wise behavior in an incompletely understood world.

Because optimizing is costly, substantive rationality requires its costs be taken into account and, if possible, avoided. This can be accomplished by alternative ways of making choices. Introspection and direct observation of individuals in various acts of choice enable us to identify several distinctly different modes in addition to explicit optimizing. These include experimentation, imitation, following an authority, habit, or tradition, following a hunch or simply searching without motivation.

In *experimentation*, a number of trial choices are made and the outcomes compared. A direction of improved decision-making might be discerned, which is used to guide further choice. At each stage in such a trial and error process, the cost of decision-making is relatively low. Given a sufficiently stable environment, improved decisions can emerge. The procedure is similar to the structure of optimizing algorithms. However, when several independent decision-makers interact, convergence may not occur. Choices may sometimes lead to better, sometimes to worse outcomes. Learning is most effective when only one of the interacting variables is varied at a time as in controlled experimentation. Then, cause and effect can be identified and appropriate directions of change determined. In situations where such a procedure could converge, the time to do so and the cost of mistakes could be considerable. The foregone benefit will depend on seemingly *ad hoc* characteristics of behavior that appear as degrees of caution or daring and the extent to which these characteristics vary in response to success or failure as experience unfolds.

Imitation of another decision-maker may reduce the effort required to think through a choice problem rationally. If a person is less skilled in choice-making than another, imitation may be the better part of wisdom. However, it need not be easy – and it may require rational thought in order to carry it out, but in many situations, it will be cheaper and safer than solving one's own problem from scratch. Industrial espionage provides an example in the business world. It may cost less and be less risky than the long process of research and development required to think through problems of product design or managerial control. Another example is provided in agriculture where imitation of a successful neighbor's crop rotation or choice of machinery is common among farmers. In virtually any occupation that requires great skill, following the practice of a master is usually the quickest way to acquire a satisfactory level of competence. Not only producers, but also consumers, especially when style and fashion are involved, often imitate one another. Indeed, imitation is so widespread a practice by consumers and producers that it seems strange to have been given so little attention by economists.

Following an authority is a common mode of behavior and most people invoke it frequently, especially if we include following the advice of a friend or the evaluation of an expert. Although such behavior may require "asking around," or even some reading and research, it may cost less than figuring out what to do for oneself. One should not suppose that this mode is costless. It is sometimes difficult to follow directions. Indeed, the instruction of an authority or expert may constitute a considerable challenge to rational thought and powers of mimicry. But expert advice can often provide a satisfactory selection of alternatives as a basis for action that short-circuits the chain of information gathering and reasoning that would otherwise be required.

Habit or following tradition is the routine repetition of past behavior. Many if not most of our actions, including routine purchase of consumption items and routine exercise of administrative procedures, fall in this category. It saves thinking and makes possible doing one thing while thinking about another. This is a profound advantage for solving costly problems and explains why great minds (one thinks of Einstein) often rely on habit, imitation, and the advice of others almost entirely in the daily routine so that they can spend most of their time thinking about deep economic, scientific, or artistic problems. Certainly, humans of any level of intelligence form habits but it is instructive to note that the most intelligent and presumably the most rational individuals rely on it as much or even more than ordinary people.

Unmotivated search is a name for behavior that is difficult to rationalize on economic grounds. It seems to be driven by curiosity, thoughtless impulse, or a sense of adventure. Small children sometimes do something merely on being exposed to the possibility. Adults who exhibit this mode might explain, "I did it just for the heck of it." This mode is perhaps easiest to identify in animals. Darwin, we recall, described "pioneer birds" who flew out to sea, presumably for no good reason and at great risk, arrived on a desolate island to initiate the evolutionary development of an identifiably unique variety of finch. Recreational sailors observe similar phenomena: lone bumble bees, miles from shore, nowhere near a flower, and none in sight. Creative scientists and business innovators are sometimes driven by a related impulse that bears no immediate reward and subjects the pioneer to unpredictable risks. In a way quite analogous to Darwin's pioneers, they provide a source of perturbation in economic evolution that can have powerful long-run effects.

A final category is *hunch*. Acting according to hunch is also some kind of nonrational mode that seems to defy explanation. Having good hunches and a willingness to act according to them is often asserted to be the basis for success in gambling, business, politics, and warfare. It may be distinguished from haberation and unmotivated search in that it may require a special intuitive faculty, quite distinct from thoughtless impulse or habit, that can be sharpened by experience. It may be especially successful in thoughtful individuals who are constantly considering problems and their solutions but who arrive at a choice by some process that has no articulation in rational terms, as in Poincaré's famous description of mathematical discovery.

Acting according to hunch may also describe some stock market investors who devote unceasing effort to examine information of many kinds and who explore every theory in whatever field that may have some bearing on economic value. Occasionally, these individuals describe their methods in best-selling books. Their imitators, however, rarely experience similar success. This suggests that *the true nature of their success is not encompassed by their analysis of it* and that it is either due to chance or due to a special intuitive faculty that they possess to a greater degree than most of us. Nelson and Winter following Polanyi call this faculty *tacit knowledge*. Pelikan (1989) and Eliasson (1990) have this in mind when they describe managerial *competence* in business.

There are, thus, seven distinct modes of action that govern economizing behavior to an important extent. They provide part of the concepts needed when attention shifts from optimality and equilibrium to procedural rationality and how economies work out-of-equilibrium. Of the seven modes, procedural rationality is probably not the most often used or necessarily the most effective. Indeed, the alternative modes make possible a focus of scarce cognitive resources and an effectual deployment of rational thought to those few problems where procedural optimizing is worth the mental effort involved.

It follows that in any given choice situation, there must be some kind of mental monitor that selects a mode of decision-making. Those who exploit rationality effectively focus it on choices that matter most and resolve the conundrum of freedom the rest of the time by behaving according to trial and error, habit, imitation, unmotivated search, authority, or hunch. Some people are much more effective than others in exercising rationality. They form models for others to imitate. Effective behavior can only be observed through time, so imitation occurs with a lag as it diffuses the benefits of rational thought.

Each mode of economizing behavior uses information. Elaborate optimizing techniques may require large numbers of parameter estimates of production and utility functions, statistical distributions, and so on. The acquisition, processing, storing, and retrieval of data take time and resources. Using too much is uneconomic and much behavior gets along with minimal information as in habit, imitation, and following tradition. Thus, *the psychological foundation of boundedly rational behavior rests itself on an economic principle applied to the activities of the mind.*

"Rational expectation" has been defined to be "the best use of all the available information." It is a seemingly unassailable assumption on the face of it, one that might reasonably be supposed to apply to any person faced with a choice. However, it involves the same paradox that rational choice itself involves. It can be a characteristic of individual equilibrium, but the act of testing it would perturb choice and reduce welfare. In other words, we cannot *know* how much information is best unless we use it all. It is the cost of doing that which is to be avoided. *This explains why we never use all the information potentially available but only a relatively tiny fraction of it.* The power of imitation, habit, and tradition is precisely that they can provide an adequate, good, or even a best choice without requiring the costly search and processing required to find and use information in the best possible way.

What information we do incorporate in our decision procedure is incorporated in a proximate framework. The adaptive, Bayesian, stochastic dynamic programming problem required by "rational expectations" could only be used for models of real problems that are *grossly simpler* than the real problems themselves. The only way competitive equilibrium could characterize economic *behavior* would be if all the agents could find and sustain it by invoking hunch and habit. Ironically, this squeezes *procedural rationality* from the economic picture entirely.

2. Cooperation, enterprise, and markets

Cooperation among individuals in the performance of production, consumption, and exchange greatly expands the range of possibilities available to individual choice. It facilitates specialization and productivity. Like decision-making, cooperation is costly and alternative ways of cooperating give scope for economizing activity. Specialized coordinating functions yield benefits just as they do in physical production. Indeed, *the performance of specialized physical and mental tasks and their coordination through management is the basis of enterprise.*

While some individuals in an enterprise focus on the development and application of physical skills, others focus on decision-making, communicating, and coordinating. This specialization requires individuals to submit to the broader purpose of the enterprise, to the mediating role of management, and to the leadership of those who organize and manage. The existence of the managerial function requires obedience to the authority of the manager. It implies a benefit to this form of specialization and cooperation. Carrying out an instruction may require a more or less challenging exercise of intellectual effort, but to do so implies a willingness to let someone else decide what instruction one is to follow: *it requires a willing suspension of one's own discretion in making choices.*

Voluntary cooperation can be induced through incentives; involuntary cooperation through some form of coercion. The former is generally the more productive in practice. In either case, the cooperating individuals must forego the freedom of self-determined action and they must exhibit forbearance in dealing with the behavior of those with whom they would cooperate. Such behavior is facilitated by group bonding, which enhances cooperation, specialization, and peaceful exchange among individuals in a group. Establishing such states of mind takes time. Individuals may achieve it by various informal interchanges or by participating in ceremonies and games. It is also produced in the process of identifying and selecting group leaders, that is to say, the mere emergence of a group leader, involves a kind of bonding. In various areas of society, such as organized religion, entertainment, sports, etc., special roles are played by individuals whose functions have something to do with bonding.

In short, cooperation based on bonding yields direct benefits that lie at the foundation of socioeconomic behavior. In complex market economies, firms exist not only to economize transactions costs in individual exchange but also to mediate specialization in work, management, and entrepreneurship. As an enterprise grows, the same principle of the division of labor that operates in physical production applies with equal force to management, and so managerial systems emerge. As they grow in complexity, the costs of deciding, communicating, coordinating, and all the other costs of transaction grow. Determining the best size for an enterprise and innovating new organizational forms and managerial practices to reduce transaction costs becomes a more and more crucial entrepreneurial activity. Eliasson has found that such costs can exceed those of direct labor and material.

Within an organization, it is in the interest of economy that rules come to play a central role. Rules proscribe behavior for repetitive situations. As they grow in complexity, systems of rules increasingly become formulated as *standard operating procedures*. Like habit and inertia, they economize intelligent discretion; they liberate cognition from trivial tasks and make it available for important problem-solving, creative innovation, and for effective bargaining and negotiation that provide the basis for voluntary cooperation. By following rules, members of a cooperative enterprise can concentrate on their several tasks, workers on their work, managers on management, bringing discretion to bear on behavior as problems arise that require it. As a corollary, however, rules reduce flexibility. They constrain individual initiative in the exercise of creativity and rational choice. The resulting inertia can impede invention and innovation.

The outcome of enterprise is the resultant of these polar effects. From the broad perspective of economic history, the bursts of creative morphogenesis and the growth of culture that characterize rapid development contrast with the atrophy of initiative and enterprise that characterize the decline of societies. Both arise from this fundamental paradox: *systems of rules that liberate intelligence also constrain its free implementation.*

Every society must have a way of establishing organizations and within each procedures for determining rules and for modifying them. The evolution of private ownership has produced a class of systems involving individual and corporate property rights and individual discretion mediated through markets for exchange. This system confers discretion to individuals and organizations for allocating effort and for using tangible and intangible assets. How does this market system work?

Markets take a great variety of concrete forms but a number of types can be identified that are characteristic. There are barter, auctions, brokerages, systems of order backlog, and/or of inventory control and price adjustment. Included in the latter are stores that are nothing more or less than inventories on display for sale at announced prices. They are adjusted from time to time in response to the volume of sales. Except for the most primitive forms of barter, these all involve economic enterprise, usually institutionalized as a licensed business, or a branch or division of a larger business organization. Markets, therefore, require work and management. They are subject to all the limits of cognition, information, and imagination outlined above. Voluntary exchange through this system is costly; it requires effort, resources, and time.

In his original statement on the nature of the firm, Coase set the firm off against "the price system" without describing what was meant by the latter. Given the foregoing observations, *a price system or market is a system of individuals, firms, and regulations that mediate individual transactions by means of prices and the exchange of purchasing power. Except for auctions and bargaining between individuals, markets are firms.*

But Coase's insights are crucial, nonetheless, and can be drawn on to explain why markets exist by turning his own argument around.[1] Consider the pure exchange with m goods and with n individuals. The Edgeworth Box describes the situation when $m = n = 2$. The lens within which voluntary exchange can occur is easily displayed; the core and the competitive equilibrium readily identified. Suppose $m = 2$ and $n = 3$. Already our geometric intuition is challenged. When $n = 4$, there is no hope of representing the theory with the aid of our spatial intuition. But think of n individuals in a large room. And as n grows large, imagine the prospects of them finding the equilibrium position in a reasonable amount of time. Consider now n individuals making plans for a lifetime involving m goods, some of which will be purchased daily, some weekly, some annually, some only a few times in a life, those times themselves to be part of the problem of choice. Now try to imagine millions of people interacting in a nation that produces thousands of goods. Think of billions of them exchanging in a world system of production and consumption.

The transaction cost of reaching mutually consistent plans rises in a combinatorial manner with the number of people and goods. For this reason, pure exchange is seldom used simply because it is uneconomic. People would starve before such a process worked itself out in the economy as a whole. In short, we use auctions, brokers, catalogs, and stores because it is economic to do so – even though *in equilibrium* we

---

[1] The classical works in transaction costs begins with Coase and includes Williamson's series of studies and those of North. I have to confess to not having read Coase's essays until this chapter was in its final stage of revision. That I came to similar views by a very much different path reinforces my confidence in my argument. In my defense, I note that Coase has not one reference to Commons, the theorist of transaction *par excellence*! The literature on this subject is, indeed, voluminous.

could be better off without them. So we derive *the disequilibrium existence theorem*:

Markets are systems of firms and units within firms that facilitate exchange when individual plans are incomplete and possibly inconsistent; they make it possible for people to get on with the tasks of production and consumption out-of-equilibrium.

The more complex the economy becomes in terms of the numbers of people, organizations, and goods, the more costly the process of search and bargaining and the greater the role for marketing enterprises. Instead of observing the gradual disappearance of these costly exchange mediators, we see instead the continuing expansion of their numbers because the cost of using them is much less than the cost of not using them.

Financial markets make possible a flexible source of purchasing power – credit – for investors whose plans cannot be perfectly coordinated with savers. They facilitate intertemporal exchanges between parties who do not yet exist. In addition, there is the special role that credit creation plays in a system where imagination is allowed to operate on the material aspects of life. We are considering now the creative potential that underlies individual acts of invention and innovation. It seems quite independent of wealth and power. It can be realized, however, only when means are placed at the discretion of those who possess it in abundance.

The emergence of a specialized role for mediating the transfer of purchasing power in exchange for promises of future repayment, and the creation of credit instruments that empower specialized enterprises to supply purchasing power when none existed before, therefore constituted economic invention of a very high order. It has rightly been made the cornerstone of the theory of economic development by Schumpeter and of the theory of development blocs by Dahmén. Thus, banking and financial intermediation generally provide mechanisms for entrepreneurship on a wide scale. In this way, they are essential instruments in the transformation of the economy. By allocating purchasing power, they facilitate and ration the application of imagination and initiative, simultaneously enabling and stabilizing change.

In effect, these institutions create an exchange between present and future consumers. The former get fewer resources and the latter receive the benefits of innovation and investment. Financial markets do this even though markets between the present and future cannot exist, and even though the future recipients have no influence whatever on the present inventive activity underlying the present creation of their consumption opportunities.

Here, as everywhere in economic life, the principle of bounded rationality is at work. Intertemperal allocations of capital can be based on forecast and hunches. Because entrepreneurship involves the hazard of discovery, the investment of capital can be and often is mistaken. Indeed, as in all managerial systems, financial intermediation is governed by the same bursts of inspired rationality, the same waves of imitation and diffusion, the same constrictions of habit and inertia, and the same unanticipated costs of imperfect expectations. Even so, it interacts with the "real" sector in a fundamental way. Far from being "neutral," the financial structure is literally the heart of the system.

3. Imagination, creativity, and imitation

As long as modern humans have existed, they have possessed the capacity to create things that could aid them in the struggle to survive; fire, tools, weapons, clothing, and the capability to domesticate other animals. From the beginning, they explored their surroundings and adjusted their way of life so that they could occupy the parts of the world their curiosity and need for living space led them to seek. This creative potential must reside to some degree in virtually every human being. We are born with no knowledge at all but must learn to cope with people and situations around us. Some are able to create things not found around them and to which others may adopt. So, culture evolves.

The ability to form and communicate images is at the foundation of human thought and language. According to Chomsky (1966), its creative character is a primitive quality even of everyday speech, which is the common heritage of all but those with special handicaps or impediments. Rational thought in general and economic rationality in particular rests on this creative capacity. Most of the choice problems that arise involve a selection among *imagined* futures, scenarios of what *might* happen, and sequences of acts that form conscious stories of what one *hopes* might be.

Managers of ongoing enterprise may possess more or less imagination. Routine operations require little of it, but the creation and choice among potential new products, new production techniques, and new forms of organization no doubt require a good deal of it. Even imitation and obedience to authority involve imagination for one must conjure up doing oneself what someone else may have done or is doing, or what one has been told to do.

Like all other human faculties, imagination and the capacity for creative endeavor is scattered asymmetrically through any population. Some are more richly endowed than others. Moreover, the uneven distribution of imagination, which provides the objects of thought among which cognition can discriminate and choose rationally, implies that rationality itself must also be unevenly distributed with some people being much better at procedurally rational thought than others. Inventors and entrepreneurs imagine things that do not exist and foresee practical steps that can make them happen just as each of us does whenever we form a plan for the future and carry it out. The choices of inventors and entrepreneurs, however, while involving conscious thought, may not always be rational in the procedural sense. They may involve hunch, the result of seemingly unmotivated search, as if their ideas come "out of the blue."

The adoption of newly invented techniques of production or management by less imaginative people follows by trial and error and by imitation. They lead to swelling waves of adoption that eventually transform the economy. Such transformations reflect the application of boundedly rational thought by the great body of managers and workers whose own endowments of creative imagination is sufficient to enable them to imitate the successful behavior of others or to follow instructions when effectively motivated. Thus, economizing and bounded rationality together explain the existence of specialized roles for invention, entrepreneurship, management, and routine work in searching out an economical allocation of resources.

The point is that *all* cognitive capacities are limited and must be rationed in carrying on the activities of life. Most people will exercise imagination and rational choice in some realm of activity but imitate others in many situations. By doing so, they take advantage of specialization and cooperation. This advantage is greatly enhanced by organizations that mediate cooperation: hence, the family, hunting, and food-collecting bands; farming villages; business firms, city—states; national governments; and administrative agencies.

4. Multiple-phase evolution

Past invention, innovation, production, and investment determine socio-economic structure and the current menu of alternative processes that can transform resources and human effort into consumer and capital goods. Choices among these processes are conditioned by current individual needs and wants, by sociopolitical institutions of collective decision-making, and by the stock of resources and capital inherited from the past. Those choices determine which activities are undertaken, what resources will be scarce, and which behavioral and social restrictions will be influential or operative. Exhaustible resources will be diminished; the stock of some capital goods increased; and productivity of some activities will be enhanced by accumulated experience. Past improvements will be embodied in more recently produced capital.

As time passes, exhaustible resources are diminished and their relative availabilities modified. New goods and technologies of production change the options available. As a result, the productivity of labor changes. Production and consumption activities evolve, some being abandoned and new ones adopted from time to time. Thus, a modified collection of activities is undertaken as the culture adopts new opportunities.

The period during which a given set of activities is undertaken and a specific set of constraints is operative constitutes an *economic phase*. As time passes, these sets of activities and constraints inevitably change as nonrenewable resources are exhausted and new technologies and commodities are created and adopted. The implication is that *economic development unfolds as a multiple-phase, evolutionary process.*

This complex process has not converged to an equilibrium or steady state and shows no sign of doing so. Instead, the pace of technological change has accelerated in the advanced economies. Many formerly backward societies have joined the process. Others are attempting to do so. It is not an objective of this chapter to speculate about the future course of this structural evolution. Certainly, it will continue to force change in patterns of behavior in all those societies entrained in the process. Certainly, also, it will precipitate new challenges for relationships among them.

Appendix A

A.1. Multiple-phase dynamics

Multiple-phase dynamic models describe the different relationships that govern behavior in differing situations of state.

In 1951, Georgescu-Roegen attributed to Le Corbeiller the idea that the theory of relaxation oscillations discussed earlier by van der Pol could give multiple-regime explanations of business fluctuations. In the same year Goodwin published his famous two-phase analysis, "Nonlinear acceleration and the persistence of business cycles," telling us of his inspiration from the same source. Georgescu's contribution was an outgrowth of Leontief's dynamic multisector model which, likewise, led to the problem of multiple regimes (Leontief, 1953, pp. 68–69). This literature, together with Simon's (1951) insightful analysis of "trigger effects" in mathematical programming, was the inspiration for my own use of multiple-phase dynamics to model structural change in microeconomic processes (Day, 1963; Day & Cigno, 1978) and in macroeconomic growth (Day & Walter, 1989). Haavelmo (1954) had already emphasized the inevitable intrusion of multiple regimes in the study of growth, and subsequently Malinvaud (1980) took the same approach in his macroeconomic reconsideration of unemployment. Despite these seminal contributions and despite the likelihood that many apparent anomalies can be explained in these terms, multiple-phase dynamics is conspicuous by its underrepresentation in the theoretical literature. This appendix provides a mathematical description of the basic concepts involved.

The formal counterpart of multiple-phase evolution can be described by a family of difference equations,

$$x_{t+1} = \theta_p(x_t), \quad x_t \in D^p, \quad p = 0, \ldots, n, \tag{A.1}$$

where each *phase domain*, D^p, belongs to an n-dimensional real vector space, $\mathbf{R}^n$. The map $\theta_p(\cdot)$ is the *p*th *phase structure*. The *p*th *regime* is the pair (θ_p, D^p). The dynamics within the several domains are described by their *phase* Equation (A.1).

In the *null domain*, D^0, the phase structure is the trivial map, $\theta_0(x)$ for all $x \in D^0$. Thus, if a trajectory enters D^0, it cannot escape.

Suppose that a trajectory enters the *p*th regime with a value $y \in D^p$. If there is a least integer n such that $\theta_p^n(y) \notin D^p$, then the trajectory emanating from y is said to *escape* regime p after n periods where the map $\theta_p^n(\cdot)$ is the *n*th iterated map of the map $\theta_p(\cdot)$. If the trajectory escapes regime p, it must switch to another regime. If it enters the null domain, the system is said to *self-destruct*.

Define the regime index at a given period by

$$I(x_t) := p \quad \text{if} \quad x_t \in D^p. \tag{A.2}$$

A history can be decomposed into a denumerable sequence of *episodes*, each one of which represents a *sojourn* within a given regime. Thus,

$$
\begin{array}{ccccccc}
s_0(x) & \leq & t & < & s_1(x), & I(\theta^t(x)) & = & p_1, \\
s_1(x) & \leq & t & < & s_2(x), & I(\theta^t(x)) & = & p_2, \\
s_2(x) & \leq & t & < & s_3(x), & I(\theta^t(x)) & = & p_3, \\
\vdots & & \vdots & & \vdots & \vdots & & \vdots
\end{array}
\tag{A.3}
$$

The state $\theta^{s_i(x)}(x)$ is the *i*th *entry state*; the sequence of integers $\{s_i(x), s_i(x)+1, \ldots, s_{i+1}(x)-1\}$ is the *i*th *sojourn*, and the number $s_{i+1}(x)-s_i(x)$ the *duration* of the *i*th episode. The sequence of regimes and episodes that generate a given trajectory is an *epochal evolution*.

If an epochal evolution has n episodes, $n < \infty$, the trajectory is trapped in the phase domain D^{p_n}. This does not imply that it converges to a stationary, steady, or periodic state, but only that the phase structure governing change does not switch once the p_n^{th} phase domain is entered. If the p_n^{th} phase zone is the null domain, the system *self-destructs*.

If for every p_i (except the last if the sequence is finite) there is a $j > i$ such that $p_j > p_i$, the history of episodes forms a *progression*. If for some $k > 0$, $p_{i+k} = p_i$, $i = 1, 2, 3, \ldots$, the evolution is *phase cyclic*. Note that a phase cycle does not imply that trajectories are periodic. Indeed, the "tent map" has two phases that are cyclic but its trajectories can be multi-periodic or periodic of any periodicity!

The general properties are illustrated in Figures 1–3. In Figure 1 after several periods of growth, the variable exhibits two-period fluctuations converging to the positive stationary state. The phase progression is simply D^1, D^2.

In Figure 2, from any initial condition except the stationary state, irregular periods of growth are followed by a single period of decline. The phases fluctuate back and forth indefinitely, D^1, D^2, D^1, D^2, ... Each phase exhibits one or more periods of growth in D^1 followed by a single decline in phase D^2.

In Figure 3, growth in phase one can be followed by a decline in phase two in a sequence of switching phases. It can be shown that, except for trajectories that hit the stationary state or a periodic cycle after a finite number of periods, trajectories escape into the null domain "almost surely," as mathematicians express it. That is, the progression is D^1, D^2, D^1, D^2, ..., D^1, D^2, D^0. Given the initial condition in the diagram, the progression is simply D^1, D^2, D^0.

These diagrams illustrate the concepts involved in the simplest possible way. Realistic models that describe economic development in agricultural and industrial sectors in both underdeveloped and developed economies have been described in *The Divergent Dynamics of Economic Growth*, published by the Cambridge University Press, 2004, 2006.

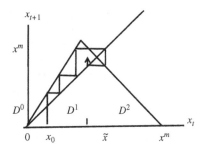

Fig. 1.   Growth and converging fluctuations.

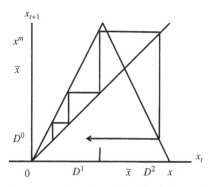

Fig. 2.   Growth with continuing fluctuations.

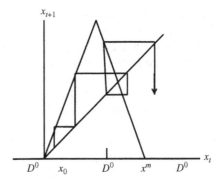

Fig. 3.   Growth, fluctuations, and demise almost surely.

A.2. An abstract adaptive society

A microeconomic multiple-phase theory of development can be outlined in abstract terms along the following lines. Begin with a set of agents (individuals, firms, and government agencies), an environmental state, and the actions that have just been taken by p agents in the system. Agents observe this situation, update their information about it, and form their plans. Actions attempt to control behavior according to plan, but contingent on the current state of the environment and on information not taken explicitly into account in the plan. Despite the attempts, actual states of the environment can cause a deviation from plans. As a result of the actions actually taken, a new state emerges. In this way, agents and environment coevolve.

Suppose there are m agents. For each agent $i \in I$, let w_t^i be the information available in period t, x_t^i be the plan for period t, and a_t^i be the action during period t. Also, let z_t represent the environmental conditions subject to which action takes place. Let $a_t = (a_t^i, \ldots, p_t^p)$ be the joint action and $w_t = (w_t^i, \ldots, w_t^p)$ be the joint information.

Begin with an environment state, z_t, a joint information, w_t, and a joint action, a_t. Each agent acquires updated information during period t,

$$w_{t+1}^i = \delta^i(a_t, w_t^i, z_t),$$

where δ^i represents the information updating procedure. While this information is being collected and processed, new plans are drawn up on the basis of the available information,

$$x_{t+1}^i = \psi^i(w_t^i),$$

where ψ^i represents the planning procedure. Given this plan, given the new information that becomes available, and given the current state, an action is taken,

$$a^i_{t+1} = \zeta^i(a^i_t, x^i_{t+1}, w^i_{t+1}, z_t),$$

where ζ^i represents the control function. Substituting for the current plan and current information, current action is seen to depend on past action, past information, and the past state of the environment,

$$a^i_{t+1} = \alpha^i(a_t, w_t, z_t) := \zeta^i(a^i_t, \psi^i(w^i_t), \delta^i(a_t, w^i_t, z_t), z_t).$$

In the meantime, a new state unfolds:

$$z_{t+1} = \omega(a_t, z_t), \tag{A.4}$$

where ω represents the environmental state transition process. Let $u_t := (a_t, w_t, z_t)$ and define the *joint information map*,

$$w_{t+1} = \delta(u_t) := (\delta^i(a_t, w^i_t, z_t))_{i \in I}. \tag{A.5}$$

Define the joint action map,

$$a_{t+1} = \alpha(u_t) := (\alpha^i(u_t))_{i \in I}.$$

The coevolution of agents and their environment boils down to the equations

$$w_{t+1} = \delta(u_t)$$
$$a_{t+1} = \alpha(w_{t+1})$$
$$z_{t+1} = \omega(a_t, z_t).$$

Define the composite map $\theta(u) := (\alpha(u), \delta(u), \omega(a,z))$. Then the complete dynamical system is summarized by

$$u_{t+1} = \theta(u_t). \tag{A.6}$$

A trajectory from an initial condition $u^0 \in U$ is represented by $u_t = \theta^t(u_0)$ where θ^t is the tth interated map of θ.

A.3. Viability

For a trajectory to exist, actions must be possible. Suppose each agent i has an *admissibility correspondence*, $A^i = \Omega_i(a_t, z_t)$, which describes the set of possible actions for agent i, given current behavior, a_t, and the external state z_t. The map $\Omega(a, z) := (\Omega^i(a, z))_{i \in I}$ defines the set of admissible joint actions for the society as a whole.

Assume there exists a *viability domain*, $U \subset \mathbf{U}$, such that

$$\theta(u) \in \Omega(a, z) \neq \varnothing \quad \text{for all} \quad u \in U. \tag{A.7}$$

The abstract adaptive society is viable in U if and only if

$$\theta(u) \in U, \quad \text{for all} \quad u \in U. \tag{A.8}$$

Condition (A.7) does not imply (A.8). It only says that each individual tries to do something. There must be a further requirement that agents' actions are compatible. To formalize this requirement, define a *compatibility correspondence*,

$$A(u) := \{(a', w')|(a', w', \omega(a, z)) \in U\},\tag{A.9}$$

where the viability condition (A.8) holds for all $u \in U$. The agents will be *compatible* for all $u \in U$ if and only if

$$(\alpha(u), \delta(u)) \in A(u) \neq \varnothing.\tag{A.10}$$

Suppose (A.8) and (A.10) *do* hold and suppose $u_0 = (a_0, \omega_0, z_0) \in U$. Then $\alpha(u_0) \in \Omega(a_0, z_0) \neq \varnothing$ because agents are admissible. Moreover, $(\alpha(u_0), \delta(u_0)) \in A(u_0) \neq \varnothing$ because agents are compatible. This implies that $(a_1, w_1, z_1) = (\alpha(u_0), \delta(u_0), \omega(a_0, z_0)) \in U$. By recursion, $\theta^t(u) \in U$ for all $u = u_0 \in U$. We therefore have the following existence requirements.

• If there exists a set U such that for all $u \in U$ (A)

    (i) $\alpha(u) \in \Omega(u) \neq \varnothing$ (agents are viable), and
    (ii) $(\alpha(u), \delta(u)) \in A(u) \neq \varnothing$ (agents are compatible),

then trajectories exist for all initial conditions $u \in U$.

Feasibility and compatibility depend on agents' information as well as on their actions. The compatibility correspondence implies that agents' actions and information cannot be independent.

To accommodate explicit economizing behavior, assume that *plans* can be represented as the solution to a multi-criterion mathematical programming problem. Thus, agents estimate the constraints that limit their actions and choose plans that satisfy those constraints according to a priority ordering amongst multiple criteria. At each stage, choices are constrained, not only to be feasible but also by the requirement that they satisfice all higher-order utility indexes. Consequently, the more criteria are satisfied, the more constrained the choice. If there is a single decision criterion, then the choice of plan is representable by a conventional constrained maximizing problem.

Formally, introduce for each agent, $i \in I$, a family of constraint functions, β_j^i, and a family of *limitation* functions, γ_j^i, $j \in J^i$. Given the information acquired, feasibility actions are represented by the correspondence

$$\Gamma^i(w_t) := \{x|\beta_j^i(x, w_t) \leq \gamma_j(w_t^i), \in J^i\}.$$

Introduce also a family of decision criteria (utility or objective functions) $\{\phi_k^i(x^i, w^i), k \in K\}$ and a family of *satisficing* functions $\{\sigma_k^i(w), k \in K\}$. Now let

$$u_k^i(x^i, w^i) := \min\{\phi_k^i(x^i, w^i), \sigma_k^i(w^i)\}, \quad k \in K.$$

Define the correspondence

$$\Psi_k^i(w) := \text{Arg} \max_{x \in \Psi_{k-1}(w)} u_k^i(x^i, w^i), \quad k \in K. \tag{A.11}$$

This is the set of perceived feasible plans for the *i*th agent that maximizes the *k*th criterion given that the preceding $k-1$ criteria in the priority order are satisfied.

Now define

$$\Psi_\ell^i(w^i) := \bigcap_{k \in K} \Psi_k^i(w^i). \tag{A.12}$$

This set is in general nonunique. For any w^i, let ψ_ℓ^i select a plan

$$\psi_\ell^i(w_t) \in \Psi_\ell^i(w_t). \tag{A.13}$$

This operator will depend on the procedure used to find a solution to the L^* problem (A.11). Call it the L^* planning operator. Notice that imitation or following an authority can be defined for any agent by

$$x_{t+1}^i = \Psi^i(w_t^i) := \min_{x^i \in \Gamma(w_t^i)} |x^i - a_t^j|.$$

That is, the *i*th agent plans to come as close as possible to what the *j*th agent actually did. Habit is represented when $j = i$, that is when one wants to "imitate" one's self.

The dependence of the decision criteria on the data allows for the adaptation of preferences to experience. The data themselves can only depend on past information actions and states, but may represent forecasts of the future so that the plan itself may represent a sequence of actions to be undertaken in the future. Anticipated actions, however, cannot depend on states that have not occurred but only projected states. Hence, by limiting the criteria to a single objective and defining Γ appropriately, the plan x_t selected at each point in time could represent a trajectory of action that would be revised from time to time on the basis of the data operator δ. It is also possible within this framework to represent optimizing plans by a Bayesian dynamic programming procedure. Moreover, by appropriate definitions of data elements in w and the information operator δ, plans could be modified at intervals longer than the unit time period, while actions could be adjusted to experience in every unit period.

Now consider the implications of L^* optimizing plans when agents adapt out-of-equilibrium in response to experience and to changes in the environment.

L^* agents are rational in that their plans optimize an L^* preference ordering given their information strategies. In the present context, the feasibility correspondence $\Gamma(w)$ is an estimate of the viability correspondence $\Omega(a,z)$. That is, what the individual considers to be feasible may be distinct from what is actually the set of viable actions. *It is essential that the control* function *make up for this possibility* and that together the information, planning, and control functions are *practical* in the sense that

$$\alpha^i(u) = (\zeta^i(a, \psi^i_\ell(w), \delta^i(a, w^i, z), z,))_{i \in I} \in \Omega^i(a, z) \tag{A.14}$$

at each stage of the process as it evolves through time. The mere requirement that $\psi^i(w^i) \in \Psi^i_\ell(w^i) \subset \Gamma^i(w)$ for all i does not guarantee this.

- If there exists a U such that for all agents $i \in I$, for all $u \in U$ (B)

  (i) $\Gamma^i(\delta^i(u)) \neq \varnothing$ (agents think they have feasible plans);
  (ii) $\psi^i(w^i) \in \Gamma^i(w^i)$ (agents select a feasible plan);
  (iii) $\alpha^i(u) = \zeta^i(\psi^i(a^i, w^i), \delta^i(w^i, z), z) \in \Omega^i(a, z)$ (agent's actions are admissible);
  (iv) $(\alpha(u), \delta(u)) \in A(\omega(u)) \neq \varnothing$ agents' joint actions and joint information are compatible)

Then trajectories exist for all initial conditions $u = u_0 \in U$.

(B) differs from (A) only by taking account explicitly of the need for rational agents to have feasible plans (otherwise they could not arrive at a decision).

A.4. Multiple-phase dynamics

Now take into account the structure of the planning problem. A plan is characterized as the solution of a programming problem. Each such plan satisfies a system of equated constraints associated with that solution. This dual system depends on the subset of constraints that are equated, the subset of the criteria that are satisfied, and on the gradient of the criterion maximized.

If the information on which plans are based changes from period to period, then this dual system may change. The characterization of each plan in terms of this system will change correspondingly. There are a finite number of possible dual systems. Let us index these sets by a subscript $p \in P^i$. Then associated with each w^i there is at least one system of equated constraints, for example, the $p^i(w)$th, a *planning rule*, $\psi^i_{p^i(w)}$, and there exists an *information zone*, $W^i_p \subset W^i$, such that for each $w^i \in W^i_p$, there exists p such that $\psi^i_p(w^i) \in \Psi^i_\ell(w^i)$.

Each situation will lead to information in one or the other of these information zones. This induces a partition $U_{p_i}, p_i \in P^i, i \in I$ on U such that for each $u \in U_{p_i}$,

$$\delta^i(u) \in W^i_p.$$

Now define for each agent the p action rules

$$\alpha^i_p(u) := \zeta^i(a^i, \psi^i_p(w^i), \delta^i(u), u), \quad u \in U_{p_i} \in P^i$$

and let $\theta_p(u)\colon = (\alpha_p(u),\ \delta(u),\ \omega(u))$. Then we arrive at the multiple-phase dynamical system

$$u_{t+1} = \theta_{p_i}(u_t), \quad u_t \in U_{p_i}, \quad p_i \in P^i, \in I.$$

As the system evolves, from time to time, u_t may cross the boundary from one phase zone to another, implying that the system of equated constraints for one or more agents will have changed. The phase structure switches endogenously. The implication is that for some agents, different constraints (e.g., associated with different resources) may be binding or a different set of needs and wants may be satisfied. The particular preferences governing choice at any time and the values imputed to the various constraining factors will therefore change. Moreover, the $\psi_p^i(w)$ may not be continuous. This means that trajectories can exhibit discrete jumps from time to time even when change may have been very gradual in between times.

A.5. Endogenous priorities

In reality, people change their minds about priorities that are reordered from time to time. To account for this phenomenon within the abstract adaptive economy framework, assume that not only the criterion and satisficing functions depend on states, but their order does also. Let $N(w)\colon = \{i_1(w),\ i_2(w),\dots\} \subset N\colon = \{1,2,\dots\} \subset N^+$. We can then refer to the jth element in $N(w)$, $i_j(w)$ by the index j. Now consider the L^* family defined in (A.8) except replace N by $N(w)$. For any information datum w, the L^* decision operator is well defined and can be characterized by a Kuhn–Tucker dual optimization problem.

Given this interpretation, the number *and* order of criteria satisfied evolve. Extended to all agents in an adaptive abstract society, this implies an endogenous evolution in the distribution of satisficed wants and needs; a possible convergence – or divergence – of social values, a development of social accord or discord. These social developments could have an important feedback effect on action and on the potential viability of a given system.

A.6. Discussion

The abstract adaptive society recognizes salient features of economic experience that have not been accounted for in formal theory, namely, the endogenous generation and switching of regimes, which is induced by the way people decide and interact. The behavior that results is based on limited and evolving knowledge which implies that adaptation out of equilibrium characterizes economic action more realistically than inter-temporal or temporary equilibrium.

138   *Richard H. Day*

Once we have gotten this far, the essence of the theoretical existence problem boils down to the nature of the data operator – which defines how agents learn about the world – and the nature of the compatibility operator that defines how a society enables the actions of its individuals to be consistent, one with another when each has scope for independent behavior. The former is both a psychological and social problem because agents learn from each other. Their values and decision criteria depend on the evolving system as a whole. Continuing evolution is a sociopolitical problem because compatibility is determined by the rules of conduct and the various institutions that are created as society evolves. This implies the existence of an evolving superstructure of coalitions among agents. That evolution depends on the need to facilitate compatibility.

To go further than these very general remarks, we need to add more specific aspects of economic structure, in particular, a more explicit distinction between stocks and flows (resources and capital, production and consumption), the incorporation of prices as components of data, and a specific provision for exchange transactions out-of-equilibrium. We should then have a multiple-phase, evolutionary analog of the Arrow and Debreu (1954) abstract economy, which would be a more realistic theoretical microfoundation for macroeconomics than is now available.

References

Arrow, K. J., & Debreu, G. (1954). Existence of an equilibrium for a competitive economy. *Econometrica, 22,* 265–290.
Chomsky, N. (1966). *Cartesian linguistics.* New York, NY: Harper and Row Publishers.
Coase, R. H. (1988). *The firm, the market and the law.* Chicago, IL: University of Chicago Press.
Commons, J. R. (1924/1959). *The legal foundations of capitalism.* Madison, WI: University of Wisconsin Press.
Cournot, A. (1838). *Researches into the mathematical principles of the theory of wealth* (N. T. Bacon, Trans.). With Irving Fishers Original Notes, 1963. Homewood, IL: Richard D. Irwin, Inc. Originally published in French.
Cyert, R. M., & March, J. G. (1963). *A behavioral theory of the firm.* Englewood Cliffs, NJ: Prentice Hall.
Dahmén, E. (1986). Schumpeterian dynamics. In R. H. Day & G. Eliasson (Eds.), *The dynamics of market economics.* Amsterdam: North-Holland Publishing, Chapter 7.
Day, R. H. (1963). *Recursive programming and production response.* Amsterdam: North-Holland Publishing Company.
Day, R. H., & Cigno, A. (1978). *Modelling economic change.* Amsterdam: Elsevier.

Day, R. H., & Walter, J.-L. (1989). Economic growth in the very long run: On the multiple-phase interaction of population, technology, and social infrastructure. In W. Barnett, J. Geweke & K. Shell (Eds.), Economic complexity: Chaos, sunspots, bubbles and nonlinearity. Cambridge: Cambridge University Press.

Eliasson, G. (1990). *The firm: Its objectives, its controls.* Stockholm: Industriens Utredningsinstitut.

Frisch,

Georgescu-Roegen, N. (1951). Relaxation phenomena in linear dynamic models. In T. C. Koopmans (Ed.), *Activity analysis of production and allocation.* New York, NY: Wiley.

Goodwin, R. (1951). The nonlinear accelerator and the persistence of business cycles. *Econometrica.*

Haavelmo, T. (1954). *A study in the theory of economic evaluation.* Amsterdam: North-Holland Publishing Company.

Leontief, W. W. (1953). Dynamic analysis. In W. Leontief (Ed.), *Studies in the structure of the American economy.* New York, NY: Oxford University Press.

Malinvaud, E. (1980). *Profitability and unemployment.* Cambridge: Cambridge University Press.

March, J., & Simon, H. (1958). *Organization.* New York, NY: Wiley.

Marshall, A. *Principles of economics* (8th ed.)

Nelson, R. R., & Winter, S. G. (1982). *An evolutionary theory of economic change.* Cambridge, MA: Harvard University Press.

North, D. (1981). *Structure and change in economic history.* New York, NY: W.W. Norton & Co.

Pelikan, P. (1989). Evolution, economic competence and the market for corporate control. *Journal of Economic Behavior and Organization, 12,* 279–304.

Polanyi, M., & Prosch, H. (1975). *Meaning.* Chicago, IL: University of Chicago Press.

Schumpeter, J. (1938). *Theory of economic development* (Rudgers Oppie, Trans.). Cambridge, MA: Harvard University Press. Originally published in German.

Siemsen, H. (2010). Unpublished correspondence.

Simon, H. (1951). Effects of technological change in a linear model. In T. Koopman (Ed.), *Activity analysis of production and allocation.* New York, NY: Wiley.

Walras, L. (1926/1954). *Elements of pure economics,* Edition Definitive (W. Jaffé and R. D. Irwin, Trans.). Homewood, IL.

Williamson, O. E. (1986). *Economic organizations: Firms, markets and policy control.* New York, NY: New York University Press.

CHAPTER 7

An Explicit Nonstationary Stochastic Growth Model

Robert Feicht[a] and Wolfgang Stummer[b,c]

[a]Chair of Economic Theory, University of Erlangen–Nürnberg, Lange Gasse 20, 90403 Nürnberg, Germany
E-mail address: robert.feicht@wiso.uni-erlangen.de
[b]Department of Mathematics, University of Erlangen–Nürnberg, Cauerstrasse 11, 91058 Erlangen, Germany
E-mail address: stummer@mi.uni-erlangen.de
[c]Affiliated Faculty Member of the School of Business and Economics, University of Erlangen–Nürnberg, Lange Gasse 20, 90403 Nürnberg, Germany

Abstract

We perform a comprehensive Monte Carlo simulation analysis of a variant of the nonstationary continuous-time stochastic growth model with Cobb–Douglas technology developed in Feicht and Stummer (2010), where for every (short-term, middle-term, long-term) time horizon the corresponding dynamic transitional sample path values were derived explicitly, that is, in closed form.

In particular, we study how much the outcoming (e.g., German empirical data adjusted) economy values are affected by changes of the involved economically meaningful parameters. Furthermore, we obtain realistically low savings rates, as well as a reasonably fast speed of recovery in situations where the abovementioned model economy is suddenly and considerably disturbed by a "crash" (macroeconomic disaster).

Keywords: Continuous-time stochastic growth, economic recovery, explicit sample-path dynamics, Monte Carlo simulations, savings rate

JEL classifications: O41, C30, C15, C60

1. Introduction

Continuous-time neoclassical stochastic growth models of Ramsey type have received growing attention for the task of modeling uncertainties in economies, see, for example, Merton (1975), Amilon and Bermin (2003), Roche (2003), Baten and Miah (2007), Smith (2007), Bucci, Colapinto,

Frontiers of Economics and Globalization
Volume 11 ISSN: 1574-8715
DOI: 10.1108/S1574-8715(2011)0000011012

Forster, and Torre (2008), Posch (2009b), as well as the books of Malliaris and Brock (1982), Turnovsky (2000), Chang (2004), Wälde (2010). Within such a one-sector economy framework which consists of a continuous-time, fully stochastic, Ramsey-type growth model with CRRA utility and Cobb–Douglas technology, we recently solved in Feicht and Stummer (2010) the inherent (extended version of the) social planner's problem in a *completely explicit* way. More detailed, we obtained in closed form

(a) the maximum expected lifetime utility of consumption under appropriate stochastic differential equation (SDE)-type constraints on capital stock K, labor-effectiveness A, and labor force L,
(b) the corresponding optimal (i.e., maximizing) consumption strategy,
(c) the dynamic transitional sample-path solutions K_t, A_t, L_t at *any* (short-term, middle-term, long-term) time horizon $t \geq 0$ of the underlying "optimized" SDEs, and hence the (nonstationary) dynamic transitional non-steady-state-equilibrium sample paths of the capital stock per effective capita described by $k_t = K_t/(A_t L_t)$,
(d) the corresponding long-term limit respectively the steady-state-equilibrium distribution of k_t.

Alternatively, (c) and (d) can also be obtained, for example, within a (nonoptimization) Solow–Swan-type context. One advantage of the outcoming total explicitness in (c), (d) is the implied ability to *precisely* analyze and simulate the stochastic dynamics of the involved economy components. This feature is especially useful in cases where these components *(re)start* from a *non-steady-state-equilibrium* distribution which applies, for example, for emerging economies like the BRICS and newly industrializing countries, as well as for scenarios of sudden economy crashes (macroeconomic disasters).

Such a comprehensive, exploratory Monte Carlo simulation analysis (ESA) – even within a slightly more general, less time-homogeneous setup than the one described above – is the main goal of the current chapter. In particular, for several economic quantities of interest we demonstrate the realistic suitability of the outcoming explicit stochastic-dynamic transitional sample paths (e.g., by comparison with German empirical data), as well as their sensitivity and robustness with respect to changes in the involved economically meaningful parameters (chosen within ranges "of broad acceptance"). One part of this ESA deals with the sample paths of the correspondingly derived implied saving rates, which stay within a realistic value-range and thus manifest a reasonable stochastic contribution to the fundamentally important question "how much should a nation save?" which was raised and extensively studied in a deterministic setup, for example, in La Grandville (2011) and the references therein.

2. The economy model

Let us fix a time horizon $0 \leq T \leq \infty$. In terms of the – at time $t \in [0, T)$ prevailing – capital stock K_t, effectiveness of labor A_t and labor force L_t, the production function for the economy is assumed to be of the Cobb–Douglas-type

$$Y_t = K_t^\gamma (A_t L_t)^{1-\gamma} \tag{1}$$

for some arbitrary but fixed capital share (output elasticity of capital stock) $\gamma \in (0, 1)$. The random dynamics of the effectiveness of labor (labor-augmenting technology level, total factor productivity) A_t evolves according to a geometric Brownian motion given by the SDE

$$dA_t = \mu_A A_t dt + \sigma_A A_t dB_t^A, \quad t \in [0, T), \quad A_0 > 0 \text{ given}, \tag{2}$$

with average growth rate $\mu_A \geq 0$ and constant volatility $\sigma_A > 0$. Moreover, the random dynamics of the labor force (labor supply) L_t is modeled by another geometric Brownian motion solving the SDE

$$dL_t = \mu_L L_t dt + \sigma_L L_t dB_t^L, \quad t \in [0, T), \quad L_0 > 0 \text{ given}, \tag{3}$$

with average growth rate $\mu_L \in (-\infty, \infty)$ and constant volatility $\sigma_L > 0$. Finally, the random dynamics of the capital stock K_t evolves according to

$$dK_t = [Y_t - \delta_t K_t - L_t c_t] dt + \sigma_K K_t dB_t^K, \quad t \in [0, T), \quad K_0 > 0 \text{ given}, \tag{4}$$

where $\sigma_K > 0$ denotes the constant volatility, c_t the random per capita consumption at time t, and $\delta_t := \delta_0 + b_\delta \cdot t \in (0, 1)$ the (time-linear) depreciation rate at time t; in case of infinite time horizon $T = \infty$ we consistently (and tacitly) assume $\tilde{b}_\delta = 0$ as well as $\delta_0 \in (0, 1)$.

At this point, let us emphasize that our quantitative findings developed below are flexible enough to allow for different nuances of interpretation of the economy components K, A, L, and Y whose time-dynamics are described by (1)–(4). However, a corresponding nuances comparison is beyond the scope of this chapter.

Notice that our model is *fully stochastic* in the sense that – due to the assumption $\sigma_A > 0$, $\sigma_L > 0$, $\sigma_K > 0$ – each of the economy values A_t, L_t, K_t (and thus, Y_t) is exposed to a source of uncertainties/shocks, here in form of independent standard Brownian motions B_t^A, B_t^L, B_t^K. A detailed comparison with similar *non-fully* stochastic models can be found in Feicht and Stummer (2010). In accordance with, for example, German empirical data, for the rest of the chapter, we confine ourselves to random per capita consumptions of the form

$$c_t = c(t, K_t, L_t) = \frac{1}{\gamma} \left\{ \frac{\gamma}{2}(1 - \gamma) \cdot (\sigma_K^2 + \sigma_L^2) - \gamma \mu_L + \rho_0 \right.$$

$$\left. + (1 - \gamma)\delta_0 + t \cdot [(2 - \gamma)\tilde{b}_\delta - 2\tilde{b}_\rho] \right\} \cdot \frac{K_t}{L_t} =: g_t \cdot \frac{K_t}{L_t} \tag{5}$$

for some linear function $\rho_t := \rho_0 - \tilde{b}_\rho \cdot t \in (0,1)$; in case of infinite time horizon $T = \infty$ we consistently (and tacitly) assume $\tilde{b}_\rho = 0$ as well as $\rho_0 \in (0,1)$. Furthermore, we assume $g_t > 0$ for all $t \in [0, T)$ which (together with (6) and (8) below) leads to $c_t > 0$. This model (1)–(5) can arise, for example, from a Solow–Swan-type setup, or alternatively, for example, from a Ramsey-type setup. The latter was shown in Feicht and Stummer (2010) for the case of constant depreciation rate $\tilde{b}_\delta = 0$ together with $\tilde{b}_\rho = 0$ to be interpreted as case of constant time-preference rate within a expected lifetime CRRA-utility-of-consumption optimizing framework; see Appendix A.3 for more details.

Explicitly solving (in a strong sense) the SDE (4) with (5) (see Appendix A.1) as well as the SDEs (2) and (3), we obtain the following economy dynamics: the random value of the capital stock at *any* (short-term, middle-term, long-term) time horizon t turns out to be uniquely given by

$$
K_t = A_0 L_0 e^{\sigma_K B_t^K + \left[\mu_L - \frac{\rho_0 + \delta_0}{\gamma} - \frac{1}{2}(2-\gamma)\sigma_K^2 - \frac{1}{2}(1-\gamma)\sigma_L^2\right]t + \frac{\tilde{b}_\rho - \tilde{b}_\delta}{\gamma} \cdot t^2} \cdot \left[\left(\frac{K_0}{A_0 L_0}\right)^{1-\gamma} + (1-\gamma) \right.
$$

$$
\left. \cdot \int_0^t e^{(1-\gamma)\left[-\sigma_K B_s^K + \sigma_A B_s^A + \sigma_L B_s^L + \frac{1}{2}\left(2\frac{\rho_0 + \delta_0}{\gamma} + 2\mu_A + (2-\gamma)\sigma_K^2 - \sigma_A^2 - \gamma\sigma_L^2\right)\cdot s + \frac{\tilde{b}_\delta - \tilde{b}_\rho}{\gamma}\cdot s^2\right]} ds \right]^{\frac{1}{1-\gamma}} > 0,
$$

$$\tag{6}$$

whereas the time-t random value of the labor effectiveness is

$$
A_t = A_0 e^{\left(\mu_A - \frac{1}{2}\sigma_A^2\right)t + \sigma_A B_t^A} > 0 \tag{7}
$$

and the time-t random value of the labor force is

$$
L_t = L_0 e^{\left(\mu_L - \frac{1}{2}\sigma_L^2\right)t + \sigma_L B_t^L} > 0. \tag{8}
$$

By using (6)–(8), one can also deduce the time-t random value of the per capita capital stock

$$
\frac{K_t}{L_t} = A_0 e^{\sigma_K B_t^K - \sigma_L B_t^L - \frac{1}{2}\left[2\frac{\rho_0 + \delta_0}{\gamma} + (2-\gamma)\sigma_K^2 - \gamma\sigma_L^2\right]t + \frac{\tilde{b}_\rho - \tilde{b}_\delta}{\gamma}\cdot t^2} \cdot \left[\left(\frac{K_0}{A_0 L_0}\right)^{1-\gamma} + (1-\gamma) \right.
$$

$$
\left. \cdot \int_0^t e^{(1-\gamma)\left[-\sigma_K B_s^K + \sigma_A B_s^A + \sigma_L B_s^L + \frac{1}{2}\left(2\frac{\rho_0 + \delta_0}{\gamma} + 2\mu_A + (2-\gamma)\sigma_K^2 - \sigma_A^2 - \gamma\sigma_L^2\right)\cdot s + \frac{\tilde{b}_\delta - \tilde{b}_\rho}{\gamma}\cdot s^2\right]} ds \right]^{\frac{1}{1-\gamma}}
$$

$$\tag{9}$$

as well as the time-t random value of the per capita effective capital stock

$$k_t = \frac{K_t}{A_t L_t} = e^{\sigma_K B_t^K - \sigma_A B_t^A - \sigma_L B_t^L - \frac{1}{2}\left(2\frac{\rho_0+\delta_0}{\gamma} + 2\mu_A + (2-\gamma)\sigma_K^2 - \sigma_A^2 - \gamma\sigma_L^2\right) \cdot t + \frac{\widetilde{b_\rho} - \widetilde{b_\delta}}{\gamma} \cdot t^2}$$

$$\cdot \left[k_0^{1-\gamma} + (1-\gamma) \int_0^t e^{(1-\gamma)\left[-\sigma_K B_s^K + \sigma_A B_s^A + \sigma_L B_s^L + \frac{1}{2}\left(2\frac{\rho_0+\delta_0}{\gamma} + 2\mu_A + (2-\gamma)\sigma_K^2 - \sigma_A^2 - \gamma\sigma_L^2\right) \cdot s + \frac{\widetilde{b_\delta} - \widetilde{b_\rho}}{\gamma} \cdot s^2 \right]} ds \right]^{\frac{1}{1-\gamma}}.$$

$$(10)$$

Accordingly, for the special case $\widetilde{b}_\rho = \widetilde{b}_\delta$ one can derive the probability density $f^{(t)}(\cdot)$ of the per capita effective capital stock k_t for any fixed (short-term, middle-term, long-term) time horizon $t \in (0, T)$ to be of the form (cf. Appendix A.2)

$$f^{(t)}(k) := \frac{1}{k^\gamma} \cdot \int_0^{(k/k_0)^{1-\gamma}} h^{(t)}\left(v, \frac{k^{1-\gamma} - v \cdot k_0^{1-\gamma}}{1-\gamma} \right) dv, \quad k \in (0, \infty), \quad (11)$$

with

$$h^{(t)}(v, z) := \frac{2\sqrt{2} \cdot e^{2\pi^2/\breve{\sigma}^2 t} \cdot v^{-b_1 - 1/2}}{\pi^{3/2}\breve{\sigma}^3 \cdot z^2 \cdot \sqrt{t}} \cdot \exp\left\{ -\frac{b_1^2 \cdot \breve{\sigma}^2 t}{2} - \frac{2(1+v)}{z \cdot \breve{\sigma}^2} \right\}$$

$$\cdot \int_0^\infty \exp\left\{ -\frac{4\sqrt{v} \cdot \cosh u}{z \cdot \breve{\sigma}^2} - \frac{2u^2}{\breve{\sigma}^2 t} \right\} \cdot \sinh u \cdot \sin\frac{4\pi u}{\breve{\sigma}^2 t} \, du \quad (12)$$

and

$$\breve{\sigma} := (1-\gamma)\sqrt{\sigma_K^2 + \sigma_A^2 + \sigma_L^2} > 0,$$

$$b_1 := \frac{2(\rho_0 + \delta_0)/\gamma + 2\mu_A + (2-\gamma)\sigma_K^2 - \sigma_A^2 - \gamma\sigma_L^2}{2 \cdot (1-\gamma) \cdot (\sigma_K^2 + \sigma_A^2 + \sigma_L^2)} > 0. \quad (13)$$

Furthermore, for the special subcase $\widetilde{b}_\rho = \widetilde{b}_\delta = 0$ we have shown in Feicht and Stummer (2010) under the two additional assumptions $T = \infty$ and

$$2\frac{\rho_0 + \delta_0}{\gamma} + 2\mu_A + (2-\gamma)\sigma_K^2 - \sigma_A^2 - \gamma\sigma_L^2 > 0 \quad (14)$$

that the long-term limit – as t tends to infinity – of the abovementioned k_t – distribution is a law $P_{\lim}$ having the density $f_{\lim}$ given by

$$f_{\lim}(k) = (1-\gamma) \cdot \frac{b_2^{2b_1}}{\Gamma(2b_1)} \cdot \exp\{-b_2 k^{\gamma-1}\} \cdot k^{-[2b_1(1-\gamma)+1]}, \quad k \in (0, \infty),$$

$$\text{with} \quad b_2 := \frac{2}{(\sigma_K^2 + \sigma_A^2 + \sigma_L^2) \cdot (1-\gamma)} > 0. \quad (15)$$

In contrast, for the same special subcase $\tilde{b}_\rho = \tilde{b}_\delta = 0$ with (14) and $T = \infty$ we have also proved that the per capita effective capital stock process $(k_t)_{t \geq 0}$ has a steady-state-equilibrium distribution P_{stea} – also known as stationary distribution respectively invariant distribution – which means in particular that if at some time $u > 0$ the distribution of k_u is equal to P_{stea}, then at any later time $v > u$ the distribution of k_v is also equal to P_{stea}.

Indeed, one gets that P_{stea} has a density f_{stea} that coincides with $f_{\lim}$. In light of this, within the special subcase there appears the effect that (at least) for long-term (but finite) time horizons u the distribution of k_u becomes close to P_{stea}, and thus at any later time horizon $v > u$ the distribution of k_v stays close to P_{stea}. Despite of this (approximative) equilibrium effect, we emphasize again that in our context the per capita effective capital stock process $(k_t)_{t \geq 0}$ *starts in non-equilibrium* – namely, with the single-valued distribution at k_0 – rather than with the steady-state-equilibrium distribution P_{stea}. Under the assumption

$$2\frac{\rho_0 + \delta_0}{\gamma} + 2\mu_A + (1 - \gamma)\sigma_K^2 - 2\sigma_A^2 - (1 + \gamma)\sigma_L^2 > 0, \tag{16}$$

which is stronger than (14), the corresponding mean μ_{stea} of the steady-state distribution P_{stea} – thus, of the limit distribution $P_{\lim}$ – can be computed as (cf. Feicht and Stummer, 2010)

$$\mu_{stea} = \left(\frac{2}{(\sigma_K^2 + \sigma_A^2 + \sigma_L^2)(1 - \gamma)}\right)^{\frac{1}{1-\gamma}}$$
$$\cdot \frac{\Gamma\left(\frac{2(\rho_0+\delta_0)/\gamma+2\mu_A+(1-\gamma)\sigma_K^2-2\sigma_A^2-(1+\gamma)\sigma_L^2}{(\sigma_K^2+\sigma_A^2+\sigma_L^2)(1-\gamma)}\right)}{\Gamma\left(\frac{2(\rho_0+\delta_0)/\gamma+2\mu_A+(2-\gamma)\sigma_K^2-\sigma_A^2-\gamma\sigma_L^2}{(\sigma_K^2+\sigma_A^2+\sigma_L^2)(1-\gamma)}\right)} < \infty. \tag{17}$$

Within the *general* setup (especially for $\tilde{b}_\rho \neq \tilde{b}_\delta$), one can derive from (6), (7), (8), and (10) further important quantities of interest such as the time-t random value of the production function

$$Y_t = K_t^\gamma \cdot (A_t L_t)^{1-\gamma} = k_t^\gamma \cdot A_t L_t$$
$$= A_0 L_0 e^{\gamma\sigma_K B_t^K + (1-\gamma)\sigma_A B_t^A + (1-\gamma)\sigma_L B_t^L + \left[(1-\gamma)\mu_A + \mu_L - \rho_0 - \delta_0 - \frac{\gamma(2-\gamma)}{2}\sigma_K^2 - \frac{1-\gamma}{2}\sigma_A^2 - \frac{1-\gamma^2}{2}\sigma_L^2\right]t + (\tilde{b}_\rho - \tilde{b}_\delta)\cdot t^2}$$
$$\cdot \left[(1-\gamma)\int_0^t e^{\left[-\sigma_K B_s^K + \sigma_A B_s^A + \sigma_L B_s^L + \frac{1}{2}\left(2\frac{\rho_0+\delta_0}{\gamma}+2\mu_A+(2-\gamma)\sigma_K^2-\sigma_A^2-\gamma\sigma_L^2\right)\cdot s + \frac{\tilde{b}_\delta-\tilde{b}_\rho}{\gamma}s^2\right]} ds\right.$$
$$\left. + \left(\frac{K_0}{A_0 L_0}\right)^{1-\gamma}\right]^{\frac{\gamma}{1-\gamma}}, \tag{18}$$

the time-t random value of the per capita production function

$$\frac{Y_t}{L_t} = k_t^\gamma \cdot A_t = A_0 e^{\gamma \sigma_K B_t^K + (1-\gamma)\sigma_A B_t^A - \gamma \sigma_L B_t^L + \left[(1-\gamma)\mu_A - \rho_0 - \delta_0 - \frac{\gamma(2-\gamma)}{2}\sigma_K^2 - \frac{1-\gamma}{2}\sigma_A^2 + \frac{\gamma^2}{2}\sigma_L^2\right]t + (\tilde{b}_\rho - \tilde{b}_\delta)\cdot t^2}$$

$$\cdot \left[(1-\gamma)\int_0^t e^{(1-\gamma)\left[-\sigma_K B_s^K + \sigma_A B_s^A + \sigma_L B_s^L + \frac{1}{2}\left(\frac{2\rho_0+\delta_0}{\gamma}+2\mu_A+(2-\gamma)\sigma_K^2 - \sigma_A^2 - \gamma\sigma_L^2\right)\cdot s + \frac{\tilde{b}_\delta - \tilde{b}_\rho}{\gamma}\cdot s^2\right]} ds\right.$$

$$\left. + \left(\frac{K_0}{A_0 L_0}\right)^{1-\gamma}\right]^{\frac{\gamma}{1-\gamma}}, \tag{19}$$

as well as the time-t random value of the per capita effective production function

$$\tilde{Y}_t := \frac{Y_t}{A_t L_t} = k_t^\gamma = e^{\gamma \sigma_K B_t^K - \gamma \sigma_A B_t^A - \gamma \sigma_L B_t^L - \left[\gamma\mu_A + \rho_0 + \delta_0 + \frac{\gamma(2-\gamma)}{2}\sigma_K^2 - \frac{\gamma}{2}\sigma_A^2 - \frac{\gamma^2}{2}\sigma_L^2\right]t + (\tilde{b}_\rho - \tilde{b}_\delta)\cdot t^2}$$

$$\cdot \left[(1-\gamma)\int_0^t e^{(1-\gamma)\left[-\sigma_K B_s^K + \sigma_A B_s^A + \sigma_L B_s^L + \frac{1}{2}\left(\frac{2\rho_0+\delta_0}{\gamma}+2\mu_A+(2-\gamma)\sigma_K^2 - \sigma_A^2 - \gamma\sigma_L^2\right)\cdot s + \frac{\tilde{b}_\delta - \tilde{b}_\rho}{\gamma}\cdot s^2\right]} ds\right.$$

$$\left. + \left(\frac{K_0}{A_0 L_0}\right)^{1-\gamma}\right]^{\frac{\gamma}{1-\gamma}}. \tag{20}$$

For the latter, within the special case $\tilde{b}_\rho = \tilde{b}_\delta$ one can proceed similarly to the treatment of per capita effective capital stock k_t and deduce for any fixed (short-term, middle-term, long-term) time horizon $t \in (0, T)$ the probability density $\tilde{f}^{(t)}(\cdot)$ to be of the form (cf. Appendix A.2)

$$\tilde{f}^{(t)}(\tilde{y}) := \frac{\tilde{y}^{\frac{1}{\gamma}-2}}{\gamma} \cdot \int_0^{\tilde{y}^{\frac{1-\gamma}{\gamma}}\cdot k_0^{\gamma-1}} h^{(t)}\left(v, \frac{\tilde{y}^{\frac{1-\gamma}{\gamma}} - v\cdot k_0^{1-\gamma}}{1-\gamma}\right) dv, \quad \tilde{y} \in (0, \infty), \tag{21}$$

with $h^{(t)}(\cdot, \cdot)$ given by (12). Furthermore, for the special subcase $\tilde{b}_\rho = \tilde{b}_\delta = 0$ it can be shown (cf. Appendix A.2) that under the assumptions (14) and $T = \infty$ the long-term limit – as t tends to infinity – of the above mentioned $\tilde{Y}_t$ – distribution is a law $\widetilde{P_{\lim}}$ having the density $\widetilde{f_{\lim}}$ given by

$$\widetilde{f_{\lim}}(\tilde{y}) = \left(\frac{1}{\gamma} - 1\right) \cdot \frac{b_2^{2b_1}}{\Gamma(2b_1)} \exp\{-b_2 \tilde{y}^{1-1/\gamma}\} \cdot \tilde{y}^{-\left[2b_1(\frac{1}{\gamma}-1)+1\right]}, \tilde{y} \in (0, \infty); \tag{22}$$

$\widetilde{P_{\lim}}$ also coincides with the corresponding steady-state-equilibrium distribution $\widetilde{P_{\text{stea}}}$ of $(\tilde{Y}_t)_{t\geq 0}$, and under the additional assumption (16) one obtains the corresponding mean $\widetilde{\mu_{\text{stea}}}$ to be

$$\widetilde{\mu}_{\text{stea}} = \left(\frac{2}{(\sigma_K^2 + \sigma_A^2 + \sigma_L^2)\left(\frac{1}{\gamma} - 1\right)} \right)^{\frac{\gamma}{1-\gamma}}$$

$$\cdot \frac{\Gamma\left(\frac{2\frac{\rho_0+\delta_0}{2-\gamma} + 2\mu_A + ((1/\gamma)-1)\sigma_K^2 - 2\sigma_A^2 - (3-(1/\gamma))\sigma_L^2}{(\sigma_K^2+\sigma_A^2+\sigma_L^2)((1/\gamma)-1)} \right)}{\Gamma\left(\frac{2\frac{\rho_0+\delta_0}{2-\gamma} + 2\mu_A + (\sigma_K^2/\gamma) - \sigma_A^2 - (2-(1/\gamma))\sigma_L^2}{(\sigma_K^2+\sigma_A^2+\sigma_L^2)((1/\gamma)-1)} \right)} < \infty. \tag{23}$$

As far as consumptions and savings are concerned, within the *general* setup (especially for $\widetilde{b}_\rho \neq \widetilde{b}_\delta$) we employ (5), (8), and (9) to end up with the time-t random value of the per capita consumption

$$c_t = \frac{1}{\gamma}\{\rho_0 + \delta_0(1-\gamma) - \gamma\mu_L + \frac{1}{2}(1-\gamma)\gamma(\sigma_K^2 + \sigma_L^2) + ((2-\gamma)\widetilde{b}_\delta - 2\widetilde{b}_\rho)\cdot t\}$$

$$\cdot A_0 e^{\sigma_K B_t^K - \sigma_L B_t^L - \frac{1}{2}\left[2\frac{\rho_0+\delta_0}{\gamma}+(2-\gamma)\sigma_K^2-\gamma\sigma_L^2\right]t+\frac{\widetilde{b}_\rho-\widetilde{b}_\delta}{\gamma}\cdot t^2} \cdot \left[\left(\frac{K_0}{A_0 L_0}\right)^{1-\gamma} \right.$$

$$\left. +(1-\gamma)\int_0^t e^{(1-\gamma)\left[-\sigma_K B_s^K + \sigma_A B_s^A + \sigma_L B_s^L + \frac{1}{2}\left(2\frac{\rho_0+\delta_0}{\gamma}+2\mu_A+(2-\gamma)\sigma_K^2-\sigma_A^2-\gamma\sigma_L^2\right)\cdot s + \frac{\widetilde{b}_\delta-\widetilde{b}_\rho}{\gamma}\cdot s^2\right]} ds \right]^{\frac{1}{1-\gamma}}, \tag{24}$$

the time-t random value of the (total) consumption

$$C_t = c_t \cdot L_t = \frac{1}{\gamma}\{\rho_0 + \delta_0(1-\gamma) - \gamma\mu_L + \frac{1}{2}(1-\gamma)\gamma(\sigma_K^2 + \sigma_L^2) + ((2-\gamma)\widetilde{b}_\delta - 2\widetilde{b}_\rho)\cdot t\}$$

$$\cdot A_0 L_0 e^{\sigma_K B_t^K + \left[\mu_L - \frac{\rho_0+\delta_0}{\gamma} - \frac{1}{2}(2-\gamma)\sigma_K^2 - \frac{1}{2}(1-\gamma)\sigma_L^2\right]t+\frac{\widetilde{b}_\rho-\widetilde{b}_\delta}{\gamma}\cdot t^2} \cdot \left[\left(\frac{K_0}{A_0 L_0}\right)^{1-\gamma} \right.$$

$$\left. +(1-\gamma)\int_0^t e^{(1-\gamma)\left[-\sigma_K B_s^K + \sigma_A B_s^A + \sigma_L B_s^L + \frac{1}{2}\left(2\frac{\rho_0+\delta_0}{\gamma}+2\mu_A+(2-\gamma)\sigma_K^2-\sigma_A^2-\gamma\sigma_L^2\right)\cdot s + \frac{\widetilde{b}_\delta-\widetilde{b}_\rho}{\gamma}\cdot s^2\right]} ds \right]^{\frac{1}{1-\gamma}},$$

which together with (18) leads to the time-t random value of the (implied) savings rate

$$s_t = 1 - \frac{C_t}{Y_t} = 1 - \frac{1}{\gamma}\left\{\rho_0 + \delta_0(1-\gamma) - \gamma\mu_L + \frac{\gamma}{2}(1-\gamma)\cdot(\sigma_K^2 + \sigma_L^2) + ((2-\gamma)\widetilde{b}_\delta - 2\widetilde{b}_\rho)\cdot t\right\}\cdot k_t^{1-\gamma}$$

$$= 1 - \frac{1}{\gamma}\left\{\rho_0 + \delta_0(1-\gamma) - \gamma\mu_L + \frac{1}{2}(1-\gamma)\gamma(\sigma_K^2 + \sigma_L^2) + ((2-\gamma)\widetilde{b}_\delta - 2\widetilde{b}_\rho)\cdot t\right\}$$

$$\cdot e^{(1-\gamma)\cdot\left[\sigma_K B_t^K - \sigma_A B_t^A - \sigma_L B_t^L - \frac{1}{2}\left(2\frac{\rho_0+\delta_0}{\gamma}+2\mu_A+(2-\gamma)\sigma_K^2-\sigma_A^2-\gamma\sigma_L^2\right)\right]\cdot t + \frac{(1-\gamma)(\widetilde{b}_\rho-\widetilde{b}_\delta)}{\gamma}\cdot t^2} \cdot \left[\left(\frac{K_0}{A_0 L_0}\right)^{1-\gamma} \right.$$

$$\left. +(1-\gamma)\int_0^t e^{(1-\gamma)\left[-\sigma_K B_s^K + \sigma_A B_s^A + \sigma_L B_s^L + \frac{1}{2}\left(2\frac{\rho_0+\delta_0}{\gamma}+2\mu_A+(2-\gamma)\sigma_K^2-\sigma_A^2-\gamma\sigma_L^2\right)\cdot s + \frac{\widetilde{b}_\delta-\widetilde{b}_\rho}{\gamma}\cdot s^2\right]} ds \right]. \tag{25}$$

From the first line in (25), one can derive – for the special case $\tilde{b}_\rho = \tilde{b}_\delta$ – the probability density $\tilde{f}^{(t)}(\cdot)$ of the savings rate s_t for any fixed (short-term, middle-term, long-term) time horizon $t \in (0, T)$ to be of the form (cf. Appendix A.2)

$$\tilde{f}^{(t)}(s) := \frac{1}{(1-\gamma) \cdot g_t} \cdot \int_0^{(1-s) \cdot g_t^{-1} \cdot k_0^{\gamma-1}} h^{(t)}\left(v, \frac{(1-s) \cdot g_t^{-1} - v \cdot k_0^{1-\gamma}}{1-\gamma}\right) dv, \quad s < 1,$$

(26)

with $h^{(t)}(\cdot, \cdot)$ given by (12), as well as with (cf. (5))

$$g_t := \frac{\rho_0 + \delta_0(1-\gamma)}{\gamma} - \mu_L + \frac{1}{2}(1-\gamma) \cdot (\sigma_K^2 + \sigma_L^2) - \tilde{b}_\delta \cdot t, \quad t \in (0, T).$$

3. Exploratory simulation analyses

In the following, we demonstrate the realistic suitability – over reasonably "long" periods – of our explicit stochastic dynamic transitional sample-paths (6)–(10), (18)–(20), (24), and (25), by evaluating them *directly* (rather than indirectly as numerically less stable SDE approximations) through a comprehensive multivariate Monte Carlo simulation analysis that is compared with corresponding German empirical data. This goal is basically achieved in two major steps: in Step 1, we choose the definite parameter constellation $T = 10$, $\gamma = 0.33$, $\delta_0 = 0.0456$, $\tilde{b}_\delta = 0.00069$, $\rho_0 = 0.0571$, $\tilde{b}_\rho = 0.00073$, $\mu_L = 0.0045$, $\sigma_L = 0.0070$, $\mu_A = 0.0088$, $\sigma_A = 0.0065$, $\sigma_K = 0.0030$, which

(G1) (except for $\tilde{b}_\delta$, $\tilde{b}_\rho$) lies within respectively "close to" a parameter range "of broad acceptance" arising from some similar, less explicit and "stochastically lower dimensional" studies quoted in Table 1,

(G2) leads to simulated dynamic transitional sample path runs which at the initial time $t = 0$ coincide with – respectively at the times (end of years) $t = 1, 2, \ldots, 10$ are very close to – the corresponding empirical data points directly taken (respectively indirectly derived) from the European Commission's Annual Macro-Economic AMECO database entries (at constant prices) about the German economy between 1995 and 2005, thus leaving out (delayed) reunification effects as well as pre-effects of the current financial crisis; notice in particular that the assumptions $\delta_0 = 0.0456$, $\tilde{b}_\delta = 0.00069$ are a good proxy for the corresponding empirical depreciation rate behavior, and $\rho_0 = 0.0571$, $\tilde{b}_\rho = 0.00073$ mirror the empirical evolution of a time preference rate, which, for example, is close to the annual yield performance of the German 10-year Federal bond within the abovementioned period.

At this point, let us emphasize that here we mainly aim for an out-of-sample simulation analysis rather than an in-sample one, and correspondingly interpret the – in all the figures as small filled circles –

Robert Feicht and Wolfgang Stummer

Table 1. Some concrete parameters in literature

Reference	ρ_0	δ_0	γ	σ_K	σ_A	μ_A	σ_L	μ_L
Acemoglu and Guerrieri (2008)	0.02	0.05	0.1–0.77					0.018
Amilon and Bermin (2003)	0.06		0.8				0.2	
Barro, Mankiw, and Sala-i Martin (1995)		0.05	0.3					0.01
Bernanke and Gürkaynak (2001)	0.07–0.12		0.36					
Braun and Nakajima (2009)	0.08		0.3					
Bucci, Colapinto, Forster, and Torre (2008)	0.04	0.05	0.33			0.0148	0.02	
Cagetti, Hansen, Sargent, and Williams (2002)	0.04	0.07	0.35			0.0192		
Cagetti and Nardi (2009)		0.06	0.33					
Caselli and Coleman (2006)			0.33					
Conesa, Kitao, and Krueger (2009)		0.0833	0.36					
Gollin, Parente, and Rogerson (2002)	0.05	0.065	0.5					
Hall (2001)		0.1						
Jensen and Richter (2007)		0.05, 0.08	0.2–0.6	0.03			0.01	0.01, 0.02
King and Rebelo (1993)		0.10	0.33					0.014
Nishide and Ohyama (2007)	0.02				0.08			
Palacios (2010)	0.001	0.05	0.36	0.12			0.017	
Posch (2009b)	0.03	0.05	0.5			0.02	0.01	
Pyyhtiä (2007)			0.33					
Schmitt-Grohe (2000)	0.04	0.1					0.016	
Williams (2004)	0.015	0.0517	0.35			0.0492	0.0176	

Note: "Blank" spaces mean no-occurrence or lacking of comparability; time-preference and depreciation are both constant in time, that is $\tilde{b}_\rho = \tilde{b}_\delta = 0$.

incorporated empirical data as a benchmark for "an economy performing in the next ten years in a similar way as the German economy did in 1995–2005". For the sake of brevity, a comprehensive statistical analysis of our model on various different data sets will appear in a forthcoming paper.

In Step 2, starting from the abovementioned concrete parameter constellation we analyze (mostly ceteris paribus, also with respect to the occuring random shocks) how strongly a change in parameter value affects the transitional sample path runs. Such changes may, for example, stem from a concrete or planned economic policy alteration, from an "internal economy regime switch", or from moving "fictitiously" between the two ends of the corresponding parameter confidence interval in the course of determining the sensitivity of statistical estimation errors (quantifying the degree of model risk).

To begin with the details of Step 1, let us first mention that for simplicity we have chosen the initial sample path values $K_0 = K_0^{\text{emp}} = 5.70793 \cdot 10^{12}$, $A_0 = A_0^{\text{emp}} = 28644$, $L_0 = L_0^{\text{emp}} = 37.601 \cdot 10^6$ (employed persons in all domestic industries, National account) to be equal with their empirical counterparts (i.e., the initial data points) $K_0^{\text{emp}}, A_0^{\text{emp}}, L_0^{\text{emp}}$. Furthermore, all the involved integrals of the type $\int_0^t \eta(s, B_s^K(\omega), B_s^A(\omega), B_s^L(\omega)) \, ds$ are approximated by sums according to either the straightforward classical Cauchy formula or the average-taking trapezoidal rule, leading to the same results.

For the capital stock dynamics K_t given by (6) we present in Figure 1 three graphs with single transitional sample path runs as well as one graph with a bunch of fifteen transitional sample path runs. Notice that for the sake of comparability and transparency, we have scaled the display of the sample paths to start at 1.0, by division through the initial empirical data point K_0^{emp}.

The last subplot with 15 sample path simulations shows that despite of the small volatility $\sigma_K = 0.0030$, there is a reasonable degree of stochastic variability in the capital stock behavior, of course mainly due to the "strong" stochasticity of the underlying Brownian motions.

As additional analyses, we also present in Figure 2 the associated annual (logarithmically taken) growth rates which for the sake of clarity are interpolated by straight lines.

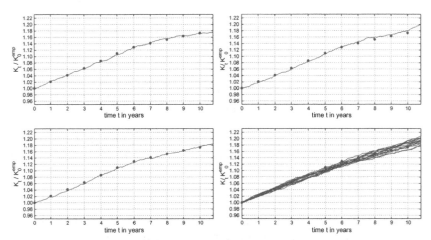

Fig. 1. *Transitional sample path simulations of the capital stock process K_t in (6) divided by K_0^{emp}.*

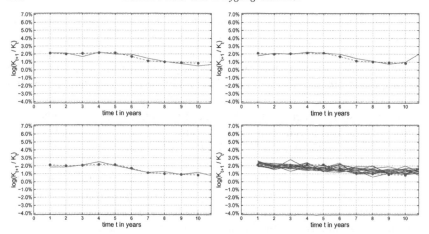

Fig. 2. *Annual growth rates of the K_t – sample-path simulations from Fig. 1.*

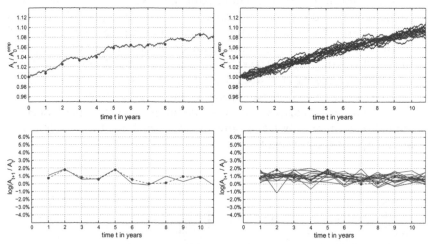

Fig. 3. *Transitional sample path simulations of the labor effectiveness process A_t in (7) divided by A_0^{emp} (first row), and associated annual growth rates (second row).*

Let us next examine the labor effectiveness dynamics A_t given by (7). Since this component is a straightforward geometric Brownian motion, for the sake of brevity we show in the first row of Figure 3 just one single and a bunch of fifteen transitional sample path runs (divided by the initial empirical data point A_0^{emp}) as well as their associated annual growth rates (second row). The corresponding empirical data (filled circles) are derived by (1) from GDP, labor force, and capital stock data together with $\gamma = 0.33$.

For the labor force dynamics L_t given by (8), which is also a straightforward geometric Brownian motion, we proceed as above which amounts to Figure 4 with just one single and a bunch of fifteen transitional sample path runs (divided by the initial empirical data point L_0^{emp}) in the first row as well as their associated annual growth rates in the second row.

To proceed with, in Figure 5 we picture three single respectively a bunch of 15 transitional sample path runs of the per capita effective capital stock evolution k_t given by (10) (divided by the initial empirical data point $k_0^{emp} = k_0$). Although we have chosen $T = 10, \tilde{b}_\rho = 0.00073, \tilde{b}_\delta = 0.00069$ – which excludes the existence of a limit (steady-state-equilibrium)

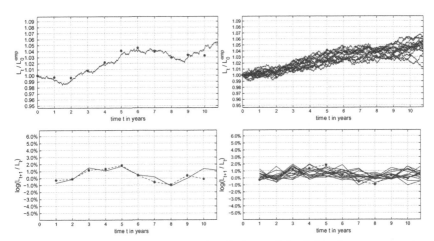

Fig. 4. *Transitional sample path simulations of the labor force process L_t in (8) divided by L_0^{emp} (first row) and associated annual growth rates (second row).*

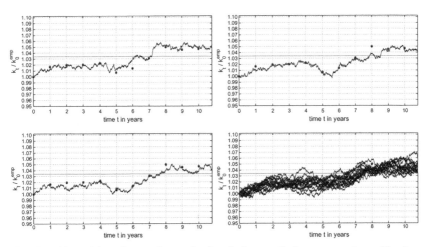

Fig. 5. *Transitional sample path simulations of the per capita effective capital stock process k_t in (10) divided by k_0^{emp}.*

distribution – for comparison reasons we also plot $\mu_{\text{stea}}/k_0^{\text{emp}} \approx 1.033$ where μ_{stea} (cf. (17)) is the mean of the limit distribution $P_{\lim}$ (respectively steady-state distribution P_{stea}) for the incompatible special case $T = \infty$, $\tilde{b}_\rho = \tilde{b}_\delta = 0$. In Figure 6 the corresponding annual growth rates are presented.

In the following, we show in Figure 7 three graphs with single respectively one graph with a bunch of 15 transitional sample path runs of the production function evolution Y_t given by (18) (divided by the initial

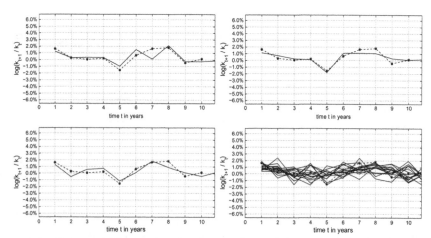

Fig. 6. *Annual growth rates of the k_t – sample-path simulations from Fig. 5.*

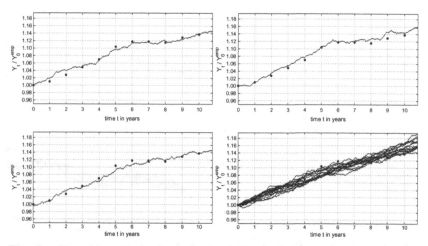

Fig. 7. *Transitional sample path simulations of the production function (GDP proxy) process Y_t in (18) divided by Y_0^{emp}.*

empirical data point $Y_0^{\text{emp}} = Y_0$), where the comparatively incorporated filled circles stem from the corresponding GDP data (as a proxy); see also Figure 8 for the associated annual growth rates.

Let us also investigate the stochastic dynamics of quantities which are closely associated with the production function (respectively GDP). Figure 9 deals with transitional sample path runs of the per capita production function Y_t/L_t in (19) (divided by the initial empirical data point $Y_0^{\text{emp}}/L_0^{\text{emp}} = Y_0/L_0$) and Figure 10 with the corresponding annual growth rates.

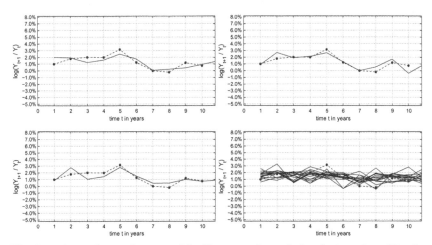

Fig. 8. *Annual growth rates of the Y_t – sample-path simulations from Fig. 7.*

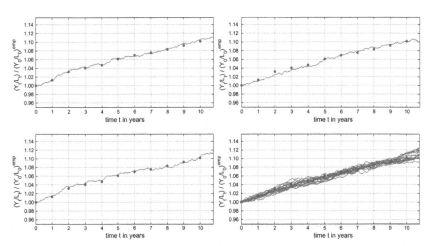

Fig. 9. *Transitional sample path simulations of the per capita production function (p.c. GDP proxy) process Y_t/L_t in (19) divided by Y_0^{emp}/L_0^{emp}.*

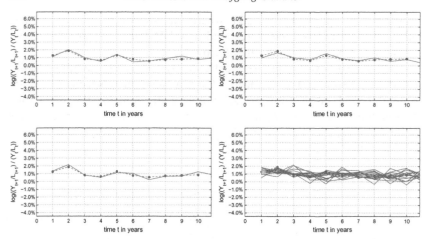

Fig. 10. *Annual growth rates of the Y_t/L_t –sample-path simulations from Fig. 9.*

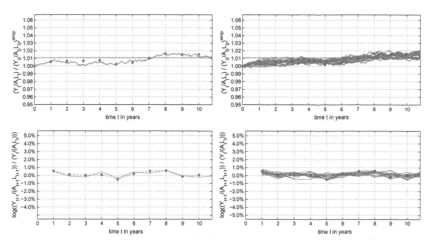

Fig. 11. *Transitional sample path simulations of the per capita effective production function (p.c.e. GDP proxy) process $Y_t/(A_t \cdot L_t)$ in (20) divided by $Y_0^{emp}/(A_0^{emp} L_0^{emp})$ (first row), and corresponding growth rates (second row).*

For the sake of brevity, we picture in the first row of Figure 11 just one single and a bunch of fifteen transitional sample path runs of the per capita effective production function $Y_t/A_t L_t$ in (20) (divided by the initial empirical data point $Y_0^{emp}/(A_0^{emp} L_0^{emp}) = Y_0/(A_0 L_0)$), together with the corresponding annual growth rates (second row). Although we have chosen $T = 10$, $\tilde{b}_\rho = 0.00073$, $\tilde{b}_\delta = 0.00069$ – which excludes the existence of a limit (steady-state-equilibrium) distribution – for comparison reasons we also plot in the first row $\widetilde{\mu_{\text{stea}}} \cdot (A_0^{\text{emp}} L_0^{\text{emp}} / Y_0^{\text{emp}}) \approx 1.011$ derived from the mean $\widetilde{\mu_{\text{stea}}}$ (cf. (23)) of the limit distribution $\widetilde{P_{\text{lim}}}$ (respectively steady-state distribution $\widetilde{P_{\text{stea}}}$) for the incompatible special case $T = \infty$, $\tilde{b}_\rho = \tilde{b}_\delta = 0$.

In order to prove the reasonability of our derived consumption rule (24), let us show in Figure 12 three single and a bunch of fifteen transitional sample path runs of c_t (divided by the initial empirical data point c_0^{emp}) and in Figure 13 the associated annual growth rates. Notice

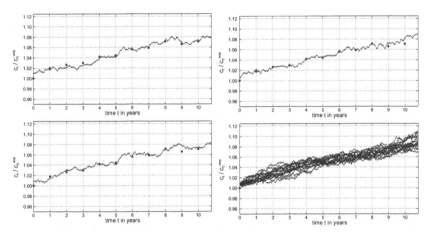

Fig. 12. *Transitional sample path simulations of the per capita consumption process c_t in (24) divided by c_0^{emp}.*

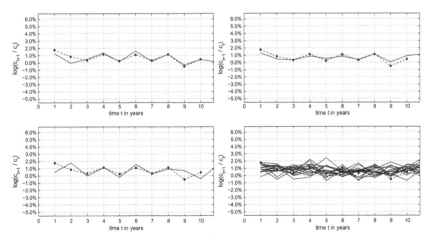

Fig. 13. *Annual growth rates of the c_t-sample-path simulations from Fig. 12.*

that the calculated initial value $c_0 = g_0 \cdot K_0/L_0$ does generally not coincide with the ("independently obtained") initial empirical consumption c_0^{emp} and hence the simulation runs typically start off 1.0.

Recall that it is well known that various different macroeconomic growth model setups suffer from unrealistically high (implicitly derived) savings rates. In order to demonstrate that this is not the case with our approach (25), we present in Figure 14 three single and a bunch of fifteen transitional sample path runs of s_t together with the corresponding empirical data displayed as filled circles. Notice that for the sake of better transparency we show directly the percentage values, i.e. there is *no* normalizing division by the initial empirical savings rate s_0^{emp}; the simulation runs typically start off s_0^{emp} for analogous reasons as the normalized c_t – paths did not begin at 1.0. The associated annual growth rates are pictured in Figure 15.

The outcoming very reasonable coincidence with the empirical data suggests that our model delivers a quite acceptable stochastic contribution to the fundamentally important question "how much should a nation save?" which was raised and extensively studied in a deterministic setup, for example, in La Grandville (2009, 2011) and the references therein.

At this point we have finished with Step 1 for proving the realistic suitability of our model, namely to identify a set of parameters for which the transitional sample-path simulations show "close" proximity to German empirical data (cf. goals (G1) and (G2)). Let us now deal with Step 2 and analyze – within a neighborhood of the parameter constellation of Step 1 – how strongly a change in parameter value affects the

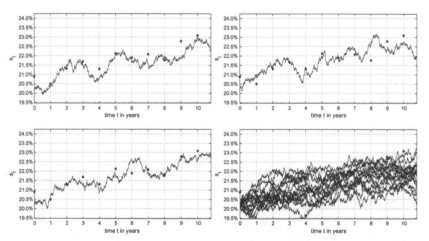

Fig. 14.   Transitional sample path simulations of the savings rate process s_t in (25).

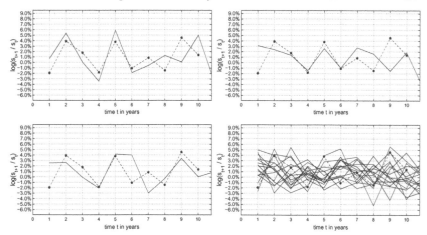

Fig. 15. Annual growth rates of the s_t-sample-path simulations from Fig. 14.

transitional sample-path simulation runs. Recall that such changes may, for example, stem from a concrete or planned economic policy alteration, from an "internal economy regime switch", or from moving "fictitiously" between the two ends of the corresponding parameter confidence interval in the course of analyzing the sensitivity of statistical estimation errors (quantifying the degree of model risk).

For our parameter sensitivity investigations, we proceed as follows: as *reference benchmark* for each of the economic quantities of interest – namely, K, A, L, k, Y, Y/L, $Y/(AL)$, c, s – we use the first single transitional sample path run (i.e., the first graph) in each of the Figures 1, 3–5, 7, 9, 11, 12, 14; this means in particular that each of the reference benchmarks carries the parameter constellation $T = 10$, $\gamma = 0.33$, $\delta_0 = 0.0456$ and $\tilde{b}_\delta = 0.00069$, $\rho_0 = 0.0571$ and $\tilde{b}_\rho = 0.00073$, $\mu_L = 0.0045$, $\sigma_L = 0.0070$, $\mu_A = 0.0088$, $\sigma_A = 0.0065$, $\sigma_K = 0.0030$, as well as the according concretely simulated exogenous random shocks $B_t^K(\omega)$ respectively $B_t^A(\omega)$ respectively $B_t^L(\omega)$, $t \in [0, 10)$. By keeping the latter three fixed – which corresponds loosely to the presumption that "the driving future-uncertainty will eventuate (i.e., occur as a statistical realization) as it will eventuate anyway" – we alter the parameters ceteris paribus and study the corresponding degree of sensitivity as well as possible (major) increasingness respectively decreasingness effects. For the sake of a well-structured discussion, let us group our parameters into volatilities σ_K, σ_A, σ_L and nonvolatilities. For the latter, we firstly summarize the qualitative sensitivity behavior in Table 2 where, for example, the entry in row K and column γ describes the qualitative type of the functional dependence $\gamma \mapsto (K_t(\gamma))_{t \in [0,10)}$ of the capital stock's transitional sample path (cf. (6)) with respect to the fixed capital share γ,

Table 2. *Qualitative sensitivity behavior with respect to nonvolatility parameters*

	ρ_0	$\tilde{b}_\rho$	δ_0	$\tilde{b}_\delta$	γ	μ_A	μ_L
K cf. (6)	h−	l+	h−	l−	h+	l+	l+
A cf. (7)	n	n	n	n	l+	l+	n
L cf. (8)	n	n	n	n	n	n	l+
k cf. (10)	h−	l+	h−	l−	h+	l−	n
Y cf. (18)	m−	l+	m−	l−	h+	l+	l+
Y/L cf. (19)	m−	l+	m−	l−	h+	l+	n
Y/(AL) cf. (20)	m−	l+	m−	l−	h+	l−	n
c cf. (24)	h+	l−	m±	l+	h−	l+	l−
s cf. (25)	h−	m+	m−	m−	h+	l+	l+

and so forth. For all entries, we have abbreviated the possible types as follows:

- *n* means "no functional dependence" (which can be seen from the associated representation formula),
- *h* means "high degree of sensitivity" (in other words, low degree of robustness),
- *l* means "low degree of sensitivity" (high degree of robustness),
- *m* means "medium degree of sensitivity" (medium degree of robustness),
- + means that the functional dependence is (mainly) increasing, that is, an upsizing respectively downsizing of the parameter (i.e., the column element) causes (mainly) an upsizing respectively downsizing of the sample path of the economic quantity of interest (i.e., the row element),
- − means that the functional dependence is (mainly) decreasing, that is, an upsizing respectively downsizing of the parameter causes (mainly) an downsizing respectively upsizing of the sample path of the economic quantity of interest,
- ± means that the change in parameter causes "a rotation around some fixed time horizon" of the sample path of the economic quantity of interest.

As a side remark, notice that a change in capital share γ triggers *indirectly* also a simultaneous change in the initial labor effectiveness level $A_0 = A_0^{\text{emp}}$ (which, e.g., also appears in the transitional sample path formula (6) for K_t) due to the fact that we have computed A_0^{emp} by the $\gamma -$ carrying formula (1) from initial GDP, labor force and capital stock data; this is particularly reflected in the (A, γ) − entry of Table 2.

In addition to Table 2, we present several selected graphs in order to illustrate the claimed parameter sensitivity effects; for the sake of a better visual comparability, we always use the same y-axis-range between 95% of the lowest empirical data point (lowest filled circle) and 105% of the highest empirical data point (highest filled circle). Let us start with the labor force process L_t being a straightforward geometric Brownian motion (8). Its sensitivity with respect to the average growth parameter μ_L is illuminated in Figure 16 as follows: the associated reference benchmark – which corresponds to the first single transitional sample path run (i.e., the first graph) in Figure 4 and which carries the parameter value $\mu_L = 0.0045$ – is drawn in the first row. In the second row, the left picture shows the ceteris paribus transformed sample path with $\mu_L = 0.0036$ which is -20% off the reference benchmark parameter value – compactly expressed as "$= -20\%$ offref" – whereas in the right picture we have used $\mu_L = 0.0054 = +20\%$ offref; one can see only a "slight upward change" which we have formalized in Table 2 as "$1+$".

Analogously, for the labor effectiveness process A_t being also a straightforward geometric Brownian motion (7), the sensitivity with respect to the parameters μ_A and γ ("indirectly" via A_0^{emp}) is indicated in Figure 17.

Let us next deal with the capital stock process K_t given by (6). Its high degree of sensitivity (and decreasingness behavior) with respect to the parameter ρ_0 is indicated in the second row of Figure 18, where in the left respectively right picture we show the transformed sample path with $\rho_0 = 0.05567 = -2.5\%$ offref respectively $\rho_0 = 0.05853 = +2.5\%$ offref. Despite the "narrow parameter range", one can see already a "substantial downward change" in the sample paths which we have formalized as "$h-$". The sensitivities with respect to the other parameters are shown in Row 3–8 of Figure 18.

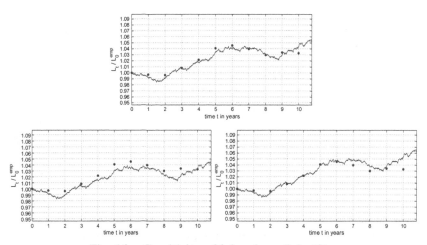

Fig. 16.   Sensitivity of labor force L in (8).
Row 1: reference benchmark with $\mu_L = 0.0045$.
Row 2: $\mu_L = 0.0036 = -20\%$ offref; $\mu_L = 0.0054 = +20\%$ offref.

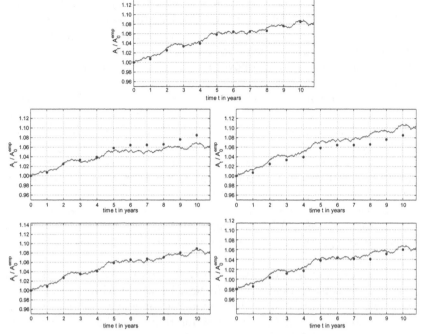

Fig. 17.   Sensitivity of labor effectiveness A in (7).
Row 1: reference benchmark with $\mu_A = 0.0088$ and $\gamma = 0.33$.
Row 2: $\mu_A = 0.00704 = -20\%$ offref; $\mu_A = 0.01056 = +20\%$ offref.
Row 3: $\gamma = 0.264 = -20\%$ offref; $\gamma = 0.396 = +20\%$ offref.

To proceed, the medium degree of sensitivity (and decreasingness behavior) of the production function process Y_t (cf. (18)) with respect to the parameter ρ_0 is visualized in the second row of Figure 19, where in the left respectively right picture we present the transformed sample path with $\rho_0 = 0.05425 = -5\%$ offref respectively $\rho_0 = 0.05996 = +5\%$ offref. Within this "medium parameter range", there is already a "substantial downward change", which we have formalized as "m−". The sensitivities with respect to the other parameters are shown in Row 3–8 of Figure 19.

The parameter sensitivities of the per capita effective capital stock process $k_t = K_t/(A_t L_t)$ (cf. (10)), the per capita production function process Y_t/L_t (cf. (19)), the per capita effective production function process $Y_t/(A_t L_t)$ (cf. (20)), the per capita consumption process (cf. (24)), and the savings rate process (cf. (25)) are presented in the Figures 20–24. Notice that in the Rows 2 and 6 of Figure 23 we have exceptionally used a parameter perturbation of $\pm5\%$ (instead of $\pm2.5\%$) to indicate a *high* degree of sensitivity, in order to better visualize the corresponding interesting "short-term-dislocation effect". Similarly, a $\pm20\%$ parameter

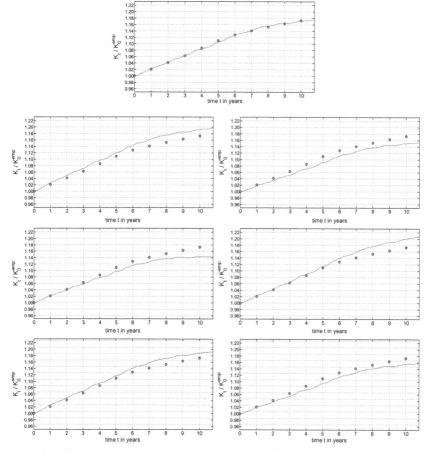

Fig. 18. **Sensitivity of capital stock K in (6) with respect to ρ, δ, γ, μ_A and μ_L.**

Row 1: reference benchmark.

Row 2: $\rho_0 = 0.05567 = -2.5\%$ offref; $\rho_0 = 0.05853 = +2.5\%$ offref.

Row 3: $\tilde{b}_\rho = 0.00058 = -20\%$ offref; $\tilde{b}_\rho = 0.00088 = +20\%$ offref.

Row 4: $\delta_0 = 0.04446 = -2.5\%$ offref; $\delta_0 = 0.04674 = +2.5\%$ offref.

Row 5: $\tilde{b}_\delta = 0.00055 = -20\%$ offref; $\tilde{b}_\delta = 0.00083 = +20\%$ offref.

Row 6: $\gamma = 0.32175 = -2.5\%$ offref; $\gamma = 0.33825 = +2.5\%$ offref.

Row 7: $\mu_A = 0.00704 = -20\%$ offref; $\mu_A = 0.01056 = +20\%$ offref.

Row 8: $\mu_L = 0.00360 = -20\%$ offref; $\mu_L = 0.00540 = +20\%$ offref.

perturbation is employed in Row 4 of Figure 23 in order to better emphasize that the per capita consumption c_t changes "in rotational way" as the initial depreciation rate δ_0 moves.

In contrast to the above considerations that involve nonvolatility parameters, let us now study the sensitivity of the transitional sample paths of our economic quantities of interest with respect to ceteris paribus

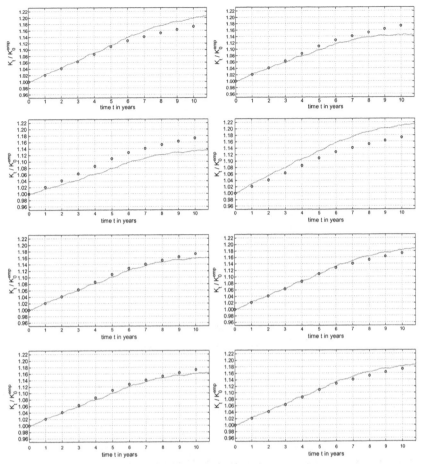

Fig. 18.   (Continued)

changes in the three volatilities σ_K, σ_A, σ_L (upwards) off their reference benchmark constellation $\sigma_K = 0.0030$, $\sigma_A = 0.0065$, $\sigma_L = 0.0070$. The corresponding *qualitative* sensitivity behavior is summarized in Table 3, where we have again used the abbreviations l, m, h, n for low, medium, high, no sensitivity – relative to each other but not relative to the above nonvolatility analyses – and for obvious reasons we have now left out the increasingness/decreasingness indicators $+$, $-$.

Supplementary to Table 3, we present in the following Figures 25–33 several selected plots in order to demonstrate the claimed parameter sensitivity effects. Because the reference-benchmark volatility values are small, their alterations are only taken upwards and of (100-fold) magnitude 250% and 500%. Notice that the transitional sample paths

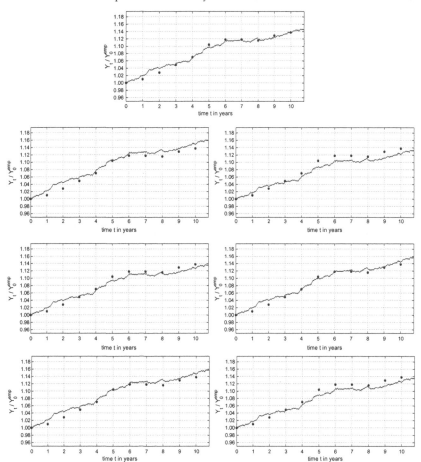

Fig. 19. *Sensitivity of production function Y in (18) with respect to* $\rho, \delta, \gamma,$ μ_A *and* μ_L.
Row 1: reference benchmark.
Row 2: $\rho_0 = 0.05425 = -5\%$ *offref;* $\rho_0 = 0.05996 = +5\%$ *offref.*
Row 3: $\tilde{b}_\rho = 0.00058 = -20\%$ *offref;* $\tilde{b}_\rho = 0.00088 = +20\%$ *offref.*
Row 4: $\delta_0 = 0.04332 = -5\%$ *offref;* $\delta_0 = 0.04788 = +5\%$ *offref.*
Row 5: $\tilde{b}_\delta = 0.00055 = -20\%$ *offref;* $\tilde{b}_\delta = 0.00083 = +20\%$ *offref.*
Row 6: $\gamma = 0.32175 = -2.5\%$ *offref;* $\gamma = 0.33825 = +2.5\%$ *offref.*
Row 7: $\mu_A = 0.00704 = -20\%$ *offref;* $\mu_A = 0.01056 = +20\%$ *offref.*
Row 8: $\mu_L = 0.00360 = -20\%$ *offref;* $\mu_L = 0.00540 = +20\%$ *offref.*

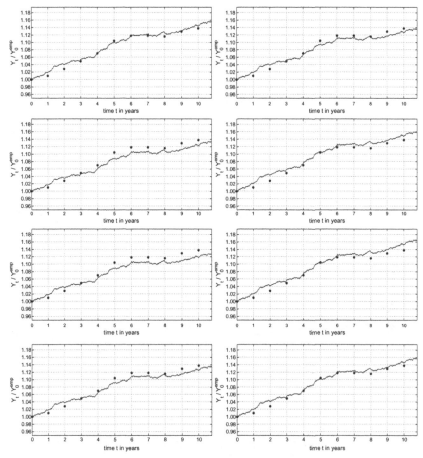

Fig. 19. *(Continued)*

show different sorts of sensitivity behavior: the changes of some parameters cause the sample paths to become more ragged but to basically stay close to the annual empirical data, whereas the changes of other parameters cause the sample paths to substantially move away from the annual empirical data.

At this point, we have finished our considerations about the sensitivities with respect to the *nonvolatility and volatility parameters*. Let us finally investigate how strongly a (direct) ceteris paribus change in the three *fundamental initial values* K_0, A_0, L_0 affects the transitional sample path runs of our economic quantities of interest. Such a (direct) change may, for example, origin from a crisis-driven sudden "crash" (macroeconomic disaster) at, say, current forecast-time $t = 0$. Let us emphasize that here we want to study the situation where all the other model parameters remain

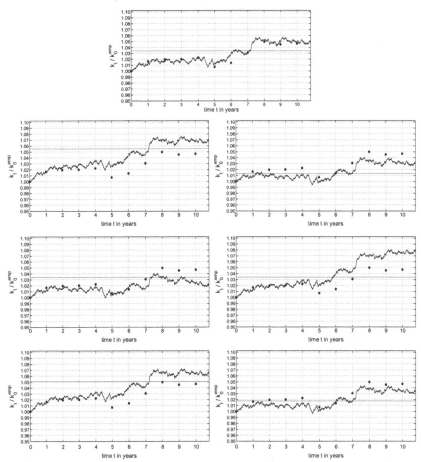

Fig. 20. ***Sensitivity of per capita effective capital stock k in (10) with***
respect to ρ, δ, γ and μ_A.
Row 1: reference benchmark.
Row 2: $\rho_0 = 0.05567 = -2.5\%$ *offref;* $\rho_0 = 0.05853 = +2.5\%$ *offref.*
Row 3: $\tilde{b}_\rho = 0.00058 = -20\%$ *offref;* $\tilde{b}_\rho = 0.00088 = +20\%$ *offref.*
Row 4: $\delta_0 = 0.04446 = -2.5\%$ *offref;* $\delta_0 = 0.04674 = +2.5\%$ *offref.*
Row 5: $\tilde{b}_\delta = 0.00055 = -20\%$ *offref;* $\tilde{b}_\delta = 0.00083 = +20\%$ *offref.*
Row 6: $\gamma = 0.32175 = -2.5\%$ *offref;* $\gamma = 0.33825 = +2.5\%$ *offref.*
Row 7: $\mu_A = 0.00704 = -20\%$ *offref;* $\mu_A = 0.01056 = +20\%$ *offref.*

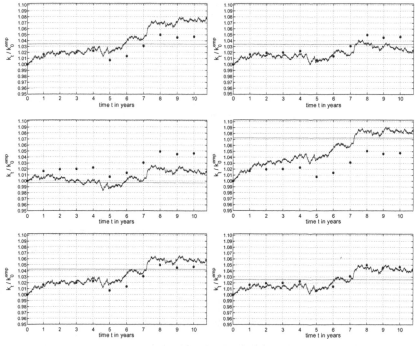

Fig. 20. *(Continued)*

the same, also covering the particular application in which there are no economic policy alterations despite of the crash. Notice the difference to the *indirect* changes in $A_0 = A_0^{\text{emp}}$ caused by a change in the capital share γ, cf. the discussion in the course of Table 2 and Row 3 in Figure 17. Accordingly, we have fixed $\gamma = 0.33$ as well as $T = 10$, $\delta_0 = 0.0456$, $\tilde{b}_\delta = 0.00069$, $\rho_0 = 0.0571$, $\tilde{b}_\rho = 0.00073$, $\mu_L = 0.0045$, $\sigma_L = 0.0070$, $\mu_A = 0.0088$, $\sigma_A = 0.0065$, $\sigma_K = 0.0030$; this will be referred to as reference benchmark in the following.

The corresponding *qualitative* sensitivity behavior is summarized in Table 4, where we have again used the abbreviations m, h, n for medium, high, no sensitivity together with the increasingness/decreasingness indicators $+$, $-$.

Additionally to Table 4, we display several selected plots in order to demonstrate the claimed initial-value sensitivity effects. For the illustration of the (mainly prevailing) *high* degree of sensitivity, we do not proceed analogously to the nonvolatility-parameter dependence case and pick a change in initial value that differs from $\pm 2.5\%$ offref, since there are several interesting "recovery-speed" respectively "graph-geometry" effects. Furthermore, for a better comparability we have kept the y-axes

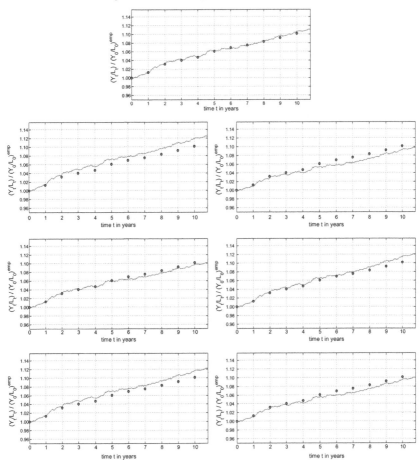

Fig. 21. Sensitivity of per capita production function Y/L in (19) with respect to ρ, δ, γ and μ_A.

Row 1: reference benchmark.

Row 2: $\rho_0 = 0.05425 = -5\%$ *offref;* $\rho_0 = 0.05996 = +5\%$ *offref.*

Row 3: $\tilde{b}_\rho = 0.00058 = -20\%$ *offref;* $\tilde{b}_\rho = 0.00088 = +20\%$ *offref.*

Row 4: $\delta_0 = 0.04332 = -5\%$ *offref;* $\delta_0 = 0.04788 = +5\%$ *offref.*

Row 5: $\tilde{b}_\delta = 0.00055 = -20\%$ *offref;* $\tilde{b}_\delta = 0.00083 = +20\%$ *offref.*

Row 6: $\gamma = 0.32175 = -2.5\%$ *offref;* $\gamma = 0.33825 = +2.5\%$ *offref.*

Row 7: $\mu_A = 0.00704 = -20\%$ *offref;* $\mu_A = 0.01056 = +20\%$ *offref.*

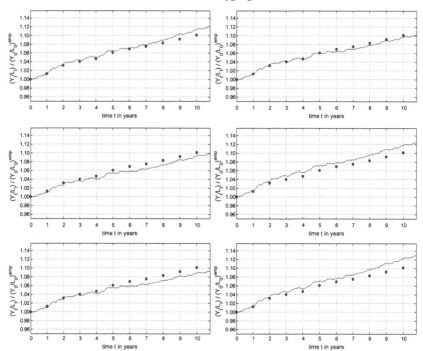

Fig. 21.   (Continued)

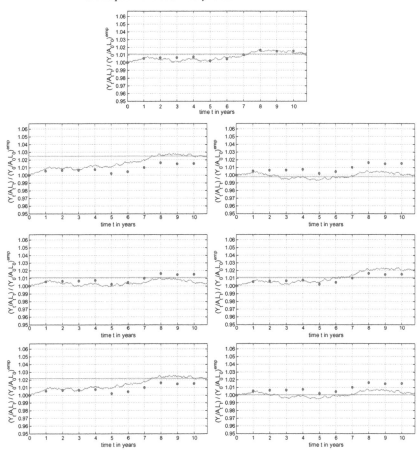

Fig. 22. *Sensitivity of per capita effective production function $Y/(AL)$ in (20) with respect to ρ, δ, γ and μ_A.*
Row 1: reference benchmark.
Row 2: $\rho_0 = 0.05425 = -5\%$ offref; $\rho_0 = 0.05996 = +5\%$ offref.
Row 3: $\tilde{b}_\rho = 0.00058 = -20\%$ offref; $\tilde{b}_\rho = 0.00088 = +20\%$ offref.
Row 4: $\delta_0 = 0.04332 = -5\%$ offref; $\delta_0 = 0.04788 = +5\%$ offref.
Row 5: $\tilde{b}_\delta = 0.00055 = -20\%$ offref; $\tilde{b}_\delta = 0.00083 = +20\%$ offref.
Row 6: $\gamma = 0.32175 = -2.5\%$ offref; $\gamma = 0.33825 = +2.5\%$ offref.
Row 7: $\mu_A = 0.00704 = -20\%$ offref; $\mu_A = 0.01056 = +20\%$ offref.

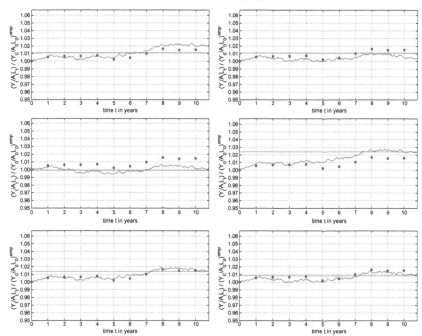

Fig. 22.   (Continued)

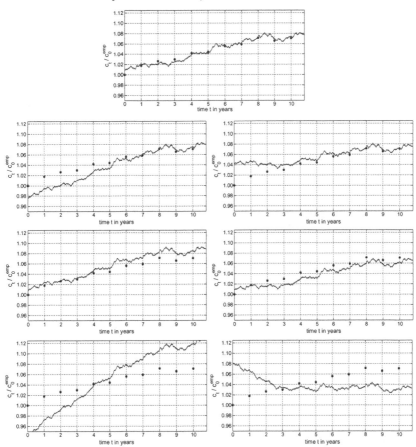

Fig. 23. *Sensitivity of per capita consumption* c *in (24) with respect to* ρ, δ, γ, μ_A *and* μ_L.
Row 1: reference benchmark.
Row 2: $\rho_0 = 0.05425 = -5\%$ *offref;* $\rho_0 = 0.05996 = +5\%$ *offref.*
Row 3: $\tilde{b}_\rho = 0.00058 = -20\%$ *offref;* $\tilde{b}_\rho = 0.00088 = +20\%$ *offref.*
Row 4: $\delta_0 = 0.03648 = -20\%$ *offref;* $\delta_0 = 0.05472 = +20\%$ *offref.*
Row 5: $\tilde{b}_\delta = 0.00055 = -20\%$ *offref;* $\tilde{b}_\delta = 0.00083 = +20\%$ *offref.*
Row 6: $\gamma = 0.31350 = -5\%$ *offref;* $\gamma = 0.34650 = +5\%$ *offref.*
Row 7: $\mu_A = 0.00704 = -20\%$ *offr;* $\mu_A = 0.01056 = +20\%$ *offr.*
Row 8: $\mu_L = 0.00360 = -20\%$ *offref;* $\mu_L = 0.00540 = +20\%$ *offref.*

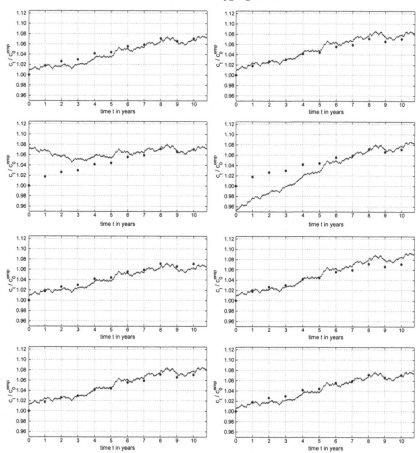

Fig. 23.　(Continued)

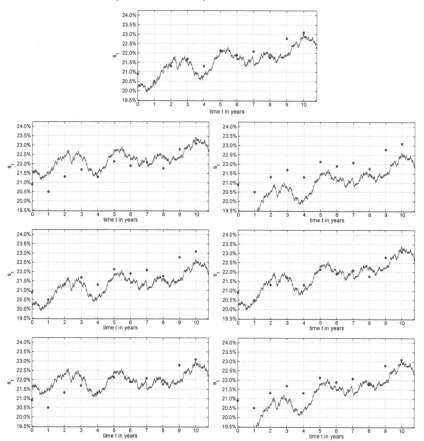

Fig. 24.   Sensitivity of savings rate s in (25) with respect to ρ, δ, γ, μ_A and μ_L.
Row 1: reference benchmark.
Row 2: $\rho_0 = 0.05567 = -2.5\%$ offref; $\rho_0 = 0.05853 = +2.5\%$ offref.
Row 3: $b_\rho = 0.00069 = -5\%$ offref; $\tilde{b}_\rho = 0.00077 = +5\%$ offref.
Row 4: $\delta_0 = 0.04332 = -5\%$ offref; $\delta_0 = 0.04788 = +5\%$ offref.
Row 5: $\tilde{b}_\delta = 0.00066 = -5\%$ offref; $\tilde{b}_\delta = 0.00072 = +5\%$ offref.
Row 6: $\gamma = 0.32175 = -2.5\%$ offref; $\gamma = 0.33825 = +2.5\%$ offref.
Row 7: $\mu_A = 0.00704 = -20\%$ offref; $\mu_A = 0.01056 = +20\%$ offref.
Row 8: $\mu_L = 0.00360 = -20\%$ offref; $\mu_L = 0.00540 = +20\%$ offref.

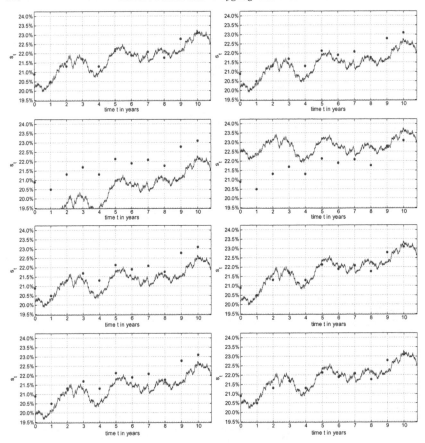

Fig. 24.   (Continued)

Table 3.   *Qualitative sensitivity behavior with respect to volatility parameters*

	σ_K	σ_A	σ_L
K cf. (6)	l	l	l
A cf. (7)	n	h	n
L cf. (8)	n	n	h
k cf. (10)	l	h	m
Y cf. (18)	l	h	l
Y/L cf. (19)	l	m	m
Y/(AL) cf. (20)	l	l	m
c cf. (24)	m	h	h
s cf. (25)	m	h	m

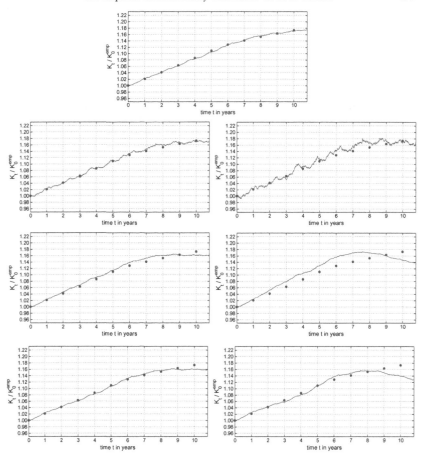

Fig. 25. *Sensitivity of capital stock K in (6) with respect to* σ_K, σ_A,
and σ_L.
Row 1: reference benchmark.
Row 2: $\sigma_K = 0.0075 = 250\%$ *offref;* $\sigma_K = 0.015 = 500\%$ *offref.*
Row 3: $\sigma_A = 0.01625 = 250\%$ *offref;* $\sigma_A = 0.0325 = 500\%$ *offref.*
Row 4: $\sigma_L = 0.0175 = 250\%$ *offref;* $\sigma_L = 0.035 = 500\%$ *offref.*

to be of exactly the same range as their corresponding abovementioned
counterparts, even if the transitional sample paths partially leave this
range and thus are cut off. Let us start with the capital stock K_t given by
(6). As it can be seen from Row 2 of Figure 34, despite of the large K_0-
perturbation $\pm 7.5\%$ offref the corresponding transitional sample path
takes roughly just about 10 years to become close to the reference
benchmark sample path values, which for themselves are annually close to
the empirical data points (filled circles). Loosely interpreted in different

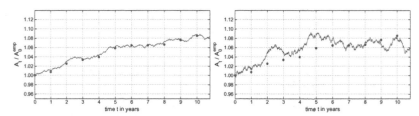

Fig. 26. Sensitivity of labor effectiveness **A** in (7) with respect to σ_A.
Row 1: reference benchmark, $\sigma_A = 0.01625 = 250\%$ offref.

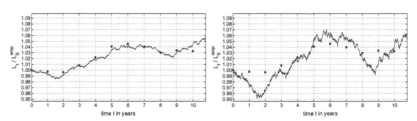

Fig. 27. Sensitivity of labor force **L** in (8) with respect to σ_L.
Row 1: reference benchmark, $\sigma_L = 0.0175 = 250\%$ offref.

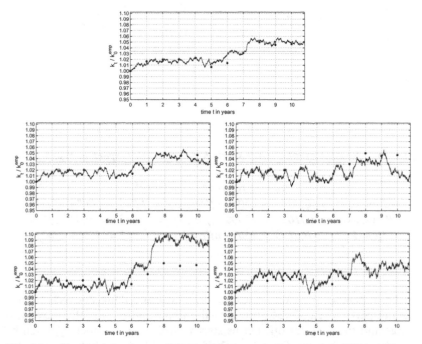

Fig. 28. Sensitivity of per capita effective capital stock **k** in (10) with
respect to σ_K, σ_A, and σ_L.
Row 1: reference benchmark.
Row 2: $\sigma_K = 0.0075 = 250\%$ offref; $\sigma_K = 0.015 = 500\%$ offref.
Row 3: $\sigma_A = 0.01625 = 250\%$ offref; $\sigma_L = 0.0175 = 250\%$ offref.

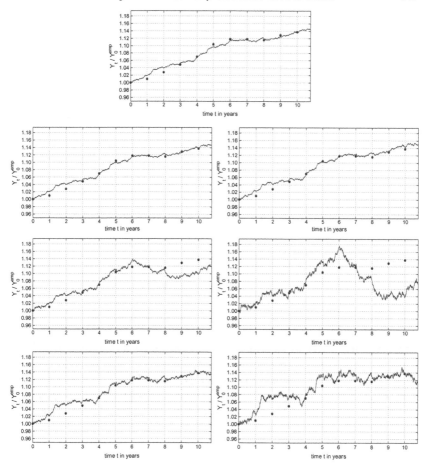

Fig. 29. *Sensitivity of production function Y in (18) with respect to* σ_K,
σ_A, *and* σ_L.
Row 1: reference benchmark.
Row 2: $\sigma_K = 0.0075 = 250\%$ *offref;* $\sigma_K = 0.015 = 500\%$ *offref.*
Row 3: $\sigma_A = 0.01625 = 250\%$ *offref;* $\sigma_A = 0.0325 = 500\%$ *offref.*
Row 4: $\sigma_L = 0.0175 = 250\%$ *offref;* $\sigma_L = 0.035 = 500\%$ *offref.*

terms, this means that in our model situation, for example, a sudden
-7.5% crash is "recovered" within 10 years *without* any economic policy
alterations (the *latter* being reflected by our ceteris paribus assumption);
yet another interpretation is that two model economies having now the
same (policy-driven) parameters but a 7.5% difference in current capital
stock K_0 will end up at nearly the same capital stock in 10 years from now,
provided that they are exposed to the same random shocks B_t^K, B_t^A, B_t^L.
This feature may, for example, serve policy makers in emerging economies
(e.g., BRICS countries and other, newly industrializing, countries) as a

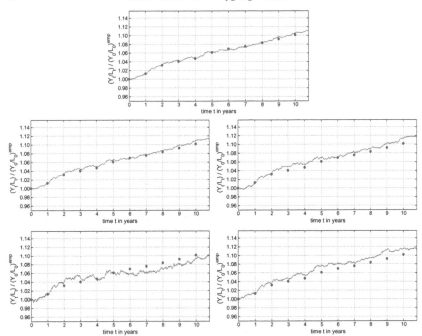

Fig. 30. *Sensitivity of per capita production function Y/L in (19) with respect to σ_K, σ_A, and σ_L.*
Row 1: reference benchmark.
Row 2: $\sigma_K = 0.0075 = 250\%$ offref; $\sigma_K = 0.015 = 500\%$ offref.
Row 3: $\sigma_A = 0.01625 = 250\%$ offref; $\sigma_L = 0.0175 = 250\%$ offref.

quantitative decision support tool to (implicitly) adjust the major economy parameters to become similar to those of (even) higher developed economies.

In contrast to the above mentioned "convergence (e.g., recovery) effect" in face of K_0-changes, the Rows 3 and 4 of Figure 34 show that changes in the other two initial values A_0 respectively L_0 cause the correspondingly transformed transitional sample path "to diverge off" the reference benchmark values (empirical data points), as time passes by.

The initial-value sensitivity analyses of the labor effectiveness A_t in (7) respectively labor force L_t in (8) lead to a straightforward parallel displacement due to their "pure (uncoupled)" geometric Brownian motion nature, see Figure 35 respectively 36.

In Figure 37, the sensitivity analyses of the per capita effective capital stock k_t in (10) with respect to the initial values K_0, A_0, L_0 show a convergence (e.g., recovery) effect which – partially up to

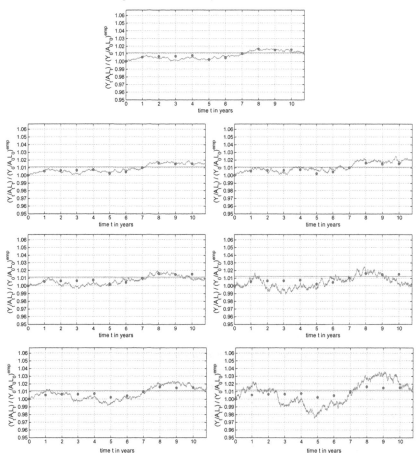

Fig. 31. *Sensitivity of per capita effective production function $Y/(AL)$ in (20) with respect to σ_K, σ_A, and σ_L.*
Row 1: reference benchmark.
Row 2: $\sigma_K = 0.0075 = 250\%$ offref; $\sigma_K = 0.015 = 500\%$ offref.
Row 3: $\sigma_A = 0.01625 = 250\%$ offref; $\sigma_A = 0.0325 = 500\%$ offref.
Row 4: $\sigma_L = 0.0175 = 250\%$ offref; $\sigma_L = 0.035 = 500\%$ offref.

Robert Feicht and Wolfgang Stummer

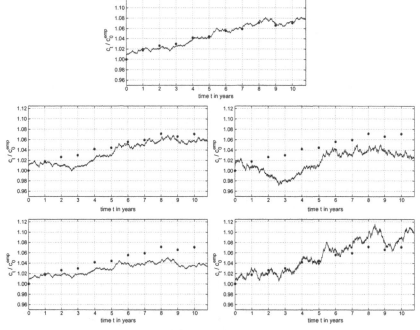

Fig. 32. *Sensitivity of per capita consumption c in (24) with respect to* σ_K, σ_A, *and* σ_L.
Row 1: reference benchmark.
Row 2: $\sigma_K = 0.0075 = 250\%$ *offref;* $\sigma_K = 0.015 = 500\%$ *offref.*
Row 3: $\sigma_A = 0.01625 = 250\%$ *offref;* $\sigma_L = 0.0175 = 250\%$ *offref.*

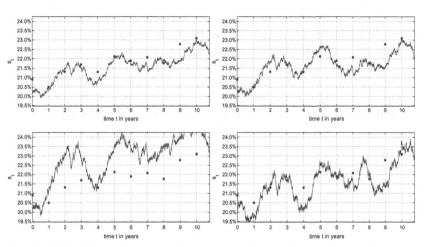

Fig. 33. *Sensitivity of savings rate s in (25) with respect to* σ_K, σ_A, *and* σ_L.
Row 1: reference benchmark; $\sigma_K = 0.0075 = 250\%$ *offref.*
Row 2: $\sigma_A = 0.01625 = 250\%$ *offref;* $\sigma_L = 0.0175 = 250\%$ *offref.*

Table 4. Qualitative sensitivity behavior with respect to initial values

	K_0	A_0	L_0
K cf. (6)	h+	h+	h+
A cf. (7)	n	h+	n
L cf. (8)	n	n	h+
k cf. (10)	h+	h−	h−
Y cf. (18)	m+	h+	h+
Y/L cf. (19)	m+	h+	m−
Y/(AL) cf. (20)	m+	m−	m−
c cf. (24)	h+	h+	h−
s cf. (25)	h−	h+	h+

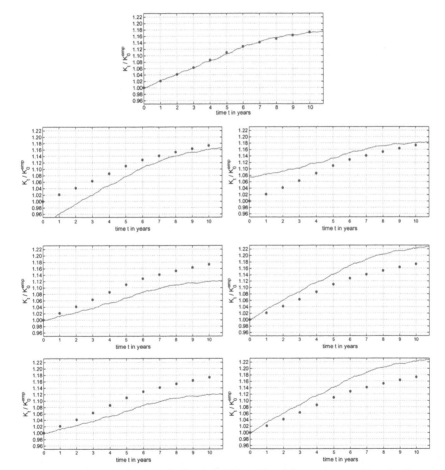

Fig. 34. *Sensitivity of capital stock K in (6) with respect to K_0, A_0, L_0.*
Row 1: reference benchmark.
Row 2: $K_0 = -7.5\%$ offref; $K_0 = +7.5\%$ offref.
Row 3: $A_0 = -5\%$ offref; $A_0 = +5\%$ offref.
Row 4: $L_0 = -5\%$ offref; $L_0 = +5\%$ offref.

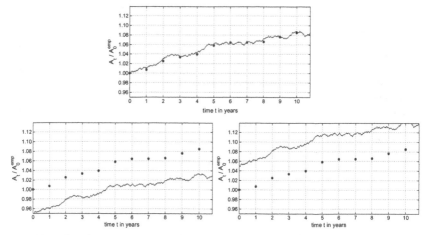

Fig. 35.   Sensitivity of labor effectiveness A in (7) with respect to A_0.
Row 1: reference benchmark.
Row 2: $A_0 = -5\%$ offref; $A_0 = +5\%$ offref.

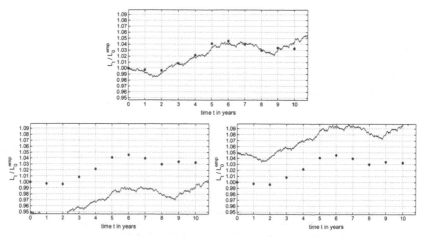

Fig. 36.   Sensitivity of labor force L in (8) with respect to L_0.
Row 1: reference benchmark.
Row 2: $L_0 = -5\%$ offref; $L_0 = +5\%$ offref.

increasingness – is similar to the K_0-dependence behavior of K_t in Row 2 of Figure 34.

To proceed, the effects of changes in the initial values K_0, A_0, L_0 on the transitional sample paths of the production function Y_t is presented in Figure 38.

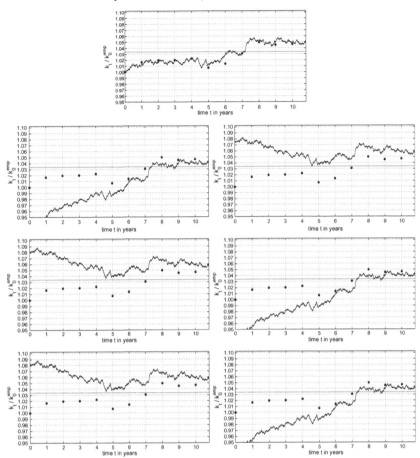

Fig. 37. Sensitivity of per capita effective capital stock k in (10) with
respect to K_0, A_0, L_0.
Row 1: reference benchmark.
Row 2: $K_0 = -7.5\%$ offref; $K_0 = +7.5\%$ offref.
Row 3: $A_0 = -7.5\%$ offref; $A_0 = +7.5\%$ offref.
Row 4: $L_0 = -7.5\%$ offref; $L_0 = +7.5\%$ offref.

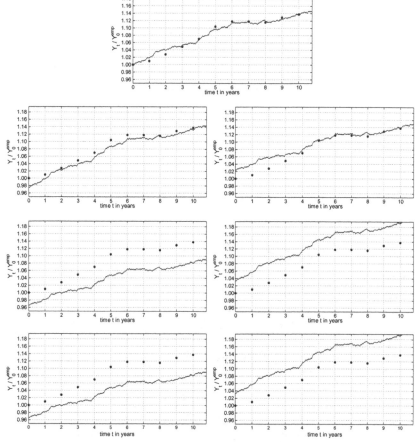

Fig. 38. *Sensitivity of production function Y in (18) with respect to* K_0, A_0, L_0.
Row 1: reference benchmark.
Row 2: $K_0 = -7.5\%$ *offref;* $K_0 = +7.5\%$ *offref.*
Row 3: $A_0 = -5\%$ *offref;* $A_0 = +5\%$ *offref.*
Row 4: $L_0 = -5\%$ *offref;* $L_0 = +5\%$ *offref.*

The initial-value-sensitivity analyses of the per capita production function Y_t/L_t respectively of the per capita effective production function $Y_t/(A_t L_t)$ are displayed in Figure 39 respectively 40.

In the following Figure 41 respectively 42 we present the initial-value-sensitivity analyses of the per capita consumption c_t respectively of the savings rate s_t.

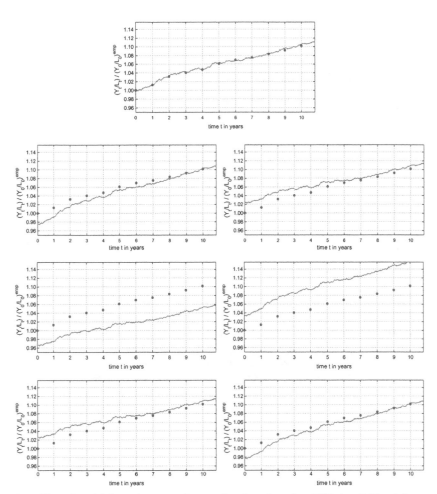

Fig. 39. *Sensitivity of per capita production function Y/L in (19) with respect to K_0, A_0, L_0.*
Row 1: reference benchmark.
Row 2: $K_0 = -7.5\%$ offref; $K_0 = +7.5\%$ offref.
Row 3: $A_0 = -5\%$ offref; $A_0 = +5\%$ offref.
Row 4: $L_0 = -7.5\%$ offref; $L_0 = +7.5\%$ offref.

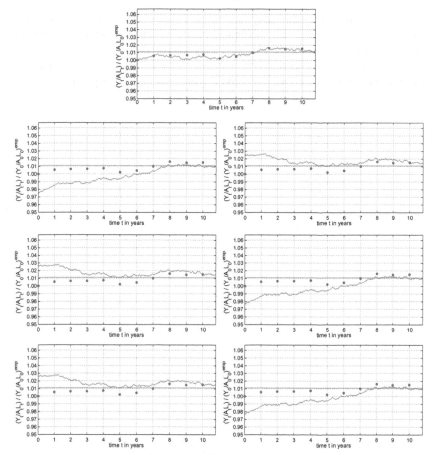

Fig. 40. *Sensitivity of per capita effective production function $Y/(AL)$ in (20) with respect to K_0, A_0, L_0.*
Row 1: reference benchmark.
Row 2: $K_0 = -7.5\%$ offref; $K_0 = +7.5\%$ offref.
Row 3: $A_0 = -7.5\%$ offref; $A_0 = +7.5\%$ offref.
Row 4: $L_0 = -7.5\%$ offref; $L_0 = +7.5\%$ offref.

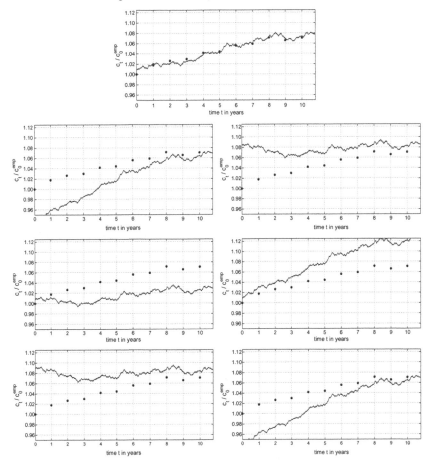

Fig. 41. **Sensitivity of per capita consumption c in (24) with respect to**
$$K_0, A_0, L_0.$$
Row 1: reference benchmark.
Row 2: $K_0 = -7.5\%$ *offref;* $K_0 = +7.5\%$ *offref.*
Row 3: $A_0 = -5\%$ *offref;* $A_0 = +5\%$ *offref.*
Row 4: $L_0 = -7.5\%$ *offref;* $L_0 = +7.5\%$ *offref.*

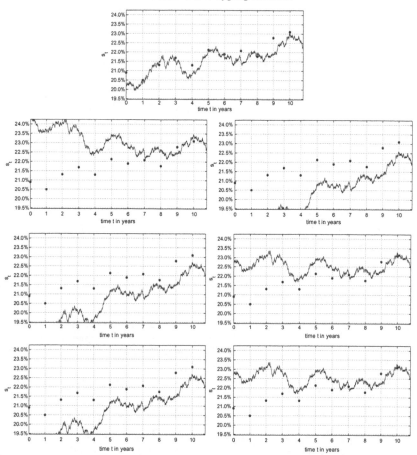

Fig. 42.   Sensitivity of savings rate s in (25) with respect to K_0, A_0, L_0.
Row 1: reference benchmark.
Row 2: $K_0 = -7.5\%$ offref; $K_0 = +7.5\%$ offref.
Row 3: $A_0 = -5\%$ offref; $A_0 = +5\%$ offref.
Row 4: $L_0 = -5\%$ offref; $L_0 = +5\%$ offref.

Let us finally mention that for the economy-value processes one can also derive some Bayesian and non-Bayesian statistical decision sensitivity results along the lines of Stummer and Vajda (2007). For the sake of brevity, this will appear in a forthcoming paper together with further analyses.

Acknowledgments

We are grateful to Olivier de La Grandville and Rainer Klump for stimulating discussions.

Appendices

A.1. Derivation of the capital stock dynamics

In terms of the constant $b_4 := (\rho_0 + \delta_0)/\gamma + \mu_A + ((1 - \gamma)/2) \cdot \sigma_K^2 - \sigma_A^2 - ((1 + \gamma)/2) \cdot \sigma_L^2$, the ("inverse geometric Brownian motion" type) auxiliary process

$$F_t(\omega) = \exp\left\{ -\sigma_K B_t^K(\omega) + \sigma_A B_t^A(\omega) + \sigma_L B_t^L(\omega) + \frac{1}{2}(\sigma_K^2 + \sigma_A^2 + \sigma_L^2) \cdot t \right\} > 0$$

as well as

$$\Upsilon_t(\omega) = e^{-b_4 t - \frac{\widetilde{b}_\delta - \widetilde{b}_\rho}{\gamma} \cdot t^2} \cdot \left[\int_0^t (1 - \gamma) \cdot F_s(\omega)^{1-\gamma} \cdot e^{(1-\gamma) \cdot \left(b_4 s + \frac{\widetilde{b}_\delta - \widetilde{b}_\rho}{\gamma} \cdot s^2 \right)} ds + k_0^{1-\gamma} \right]^{\frac{1}{1-\gamma}} > 0,$$

one can rewrite the time-t random value k_t of the per capita effective capital stock given in (10) as $k_t(\omega) = \Upsilon_t(\omega)/F_t(\omega) > 0$. Furthermore, for fixed ω one can straightforwardly verify

$$\frac{d\Upsilon_t(\omega)}{dt} = F_t(\omega)^{1-\gamma} \cdot \Upsilon_t(\omega)^\gamma - \left(b_4 + 2\frac{\widetilde{b}_\delta - \widetilde{b}_\rho}{\gamma} \cdot t \right) \cdot \Upsilon_t(\omega)$$

$$= F_t(\omega) \cdot \widetilde{g}(t, k_t(\omega)), \quad Y_0 = k_0,$$

with $\widetilde{g}(t, z) := z^\gamma - \left(b_4 + 2((\widetilde{b}_\delta - \widetilde{b}_\rho)/\gamma) \cdot t \right) \cdot z$. Hence, one can apply Lemma 1 of Feicht and Stummer (2010) to conclude (with suppression of ω) that k_t is a (strong) solution of the SDE

$$dk_t = \left[k_t^\gamma - \left(b_4 + 2\frac{\widetilde{b}_\delta - \widetilde{b}_\rho}{\gamma} \cdot t \right) \cdot k_t \right] dt$$

$$+ k_t \cdot [\sigma_K dB_t^K - \sigma_A dB_t^A - \sigma_L dB_t^L], \quad k_0 > 0, t \in [0, T). \tag{27}$$

The (pathwise) uniqueness of (strong) solutions of (27) can be seen, for example, as follows: let $\widetilde{k}_t > 0$ be another (strong) solution of (27) with initial value $\widetilde{k}_0 = k_0$. Then by Ito's formula one gets

$$dX_t := d(\log k_t) = \left[e^{(\gamma-1)\cdot X_t} - b_4 - \frac{1}{2}(\sigma_K^2 + \sigma_A^2 + \sigma_L^2) - 2\frac{\widetilde{b}_\delta - \widetilde{b}_\rho}{\gamma} \cdot t \right] dt$$

$$+ [\sigma_K dB_t^K - \sigma_A dB_t^A - \sigma_L dB_t^L], \quad X_0 := \log k_0 \in (-\infty, \infty), \quad t \in [0, T),$$

as well as

$$d\widetilde{X}_t := d(\log \widetilde{k}_t) = \left[e^{(\gamma-1)\cdot \widetilde{X}_t} - b_4 - \frac{1}{2}(\sigma_K^2 + \sigma_A^2 + \sigma_L^2) - 2\frac{\widetilde{b}_\delta - \widetilde{b}_\rho}{\gamma} \cdot t \right] dt$$

$$+ [\sigma_K dB_t^K - \sigma_A dB_t^A - \sigma_L dB_t^L], \quad \widetilde{X}_0 = X_0 \in (-\infty, \infty), t \in [0, T).$$

Hence, one can apply a general (pathwise) SDE uniqueness result of Gyöngy and Martinez (2001) to conclude that $X_t = \widetilde{X}_t$ for all $t \in [0, T)$ with probability one. Consequently, $k_t = \widetilde{k}_t$ for all $t \in [0, T)$ with probability one.

In order to achieve the dynamics of the time-t random value K_t of the capital stock given in (6), one can use (10) as well as the appropriate three-dimensional version of Ito's formula together with the SDEs (2), (3), (27) to compute

$$dK_t = d(k_t A_t L_t) = A_t L_t dk_t + A_t k_t dL_t + L_t k_t dA_t$$
$$+ k_t dA_t dL_t + A_t dk_t dL_t + L_t dk_t dA_t + dk_t dA_t dL_t$$
$$= A_t L_t \left\{ \left[k_t^\gamma - \left(b_4 + 2\frac{\widetilde{b}_\delta - \widetilde{b}_\rho}{\gamma} \cdot t \right) \cdot k_t \right] dt + k_t [\sigma_K dB_t^K - \sigma_A dB_t^A - \sigma_L dB_t^L] \right\}$$
$$+ A_t k_t \{ \mu_L L_t dt + \sigma_L L_t dB_t^L \} + L_t k_t \{ \mu_A A_t dt + \sigma_A A_t dB_t^A \} + k_t \cdot 0$$
$$+ A_t \cdot \{ -\sigma_L^2 L_t k_t dt \} + L_t \cdot \{ -\sigma_A^2 A_t k_t dt \} + 0$$
$$= \left[K_t^\gamma (A_t L_t)^{1-\gamma} - \left(b_4 - \mu_A - \mu_L + \sigma_A^2 + \sigma_L^2 + 2\frac{\widetilde{b}_\delta - \widetilde{b}_\rho}{\gamma} \cdot t \right) \cdot K_t \right] dt + \sigma_K K_t dB_t^K$$
$$= [K_t^\gamma (A_t L_t)^{1-\gamma} - (g_t + \delta_t) \cdot K_t] dt + \sigma_K K_t dB_t^K \tag{28}$$

where for the last equality we have employed (5). Thus, K_t is a (strong) solution of (4). The (pathwise) uniqueness follows similarly to the abovementioned considerations, by letting $\widetilde{K}_t > 0$ be another (strong) solution of (28) with initial value $\widetilde{K}_0 = K_0$, and by applying Ito's formula to obtain

$$d\widetilde{k}_t := d\frac{\widetilde{K}_t}{A_t L_t} = \frac{1}{A_t L_t}\{[\widetilde{K}_t^{\gamma}(A_t L_t)^{1-\gamma} - (g_t + \delta_t) \cdot \widetilde{K}_t]dt + \sigma_K \widetilde{K}_t dB_t^K\}$$

$$-\frac{\widetilde{K}_t}{A_t^2 L_t}[\mu_A A_t dt + \sigma_A A_t dB_t^A]$$

$$-\frac{\widetilde{K}_t}{A_t L_t^2}[\mu_L L_t dt + \sigma_L L_t dB_t^L] + \frac{\widetilde{K}_t}{A_t^3 L_t}\sigma_A^2 A_t^2 dt + \frac{\widetilde{K}_t}{A_t L_t^3}\sigma_L^2 L_t^2 dt$$

$$= \left[\widetilde{k}_t^{\gamma} - \left(b_4 + 2\frac{\widetilde{b}_\delta - \widetilde{b}_\rho}{\gamma} \cdot t\right) \cdot \widetilde{k}_t\right]dt + \widetilde{k}_t \cdot \left[\sigma_K dB_t^K - \sigma_A dB_t^A - \sigma_L dB_t^L\right]$$

which gives the desired result from the (pathwise) uniqueness assertion for (27).

A.2. Distributions

In this entire section, we suppose $\widetilde{b}_\rho = \widetilde{b}_\delta$. In terms of the constant $\breve{\mu} :=$ $((\gamma - 1)/2) \cdot \left\{2(\rho_0 + \delta_0)/\gamma + 2\mu_A + (2 - \gamma)\sigma_K^2 - \sigma_A^2 - \gamma\sigma_L^2\right\}$ and the auxiliary process

$$Z_t := (1 - \gamma) \cdot (\sigma_K B_t^K - \sigma_A B_t^A - \sigma_L B_t^L) + \breve{\mu} \cdot t$$

one can rewrite the time t random value k_t of the per capita effective capital stock given in (10) as

$$k_t = \left[(1 - \gamma) \cdot e^{Z_t} \cdot \int_0^t e^{-Z_s}ds + e^{Z_t} \cdot k_0^{1-\gamma}\right]^{\frac{1}{1-\gamma}}.$$

Since (in terms of distributional equality $\overset{\text{dist}}{=}$) there holds $Z_t \overset{\text{dist}}{=} \breve{\sigma} \cdot \widetilde{B}_t +$ $\breve{\mu} \cdot t$ with some Brownian motion $\widetilde{B}_t$ and $\breve{\sigma}$ defined by (13), one can apply a general result of Carmona, Petit, and Yor (1997) on Levy processes to conclude that $\left(e^{Z_t}, e^{Z_t} \cdot \int_0^t e^{-Z_s}ds\right) \overset{\text{dist}}{=} \left(e^{Z_t}, \int_0^t e^{Z_s}ds\right)$. For fixed $t \in (0, T)$, the joint distribution of the latter has the density $h^{(t)}(\cdot, \cdot)$ given by (12), which can be derived, for example, by using the general formula 1.8.8 of Borodin and Salminen (2002, p. 613). Consequently, one can show by straightforward calculations that

$$k_t \overset{\text{dist}}{=} \left[(1 - \gamma) \cdot \int_0^t e^{Z_s}ds + e^{Z_t} \cdot k_0^{1-\gamma}\right]^{\frac{1}{1-\gamma}}$$

has the density $f^{(t)}(\cdot)$ proposed in (11), that the time-t random value of the per capita effective production function $Y_t/(A_t L_t) = k_t^{\gamma}$ (cf. (20)) has the density $\widetilde{f}^{(t)}(\cdot)$ given by (21), and that the savings rate $s_t = 1 - g_t \cdot k_t^{1-\gamma}$ (cf. (25), (5)) has the density $\widetilde{\widetilde{f}}^{(t)}(\cdot)$ mentioned in (26).

For the rest of this section, we suppose $T = \infty$, $\tilde{b}_\rho = \tilde{b}_\delta = 0$ and that the assumption (14) is satisfied. Within this setup, we have shown in Feicht and Stummer (2010) that the long-term limit – as t tends to infinity – of the per capita effective capital stock k_t-distribution is a law $P_{\lim}$ having the density $f_{\lim}$ given by (15); furthermore, $P_{\lim}$ coincides with the steady-state-equilibrium distribution P_{stea}. From these investigations, one can derive by "direct computations" that the long-term limit distribution $\widetilde{P}_{\lim}$ of the per capita effective production function $\widetilde{Y}_t = Y_t/(A_t L_t) = k_t^\gamma$ has the density $\widetilde{f}_{\lim}(\cdot)$ given by (22), and that $\widetilde{P}_{\lim}$ coincides with the corresponding steady-state-equilibrium distribution $\widetilde{P}_{\text{stea}}$. In the following, we show how to obtain these assertions by an alternative method. To start with, let us recall that k_t is a solution of (27) (with $\tilde{b}_\rho = \tilde{b}_\delta = 0$) and accordingly employ Ito's formula to characterize the dynamics of $\widetilde{Y}_t$ as

$$d\widetilde{Y}_t = d(k_t^\gamma) = \left[\gamma k_t^{\gamma-1} \cdot (k_t^\gamma - b_4 k_t) + \frac{\gamma \cdot (\gamma - 1)}{2} \cdot k_t^{\gamma-2} \cdot k_t^2 \cdot (\sigma_K^2 + \sigma_A^2 + \sigma_L^2) \right] dt$$

$$+ \gamma k_t^{\gamma-1} \cdot k_t \cdot [\sigma_K dB_t^K - \sigma_A dB_t^A - \sigma_L dB_t^L]$$

$$= [\gamma \widetilde{Y}_t^{\frac{2\gamma-1}{\gamma}} - b_5 \widetilde{Y}_t] dt + \widetilde{Y}_t \cdot [\gamma \sigma_K dB_t^K - \gamma \sigma_A dB_t^A - \gamma \sigma_L dB_t^L],$$

$$\widetilde{Y}_0 = k_0^\gamma > 0, t \in [0, \infty), \tag{29}$$

with $b_5 := \gamma b_4 + (\gamma/2)(1 - \gamma) \cdot (\sigma_K^2 + \sigma_A^2 + \sigma_L^2)$. Hence, one can apply (an adaption of) the corresponding general "ergodic" theory of one-dimensional SDEs, see, for example, Karatzas and Shreve (1991), Kallenberg (2002). Correspondingly, let us first observe that in (29) both the drift term and the diffusion term are bounded on compact subintervals of the domain $I = (0, \infty)$. By this and the nondegeneracy $\gamma^2 \cdot (\sigma_K^2 + \sigma_A^2 + \sigma_L^2) > 0$, all the following quantities are well defined. It is crucial to study the boundary behavior of the scale function

$$S(\tilde{y}) := \int_1^{\tilde{y}} \exp \left\{ -2 \int_1^\xi \frac{\gamma z^{2-1/\gamma} - b_5 z}{\gamma^2 \cdot (\sigma_K^2 + \sigma_A^2 + \sigma_L^2) \cdot z^2} dz \right\} d\xi$$

$$= \int_1^{\tilde{y}} \exp \left\{ b_2 \cdot \left[\xi^{1-1/\gamma} + \frac{1-\gamma}{\gamma^2} \cdot b_5 \cdot \ln \xi - 1 \right] \right\} d\xi$$

$$= \frac{\gamma}{\gamma - 1} e^{-b_2} \int_1^{\tilde{y}^{1-1/\gamma}} \exp\{b_2 \zeta - b_6 \ln \zeta\} d\zeta, \quad k \in (0, \infty),$$

with

$$b_2 := \frac{2}{(\sigma_K^2 + \sigma_A^2 + \sigma_L^2) \cdot (1 - \gamma)} > 0 \quad (\text{cf. (15)})$$

and

$$b_6 := \frac{2b_5}{\gamma \cdot (1 - \gamma) \cdot (\sigma_K^2 + \sigma_A^2 + \sigma_L^2)} + \frac{\gamma}{1 - \gamma} + 1$$

$$= \frac{2b_4}{(\sigma_K^2 + \sigma_A^2 + \sigma_L^2) \cdot (1 - \gamma)} + \frac{1}{1 - \gamma} + 1$$

where $b_6 > 1$ because of (14). It is easy to see that

$$\lim_{\tilde{y} \to 0+} S(\tilde{y}) = -\infty \quad \text{and} \quad \lim_{\tilde{y} \to \infty} S(\tilde{y}) = +\infty$$

hold. From the scale function one can deduce the speed measure density

$$m(\tilde{y}) := \frac{2}{S'(\tilde{y}) \cdot \gamma^2 \cdot (\sigma_K^2 + \sigma_A^2 + \sigma_L^2) \cdot \tilde{y}^2}$$

$$= \frac{2}{\exp\left\{ b_2 \cdot \left[\tilde{y}^{1-1/\gamma} + \frac{1-\gamma}{\gamma^2} \cdot b_5 \cdot \ln \tilde{y} - 1 \right] \right\} \cdot \gamma^2 \cdot (\sigma_K^2 + \sigma_A^2 + \sigma_L^2) \cdot \tilde{y}^2}, \quad \tilde{y} > 0.$$

(30)

The total mass of the associated speed measure $\hat{m}$ with density $m(\cdot)$ can be computed in terms of the gamma function $\Gamma(\cdot)$ and b_1 given by (13) as

$$\hat{m}[(0, \infty)] = \int_0^\infty m(\tilde{y}) \, d\tilde{y} = \frac{b_2}{\gamma} \cdot e^{b_2} \int_0^\infty e^{-b_2 \tilde{y}} \cdot \tilde{y}^{2b_1 - 1} \, d\tilde{y}$$

$$= \frac{b_2^{1-2b_1}}{\gamma} \cdot e^{b_2} \cdot \Gamma(2b_1) < \infty.$$

(31)

Since by (21) every k_t^γ ($t \in (0, \infty)$) has a density, one can apply a result of Pollak and Siegmund (1985) (see also Karatzas and Shreve 1991, p. 352) to obtain the desired limit distribution density (22) by

$$\widetilde{P_{\lim}}[(0, a)] = \lim_{t \to \infty} P\left[\frac{Y_t}{A_t L_t} \le a \right] = \lim_{t \to \infty} P[k_t^\gamma \le a] = \frac{\hat{m}[(0, a)]}{\hat{m}[(0, \infty)]}$$

$$= \frac{\gamma \cdot \int_0^a m(\tilde{y}) \, d\tilde{y}}{b_2^{1-2b_1} \cdot e^{b_2} \cdot \Gamma(2b_1)} = \frac{(1 - \gamma) \cdot b_2^{2b_1}}{\gamma \cdot \Gamma(2b_1)} \int_0^a \exp\left\{ -b_2 \tilde{y}^{1-1/\gamma} \right\}$$

$$\cdot \tilde{y}^{-[1+2b_1(1-\gamma)/\gamma]} \, d\tilde{y}, \quad a \in (0, \infty),$$

where we have used (30) and (31). Furthermore, the equality between steady-state-equilibrium distribution and the limit distribution (i.e., $\widetilde{P_{\text{stea}}} = \widetilde{P_{\lim}}$) follows by standard techniques, see, for example, Kallenberg (2002, Chap. 23).

Let us finally mention that one can proceed similarly in order to derive the limit distribution and the steady-state-equilibrium distribution of the savings rate process $(s_t)_{t \in (0, \infty)}$, which for the sake of brevity is omitted here.

A.3. Consumption (5) within a Ramsey-type setup

In this entire section, we suppose $\tilde{b}_\rho = \tilde{b}_\delta = 0$ as well as $T = \infty$ and indicate how the random per capita consumption (5) can for instance arise from the following continuous-time "fully-stochastic" Ramsey-type setup (see Feicht and Stummer, 2010):

In addition to the economy components given by the Cobb–Douglas-type production function Y_t in (1), the effectiveness of labor A_t in (2), the labor force L_t in (3) and the capital stock K_t in (4), we suppose a representative consumer that has a constant rate $\rho_0 \geq 0$ of time-preference and CRRA utility

$$u(c) = \frac{c^{1-\tilde{\gamma}} - 1}{1 - \tilde{\gamma}}$$

with coefficient of relative risk aversion (respectively, the reciprocal of the intertemporal elasticity of substitution) $\tilde{\gamma}$. Furthermore, let the technical requirement $(1 - \tilde{\gamma})\mu_A + \mu_L < \rho_0$ be satisfied. Additionally, we confine ourselves (mathematically without (much) loss of generality) to random per capita consumptions of the form $c_t = c(K_t, A_t, L_t)$ for some deterministic, nonnegative consumption rule $c(\cdot)$ in the class $\mathscr{C}$ of all admissible (i.e., technically adequate) consumption strategies. Within the abovementioned economy framework, the social planner is supposed to solve the following optimization problem for fixed capital share $\gamma \in (0,1)$, depreciation rate $\delta_0 \geq 0$, time-preference rate $\rho_0 \geq 0$, coefficient of relative risk aversion $\tilde{\gamma} \geq 0$, volatilities $\sigma_K, \sigma_A, \sigma_L > 0$, and average growth rates $\mu_A \geq 0$, $\mu_L \in (-\infty, \infty)$.

Social Planner's Problem (SPP): For prevailing economy values $K_0, A_0, L_0 > 0$ at current time $s = 0$, maximize over all admissible nonnegative per capita consumption rules $c(\cdot) \in \mathscr{C}$ the expected (discounted) lifetime utility of consumption

$$E\left[\int_0^\infty e^{-\rho_0 t} \frac{(c(K_t, A_t, L_t))^{1-\tilde{\gamma}} - 1}{1 - \tilde{\gamma}} \, L_t \, dt \,\middle|\, K_0, A_0, L_0 \right]$$

subject to the three constraints (2), (3) and

$$dK_t = [K_t^\gamma (A_t L_t)^{1-\gamma} - \delta_0 K_t - L_t \, c(K_t, A_t, L_t)] \, dt + \sigma_K K_t dB_t^K, \quad K_0 \text{ given.}$$
(32)

As usual, by $E[\,\cdot\,|\,K_0, A_0, L_0\,]$ we denote the expectation conditioned on the initial economy values K_0, A_0, L_0. As extension of SPP, there are several additional tasks which should be investigated too:

Social Planner's "Extended" Problem (SPEP): For arbitrarily given initial economy values $K_0, A_0, L_0 > 0$, find

(SPEP1) the maximum expected (discounted) lifetime utility of consumption

$$V(K_0, A_0, L_0) := \max_{c(\cdot) \in \mathscr{C}} E\left[\int_0^\infty e^{-\rho_0 t} \frac{(c(K_t, A_t, L_t))^{1-\tilde{\gamma}} - 1}{1 - \tilde{\gamma}} L_t dt \,\middle|\, K_0, A_0, L_0\right]$$

subject to the economy-value-evolution constraints (2), (3), (32),

(SPEP2) the corresponding maximizing per capita consumption **rule** $c^{\max}(\cdot)$ (including a proof of uniqueness),

(SPEP3) for each time t the **explicit closed-form** of the economy values K_t, A_t, L_t and consequently of the maximizing per capita consumption **strategy** $c_t^{\max} = c^{\max}(K_t, A_t, L_t)$,

(SPEP4) the **explicit closed-form** of the per capita effective capital stock $k_t = K_t/(A_t L_t)$ and its **non-steady-state-equilibrium** distribution,

(SPEP5) the **long-term limit** (as t tends to infinity) of the k_t–distribution, which turns out to be equal to the **steady-state-equilibrium distribution**.

In Table 5 we exemplarily mention some studies about continuous-time stochastic growth models (mainly with Cobb–Douglas-type technology), which are similiar but of lower-dimensional "uncertainty" and of less "explicitness" than our framework; for comparison, we have also included some Solow–Swan-type studies.

In line with, for example, Chang (1988), Xie (1991, 1994), Boucekkine and Ruiz-Tamarit (2004), Smith (2006, 2007), Boucekkine and Ruiz-Tamarit (2008), Ferrara and Guerrini (2009a, 2009b), Posch (2009a, 2009b), Posch and Wälde (2009), Wälde (2009), we assume that the coefficient of relative risk aversion is equal with the capital share, that is, $\tilde{\gamma} = \gamma$. As a corresponding side remark, let us briefly mention that within

Table 5. *Some literature comparison*

Reference	σ_K	σ_A	μ_A	σ_L	μ_L	Type
Amilon and Bermin (2003)	= 0			> 0	$\in (-\infty, \infty)$	Ramsey
Baten and Miah (2007)	= 0			> 0	$\in (-\infty, \infty)$	Ramsey
Bourguignon (1974)	> 0			> 0	$\in (-\infty, \infty)$	Solow–Swan
Bucci et al. (2008)	= 0	> 0	$\in (-\infty, \infty)$	= 0	$\in (-\infty, \infty)$	Ramsey
Jensen and Richter (2007)	> 0			> 0	$\in (-\infty, \infty)$	Solow–Swan
Merton (1975)	= 0			> 0	$\in (-\infty, \infty)$	Solow–Swan&Ramsey
Posch (2009b)	= 0	> 0	$\in (-\infty, \infty)$			Ramsey
Roche (2003)	> 0			> 0	$\in (-\infty, \infty)$	Ramsey
Smith (2007)	= 0	> 0	$\in (-\infty, \infty)$			Ramsey
Smith (2007)	= 0			> 0	$\in (-\infty, \infty)$	Ramsey
this chapter	> 0	> 0	$\in (-\infty, \infty)$	> 0	$\in (-\infty, \infty)$	Ramsey

Note: "Blank" spaces mean no-occurrence; eventual parameter restrictions are not mentioned here.

the range of the German empirical data used in Section 3 one has the
following effect: suppose that the capital share is $\gamma = 1/3$ and consider the
four different utility functions

$$u_0(c) = \frac{c^{1-1/3} - 1}{1 - 1/3} = \frac{3}{2} \cdot (c^{2/3} - 1), \quad u_1(c) = \frac{2}{3} \cdot u_0(c) + 1 = c^{2/3}, \quad \text{that is, } \tilde{\gamma} = 1/3,$$

$$u_2(c) = 25913 \cdot \frac{c^{1-4/3} - 1}{1 - 4/3} - 74286, \quad u_3(c) = \frac{c^{1-4/3} - 1}{1 - 4/3} = 3 \cdot (1 - c^{-1/3}),$$

that is, $\tilde{\gamma} = 4/3$.

Clearly, the maximization of the expected (discounted) lifetime utility of
consumption

$$E\left[\int_0^\infty e^{-\rho_0 t} u_i(c(K_t, A_t, L_t)) L_t \mathrm{d}t \,\Big|\, K_0, A_0, L_0\right] \quad (i = 0, 1, 2, 3)$$

– subject to the three constraints (2), (3), (32) – leads in both cases $i = 0$
and $i = 1$ to the identical maximum consumption rule (say) $c_1^{\max}(\cdot)$;
furthermore, in both cases $i = 2$ and $i = 3$ the maximum consumption rule
is also identical, (say) $c_2^{\max}(\cdot)$. Within the range of the German empirical
data used in Section 3, the per capita (in the sense of per worker)
consumption is typically about 40000 Euros, around which the two utility
functions u_1 and u_2 are close to each other, see Figure 43.

In the following, we indicate the solutions to (SPEP1) and (SPEP2) (cf.
Feicht and Stummer, 2010), which leads to random per capita consump-
tions of the form (5) with $\tilde{b}_\rho = \tilde{b}_\delta = 0$. Consequently, the solutions to
(SPEP3), (SPEP4), and (SPEP5) appear indirectly as a special case of our
more general investigations in Section 2 which can also arise within a
Solow–Swan-type setup (rather than a Ramsey-type setup).

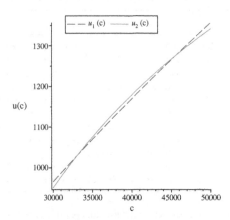

Fig. 43.   Comparison of utility functions u_1 and u_2.

To start with, the corresponding Hamilton-Jacobi-Bellman (HJB) equation has the form – in terms of $X = (K, A, L) > 0$ –

$$\sup_{v \in [0,\infty)} \left\{ \frac{v^{1-\gamma} - 1}{1 - \gamma} L - \rho_0 W(X) + [K^\gamma (AL)^{1-\gamma} - \delta_0 K - Lv] \frac{\partial W(X)}{\partial K} + \mu_A A \frac{\partial W(X)}{\partial A} \right.$$

$$\left. + \mu_L L \frac{\partial W(X)}{\partial L} + \frac{1}{2} \sigma_K^2 K^2 \frac{\partial^2 W(X)}{\partial K^2} + \frac{1}{2} \sigma_A^2 A^2 \frac{\partial^2 W(X)}{\partial A^2} + \frac{1}{2} \sigma_L^2 L^2 \frac{\partial^2 W(X)}{\partial L^2} \right\} = 0$$

which by maximization of the left-hand side induces

$$v = \left(\frac{\partial W(X)}{\partial K} \right)^{-\frac{1}{\gamma}} =: v^{\max}(X) \tag{33}$$

and thus

$$\frac{\left(\frac{\partial W(X)}{\partial K} \right)^{-\frac{1-\gamma}{\gamma}} - 1}{1 - \gamma} L - \rho_0 W(X) + \left[K^\gamma (AL)^{1-\gamma} - \delta_0 K - L \cdot \left(\frac{\partial W(X)}{\partial K} \right)^{-\frac{1}{\gamma}} \right] \frac{\partial W(X)}{\partial K}$$

$$+ \mu_A A \frac{\partial W(X)}{\partial A} + \mu_L L \frac{\partial W(X)}{\partial L} + \frac{1}{2} \sigma_K^2 K^2 \frac{\partial^2 W(X)}{\partial K^2}$$

$$+ \frac{1}{2} \sigma_A^2 A^2 \frac{\partial^2 W(X)}{\partial A^2} + \frac{1}{2} \sigma_L^2 L^2 \frac{\partial^2 W(X)}{\partial L^2} = 0.$$

By plugging in the educated guess

$$W(X) := a_1 K^{1-\gamma} L^\gamma + a_2 A^{1-\gamma} L + a_3 L \tag{34}$$

for some constants $a_1, a_2, a_3 \in (-\infty, \infty)$, one arrives at the following three conditions to be fulfilled:

$$a_4 := [(1-\gamma) a_1]^{-\frac{1}{\gamma}} = \frac{1}{\gamma} [\rho_0 + \delta_0 (1-\gamma) - \mu_L \gamma + \frac{1}{2} (1-\gamma) \gamma (\sigma_K^2 + \sigma_L^2)], \tag{35}$$

$$a_2 = \frac{a_1 (1-\gamma)}{\rho_0 - \mu_A (1-\gamma) - \mu_L + \frac{1}{2} \sigma_A^2 (1-\gamma) \gamma},$$

$$a_3 = -\frac{1}{(1-\gamma)(\rho_0 - \mu_L)}.$$

From (33), (34) and (35) one obtains

$$v^{\max}(X) = v^{\max}(K, A, L) = a_4 \frac{K}{L} =: c^{\max}(K, A, L) > 0$$

which "coincides" (i.e., is consistent) with (5) in the current constellation $\tilde{b}_\rho = \tilde{b}_\delta = 0$. Finally, as usual, one has to run through a corresponding verification procedure including in particular a transversality condition. For details, the reader is referred to Feicht and Stummer (2010).

References

Acemoglu, D., & Guerrieri, V. (2008). Capital deepening and nonbalanced economic growth. *Journal of Political Economy*, *116*(3), 467–498.

Amilon, H., & Bermin, H.-P. (2003). Welfare effects of controlling labor supply: An application of the stochastic Ramsey model. *Journal of Economic Dynamics and Control*, *28*(2), 331–348.

Barro, R. J., Mankiw, N. G., & Sala-i Martin, X. (1995). Capital mobility in neoclassical models of growth. *American Economic Review*, *85*(1), 103–115.

Baten, A., & Miah, S. (2007). Optimal consumption in a growth model with the CES production function. *Stochastic Analysis and Applications*, *25*(5), 1025–1042.

Bernanke, B. S., & Gürkaynak, R. S. (2001). Is growth exogenous? Taking Mankiw, Romer, and Weil seriously. In B. S. Bernanke & K. Rogoff (Eds.), *NBER Macroeconomics Annual 2001* (Vol. 16, pp. 11–57). Cambridge, MA: MIT Press.

Borodin, A. N., & Salminen, P. (2002). *Handbook of Brownian Motion: Facts and Formulae* (2nd ed.). Basel: Birkhäuser.

Boucekkine, R., & Ruiz-Tamarit, J. (2004). Imbalance effects in the Lucas model: An analytical exploration. *Topics in Macroeconomics*, *4*(1), Article 15.

Boucekkine, R., & Ruiz-Tamarit, J. (2008). Special functions for the study of economic dynamics: The case of the Lucas-Uzawa model. *Journal of Mathematical Economics*, *44*(1), 33–54.

Bourguignon, F. (1974). A particular class of continuous-time stochastic growth models. *Journal of Economic Theory*, *9*(2), 141–158.

Braun, R. A., & Nakajima, T. (2009). *How large is the intertemporal elasticity of substitution?* Unpublished Working Paper, University of Tokyo/Kyoto University.

Bucci, A., Colapinto, C., Forster, M., & Torre, D.L. (2008). *On human capital and economic growth with random technology shocks.* Departemental Working Paper No. 2008-36, State University of Milan, Department of Economics. Available at http://air.cilea.it/bitstream/ 2434/53795/1/WP.pdf

Cagetti, M., Hansen, L. P., Sargent, T., & Williams, N. (2002). Robustness and pricing with uncertain growth. *Review of Financial Studies*, *15*(2), 363–404.

Cagetti, M., & Nardi, M. D. (2009). Estate taxation, entrepreneurship, and wealth. *American Economic Review*, *99*(1), 85–111.

Carmona, P., Petit, F., & Yor, M. (1997). On the distribution and asymptotic results for exponential functionals of Levy processes. In M. Yor (Ed.), *Exponential functionals and principal values related to Brownian motion* (pp. 73–126). Madrid: Biblioteca de la Revista Matematica Iberoamericana.

Caselli, F., & Coleman, W. J. (2006). The world technology frontier. *American Economic Review*, *96*(3), 499–522.

Chang, F.-R. (1988). The inverse optimal problem: A dynamic programming approach. *Econometrica, 56*(1), 147–172.

Chang, F.-R. (2004). *Stochastic Optimization in Continuous Time.* Cambridge: Cambridge University Press.

Conesa, J. C., Kitao, S., & Krueger, D. (2009). Taxing capital? Not a bad idea after all! *American Economic Review, 99*(1), 25–48.

Feicht, R., & Stummer, W. (2010). *Complete closed-form solution to a stochastic growth model and corresponding speed of economic recovery.* IWQW Discussion Paper 5/2010, University of Erlangen-Nürnberg. Available at http://www.iwqw.rw.uni-erlangen.de/forschung/05-2010.pdf

Ferrara, M., & Guerrini, L. (2009a). The Ramsey model with logistic population growth and Benthamite felicity function revisited. *WSEAS Transactions on Mathematics, 8*(3), 97–106.

Ferrara, M., & Guerrini, L. (2009b). *A closed form solution to the transitional dynamics of a modified Ramsey model.* Working Paper No. 2009/6, University Spiru Haret, Facultatea de Finante si Banci, Centrul de Cercetari Economico-Financiare Avansate.

Gollin, D., Parente, S., & Rogerson, R. (2002). *Structural transformation and cross-country income differences.* Levine's Working Paper Archive 506439000000000259.

Gyöngy, I., & Martinez, T. (2001). On stochastic differential equations with locally unbounded drift. *Czechoslovak Mathematical Journal, 51*(126), 763–783.

Hall, R. E. (2001). The stock market and capital accumulation. *American Economic Review, 91*(5), 1185–1202.

Jensen, B. S., & Richter, M. (2007). Stochastic one-sector and two-sector growth models in continuous time. In B. S. Jensen & T. Palokangas (Eds.), *Stochastic Economic Dynamics* (pp. 167–216, Part 5). Copenhagen: Business School Press.

Kallenberg, O. (2002). *Foundations of Modern Probability* (2nd ed.). New York, NY: Springer.

Karatzas, I., & Shreve, S. E. (1991). *Brownian Motion and Stochastic Calculus* (2nd ed.). New York, NY: Springer.

King, R. G., & Rebelo, S. T. (1993). Transitional dynamics and economic growth in the neoclassical model. *American Economic Review, 83*(4), 908–931.

La Grandville, O. de (2009). *Economic Growth-A Unified Approach.* Cambridge: Cambridge University Press.

La Grandville, O. de (2011). How much should a nation save? A new answer. To appear in *Studies in Nonlinear Dynamics & Econometrics.*

Malliaris, A. G., & Brock, W. A. (1982). *Stochastic Methods in Economics and Finance.* Amsterdam: North-Holland.

Merton, R. C. (1975). An asymptotic theory of growth under uncertainty. *Review of Economic Studies, 42*(3), 375–393.

Nishide, K., & Ohyama, A. (2007). *Timing an environmental policy optimally under economic considerations*. Discussion Paper No. 126, Kyoto University, Interfaces for Advanced Economic Analysis. Available at http://www.kier.kyoto-u.ac.jp/coe21/dp/121-130/21COE-DP126.pdf

Palacios, M. (2010). *Human capital as an asset class: Implications from a general equilibrium model*. Working Paper, Vanderbilt University, Owen Graduate School of Management. http://www2.owen.vanderbilt.edu/miguel.palacios/PalaciosValueHC.pdf

Pollak, M., & Siegmund, D. (1985). A diffusion process and its applications to detecting a change in the drift of Brownian motion. *Biometrika, 72*(2), 267–280.

Posch, O. (2009a). *Explaining output volatility: The case of taxation*. CESifo Working Paper No. 2751. To appear in *Journal of Public Economics*.

Posch, O. (2009b). Structural estimation of jump-diffusion processes in macroeconomics. *Journal of Econometrics, 153*(2), 196–210.

Posch, O., Wälde, K. (2009). *On the non-causal link between volatility and growth*. CREATES Economics Working Paper No. 2009-10. Available at ftp://ftp.econ.au.dk/afn/wp/09/wp09_10.pdf. To appear in *Journal of Economic Growth*.

Pyyhtiä, I. (2007). *Why is Europe lagging behind?* Bank of Finland, Research Discussion Paper No. 3/2007.

Roche, H. (2003). Stochastic growth: A duality approach. *Journal of Economic Theory, 113*(1), 131–143.

Schmitt-Grohe, S. (2000). Endogenous business cycles and the dynamics of output, hours, and consumption. *American Economic Review, 90*(5), 1136–1159.

Smith, W. T. (2006). A closed form solution to the Ramsey model. *Contributions to Macroeconomics, 6*(1), Article 3.

Smith, W. T. (2007). Inspecting the mechanism exactly: A closed-form solution to a stochastic growth model. *The B.E. Journal of Macroeconomics, 7*(1), Article 30.

Stummer, W., & Vajda, I. (2007). Optimal statistical decisions about some alternative financial models. *Journal of Econometrics, 137*(2), 441–471.

Turnovsky, S. J. (2000). *Methods of Macroeconomic Dynamics* (2nd ed.). Cambridge, MA: MIT Press.

Wälde, K. (2005). Endogenous growth cycles. *International Economic Review, 46*(3), 867–894.

Wälde, K. (2010). *Applied Intertemporal Optimization*. Lecture notes, Mainz University Gutenberg Press.

Williams, N. (2004). Small noise asymptotics for a stochastic growth model. *Journal of Economic Theory, 119*(2), 271–298.

Xie, D. (1991). Increasing returns and increasing rates of growth. *Journal of Political Economy, 99*(2), 429–435.

Xie, D. (1994). Divergence in economic performance: Transitional dynamics with multiple equilibria. *Journal of Economic Theory, 63*(1), 97–112.

CHAPTER 8

Growth Volatility and the Structure of the Economy

Davide Fiaschi[a] and Andrea Mario Lavezzi[b]

[a]*Dipartimento di Scienze Economiche, University of Pisa, Via Ridolfi 10, 56124 Pisa, Italy*
E-mail address: dfiaschi@ec.unipi.it
[b]*Dipartimento di Studi su Politica, Diritto e Società, University of Palermo, Piazza Bologni 8, 90134 Palermo, Italy*
E-mail address: mario.lavezzi@unipa.it

Abstract
The aim of the chapter is twofold: (i) to propose a methodology to compute the growth rate volatility of an economy and (ii) to investigate the relationship between growth volatility and economic development through the lenses of the structural characteristics of an economy. We study a large cross-section of countries in the period 1970–2009, controlling for the stability of the estimates in two subperiods: 1970:1989 (Period I) and 1990:2009 (Period II). Our main findings are (i) the degree of trade openness has a destabilizing effect, while the degree of financial openness has not a significant effect; (ii) the size of the public sector displays a U-shaped relationship with growth volatility, but only in Period II; and (iii) the level of financial development has a negative effect on growth volatility, but only in Period I. Therefore, the dominant policy orientations in the recent decades contained emphasis on potential sources of instability, for example, on the increase in openness and on the reduction of the size of the public sector.

Keywords: Growth volatility, economic development, economic structure, nonparametric methods

JEL classifications: O11, O40, C14, C21

1. Introduction

The volatility of the growth rate of economies has attracted the interest of many researchers, with the emerging stylized fact in the literature that poor countries display a much higher degree of volatility than rich countries (see, e.g., Durlauf, Johnson, & Temple, 2005, p. 575; Pritchett, 2000).

Frontiers of Economics and Globalization
Volume 11   ISSN: 1574-8715
DOI: 10.1108/S1574-8715(2011)0000011013

Some authors have, moreover, argued that there exists a causal relationship going from high growth volatility to low long-run growth (see the pioneering paper by Ramey & Ramey, 1995). In addition to these pieces of evidence, in recent years, developed countries have experienced an abrupt end of the period of the so-called "Great Moderation", that is, a period characterized by a remarkable reduction of growth volatility started in the 1980s (see, e.g., Stock & Watson, 2002, on the United States).

The aim of the chapter is twofold: (1) to propose a methodology to compute the growth rate volatility of per capita GDP (GRV henceforth), which preserves both the time-series and cross-section dimensions, a feature typically overlooked in the literature with the notable exception of Pritchett (2000); and (2) to investigate the relationship between GRV and economic development through the lenses of the *structural characteristics* of an economy, that is (i) the *size* of the economy; (ii) the degree of *trade and financial openness*; (iii) the *size of the public sector*; (iv) the level of *financial development*; and (v) the *composition of* GDP. This chapter considers a large cross-section of countries in the period 1970–2009, controlling for the stability of the estimates in two subperiods: 1970:1989 (Period I) and 1990:2009 (Period II). When possible, we use different measures for each structural characteristics. Our findings can be summarized as follows:

(i) The size of the economy exerts a stabilizing role at low levels in terms of both total GDP and total population. This finding, however, differs across the two subperiods: in particular, only in Period II, total GDP has a significant effect. In the literature, the size of an economy is expected to be negatively related to growth volatility because "individual" volatility (of, e.g., firms and sectors) should be smoothed out by averaging across an increasing number of units (Canning, Amaral, Lee, Meyer, & Stanley, 1998; Scheinkman & Woodford, 1994), and large countries can provide regional "insurance" by fiscal transfers (Alesina & Spolaore, 2003, p. 4). The density of population has an inverted U-shaped effect, in contrast with the expected destabilizing effect suggested by Collier (2007).

(ii) The degree of trade openness, measured by imports plus exports on GDP, has a destabilizing effect, while the degree of financial openness, measured by the net flow of foreign direct investment on GDP, has not a significant effect. The concentration of exports by trade partner, a novel measure introduced to further qualify the degree of trade openness, has a positive effect effect on GRV but only at low levels. In general, the degree of trade and financial openness has an ambiguous effect on volatility because it allows to smooth internal shocks through trade and financial interactions with other countries but, at the same time, it exposes a country to external shocks (see, e.g., Di Giovanni & Levchenko, 2009; Easterly, Islam, & Stiglitz, 2000). Malik and Temple (2009, p. 166), moreover, argue that the vulnerability to external shocks is higher when trade is concentrated in few goods.

(iii) The size of the public sector, measured by government consumption on GDP, has a statistically significant effect only in Period II, displaying a U-shaped relationship with GRV, with a minimum around 20% of GDP. This value should represent the optimal size of a government aiming at minimizing growth volatility. A large public sector should indeed reduce volatility as it can act as an automatic stabilizer (see, e.g. Galí, 1994; Fatás & Mihov, 2001). Rodrick (1998) discusses a possible positive relationship between openness and the size of government, arguing that more open economies choose large public sectors to counterbalance the increased instability due to their higher degree of openness.

(iv) The level of financial development, measured by the stock of domestic credit to private sector on GDP, has a negative effect on GRV, but only in Period I. Our measure of financial development, however, may not be fully adequate to capture the actual level of financial development in more recent years. In principle, financial development can have an ambiguous effect on growth volatility because, as argued by Easterly et al. (2000, p. 202), "developed financial systems offer opportunities for stabilization, [but] they may also imply higher leverage of firms and thus more risk and less stability ... As the financial system grows relative to GDP, the increase in risk becomes becomes more important and acts to reduce stability."

(v) The composition of GDP, measured by the rents from natural resources on GDP, has a positive effect on GRV but only at high levels and in Period II. There exist many contributions discussing how different sectors display different levels of volatility; for example, Fiaschi and Lavezzi (2005) show that a higher share of agricultural GDP is associated to higher volatility, and Koren and Tenreyro (2007, p. 262) show that sectors can be ranked in terms of their volatility: agriculture, mining, and quarrying have high volatility, manufactures have intermediate volatility and services have low volatility. The presence of some sectors with high rents from metals, oil, and so on, moreover, can increase volatility as they favor the onset of social conflicts and civil wars (see, e.g., Collier, 2007).

Among the controls, those with explanatory power on GRV are the quality of the institutions, measured by constraint on executives (we find a negative effect, but only in Period I, see Acemoglu, Johnson, Robinson, & Thaicharoen, 2003 for a similar finding); a measure of the fertility of soil (positive effect at low/medium levels, but only in Period II, see Malik & Temple, 2009); the mean distance to the nearest coastline or sea-navigable river (positive effect, but only in Period II, see, again, Malik & Temple, 2009). Measures of aggregate volatility, as the volatility of world prices of food, or minerals, ores and metals, are statistically significant only in the whole period, suggesting that a change of regime of volatility occurred between Periods I and II, while within each period, aggregate shocks played a marginal role.

The chapter is organized as follows. Section 2 discusses the methodology for the computation of growth volatility; Section 3 contains the description of the database and the results from the empirical analysis; Section 4 concludes.

2. The estimation of growth volatility

In this section, we propose a methodology for the estimation of GRV, which exploits its both cross-sectional and time-series dimensions.[1] Then, we apply this methodology to the growth rate of per capita GDP of a large sample of countries, discussing the main characteristics of the estimated growth volatilities.[2]

2.1. The methodology

Following Barro and Sala-i-Martin (1998, p. 37), consider the log-linear approximation around the steady state of the growth rate of per capita income of country j at time t:

$$\tilde{\gamma}_{jt} \approx -\beta(\log \tilde{y}_{jt} - \log \tilde{y}_j^{SS}),$$ (1)

where $\tilde{\gamma}_{jt}$ is the growth rate of per capita income in efficiency units, that is, normalized with respect to the growth rate of exogenous technological progress γ_A, that is, $\tilde{\gamma}_{jt} = \gamma_{jt} - \gamma_A$, where γ_{jt} is the growth rate of per capita income; $\beta > 0$ measures the speed of convergence to steady state, $\tilde{y}_t^j$ is per capita income in efficiency units, and $\tilde{y}_j^{SS}$ is the steady-state level of per capita income in efficiency units of country j. From Equation (1), taking $\tilde{\gamma}_{jt} \approx \log \tilde{y}_{jt}/\tilde{y}_{j,t-1}$, we obtain,

$$\tilde{\gamma}_{jt} \approx \left(\frac{1}{1+\beta}\right)\tilde{\gamma}_{jt-1},$$ (2)

---

[1] This is in line with the remark of Galí (2002, p. 224) which, with respect to the US experience, observes, "SW [Stock and Watson (2002)] paper ... studies the phenomenon of changes in the business cycle from a time-series perspective. But measures of macroeconomic volatility appear to vary across countries no less than they vary over time. Can we learn anything from the cross-country evidence regarding the sources of the observed changes (*over time*) in the U.S. business cycle?" (emphasis added).

[2] Data of per capita GDP are from the Penn World Table 7.0. We used the growth rate of PPP converted GDP chain per capita (PWT code: grgdpch).

and, therefore, in terms of the growth rate of per capita income:

$$\gamma_{jt} \approx \left(\frac{\beta}{1+\beta}\right)\gamma_A + \left(\frac{1}{1+\beta}\right)\gamma_{jt-1}. \tag{3}$$

Adding a stochastic term to Equation (3), we obtain a representation of the dynamics of the growth rate as an AR(1) process:

$$\gamma_{jt} \approx \left(\frac{\beta}{1+\beta}\right)\gamma_A + \left(\frac{1}{1+\beta}\right)\gamma_{j,t-1} + \varepsilon_{jt}, \tag{4}$$

where ε_{jt} is assumed to be normally distributed with zero mean and standard deviation σ_{jt}^ε. Writing Equation (4) in the standard AR(1) form, that is,

$$\gamma_{jt} = \mu_j + \phi_1 \gamma_{j,t-1} + \varepsilon_{jt}, \tag{5}$$

we derive the standard deviation of the growth rate γ_{jt} (see, e.g., Hamilton, 1994, p. 53):

$$\sigma_{jt}^\gamma = \frac{\sigma_{jt}^\varepsilon}{\sqrt{1 - \phi_1^2}}. \tag{6}$$

The unbiased estimator of σ_{jt}^ε is proportional to the estimated absolute value of residuals from the estimation of Equation (5) (see McConnell & Perez-Quiros, 2000, p. 1466; Stock & Watson, 2002, pp. 207–208), that is,

$$\hat{\sigma}_{jt}^\varepsilon = \sqrt{\frac{\pi}{2}}|\hat{\varepsilon}_{jt}|. \tag{7}$$

Taking as measure of GRV the standard deviation of the growth rate, from Equations (6) and (7) we have that

$$\hat{\mathrm{GRV}}_{jt} = \hat{\sigma}_{jt}^\gamma = \frac{\sqrt{\pi/2}|\hat{\varepsilon}_{jt}|}{\sqrt{1 - \hat{\phi}_1^2}}. \tag{8}$$

This method of computation of GRV can be easily extended to higher-order AR models,[3] which correspond to the case where the log-linear

---

[3] For an AR(3), the maximum lag considered in the empirical analysis, we have (see Hamilton, 1994, pp. 58–59):

$$\mathrm{GRV}_{jt} = \frac{\sigma_{jt}^\varepsilon}{\sqrt{1 - \rho_1 \phi_1^2 - \rho_2 \phi_2^2 - \rho_3 \phi_3^2}},$$

where,

$$\rho_1 = \frac{\phi_1 + \phi_2 \phi_3}{1 - \phi_2 - \phi_3(\phi_1 + \phi_3)};$$

$$\rho_2 = \frac{\phi_1(\phi_1 + \phi_3) + \phi_2(1 - \phi_2)}{1 - \phi_2 - \phi_3(\phi_1 + \phi_3)}, \text{and}$$

$$\rho_3 = \phi_1 \rho_2 + \phi_2 \rho_1 + \phi_3.$$

approximation in Equation (1) includes other terms with lagged values of (normalized) per capita income.[4] In the empirical analysis, we select the order of AR for each country in our sample (among which the AR of order 0, that is, the case of growth rate processes that can be represented by their means plus a random error) by a small-sample version of the Akaike Information Criterion (AIC), indicated as AIC_c (see Burnham & Anderson, 2004, p. 66). The list of the selected order of ARs for the 69 countries of the sample used in the analysis is reported in the appendix.

Country j's GRV can be decomposed in aggregate shocks, that is, shocks affecting all countries in the same period,[5] and country-specific (idiosyncratic) shocks deriving from country-specific characteristics, that is,

$$\varepsilon_{jt} = \lambda_t + u_{jt}, \tag{9}$$

where λ_t is an aggregate shock, normally and independently distributed with zero mean and standard deviation σ_t^λ, and u_{jt} is a country-specific normally distributed random shock with zero mean and standard deviation σ_{jt}^u. Therefore,

$$\sigma_{jt}^\varepsilon = \sqrt{(\sigma_t^\lambda)^2 + (\sigma_{jt}^u)^2}. \tag{10}$$

The standard deviation of the country-specific shock can be expressed as follows:

$$\sigma_{jt}^u = \sigma^u(\mathbf{Z}_{jt}), \tag{11}$$

where the vector $\mathbf{Z}_{jt}$ contains the country-specific variables, such as size of the economy, trade, and financial openness.

---

[4] For an AR(3), we have,

$$\tilde{\gamma}_{jt} \approx -\beta_0(\log \tilde{y}_{jt} - \log \tilde{y}_j^{SS}) - \beta_1(\log \tilde{y}_{j,t-1} - \log \tilde{y}_j^{SS})$$
$$- \beta_2(\log \tilde{y}_{j,t-2} - \log \tilde{y}_j^{SS}) - \beta_3(\log \tilde{y}_{j,t-3} - \log \tilde{y}_j^{SS}),$$

from which,

$$\gamma_{jt} \approx \left(\frac{\beta_0 + \beta_1 + \beta_2 + \beta_3}{1 + \beta_0}\right)\gamma_A + \left(\frac{1}{1 + \beta_0}\right)[(1 - \beta_1)\gamma_{j,t-1} + \beta_2\gamma_{j,t-2} + \beta_3\gamma_{j,t-3}].$$

[5] "[T]he price of a major input in production, such as steel ... may affect the productivity of sectors that are steel-intensive. More generally, technology- and price-shocks that affect a sector or a group of sectors across countries will fall in this category" (Koren & Tenreyro, 2007, p. 248).

Hence, we rewrite Equation (8) in the light of Equations (10) and (11) as follows:

$$\hat{\mathrm{GRV}}_{jt} = \sqrt{\frac{(\hat{\sigma}_t^\lambda)^2 + (\hat{\sigma}_{jt}^u)^2}{1 - \hat{\phi}_1^2}} = f(\mathbf{X}_t, \mathbf{Z}_{jt}), \tag{12}$$

where $\mathbf{X}_t$ is a vector of variables capturing the effect of global shocks on GRV. Equation (12) represents the structure of our baseline econometric model when the order of the AR process is 1.[6] Specifically, in the empirical analysis, the aggregate shocks will be captured by time dummies and by the volatility of world prices of broad categories of goods, such as food and metals, while the impact of country-specific variables will be estimated by a semiparametric specification.

This approach has important advantages with respect to the methods commonly used in the literature, deriving from the exploitation of *both* the cross-sectional and the time-series dimensions of GRV. The most popular methodology consists in calculating GRV by the standard deviation of the time series of country *j*'s growth rates of per capita or per worker GDP (see, e.g., Di Giovanni & Levchenko, 2009; Easterly et al., 2000; Malik & Temple, 2009). The main drawback of this method is that many variables potentially included in $\mathbf{Z}$ in Equation (12) are likely to vary over time. In other words, this approach omits the possible changes of within-country volatility in time which, following our representation, may depend of the variation in time of the elements of $\mathbf{Z}$.

Differently, Canning et al. (1998) pool the residuals from a panel estimation of the following model:[7]

$$g_{jt} = \gamma_j + \lambda_t + u_{jt}, \tag{13}$$

partition them into different classes on the basis of the level of total GDP and calculate the standard deviation within each class. This amounts to assume that $\mathbf{Z}$ in Equation (12) includes only total GDP and that the effect of global shocks can be captured by a time dummy. A similar procedure is also followed by Acemoglu and Zilibotti (1997, p. 715), who partition the residuals in classes defined on the basis of per capita GDP.

Finally, papers such as Head (1995) apply the Hodrick–Prescott filter to countries' growth rates and then compute GRV as the standard deviation of growth rate residuals with respect to the smoothed series. This amounts to assume that growth rates follow a (possibly nonlinear) autoregressive stochastic process as in our methodology but, also in this case, the time-series dimension of GRV is completely lost.

---

[6] We adjust the denominator of Equation (12) according to the order of the AR process (see Footnote 3, this chapter).

[7] A similar method to compute volatility is followed also by Koren and Tenreyro (2007, p. 252) and Acemoglu and Zilibotti (1997, p. 714).

2.2. A look at the estimated growth volatilities

Figure 1 reports the sample average GRV for the period 1970:2009 for each year and the relative five-year averages, for our sample of 69 countries (GRV is reported in percentage points).[8]

We notice a clear downward trend from 1970 to 2000, a period in which the sample average GRV almost halves. This piece of evidence is consistent with the literature on the "Great Moderation" in the growth pattern of developed countries (see, e.g., McConnell & Perez-Quiros, 2000; Stock & Watson, 2002, for the United States). After 2000, however, the trend reverted and GRV reaches a peak in 2009, the last year that we consider in our analysis.

Figure 2 shows that significant differences also emerge from the dynamics of the cross-country distributions of five-year averages of GRV. The distribution with the highest average GRV is that of the period 1975:1979, characterized by the oil shocks. This distribution displays a peak at a value not very different from the values of the peaks of the other two distributions, but it has a very broad shape, highlighting that a

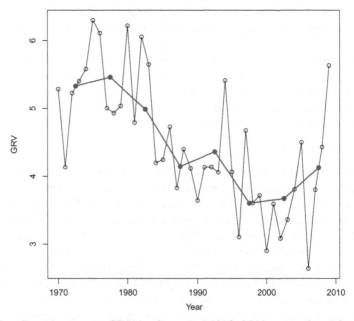

Fig. 1.   Sample average GRV in the period 1970–2009: annual and five-year averages.

---

[8] All computations are performed with R (Development Core Team, 2010). Datasets and codes are available on authors' website (http://www-dse.ec.unipi.it/persone/docenti/fiaschi/ WorkingPapers.html).

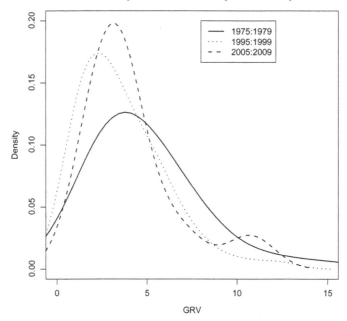

Fig. 2. **Cross-section distribution of five-year GRV for the periods 1975:1979, 1995:1999, and 2005:2009.**

remarkable number of countries experimented very large shocks. The distribution of 1995:1999, corresponding to the lowest average volatility appears, on the contrary, very concentrated around its peak, with a negligible mass in the top tail. Finally, the distribution of 2005:2009 displays two peaks, suggesting the existence of two distinct clusters of countries in terms of growth volatilities.

Table 1 reports the transition matrix across five classes of GRV, defined to contain the same number of observations in each class. GRV appears characterized by persistence, especially in the extreme classes *I* and *V*, where the probability to remain in the same GRV class is equal to 0.51 and 0.45, respectively.[9] This suggests the presence of two clusters of countries, one with a persistent low volatility, as opposed to another with high volatility. Figures 3–6, presenting the dynamics of GRV for selected individual countries confirm this intuition.

In particular, GRV of United States and Italy follows a similar U-shaped pattern over time within approximately the same interval, ranging from about 4 in the 1970s to about 1 in the period 1985:2000 for five-year averages (see Figures 3 and 4). Argentina (Figure 5), instead, shows a moderate and persistent level of GRV around 6 points from 1980. Finally, Nigeria (Figure 6) displays on average a very high GRV of about

---

[9] Also notice that the off-diagonal elements are relatively high.

Table 1.   Transition matrix for GRV 1970–2009 with five-year averages

Range of GRV		I	II	III	IV	V
I	[0:1)	0.51	0.22	0.19	0.04	0.04
II	[1:2.2)	0.29	0.25	0.22	0.16	0.09
III	[2.2:3.8)	0.18	0.23	0.30	0.22	0.07
IV	[3.8:6.7)	0.06	0.18	0.25	0.28	0.24
V	[6.7:∞)	0.03	0.13	0.11	0.27	0.45

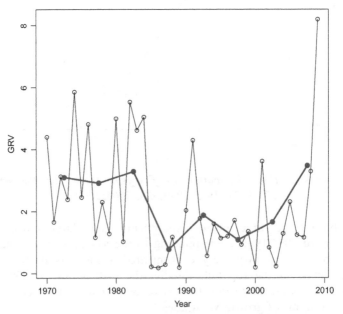

Fig. 3.   Growth volatility 1970–2009: United States.

10, with wide fluctuations. Overall, these pieces of evidence suggest that GRV is changing in time within each country, as well as in terms of its distribution dynamics across countries, providing support to our methodological approach. In the next section, we study the determinants of GRV.

3. Empirical analysis

In this section, we test the explanatory power of the structural characteristics of an economy as possible determinants of GRV. In particular, following the literature, we consider (i) the size of the economy; (ii) the degree of trade and financial openness; (iii) the size of the public sector; and (iv) the composition of output. In addition, we control for institutional/cultural characteristics and geography. The possible presence of aggregate shocks is controlled by time dummies (see, e.g., or Canning

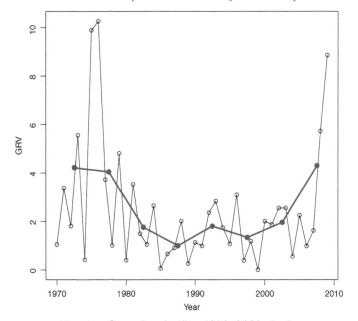

Fig. 4.   Growth volatility 1970–2009: Italy.

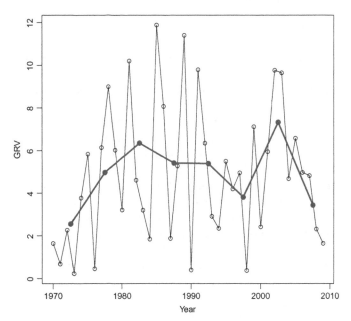

Fig. 5.   Growth volatility 1970–2009: Argentina.

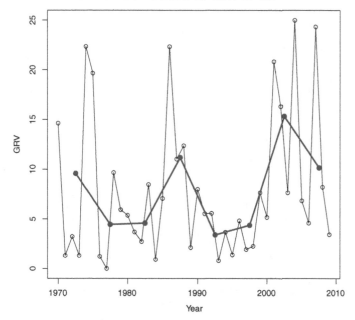

Fig. 6.   Growth volatility 1970–2009: Nigeria.

et al., 1998, p. 336, or Koren & Tenreyro, 2007, p. 248) and by the volatility of the world prices of food, agricultural products, and metals.

3.1. The dataset

Table 2 contains the list of variables used in the analysis, their sources, and the relevant references.

The selection of the variables was dictated by the choice to have a balanced panel with a relatively high number of observations for each country, to keep track of the within-country dynamics of GRV. This choice prevented us from considering, for example, alternative measures of output composition, such as the share of agriculture (see Fiaschi & Lavezzi, 2005) and manufacturing and services on GDP, of exports (i.e., the export concentration index used by Malik & Temple, 2009), of institutions (i.e., the settlers' mortality rate used by Acemoglu, Johnson, & Robinson, 2001), and so on, because this would have implied a substantial reduction in the number of observations, especially in the time series dimension.

Considering five-year averages of yearly observations to reduce measurement errors and the effect of cyclical components,[10] we obtain a

---

[10] Given that the variables that we use are relatively stable in time, to enlarge as much as possible the sample the data for a five-year average was calculated also in the limiting case when only an observation out of five was available. In addition, we assume that variables available for one year are representative of the values for the whole period.

Table 2.   List of variables used in the analysis

Variable	Code	Description and source	References
Size of the economy	TOTGDP	Total GDP. PPP converted GDP per capita (Chain series, 2005 constant prices). PWT 7.0	Canning et al. (1998), Scheinkman and Woodford (1994), Alesina and Spolaore (2003)
	POP	Population. PWT 7.0	Collier (2007)
	DENSITYPOP	Population per km^2. PWT 7.0 and http://www.cid.harvard.edu	
Trade and financial openness	OPENNESS	Exports + imports as % of GDP. PWT 7.0	Easterly et al. (2000), Di Giovanni and Levchenko (2009)
	EXPCONCTRADEPARTNER	Herfindahl index of concentration of exports by trade partner. Correlates of War Project (http://www.correlatesofwar.org)	Malik and Temple (2009)
	NETFDI	Net flow of foreign direct investments as share of GDP. UNCTAD	
Size of public sector	GOVSHARE	Government consumption share of PPP converted GDP per capita at 2005 constant prices. PWT 7.0	Fatás and Mihov (2001), Galí (1994), Rodrick (1998)
Size of financial sector	CREDIT	Domestic credit to private sector (% of GDP). WDI 2011	Easterly et al. (2000)
Output composition	NATRESOURCESRENTS	Total natural resources rents (% of GDP). WDI 2011	Acemoglu and Zilibotti (1997), Fiaschi and Lavezzi (2005), Koren and Tenreyro (2007)
Geography	SOILSUITMEDIUM	Percentage of each soil type that is moderately suitable for six rain-fed crops in 1995. http://www.cid.harvard.edu	Malik and Temple (2009)

Table 2. (Continued)

Variable	Code	Description and source	References
	AVDISTANCECOSTLINERIVER	Mean distance to nearest coast line or sea-navigable river. http://www.cid.harvard.edu	Malik and Temple (2009)
Institutions and culture	CONSTRONEXECUTIVE	Executive constraint. 1: unlimited authority, 7: executive Parity or Subordination. POLITY IV	Acemoglu et al. (2003), Glaeser, La Porta, Lopez-de-Silanes, and Schleifer (2004)
	ETHNOLINGDIVERSITY	Ethnolinguistic diversity (1960). Collier and Hoeffler (2004)	Malik and Temple (2009), Collier (2007), Hegre and Sambanis (2006)
	ETHNICDOMINANCE	Ethnic dominance measure (dummy) (1964). Dummy = 1 if the largest ethnic group constitutes 45%–90% of the population. Collier and Hoeffler (2004)	
Aggregate shocks	VOLFOODPRICE	Estimated volatility of food price at world level (estimated using the same methodology for GRV). UNCTAD	
	VOLAGRIPRICE	Estimated volatility of agriculture raw materials price at world level (estimated using the same methodology for GRV). UNCTAD	
	VOLMETALPRICE	Estimated volatility of minerals, ores and metals price at world level (estimated using the same methodology for GRV). UNCTAD	
	VOLOILPRICE	Estimated volatility of oil price at world level (estimated using the same methodology for GRV). UNCTAD	

sample of 69 countries for the period 1970–2009 (the total number of observations is therefore $69 \times 8 = 552$).[11]

Figures 7–18 present the estimates of the univariate relationships between some selected variables and GRV.[12] We also show the estimation of the univariate relationship between GRV and per capita GDP (denoted PERCAPITAGDP). As noted, a typical stylized fact is that GRV decreases with the level of development, and per capita GDP is the common proxy for development (see, e.g., Acemoglu & Zilibotti, 1997; Fiaschi & Lavezzi, 2005; Koren & Tenreyro, 2007). In the multivariate analysis, however, we do not include per capita GDP among the regressors because it does not add significant information to the analysis once we control in the regression for the structural characteristics of an economy.[13]

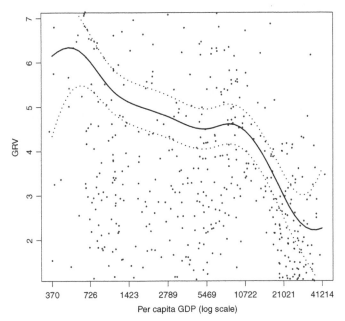

Fig. 7.   Nonparametric regression of GRV on PERCAPITAGDP.

---

[11] The country list is reported in the appendix.
[12] Each figure contains the result of a nonparametric estimation and its 95% confidence band made by the package "sm" in R. In particular, we run a Nadaraya–Watson kernel regression, using the *Generalized Cross Validation* as method of selection of the bandwidth (see Bowman & Azzalini, 2010).
[13] For example, Fiaschi and Lavezzi (2005) show that per capita GDP loses its explanatory power when the size of the economy, openness, and output composition are taken into account. Moreover, here, per capita GDP is highly correlated with CREDIT and CONSTRONEXECUTIVE (the correlation coefficients are, respectively, 0.74 and 0.80).

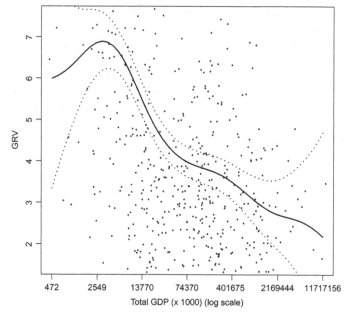

Fig. 8. *Nonparametric regression of GRV on TOTGDP.*

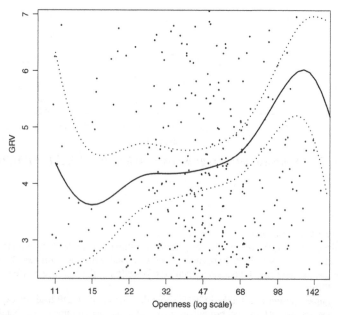

Fig. 9. *Nonparametric regression of GRV on OPENNESS.*

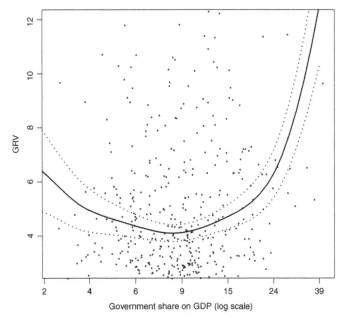

Fig. 10.   *Nonparametric regression of GRV on GOVSHARE.*

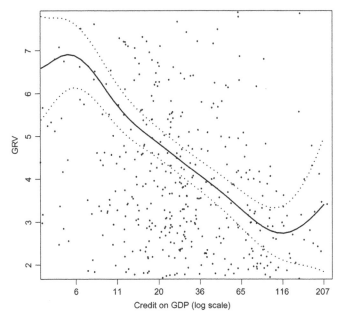

Fig. 11.   *Nonparametric regression of GRV on CREDIT.*

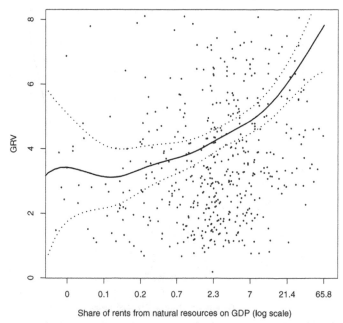

Share of rents from natural resources on GDP (log scale)

Fig. 12. *Nonparametric regression of GRV on NATRESOURCERENTS.*

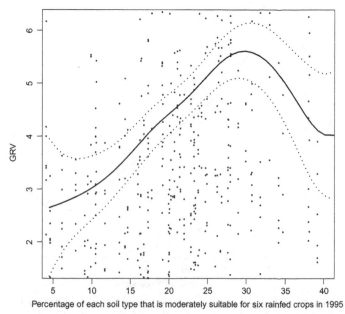

Percentage of each soil type that is moderately suitable for six rainfed crops in 1995

Fig. 13. *Nonparametric regression of GRV on SOILSUITMEDIUM.*

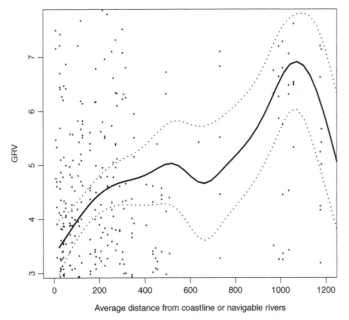

Fig. 14.   *Nonparametric regression of GRV on AVDISTANCECOAST.*

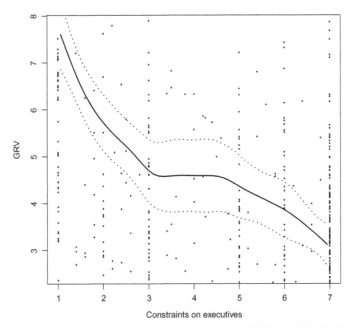

Fig. 15.   *Nonparametric regression of GRV on CONSTEXECUTIVE.*

PERCAPITAGDP, TOTGDP, CREDIT, and CONSTRONEXECU-
TIVE display a clear negative relationship with GRV. On the contrary,
NATRESOURCERENTS, OPENNESS, AVDISTANCECOAST, SOIL-
SUITMEDIUM, and VOLFOODPRICE seem to have a substantially
positive relation (with the presence of nonlinearities, in particular for
VOLFOODPRICE). GOVSHARE, instead, displays a U-shaped relation-
ship, although the increasing part of the relation corresponds to few
observations with very high values of government consumption. Also,
ETHNOLINGDIVERSITY displays a U-shaped relationship. Finally,
GRV and VOLMETALSPRICE exhibit an inverted U-shaped relationship,
but the negative part seems to be due to the observations of one period only
(the one with the highest price volatility).

The literature on growth volatility largely agrees with the estimated
relationships between GRV and, respectively, PERCAPITAGDP,
TOTGDP, CONSTEXECUTIVE, NATRESOURCERENTS, and
AVDISTANCECOAST (see, e.g., Koren & Tenreyro, 2007; Malik &
Temple, 2009). The main novelty is in the existence of a clear relationship
also between GRV and CREDIT, GOVSHARE, and OPENNESS, issues
still debated in the literature (see, e.g., Easterly et al., 2000; Fatás &
Mihov, 2001; Galí, 1994). So far, to the best of our knowledge, the
relationship between GRV and ETHNOLINGDIVERSITY and

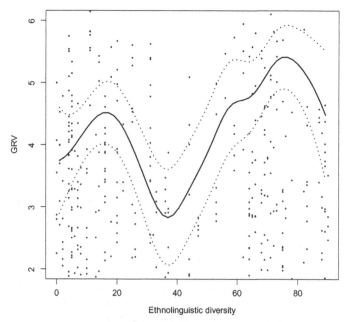

*Fig. 16. Nonparametric regression of GRV on ETHNOLINGUISTIC-
DIVERSITY.*

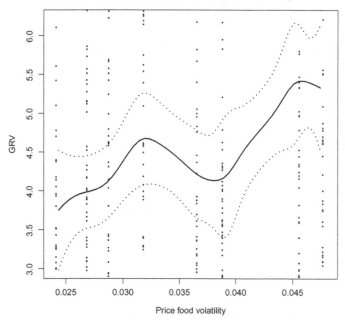

Fig. 17. *Nonparametric regression of GRV on VOLFOODPRICE.*

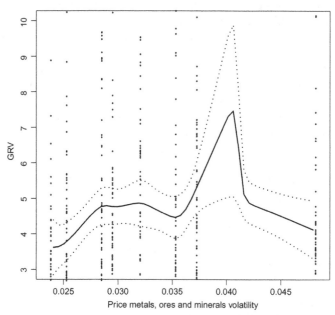

Fig. 18. *Nonparametric regression of GRV on VOLMETALSPRICE.*

SOILSUITMEDIUM has been analyzed only by Malik and Temple (2009), who find a negative impact for both.[14] The evidence for VOLFOODPRICE and VOLMETALSPRICE, variables so far neglected in the literature, suggests that also aggregate shocks may play a role in the explanation of GRV. In the next section, we test whether these relationships survive in a multivariate analysis.

3.2. GAM estimation

We estimate the relationships between GRV and the variables reported in Table 2 by nonparametric methods. In particular, we estimate the following *generalized additive model* (GAM) (see Wood, 2006) based on Equation (12):

$$GRV_{jt} = \beta_0 + f_1(\text{Size of the economy}_{jt})$$
$$+ f_2(\text{Trade and financial openness}_{jt}) + f_3(\text{Size of public sector}_{jt})$$
$$+ f_4(\text{Size of financial sector}_{jt}) + f_5(\text{Output composition}_{jt})$$
$$+ Controls_{jt} + \text{Aggregate shocks}_t + \xi_{jt}, \qquad (14)$$

where i and t index, respectively, countries and periods; the functions $f_j(\cdot)$, with $j = 1,..., 5$, are smooth functions of the explanatory variables; *Controls* is a vector including controls for institutional and cultural factors, and geography; aggregate shocks refer to the effect of variables that may affect GRV in different countries in the same period; and ξ is a normally distributed random variable with zero mean and standard deviation σ^ξ.

Table 3 contains the results from the estimation of different specifications of Equation (14). For any estimated term, we report either the *estimated degrees of freedom* (EDF)[15] or, when the EDF of the term are equal to one, the estimated linear coefficient in square brackets.[16] The goodness of fit is measured by the *generalized cross validation* (*GCV*) score (see Wood, 2006, p. 132). For each model, it is also reported the proportion of deviance explained, a measure comparable to R^2 for linear models (see Wood, 2006, p. 84). Each model in Table 3 represents the preferred specification, which is obtained by recursively eliminating the least significant term until the lowest level of the GCV score is reached.[17]

---

[14] Ethnic diversity and the presence of a not very large ethnic majority (ETHNIC-DOMINANCE) should be positively associated to rebellion and social conflicts and therefore to instability (Collier, 2007).

[15] The EDF reflect the nonlinear impact of the variable on GRV.

[16] See Wood (2006, pp. 170–172), for more details.

[17] NETFDI and ETHNICDOMINANCE are never statistically significant and therefore do not appear in Table 3.

Table 3.   Estimation of Equation (14)

Model	I	II	III	IV
Time dummies	YES	YES	YES	NO
Constant	5.0423	7.2702	1.4508	5.1985
	(0.000)	(0.000)	(0.000)	(0.000)
log(TOTGDP)	4.996	–	–	–
	(0.0005)			
log(OPENNESS)	1.916	1.894	1.894	2.244
	(0.0000)	(0.0000)	(0.0000)	(0.0001)
log(GOVSHARE)	6.708	6.600	6.600	6.312
	(0.0000)	(0.0035)	(0.0035)	(.0023)
log(CREDIT)	8.020	[−0.5770]	[−0.5770]	[−0.5392]
	(0.0002)	(0.0085)	(0.0085)	(0.0120)
log(NATRESOURCESRENTS)	2.884	–	–	–
	(0.0212)			
log(POP)	–	7.191	7.191	6.952
		(0.0005)	(0.0005)	(0.0010)
log(DENSITYPOP)	8.239	7.090	7.090	7.475
	(0.0000)	(0.0000)	(0.0000)	(0.0000)
log(EXPCONCTRADEPARTNER)	3.498	3.405	3.405	3.494
	(0.2159)	(0.1035)	(0.1035)	(0.1035)
CONSTRONEXECUTIVE	–	2.602	2.602	2.704
		(0.0043)	(0.0043)	(0.0009)
ETHNOLINGDIVERSITY	–	[−0.0103]	[−0.0103]	–
		(0.0754)	(0.0754)	
SOILSUITMEDIUM	–	2.927	2.927	2.941
		(0.0021)	(0.0021)	(0.0026)
AVDISTANCECOSTLINERIVER	–	3.655	3.655	3.871
		(0.0022)	(0.0022)	(0.0117)
VOLMETALPRICE	–	–	[0.7393]	–
			(0.0006)	
VOLFOODPRICE	–	–	[0.7793]	[0.3057]
			(0.0000)	(0.0543)
GCV score	8.1433	7.8434	7.8434	7.7893
Deviance explained	39.3%	41.8%	41.8%	40.8%
Number of obs.	552	552	552	552

Notes: Dependent variable is GRV. EDF or estimated linear coefficients (in square brackets) of the preferred specifications (*p*-values in parenthesis)

Model I only includes the five explanatory variables on the structure of the economy. All the variables but POP are present in the preferred specification, and their impacts appear nonlinear (in Table 3, the values of EDF range from 1.92 for OPENNESS to 8.02 for CREDIT).[18]

---

[18] For lack of space, we do not report figures with the impact of the individual variables. These effects are very similar to those reported below for the other models.

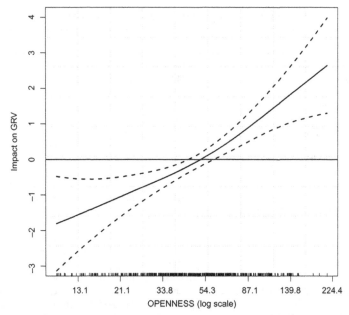

**Fig. 19. Estimated impact of OPENNESS on GRV in Models II and III.
Period 1970:2009.**

Model II adds to Model I the controls for institutional, cultural, and
geographical characteristics. In the preferred specification, TOTGDP and
NATRESOURCESRENTS are not included. OPENNESS has, instead, a
highly significant impact, as shown in Figure 19 (see Di Giovanni &
Levchenko, 2009, for a similar result): countries more open to world trade
display a higher level of GRV. As for the magnitude of the effect, we find
that a country with OPENNESS of about 100 has GRV higher of about 1.5
percentage points than a country with a level of OPENNESS of about 50.

Government consumption does not seem to statistically affect GRV at
low levels (see Figure 20). At medium/high levels (around 20 percentage
points of GDP), however, it exerts a slightly negative influence as expected
(see, e.g., Fatás & Mihov, 2001), which becomes strongly positive around a
value of 30 percentage points.[19] We conjecture that very high levels of
GOVSHARE are indicators of bad macroeconomic policy, whose
consequences could also be higher instability (see Collier, 2007). The
analysis suggests that there exits an optimal size of government
consumption that may act as economic stabilizer of about 20; in terms

---

[19] A value found for Gambia, Nicaragua, and Rwanda.

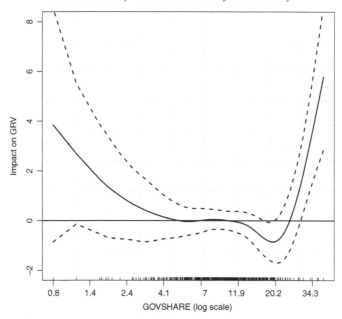

Fig. 20.   Estimated impact of GOVSHARE on GRV in Models II and III. Period 1970:2009.

of policy, this finding should be compared with the possible negative effect on the average growth rate (Barro, 1991).

The size of credit on GDP has a statistically significant and negative (linear) effect. As to the magnitude, the average increase in CREDIT from 25.15 in 1970 to 69.93 in 2000 has reduced the overall volatility on average of 0.59 percentage points. This evidence contrasts with the nonlinear effect found by Easterly et al. (2000, p. 202).

Low-population countries appear subject to higher GRV (see Figure 21). The impact of POP, however, already vanishes for countries with more than 3 millions of inhabitants (in 2009, the only countries with less than 3 millions of inhabitants are Gabon, Gambia, Jamaica, and Trinidad and Tobago). This finding supports the existence of a size effect on GRV, by which an increasing size of the country in terms of population reduces volatility. The surprising result, however, is that the minimum size after which the effect vanishes is very low (see Alesina & Spolaore, 2003, for a thorough discussion of the possible relevance of the size of population for countries' volatility).

Figure 22 highlights that the density of population has a nonlinear relationship with GRV. At low/medium values, population density decreases volatility, while in the intermediate range (around 0.015, i.e., 15 inhabitants per km^2), the positive effect on GRV is the highest. The

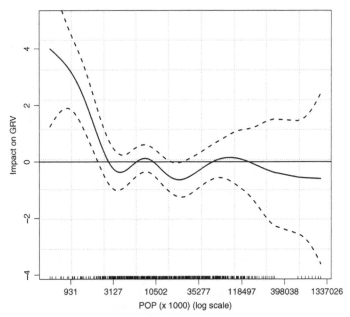

Fig. 21. *Estimated impact of POP on GRV in Models II and III. Period 1970:2009.*

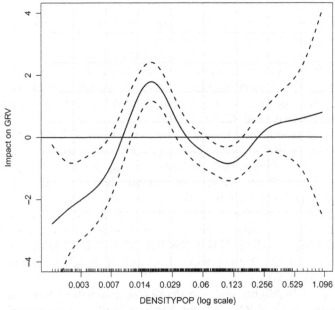

Fig. 22. *Estimated impact of DENSITYPOP on GRV in Models II and III. Period 1970:2009.*

expected result was a positive relationship, on the assumption that a high population density puts pressure on available resources, so favoring social conflict and instability (see Collier, 2007). Indeed, in 2009, this holds for some low-medium income countries from South America (Argentina, Brazil, Chile, Peru, and Uruguay) and sub-Saharan Africa (Republic of Congo, Mali, Niger, and Zambia), belonging to the intermediate range of population density (between 0.01 and 0.025).[20] However, it remains to be explained how the increase in population density leads to a decrease in GRV at higher population density levels.

Figure 23 gives only partial support to the expected positive relationship between the EXPCONCTRADEPARTNER and GRV (in particular, in the range 0–0.2). At medium levels (approximately around 0.2), concentration of trade has a statistically significant and positive impact on GRV while, on the contrary, at low and high levels, it does not appear to exert any significant effect.

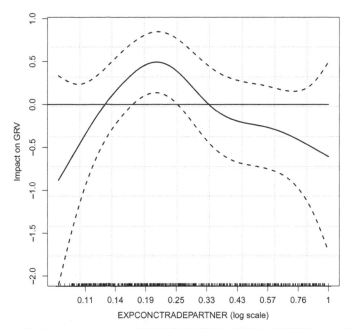

Fig. 23. *Estimated impact of EXPCONCTRADEPARTNER on GRV in Models II and III. Period 1970:2009.*

---

[20] In this range, we also find Finland, New Zealand, and Sweden, even though their population density strongly depends on geography.

The measure for the quality of institutions, CONSTRONEXECU-TIVE, has the expected negative effect (see Acemoglu et al., 2003), but its effect is statistically significant only at low/medium levels (see Figure 24). ETHNOLINGDIVERSITY has a negative and moderately significant (linear) impact like in Malik and Temple (2009, p. 172, 176), who, however, find a positive impact when this variable is interacted with a dummy for war.[21] This evidence contrasts also with the idea discussed in Alesina and Spolaore (2003) that more fractionalized societies are more subject to instability.

The fertility of soil has a statistically significant and increasing impact on volatility in the low/medium range, while it is not significant at higher levels (see Figure 25). This contrasts with Malik and Temple (2009, p. 176) who find that the fertility of soil has a negative effect on volatility. We conjecture that high fertility favors the increase in the share of output from agriculture, which, as shown by Fiaschi and Lavezzi (2005), has an volatility-enhancing effect. The correlation between SOILSUITMEDIUM

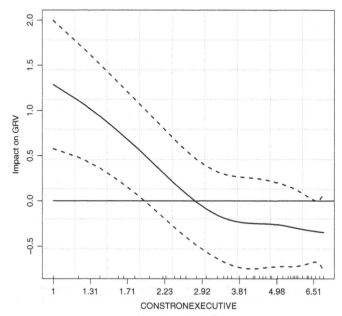

Fig. 24. Estimated impact of CONSTRONEXECUTIVE on GRV in Models II and III. Period 1970:2009.

[21] Malik and Temple (2009) actually consider ethnic fractionalization. In this chapter, we use ethnolinguistic diversity because Hegre and Sambanis (2006) show that it is significantly related to the onset of civil wars.

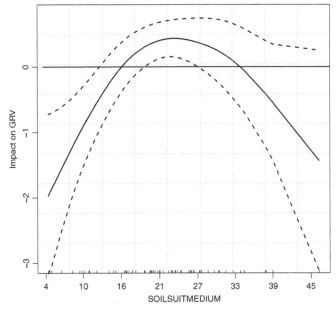

Fig. 25. Estimated impact of SOILSUITMEDIUM on GRV in Models II and III. Period 1970:2009.

and the average value of the share of agriculture on GDP for the available observations in WDI 2011 is indeed positive and equal to 0.37. As noticed, unfortunately, lack of data prevents us to use the agricultural share on GDP in the present analysis.

Finally, as expected, AVDISTANCECOSTLINERIVER (Figure 26) has a positive effect on volatility, a result consistent with Malik and Temple (2009), who argue that distance from the sea coast or a river is associated to high concentration in terms of exported goods, which in turns exposes the country to volatility of terms of trade and therefore causes output volatility.[22]

Model III adds to Model II two measures of aggregate shocks calculated on the price of food and metals, minerals and ores: VOLFOODPRICE and VOLMETALPRICE respectively.[23] In the preferred specification, both variables have a positive and statistically

---

[22] In the analysis, we could utilize neither the export concentration index from UNCTAD, as noted, nor the terms of trade volatility index from WDI 2011, both used by Malik and Temple (2009), because this would have implied a sharp reduction of the number of available observations.

[23] VOLFOODPRICE and VOLAGRIPRICE have a correlation coefficient equal to 0.91. Although the price of agricultural products can have an effect on the volatility of countries with large agricultural sectors, VOLFOODPRICE produces a slightly better fit. Results, not reported here, show that also VOLAGRIPRICE has a positive and significant effect on volatility. VOLOILPRICE is neglected in the analysis, instead, because its inclusion did not lead to an improvement in the estimates.

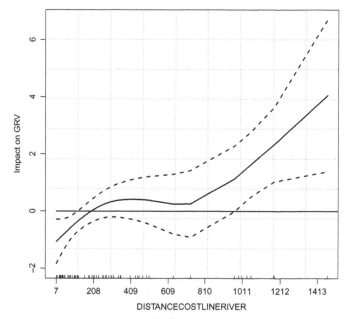

Fig. 26. *Estimated impact of AVDISTANCECOSTLINERIVER on GRV in Models II and III. Period 1970:2009.*

significant coefficient, capturing a large part of the explanation that in Model II was imputed to the intercept.

Finally, to evaluate the robustness of our estimates to time effects, and the explanatory power of VOLFOODPRICE and VOLMETALPRICE, we estimate Model IV derived from Model III by removing the time dummies. ETHNOLINGDIVERSITY and VOLMETALPRICE are dropped in the preferred specification, but the estimates of the other regressors are unchanged.[24]

3.2.1. On the stability of the estimates

Figures 1 and 2 suggest that aggregate behavior of GRV underwent relevant changes in time. For this reason, we control for the robustness of the estimates by considering two 20-year subperiods: 1970:1989 (Period I) and 1990:2009 (Period II). In Table 4, we report the results of the estimation of Model III in the whole period and in the two subperiods.[25]

The goodness of fit in Period II is remarkably higher with respect to both the entire period and the Period I (the deviance explained is 61.5%

---

[24] The figures of the estimates are available upon request.
[25] We choose Model III because it contains all the variables of interest. Comparison of the remaining models does not add significant differences to the results presented.

Table 4.   Estimation of Equation (14)

Model	III	III	III
Period	1970:2009	1970:1989	1990:2009
Time dummies	YES	YES	YES
Constant	1.4508	−0.6145	1.0798
	(0.000)	(0.8767)	(0.5613)
log(TOTGDP)	–	[0.4945]	6.123
		(0.0520)	(0.0010)
log(OPENNESS)	1.894	1.923	[0.7860]
	(0.0000)	(0.0000)	(0.0746)
log(GOVSHARE)	6.600	–	8.752
	(0.0035)		(0.0000)
log(CREDIT)	[−0.5770]	[−0.9803]	–
	(0.0085)	(0.0034)	
log(NATRESOURCESRENTS)	–	–	3.115
			(0.0100)
log(POP)	7.191	2.052	–
	(0.0005)	(0.1115)	
log(DENSITYPOP)	7.090	3.475	8.007
	(0.0000)	(0.0018)	(0.0000)
log(EXPCONCTRADEPARTNER)	3.405	2.915	[0.3848]
	(0.1035)	(0.0793)	(0.1134)
NETFDI	–	2.080	4.601
		(0.0505)	(0.1709)
CONSTRONEXECUTIVE	2.602	2.751	–
	(0.0043)	(0.0000)	
ETHNOLINGDIVERSITY	[−0.0103]	–	–
	(0.0754)		
SOILSUITMEDIUM	2.927	–	2.864
	(0.0021)		(0.0030)
AVDISTANCECOSTLINERIVER	3.655	–	[0.0023]
	(0.0022)		(0.0011)
VOLMETALPRICE	[0.7393]	–	–
	(0.0006)		
VOLFOODPRICE	[0.7793]	–	–
	(0.0000)		
GCV score	7.8434	8.1799	5.3462
Deviance explained	41.8%	42.2%	61.5%
Number of obs.	552	276	276

Notes: Dependent variable is GRV. EDF or estimated linear coefficients (reported in squared brackets) of the best specifications of Model III (*p*-values in parenthesis)

against 41.8% and 42.2%, respectively). Period I, as we showed, was characterized by higher turbulence and by phenomena of extreme volatility (see Figure 2).

TOTGDP, absent in the preferred specification for the whole period, has a positive, significant, and linear impact in Period I. In Period II, instead, it has a statistically significant positive impact at low levels, negative in an intermediate range, and becomes nonsignificant afterwards (see Figure 27). This suggests the possible existence of an optimal size of the economy in terms of total GDP for the minimization of volatility.

OPENNESS has a positive effect in both periods, even though in Period II, its significance is lower (see Table 4 and Figure 28). In addition, the magnitude of the effect is substantially lower in Period II: for example, increasing OPENNESS from 50 to 75 in Period I implies an increase in GRV of about 1 percentage point, while the same increase in Period II is associated to an increase of 0.32 percentage points only (Figure 28).

GOVSHARE is not present in the best specification in Period I, while in Period II, it is highly statistically significant. Figure 30 shows that there exists an optimal size of government consumption, which minimizes GRV, as in the analysis of the whole period; in particular, in the range 15–23, the magnitude of the negative effect on GRV appears sizeable (around −2 percentage points).

The stabilizing effect of CREDIT found for the whole period holds only for Period I. We conjecture that the absence of a significant effect in Period II may depend on a higher degree of "financialization" of the economy, which qualitatively changed what "the amount of credit" measures. In particular, anecdotal evidence hints at an increasing use of financial

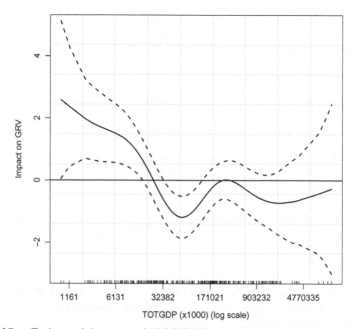

Fig. 27. Estimated impact of TOTGDP on GRV in Model II. Period 1990:2008.

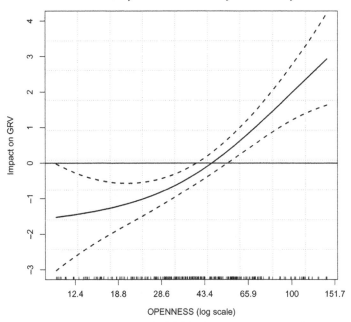

Fig. 28. **Estimated impact of OPENNESS on GRV in Model II. Period 1970:1989.**

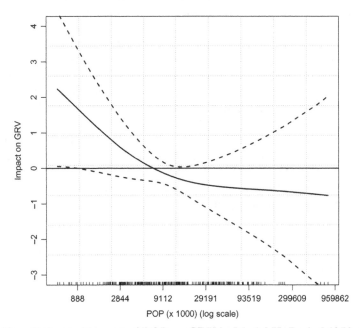

Fig. 29. **Estimated impact of POP on GRV in Model II. Period 1970:1989.**

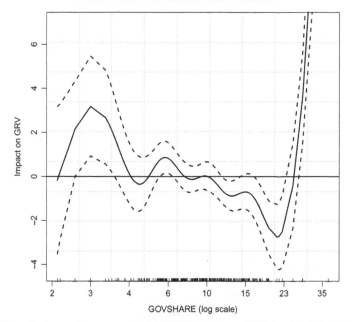

Fig. 30. Estimated impact of GOVSHARE on GRV in Model II. Period 1990:2008.

resources not for smoothing the effects of the business cycle but for pure financial operations. A more detailed analysis of this aspect remains for future research.

In Period II, NATRESOURCESRENTS has the expected positive impact on GRV, at least after a threshold, as shown in Figure 31. However, NATRESOURCESRENTS is not present in the preferred specification in Period I. It is worth to remark that in Period II, NATRESOURCESR-ENTS results highly correlated to the share of primary goods (ores and metals, agricultural raw materials, food and fuel) on total merchandise exports (the correlation coefficient is equal to 0.69), suggesting that a part of explanation of the positive impact could be attributed to the composition of exports (see also Malik & Temple, 2009, p. 166).[26]

The estimated effect of POP in Period I resembles the one for the whole period, but its statistical significance is very low (see Figure 29). POP is instead absent in the best specification of Period II where, however, the size of the economy is proxied by TOTGDP. The estimate of DENSITYPOP appears significant in both periods, with substantially the same shape (see Figures 32 and 33).

---

[26] The lack of data for the whole period prevented us from using the composition of exports in the analysis.

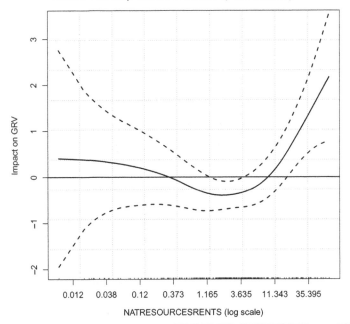

Fig. 31. *Estimated impact of NATRESOURCESRENTS on GRV in Model II. Period 1990:2008.*

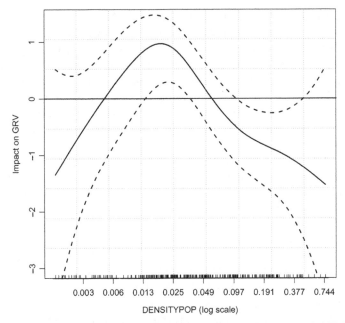

Fig. 32. *Estimated impact of DENSITYPOP on GRV in Model II. Period 1970:1989.*

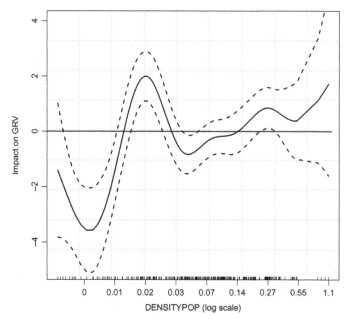

Fig. 33.   Estimated impact of DENSITYPOP on GRV in Model II. Period
1990:2008.

In Period I, EXPCONCTRADEPARTNER has the expected positive relationship at low and medium levels of concentration; subsequently, the effect becomes nonsignificant (see Figure 34). Differently, in Period II, the estimated impact is positive and linear, albeit with poor statistical significance. The magnitude of the impact on GRV is lower in Period II in the range 0–0.25, where the relationship is significant (an increase from 0.11 to 0.25 of concentration in Period I implies a 1.5 percentage points increase in GRV, against a value of 0.32 points in Period II).

NETFDI is in the preferred specification in both Period I and Period II. However, even though the relationship is similar in the two periods (in particular, for the decreasing part at low levels, see Figures 35 and 36), the estimate is very imprecise, preventing us from drawing conclusions on the effect of this variable on GRV.

CONSTRONEXECUTIVE has a clear negative effect on GRV in Period I (Figure 37), while it is not in the preferred specification in Period II. ETHNOLINGDIVERSITY is not significant in the two subperiods; the effect of SOILSUITMEDIUM is negative at low levels and positive at medium levels and then nonstatistically significant (see Figure 38), as in the estimate for the whole period; AVDISTANCE-COSTLINERIVER has a positive, linear, and significant effect in Period II, but not in Period I.

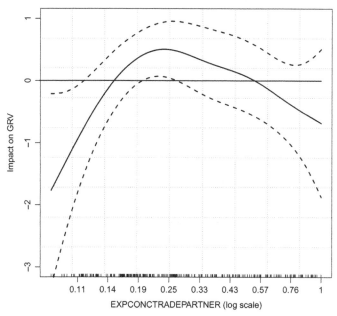

Fig. 34. Estimated impact of EXPCONCTRADEPARTNER on GRV in Model II. Period 1970:1989.

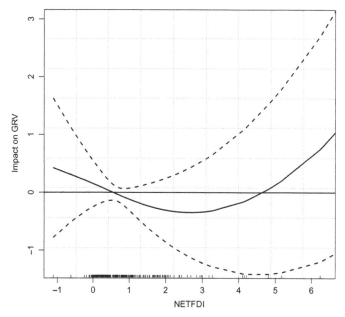

Fig. 35. Estimated impact of NETFDI on GRV in Model II. Period 1970:1989.

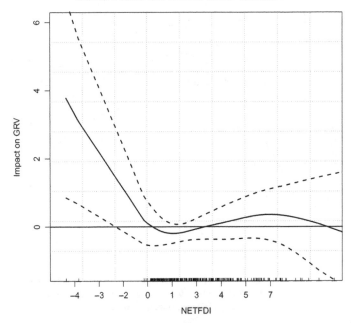

Fig. 36. *Estimated impact of NETFDI on GRV in Model II. Period 1990:2008.*

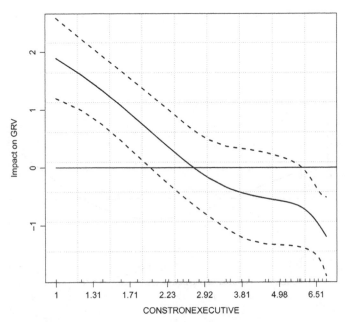

Fig. 37. *Estimated impact of CONSTRONEXECUTIVE on GRV in Model II. Period 1970:1989.*

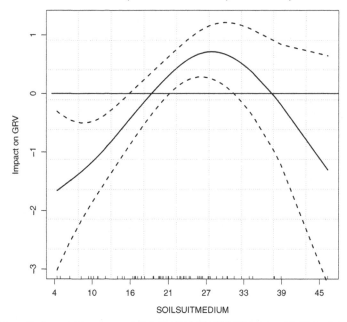

Fig. 38. **Estimated impact of SOILSUITMEDIUM on GRV in Model II.**
Period 1990:2008.

Finally, the indicators of aggregate shocks, VOLMETALPRICE and VOLFOODPRICE, are not statistically significant in the two superiods, pointing out that the explanatory power we found for the whole period was due to the difference in volatility between the two subperiods.

4. Concluding remarks

In this chapter, we have analyzed the role of the structural characteristics of an economy in the explanation of growth volatility in the period 1970:2009. We first proposed a novel methodology to measure growth volatility, which allows to preserve the time-series and cross-country dimensions of the phenomenon, controlling for the stability of the estimates in two subperiods: 1970:1989 and 1990:2009.

These results provide insights on the onset of the "Great Moderation," in particular through the change in output composition and the development of the financial sector, and on its end, in particular, through the increase in openness and the reduction of the size of the public sector. Therefore, we submit that the dominant policy orientations in the recent decades contained emphasis on potential sources of instability.

Two issues, finally, should be remarked. First, the comparison between the estimates of the two subperiods highlights how the effect on volatility

Davide Fiaschi and Andrea Mario Lavezzi

of the integration of economy in the world markets has remarkably changed over time: besides the *amount* of trade, the *structure* of trade has gained importance, suggesting the need for a closer investigation of the latter aspect. Second, the amount of credit has a significant stabilizing effect in the first period, but not in the second. This finding indicates that, to fully evaluate the role of the financial sector, more specific measures are needed, reflecting not only the *quantity* of credit but also the very different *quality* of the uses of the financial resources available in the economy.

Acknowledgment

We thank Gabriele Fiorentini for very useful suggestions and Michele Battisti for comments. The usual disclaimers apply.

Appendix

Table A1.   List of countries and selected AR order by AIC_c

Country code	Country Name	AR order selected by AIC_c
ARG	Argentina	1
AUS	Australia	0
AUT	Austria	0
BDI	Burundi	0
BEN	Benin	1
BFA	Burkina Faso	1
BGD	Bangladesh	0
BOL	Bolivia	0
BRA	Brazil	1
CAF	Central African Republic	0
CAN	Canada	1
CHL	Chile	1
CMR	Cameroon	3
COG	Congo, Rep.	1
COL	Colombia	0
CRI	Costa Rica	2
DNK	Denmark	0
DOM	Dominican Republic	0
ECU	Ecuador	1
EGY	Egypt, Arab Rep.	0
ESP	Spain	1
FIN	Finland	2
FRA	France	1
GAB	Gabon	1
GBR	United Kingdom	2
GHA	Ghana	3

Table A1. (Continued)

Country code	Country Name	AR order selected by AIC$_c$
GMB	Gambia, The	0
GRC	Greece	3
GTM	Guatemala	2
HND	Honduras	0
IND	India	0
IRL	Ireland	2
IRN	Iran, Islamic Rep.	1
ISR	Israel	2
ITA	Italy	1
JAM	Jamaica	1
JOR	Jordan	0
JPN	Japan	1
KEN	Kenya	0
KOR	Korea, Rep.	0
LKA	Sri Lanka	0
MEX	Mexico	1
MLI	Mali	0
MYS	Malaysia	0
NER	Niger	0
NGA	Nigeria	1
NIC	Nicaragua	0
NLD	Netherlands	1
NPL	Nepal	1
NZL	New Zealand	0
PAK	Pakistan	0
PER	Peru	2
PHL	Philippines	0
PRT	Portugal	1
RWA	Rwanda	2
SEN	Senegal	0
SLV	El Salvador	1
SWE	Sweden	2
SYR	Syrian Arab Republic	1
TGO	Togo	1
THA	Thailand	1
TTO	Trinidad and Tobago	2
TUR	Turkey	0
UGA	Uganda	1
URY	Uruguay	2
USA	United States	1
VEN	Venezuela, RB	0
ZAF	South Africa	1
ZMB	Zambia	1

References

Acemoglu, D., Johnson, S., & Robinson, J. (2001). The colonial origins of comparative development: An empirical investigation. *The American Economic Review, 91*, 1369–1401.

Acemoglu, D., Johnson, S., Robinson, J., & Thaicharoen, Y. (2003). Institutional causes, macroeconomic symptoms: Volatility, crises and growth. *Journal of Monetary Economics, 50*, 49–123.

Acemoglu, D., & Zilibotti, X. (1997). Was Prometheus unbound by chance? Risk, diversification, and growth. *Journal of Political Economy, 105*, 709–751.

Alesina, A., & Spolaore, E. (2003). *The size of nations.* Cambridge, MA: MIT Press.

Barro, R. (1991). Economic growth in a cross-section of countries. *Quarterly Journal of Economics, 106*, 407–443.

Barro, R., & Sala-i-Martin, X. (1998). *Economic growth.* Cambridge: MIT Press.

Bowman, A. W., & Azzalini, A. (2010). *R package 'sm': Nonparametric smoothing methods (version 2.2-4).*

Burnham, K., & Anderson, D. (2004). Multimodel inference. Understanding AIC and BIC in model selection. *Sociological Methods & Research, 33*, 261–304.

Canning, D., Amaral, L., Lee, Y., Meyer, M., & Stanley, H. (1998). Scaling the volatility of GDP growth rate. *Economics Letters, 60*, 335–341.

Collier, P. (2007). *The bottom billion.* Oxford, NY: Oxford University Press.

Collier, P., & Hoeffler, A. (2004). Greed and grievance in civil war. *Oxford Economic Papers, 56*, 563–595.

di Giovanni, J., & Levchenko, A. A. (2009). Trade openness and volatility. *Review of Economics and Statistics, 91*, 558–585.

Development Core Team. (2010). *R: A language and environment for statistical computing. R Foundation for Statistical Computing.* Vienna, Austria. ISBN 3-900051-07-0. Retrieved from http://www.R-project.org

Durlauf, S. N., Johnson, P. A., & Temple, J. R. W. (2005). Growth econometrics. In Durlauf, S.N. & Aghion, P. (Eds.), *Handbook of economic growth.* The Netherlands: Elsevier.

Easterly, W., Islam, R., & Stiglitz, J. E. (2000). Shaken and stirred. Explaining growth volatility. *The Annual World Bank Conference on Development*, Washington DC, USA.

Fatás, A., & Mihov, I. (2001). Government size and automatic stabilizers: International and intranational evidence. *Journal of International Economics, 55*, 3–28.

Fiaschi, D., & Lavezzi, A. M. (2005). *On the determinants of growth volatility: A nonparametric approach.* Mimeo. University of Pisa, Pisa, Italy.

Galí, J. (1994). Government size and macroeconomic stability. *European Economic Review, 38*, 117–132.

Galí, J. (2002). Comment to: Has the business cycle changed and why? In Gertler, M. & Rogoff, K. (Eds.), *NBER Macroeconomics Annual 2002, Volume 17.* Cambridge: MIT Press.

Glaeser, E. L., La Porta, R., Lopez-de-Silanes, F., & Schleifer, A. (2004). Do institutions cause growth? *Journal of Economic Growth, 9*, 271–303.

Hamilton, J. (1994). *Time series analysis.* Princeton, NJ: Princeton University Press.

Head, A. C. (1995). Country size, aggregate fluctuations, and international risk sharing. *Canadian Journal of Economics, 28*, 1096–1119.

Hegre, H., & Sambanis, N. (2006). Sensitivity analysis of empirical results on civil war onset. *Journal of Conflict Resolution, 50*, 508–535.

Koren, M., & Tenreyro, S. (2007). Volatility and development. *Quarterly Journal of Economics, 55*, 244–287.

Malik, A., & Temple, J. R. W. (2009). The geography of output volatility. *Journal of Development Economics, 90*, 163–178.

McConnell, M., & Perez-Quiros, G. (2000). Output fluctuations in the United States: What has changed since the early 1980s? *The American Economic Review, 90*, 1464–1476.

Pritchett, L. (2000). Understanding patters of economic growth: Searching for hills among plateaus, mountains, and plains. *The World Bank Economic Review, 14*, 221–250.

Ramey, G., & Ramey, V. A. (1995). Cross-country evidence on the link between volatility and growth. *The American Economic Review, 85*, 1138–1151.

Rodrick, D. (1998). Why do more open economies have bigger governments? *Journal of Poltical Economy, 106*, 997–1032.

Scheinkman, J., & Woodford, M. (1994). Self organized criticality and economic fluctuations. *The American Economic Review, 84*, 417–421.

Stock, J., & Watson, M. (2002). Has the business cycle changed and why? In Gertler, M. & Rogoff, K. (Eds.), *NBER Macroeconomics Annual 2002, Volume 17.* Cambridge: MIT Press.

Wood, S. N. (2006). *Generalized additive models. An Introduction with* London: R. Chapman & Hall.

CHAPTER 9

Stability of Growth Models with Generalized Lag Structures

Donald A.R. George[a,b]

[a]School of Economics, University of Edinburgh, UK
[b]Department of Economics, University of Canterbury, New Zealand
E-mail address: D.George@ed.ac.uk

Abstract
This chapter considers the lag structures of dynamic models in economics, arguing that the standard approach is too simple to capture the complexity of actual lag structures arising, for example, from production and investment decisions. It is argued that recent (1990s) developments in the the theory of functional differential equations provide a means to analyze models with generalized lag structures. The stability and asymptotic stability of two growth models with generalized lag structures are analyzed. The chapter's penultimate section includes a speculative discussion of time-varying parameters.

Keywords: Economic growth, AK model, lag structure

JEL classifications: C62, O40, O41

1. Introduction

Economic models often generate dynamic processes in which the current rate of change of a variable depends on the current and lagged levels of that variable. For simplicity the lag is usually taken to be constant, but this radically oversimplifies most economic problems. In this chapter attention is focussed on dynamic processes with a generalized lag structure: such a process can be summarized by the following equation:

$$\dot{X}(t) = A(t)X(t) + B(t)X(t - \lambda(t)) + C(t)\dot{X}(t - \lambda(t))$$

with

$$X(0) = X_0 \quad \text{given} \tag{1}$$

Frontiers of Economics and Globalization
Volume 11 ISSN: 1574-8715
DOI: 10.1108/S1574-8715(2011)0000011014

The function $\lambda(.)$ is called the *lag* function: it is assumed to be continuous and to satisfy:

$$0 \le \lambda(t) \le t \tag{2}$$

Moreover the functions $A(t)$, $B(t)$, and $C(t)$ are assumed continuous with:

$$A(t) \le 0 \quad \text{and} \quad |C(t)| \le C^* < 1 \tag{3}$$

Note that this specification allows for three generalizations of the standard dynamic processes that arise in economics:

(i)   It allows time-varying coefficients $(A(t), B(t), C(t))$
(ii) It allows variable lags (via the function $\lambda(t)$)
(iii) It allows dependence on lagged rates of change as well as lagged levels of variables.

Equation (1) may be generalized to cover many variables by allowing X to be a vector and A B and C to be matrices. The particular case in which $t - \lambda(t) = \mu t$ where μ is constant and $0 < \mu < 1$ is analyzed by Iserles (1993). Feldstein, Iserles, and, Levin (1995) consider a further generalization of (1) and develop a numerical approach.

Examples of this kind of problem can be found in the theory of economic growth and in investment theory. Bar-Ilan and Strange (1996) analyze models of irreversible investment which allow for the fact that most investments take time. Majd and Pindyck (1987) report that this problem is particularly pronounced in the aircraft industry where a new model requires several stages of activity, including prototype production, testing, and final tooling. Together these can introduce production lags of 8–10 years. Sequeira (2008) develops an endogenous growth model with an erosion effect, paying particular attention to its transitional dynamics. Li (2002) explores the empirical validity of AK-type growth models, introducing complex lag structures. He introduces these complex lag structures in a more or less ad hoc way, aiming at a good empirical fit, conluding that the long-run relationship between growth and investment is consistent with the AK model. In this chapter we modify the AK model in such a way as to provide theoretical underpinnings for a complex lag structure. The resulting dynamics are analyzed using the theory of functional differential equations.

2. Stability, asymptotic stability, and convergence

In this chapter we analyze the *stability* and *asymptotic stability* of two growth models. These two properties are defined below:

DEFINITION 1. The function $X(t)$ will be called stable if $|X(t)|$ is bounded.

DEFINITION 2. The function $X(t)$ will be called asymptotically stable if it is stable and $\lim_{t\to\infty} X(t) = 0$.

Note that it may be useful to think of $X(t)$ as the divergence of some economic variable (such as the capital/labour ratio $k(t)$) from its long-run equilibrium value, k^*, so that $X(t) = k(t) - k^*$. Clearly asymptotic stability is stronger than stability and is the convergence concept typically employed in economic growth theory. It is generally considered a desirable property of growth models, largely to ensure that the method of comparative dynamics can be validly employed. This method involves analyzing the effects of shocks (e.g., tax changes, productivity increases, etc.) by comparing the new (post-shock) equilibrium with the old (pre-shock) equilibrium. This procedure makes sense only if the economy can be relied on to converge to its new equilibrium when displaced from its old one. The weaker property of stability only guarantees that the variable of interest stays within a neighborhood of its equilibrium value, but nonetheless may still be useful in model construction, econometric analysis, or simulation. The theorist may be satisfied that his model cannot diverge to infinity and the econometrician, with limited data available, may be satisfied with boundedness.

The standard approach necessary to ensuring convergence (asymptotic stability) in growth theory is to assume the economy is controlled by a single ("representative") agent maximizing an infinite horizon Ramsey utility function such as:

$$\int_0^\infty U(c(t))e^{(n-\rho)t}\,dt \tag{4}$$

where $c(t) = $ consumption per head, $n = $ population growth rate, $\rho = $ discount rate and U is concave. Equation (4) can be modified to make U a function of more variables (perhaps including human capital for example) but it is usually necessary to assume $\rho > n$ to ensure existence of the integral. Maximizing (4) subject to the relevant (differential equation) constraints typically leads to saddlepoint dynamics and the imposition of a transversality condition such as:

$$p(t).k(t) \to 0 \text{ as } t \to \infty \tag{5}$$

where $p(t)$ is the costate variable associated with the state variable $k(t)$ (capital per head). The costate variable usually has the interpretation of a discounted shadow price of the corresponding state variable, so that the transversality condition (5) requires that the discounted shadow value of the capital stock tends to zero as t tends to infinity. This approach has a number of significant difficulties:

1. It relies on assuming the existence of a controlling agent with a particular type (Ramsey) of utility function. Such an assumption is usually completely orthogonal to the rest of the model. For example, it

may be a plausible working hypothesis to assume rational expectations but, in the absence of central planning (which, presumably, is not what the theorist has in mind), it is going much further to assume the existence of single controlling agent of the requisite type.

2. The transversality condition is not, in general, a necessay condition for a maximum of (4) (see Halkin, 1971). Moreover, it only guarantees convergence in the infinite horizon case. The finite horizon version of (5), $p(T).k(T) = 0$, could easily be satisfied on a divergent path.

3. Even when the transversality condition does guarantee convergence, it does not explain how convergence is re-established after a shock is applied to the model. In practice this is achieved by invoking the implausible notion of "jump variables" which, as if by magic, adjust instantaneouly to ensure that the model is always on a convergent path (i.e., one lying in the stable manifold). Although some variables, such as prices, might be thought to jump in reality, the jump variables invoked in growth theory, for example, are usually quantities such as consumption. Jumps in quantity variables such as consumption are clearly less plausible than jumps in prices.

4. In practice the transversality condition/jump variables approach is applied to a local linearization of the model that holds only in a neighborhood of an equilibrium. Such a linearization obscures potentially important behavior of the model away from the particular equilibrium under consideration. Moreover it has problematic implications for the jump variables mentioned above. For example the linearization may call for an upward jump under exactly the same conditions that the original (nonlinear) model requires a downward jump. This raises insuperable difficulties for empirical testing.

These issues are discussed in George, Oxley, and Carlaw (2003), George and Oxley (2005), and Buiter (2009). We dispense with the Ramsey/Pontryagin framework in this chapter and focus directly on the issue of convergence (stability and asymptotic stability).

3. Economic growth with a variable production lag

It is widely assumed in growth theory that investment projects contribute to output as soon as the investment decision is taken. In reality there is usually a significant delay between investment decision and increased output. Sometimes referred to as "construction lags" or "time to build," these delays can be long and/or highly variable. Wheaton (1987) discovers that, for the United States, there is a lag between receiving a construction permit and completing the building that varies between 18 and 24 months. Macrae (1989) describes lags of 6–10 years in the construction of power stations and Pindyck (1991) notes similar delays in the aerospace and pharmaceutical sectors. The complexity of protoype production, testing, and certification (e.g., in pharmaceuticals) all contribute to this problem. There are reasons to believe that actual lags in all these cases are even longer and/or more variable than these authors describe. They only consider a subset of the lags applicable to any particular investment project.

The standard AK growth model, with a Ramsey utility function, leads to the reduced form dynamical system:

$$\dot{k} = (A - n - \delta)k - c \tag{6}$$

$$\dot{c} = c \left[\frac{A - \delta - \rho}{\theta} \right] \tag{7}$$

where k = capital per head, c = consumption per head, A = productivity parameter, n = population growth rate, δ = depreciation rate, ρ = discount rate, $1/\theta$ = intertemporal elasticity of substitution. Establishing this reduced form requires use of the transversality condition. There are no lags in the model, and its solution is simply exponential growth (of all variables) at a rate $g = (A - \rho - \delta/\theta)$. A condition for asymptotic stability is therefore $g < 0$.

In this section and the next, we develop simple AK-type growth models with complex lag structures. Their dynamics are analyzed by appeal to the theory of functional differential equations. In this section we focus on a model with a variable production lag.

DEFINITION 3. Let $\mu(t) = t - \lambda(t)$. Note that $\mu(t)$ is continuous and $0 \le \mu(t) \le t$, from (2). No further restrictions are imposed on $\mu(t)$, allowing for a completely general lag structure.

Now assume a variable production lag, so that:

$$Y(t) = AK(\mu(t)) \tag{8}$$

where $Y(t)$ = output, $K(t)$ = capital stock and A = constant. Assume growth of population ($N(t)$) is exponential:

$$\dot{L}(t) = nL(t) \tag{9}$$

where n = constant. Assume also that depreciation occurs at a constant rate (δ):

$$\text{depreciation} = -\delta K(t) \tag{10}$$

Then:

$$\dot{K}(t) = sY(t) - \delta K(t) = sAK(\mu(t)) - \delta K(t) \tag{11}$$

where s = savings rate (assumed constant).

We now derive a differential equation in the capital/labour ratio $(k(t) = (K(t)/L(t)))$. Logarithmic differentiation together with Equation (9) yield:

$$\dot{k}(t) = \frac{\dot{K}(t)}{L(t)} - nk(t) \tag{12}$$

Equations (10)–(12) yield:

$$\dot{k}(t) = \frac{sAK(\mu(t)) - \delta K(t)}{L(t)} - nk(t) = \frac{sAK(\mu(t))}{L(t)} - (n + \delta)k(t) \Rightarrow \tag{13}$$

$$\dot{k}(t) = \left[\frac{sAK(\mu(t))}{L(\mu(t))}\right] \cdot \left[\frac{L(\mu(t))}{L(t)}\right] - (n + \delta)k(t) \Rightarrow \tag{14}$$

$$\dot{k}(t) = sAk(\mu(t))e^{(\mu(t)-t)n} - (n + \delta)k(t) \tag{15}$$

Equation (15) relates $\dot{k}(t)$ to current and lagged values of $k(t)$. It has the form of Eq. (1) in its scalar form. Adopting lower case letters (to represent scalars) let:

$$a(t) = -(n + \delta), \quad b(t) = sAe^{(\mu(t)-t)n}, \quad c(t) = 0 \tag{16}$$

Now define the *aggregate coefficient* $\omega(t)$:

DEFINITION 4. The aggregate coefficient $\omega(t)$ is defined as $\omega(t) = b(t) + a(t - \lambda(t))c(t)$

Standard approaches to determining stability fail because of the completely general form of the lag function $\lambda(t)$ (generating a completely general form for $\mu(t)$) but progress can be made by appeal to the theory of functional differential equations (see Azbelev, Maksimov, & Rakhmatullina, 2007 for an introduction). In particular Theorem 2 of Iserles and Terjeki (1995) provides a useful means to identify sufficient conditions for the stability and asymptotic stabilty (in the sense of Section 2) of $k(t)$. It is relatively straightforward to confirm that the conditions of this theorem are satisfied by our growth model.

The coefficient $b(t)$ is depicted in Figure 1.

Clearly Re $a(t) < 0$ (note that $a(t)$ is real so Re $a(t) = a(t)$) and $b(t)$ is continuous. Moreover $|c(t)| \leq c^* < 1$, taking $c^* = 0$. Furthermore, the aggregate coefficient $\omega(t)$ is given by:

$$\omega(t) = sAe^{(\mu(t)-t)n} \tag{17}$$

Hence

$$\omega^*(t) = \max_{\tau \in [0,t]} b(\tau) = sA \tag{18}$$

because $e^{(\mu(t)-t)n} \leq 1$ and $e^{(\mu(t)-t)n} = 1$ at $t = 0$. The theorem now provides a sufficient condition for the stabilty (in the sense of Section 2) of $k(t)$. That condition is:

$$\omega^*(t) + Re\ a(t)(1 - c^*) \leq 0; \quad \text{for} \quad \forall t \geq 0 \tag{19}$$

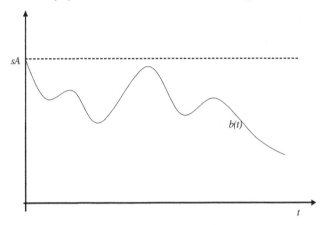

Fig. 1.   The coefficient b(t).

this is (from Equations (16) and (18)):

$$sA - (n + \delta) \leq 0 \tag{20}$$

Note that this a sufficient condition for stability in the sense of Section 2. That is it guarantees the uniform boundedness of $k(t)$.

However, (20) does not provide a sufficient condition for the stronger property of asymptotic stability in the sense of Section 2. Theorem 3 of Iserles and Terjeki (1995) does provide such conditions. Consider conditions (iv), (v), and (vi) of that theorem.

Condtion iv.

The condition: $\omega^*(t) + Rea(t)(1 - c^*)\kappa \leq 0 \ (0 < \kappa < 1)$ becomes:

$$sA - (n + \delta)\kappa \leq 0 (0 < \kappa < 1) \tag{21}$$

Since s, A, n,, and δ are constants, this is equivalent to:

$$sA - (n + \delta) < 0 \tag{22}$$

Condition v.

The condition: $\int_0^\infty Rea(s)ds = -\infty$ becomes:

$$\int_0^\infty -(\delta + n)ds = -\infty \tag{23}$$

in terms of our model, and is clearly satisfied.

Condition (vi)

In terms of our model this becomes:

$$\mu(t) \to \infty \ \text{as} \ t \to \infty \tag{24}$$

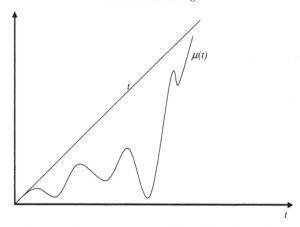

Fig. 2. Lag structure satisfying Equation (24).

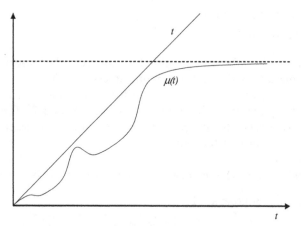

Fig. 3. Lag structure violating Equation (24).

Imposing this last condition (24), in addition to the other assumptions, will therefore guarantee asymptotic stabilty of $k(t)$. This condition admits a wide variety of lag structures (Figure 2) but rules out others. For example, Figure 3 depicts a function $\mu(t)$ that tends to some finite limit as $t \to \infty$. Another example is given by the function:

$$\mu(t) = t\sin^2 t \tag{25}$$

depicted in Figure 4. This function does not tend to a finite limit, but continues to oscillate as $t \to \infty$, violating condition (24).

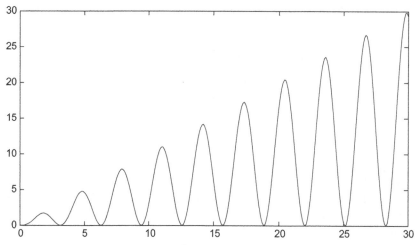

Fig. 4. *The function μ(t) = t sin² t. This lag structure violates Equation (24).*

4. Economic growth with an accelerator investment function

It has been widely assumed that aggregate investment depends on the rate of change of output and not on its level, leading to an exponential *accelerator* investment function. For similar reasons to those discusssed in Section 3, it is reasonable to suppose that this relationship operates with a variable lag so that:

$$I(t) = s\,\dot{Y}(\mu(t)) \tag{26}$$

where $I(t)$ = gross investment, $Y(t)$ = output, s = constant and $\mu(t) = t - \lambda(t)$, where $\lambda(t)$ is the lag function, as before. As before, take depreciation = $-\delta K(t)$, an AK production $Y(t) = AK(t)$, and exponenential population growth $\dot{L}(t) = nL(t)$. Then

$$\dot{K}(t) = I(t) - \delta K(t) = s\,\dot{Y}(\mu(t)) - \delta K(t) = sA\dot{K}(\mu(t)) - \delta K(t) \tag{27}$$

As before, we seek a differential equation in $k(t)$, the capital labour ratio. Logarithmic differentiation yields:

$$\dot{k}(t) = \frac{\dot{K}(t)}{L(t)} - nk(t) \tag{28}$$

Using Equation (26) this yields:

$$\dot{k}(t) = \frac{sA\dot{K}(\mu(t))}{L(t)} - (n + \delta)k(t) \tag{29}$$

Noting that Equation (9) holds for the lagged variable $\mu(t)$, that is, $\dot{L}(\mu(t)) = nL(\mu(t))$, Equation (29) yields:

$$\dot{k}(t) = sAe^{n(\mu(t)-t)}\dot{k}(\mu(t)) + sAne^{n(\mu(t)-t)}k(\mu(t)) - (\delta + n)k(t) \qquad (30)$$

As before, we seek sufficient conditions for the stability and asymptotic stability of Equation (30) by appeal to Iserles and Terjeki (1995) Theorem 2. Let:

$$a(t) = -(\delta + n), b(t) = sAne^{n(\mu(t)-t)}, c(t) = sAe^{n(\mu(t)-t)} \qquad (31)$$

Clearly the function $a(t)$ satisfies the conditions of Iserles and Terjeki (1995) Theorem 2 because $a(t) < 0$. To satisfy the conditions of the theorem we require that $|c(t)| \leq c^* < 1$ but, in contrast to the model of Section 3, in this case $c(t) \neq 0$. In this model $c(t) = sAe^{n(\mu(t)-t)}$, so by taking $c^* = sA$ and assuming:

$$sA < 1 \qquad (32)$$

the condition on $c(t)$ is satisfied. Figure 5 depicts $c(t)$ with condition (32) satisfied.

In this model the aggregate coefficient $\omega(t)$ is given by $\omega(t) = -\delta sAe^{n(\mu(t)-t)}$ so that $\omega^*(t) = \max_{\tau \in [0,t]} \delta sAe^{n(\mu(\tau)-\tau)} = \delta sA$. So the additional condition for stability is:

$$\omega^*(t) + \alpha(t)(1 - c^*) \leq 0 \qquad (33)$$

which becomes (noting that $c^* = sA$ in this model) $\delta sA - (\delta + n)$ $(1 - sA) \leq 0$. Rearranging yields:

$$(2\delta + n)sA - \delta - n \leq 0 \qquad (34)$$

Turning now to the conditions for asymptotic stability:
Condition iv.

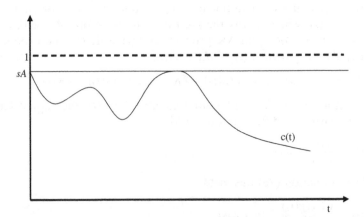

Fig. 5. The function c(t) shown satisfying condition (32).

The condition $\omega^*(t) + \alpha(t)(1 - c^*)\kappa \leq 0$ (where $0 < \kappa < 1$) is a stricter version of Equation (33) and may therefore be treated as technical. It yields a stricter version of (34) namely:

$$\delta sA - (\delta + n)(1 - sA)\kappa \leq 0 \quad (\text{where } 0 < \kappa < 1) \tag{35}$$

Condition v.

As in the production lag model of Section 3, the condition: $\int_0^\infty \text{Re } a(s)\,ds = -\infty$ becomes:

$$\int_0^\infty -(\delta + n)\,ds = -\infty \tag{36}$$

in this model, and is clearly satisfied.

Condition vi.

As in the production lag model this becomes:

$$\mu(t) \to \infty \quad \text{as } t \to \infty \tag{37}$$

Once again this is the crucial condition for asymptotic stability. Figure 2 shows a lag structure satisfying this condition and Figures 3 and 4 show lag structures violating it.

5. Time-varying parameters

The approach adopted above is general enough to admit time-varying parameters. As an example consider the production lag model of Section 3 with a time-varying productivity parameter $A(t)$ (perhaps arising from exogenous technical progress) and depreciation rate $\delta(t)$. For simplicity we keep population growth (n) and the savings ratio (s) constant. Now $\omega^*(t)$

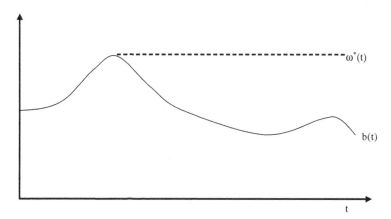

Fig. 6.   The relationship between b(t) and $\omega^*(t)$ with a time-varying productivity parameter.

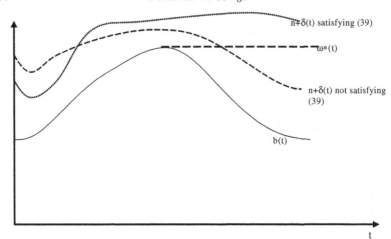

Fig. 7.   Convergence condition with time-varying parameters.

takes a slightly more complicated form. The production function is now
$Y(t) = A(\mu(t))K(\mu(t))$ and $\omega(t) = b(t) = sA(\mu(t))e^{(\mu(t)-t)n}$ so that:

$$\omega^*(t) = \max_{\tau \in [0,t]} sA(\mu(\tau))e^{(\mu(\tau)-\tau)n} \tag{38}$$

Because $A(\mu(t))$ is a now function of time, the relationship between $\omega^*(t)$ and $b(t)$ is now more complicated than in the model of Section 3. This relationship is illustrated in Figure 6.

Condition (19) of Section 3 now becomes:

$$\omega^*(t) - (n + \delta(t)) \leq 0 \tag{39}$$

This need not be satisfied even if $s.A(0) \leq 0$. Figure 7 shows both cases (satisfying (39) and violating it).

6. Conclusions

Economic models often generate complicated lag structures that cannot be captured with the standard modeling techniques. This is particularly true in the theory of economic growth. Recent (1990s) developments in the theory of functional differential equations however provide a useful approach to this problem. Two growth models with generalized lag sructures are analyzed, involving production lags and an accelerator investment function respectively. By applying the theory of functional differential equations, sufficient conditions for stability and asymptotic stability can be obtained. In both cases an important extra condition required to guarantee asymptotic stability (convergence) is that $\mu(t) \to \infty$ as $t \to \infty$, where $\mu(t) = 1 - \lambda(t)$ for any lag function $\lambda(t)$.

The approach adopted can be extended to cover time-varying parameters and vector-valued equations (using matrix algebra). These extensions should encompass most nonlinearities arising in economic modeling. However, the approach through functional differential equations can be extended to full nonlinearity at the expense of increased mathematical complexity.

It is not confined to models with an AK production function nor to those with production/investment lags. Any plausible production function can be employed and generalized lags can enter the model through many different routes apart from those discussed here. For example, given the complexities of education and training, there may easily be a lag between human capital being accumulated and its effect on output. The R&D process is at least as complex as education and training, so there is likely to be significant lag between acquiring new knowledge, its embodiment in new capital, and its eventual impact on output. The techniques discussed above can readily be extended to many variables, by allowing X to be a vector and A B and C to be matrices, in Equation (1). A model including features such as these may require a nonlinear analysis, and this too can developed, at the expense of increased mathematical complexity. For example, Iserles and Terjeki (1995) analyze the separably nonlinear system:

$$\dot{y}(t) = f(t, y(t)) + g(t, y(\mu(t))) + C(t)\dot{y}(\mu(t)) \qquad \text{with } y(0) = y_0 \qquad (40)$$

where the functions f and g are continuous and locally Lipschitz, and C is a continuous matrix funcion. However, to use this technique it is necessary to drop the "saddlepoint plus jump variables" approach discussed in Section 2. Since the standard Ramsey/Pontryagin setup typically leads to saddlepoints and jump variables, it would have to be abandoned if the techniques discussed in this chapter are to be employed.

Acknowledgments

This chapter originated from discussions with Clive Granger and Les Oxley, to both of whom I am indebted. These discussions took place while I was on leave at the University of Canterbury, New Zealand, to whom I am grateful for a positive and constructive research environment. I am also indebted to Vela Velupillai, Stefano Zambelli, Carl Chiarella, and Peter Flaschel. Thanks also to the Carnegie Foundation for a research grant that supported this research. Any remaining errors or omissions are entirely mine.

References

Azbelev, N. V., Maksimov, V. P., & Rakhmatullina, L. F. (2007). *Introduction to the theory of functional differential equations: Methods and applications.* Hindawi Publishing Corporation, New York, NY.

Bar-Ilan, A., & Strange, W. C. (1996). Investment lags. *American Economic Review, 86*, 610–622.

Buiter, W. (2009). The unfortunate uselessness of most 'state of the art' academic monetary economics. Retrieved from http://www.voxeu.org/index.php?q = node/3210

Feldstein, A., Iserles, A., & Levin, D. (1995). Embedding of delay equations into an infinite-dimensional ODE system. *Journal of Differential Equations, 117*, 127–150.

George, D. A. R., & Oxley, L. T. (2005). La dinamica de las expectivas racionales: una critica metodologica. *Investigacion Economica, LXIV*, 71–89.

George, D. A. R., Oxley, L. T., & Carlaw, K. I. (2003). Economic growth in transition. *Journal of Economic Surveys, 17*, 227–237.

Halkin, H. (1971). Necessary conditions for optimal control problems with infinite horizons. *Econometrica, 42*, 267–272.

Iserles, A. (1993). On the generalized pantograph functional-differential equation. *European Journal of Applied Mathematics, 4*, 1–38.

Iserles, A., & Terjeki, J. (1995). Stability and asymptotic stability of functional-differential equations. *Journal of the London Mathematical Society, 51*, 559–572.

Li, D. (2002). Is the AK model still alive? The long-run relation between growth and investment re-examined. *Canadian Journal of Economics, 35*, 92–114.

Macrae, K. M. (1989). *Critical issues in electric power planning in the 1990s* (Vol. 1). Canadian Energy Research Institute, Calgary, Alberta, Canada.

Majd, S., & Pindyck, R. (1987). Time to build, option value and investment decisions. *Journal of Financial Economics, 18*, 7–27.

Pindyck, R. (1991). Irreversibility, uncertainty and investment. *Journal of Economic Literature, 29*, 1110–1148.

Sequeira, T. N. (2008). Transitional dynamics of an endogenous growth model with an erosion effect. *The Manchester School, 76*, 436–452.

Wheaton, W. (1987). The cyclic behavior of the national office market. *Journal of the American Real Estate and Urban Economics Association, 15*, 281–299.

CHAPTER 10

On the Track of the World's Economic Center of Gravity

Jean-Marie Grether[a] and Nicole Andréa Mathys[b]

[a]*University of Neuchâtel, Institute of Economic Research, Pierre-a-Mazel 7, CH-2000 Neuchatel, Switzerland*
E-mail address: jean-marie.grether@unine.ch
[b]*Swiss Federal Office of Energy in Berne and University of Neuchâtel, Institute of Economic Research, Pierre-a-Mazel 7, CH-2000 Neuchâtel, Switzerland*
E-mail address: nicole.mathys@gmail.com

Abstract
This chapter proposes a refined and updated measurement of the World's Economic Center of Gravity over the 1950–2008 period, based on historical data provided by Maddison (2010) and on the detailed grid data of the G-Econ (Nordhaus, 2006) database. The economic center of gravity is located in the vicinity of Iceland during the first three decades, and then heads strongly toward the East since 1980. Regarding geographic concentration, world production is less concentrated than population across the Earth's surface, and becomes even less so over time. A new decomposition technique is proposed, which suggests a structural break at the end of the 1970s. Measures of R&D activity, education expenditures and literacy as growth related indicators depict a spatial pattern that is consistent with the Eastern shift of the world economic center of gravity.

Keywords: Spatial distribution, economic growth

JEL classifications: R12, 040

1. Introduction

Many would agree with the assertion of French (2005) that the recent growth performance of China and India has been pulling "the globe's economic center of gravity decidedly towards Asia." But by how much? How fast? And since when? A first objective of this chapter is to answer those questions relying on the concept of the world's economic center of gravity (WECG) introduced by Grether and Mathys (2010) and further

Frontiers of Economics and Globalization
Volume 11   ISSN: 1574-8715
DOI: 10.1108/S1574-8715(2011)0000011015

applied by Quah (2011). While the previous attempts were limited to the past 30 years, here the observation period is expanded back to 1950 (and forward to 2008), which provides evidence that the strong Asian shift initiated at the end of the 1970s. A second objective is to increase the precision of estimates: while previous attempts were based on less than 1,000 location points, calculations are based here on the spatial grid established by Nordhaus et al. (2006), which provides information on the distribution of economic activity across the globe for more than 27'000 different grid cells. A third objective of this chapter is to better document this trend by analyzing a characteristic of the WECG that has been neglected so far, namely the length of the vector of the corresponding center of gravity, which is a measure of how economic production is concentrated upon the Earth's surface. As it turns out, this length has been decreasing across the sample period, which means that production has become geographically more evenly spread.[1] This is confirmed by a new decomposition technique that identifies the sources of change along the three dimensional space. Finally, a fourth objective is to apply the same methodology to other growth-related indicators such as R&D expenditures, education expenditures, and the number of literate people. The same trends are identified in terms of mean direction and concentration, although innovation and education efforts appear to be geographically more concentrated at the beginning of the sample period than economic activity.

Section 2 defines the theoretical concepts of mean direction and mean concentration on a sphere, Section 3 presents results and discusses the evolution of the different centers of gravity, and Section 4 concludes.

2. Measuring the world's economic center of gravity

This section provides a brief recap of how the WECG is calculated, then proposes and discusses a new decomposition of the concentration index represented by the length of the WECG vector. For a detailed description of the concepts, see Appendix B.

2.1. Mean direction and mean concentration on a sphere

As exposed by Grether and Mathys (2010), socioeconomic centers of gravity, or centers of mass, can be defined by assuming that the Earth is a perfect sphere and that "mass" is represented by a socioeconomic variable, V, which is GDP in the case of the world *economic* center of gravity (WECG, $V = E$), human population in the case of the world *demographic* center of gravity (WDCG, $V = D$), and land in the case of the world

---

[1] In this chapter the units of observation are always grid cells on the Earth surface, not people. Therefore the reported evidence is not appropriate to discuss per capita income inequalities.

geographic center of gravity (WGCG, $V = G$). We assume that the Earth's surface is covered by a regular lattice defining n location points $i = 1,...,n$ and that all Cartesian coordinates are expressed as a fraction of the Earth's radius (so that all reported distances should be multiplied by 6371 to get the corresponding value in kilometer). The weight of each location point is given by the share of that location in the world total of the corresponding socioeconomic variable, so that the position vector of the world center of gravity is given by:

$$\overrightarrow{OG^V} = \left(\sum_{i=1}^{n} \theta_i^V x_i, \sum_{i=1}^{n} \theta_i^V y_i, \sum_{i=1}^{n} \theta_i^V z_i \right)^{\mathrm{T}} \tag{1}$$

where θ_i^V represents the share of location i in total land in the case of the WGCG, in total population in the case of the WDCG, and in total production in the case of the WECG.

The center of gravity encapsulates the two major descriptive dimensions commonly used in spherical statistics (see, e.g., Mardia & Jupp, 2000). On the one hand, it indicates a direction in space, which is usually extended to its projection onto the Earth's surface[2] and referred to as the *mean direction*. The mean direction vector is simply the normalized gravity vector, that is:

$$\overrightarrow{OG_0^V} = \frac{\overrightarrow{OG^V}}{\|\overrightarrow{OG^V}\|} \tag{2}$$

This will be the direction indicator reported and discussed below.[3]

On the other hand, the length of the vector of the center of gravity, usually referred to as the *mean resultant length*, is an indicator of the concentration of the weighting variable upon the Earth's surface (at the limit, if all the weight is concentrated on a single point, the length is 1). We will denote this length by c_V, so that its square is given by:

$$c_V^2 = \|\overrightarrow{OG^V}\|^2 = \left(\sum_{i=1}^{n} \theta_i^V x_i \right)^2 + \left(\sum_{i=1}^{n} \theta_i^V y_i \right)^2 + \left(\sum_{i=1}^{n} \theta_i^V z_i \right)^2 \tag{3}$$

This will be our concentration measure.[4]

---

[2] Note that the convention followed by Quah (2011) is different as he orthogonally projects the center of gravity onto the cylinder wrapping up the Earth around the equator. We discarded that alternative projection technique in our context, because it mixes the influence of the two dimensions of the center of gravity vector that we want to disentangle (i.e., direction and length).

[3] If the Cartesian coordinates of the mean direction vector are denoted by (x_0, y_0, z_0) then the corresponding polar coordinates are given by: $(\pi/2)-\cos^{-1}(z_0)$ for the latitude, and $\tan^{-1}(y_0/x_0)$ for the longitude.

[4] As concentration and dispersion are mirror images of the same reality, some authors propose $2(1-c_V)$ or $1 - c_V^2$ as a measure of spherical variance (e.g., Mardia & Jupp, 2000, p. 164).

2.2. From land to population and from population to production

If production activity is clustered in particular spots on the Earth's surface, it is in good part because human population is also concentrated in particular areas. And if human population is concentrated in specific places, it is also partly because a substantial share of the Earth's surface is inhospitable to human settlements. To clarify this chain of links between the three indicators of economic (c_E), demographic (c_D), and geographic (c_G) concentration, let us first note that, as all location points are regularly spread across the Earth's surface, the sum of the Cartesian coordinates is zero (e.g., $\sum_{i=1}^{n} x_i = 0$). This implies that each one of the squared elements that appears in equation (3) can be written as a simple covariance [e.g., $\sum_{i=1}^{n} \theta_i^V x_i = n\text{cov}(\theta_i^V, x_i)$], so that the concentration index can be rewritten:

$$c_V^2 = n^2 \left\{ \left[\text{cov}(\theta_i^V, x_i)\right]^2 + \left[\text{cov}(\theta_i^V, y_i)\right]^2 + \left[\text{cov}(\theta_i^V, z_i)\right]^2 \right\} \qquad (4)$$

Second, define μ_X^G, μ_Y^G, μ_Z^G as the share of each directional element in the geographic concentration index (e.g., $\mu_X^G \equiv [n\text{cov}(\theta_i^G, x_i)]^2/c_G^2$ and similarly for μ_Y^G and μ_Z^G), g_D as the *densification rate* of c_D^2 with respect to c_G^2, that is, $c_D^2 = c_G^2(1 + g_D)$, and $g_{D,X}$ as the directional densification rate of the x-dimensional element of the concentration index when switching from the geographic to the demographic case, that is, $g_{D,X} = [\text{cov}(\theta_i^D, x_i)/\text{cov}(\theta_i^G, x_i)]^2 - 1$ and similarly for $g_{D,Y}$ and $g_{D,Z}$. If we adopt similar notational conventions to define the densification rate when switching from demographic to economic concentration [i.e., $c_E^2 = c_D^2(1 + g_E)$], then simple algebra combining equations (3) and (4) shows that:

$$g_D = g_{D,X}\mu_X^G + g_{D,Y}\mu_Y^G + g_{D,Z}\mu_Z^G \qquad (5a)$$

$$g_E = g_{E,X}\mu_X^D + g_{E,Y}\mu_Y^D + g_{E,Z}\mu_Z^D \qquad (5b)$$

Equations (5a) and (5b) state that the densification rate of the concentration index is a weighted average of the three directional densification rates. Each directional densification rate reflects the effect of increased concentration along a particular dimension. For example, a positive $g_{D,X}$ means that population tends to be more polarized along the x dimension than land is, so that it reinforces the concentration pattern along that dimension. Similarly, directional densification rates in (5b) reflect the impact of production distribution across persons, that is, if $g_{E,X}$ is positive, it means that along the x-axis, production tends to concentrate where people are already concentrated.

Let us illustrate these relationships on the basis of a very stylized example in which a single direction is relevant. Assume that land, people, and production are homogenously allocated across the surface of four concentric slices of a given hemisphere obtained by cutting the Earth along planes parallel to the equator, as if we were preparing a sauce and slicing half an onion in four slices of equal thickness. As all dots are uniformly spread around the common axis, only the vertical dimension is relevant (i.e., in terms of equations (5a) and (5b), we have $\mu_Z^G = 1$ and $\mu_X^G = \mu_Y^G = 0$). Another convenient property of that example is that the surface of a slice is proportional to its thickness, so that each slice has the same weight of $1/4$, which makes concentration indices straightforward to calculate (see Section 4.1 in Appendix B for more details). Let us assume first a pattern of increasing concentration in the sense that, starting from the equator, there is nothing on the first slice, only land in the second one, land and people on the third one and land, people and production on the fourth one reaching the pole. As each variable is homogenously spread across the surface of each slide, we obtain easily[5] that $c_G = 0.625$, $c_D = 0.75$, and $c_E = 0.875$, from which we get $g_D = 44\%$ and $g_E \cong 7\%$. As an alternative pattern, consider that land and population distributions are kept unchanged with respect to the first case but that production locates in the third slice, that is, spreading away from the core. The new values are $c'_E = 0.625$ and $g'_E \cong -31\%$, that is, illustrating first a magnification effect from geographic to demographic concentration and then a dilution effect from demographic to economic concentration. Of course what makes things more interesting in the real world is that we have three dimensions and nonhomogenous distributions, which is what we want to analyze now, but keeping in mind this simple example, which will turn out to be quite close to what happened in reality.

3. Tracking the centers of gravity

To estimate the centers of gravity defined in the previous section, detailed data on production, population, and land area are needed over a long time horizon and on a geographically detailed grid basis. These data are not readily available. Hence we propose to combine two international databases to construct the information needed (for another approach based on city data see Grether & Mathys, 2010). The first dataset, the G-Econ database (for a description see Chen, 2008 and Nordhaus et al., 2006, for an application to macroeconomics see Nordhaus, 2006) reports the gross cell product and population for the years 1990, 1995, 2000, and 2005 at a 1° longitude by 1° latitude resolution at a global scale (roughly 27,000 cells). To extend the time-dimension of our computations, we combine this geographically detailed data with the dataset prepared by Maddison (2010) reporting GDP and population data for 159 countries

---

[5] The average location along the vertical axis is 0.125 for the first slice (average between 0 and 0.25) and 0.375, 0.625, and 0.875 for the three following ones. The positions of the centers of gravity are obtained by taking the average of the last three numbers for c_G, of the last two for c_D, and by considering only the last number for c_E.

from 1950 to 2008. National population and GDP figures are allocated across grid cells according to their shares in 1990. The selected sample of 159 countries represents 99.8% of world population, 99.6% of world GDP, and 89.7% of emerged land in 1990, the smaller representativeness for land being due to the voluntary exclusion of Antarctica, a continent with neither production nor human population.

3.1. Moving eastward: mean direction trends 1950–2008

Figure 1 shows the projection on the Earth surface of all three centers of gravity and over time for the population and economic center (the geographic one remains fixed by definition). Almost all identified centers (except in the 1950s for the economic center) lie on the same quarter of the northern hemisphere, where coordinates for all three dimensions (x, y, z) are positive. The geographic center, a fixed point located in the Black sea, has no interest by itself but is rather used as a point of comparison, showing the hypothetical economic or demographic center if all people and all economic activity were allocated homogeneously on all land slots. The demographic center of gravity is located roughly at the same latitude as the geographic center but almost 5,000 km more to the East. If economic activity would have been distributed on a per capita basis (i.e., equal per capita incomes, denoted as the "flat-world" in Quah, 2011), the economic center would coincide with the

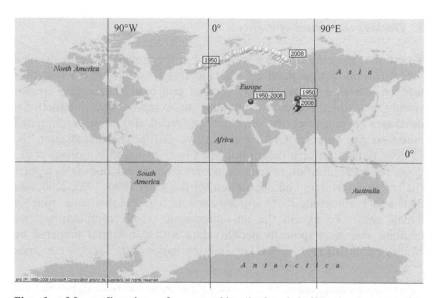

Fig. 1. Mean direction of geographic (isolated balloon), demographic (dark) and economic (pale) center of gravity, 1950–2008. Copyright © and (p) 1988–2009 Microsoft Corporation and/or its suppliers. All rights reserved.

demographic center. Given the observed income distribution over the period 1950–2008, the WECG has been located more to the North and more to the West than the demographic center, although its eastward shift is remarkable.

Figure 2 depicts more clearly the trajectory of the demographic center, lying in Kazakhstan in 1950, moving clearly to the South over the whole period, and since the 1970s also west-wards, mainly due to the increased share in population of South America, Sub-Saharan Africa and South Asia (see Table A1 for average regional shares for land, population, and production). In 2008 the demographic center has crossed Kyrgyzstan and Tajikistan and is heading toward Afghanistan.

This shift to the South at the global level is also supported by a simple analysis of the share of the main regions/countries in the demographic center as drawn in Figure 3. It can be seen that while India and the Rest of the World are increasing their shares, the share of the EU is significantly decreasing. China has had an increase in its share up to 1980 but saw its share decrease thereafter.

Figure 4 gives the details on the trajectory of the WECG. In the 1950s the center sets off from the coast of Iceland and is up to 1980 moving slowly and afterwards quickly toward Russia where it reaches the mainland in 2008. This shift to the East is faster than what had been predicted in Grether and Mathys (2010). Note also that the trend toward

Fig. 2.   Mean direction of the demographic center of gravity, 1950–2008.
**Copyright © and (p) 1988–2009 Microsoft Corporation and/or its suppliers.
All rights reserved.**

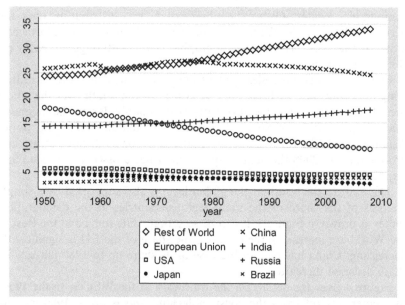

Fig. 3. *Average share in demographic center of gravity by large regions and countries.*

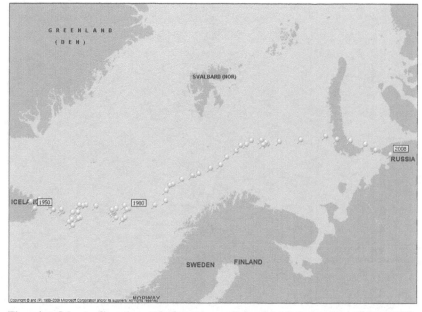

Fig. 4. *Mean direction of the economic center of gravity, 1950–2008.*
Copyright © and (p) 1988–2009 Microsoft Corporation and/or its suppliers.
All rights reserved.

the North that can be observed from 1950 to 2000 is not pursued; instead the "new" trend is rather to the South. The demographic and economic centers end up roughly on the same longitude but with the demographic center being much more to the South than the economic one.

Figure 5 shows the evolution of the average shares of main regions/ countries in the WECG. As one would expect, the EU and the USA display strongly decreasing shares while China and India report increasing shares mainly since the 1980s. Japan has seen its share increase from 1960 to 1990 but reports a decreasing share afterwards. The average share of the rest of the world is weakly increasing.

To sum up, we can put forward three findings. First, all socio-economic centers of gravity locate in the Northern Hemisphere, and while the geographic and demographic centers locate both to the East of the Greenwich Meridian (and more so for the latter), the economic center has been to the West for the period 1950–1975 but to the East afterwards. Second, the demographic center displays a clear shift to the South with a less pronounced shift to the West since the 1980s. Third, the WECG is shifting since 1980 quickly to the East and since 2000 also to the South. Does the movement of the economic center of gravity towards the demographic center of gravity mean that GDP distribution is becoming more equal? This question is addressed in the next section.

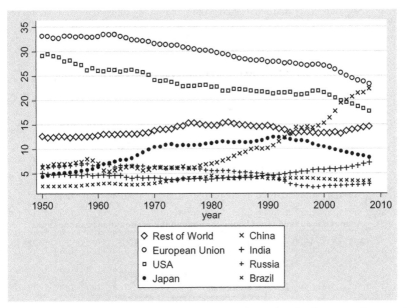

Fig. 5. Average share in economic center of gravity by large regions and countries.

3.2. Mean concentration decomposition 1950–2008

Complementary to the analysis on the mean direction trends, this section reports the evolution of the concentration indices defined in Section 2. Figure 6 depicts the evolution of the concentration indices over time for the three variables: land, population, and production (see Table A2 for regional shares in concentration). Concentration is highest for population over the whole sample period although there is a weak downward trend. The concentration index for production is just below the demographic one at the beginning of the period but is significantly decreasing over time since 1968 with a weak rebound since 1997. This means that production tends to be less concentrated than population across the Earth's surface and that it becomes even less so over time. The concentration index for land, as a benchmark, is several orders of magnitude smaller, suggesting that land is a lot more homogenously spread than production or people.

Figure 7 reports the evolution of the densification rates g_D and g_E. The hollow dots indicate that people are much more concentrated than land areas on the globe. The solid dots indicate that production is less concentrated than people (i.e., the distribution of production is biased toward less densely populated areas) and that this tendency is reinforced over time.

To better understand the evolution of the concentration index, we decompose it along the three different axes, starting with the shift from geographic to demographic concentration (i.e., equation (5a)). To clarify

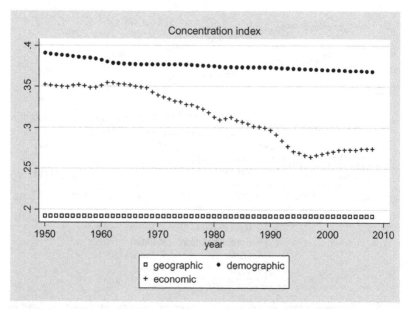

Fig. 6.   Average concentration indices.

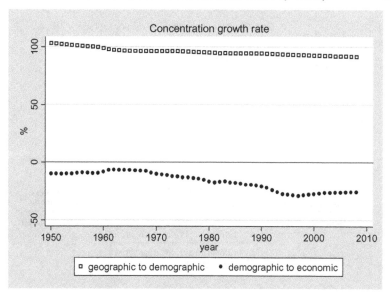

Fig. 7. Average densification rates.

the spatial interpretation, we take the view of an Euro-centric observer who is facing the prime meridian at the level of the equator, with two obvious directions: North/South (z-axis) and East/West (y axis), and a third one that is hidden behind the prime meridian denoted by close/away (x axis, with decreasing values indicating a location getting further away from the observer, deep into the Earth). The contributions of each axis to the geographic center of gravity (i.e., μ_X^G, μ_Y^G, μ_Z^G) do not change over time and should be taken as a benchmark (that is why no figure is worth reporting in this case). The North/South dimension turns out to be the most important (61%), the East/West dimension intermediate (30%) and the close/away dimension the least important (9%), meaning that the corresponding vector is pretty close to the plane that cuts the Earth along the 90° Meridian. In short, what matters most in terms of land distribution is its concentration into the Northern hemisphere.

    Figure 8 plots the densification rates $(g_{D,X}, g_{D,Y}, g_{D,Z})$ when moving from the geographic to the demographic center of gravity. By far the largest effect is the one reported along the East/West axis, with an order of magnitude close to 1000% (while the other two effects are a lot smaller and tend to cancel each other out). This may come as a surprise because at first sight, on Figure 1, the demographic center does not seem so much further to the East than the geographic center. However one should keep in mind that Figure 1 only reports the mean *orientation*, that is, the projection onto the Earth's surface. The densification rate along the y-axis (i.e., East/West) also takes into account the fact that geographic *concentration* is a lot

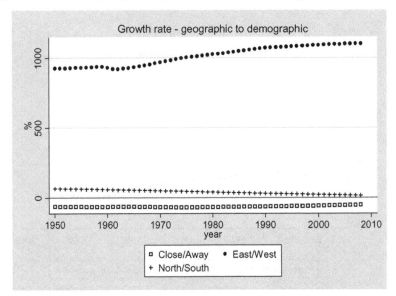

Fig. 8. Densification rate of concentration: from geographic to demographic.

smaller, that is, the effective geographic center is a lot closer to the Earth's center than the demographic center, which explains why the densification rate is so large. Thus, the outstanding result in this figure is that population is a lot more concentrated than land, and this is particularly telling along the East/West axis, meaning that population density is relatively more important in the East compared to land density.

Next let us turn to the move from the demographic concentration measure to the economic concentration measure (Equation (5b)). Figure 9 reports the importance of the three dimensions in the location of the demographic center (i.e., μ_X^D, μ_Y^D, μ_Z^D). Given the shift to the South of the center, shares are modified over time. However the basic picture remains one in which two dimensions of roughly equal magnitude, North/South and East/West drive the result, while the close/away dimension has no significant contribution. In short, and keeping in mind that concentration is larger in this case than for the geographic center (Figure 6), these shares basically illustrate that human population is concentrated in the Eastern side of the Northern hemisphere.

Figure 10 draws the densification rates when going from demographic to economic concentration (i.e., $g_{E,X}$, $g_{E,Y}$, $g_{E,Z}$). This time the pattern is more varied and changing than in the geographic–demographic comparison where Eastern densification is the major driver. Along the East–West axis, production appears to be a lot less concentrated than people, with a drop of close to 100%. However, production is more concentrated up North (z-axis) and, at least at the beginning of the period, closer to our

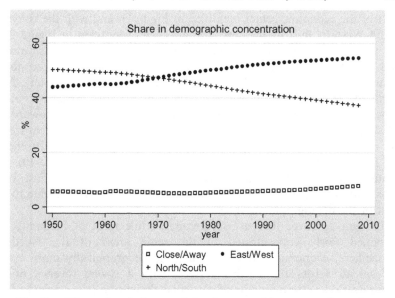

Fig. 9. Dimensional shares of the demographic center of gravity.

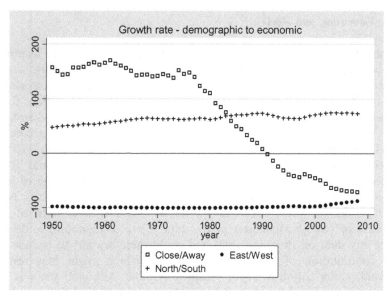

Fig. 10. Densification of the concentration rate from demographic to economic.

Euro-centric observer (x-axis). This pattern changes remarkably over time. Starting in 1976, there is a progressive drop of the close/away densification rate, which is associated with both the acceleration of the North-Eastern shift of the economic center identified in Figure 3, and with the converse South-Western shift of the demographic center identified in Figure 2. A few years after 1990, the relative magnitude of the covariances is reversed and the close/away densification rate becomes negative (the economic center is now deeper into the Earth than the demographic center). As a result, at the end of the sample period, there are now two dimensions along which production appears to be less concentrated than people: toward the West and further away from the observer. Note also that if current trends are pursued in the following decades (extrapolating the upward trend of the Eastern densification rate at the end of the period in Figure 10), one should expect that a similar reversal would affect the East–West densification rate (when the economic center will eventually locate to the East of the demographic center).

To sum up, over the past six decades, while most of humanity has remained fairly concentrated in the same areas of the Northern hemisphere, economic activity has become geographically more evenly widespread across the Earth's surface, with a strong reversal of the concentration pattern along one particular dimension (close/away) of the three-dimensional space.

3.3. Education and R&D

In the growth literature a large number of variables have been identified to be closely related to GDP growth. The location and shifts in the center of gravity for some important variables with this respect are analyzed. The variables used are: public expenditure in education, R&D expenditures, and the number of literate adults. The data are taken from the World Development Indicators (2010), are available at the country level and have been averaged over five 10-year periods from 1960 to 2009. Production shares have been used to allocate national R&D expenditure at the intra-national sublevel, while population shares have been used for public expenditures on education and literate adults. Note that results for these variables should be taken with a grain of salt because of two shortcomings in the data. First, some countries do not have any data on these variables and could therefore not be included in the computation of the center of gravity, which might bias results. Second, some countries report suspicious data. Although there is not much we can do about that, it has to be recognized that this may have biased the location of the centers of gravity. However, as most large (and hence influential in terms of the center of gravity) countries do provide reliable data, we believe that the main results reported here are reasonably robust.

Figure 11 shows the location of the center of gravity of R&D and education expenditures and literate adults. The number of literate adults

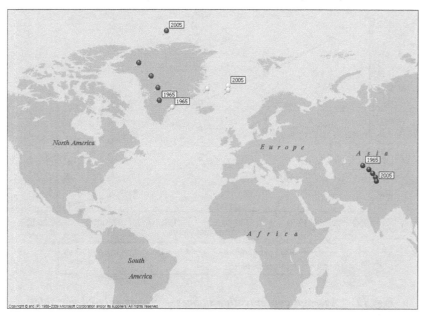

Fig. 11. Center of gravity 1965–2005 for literate adults (dark right balloons), R&D expenditures (dark left) and public education expenditures (pale). **Copyright © and (p) 1988–2009 Microsoft Corporation and/or its suppliers. All rights reserved.**

follows closely the location of the demographic center of gravity reported in Figure 1. The center of gravity for R&D expenditures locates more to the North and to the West than the economic center and is taking the shortest way to Tokyo. The center of gravity of public expenditures on education is not far from the economic center and is also moving eastwards.

The corresponding concentration indices are reported in Figure 12. As for the location analysis, we find that the time pattern for R&D and education expenditures is similar to the time pattern for economic activity, i.e. a decreasing geographic concentration (or increasing geographic dispersion) over time, while literacy concentration is quite stable, as in the case for the population at large. However, note that the initial level of concentration is larger for R&D and education expenditures, which suggests that at the beginning of the sample period innovation and human capital investment activities were quite concentrated amongst industrial countries.

To sum up, we computed the center of gravity for several growth related variables and found that R&D expenditures and public expenditures on education follow relatively closely the mean direction of the WECG (the center for R&D expenditures is however more to the West) and display also decreasing geographic concentration but at a higher level than the one

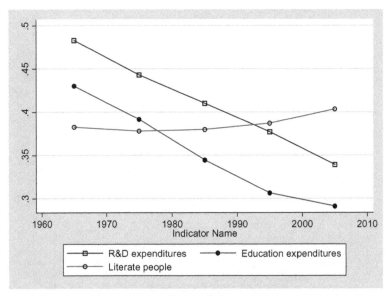

Fig. 12.   Average concentration indices – growth-related variables.

measured for economic activity. The mean direction for literate people follows the mean direction of the population, and concentration levels are also of comparable magnitude, although the one for literate people exhibits a slightly increasing trend.

4. Conclusion

This chapter presented estimates of the location of the world center of gravity of land, population, production, R&D, education expenditure and literate people and the associated concentration of these variables. The identified trends are broadly consistent with the common perception of centers of gravity shifting to the East. The demographic center of gravity is moving South and West-wards from Kazakhstan toward Afghanistan. The economic center of gravity starts off on the coast of Iceland and is heading East first very slowly and then very quickly towards the coast of Russia. During the last few years a small tendency toward the South can also be observed. During the 1950s, economic activity was already more geographically widespread than human population. It has become even more so over time, along two out of three spatial dimensions, and with a structural break that seems to coincide with the second oil shock at the end of the 1970s. The growth-related variables present a spatial pattern that is consistent with these stylized facts, with education and R&D expenditures exhibiting a strong correlation with overall output, while literate people and total population are closely linked.

This chapter includes information on the entire spatial distribution of population and economic activity and condensates it to a simple, tractable measure. This allows tracking the demographic and economic power balance at the world-wide level and taking geography into account, which in turn allows for a better understanding of past, present, and future distribution of political and economic power. Any field depending on global policies, such as trade, the financial and monetary system, environmental protection, global security and justice and also economic growth, have been and will be affected by the global distribution of economic power (see Quah, 2010).

It would be of interest in future research to test in which way the shift of the center of gravity influences international negotiations or regional development. The measure of the distance to the center of gravity could also be used in gravity equations of international trade (see Antweiler, 2008 for an application with time-varying distances) or in growth equations. Finally, two caveats should be kept in mind and could nurture further refinements. First, as was made clear upfront, this chapter focuses on economic concentration in a geographic sense, that is, in terms of dollars of production per square kilometer, which is related but different from economic concentration across people, that is, in terms of dollars of production per capita. Second, the fact that production turns out to be substantially less concentrated than human population is interesting per se but also calls for an explanation that would ideally encompass both policies (i.e., obstacles to the international mobility of factors of production) and economic incentives (in particular the agglomeration effects evidenced by the economic geography literature).

Acknowledgments

We thank Paul Cotofrei for his technical advice, Delphine Troyon-Guédat for excellent research assistance, and Olivier de La Grandville for his enthusiastic and inspiring support. The usual disclaimers apply.

Appendix A

Table A1.   *Average regional shares (%)*

	1950s	1960s	1970s	1980s	1990s	2000s
Area						
Oceania & Pacific Islands	6.05	6.05	6.05	6.05	6.05	6.05
North & Central America	16.73	16.73	16.73	16.73	16.73	16.73
South America	13.17	13.17	13.17	13.17	13.17	13.17
Europe (excl. FSU)	3.63	3.63	3.63	3.63	3.63	3.63
Former Soviet Union	17.01	17.01	17.01	17.01	17.01	17.01
Middle East & North Africa	8.49	8.49	8.49	8.49	8.49	8.49
Sub-Saharan Africa	17.61	17.61	17.61	17.61	17.61	17.61
South Asia	5.57	5.57	5.57	5.57	5.57	5.57
South East Asia	2.88	2.88	2.88	2.88	2.88	2.88
East Asia	8.86	8.86	8.86	8.86	8.86	8.86
Population						
Oceania & Pacific Islands	0.41	0.42	0.41	0.4	0.38	0.38
North & Central America	8.77	8.85	8.5	8.19	8.01	7.92
South America	4.58	5	5.28	5.54	5.67	5.78
Europe (excl. FSU)	14.8	13.37	11.73	10.23	8.99	8.1
Former Soviet Union	7.08	6.91	6.3	5.77	5.16	4.49
Middle East & North Africa	3.62	3.88	4.12	4.62	5.06	5.5
Sub-Saharan Africa	7.33	7.72	8.25	9.18	10.25	11.46
South Asia	20.08	20.6	21.26	22.45	23.54	24.6
South East Asia	6.53	6.87	7.17	7.51	7.73	7.84
East Asia	26.81	26.37	26.98	26.12	25.2	23.94
Production						
Oceania & Pacific Islands	1.37	1.34	1.3	1.26	1.28	1.26
North & Central America	30.31	28.46	26.37	26.11	26.04	24.55
South America	5.65	5.67	6.26	6.14	5.9	5.36
Europe (excl. FSU)	29.69	30.19	28.62	26.04	23.29	20.56
Former Soviet Union	9.59	9.9	9.34	8.21	4.56	3.98
Middle East & North Africa	2.57	2.82	3.57	4.01	3.98	3.99
Sub-Saharan Africa	2.76	2.58	2.52	2.24	2.03	2.04
South Asia	5.75	5.46	5.37	5.62	6.88	8.36
South East Asia	2.61	2.47	2.8	3.39	4.64	4.81
East Asia	9.71	11.1	13.84	16.99	21.4	25.1

Table A2. *Average regional shares in concentration (%)*

	1950s	1960s	1970s	1980s	1990s	2000s
Area						
Oceania & Pacific Islands	7.25	7.25	7.25	7.25	7.25	7.25
North & Central America	16.3	16.3	16.3	16.3	16.3	16.3
South America	13.64	13.64	13.64	13.64	13.64	13.64
Europe (excl. FSU)	4.06	4.06	4.06	4.06	4.06	4.06
Former Soviet Union	15.3	15.3	15.3	15.3	15.3	15.3
Middle East & North Africa	9.62	9.62	9.62	9.62	9.62	9.62
Sub-Saharan Africa	16.3	16.3	16.3	16.3	16.3	16.3
South Asia	5.71	5.71	5.71	5.71	5.71	5.71
South East Asia	2.59	2.59	2.59	2.59	2.59	2.59
East Asia	9.22	9.22	9.22	9.22	9.22	9.22
Population						
Oceania & Pacific Islands	0.49	0.51	0.5	0.48	0.47	0.47
North & Central America	7.2	7.27	6.99	6.78	6.67	6.67
South America	4.63	5.03	5.3	5.54	5.66	5.75
Europe (excl. FSU)	16.74	15.3	13.6	12.02	10.69	9.71
Former Soviet Union	7.81	7.69	7.08	6.57	5.94	5.22
Middle East & North Africa	4.25	4.59	4.91	5.54	6.12	6.67
Sub-Saharan Africa	6.71	7.08	7.56	8.38	9.31	10.4
South Asia	17.84	18.31	18.9	20.06	21.2	22.3
South East Asia	5.24	5.52	5.73	5.97	6.14	6.23
East Asia	29.1	28.7	29.43	28.66	27.81	26.58
Production						
Oceania & Pacific Islands	1.64	1.57	1.51	1.46	1.51	1.51
North & Central America	26.08	24.56	22.72	22.14	21.68	20.22
South America	6.07	6.06	6.59	6.48	6.12	5.56
Europe (excl. FSU)	31.17	31.19	29.21	26.95	24.7	22.37
Former Soviet Union	9.87	10.15	9.55	8.4	4.79	4.07
Middle East & North Africa	3.05	3.3	4.1	4.66	4.66	4.74
Sub-Saharan Africa	2.87	2.63	2.49	2.23	2.02	2.05
South Asia	5.64	5.42	5.36	5.44	6.48	7.69
South East Asia	2.44	2.33	2.54	3	3.92	4.01
East Asia	11.17	12.79	15.92	19.25	24.11	27.79

Appendix B. : The world economic center of gravity explained

Delphine A. Troyon-Guédat

B.1. How is a center of gravity measured?

In physics, the *center of mass* of a body formed by n individual point masses is the point where all the mass of the object can be considered to be concentrated. When the body is subject to a uniform gravitational field, as we assume here, its center of mass coincides with its *center of gravity*.

Consider first the case of a *discrete* distribution of n point masses located at coordinates (x_i, y_i), $i = 1, \ldots n$. The coordinates (x_{cg}, y_{cg}) of the center of gravity of this collection of points are given by the following formulas:

$$x_{cg} = \sum_{i=1}^{n} \frac{m_i}{m} x_i, \text{ and } y_{cg} = \sum_{i=1}^{n} \frac{m_i}{m} y_i \tag{B.1}$$

where m_i is the mass of point i and $m = \sum_{i=1}^{n} m_i$ is the total mass (in kilogram, or dollars for the WECG). In other words, the coordinates of the center of gravity are equal to the mass-weighted average of the coordinates of the individual points. Figure A1 represents the case of two point masses.

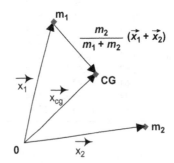

Fig. A1.   Center of gravity of a system with two point masses.

For a *continuous* mass distribution, the weighted average formulas are replaced by the following integral forms:

$$x_{cg} = \frac{\int x\rho(x)dx}{m} \text{ and } y_{cg} = \frac{\int y\rho(y)dy}{m} \tag{B.2}$$

Where $\rho(x)$ [or $\rho(y)$] is the mass per unit length (or density) of the body along the x (or y) dimension.

B.2. Location on a sphere: polar and Cartesian coordinates

B.2.1. Conversion between polar coordinates and Cartesian coordinates

Consider a system of polar (or spherical) coordinates where r represents the radius, θ the inclination angle (i.e., the angle between the zenith direction and the considered line segment) and φ the azimuth angle (i.e., the angle between the azimuth direction and the projection of the line segment on the reference plane). Then for any point, the polar coordinates (r, θ, φ) can be obtained from the Cartesian coordinates (x, y, z) by the following formulas:

$$r = \sqrt{x^2 + y^2 + z^2} \tag{B.3}$$

$$\theta = \cos^{-1}\left(\frac{z}{r}\right) \tag{B.3'}$$

$$\varphi = \tan^{-1}\left(\frac{y}{x}\right) \tag{B.3''}$$

Conversely, Cartesian coordinates may be retrieved from polar coordinates (r, θ, φ) where $r \in [0, \infty]$, $\theta \in [0, \pi]$ $\varphi \in [0, 2\pi]$, by:

$$x = r\ \sin(\theta)\cos(\varphi) \tag{B.4}$$

$$y = r\sin(\theta)\sin(\varphi) \tag{B.4'}$$

$$z = r\cos(\theta) \tag{B.4''}$$

These formulas assume that the two systems have the same origin, that the spherical reference plane is the Cartesian x-y plane, that θ is the inclination from the z direction, and that the azimuth angles are measured from the Cartesian x axis (so that the y axis has $\varphi = +90°$). If θ measures elevation from the reference plane instead of inclination from the zenith, $\cos^{-1}$ becomes $\sin^{-1}$, and the $\cos(\theta)$ and $\sin(\theta)$ above are switched.

B.2.2. Geographic coordinates

Geographic coordinates are a particular type of polar coordinates when all points locate on the surface of a planet (normally the Earth). They are measured in degrees and represent angular distances calculated from the center of the Earth.

It is important to note that the value of the angle depends on the choice of the origin (North or East, for example) and the sense of rotation (counter-clockwise or clockwise). Therefore, the conventions adopted for calculations should be clearly mentioned.

Latitude (θ) is used in degrees North (90°) or South (−90°) of the equator plane (0°) in the range $-90° \leq \theta \leq 90°$. It is an elevation instead of an inclination angle (see B.2.1).

Longitude (φ) is measured in degree East (180°) or West (−180°) from the conventional Greenwich reference meridian and its range is $-180° \leq \varphi \leq 180°$.

For positions on the Earth, the reference plane is usually taken to be the plane perpendicular to the axis of rotation. The zenith angle or inclination, which is (90°−θ) and ranges from 0 to 180°, is called colatitude in geography. The radial distance is the distance between the planet's center and some surface reference like for example sea level, which is approximately 6,371 km for the Earth.

B.3. Descriptive statistics on a sphere

Applying classical arithmetic averages to angles does not make sense. For example, the mean between 1° and 359° cannot be 180°. This is due to the property that the beginning and the end of the scale coincide (0° = 360°). To control for that property, which also affects the center of gravity calculations, we have to introduce two notions. The first one is the *mean direction*, which indicates the average direction in space of any distribution of point masses. The second one is the *mean resultant length*, which indicates the concentration of those points.

B.3.1. Circle

Let us start with the circle (or circular data), by considering the distribution of n points of equal mass along a trigonometric circle of unit radius. Those points are given by unit vectors $\vec{x}_i$, to $\vec{x}_n$, with Cartesian coordinates (x_1, y_1) to (x_n, y_n) and corresponding angles θ_1 to θ_n [$x_i = \cos(\theta_i)$, $y_i = \sin(\theta_i)$]. They are represented by the solid squares in Figure A2.

As all points have equal weights, applying formula (B.1), we get the following Cartesian coordinates for the center of gravity:

$$x_{cg} = \frac{1}{n}\sum_{i=1}^{n}\cos(\theta_i), \text{ and } y_{cg} = \frac{1}{n}\sum_{i=1}^{n}\sin(\theta_i) \tag{B.5}$$

The *mean direction* (or circular mean) is the angle between the center of gravity vector, $\vec{x}_{cg}$, and the horizontal axis. It is given by:

$$\bar{\theta} = \begin{cases} \tan^{-1}\left(\frac{y_{cg}}{x_{cg}}\right) & \text{if } x_{cg} \geq 0 \\ \tan^{-1}\left(\frac{y_{cg}}{x_{cg}}\right) + \pi & \text{if } x_{cg} < 0 \end{cases} \tag{B.6}$$

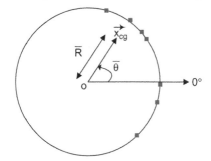

Fig. A2. Mean direction and mean resultant length on a circle.

The *mean resultant length* is the length of the center of gravity vector, given by:

$$\overline{R} = ||\vec{x}_{cg}|| = \sqrt{(x_{cg})^2 + (y_{cg})^2} \tag{B.7}$$

The unit vector of angle $\overline{\theta}$ can be referred to as the *mean direction vector* ($\vec{x}_0$). It corresponds to the normalized center of gravity vector ($\vec{x}_0 = \vec{x}_{cg}/||\vec{x}_{cg}||$).

If points are tightly clustered then $\overline{R}$ will be almost 1. In contrast, if points are widely and uniformly dispersed then $\overline{R}$ will be almost 0. The mean resultant length $\overline{R}$ is the most common (inverse) indicator of circular dispersion. However, as it is a concentration index, not a direct measure of dispersion, some authors prefer to refer to the circular variance, often defined as $1-\overline{R}^2$.

B.3.2. Sphere

When we work in a three-dimensional framework the same principles apply, except that the mean direction will be defined by two angles rather than one. Let us analyze then a distribution of n equally weighted points on the surface of a sphere with a unit radius. Each point i can be associated with a unit vector $\vec{x}_i$ with polar coordinates $(1, \theta_i, \varphi_i)$ and Cartesian coordinates (x_i, y_i, z_i) (Figure A3).

Following expression (B.1), the Cartesian coordinates of the center of gravity are given by:

$$x_{cg} = \frac{1}{n}\sum_{i=1}^{n}\sin(\theta_i)\cos(\varphi_i), \quad y_{cg} = \frac{1}{n}\sum_{i=1}^{n}\sin(\theta_i)\sin(\theta_i)\sin(\varphi_i),$$

$$z_{cg} = \frac{1}{n}\sum_{i=1}^{n}\cos(\theta_i) \tag{B.8}$$

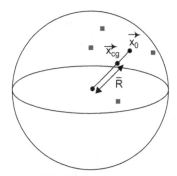

Fig. A3.   Mean direction and mean resultant length on a sphere.

where θ represents the colatitude so that $90°-\theta$ denotes latitude and φ denotes longitude.

We can retrieve the polar coordinates of the center of gravity, which reflect the *mean direction*, applying the following expressions (i.e., equations (B.6) adapted to the three dimensional case):

$$\theta_{cg} = \cos^{-1}(z_{cg}). \tag{B.9}$$

$$\varphi_{cg} = \begin{cases} \tan^{-1}\left(\frac{y_{cg}}{x_{cg}}\right) & \text{if } x_{cg} \geq 0 \\ \tan^{-1}\left(\frac{y_{cg}}{x_{cg}}\right) + \pi & \text{if } x_{cg} < 0 \end{cases} \tag{B.9'}$$

And the *mean resultant length* is given by:

$$\overline{R} = \|\vec{x}_{cg}\| = \sqrt{(x_{cg})^2 + (y_{cg})^2 + (z_{cg})^2} \tag{B.10}$$

As before regarding the circle, equation (B.10) is a measure of the concentration of the distribution on the surface of the sphere. Note also that the *mean direction vector*, $\vec{x}_0$, obtained as the normalized center of gravity vector, that is,

$$\overline{x}_0 = \frac{1}{\|\overline{x}_{cg}\|} \overline{x}_{cg} \tag{B.11}$$

corresponds to the projection of the center of gravity vector upon the surface of the sphere, as illustrated by Figure A3.

B.4. Specific cases

In this section we consider particular cases of centers of gravity calculations on spheres, which are useful to analyze the results reported in the chapter.

B.4.1. Spherical caps

Let us remind first that the surface of a spherical cap, as the one represented by Figure A4, is given by:

$$S = 2\pi r\, h = \pi(a^2 + h^2) \tag{B.12}$$

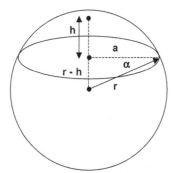

Fig. A4.   A spherical cap.

Where h is the height of the spherical cap, r the radius of the sphere, and a the radius of the spherical cap. This simple formula has important consequences for center of gravity calculations.

To see why, assume now that we slice this spherical cap into m spherical rings, parallel to the equator plane, and of equal "thickness" along the height dimension. A corollary of formula (B.12) is that the surface of each one of these rings is strictly identical. This may appear slightly surprising at first sight, as the radius of the ring becomes smaller and smaller when one gets closer to the pole. However, working oppositely is the fact that the difference between the inner and outer circle of each ring becomes bigger and bigger, which exactly compensates the first effect.

Let us finally cover this spherical cap by points of equal weight uniformly, in the sense that the number of points per unit of surface remains constant. Consider calculating the Cartesian coordinates of the center of gravity of this spherical cap. As the cap is perfectly symmetric along the polar axis, all points perfectly compensate each other along the x and y dimensions when applying formula (B.1), that is, $x_{cg} = 0$ and $y_{cg} = 0$. What remains is the height, or the z dimension, but for which we know that we can decompose the cap into m slices of equal weight, and whose distance to the origin vary between $(r-h)$ and r. At the end of the day the mean direction is only determined by the average distance of the cap with respect to the origin, namely:

$$x_{cg} = 0, \quad y_{cg} = 0, \quad z_{cg} = r - \frac{h}{2} \tag{B.13}$$

For example, if we consider the spherical cap which slices the northern hemisphere into two equal parts, with a height equal to just half of the radius, then the corresponding center of gravity vector will have coordinates (0,0,0.75r).

B.4.2. A case of three spherical caps

To conclude, consider the three caps case represented in Figure A5. Those caps are not perfectly symmetrical nor aligned along the polar axis, but we assume that we can apply the above principles to estimate their centers of gravity. Those caps are named after the three main economic zones (USA, EU, Asia) that matter most in terms of world GDP or population. Thus, although very sketchy, Figure A5 may serve as a reference diagram to analyze the actual shifts of the WECG and WDCG.

Each pale point represents the projection of the WECG upon the Earth's surface (or the extremity of the mean direction vector) for a given year. The corresponding world center of gravity vector is a weighted average of the center of gravity vectors of each cap. The pale points are shifting to the East, because the economic weight of Asia is continuously increasing along time. A similar construction lies behind the dark points, which represent the projections of the WDCG on the Earth's surface. Here again, there is a temporal shift, first towards the South-East, then toward

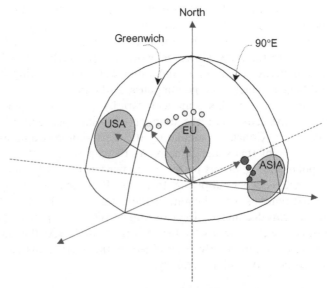

Fig. A5.   A stylized vision of the world.

the South-West, a reversal that would be best explained by enriching the diagram with other continents (see the main text for more details).

References

Antweiler, W. (2008). *Internal and external distance: Gravity depends on it.* Mimeo.

Chen, X. (2008). *Description of Gecon 2.11.* Mimeo. Retrieved from http:// gecon.yale.edu/.

French, H. W. (2005, April 9). China meets India, hints of a global shift. *New York Times.*

Grether, J. M., & Mathys, N. A. (2010). Is the world's economic center of gravity already in Asia?. *Area, 42*(1), 47–50.

Maddison, A. (2010). Statistics on world population, GDP and per capita GDP. Retrieved from http://www.ggdc.net/MADDISON/.

Mardia, K. V., & Jupp, P. E. (2000). *Directional statistics.* Wiley, New York.

Nordhaus, W. (2006). Geography and macroeconomics: New data and new findings. *Proceedings of the National Academy of Sciences (US), 103*(10), 3510–3517.

Nordhaus, W., Azam, Q., Corderi, D., Hood, K., Makarova, N., Mohammed, M., Miltner, A., Weiss, J. (2006). The G-Econ database on gridded output: Methods and data. Retrieved from http:// gecon.yale.edu/.

Quah, D. (2011). The global economy's shifting centre of gravity. *Global Policy, 2*(1), 3–9.

World Development Indicators.(2010). Retrieved from http://databank. worldbank.org/ddp/home.do. The World Bank, Washington DC.

CHAPTER 11

Homothetic Multisector Growth Models

Bjarne S. Jensen[a] and Ulla Lehmijoki[b]

[a]*Department of Environmental and Business Economics, University of Southern Denmark, Niels Bohrs Vej 9, DK-6700 Esbjerg, Denmark*
E-mail address: bsj@sam.sdu.dk
[b]*Department of Political and Economic Studies, University of Helsinki, P.O. Box 17 (Arkadiankatu), FIN-00014 Helsinki, Finland*
E-mail address: ulla.lehmijoki@helsinki.fi

Abstract
Multisector growth (MSG) models have a special aura that is shared with computable general equilibrium (CGE) models. Both of them, with their many sectors (industries and goods), are known as trying to convert Walrasian general equilibrium systems from an abstract economy representation into workable models with industrial structures changing as actually observed. Yet, they are plagued by severe problems. First, they are difficult subjects involving systems of nonlinear equations. Second, their prevalent numerical (algorithmic) methodology offers little in the way of showing a clear overall picture and understanding the plethora of numbers pouring out from model simulations. The great wood is not seen for all the trees. Hence, the main objective is to set out comparative static and dynamic systems for succinctly stating and explicitly solving MSG models. The Walrasian general equilibrium is completely stated by one equation and the multisector dynamics by one differential equation. Benchmark solutions are shown for three Constant Elasticity of Substitution (CES) parameter regimes of a 10-sector general equilibrium model.

Keywords: Neoclassical growth models, multisector models, computable general equilibrium models

JEL classifications: O40, O41, C68

1. Introduction

Naturally, through more than 50 years, the basic one-sector growth model of Solow (1956) has been extended in many directions (Solow, 1999, 2000). Earlier, there were explorations to equip the macro model with an industrial structure by including more sectors (goods and industries).

Frontiers of Economics and Globalization
Volume 11   ISSN: 1574-8715
DOI: 10.1108/S1574-8715(2011)0000011016

The seminal work on two-sector growth models with flexible sector technologies was done by Uzawa (1961/1962, 1963). In this work, a framework for efficient factor allocation using the price mechanism is set up – referred to as a "miniature Walrasian general equilibrium system" (Solow, 1961/1962, p. 49; Walras, 1954). However, in contrast to Solow (1956) – where the benchmark examples of the explicit solutions of the basic dynamic model were rigorously established for the CES technology parameter values of the factor substitution elasticity, $\sigma = 0,1,2$, allowing alternatively for steady-state growth or persistent growth per capita – there was no explicit (parametric) sectorial production functions used in these two-sector growth models (Uzawa, 1961/1962, 1963; Jensen, 1994). The qualitative analysis and the subsequent focus on various sufficient conditions for the stability of the steady states (Inada, 1964) hampered further progress and extensions toward multisector growth (MSG) models. But the allocation aspects of two-factor, two-sector general equilibrium model were given due to attention in trade theory by Jones (1965). The implications of heterogeneous capital in a two-sector neoclassical vintage growth model with embodied Harrod-neutral technological progress and with a constant saving rate were investigated by Stiglitz (1969). It was shown that the labor-intensive sector would attract all the newer (better) machines. However, the analysis was qualitative with emphasis on the existence and uniqueness of momentary equilibrium and steady states, using the Inada restrictions upon the sectorial production functions.

So far, most extensions of Solow (1956) have dealt with the multifactor elaborations of the aggregate growth model (Taylor & Woodford, 1999; Jensen, 2009). The human capital augmented macro model with the Cobb–Douglas (CD) technology was studied in Mankiw, Romer, and Weil (1992); it is with constant and/or optimal saving rates included in the standard textbooks of growth theory and macroeconomics (Barro & Sala-i-Martin, 2004; Romer, 2001). On schooling and externalities, see Carstensen, Gundlach, and Hartman (2009). Further augmentation with several types of capital goods was analyzed by Nonneman and Vanhoudt (1996). Parametric solutions with multifactor CD and CES technologies were examined in Jensen, Alsholm, Larsen, and Jensen (2005), particularly related to the exposition in Romer (2001).

Much of the endogenous growth theory with emphasis on innovation-driven growth and modeling technological progress – R&D (human capital) producing new (better) varieties (or larger numbers) of inter-mediate goods for the production function of the final output – can be seen as the particular multiple input extensions of the one-sector two-factor growth model. Thus, the textbooks of Barro and Sala-i-Martin (2004) and Aghion and Howitt (1998) do not go beyond two final goods (industries).

The latest handbook on economic growth (Aghion & Durlauf, 2005) can neither report on much attention to multisectoral growth patterns. Regarding territories into which growth theory has not expanded, Solow (2005, p. 4) noted "I suspect that early on one would have expected much more work on multi-sector growth models than there has been." Long ago, Kuznets (1966, p. 1) wrote, "We identify the economic growth of a nation as a sustained increase in per capita or per worker product, most often accompanied by an increase in population and usually by sweeping structural changes."

The economic literature contains an early genuine N-sector extension of Solow (1956), that of Dhrymes (1962). This MSG model used CD sectoral production functions, and the demand functions employed were of the Graham type – which had long been used in trade models (McKenzie, 1954, p. 149). The "Graham type" demand functions imply that a constant proportion (share) of total income (consumer expenditures) is devoted to each final good regardless of its price. In other words, the price and income elasticities of consumer demand (Marshallian) are unity; hence, the implied preferences are given by the ordinal utility function of CD form. Thus, Dhrymes (1962) is a fully fledged MSG model parameterized by CD specifications. The CD assumptions have always been used first in obtaining explicit static and dynamic model solutions. Although the sectorial capital-labor ratios, the wage-rental ratio, and the overall factor-endowment (capital-labor) ratio are changing in this multisector CD economy, they all change at the same rate and leave the sectorial allocation fractions of labor and capital unchanged. This invariance of the occupational industrial structure is evidently counterfactual consequences of the CD assumptions.

The CD growth model of Dhrymes (1962) serves us mainly as the simplest benchmark case within the economically much richer CES parameter family of consumer preferences and sector technologies. Thus, our main objective is to establish the comparative static and dynamic systems for explicitly solving the CES MSG model. Numerical illustrations are shown for three CES parameter regimes of a 10-sector general equilibrium model – continuing the seminal work within the traditions of the Solow – Uzawa legacy.

Attention to dynamic general equilibrium models with the industrial patterns of structural change is given in Echevarria (1997) and Kongsamut, Rebelo, and Xie (2001); both papers study three-sector growth models. But the sectorial production functions in Kongsamut et al. (2001) are identical up to proportionality constant, and hence, the relative prices of three different goods are not affected by factor prices, factor allocations, or change over time. The factor reallocations and sectorial changes in output composition are entirely driven by differences in the income elasticities of demand (here the linear expenditure system and its nonhomothetic preferences are used in an intertemporal optimization). Echevarria (1997) uses three CD technologies and nonhomothetic preferences that converge to CD preferences. The time paths in this three-sector model are asymptotically equivalent to the steady-state values in the CD growth model of Dhrymes (1962) with unitary demand elasticities.

Our analytic N-sector- and simulated 10-sector CES growth models intend to fully show how – in the short and long run – the time paths of the

CES solutions for relative prices as the invisible hand (the general equilibrium prices of commodities and factors) perform its allocative and market clearing role (Arrow, 1974, p. 253) on the tendency of goods and factor markets to balance "When all due allowances are made, the coherence of individual economic decisions is remarkable. As income rise and demand shifts, for example from food to clothes and housing, the labor force and productive facilities follow suit. Similarly, even more surprising to the layman, there is mutual interaction between shifts in technology and the allocation of the labor force. As technology improves exogenously, through innovations, the labor made redundant does not become permanently unemployed, but find its place in the economy. It is truly amazing that the lessons of both theory and over a century of history are still so misunderstood. On the other hand, a growing accumulation of the instruments of production raises real wages and in turn induces a rise in the prices of labor-intensive commodities relative to those which use little labor. All these phenomena show that by and large and in the long view of history, the economic system adjusts with a considerable degree of smoothness and indeed of rationality to changes in the fundamental facts within which it operates."

The chapter is organized as follows. Section 2 starts with the central theoretical core of the growth theory consisting of production, cost, and utility functions. The national income and product accounting of a multisector economy and resource accounting must next be carefully integrated to satisfy Walras's law and general equilibrium conditions. In Section 3, the general equilibrium of the homothetic multisector economy with two primary factors (labor and capital) is expressed compactly by just one equation. The operating invisible hand – the correspondence between relative commodity prices and relative factor prices – is parametrically fully illustrated. Section 4 introduces the equations of factor accumulations, which give the laws of motions that must be solved. The dynamics of our homothetic multisector economy can be expressed by one differential equation. Section 5 presents in detail the benchmark solutions of the general equilibrium dynamics for the CES 10-sector economy with three different parameter regimes. Section 6 offers final comments.

2. Structure of homothetic multisector economies

2.1. CES sector technologies and cost functions

Consider an economy consisting of N industries (sectors). Sectoral technologies, $F_i(L_i, K_i)$, are described by nonnegative smooth concave homogeneous production functions with constant returns to scale in labor and capital,

$$Y_i = F_i(L_i, K_i) \equiv L_i f_i(k_i) \equiv L_i y_i; \quad L_i \neq 0; \quad F_i(0,0) = 0; \quad i = 1, \ldots, N \quad (1)$$

where $f_i(k_i)$, is strictly concave and monotonically increasing in the capital-labor ratio $k_i \in [0, \infty]$. The CES forms – (Arrow, Chenery, Minhas, & Solow, 1961, p. 230), de La Grandville (2009, p. 90) – of $F_i(L_i, K_i)$, (1), $\gamma_i > 0$, $0 < a_i < 1$, $\sigma_i > 0$, are

$$Y_i = F_i(L_i, K_i) = \gamma_i L_i^{1-a_i} K_i^{a_i} \equiv L_i f_i(k_i) \equiv L_i y_i \tag{2}$$

$$Y_i = F_i(L_i, K_i) = \gamma_i[(1-a_i)L_i^{\sigma_i-1/\sigma_i} + a_i K_i^{\sigma_i-1/\sigma_i}]^{\sigma_i/\sigma_i-1} \equiv L_i f_i(k_i) \equiv L_i y_i \tag{3}$$

where the CES forms of $f_i(k_i)$ and $f_i'(k_i)$ are

$$\sigma_i = 1, \quad f_i(k_i) = \gamma_i k_i^{a_i}, \quad f_i'(k_i) = \gamma_i a_i k_i^{a_i-1} \tag{4}$$

$$\sigma_i \neq 1, \quad f_i(k_i) = \gamma_i[(1-a_i) + a_i k_i^{(\sigma_i-1)/\sigma_i}]^{\sigma_i/(\sigma_i-1)} \tag{5}$$

$$\sigma_i \neq 1, \quad f_i'(k_i) = \gamma_i a_i[a_i + (1-a_i)k_i^{-(\sigma_i-1)/\sigma_i}]^{1/(\sigma_i-1)} \tag{6}$$

By evaluating (5) and (6), the limits of $f_i(k_i)$, $f_i'(k_i)$ are $[\sigma \gtrless 1 \Rightarrow a^{\sigma/(\sigma-1)} \lessgtr 1]$:

$$\sigma_i < 1 \quad : \quad \lim_{k_i \to \infty} f_i(k_i) = \gamma_i(1-a_i)^{\sigma_i/\sigma_i-1}; \lim_{k_i \to \infty} f_i'(k_i) = 0 \tag{7}$$

$$\sigma_i > 1 : \lim_{k_i \to \infty} f_i(k_i) = \infty; \quad \lim_{k_i \to \infty} f_i'(k_i) = \gamma_i a_i^{\sigma_i/\sigma_i-1} \tag{8}$$

In each sector, we have the competitive producer equilibrium equations,

$$w = P_i \cdot MP_{L_i} = P_i \cdot [f_i(k_i) - k_i f_i'(k_i)]; \quad r = P_i \cdot MP_{K_i} = P_i \cdot f_i'(k_i) \tag{9}$$

$$P_i Y_i = w L_i + r K_i; \quad P_i = \frac{(w + r k_i)}{y_i} = \frac{r(\omega + k_i)}{y_i}; \quad \omega = \frac{w}{r} \tag{10}$$

$$\varepsilon_{L_i} = \frac{w L_i}{P_i Y_i} = \frac{\omega}{\omega + k_i}; \quad \varepsilon_{K_i} = \frac{r K_i}{P_i Y_i} = \frac{f_i'(k_i)}{f_i(k_i)/k_i} = \frac{k_i}{\omega + k_i}; \quad \varepsilon_{K_i} + \varepsilon_{L_i} = 1 \tag{11}$$

The marginal rates of technical substitution (MRTS) – $\omega_i(k_i)$ – are monotone increasing functions,

$$\left(\frac{w}{r}\right)_i = \omega_i = \omega_i(k_i) = \frac{MP_{L_i}}{MP_{K_i}} = \frac{f_i(k_i)}{f_i'(k_i)} - k_i \tag{12}$$

With the CES technologies, (4) and (6), the monotone relations between (ω_i), (12), and the sectorial factor ratios (k_i) and ε_{K_i}, (11), have the parametric forms:

$$\omega_i = \frac{1-a_i}{a_i} k_i^{1/\sigma_i}; \quad k_i = \frac{1}{c_i}(\omega_i)^{\sigma_i}; \quad c_i = \left[\frac{1-a_i}{a_i}\right]^{\sigma_i}; \quad \omega_i, k_i \in [0, \infty) \tag{13}$$

$$\varepsilon_{K_i} = \left[1 + \frac{1-a_i}{a_i}k_i^{1-\sigma_i/\sigma_i}\right]^{-1} = \frac{1}{1+c_i\omega^{1-\sigma_i}}; \quad \varepsilon_{L_i} = \frac{c_i\omega^{1-\sigma_i}}{1+c_i\omega^{1-\sigma_i}} \quad (14)$$

The dual CES cost function $C_i(w, r, Y_i)$ to CES technology $F_i(L_i, K_i)$, (3) is,

$$C_i(w, r, Y_i) = r/\gamma_i[a_i^{\sigma_i} + (1-a_i)^{\sigma_i}(w/r)^{1-\sigma_i}]^{1/1-\sigma_i} Y_i \quad (15)$$

Hence, the unit (average/marginal) cost (commodity price) functions are:

$$P_i = AC_i(w, r) = MC_i(w, r) = r/\gamma_i[a_i^{\sigma_i} + (1-a_i)^{\sigma_i}(w/r)^{1-\sigma_i}]^{1/1-\sigma_i} \quad (16)$$

$$MC_i(w/r) = (1/\gamma_i)\,a_i^{\sigma_i/(1-\sigma_i)}\left[1 + c_i(w/r)^{1-\sigma_i}\right]^{1/1-\sigma_i}; \quad c_i = \left[\frac{1-a_i}{a_i}\right]^{\sigma_i} \quad (17)$$

By (15)–(17), the relative CES cost functions (relative commodity prices) are:

$$p_{ij} = \frac{P_i}{P_j} = \frac{MC_i(w/r)}{MC_j(w/r)} = \frac{(1/\gamma_i)a_i^{\sigma_i/(1-\sigma_i)}[1 + c_i(w/r)^{1-\sigma_i}]^{1/1-\sigma_i}}{(1/\gamma_j)a_j^{\sigma_j/(1-\sigma_j)}[1 + c_j(w/r)^{1-\sigma_j}]^{1/1-\sigma_j}} \quad (18)$$

$$= \frac{\gamma_j a_j^{\sigma_j/(\sigma_j-1)}\left[1 + c_j(w/r)^{1-\sigma_j}\right]^{1/(\sigma_j-1)}}{\gamma_i a_i^{\sigma_i/(\sigma_i-1)}\left[1 + c_i(w/r)^{1-\sigma_i}\right]^{1/(\sigma_i-1)}} = \Phi\left[\frac{w}{r}\right]; \quad \frac{w}{r} = \omega \in [0, \infty) \quad (19)$$

With $\sigma_i = \sigma_j = \sigma$, we get, cf. (19),

$$p_{ij} = \Phi(w/r) = \frac{\gamma_j}{\gamma_i}\left[\left[\frac{a_j}{a_i}\right]^\sigma \frac{1 + c_j(w/r)^{1-\sigma}}{1 + c_i(w/r)^{1-\sigma}}\right]^{1/\sigma-1}; \quad c_i = \left[\frac{1-a_i}{a_i}\right]^\sigma \quad (20)$$

In the limit case of (20) with $\sigma = 1$ (Cobb–Douglas), we obtain:

$$p_{ij} = \Phi(w/r) = \frac{\gamma_j a_j^{a_j}(1-a_j)^{1-a_j}}{\gamma_i a_i^{a_i}(1-a_i)^{1-a_i}}\left[\frac{w}{r}\right]^{a_j-a_i}; \quad w/r = \omega \in [0, \infty) \quad (21)$$

2.2. CES preferences and consumer demands

As we are setting up a multisector (N) growth model with sector technologies using two primary factors, labor and capital (physical), we need at least one capital good sector. Let sector 1 be the capital good industry.

The consumer demand in the multisector economy is here governed by homothetic preferences, and they are expressed by parametric ordinal utility functions. We use the expenditure shares (e_i) derived from the CES class, (3):

$$U(Y_2, \ldots, Y_N) = \gamma_u; \quad \sum_{i=2}^{N} \alpha_i \, Y_i^{\sigma_u - 1/\sigma_u}; \quad \alpha_i > 0, \quad \sum_{i=2}^{N} \alpha_i = 1; \quad \sigma_u > 0 \qquad (22)$$

$$e_i = \frac{P_i Y_i}{\displaystyle\sum_{i=2}^{N} P_i Y_i} = \frac{\alpha_i^{\sigma_u} P_i^{1-\sigma_u}}{\displaystyle\sum_{j=2}^{N} \alpha_j^{\sigma_u} P_j^{1-\sigma_u}} = \left[\sum_{j=2}^{N} \left[\frac{\alpha_j}{\alpha_i} \right]^{\sigma_u} p_{ij}^{\sigma_u - 1} \right]^{-1}; \quad i = 2, \ldots, N \qquad (23)$$

$$e_i = e_i(p_{i2}, \ldots, p_{iN}) = \left[1 + \sum_{j=2, j \neq i}^{N} \left[\frac{\alpha_j}{\alpha_i} \right]^{\sigma_u} p_{ij}^{\sigma_u - 1} \right]^{-1}; \quad i = 2, \ldots, N \qquad (24)$$

Linking the relative consumer prices in e_i (24) to the cost prices, (18)–(19), we get

$$e_i(\omega) = \left[1 + \sum_{j=2, j \neq i}^{N} \left[\frac{\alpha_j}{\alpha_i} \right]^{\sigma_u} p_{ij}(\omega)^{\sigma_u - 1} \right]^{-1}; \quad i = 2, \ldots, N; \quad \sum_{i=2}^{N} e_i(\omega) = 1 \qquad (25)$$

for $\alpha_i = 1/N$ and equal e_i, (25) (Dixit & Stiglitz, 1977, p. 298). Price and income (expenditure) elasticities of the CES system of the Marshallian demands (22)–(24) are (Chung, 1994, p. 58; Shoven & Whalley, 1992, p. 96),

$$E(Y_i, P_i) = -\sigma_u(1 - e_i) - e_i; \quad E(Y_i, P_j) = (\sigma_u - 1)e_j; \quad E(Y_i, C) = 1 \qquad (26)$$

Although there are only $N-1$ relative commodity prices involved in a N-sector economy, we need, in a multisectorial setting, to be careful about including all the relevant cross-price (relative) ratios from (19) into the respective budget shares in (24)–(25).

Thus for the 9 budget shares used in our 10-sector model below, we state:

$$e_2 = e_2(p_{22}, \ldots, p_{210}) = \left[1 + \sum_{j=2, j \neq i}^{10} \left[\frac{\alpha_j}{\alpha_2} \right]^{\sigma_u} p_{2j}^{\sigma_u - 1} \right]^{-1} \qquad (27)$$

$$e_3 = e_3(p_{32}, \ldots, p_{310}) = \left[1 + \sum_{j=2, j \neq i}^{10} \left[\frac{\alpha_j}{\alpha_3} \right]^{\sigma_u} p_{3j}^{\sigma_u - 1} \right]^{-1} \qquad (28)$$

$$e_{10} = e_{10}(p_{102}, \ldots, p_{1010}) = \left[1 + \sum_{j=2, j \neq i}^{10} \left[\frac{\alpha_j}{\alpha_{10}} \right]^{\sigma_u} p_{10j}^{\sigma_u - 1} \right]^{-1} \qquad (29)$$

2.3. Factor endowments, allocation fractions, and GDP

The factor endowments, total labor force (L) and the total capital stock (K), are inelastically supplied and are fully employed, that is,

$$L = \sum_{i=1}^{N} L_i; \quad \sum_{i=1}^{N} \frac{L_i}{L} \equiv \sum_{i=1}^{N} \lambda_{L_i} = 1 \tag{30}$$

$$K = \sum_{i=1}^{N} K_i; \quad \sum_{i=1}^{N} \frac{K_i}{K} \equiv \sum_{i=1}^{N} \lambda_{K_i} \equiv 1 \tag{31}$$

$$\frac{K}{L} \equiv k \equiv \sum_{i=1}^{N} \lambda_{L_i} k_i \tag{32}$$

where λ_{L_i}, λ_{K_i} (30)–(31) are the factor allocation fractions.

Free factor mobility between multiple sectors (industries) and efficient factor allocation impose the common MRTS condition, cf. (12), (9),

$$\omega = \omega_i = \omega_i(k_i); \quad i = 1, \dots, N \tag{33}$$

Gross domestic product (GDP), Y, is the total of sectorial producer revenues [monetary value of sector outputs, $Y_i = F_i(L_i.K_i) = L_i y_i$, (3)],

$$Y_i = L \lambda_{L_i} y_i; \quad Y \equiv \sum_{i=1}^{N} P_i Y_i = L \left[\sum_{i=1}^{N} P_i \lambda_{L_i} y_i \right] \equiv L y \tag{34}$$

With perfect competition, (9)–(10), Y is equal to the total factor income

$$Y = wL + rK = L(w + rk) = Lr(\omega + k) = Ly \tag{35}$$

The factor income distribution shares, $\delta_K + \delta_L = 1$, become, cf. (35), (11),

$$\delta_K \equiv \frac{rK}{Y} = \frac{rk}{y} = \frac{k}{\omega + k}; \quad \delta_L \equiv \frac{wL}{Y} = \frac{w}{y} = \frac{\omega}{\omega + k} \tag{36}$$

Thus, by (36),

$$\frac{\delta_K}{\delta_L} \equiv \frac{k}{\omega} \Leftrightarrow k \equiv \frac{\omega}{\delta_L} \frac{\delta_K}{\delta_L} \tag{37}$$

The composition of GDP (34) as final expenditure shares, s_i, are

$$s_i = \frac{P_i Y_i}{Y}; \quad \sum_{i=1}^{N} s_i \equiv \sum_{i=1}^{N} \frac{P_i Y_i}{Y} = 1 \tag{38}$$

LEMMA 1. The macro factor income shares δ_L, δ_K (36) are final expenditure-weighted (38) combinations of the sectorial factor (cost) shares, ε_{L_i}, ε_{K_i},

$$\delta_L = \sum_{i=1}^{N} s_i \varepsilon_{L_i}; \quad \delta_K = \sum_{i=1}^{N} s_i \varepsilon_{K_i}; \quad \delta_K + \delta_L = 1 \tag{39}$$

The factor allocation fractions (30)–(31) are obtained by

$$L_i/L = \lambda_L = s_i \varepsilon_L / \delta_L; \quad \frac{K_i}{K} = \lambda_{K_i} = \frac{s_i \varepsilon_{K_i}}{\delta_K} \tag{40}$$

The total factor-endowment ratio, K/L, satisfies the identity, cf. (37), (39):

$$\frac{K}{L} = k = \frac{\omega \delta_K}{\delta_L} = \frac{\omega \sum_{i=1}^{N} s_i \varepsilon_{K_i}}{\sum_{i=1}^{N} s_i \varepsilon_{L_i}} \tag{41}$$

which is a convenient representation of the Walras's law (identity) and (32).

PROOF. By definition, we have

$$\delta_L = \frac{wL}{Y} = \frac{[wL_1 + wL_2 + \cdots + wL_N]}{Y} \tag{42}$$

$$\delta_K = \frac{rK}{Y} = \frac{[rK_1 + rK_2 + \cdots + rK_N]}{Y} \tag{43}$$

From (10) and (38), we get

$$wL_i = \varepsilon_{L_i} P_i Y_i = s_i \varepsilon_{L_i} Y,; \quad rK_i = \varepsilon_{K_i} P_i Y_i = s_i \varepsilon_{K_i} Y \tag{44}$$

Hence, by (42)–(43) and (44), we obtain (39). Next, as stated in (40), we have

$$\lambda_{L_i} = \frac{L_i}{L} = \frac{wL_i}{wL} = \frac{s_i \varepsilon_{L_i} Y}{\delta_L Y} = \frac{s_i \varepsilon_{L_i}}{\delta_L} \tag{45}$$

$$\lambda_{K_i} = \frac{K_i}{K} = \frac{rK_i}{rK} = \frac{s_i \varepsilon_{K_i} Y}{\delta_K Y} = \frac{s_i \varepsilon_{K_i}}{\delta_K} \tag{46}$$

as in Jensen and Larsen (2005, p. 24).

With one capital good industry (sector 1), the final demand decomposition of the aggregate expenditures, GDP (Y), into gross investment expenditures (I) and total consumption expenditures (C) becomes,

$$I = P_1 Y_1; \quad C = \sum_{i=2}^{N} P_i Y_i; \quad Y = C + I; \quad s_1 = \frac{I}{Y} \tag{47}$$

Evidently, the connection between the GDP shares (38), (47), and (23)–(25) is

$$s_i(\omega) = (1 - s_1)e_i(\omega) \ ; \quad i = 2, \ldots, N \tag{48}$$

3. Walrasian equilibrium of two-factor-multisector economies

The demand side of the multisector economy is expressed by the GDP expenditure shares, s_i: (38), (47)–(48), and (25). The supply side of the economy – operating with full (30)–(31) and efficient factor utilization, (33)– is always summarized by the sectorial factor allocation fractions λ_{L_i}, λ_{K_i}, (40), which, in turn, are determined by $s_i(\omega)$ (47)–(48), (25), and the sectorial cost shares $\varepsilon_{L_i}(\omega)$, $\varepsilon_{K_i}(\omega)$, (14). Thus, we have established:

THEOREM 1. The Walrasian equilibrium (competitive general equilibrium) states, by market clearing prices on the commodity and factor markets and Pareto efficient endowments allocations, are – with homogeneous production functions of degree one, and with any homothetic preferences – given by: $\forall \ k, \ \omega \in R_+,$

$$k = \frac{\omega \ \delta_K(\omega)}{\delta_L(\omega)} = \frac{\omega \sum_{i=1}^{N} s_i(\omega)\varepsilon_{K_i}(\omega)}{\sum_{i=1}^{N} s_i(\omega)\varepsilon_{L_i}(\omega)} = \Psi(\omega) \tag{49}$$

COROLLARY 1.1. With CES sector technologies and any homothetic utility function, the Walrasian equilibrium $k = \Psi(\omega)$ becomes by (49) and (14):

$$k = \frac{\omega \sum_{i=1}^{N} s_i(\omega)(1 + c_i\omega^{1-\sigma_i})^{-1}}{1 - \sum_{i=1}^{N} s_i(\omega)(1 + c_i\omega^{1-\sigma_i})^{-1}} = \Psi(\omega); \quad \lim_{\omega \to 0} \Psi(\omega) = 0; \quad \lim_{\omega \to \infty} \Psi(\omega) = \infty$$

$$\tag{50}$$

By (49)–(50), the competitive general equilibrium of the two-factor and N-sector ($2 \times N$) economy is by composite functions reduced to a *single* equation (link) between the factor-endowment ratio (k) and the factor price ratio (ω). Experiments in comparative statics are straightforward.

But having obtained (ω) from (50), we can go back through, (19), (25) (14), (39), (40), and (34) to get the associated general equilibrium values of

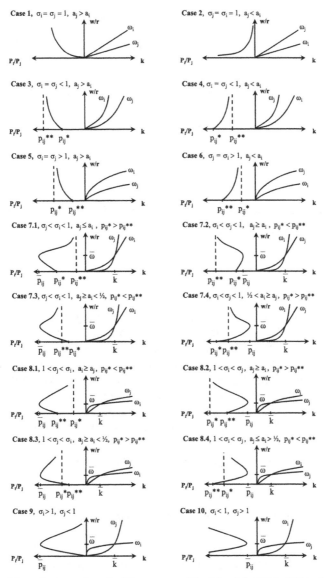

Fig. 1. *The relative prices* $P_i/P_j = p_{ij} = \Phi(w/r)$ *with CES, (19)–(21), and the isoelastic pair* $\omega_i(k_i)$, $\omega_j(k_j)$ *and (13).*

all other variables – the relative commodity prices, factor allocation fractions, income shares, sectorial capital – labor ratios and the outputs.

The relative CES commodity prices, $p_{ij} = \Phi(w/r)$, (19), together with their CES pairs, $\omega_i(k_i)$, $\omega_j(k_j)$, (13), are shown in Figure 1. With $\sigma_i \neq \sigma_j$, there will be one (and only one) intersection point of (13),

$(k_i, \omega_i) = (k_j, \omega_j) = (\overline{k}_{ij}, \overline{\omega}_{ij}), \ [a_i = a_j = a : (\overline{k}_{ij}, \overline{\omega}_{ij}) = (1, (1-a)/a] :$

$$\sigma_i \neq \sigma_j; \ \ \overline{k}_{ij} = \left[\frac{a_i(1-a_j)}{a_j(1-a_i)}\right]^{\sigma_i\sigma_j/\sigma_j-\sigma_i} = \left[\frac{c_j^{\sigma_i}}{c_i^{\sigma_j}}\right]^{\frac{1}{\sigma_j-\sigma_i}}; \ \ \overline{\omega}_{ij} = \left[\frac{c_j}{c_i}\right]^{\frac{1}{\sigma_j-\sigma_i}} \tag{51}$$

With (51), $p_{ij}(\omega) = \Phi(w/r)$, (19), has a unique reversal price ratio:

$$\overline{p}_{ij} = p_{ij}(\overline{\omega}_{ij}) = \frac{\gamma_j a_j^{\sigma_j/(\sigma_j-1)}\left[1 + c_j[c_j/c_i]^{1-\sigma_j/\sigma_j-\sigma_i}\right]^{\frac{1}{\sigma_j-1}}}{\gamma_i a_i^{\sigma_i/\sigma_i-1}\left[1 + c_i[c_j/c_i]^{\frac{1-\sigma_i}{\sigma_j-\sigma_i}}\right]^{1/\sigma_i-1}}; \ \ a_i = a_j : \overline{p}_{ij} = \frac{\gamma_j}{\gamma_i}$$

$$\tag{52}$$

The limits – for $\omega = w/r$, going to zero and infinity – of the relative price (cost) functions, $p_{ij} = \Phi(w/r)$, (19) become either

$$p_{ij}^* \equiv \frac{\gamma_j \, a_j^{\sigma_j/(\sigma_j-1)}}{\gamma_i \, a_i^{\sigma_i/(\sigma_i-1)}}; \ \ p_{ij}^{**} \equiv \frac{\gamma_j \, (1-a_j)^{\sigma_j/(\sigma_j-1)}}{\gamma_i \, (1-a_i)^{\sigma_i/(\sigma_i-1)}} \tag{53}$$

and (51)–(53) are depicted in Figure 1.

The proper literature reference to interpreting the correspondence between the relative commodity prices and the relative factor prices, $p_{ij} = \Phi(w/r)$, (19), as the *"Invisible Hand"* is Samuelson (1949, p. 186), where the idea of the left/right panels in Figure 1 was first explained.

The graphs of the Walrasian equilibrium, $k = \Psi(\omega)$, (49)–(50), could be depicted in the right panels of Figure 1. Only in two-sector models will $k = \Psi(\omega)$ pass through the intersection points, (51), when the latter exists; Jensen (2003, p. 61). These graphs of the Walrasian equilibria, $k = \Psi(\omega)$, (49)–(50), will geometrically be trajectories of the Walrasian multisector general equilibrium dynamics with factor (labor and capital) accumulation.

4. Dynamics and evolution of homothetic multisector economies

The equations of factor accumulation for MSG models, with two primary factors and flexible constant return-to-scale sector technologies, are formally given by

$$\frac{dL}{dt} \equiv \dot{L} = nL \tag{54}$$

$$\frac{dK}{dt} \equiv \dot{K} = Y_1 - \delta K = Ly_1\lambda_{L_1} - \delta K = L\{f_1(k_1)\lambda_{L_1} - \delta k\} \tag{55}$$

where Y_1 is the output of capital good sector 1, δ the depreciation rate of capital and n the growth rate of labor. The variables k_1 and λ_{L_1} in (55) are through ω, (33), and (49), uniquely determined by the factor-endowment ratio $k : \omega(k) = \Psi^{-1}(k)$. Hence, the accumulation equation (55) becomes an autonomous differential equations in the state variables L and K,

$$\dot{K} = L\{f_1(k_1[\omega(k)])\lambda_{L_1}[\omega(k)] - \delta k\} \equiv Lg(k); \quad L \neq 0 \tag{56}$$

As (56) is an intricate function of k, we rewrite $g(k)$ by (47), (35)–(36), (9), as

$$\dot{K} = I/P_1 - \delta K = s_1 Y/P_1 - \delta K = Ls_1(\omega + k)f_1'(k_1) - \delta K \tag{57}$$

$$= Lk\left\{\frac{s_1 f_1'(k_1)}{\delta_K} - \delta\right\} = Lg(k); \quad Lk = K \tag{58}$$

From the governing functions, (58) and (54), the director function, $h(k)$, that controls for $dk/dt \equiv \dot{k}$ becomes, $h(k) \equiv g(k) - nk$,

$$\dot{k} = h(k) = k\left[\frac{s_1 f_1'[k_1[\omega(k)]]}{\delta_K[\omega(k)]} - (n+\delta)\right]; \quad \omega(k) = \Psi^{-1}(k) \tag{59}$$

The dynamic system (59) in k is difficult to evaluate quantitatively and analytically intractable; for example, if $\sigma_i \neq \sigma_j$, then, $k = \Psi(\omega)$, (50), cannot be inverted (although Ψ^{-1} exists) in a closed form.

Nevertheless, $k = \Psi(\omega)$, (49), is a continuously differentiable function of ω, and the dynamics of k can be converted into the dual autonomous dynamics in ω:

$$\dot{\omega} = \frac{\dot{k}}{dk/d\omega} = \frac{h(k)}{dk/d\omega} = \frac{h(\Psi[\omega])}{\Psi'(\omega)} \equiv \hbar(\omega) \tag{60}$$

Hence, we get, cf. (59),

$$\hbar(\omega) = \frac{\Psi(\omega)}{\Psi'(\omega)}\left[\frac{s_1 f_1'[k_1(\omega)]}{\delta_K(\omega)} - (n+\delta)\right] \tag{61}$$

Thus, with CES preferences and technologies, we get from (61), (48), (39), (13)–(14) and (6)

$$\dot{\omega} = \hbar(\omega) = \frac{\Psi(\omega)}{\Psi'(\omega)}\left[\frac{s_1\gamma_1 \, a_1^{\sigma_1/\sigma_1-1}\left[1 + c_1\omega^{1-\sigma_1}\right]^{1/(\sigma_1-1)}}{\sum_{i=1}^{N} s_i(\omega)[1 + c_i\omega^{1-\sigma_i}]^{-1}} - (n+\delta)\right] \tag{62}$$

with the CES expression for $\Psi(\omega)$ as given in (50).

Although the pair of time paths, $k(t), \omega(t) = \Psi^{-1}[k(t)]$, obtained from (59) is the same as the pair, $\omega(t), \ k(t) = \Psi[\omega(t)]$, given by the solution of (62), the latter turns out to be computationally more convenient, because the numerical calculation of the derivative $\Psi'(\omega)$ in (62) is much quicker than getting the inverse function values in (59). Moreover, most of our variables are given directly in the factor price ratio (ω) rather than in the factor-endowment ratio (k). Thus, the solution $\omega(t)$ of (62) is what is needed to get all other time paths of the multisector economy.

5. Solving the multisector growth – (2 × 10) – model

To provide the concrete benchmark solutions of the general equilibrium dynamics, (62), we use a 10-sector model, in which sector 1 produces the capital good and sectors 2–10 produce consumption goods.

5.1. CES parameter sets of $U(Y_2, \ldots, Y_{10})$ and $F_i(L_i, K_i)$

For the CES utility function we use the substitution elasticity, $\sigma_u = 0.8$, (price inelastic), and the commodity parameters α_i in column 1, Table 1. With $\sigma_u < 1$, all sectoral outputs Y_i, goods (22)–(23), will be strictly positive, cf. isoquant map in appendix. About σ_u for CES demands, see de La Grandville (1989, p. 473). As to the other model parameters, we adopt a fixed saving rate $s_1 = 0.2$, a depreciation $\delta = 0.04$, and a population (labor) growth rate $n = 0.01$, that is,

$$\sigma_u = 0.8, \quad s_1 = 0.2, \quad \delta = 0.04, \quad n = 0.01; \quad \gamma_i = 1, \quad i = 1, \ldots, 10 \quad (63)$$

The CES technology is applied in each sector (γ_i, (63)) with some variation in the CES parameters, a_i and σ_i, as seen in Table 1 for the three Cases I–III.

Only few comments are needed upon the CES technology parameters and the three technology regimes given by Cases I–III. The CES parameter, (a_i), (13) is traditionally referred to as a "distribution parameter," technologically a misnomer. The effect of an increase in a_i is seen from (13) as a rightward shift of the ω_i curve in Figure 1, right panels, (or all isoquant tangents, $\omega = |dK/dL|$, smaller/flatter) that is, a

Table 1. *The CES parameters of $U(Y_2, \ldots, Y_{10})$ and $F_i(L_i, K_i)$,*
Cases I–III

i	α_i	a_i	σ_i I	σ_i II	σ_i III
1	—	0.5	0.8	1.2	2.0
2	0.15	0.3	0.9	1.5	2.5
3	0.10	0.4	0.7	1.1	1.5
4	0.20	0.5	0.9	0.9	0.8
5	0.10	0.2	0.8	0.8	0.8
6	0.15	0.4	0.6	1.3	1.3
7	0.10	0.7	0.7	0.7	0.7
8	0.10	0.6	0.5	0.7	1.1
9	0.05	0.2	0.5	1.5	2.5
10	0.05	0.6	0.6	1.1	1.5

higher capital-labor ratio k_i for any factor price ratio. Hence, a_i is aptly characterized as a capital-intensity parameter (Uzawa, 1959, p. 459). A high capital-labor ratio can alternatively be due to a movement along the ω_i curve, (or isoquants, cf. appendix), the effect of which is determined by the substitution (flexibility) parameter σ_i cf. de La Grandville (1997). As to obtaining high k_i over time, the effect of σ_i will eventually dominate the effect of a_i. The main parameter (determinant) of economic growth is σ_i, and its size characterizes the three technological regimes in Table 1.

With, $0 \leq \sigma_1 \leq 1$, all transition paths will eventually reach the steady state. If some, $\sigma_i \geq 1$, (including σ_1), persistent "endogenous" growth may occur, depending on the mixture of a_i and σ_i. The threshold parameter values for persistent growth are satisfied with Case III, Table 1, cf. (8)

5.2. MSG time paths of the CES 10-sector growth model

Corresponding to the selected parameter values in Table 1, Cases I–III and (63), the solutions $\omega(t)$ of (62) are shown in Figure 2 up to $t = 100$ – together with $k(t) = \Psi[\omega(t)]$ – as well as their respective growth rates, looking fairly reasonable. The actual picture displayed in Figure 2 contains no surprises. With factor accumulation, rising $k(t)$ and increasing wage-rental ratios $\omega(t)$ go together in a 10-sector economy as well. For the parameters in Cases I–II, (62) has a critical point – a unique steady state – which is, respectively,

$$\omega_I^* = 32.83, \quad k_I^* = 11.46; \quad \omega_{II}^* = 29.17, \quad k_{II}^* = 27.98 \tag{64}$$

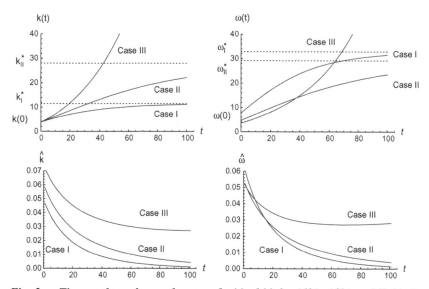

Fig. 2. Time paths and growth rates of $\omega(t)$, $k(t)$ by (62)–(63) and Table 1.

In Case III, no steady state exists and persistent economic growth takes place, as seen below, when the solution of (62) is extended beyond the time horizon of Figure 2. The trajectories – (k,ω) locus – of the time paths in Figure 1 are shown in the left panel of Figure 3. The right panel of Figure 3 exhibits the locus of the Walrasian equilibria (comparative statics independent of time).

All the solutions in Figure 2 and Figures 4–11 start from the initial time value: $K(0)/L(0) = k(0) = 3.82 = k_I^*/3$, cf. (64). The corresponding three initial time values of $\omega(0)$ for all solutions in Figures 4–11 are depicted in Figure 2. The absolute size of $K(0)$ and $L(0)$ can be arbitrarily chosen; all solutions apply for small and large economies. With our $\gamma_i = 1$: $y_i = f_i(1) = 1$, (5).

The time paths of the sectorial capital-labor ratios, $k_i(t)$, are exhibited in Figure 4. Obviously, with a rising $\omega(t)$, all 10 $k_i(t)$ are increasing, too, but an underlying distinct sectorial pattern evidently appears, calling for attention. However, essentially a common economic mechanism is involved behind the pattern in Figure 4. In Table 1, the ranking order of the substitution elasticities σ_i (combined with a similar ranking of the intensity parameters a_i) corresponds to the vertical orders of $k_i(t)$ in Figure 4 for $t > 50$. Thus, in Table 1, Case I, the sectors 4,7,1 have high σ_i (backed up with high a_i) corresponding to the vertical order in Case I (Figure 4). For Case II, an analogous ranking and vertical order occurs with sectors 10,1,6,2. In Case III, this ranking/order pattern is repeated with sectors

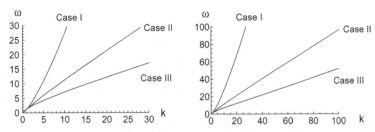

Fig. 3.   Left: The (ω, k) locus of Figure 2. Right: $k = \Psi(\omega)$ by (50), Table 1.

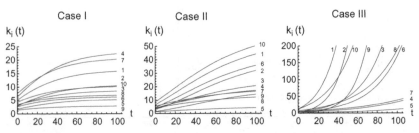

Fig. 4.   The sectorial $k_i(t)$ by (13) and $\omega(t)$, (62)–(63), Table 1, Fig. 2.

1,2,10,9,3. In short, the sectors with high σ_i (and high a_i) become mechanized – thus increasing $k_i(t)$ by attracting both new capital and capital from other sectors with lower σ_i (and a_i). This sectorial order of attraction and reallocation of capital – as evident in Figure 4 – will also be reflected in the time paths of the allocation fractions, $\lambda_{K_i}(t)$ of capital in Figure 7. But these sectorial evolutions of $\lambda_{K_i}(t)$ in Figure 7 are partly modified by their respective magnitudes of α_i (Table 1) from the demand side of the multisector economy. The demand side composition of the economy exerts a particular powerful influence on the time paths of the allocation fraction of capital in sector 1, $\lambda_{K_1}(t)$, as shown for Cases I–III in Figure 5. Below, we return to the paths of Figure 5, and the sizes of the factor income shares exhibited in Figure 6. Evidently, the allocation fractions of labor in Figure 7 reflect reallocation of labor toward the labor-intensive sectors, cf. their parameters in Table 1.

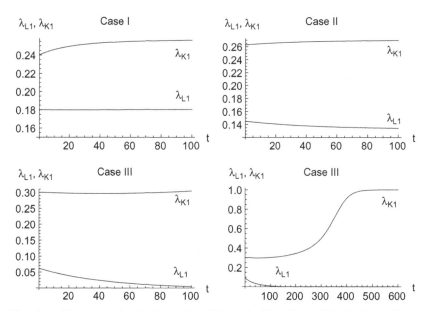

Fig. 5.   Allocations $\lambda_{L_1}(t), \lambda_{K_1}(t)$ by (40) and $\omega(t)$, (62)–(63), Table 1, Fig. 2.

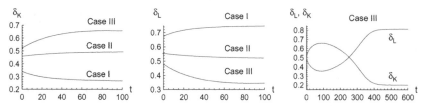

Fig. 6.   Factor shares $\delta_L(t), \delta_K(t)$ by (39) and $\omega(t)$, (62)–(63), Table 1.

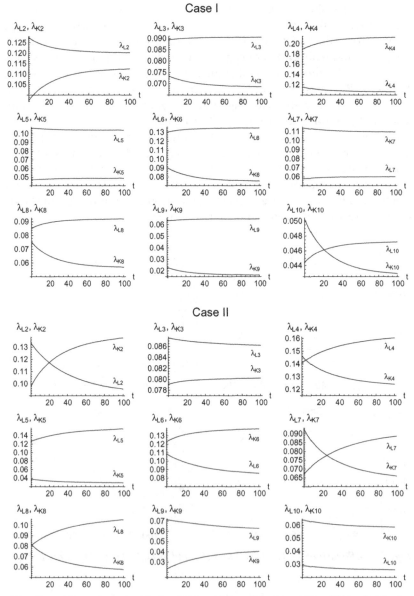

Fig. 7. *Allocations* $\lambda_{L_i}(t), \lambda_{K_i}(t)$ *by (40) and* $\omega(t)$, *(62)–(63), Table 1.*

With commodity 2 as the numeraire, the time paths of our nine relative prices, $p_{i2}(t)$, $i = 1, 3, \ldots, 10$, are seen in Figure 8, Cases I–III. As these relative general equilibrium prices play the fundamental allocative role ("invisible hand") in multisector economies, it is important that the sizes

Case III

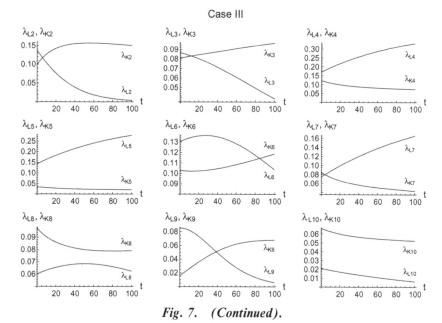

Fig. 7. *(Continued).*

and the overall picture for all these price numbers (rising/falling) can be checked easily, which is seldom offered for the users of the CGE models. Here, Figure 1 can serve as a "road map" for checking the direction and the turning points of the nine prices in Cases I–III (Figure 8).

Hence, we calibrate Figure 1 with the intersection/reversal points according to the parameters in Table 1. Only the technology parameters affect the price reversals or limits for Cases I–III in Table 2. In Figure 8, we note reversals for $p_{32}(t)$, $p_{82}(t)$ in Case I; by Table 2, the reversal prices are: $\overline{p}_{32} = 0.935$, $\overline{p}_{82} = 0.816$, confirming the time paths in Figure 8 by Figure 1, Case 7.4. Some reversal points occurs either for lower $\omega(0)$ or higher t than shown here.

All the paths $p_{i2}(t)$ seen in Figure 8 can be checked with Figure 1 and Table 2.

All calculations of the time paths are performed by Mathematica (version 7.0) and are available on request.

The time paths of the nine budget shares $e_i(t)$ are shown in Figure 9. The evolution of $e_i(t)$ depends on the evolution of own- and cross prices. Since the numeraire commodity 2 is produced by a technology with a relative high σ_2 (especially in Cases I and III), its costs (price) will, with increased $\omega(t)$ and mechanization, become relatively cheap, or equivalently, the other commodities become more expensive in terms of commodity 2. Accordingly, many time paths for $p_{i2}(t), i > 2$, in Figure 8 are rising, especially in Case III.

308   *Bjarne S. Jensen and Ulla Lehmijoki*

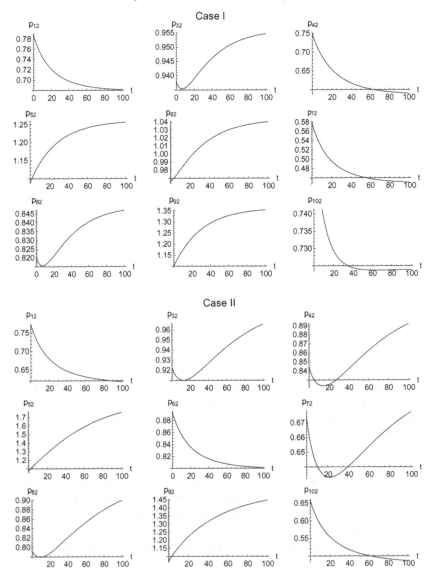

Fig. 8. ***Relative prices $p_i2(t)$ by (19), $\omega(t)$, (62)–(63), Tables 1 and 2, Figures 1 and 2.***

With generally inelastic demand curves due to $\sigma_u = 0.8$, the higher (lower) own price $p_{i\,2}(t)$, implies a higher (lower) budget share $e_i(t)$. Hence, we have roughly the connection between rising consumption prices $p_{i2}(t), i > 2$ in Figure 8 and rising $e_i(t)$ in Figure 9. The budget shares are not changing much (three-four decimals) in Figure 9. With $\sigma_u = 0.8$, all

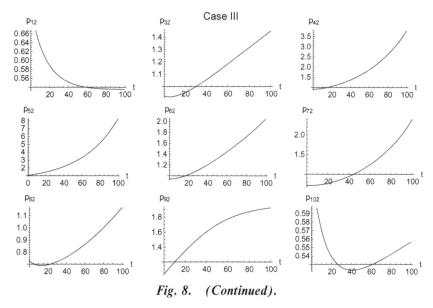

Case III

Fig. 8. (Continued).

Table 2. Points of intersection/reversal $(\bar{k}_{i2}, \bar{\omega}_{i2})$, (51), $(\bar{p}_{i2})$, (52), limits, (p^*_{i2}, p^{**}_{i2}), (53), by Table 1, $\gamma_i = 1$

	$\bar{k}_{i2}$			$\bar{\omega}_{i2}$			$\bar{p}_{i2}$			p^*_{i2}			p^{**}_{i2}		
i	I	II	III	I	II	III	I	II	III	I	II	III	I	II	III
1	446	161	4783	2050	69	69	0.578	0.593	0.535	3175	1.73	0.54	1.55	21.95	2.21
2															
3	4.02	6.19	5.24	10.95	7.86	4.52	0.935	0.910	0.916	5989	644	2.10	7.52	95	2.55
4	–	6.73	2.71	–	8.32	3.48	–	0.823	0.724	99.2	–	–	0.05	–	–
5	0.02	0.40	0.53	0.03	1.26	1.81	0.806	0.955	0.969	81.3	–	–	10.15	–	–
6	2.22	74.3	3.31	5.65	41.2	3.77	0.962	0.795	0.939	12852	1.43	7.13	11.52	3.14	5.05
7	208	9.25	5.19	879	10.28	4.51	0.362	0.632	0.712	22104	–	–	1.49	–	–
8	4.09	5.18	11.71	11.17	6.98	6.24	0.816	0.779	0.687	30483	–	37.05	9.91	–	13157
9	0.55	–	–	1.19	–	–	0.968	–	–	10161	3.38	1.97	19.82	0.67	0.80
10	9.54	175	110	28.6	73	15.3	0.724	0.458	0.523	23612	7.44	0.62	6.27	8178	8.62

consumer goods are net (Hicksian) substitutes $[E(H_i, P_i) = -\sigma_u(1 - e_i)$, $E(H_i, P_j) = \sigma_u e_j]$, but they are also gross complements, cf. (26), which stabilizes the budget shares to cross-price changes. At the bottom of Figure 9, it is seen that all the calculated paths of the budget shares $e_i(t)$ do add up to one, anytime.

Besides prices, $p_{i2}(t)$, and the shares, $e_i(t)$, it is instructive to check and examine the time paths of the "real consumption" (demand = output) of various goods in the multisector economy. The time paths of the per capita outputs of the nine consumer goods and the capital good are seen in Figure 10.

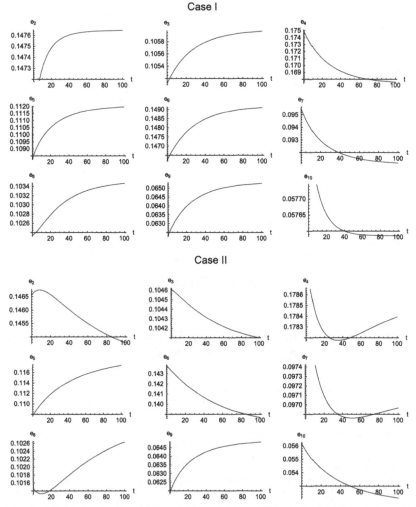

Fig. 9.   Budget shares $e_i(t)$ by (25) and $\omega(t)$, (62)–(63), Table 1, Figure 8.

In Table 1, the CES preference parameters (α_i, weights) are largest for $i = 4,6,2$. In Cases I–II, these consumer goods are also in Figure 10 among the major outputs on the whole time horizon toward the steady state. In Cases I–II, the price and budget changes cause minor structural changes in factor allocations (Figure 7), hence neither much in structure of outputs (Figure 10).

In Case III, even on a short horizon ($t < 100$), we see considerable changes in the relative prices (Figure 8) and factor reallocations (Figure 7), hence also in the output compositions Figure 10) where it is already seen

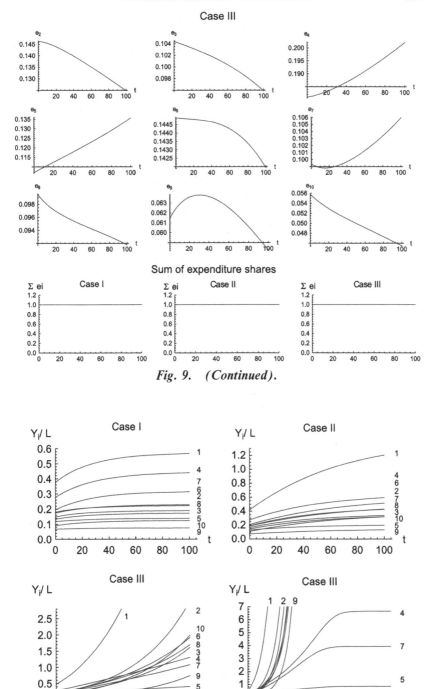

Case III

Sum of expenditure shares

Fig. 9. (Continued).

Fig. 10. Per capita outputs Y_i/L (t) by (34) and $\omega(t)$, (62)–(63), Figures 4–7.

$(t < 100)$ that the output (consumption) per capita, $Y_i/L(t)$, for those industries where $\sigma_i < 1$, $(i = 4,7,5)$, are stagnating, which is evident for $t > 100$ (Figure 10). The sectorial labor productivities $y_i(t)$ are bounded above for $\sigma_i < 1$, see (7).

For parameter Case III, these structural output changes for $t > 100$ (Figure 10) are dramatically underscored by the concomitant evolution of the occupational structure, $\lambda_{L_i}(t)$, as seen by the factor allocations in Figure 11; the three industries with $\sigma_i < 1$, $(i = 4,7,5)$, employ almost the entire labor force ("service industries," without much mechanization, Figure 4, Case III).

The complement to the allocations for the consumer goods in Figure 11 is the allocation fractions to the capital good sector, shown in Figure 5, Case III. The anomalous time paths of $\lambda_{K_1}(t)$ and $\delta_K(t)$ in Figures 5 and 6, Case III require a mathematical-economic justification, and they pose the question:

what are the asymptotic limits $[k(t) \rightarrow \infty]$ for: $\delta_K(t)$ (39), $\lambda_{K_1}(t)$ (40)?

Although analytic expressions for these limits are hard to establish, some approximate answers are available, Jensen et al. (2005, p. 51), viz.,

$$\lim_{k(t) \to \infty} \delta_K(t) \approx s_1 + \varepsilon_\delta \quad \lim_{k(t) \to \infty} \lambda_{K_1}(t) \approx \frac{s_1}{(s_1 + \varepsilon_\lambda)} \tag{65}$$

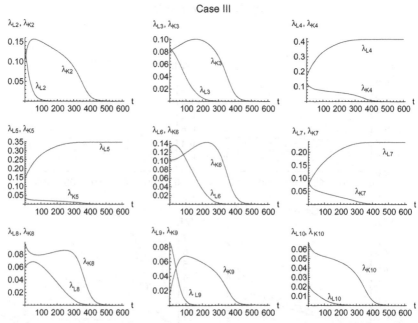

Fig. 11. **Long-run allocations** $\lambda_{L_i}(t)$, $\lambda_{K_i}(t)$ **by (40) and** $\omega(t)$, **Figures 5, 7 and 10.**

with ε_δ, ε_λ, as infinitesimals. Thus with s_1 (63) and (65), we get

$$\lim_{k(t)\to\infty} \delta_K(t) \approx 0.2, \quad \lim_{k(t)\to\infty} \lambda_{K_1}(t) \approx 1 \tag{66}$$

which is in line with: $\delta_K(t)$ and $\lambda_{K_1}(t)$ in Figures 5 and 6, Case III, $t = 600$.

But obviously the limits (65) required persistent growth of $k(t)$, that is, no critical (steady-state) point in (59). The necessary and sufficient parametric conditions for absence of critical points in, (59), (62), are:

$$\forall i \; \sigma_i > 1 : \gamma_1 a_1^{\sigma_1/\sigma_1 - 1} > \frac{(n+\delta)}{s_1}; \quad \text{only } \sigma_1 > 1 : \; \gamma_1 a_1^{\sigma_1/\sigma_1 - 1} > n + \delta \tag{67}$$

compare the large bracket (62). The distinction in (67) derives from the bracket denominator of (62), which takes the values 1 or s_1 for $\omega \to \infty$, depending on the size of all σ_i; (see Jensen et al., 2005, p. 44).

Then, from Table 1, (63), (67), and (8), we obtain

$$\gamma_1 a_1^{\sigma_1/\sigma_1 - 1} = 0.25; \quad \frac{(n+\delta)}{s_1} = 0.25; \quad n + \delta = 0.05 \tag{68}$$

By inspecting (67)–(68), it is clear that if we had, $\sigma_i > 1$, for *all* 10 sectors in Table 1, then the strict inequality (67) is violated, and we could not have obtained the persistent MSG solutions for Case III, Figures 2–11. If we only had $\sigma_1 > 1$, then inequality, (67)–(68), is easily satisfied, but the time paths for the levels of consumer goods per capita would be bounded, as in Figure 10 for sectors 4,7,5.

It is noteworthy that the, $\forall i \; \sigma_i > 1$, condition in (67) corresponds to the macro CES threshold condition. For the combinations of the CES parameters satisfying the macro threshold values, see (de La Grandville, 1989, p. 479; de La Grandville, 2009, p. 125; Jensen & Larsen, 1987, p. 234; Jensen et al., 2005, p. 78; Klump & de La Grandville, 2000, p. 282).

Thus, we see by (67)–(68) that it is "easier" to generate persistent growth within CES 10-sector models than within CES 1–2 sector models. The main economic and dynamic reason for this paradoxical result is that the occupational structure by $\lambda_{L_1}(t)$, (55)–(56), and hence all the sectorial allocations $\lambda_{L_i}(t), \lambda_{K_i}(t)$ are endogenous variables, and this continuous factor reallocation as implemented by the time paths of the relative factor and commodity prices reinforces – as we have seen with our solutions of (62)–(63) – capital allocation toward the capital good sector.

Especially, regarding changes in the prices of the capital good and consumer goods, we note that the relative price of the capital good, $p_{12}(t)$, is declining in Figure 8 for all three Cases I–III. For $p_{12}(t)$, the Case I, Table 1, corresponds to Case 7.4, Figure 1; Cases II–III correspond to Case 8.4, Figure 1. Since $\omega_I^* = 32.83$, $\omega_{II}^* = 29.17$, cf. (64), are far below the reversal points, $\overline{\omega}_{12}$: (2050, 69), Table 2, any rising values of $p_{12}(t)$ will not be observed before the steady states in Case I–II.

We get in Case III $\overline{\omega}_{12} = 69$, Table 2 (exactly as Case II, with any decimals). In Table 2, Case III, we see that $\overline{p}_{12} = 0.535$ is very close to $p_{12}^* = 0.54$; thus the rising part in Case 8.4, Figure 1 is very short, and $p_{12}(t)$ reaches this lower zone already at $t = 60$ in Figure 8. A glimpse of the role for the capital good price P_1 in obtaining persistent growth is evident in (57). For empirical evidence on the relative price decline of capital goods (equipment), see the pioneering study of Greenwood, Hercowitz, and Krusell (1997, p. 343).

The evolution of relative shares of capital and labor in Case III, Figure 6, deserves special attention. With mechanization of this 10-sector CES economy, we see an initial stage with a rising capital share, $\delta_K(t)$; economic history has adduced to such initial phase for $\delta_K(t)$. In (59) with $N = 1$ and $\delta_K = \varepsilon_{K_1}, (11)$, the share $\varepsilon_{K_1}(t), (14,)$ rises toward one with $\sigma_1 = \sigma > 1$. But with the extension to $N = 10$, the evolution and the convergence value of $\delta_K(t)$, Case III, Figure 6 are much closer to the recorded economic time series.

6. Final comments

Decentralization with dispersion of factor endowment and decision-making authority is the main principle underlying the general economic assumption of competitive markets with individual maximizing agents. Momentary and moving general equilibria of commodity and factor markets have been involved in the parametric solutions of the CES 10-sector growth model and in the analytical system for the N-dimensional homothetic economy.

A natural topic for future research on the MSG models is extensions to include nonhomothetic preferences, allowing for nonunitary income elasticities of demand for the different goods. CDES preferences generalize CES, cf. Jensen, de Boer, van Daal, and Jensen (2011).

Other extensions of general equilibrium dynamics could include financial assets, portfolio analysis, and stochastic dynamics. Stochastic and deterministic MSG models should together contribute to a better understanding of the historical time series in economics and other disciplines (cf. de La Grandville, 2001; Jensen & Palokangas, 2007).

Acknowledgment

B.S. Jensen is grateful to Springer Verlag for permission to use former results published in *Journal of Economics* (2005), Suppl. 10. I am also grateful to Blackwell Publ. for permission to make use of earlier work published in *German Economic Review* (2003), vol. 4.

We would like to thank Olivier de La Grandville for useful comments upon an earlier version.

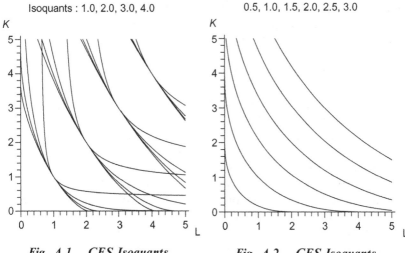

Isoquants : 1.0, 2.0, 3.0, 4.0   0.5, 1.0, 1.5, 2.0, 2.5, 3.0

Fig. A.1. CES Isoquants.   **Fig. A.2. CES Isoquants.**

$\gamma_i = 1$ $\gamma_i = 1$

$a_i = 0.4;\ \sigma_i = 0.5,\ 1.5,\ 2.5,\ 3.5$ $a_i = 0.5;\ \sigma_i = 2.0$

Appendix:. CES isoquant map

If $\sigma > 1$, the isoquants of (3) reach the axes, and the interception points $(\overline{L}, 0)$ and $(0, \overline{K})$ are given by :

$$\overline{L} = \left(\frac{Y}{\gamma}\right)(1 - a)^{\sigma/1-\sigma}; \quad \overline{K} = \left(\frac{Y}{\gamma}\right)(a)^{\sigma/1-\sigma} \tag{69}$$

that is, for the unit isoquant in Figure A.2, $Y = 1$: $\overline{L} = 4, \overline{K} = 4$.

If $\sigma < 1$, the CES isoquants have vertical and horizontal asymptotes. Their intersection point, $(\overline{L}, \overline{K})$, is formally given by the same expressions (69). The slopes of all CES isoquants, $\omega = |dK/dL|$, range from zero to infinity, neither of which are reached in finite time for $\omega(t)$ solutions in Figures 2–11.

References

Aghion, P., & Durlauf, S. (Eds.). (2005). *Handbook of economic growth 1.* Amsterdam: Elsevier.

Aghion, P., & Howitt, P. (1998). *Endogenous growth theory.* Cambridge, MA: M.I.T. Press.

Arrow, K. J., Chenery, H. B., Minhas, B. S., & Solow, R. M. (1961). Capital-labour substitution and economic efficiency. *Review of Economics and Statistics*, *43*, 225–250.

Arrow, K. J. (1974). General economic equilibrium: Purpose, analytic techniques, collective choice. *American Economic Review*, *64*, 253–272.

Barro, R. J., & Sala-i-Martin, X. (2004). *Economic Growth Theory* (2nd ed.). Cambridge, MA: M.I.T. Press.

Carstensen, K., Gundlach, E., & Hartman, S. (2009). The augmented solow model with mincerian schooling and externalities. *German Economic Review*, *10*, 448–463.

Chung, J. W. (1994). *Utility and production functions*. Oxford: Blackwell.

de La Grandville, O. (1989). In quest of the slutsky diamond. *American Economic Review*, *79*, 468–481.

de La Grandville, O. (1997). Curvature and the elasticity of substitution: Straightening it out. *Journal of Economics*, *66*, 23–34.

de La Grandville, O. (2001). *Bond pricing and portfolio analysis*. Cambridge, MA: The MIT Press.

de La Grandville, O. (2009). *Economic growth – A unified approach*. Cambridge: Cambridge University Press.

Dhrymes, P. J. (1962). A multisectoral model of growth. *Quarterly Journal of Economics*, *76*, 264–278.

Dixit, A. K., & Stiglitz, J. E. (1977). Monopolistic competition and optimum product diversity. *American Economic Review*, *67*, 297–308.

Echevarria, C. (1997). Changes in sectoral composition associated with economic growth. *International Economic Review*, *38*, 431–452.

Greenwood, J., Hercowitz, Z., & Krusell, P. (1997). Long-run implications of investment-specific technological change. *American Economic Review*, *87*, 342–362.

Inada, K. (1964). On the Stability of Growth Equilibria in Two-Sector Models. *Rev. Econ. Stud.*, *31*, 127–142.

Jensen, B. S. (1994). *The dynamic systems of basic economic growth models*. Dordrecht: Kluwer Academic Publishers.

Jensen, B. S. (2003). Walrasian general equilibrium allocations and dynamics in two-sector growth models. *German Economic Review*, *4*, 53–87.

Jensen, B. S. (Ed.) (2009). Dynamic extensions of the Solow growth model (1956): Editorial, *German Economic Review*, *10*, 378–383.

Jensen, B. S., Alsholm, P. K., Larsen, M. E., & Jensen, J. M. (2005). Dynamic structure, exogeneity, phase portraits, growth paths, and scale and substitution elasticities. *Review of International Economics*, *13*, 59–89.

Jensen, B. S., de Boer, P., van Daal, J., & Jensen, P. E. (2011). Global restriction on the parameters of the CDES indirect utility function. *Journal of Economics*, *102*, 217–235.

Jensen, B. S., & Larsen, M. E. (1987). Growth and long-run stability. *Acta Applicandae Mathematicae, 9,* 219–237.

Jensen, B. S., & Larsen, M. E. (2005). General equilibrium dynamics of multi-sector growth models. *Journal of Economics, S10,* 17–56.

Jensen, B. S., & Palokangas, T. (Eds.). (2007). *Stochastic economic dynamics.* Denmark: Copenhagen Business School Press.

Jones, R. W. (1965). The Structure of Simple General Equilibrium Models. *J. Political Economy, 73,* 557–572.

Klump, R., & de La Grandville, O. (2000). Economic growth and the elasticity of substitution: Two theorems and some suggestions. *American Economic Review, 90,* 282–291.

Kongsamut, P., Rebelo, S., & Xie, D. (2001). Beyond balanced growth. *Review of Economic Studies, 68,* 869–882.

Kuznets, S. (1966). *Modern economic growth – Rate, structure and spread.* New Haven, CT: Yale University Press.

Mankiw, N. G., Romer, D., & Weil, D. N. (1992). A contribution to the empirics of economic growth. *Quarterly Journal of Economics, 107,* 407–437.

McKenzie, L. (1954). On equilibrium in grahamic model of world trade and other competitive sytems. *Econometrica, 22,* 147–161.

Nonneman, W., & Vanhoudt, P. (1996). A further augmentation of the solow model and the empirics of economic growth for OECD countries. *Quarterly Journal of Economics, 111,* 943–953.

Romer, D. (2001). *Advanced Macroeconomics* (2nd ed.). Boston: McGraw-Hill.

Rosenberg, N. (1963). Capital goods, technology, and economic growth. *Oxford Economic Papers, 15,* 217–227.

Samuelson, P. A. (1949). International Factor Price Equalisation Once Again. *Economic Journal, 59,* 181–197.

Shoven, J. B., & Whalley, J. (1992). *Applying general equilibrium.* Cambridge, UK: Cambridge University Press.

Solow, R. M. (1956). A contribution to the theory of economic growth. *Quarterly Journal of Economics, 70,* 65–94.

Solow, R. M. (1961–62). Note on uzawa's two-sector model of economic growth. *Review of Economic Studies, 29,* 48–50.

Solow, R. M. (1999). Neoclassical growth theory, Chapter 9. In Taylor & Woodford (eds.). Handbook of Macroeconomics (Vol. 1). Amsterdam: Elsevier.

Solow, R. M. (2000). *Growth theory* (2nd ed.). Oxford: Oxford University Press.

Solow, R. M. (2005). Reflections on growth theory, 3–10. Introduction in Aghion and Durlauf (eds.). Handbook of economic growth (Vol. 1). Amsterdam: Elsevier.

Stiglitz, J. E. (1969). Allocation of heterogeneous capital goods in a two-sector economy. *International Economic Review, 10,* 379–390.

Taylor, J. B., & Woodford, M. (Eds.). (1999). *Handbook of Macroeconomics* (Vol. 1). Amsterdam: Elsevier.

Uzawa, H. (1959). Prices of the factors of production in international trade. *Econometrica, 27,* 448–468.

Uzawa, H. (1961). On a two-sector model of economic growth: I. *Review of Economic Studies, 29,* 40–47.

Uzawa, H. (1963). On a two-sector model of economic growth: II. *Review of Economic Studies, 30,* 105–118.

Walras, L. (1954). Elements of pure economics. Jaffic, W. (trans.), George Allen and Unwin, London.

CHAPTER 12

Medium-Term Growth: The Role of Policies and Institutions

Michał Jerzmanowski[a] and David Cuberes[b]

[a]*Department of Economics, Clemson University, Clemson, SC 29634, USA*
E-mail address: mjerzma@clemson.edu
[b]*Department of Economics, University of Sheffield, Sheffield, South Yorkshire,*
S1 4DT, United Kingdom
E-mail address: d.cuberes@sheffield.ac.uk

Abstract

In this chapter we review the recent and growing literature on medium-term growth patterns. This strand of research emerged from the realization that for most countries economic development is a highly unstable process; over a course of a few decades, a typical country enjoys periods of rapid growth as well episodes of stagnation and economic decline. This approach highlights the complex nature of growth and implies that studying transitions between periods of fast growth, stagnation, and collapse is essential for understanding the process of long run growth. We document recent efforts to characterize and study such growth transitions. We also update and extend some of our earlier research. Specifically, we use historical data from Maddison to confirm a link between political institutions and propensity to experience large swings in growth. We also study the role of institutions and macroeconomic policies, such as inflation, openness to trade, size of government, and real exchange rate overvaluation, in the context of growth transitions. We find surprisingly complex effects of some policies. For example, trade makes fast growth more likely but also increases the frequency of crises. The size of government reduces the likelihood of fast miracle-like growth while at the same time limiting the risk of stagnation. Moreover, these effects are nonlinear and dependent on the quality of institutions. We conclude by highlighting potentially promising areas for future research.

Keywords: Economic growth, institutions, macroeconomic policies, medium-term growth, volatility

JEL classifications: O43, O57, O11

Frontiers of Economics and Globalization
Volume 11   ISSN: 1574-8715
DOI: 10.1108/S1574-8715(2011)0000011017

Michał Jerzmanowski and David Cuberes

1. Introduction

The revival of research on economic growth that began in the last decades of the 20th century was spurred on by both theoretical and empirical contributions. On the theoretical front the papers by Romer (1986, 1990), Lucas (1988), and later Grossman and Helpman (1991), and Aghion and Howitt (1992) provided new ways of modeling endogenous growth and technological progress. On the empirical side, the availability of a large cross-country data set, the Penn World Table, and early papers exploiting it (Barro & Sala-i-Martin, 1992; Mankiw, Romer, & Weil, 1992) gave impetus for researchers to test old and new theories of growth against the facts.

Following the early contributions (Barro, 1991; Barro & Sala-i-Martin, 1992) most researchers adopted the approach of using long run, 20 years or more, averages of growth of GDP per capita (or per worker) as the variable to be explained in the empirical analysis. There is enormous variation in long run growth rates. For example, Jordan's income per capita increased by only 30% between 1970 and 2000 while that of Singapore increased sevenfold. In much of the growth literature of the last two decades researchers tried to explain such difference by looking for factors – openness to trade, protection of property rights, high investment rates, etc. – that are necessary for growth and that Jordan lacks while Singapore has in abundance. This literature has delivered many important insights but has also come under severe criticism for difficulties with establishing causality and the lack of robustness of many results (e.g., the effect of trade on growth). However, there is another reason why the overall balance of this empirical approach is quite disappointing. While focusing on explaining long run average growth rates is a sensible starting point, when one wants to isolate long run tendencies from higher frequency phenomena such as business cycle fluctuations, it also removes the information about how economic growth changed within a country over time. This would not be a great loss if countries behaved like in the growth models where economies approach balanced growth paths (BGPs) in smooth monotonic fashion. Unfortunately, most countries' growth experiences are far from smooth; they often experience long stretches of tepid growth interrupted by 5- or 10-year periods of rapid development only to later fall victim to decades of stagnation or years of decline. Long-term averages remove these patterns and preclude us from using this variation to learn about the nature of the process of economic growth. Lant Pritchett, a leading development economist, has been one of the first to point out the disconnect between the prevailing empirical approach and reality of economic growth. In one of the papers (Pritchett, 2000) he writes:

The historical path of gross domestic product (GDP) per capita in the United States is, except for the interlude of the Great Depression, well characterized by reasonably stable exponential trend growth with modest cyclical deviations: graphically, it is a modestly sloping, slightly bumpy hill. However, almost nothing that is true of U.S. GDP per capita (or that of other countries of the Organization for Economic Co-operation and Development) is true of the growth experience of developing countries. A single time trend does not adequately characterize the evolution of GDP per capita in most developing countries. Instability in growth rates over time for a single country is great, relative to both the average level of growth and the variance across countries.

These observation led Pritchett to list the fact that "Growth has been enormously variable within developing countries and there is little persistence of economic growth rates" as one of his seven stylized facts of the international growth experience. To make things concrete, consider again Jordan and Singapore. Their growth paths are plotted in Figure 1. It is apparent that the performance of the two countries is radically different, with Singapore experiencing a spectacular period of rapid growth, and Jordan suffering a dramatic stagnation. However, when inspecting Jordan's growth in greater detail, as is done in Figure 2, it becomes apparent that the forty years of its economic history are more than just a period of uninterrupted stagnation. The years 1960–1975, and even more so the periods 1985–1990 and 1995–2000 have been relatively successful while the years 1975–1985 and 1990–1995 brought a large decline in income level. As it turns out Jordan did not perpetually stagnate but

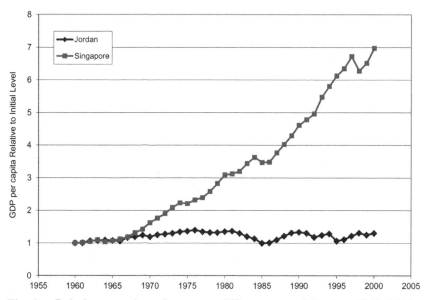

Fig. 1. *Relative growth performance of Singapore and Jordan, 1960–2000. Initial GDP per capita normalized to 100.*

Fig. 2. *Jordan's growth performance 1960–2000. Initial GDP per capita normalized to 100.*

instead had periods of rapid growth and also of dramatic decline; its economic growth seems to wax and wane. Explaining such medium-term cycles in economic performance seems key to understanding long run economic growth and discovering the right set of policies for development and stability.

To see even more directly how average growth studies can be misleading consider Figure 3, which illustrates the paths of output per worker in three countries, the Republic of Congo, Gabon and Portugal, over the period 1960–1995. The values have been normalized to equal one at the beginning of the period. The growth experiences of these three countries differ vastly: Portugal experienced a period of rapid growth followed by a mild slowdown and a return to fairly rapid growth, Congo went through a long period of rapid growth and then a period of equally rapid decline. Finally, Gabon grew faster than the two remaining countries until late 1970s, but stagnated thereafter. Yet after 40 years all three countries have grown by a surprisingly similar amount, roughly tripling their GDP per capita. If we look at average performance only, we conclude that Congo, Gabon, and Portugal's growth looks the same.

Why is understanding these patterns important? As a number of the papers described in this chapter emphasize, starting rapid growth and sustaining it are two different phenomena. We do not yet understand either of them very well. For example, increases in the variables usually found to be strongly correlated with average long-run growth, such as investment rates or trade openness, do not seem to initiate accelerations of

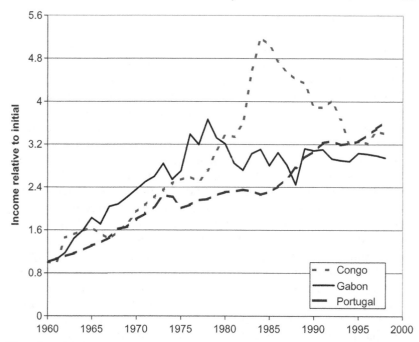

Fig. 3. *Different growth paths lead to similar average outcomes; Democratic Republic of Congo, Gabon, and Portugal.*

economic growth. This suggests that what the standard literature identifies as correlates of growth may not in fact be the factors that are needed to ignite it.

This chapter is an overview of the recent literature that studies the within-country growth patterns and tries to, among other things, learn about the nature of the growth process from analyzing differences in growth patterns such as those in Figure 3. This approach highlights the complex nature of growth and implies that studying "growth transitions", that is, switches between periods of fast growth, stagnation, and collapse is essential for understanding the process of long run growth. We begin by discussing early research that emphasized the lack of persistence of growth and the diversity of growth experiences among developing countries. We then summarize a series of more recent papers that look at growth transitions. Here we extend one of our earlier contributions to look at growth transitions going back to the late 19th century. We also discuss the idea of modeling growth in a nonlinear structure of multiple growth regimes and transitions between them. Here too, we extend our earlier work by studying the role of macroeconomic policies in shaping growth patterns. We conclude by highlighting the achievements of the literature so far and pointing to potentially fruitful avenues for future research.

2. Lack of growth persistence

The traditional analysis of growth assumes that there exist certain characteristics of countries which are conducive to development. They either affect the growth rate of the economy along a BGP or the level of the BGP, or both. Among such factors suggested by theory and explored empirically are investment rates, population growth rates, quality of institutions, development of financial markets, quality of macroeconomic policies, openness to trade and many more. To keep our discussion general we will refer to any such growth-enhancing factor as X. An increase in X will therefore shift the BGP up or increase its slope. In either case a monotonic convergence to the new BGP follows. Once on the BGP of course the economy will grow at a constant rate. It is instructive to start by asking why, in this framework, would the growth rate of an economy change. Most models predict that if a country is not on its BGP but is approaching it from below, growth will fall monotonically. This suggests both of these possibilities suggest smoothly evolving growth and a fairly large degree of persistence of growth rates. Leaving aside for now the possibility of frequent shocks that move the economy away from the BGP, the only way to get growth to change nonmonotonically is to have changes in X, that is, to have changes that affect the BGP. If the variable X that determines the position and slope of the BGP jumps around a lot, so will growth. Conversely, if X is fairly stable we would expect growth rates to be stable, too. Yet they aren't. One of the first papers to draw attention to the variability of the growth process was Easterly, Kremer, Pritchett, and Summers (1993). Specifically, they computed the correlation of growth rates across decades (e.g., 1960–1970 and 1970–1980) as well as longer timer periods (20 and 30 years) in a sample of Penn World Table countries and found it to be quite low: depending on sample and period the correlation coefficient was around 0.2–0.3. That is countries that developed rapidly in one decade are not very likely to be found in the group of fast growers in the following 10 years and conversely, slow growers are likely to pick up speed.

Here we re-do the same exercise using more recent data. In Figure 4 we plot the average growth of GDP per worker between 1985 and 1995 on the horizontal axis against the average growth in the following decade using 150 countries in the PWT 6.3 data set. Just like Easterly and his coauthors we find very little persistence; the correlation coefficient is only 0.3.[1] In Table 1 we report the results of regressing growth in given decade on growth in the previous one. While the relationship is positive (although

---

[1] It is even lower when we keep two outliers: Liberia (whose output declined by an average 22% per year between 1985 and 1995) and Equatorial Guinea (whose output increased by 28% annually during the decade following 1995).

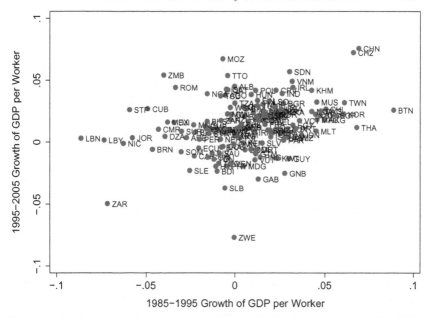

Fig. 4. *Lack of growth persistence. Growth in GDP per capita 1985–1995 versus 1995–2005.*

Table 1. *Growth over a decade regressed on growth during previous decade (update on Easterly et al., 1993)*

	1995–2005	1985–1995	1975–1985
Growth in previous decade	0.226	0.326	0.121
	(0.059)	(0.075)	(0.109)
Constant	0.012	0.004	0.006
	(0.002)	(0.002)	(0.004)
R-squared	0.086	0.110	0.002
No. of observations	150	146	112

not always significant) the explanatory power of the regression never exceeds 11%.

Perhaps then the growth determinants – the X's which much of the empirical growth literature sought to identify – vary over time. Easterly et al. consider this possibility but as they point out most growth determinants suggested by theory are very persistent: investment rates, trade openness, and even government policies don't vary much decade to decade. In fact, one of the most robust correlates of development is the quality of institutions, a characteristic which is usually thought to be a deep-rooted and very slow-moving variable.

This leaves the possibility that the growth rates we observe is just a consequence of random shocks pushing countries out of steady states and the transitional dynamics that follows such shocks. However, Pritchett (2000) looks more closely at growth in developing countries and concludes that a complex set of growth patterns can indeed be identified. These patterns often do not resemble a shock-and-monotonic-transition-back-to-BGP scenario. Pritchett writes "[S]hifts in growth rates lead to distinct patterns. While some countries have steady growth (hills and steep hills), others have rapid growth followed by stagnation (plateaus), rapid growth followed by decline (mountains) or even catastrophic falls (cliffs), continuous stagnation (plains), or steady decline (valleys)." He concludes that the empirics of growth should focus on identifying factors that initiate and stop growth, instead of analyzing what explains average growth.

3. Growth transitions

Following the contributions by Easterly et al. (1993) and Pritchett (2000) several recent papers have focused attention on growth transitions, that is, points in time when a large shift in growth occurs, such as an acceleration when the rate of expansion of GDP per capita suddenly picks up significantly for an extended period of time. The main focus of these papers is to identify such turning points.[2] The common finding in all these papers is that such large growth changes are a common phenomenon in both rich and poor countries. In particular, growth accelerations – defined in one paper as periods of rapid growth in excess of 3.5% per year (but usually much higher) – are quite common even among countries that are regarded as unsuccessful developers. That is, now and then even poor countries grow rapidly for a significant period of time. One of the key conclusions from this research is that igniting rapid growth and sustaining it are two very different enterprises and that the latter seems much more difficult (see Rodrik, 2005). This is an important finding for policy makers but also for the field of economic growth because it casts doubt on the applicability of standard growth models to the question of economic development. The obvious next step in this literature is to determine what forces lead to growth accelerations and how they can be sustained. Here the literature has been less successful. Each of the contributions described below attempts to shed some light on the causes of growth transitions but our understanding of this phenomenon is still limited.

---

[2] In this chapter we focus on papers employing statistical methods to detect and analyze growth transitions. Another approach is to look at case studies, that is, analyze the history of development of a single country at a time with a close attention to economic, political and social changes. While important, this approach offers limited possibility for generalization of results and we view it as complementary to the systematic statistical approach. See the volume edited by Dani Rodrik (2003).

Hausmann, Pritchett, and Rodrik (2005) are the first to develop a formal methodology for identifying growth accelerations. They define "growth acceleration" as an episode satisfying three criteria: (1) growth of GDP per capita exceeds 3.5% per year, (2) the increase in growth rate exceeds 2 percentage points, and (3) after seven years output per capita exceeds the highest level attained prior to the episode. They use a spline regression to identify such episodes in a large sample of countries between 1950 and 2000. To their surprise they find a great many accelerations; there are a total of 83 accelerations in their sample during the 36 years where their methodology allowed for accelerations to occur. This implies that an average country would have about a 25% chance of experiencing a growth acceleration per decade. In fact, 60% of the countries in the sample had at least one episode of acceleration and 23% had at least two. The accelerations were also large in magnitude with an average of 4.7 percentage points increase in growth. Hausmann and co-authors also investigate the causes of growth accelerations. They run a probit where the dependent variable is a dummy that takes the value of 1 around the time of a growth acceleration and 0 otherwise. The list of covariates in their regressions includes a terms-of-trade shock, political regime change, and economic liberalization. They find many results consistent with the common wisdom in the growth literature: episodes of financial liberalization are positively correlated with the probability of experiencing a growth acceleration, economic reforms help produce more sustained accelerations, while shocks tend to produce short-lived growth. Additionally, they find that the negative impact of a movement towards autocracy is much larger than the positive impact of a movement towards democracy. However, many growth accelerations do not appear to be spurred by any obvious changes in standard growth determinants and, equally interestingly, many instances of reform fail to produce fast growth. As the authors emphasize, growth accelerations are surprisingly hard to explain, that is, even if some of the variables have a statistically significant effect, the overall predictive power of these regressions remains quite low.[3]

---

[3] de Haan and Jong-A-Pin (2007) use a different indicator of growth accelerations and find that they tend to be preceded by economic reforms and that they are more likely to take place after the start of a new political regime. In a related paper, Jones and Olken (2005) study in more detail the impact of the accidental death of a political leader on the subsequent growth performance of the country he was ruling. They find robust evidence that the impact of the death of a leader, particularly in an autocracy, has a positive and large impact on growth. Imam and Salinas (2008) study growth accelerations in Sub-Saharan Africa and find that they are mostly associated with external shocks, episodes of economic liberalization, political stability, and geographical variables such as proximity to the coast. On the other hand, high levels of corruption, as well as falling domestic credit seem to be correlated with sharp growth decelerations. Aizenman and Spiegel (2010) focus on take-off from stagnation to rapid growth (i.e., they exclude accelerations from already rapid growth to even higher one) and explore, among other factors, the composition of the country's output.

Jones and Olken (2008) extend the analysis of Hausmann et al. to include both accelerations and decelerations in growth episodes. They identify growth transitions using the Bai–Perron test (Bai & Perron 1998).[4] Their findings confirm that such episodes are frequent for most rich and developing countries; they detect 73 structural breaks in 48 of the 125 countries with at least 20 years of Penn World Table data. Of these transitions, 43 are "up-breaks" or accelerations, and 30 are "down-breaks" or collapses. The breaks identified by the Bai–Perron test are large: the mean change in growth during a break is 6.8 percentage points for "up-breaks" and –6 percentage points for "down-breaks." Since their test seems to set the bar for identifying an acceleration higher, they find fewer of them than Hausmann et al. (2005). To better understand the nature of growth transitions, Jones and Olken (2008) look for significant changes in main macroeconomic variables and measures of institutions around the time of the transition. First, they perform a standard growth decomposition separating growth of GDP into that of physical capital and the residual (TFP) and find an interesting asymmetry whereby accelerations are associated with rapid TFP growth but not significantly faster capital accumulation. "Down-breaks" are associated with declines in both TFP and capital accumulation. They fail to find any significant change in institutional variables at the time of growth breaks. Of the macroeconomic variables, accelerations appear to be associated with a significant increase in trade (both imports and exports) while collapses coincide with increases in nominal instability (increase in inflation and nominal exchange rate depreciation).

In Cuberes and Jerzmanowski (2009) we follow a similar approach. We also start by identifying and documenting structural breaks in the growth process using the Bai–Perron approach in the following specification

$$y_t = \alpha_n + g_n t + \varepsilon_t \quad \text{for} \quad t_n < t \le t_{n+1}, \forall t = 1, \dots T \tag{1}$$

where y_t represents the logarithm of real output per worker relative to the United States, the variable t indexes time, while n indexes growth breaks, g_n represents the trend growth following n-th break, and ε_t is the error term. That is, each time a break occurs, there can potentially be a change in the intercept parameter, the slope, or both. We focus our attention on the changes in growth rates (the slope parameter).

We use data on real output per worker from the Penn World Table (Heston, Summers, & Aten, 2006) for the period 1950–2000. We find a total of 208 breaks, which corresponds to 1.8 breaks per country. Of these breaks, 49% represent increases in the growth rate. Figure 5 shows the case of Argentina, where the Bai–Perron methodology finds two structural breaks. The first break occurs around 1980, and it corresponds to a large

---

[4] See also Ben-David, Lumsdaine, and Papell (2003).

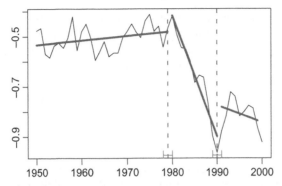

Fig. 5. Argentina's log real output per worker relative to the United States.
Notes: *Bai–Perron break dates are indicated by the vertical dashed lines. The solid lines show the estimate of the trend part of* $y_t = \alpha_n + g_n t$. *The figure also shows the confidence intervals around the estimated break dates.* **Source:** *Cuberes and Jerzmanowski (2009).*

decline in Argentina's growth rate, which moves from positive (catching up to the United States) to negative (falling behind it). The second break occurs around 1990, and this time growth becomes less negative without changing its sign. The graph also shows the confidence intervals of the estimated break dates.[5]

Next we analyze the patterns in the trend-growth changes we have identified. We are particularly interested in the link between political institutions and the magnitude of growth swings. We are motivated by the strong evidence that democratic countries are less volatile (Quinn & Woolley, 2001; Rodrik, 2000). This interesting correlation proved to be much more robust than the democracy–growth relationship: while various studies find that the effect of democracy on growth is rather weak (Barro & Sala-i-Martin, 2003; Przeworski & Limongi, 1993), the link between a greater degree of democracy and lower economic instability appears very robust (Rodrik, 1999). However, this literature usually measures volatility of per-capita GDP growth as the standard deviation of annual growth rates. Having uncovered large and frequent medium-term swings in

---

[5] One concern about the Bai–Perron test of structural breaks is that it relies on asymptotic properties. Since we use relatively short time series throughout the analysis, one may be concerned about inference based on asymptotic results. To check the robustness of our break detection results, we employ a Bayesian approach based on Wang and Zivot (2000) to estimate these breaks and compare our results with the ones obtained using the Bai–Perron method. Our comparison focuses on the years at which breaks occur with each method. The average difference (in absolute value) between the two estimates is 0.33 years, and its standard deviation is 3.23. In 67% of the cases, the break dates are identical, and the difference is no larger than five years 92% of the time.

growth we investigate whether this sort of medium-term volatility is also related to political institutions. In particular, we estimate: (i) how the magnitude of trend-growth changes varies with the degree of the country's democracy, and (ii) whether democracy affects the likelihood of experiencing large trend-growth swings.

To analyze the dynamics of growth transitions we estimate the following regression

$$g_{in} = \beta_0 + \beta_1 g_{in-1} + \varepsilon_{in} \tag{2}$$

where g_{in} represents the growth rate in country i after break n-th break estimated from (1). We are interested in the coefficient β_1, that is, the existence and direction of a relation between pre-break and post-break growth rates. Depending on the value of the β_1 parameter, we can have three interesting cases. First, if $\hat{\beta}_1 = 0$, then, on average, the growth rate before a break does not help predict the growth rate after it. If $\hat{\beta}_1 \in (0,1)$, then there is monotonic convergence in growth rates. This is a reversion-to-the-mean dynamic; that is, exceptionally fast growers before the break still grow fast after the break, just slightly less so; in the long run, there is convergence to the BGP. Figure 5 illustrates the dynamics of this system for the case where initial growth is above the long-run equilibrium value. When interpreting the figure, recall that "periods" here are not calendar years but break dates. Thus growth may remain constant for a long period of time, but when a break occurs, the adjustment is as illustrated in the figure. Figure 5 shows the case in which $\hat{\beta}_1 \in (-1,0)$ and growth fluctuates from above and below the BGP during its transition, in other words the process is characterized by growth cycles or reversals.

To see whether the degree of democracy affect the dynamics of growth transition, we split the sample into high and low democracy groups and estimate Equation (2) separately for each group.[6] We use the variable *polity2* from the dataset *POLITY IV* (Marshall & Jaggers, 2002) as our measure of democracy.[7] As additional covariates in the estimated version of (2), we also include the level of democracy and the log of initial income (to capture the standard convergence dynamics) and decade dummies. We use alternative panel data estimators but in Table 2 we only report the estimates obtained using the dynamic Arellano-Bond estimator (Arellano & Bond, 1991). While among the democratic countries we find no significant relationship between the pre- and post-break growth rates ($\beta_1 \approx 0$), in the less democratic sample we see evidence of growth reversals ($\beta_1 < 0$). That

---

[6] In Cuberes and Jerzmanowski (2009) we use an interaction to avoid picking an arbitrary cut-off level of democracy to split the sample.

[7] *polity2* is an average of autocracy and democracy scores. It ranges from -10 to 10 ($-10 =$ high autocracy; $10 =$ high democracy) and includes specific indexes meant to capture constraints on the executive, the degree of political competition, the legislature effectiveness, etc.

Table 2. Growth reversals in the PWT data

	Low democracy	High democracy
Growth before break	-0.374^{**}	0.083
	(0.146)	(0.202)
Initial income	-0.074^{**}	-0.069^{***}
	(0.036)	(0.018)
Democracy	0.00	0.000
	(0.001	(0.001)
Constant	-0.006	0.003
	(0.005)	(0.005)
Obs.	84	49

$^{**}p<0.5, ^{***}p<0.01.$

is, periods of exceptionally high growth are, on average, followed by periods of exceptionally low growth, and vice versa. Growth rates in less democratic economies are not monotone; rather, they cycle between high and low (or even negative) values as in Figure 6(b). Interestingly, the income level does not affect the propensity to experience growth reversals.

Using a probit and linear probability models we also find that the propensity to experience large swings of trend-growth is not uniform across countries – less democratic countries are more susceptible to it. When compared with factors commonly associated with volatility, such as measures of quality of institutions, macroeconomic policies, and financial development, as well as income level, we find that democracy is the most robust predictor of a country's propensity for growth reversals. Finally, we test whether our results can be explained by the fact that countries that rely heavily on natural resources tend to be less democratic and also exposed to large shocks (in the form of large swings of world prices of the resources

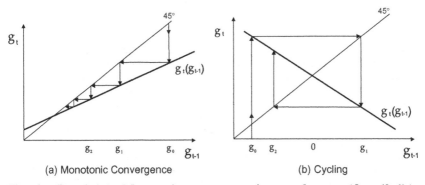

Fig. 6. Panel (a): Monotonic convergence in growth rates ($\beta_1 \in (0,1)$). Panel (b): Growth reversals ($\beta_1 \in (-1,0)$). Source: Cuberes and Jerzmanowski (2009).

332   Michał Jerzmanowski and David Cuberes

they export). While shocks to prices of natural resources appear to contribute to the propensity for growth reversals, they do not account for the effect of democracy.[8]

In the above analysis, taken from Cuberes and Jerzmanowski (2009), we use data on output per worker from the Penn World Table covering, for most countries, the period 1960–2000. Here, to explore the presence and dynamics of growth transitions in a longer time series, we extend our analysis to the historical figures on output per capita from Maddison (1995, 2001), which covers the period 1870–1994.[9] We again use the Bai–Perron test for structural breaks, and we exploit the same measures of democracy.[10] We find that during this period the average number of breaks per country in the Maddison sample is around 4. In 48% of the cases these breaks represent an increase in growth. The lowest number of breaks per country is 2, and the largest is 8. Figure 7 presents an histogram of the changes in growth rates at the time of the structural break. Since in the Maddison data the number of countries with available information on income changes significantly over time, going from 14 countries in the 1870s, to 29 in the 1920s, to 54 after 1960, we divide the number of breaks by the number of countries in each year.

The first observation is that the frequency of breaks does not show a very clear trend if one considers the entire period. The incidence of breaks was quite large in the 1880s, and in most cases they represented sudden increases in growth. After that decade, the frequency of breaks decreased and then rose again until the 1920s. The vast majority of structural breaks that we detect in the 1930s were negative, indicating the economic turbulence of the Great Depression. The opposite happens in the aftermath of WW2 (1940s), a period of very frequent growth accelerations that reflect the economic recovery in many of the countries in our sample. The number of breaks dropped drastically in the 1950s and rose again in the last three decades of the studied period. It is noticeable that in these decades growth decelerations were more common than accelerations. The

---

[8] One may think that greater growth variability in less democratic countries is a reflection of more frequent regime changes: that is, whenever a ruler changes there is an abrupt change in growth. While Jones and Olken's (2005) result suggest leaders do matter for growth in less democratic countries, the average time between breaks is usually shorter than many autocrats' tenure. Easterly (2011) studies this question directly and concludes that growth is equally variable within autocrats' tenure as between them.

[9] The 112 countries in Maddison's unbalanced panel are: Argentina, Australia, Austria, Belgium, Bangladesh, Bulgaria, Brazil, Canada, Chile, China, Colombia, Cote d'Ivoire, Congo Rep., Czech Republic, Denmark, Egypt, Ethiopia, Finland, France, Germany, Ghana, Greece, Hungary, India, Indonesia, Ireland, Italy, Japan, Kenya, Korea Rep., Mexico, Morocco, Netherlands, New Zealand, Nigeria, Norway, Pakistan, Peru, Philippines, Poland, Portugal, Romania, Russia, South Africa, Spain, Sweden, Switzerland, Taiwan, Tanzania, Thailand, Turkey, United Kingdom, Venezuela, and Yugoslavia.

[10] Using the Bayesian methodology of Wang and Zivot (2000) we get similar results.

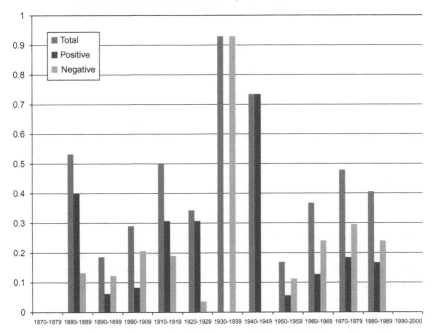

Fig. 7.   *Frequency of growth breaks in the Maddison data set.*

key conclusion we draw from this exercise is that the phenomenon of growth transitions is not unique to the modern period studied by most papers in this literature.

Next we ask whether, as was the case in the modern period PWT data, there is a tendency for less democratic countries to experience larger growth swings. As we did in Cuberes and Jerzmanowski (2009) we split countries in two groups: those with high democracy and those with low democratic scores.[11] We then estimate an Equation (2) including as regressors initial income, the initial level of democracy, and time dummies for each decade. Table 3 displays the results obtained using the Arellano-Bond dynamic fixed effects estimator.

In the entire sample there is evidence of growth reversals even after controlling for initial income (column 3), although it is not statistically significant once we include initial democracy as an additional control (column 4). Columns 5 and 6 show that democratic countries exhibit no cycling. The coefficient associated with growth before the break is not

---

[11] In both cases, the cut-off here is chosen to be the median value of polity2 in the sample, that is, countries with a democracy score equal or larger than this threshold are labeled "high democracies" and below it they are considered "low democracies." Alternative cutoffs deliver very similar results.

Table 3.   Growth reversals in the Maddison data

	All countries		High democracy		Low democracies	
Growth before break	-0.307^{***}	-0.157	-0.223	0.174	-0.388^{***}	-0.468^{***}
	(0.095)	(0.1)	(0.148)	(0.157)	(0.113)	(0.134)
Initial income	-0.029	-0.075^{***}	-0.03	-0.109^{***}	-0.048^{***}	-0.062^{***}
	(0.018)	(0.023)	(0.027)	(0.038)	(0.015)	(0.017)
Democracy		0.000		-0.001		0.001
		(0.001)		(0.001)		(0.001)
No. of observations	130	85	74	46	56	39

$^{***}p<0.01.$

significant and it even turns positive. On the contrary, nondemocracies experience growth reversals. Columns 6 and 7 show that, in these countries periods of rapid growth are followed by periods of much slower growth, and vice versa. This is very much consistent with the results obtained using the PWT data for the period 1950–2000.[12]

The above exercise gives us further confidence in the phenomenon of growth reversals first described in Cuberes and Jerzmanowski (2009). Of course, the natural question to ask is why do less democratic institutions lead to larger growth swings? We hypothesize, following arguments made by Acemoglu (2008) and Aghion, Alesina, and Trebbi (2007), that less democracy implies larger barriers to entry for firms and thus a larger degree of concentration in production. With less diversification comes the potential for larger growth swings. Using data on manufacturing concentration from the U.N's Industrial Statistics Database (revision 2), we find support for this argument. Specifically, we first calculate the Herfindahl–Hirschmann index of concentration for the manufacturing industry in each of the 181 countries in our sample during the period 1963–2003.[13] We then regress this index against the POLITY IV measure of democracy as well as per capita GDP and its square. Table 4 shows that the coefficient on democracy is negative and significant at conventional levels, indicating that the manufacturing sector is indeed less concentrated in more democratic countries, even after controlling for income effects.

Another reason less democratic countries may experience growth reversals is due to social conflict. For example, Rodrik (1999) shows that the growth slowdowns of the 1970s were larger in less democratic and more ethno-

---

[12] It is also noticeable that in all cases, richer countries tend to experience more slow growth in the next regime, indicating some degree of neoclassical convergence. The initial level of democracy, on the contrary, is uncorrelated with future rates of growth.

[13] The dataset contains information on 29 manufacturing categories at the three-digit level of disaggregation.

Table 4. Democracy and industrial concentration

	Value added	Output	Value added	Output
Democracy	−0.159***	−0.166***	−0.111*†	−0.121**
	(0.052)	(0.048)	(0.070)	(0.061)
GDP p.c.			−0.386	−0.623**
			(0.269)	(0.263)
GDP p.c. squared			0.019	0.034**
			(0.018)	(0.017)
Constant	2.880***	2.739***	4.629***	5.402***
	(0.136)	(0.127)	(1.060)	(1.037)
R^2	0.072	0.084	0.109	0.127
No. of observations	2695	2623	2649	2591

Source: Cuberes and Jerzmanowski (2009).
Notes: Pooled OLS regression of the Herfindahl-Hirschman index in manufacturing on democracy, GDP per capita, and GDP per capita squared. Standard errors clustered by country. *†$p < 0.12$, **$p < 0.05$, ***$p < 0.01$.

linguistically fictionalized countries. He argues that both of these characteristics lead to more internal conflict because there are more groups in the society who may have opposing interests and the lack of democracy prevents peaceful resolution of disputes among them. It is plausible that a mechanism like this could lead to growth reversals. In early stages of rapid growth, its benefits are usually distributed unevenly among the various groups in the society (workers vs. capital owners, exporters vs. import-competing producers, educated vs. uneducated workers, etc.). If the rising income inequality leads to social tension and conflict, and there are no peaceful resolution mechanisms, internal turmoil and a growth collapse may be a direct consequence of the preceding rapid growth. While logically appealing, this hypothesis has not been formally tested as far as we know.

An interesting alternative explanation for growth reversals has recently been suggested by Boucekkine and Pintus (2011). They develop an AK model of a small open economy with borrowing constraints that allows for both leapfrogging and growth reversals. In their model, economies have access to the international capital market but there exists a borrowing limit determined by the amount of available collateral. The novel element comes for the fact that, if it is not possible for the borrower to commit to a future investment plan, the lender uses the borrower's past stock of capital as collateral. This assumption leads to interesting history dependence: the BGP of the economy depends not only on the initial level of capital but also on its past growth path. This dependence of the borrowing limit on lagged capital stock is also key to generating growth reversals and/or leapfrogging. If the delay – the lag with which capital becomes collateral – is short, then history does not matter much. Therefore, a rich country that had a recent slow growth will receive a low amount of credit, and therefore, it will grow slowly in the future. In this case, there will be leapfrogging and no growth reversals (the country that was performing poorly will continue to do so in the future). Growth reversals (instances when growth goes from above BGP value to below it) are also possible. They occur when a fast growing country faces the borrowing constraint with a sufficiently long lag. Since its capital stock was low in the past, its current debt limit is low and the lack of foreign capital inflow leads to a growth slowdown. There is also an intermediate case where both leapfrogging and growth reversals are possible. The authors argue that under reasonable parameter values the model is able to replicate characteristics of growth reversals reported in Cuberes and Jerzmanowski (2009). The paper by Boucekkine and Pintus is especially noteworthy because it represents one of the first attempts to construct a theory of growth transitions.[14]

Finally, we should note that the theories of poverty traps would appear to be natural explanations for growth transitions. After all, most of such models predict a long period of stagnation or slow growth (poverty trap) and a sudden acceleration of growth once the economy escapes the trap. However, most of these theories also imply that the escape from the trap is once and for all. Easterly (2006) uses the Bai–Perron test to identify episodes of permanent growth take-off, that is, growth permanently transiting from zero to positive value, which he interprets as evidence of emergence from a poverty trap. He finds very few such episodes. This is consistent with our findings that growth accelerations, especially in non-democratic countries, are ultimately reversed.

One conclusion reiterated in the papers discussed above is that initiating growth and sustaining it require different policies and/or environments. For example, Hausmann et al. (2005) show that standard economic and political fundamentals (economic reform, political regime change, terms of trade shocks, etc.) do rather poorly at explaining the timing of growth accelerations. A paper by Berg, Ostry, and Zettelmeyer (2008) asks a very natural complementary question: what is the role of standard growth determinants in sustaining growth? Of course, knowing what makes growth sustained is key for policymakers in developing world, perhaps more important than knowing how to start it, since accelerations happen quite often (even if we don't fully understand why). To investigate duration of growth spells Berg and coauthors estimate a proportional hazard model using a host of potential determinants including shocks (world interest rate, terms of trade), institutions, macroeconomic stability, social and economic homogeneity, human capital, and trade and financial openness (including

---

[14] Aghion, Bacchetta, and Banerjee (2004) are motivated by more high frequency volatility but their model, in which periods of economic boom put upward pressure on price of the scarce domestic factor of production that leads to a slowdown, suggest another interesting mechanism for generating growth reversals.

structure of exports and capital inflows). Where appropriate and possible the authors include the initial level as well as the change during the spell for the explanatory variables. To measure growth spell duration they use a combination of the Hausmann et al. (2005) and Jones and Olken (2008) approaches to dating growth accelerations. Specifically, the authors focus their attention on episodes of growth acceleration to above 2% followed by deceleration to below 2% (complete spells) or end of sample (incomplete spells). Among their findings they report that democracy, income equality, macroeconomic stability as well as export orientation (including propensity to export manufactures, openness to FDI, and avoidance of exchange rate overvaluation) all help sustain growth spells. Perhaps surprisingly, violent conflict doesn't appear to matter. Conditional on the covariates the authors usually find a positive but often not significant duration dependence.[15]

4. Growth regimes

Just as averaging growth over long periods of time masks the diverse experience of growth accelerations and collapses, the binary classification of a growth transition (acceleration versus its absence) removes some important variation across countries and time. In fact, in Pritchett's analysis cited above he distinguished multiple growth patterns, of which accelerations (and collapses) were just one example. In another paper, Pritchett (2003) suggests that an appropriate way to think about growth is to imagine that there exist multiple growth states, or regimes, each of which represents a distinct growth behavior.

Pritchett illustrates his idea with a simulation of a simple model with four states: a stagnation state with constant growth of 0.5%, a convergence state with rapid growth, an implosion state with negative growth, and a state of steady growth at 1.8%. He assumes that the state characteristics (growth rates in each state) and that transition are probabilistically constant and identical for all developing countries. He then calibrates the transition matrix in so that the world economy with 103 developing countries and 14 developed countries (which are restricted to always be in the steady growth regime) matches the observed dispersion of GDP per capita in 1995. His main message is that a model of this kind has the potential to generate a wide range of growth patterns among developing countries as well as account for low persistence of growth discussed above. Notice that in this model it is only the randomness of the (common) transition dynamics that generates the diversity of growth patterns across developing countries. However, in practice, there is no particular reason to think that transition probabilities are the same for all countries. The idea that country-specific characteristics affect growth by determining transition probabilities leads to some interesting possibilities.

---

[15] See also Johnson, Ostry, and Subramanian (2007).

To illustrate the idea consider the following simple example. Suppose that there are only two possible states of the world – one in which the economy stagnates and another in which it grows at 3% per year. If over time a country switches between regimes, growth will be an uneven process. This is of course what growth looks like for many countries. For example, Japan accelerated in the 1950s and 1960s and the stagnated in the 1990s while India grew slowly until it took off in the 1990s. If we further assume that these transition probabilities themselves depend on some country-specific characteristic X (e.g., quality of institutions), we have a model where country characteristics, such as policies or institutional quality, shape long run growth by affecting the frequency of the two regimes.

Within a standard approach to growth, if a characteristic X is "good" for growth, then countries with a high level of X are expected to be growing fast (say, at 3% per year) and countries with low levels of X are expected, all else equal, to be growing slowly (say, stagnate); this is a world where "you either have what it takes for growth or you don't." In the regimes approach it becomes possible for country characteristics to be favorable to growth by affecting the transition probabilities; good X means more frequent episodes of growth but it is possible for the high-X country to stagnate just as it is possible for the low-X country to grow from time to time. A stylized illustration of the switching process of growth for two countries is presented below in Figure 8.

Country 1 has a lower level of the growth-conducive characteristic X, and so it spends more time in the stagnation regime. However, it is capable of periods of fast growth. In fact, when it is growing, it grows as fast as country 2. Of course, country 2 with high X visits the growth regime more frequently, and so in the long run it will grow faster. However, it too stagnates from time to time. What determines the long run growth performance of an economy is the within-regime dynamics (3% vs. 0), and the frequency of visits to the two growth regimes. The growth regimes approach calls for identifying the regimes as well as the properties of transitions, including the set of X's that may include present day economic and political characteristics of the country, regional or world variables, the country's history, etc.

Jerzmanowski (2006) estimates a model where transition probabilities are allowed to differ across countries, as was the case in the example of Figure 8. He builds on Pritchett's insights and applies the framework of Markov-switching regression to identify the regimes. Assuming that there are four regimes, each with a distinct AR(1) growth process leads to the following model[16]

---

[16] Unfortunately the correct number of regimes cannot be tested with the simple likelihood ratio test. See Hamilton (1994) for discussion and references. The informal procedure followed by Jerzmanowski (2006) was to start with two regimes and increase the number of regimes as long as all estimated regimes appeared distinct.

Country 1

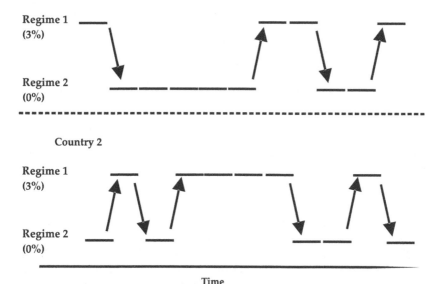

Fig. 8. *A stylized illustration of the switching process of growth.* **Notes:** *Some country-specific characteristic* X *makes the growth regime more likely (e.g. good institutions). Country 1 has low value of* X *and so it spends more time in the stagnation regime. However, it is capable of periods of fast growth. Country 2 has high* X *and so it visits the growth regime more frequently. However it too stagnates from time to time.*

$$\hat{y}_{it} = \alpha_{s_t} + \beta_{s_t}\hat{y}_{it-1} + \varepsilon_{it}^{s_t} \tag{3}$$

$$\varepsilon_{it}^{s_t} \sim i.i.d.N(0, \sigma_{s_t}^2) \tag{4}$$

where $\hat{y}_{ti}$ is the growth rate of country i in period t and s_t indicates the regime that is in effect at time t, that is for every t, $s_t \in \{1, 2, 3, 4\}$.

The growth process is fully characterized by the above within regime dynamics (3)–(4) and the evolution of regimes, which is assumed to follow a 4-state Markov process where the transition probabilities are allowed to depend on the country's quality of institutions. That is, $P\{s_{it} = k | s_{it-1} = j\} \equiv p_{jk} = p_{jk}(z_i)$ for $j, k = 1, \ldots, 4$, where z_i is a measure of the quality of institutions in country i. Thus unlike in Pritchett's simple simulation, transition probabilities are country specific. This model is estimated using maximum likelihood (see Jerzmanowski, 2006, for details). The resulting estimates consist of the within-regime parameters (α's, β's, and σ's), the

Michał Jerzmanowski and David Cuberes

Table 5.   Parameter estimates of the regime switching model

	Constant (α_s)	AR coeff. (β_s)	Std. dev.(σ_s)	Long-run growth
Stable growth	0.0132**	0.3761**	2.11%	2.12%
Stagnation	0.0010	0.1799**	4.56%	0.12%
Crisis	−0.0101**	−0.0045	13.16%	−1.00%
Miracle growth	0.0536**	0.1417**	2.71%	6.25%

Source: Jerzmanowski (2006).
Note: The first column shows the constant term, the second is the autoregressive coefficient and the third is the estimate of the standard deviation of the error component. The last column shows the implied long-run growth. Parameter estimates of the regime switching model, ** significance at 5% level.

parameters of the transition matrix $p_{jk}(z_i)$ for $j, k = 1, \ldots, 4$, and the inference about regimes s_t for $t = 1, \ldots T$. We discuss them in turn.

Table 5 shows the parameter estimates. Each of the four AR(1) processes implies a different long-run growth rate, that is, the average growth rate that would obtain if the economy were to remain in that regime indefinitely, given by $\alpha/(1 - \beta)$ and shown in the last column. Notice that these average long run growth rates (from which we derive the regime labels) do not fully characterize the regimes. In addition to the long run average performance, regimes differ significantly in volatility of growth (σ) and persistence of growth shocks (β).[17] The stable regime corresponds to the growth experience predominant among developed economies, with long run average growth of about 2%. The volatility is relatively low and there is a great deal of persistence in the growth process. The stagnation regime is characterized by no growth on average and larger volatility of growth shocks. In this regime, periods of growth and decline occur but are not very persistent. The crisis regime is an episode of large shocks to growth. While these shocks tend on average to be negative reflecting economic crises, the dispersion is very large and positive shocks are also possible. These shocks have no persistence. Finally, there exists the regime of fast, miracle-like growth with a long run average growth of 6% and modest volatility.

Figure 9 summarizes the estimates of transition matrices. Each of the four boxes plots the probability of moving from a given state to each of the four states as a function of the institutions index. For example, the upper

---

[17] Note that the within-regime persistence of the growth process β, say 0.3761 for the stable growth regime, should not be confused with the persistence of the stable growth regime itself. The former is assumed to be a property of the stable growth process common to all countries, whereas the latter depends on the country-specific transition probabilities, which will be discussed below.

left hand side box shows the probability of moving from the stable growth state to each of the four states. The solid line shows the probability of moving to the stable state (i.e., in this case remaining in the same state), the dash-dot line shows the probability of moving to stagnation while the dashed and dotted lines show the same for crisis and miracle regimes, respectively. The upper right hand side box shows the same set of plots conditional on the current state being stagnation and so on.

The stable growth regime is very persistent for all values of the institutions index but the persistence does increase with the quality of institutions. Stagnation is very persistent for weak-institutions countries but this persistence falls off markedly with the quality of institutions above

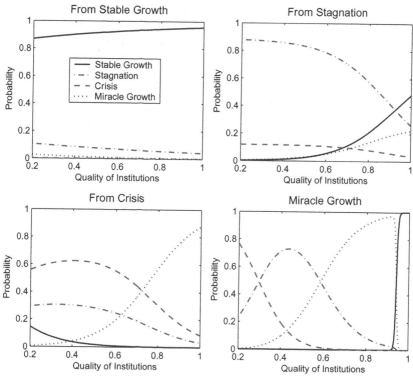

Fig. 9. Transition probabilities as a function of the quality of institutions. **Notes:** *The upper left hand side box shows plots of the probability of moving from state 1 to each of the four states. The solid line shows the probability of moving to state 1 (i.e., probability of remaining in the same state), the dash-dot line shows the probability of moving to state 2 while the dashed and dotted lines show the same for states 3 and 4, respectively.* **Source:** *Jerzmanowski (2006).*

0.6 (e.g., Turkey). For countries with high quality of institutions stagnation is more likely to be followed by a reversal to stable growth. The lower left hand side graph shows the probability of changing regimes conditional on current state being the growth shock (crisis) state. Finally, the lower right hand side graph shows the probability of changing regimes conditional on current state being the fast growth state. For low quality countries a period of fast growth is very likely followed by a growth shock state. Intermediate quality countries are also not likely to remain in the growth regime for long and most likely revert to stagnation. However for mid-to high institutions countries the fast growth regime is very persistent.

Figure 10 shows the plots of the ergodic distribution of states for different levels of institutional quality. The most important feature is that countries with low quality of institutions spend about 60% of the time in stagnation, and only around 15–20% of the time growing at positive and sustained but moderate rates. For values of the quality of institutions above 0.4 time spent stagnating starts decreasing while the fraction of time spent growing increases. However quality of institutions must be above 0.6 for stagnation to no longer be the most frequent state. Improving institutions also increases the time spent growing fast (miracle growth).

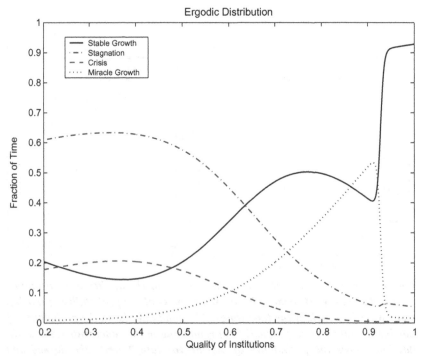

Fig. 10.   Ergodic probabilities of the four regimes as functions of the quality of institutions. Source: Jerzmanowski (2006).

For values of index above 0.7 (e.g., Mauritius) more time is spent growing fast than stagnating.

These estimated transition probabilities imply that institutions are more important in sustaining growth than in igniting it. In particular, low quality of institutions countries have significant probability of entering growth regimes, however, the probability of exit is high. In the long run regimes follow an ergodic distribution where low quality of institutions leads to frequent stagnation and crisis whereas high quality, while not ruling out stagnation or crises, reduces their frequency and increases that of the growth regimes.

These results suggest that randomness of the transition between regimes is not the only factor accounting for differences in growth patterns across countries. In particular, the quality of institutions, widely believed to be an important growth determinant, affect the transition dynamics. High quality of institutions, such as strong rule of law and protection of private property, increase the frequency of visits to favorable regimes but most importantly make them more persistent; countries with weak institutions are capable of growth takeoffs, however, they are unable to sustain them.

5. Policies, institutions, and regime switching

Pritchett's (2003) simple simulation illustrated that a model that includes multiple growth regimes and random transitions between them can account for the large diversity of growth patterns. Jerzmanowski (2006) extends this insight by explicitly estimating a regime-switching growth model and allowing the transition probabilities to depend on quality of country's institutions. This raises a natural question about what other country characteristics influence the probability of transitions between regimes. In this section we provide a novel analysis of this question. We focus on the role of macroeconomic policies.

The question whether macroeconomic policies such as inflation, government spending, real exchange rate overvaluation, and trade openness matter for long-run economic growth has a long history in empirical growth literature. Early research on determinants of growth in a cross-section of countries found significant effects of macroeconomic policies on long-run growth (e.g., Barro, 1991; Dollar, 1992; Sachs & Warner, 1995). However, much of the recent literature is more skeptical. Easterly and Levine (2003) argue that, after controlling for institutions, policies do not affect the level of income. Easterly (2005) shows that the findings of significant effects of policies on growth are driven by extreme outliers. Finally, Acemoglu, Johnson, Robinson, and Thaichoren (2003) argue that once institutions are controlled for, policies do not matter much for growth and volatility. Here we re-examine the question of policies and growth, while explicitly accounting for within-country variation in the growth process. This framework is richer than the standard average growth analysis since it allows policies to work through multiple channels by differentially affecting the likelihood of growth accelerations, stagnation and crisis. We use the regime probabilities obtained by Jerzmanowski (2006) to estimate the effects of policies on the frequency of the four growth regimes. We ask whether some policies are associated with a country spending more time in periods of growth, stagnation or crisis.

To study the joint effect of institutions and policies on growth through their effect on regimes changes, one could follow the same approach as Jerzmanowski (2006) and extend the vector z in the transition probabilities matrix $p(z)$ to include measures of policy. In practice, the estimation is quite computationally intensive even with only one variable. Instead, we use the inference about likelihood of regimes obtained from the estimation of the baseline model. The logic of the approach is as follows.

Since the true value of the regime is unobservable we can never know with certainty whether a given country is in any given state. However, conditional on the model, the estimated parameters and all the observations for a given country, we can form inference about the probability of the regimes during the sample period. These *smoothed probabilities*, denoted by $\hat{P}(s_t = j | \mathscr{Y}_{mT})$, where $\mathscr{Y}_{mT}$ stands for the entire time series for country m, give us an estimate of the likelihood of each of the four regimes for country m at all sample dates t. For example, $\hat{P}(s_{1979} = 1 | \mathscr{Y}_{UST})$ tells us the (conditional) probability that the U.S. was in the stable growth regime in 1979. Figures 11 and 12 plot examples of the smoothed regime probabilities.

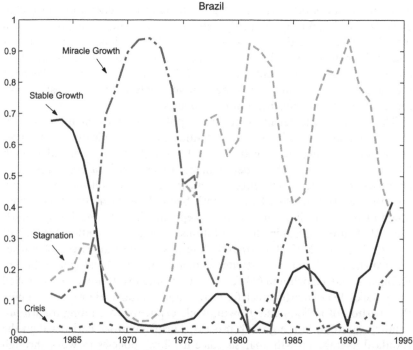

Fig. 11.   Regime probabilities: Brazil. Source: *Jerzmanowski (2006).*

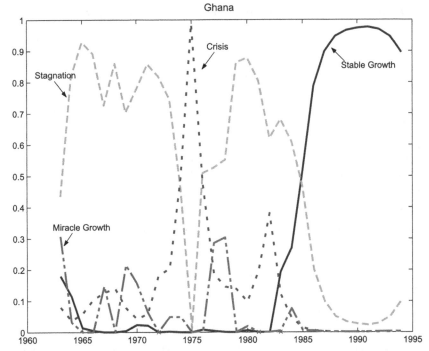

Fig. 12.   Regime probabilities: Ghana. Source: *Jerzmanowski (2006).*

Table 6 presents the smoothed probabilities averaged over the sample period 1970–1994 for each of the regimes for a selected group of countries. That is, for each country the first column gives the average probability of the stable growth regime $(1/T) \sum_{l=1}^{T} \hat{P}(s_l = 1|\mathcal{Y}_T)$, the second column gives the average probability of stagnation $(1/T) \sum_{l=1}^{T} \hat{P}(s_l = 2|\mathcal{Y}_T)$, and so on. These probabilities tell us what is the average (over sample years) probability that a country was in a given regime. For example, on average the probability that Japan was in the miracle growth regime is 33% while the average probability that it was stagnating is 5%.

We assume that the average frequencies approximate the ergodic regime distribution and use them to compute the average number of occurrences of each regime during the sample period. We then ask how the country's quality of institutions and macroeconomic policies affect the regime probabilities. In particular, we average the estimated probabilities over two subperiods, 1970–1982 and 1983–1994, and run a pooled multinomial logit. If, as was assumed by Jerzmanowski (2006), quality of institutions is the only variable determining transition probabilities, we would expect to

Table 6. *Smoothed probabilities averaged over the period 1970–1994*

Country	Stable growth	Stagnation	Crisis	Miracle growth	Avg. growth
Hong Kong	0.04	0.17	0.06	0.72	5.56%
Japan	0.62	0.05	0.00	0.33	4.31%
Thailand	0.13	0.33	0.03	0.51	4.36%
Portugal	0.51	0.13	0.01	0.36	3.92%
Malaysia	0.31	0.24	0.03	0.42	3.48%
Egypt	0.50	0.40	0.05	0.06	2.20%
India	0.37	0.51	0.03	0.09	2.10%
USA	0.89	0.07	0.00	0.03	2.04%
Mexico	0.52	0.35	0.02	0.11	1.68%
Chile	0.05	0.45	0.16	0.34	1.64%
Zimbabwe	0.05	0.72	0.15	0.08	1.03%
New Zealand	0.74	0.21	0.01	0.04	0.90%
Bolivia	0.45	0.43	0.08	0.03	0.10%
Cote d'Ivoire	0.02	0.61	0.15	0.22	0.07%

Source: Jerzmanowski (2006).

Notes: Let $\hat{P}(s_t = 1|Y_T)$, the smoothed inference about the likelihood that regime 1 was in effect in period t. Column 1 is $(1/T)\sum_{l=1}^{T}\hat{P}(s_l = 1|Y_T)$, column 2 is $(1/T)\sum_{l=1}^{T}\hat{P}(s_l = 2|Y_T)$, and so on.

replicate the estimates of the relationship between the ergodic distribution of regimes and the institutional quality presented in Figure 10, with departures from this distribution being purely random and unrelated to policies. Alternatively, if policies do matter, they will add additional explanatory power in fitting the observed regime distributions.[18]

To determine the relationship between policies and institutions and regime frequencies we estimate the following multinomial logit model.

$$\Pr(\text{regime} = j)_i = \frac{\exp(X_i\beta_j)}{\sum_{s=1}^{4} \exp(X_i\beta_s)}, \tag{5}$$

for $j = 1, 2, 3, 4$. $\Pr(\text{regime} = j)$ is the average probability of regime j during the sample periods, and X_i is a vector of country specific characteristics including initial income, quality of institutions and four policy measures: log of average inflation, real exchange rate overvaluation,

---

[18] See Kerekes (2009) for an innovative way to extend the approach in Jerzmanowski (2006) 45 to multivariate transition probabilities.

share of government's consumption in GDP, and trade to GDP ratio. Quality of institutions is measured using the rule of law index from Kaufmann, Kraay, & Mastruzzi (2003). Policy variables are averaged over the relevant period and are taken from World Bank economic indicators, except the real exchange rate overvaluation, which comes from Dollar (1992).

This model is a simple multinomial logit model with four (unordered) outcomes: stable growth, stagnation, collapse, and miracle growth. Of course, as discussed above, we do not actually observe whether a country is in a given regime in any given year but instead we have the (estimated) probabilities of regime occurrences. To proceed with the logit estimation, we convert the data on regime probabilities into counts of regime occurrences by multiplying the probabilities by the number of years in the sample. For example, the data in Table 6 corresponds to the period 1970–1994 and so multiplying the entries in the first row we attribute to Hong Kong one year of stable growth, four years of stagnation, one year of crisis, and 17 years of miracle growth.[19]

We estimate the above model using pooled data for the subperiods 1970–1982 and 1983–1994. Since the coefficient estimates are not easily interpreted, we do not report them here, instead we tabulate the estimated marginal effects at the median. Below we also examine how these effects vary over the entire distribution of the right hand side variables. This is important since, as Easterly (2005) points out, there are often significant outliers in the policy measures.

Table 7 shows the marginal effects of institutions, policies and income on the probability of each of the four regimes for a hypothetical country with all the right-hand side variables equal to the sample median (we refer to it as "median country"). The quality of institutions increase the probability of favorable outcomes – miracle growth and stable growth, while reducing the chances of unfavorable regimes – stagnation and crisis. The size of government lowers the likelihood of miracle growth but compensates this effect by increasing the chances of stable growth and reducing the probability of stagnation and crisis. Trade lowers the probability of stable growth while increasing that of miracle growth; it also increases the chances of crisis and stagnation. Both distortionary policies, inflation and real exchange rate overvaluation, increase the chances of stagnation and crisis, and lower the chances of stable growth, although the effect of inflation is not statistically significant. Their effect on miracle

---

[19] An alternative strategy, would be to estimate a linear model of the log odds-ratios, which are given by ln Pr(regime = j)$_i$/Pr(regime = 4)$_i$ = $X_i\beta_j$ for j = 1,2,3 where we have normalized β_4 = 0. Here we could use the probabilities of regime occurrences (Table 6) without the need to compute regime counts. This approach gives very similar results but has the disadvantage of considerably over-predicting (in sample) the probability of miracle growth and we do not pursue it.

Michał Jerzmanowski and David Cuberes

Table 7. Multinomial logit: marginal effects at the median

Variable	Stable growth	Stagnation	Crisis	Miracle growth
Rule of law	0.202*** (0.026)	−0.199*** (0.026)	−0.064*** (0.012)	0.060*** (0.015)
Inflation	−0.110 (0.100)	0.058 (0.073)	0.015 (0.014)	0.037 (0.027)
Overvaluation	−0.310*** (0.065)	0.240*** (0.057)	0.043** (0.018)	0.026 (0.031)
Government	2.086*** (0.445)	−0.806** (0.394)	−0.056 (0.153)	−1.224*** (0.400)
Trade	−0.434*** (0.072)	0.228*** (0.071)	0.046 (0.032)	0.161*** (0.034)
Initial Income	0.132*** (0.028)	−0.078*** (0.025)	−0.018** (0.008)	−0.035** (0.016)

Note: Standard errors in parentheses. Significance levels: ** 5%, *** 1%.

growth is also insignificant. Finally, the level of development as captured by initial income has an independent influence on regimes; it lowers the probability of miracle growth, which is the familiar convergence effect, albeit in a probabilistic sense. That is richer countries are less likely to grow at very rapid rates as predicted by the neoclassical model as well as technology catch-up models. This effect is, however, mitigated by the fact that income also increases the chances of stable growth. Higher income countries also appear to stagnate less and have less frequent crises. We can use the marginal effect to calculate the change in the probability of each regime given a one standard deviation change in the right hand side variables. These results are displayed in Figure 13.

Clearly, institutions not only deliver the desirable effects (more frequent growth states, less stagnation and crises) but quantitatively also have a large impact. However, the effects of government size and trade openness are also nontrivial but they are, to some extent, off-setting across regimes. For example, a one standard deviation increase in trade share means 3.5% more time spent growing fast and 10% less time growing at moderate stable rates. To translate the effects on probabilities of regimes into effects on long run growth we can multiply the effects from Figure 13 by the average long-run growth numbers for each regime, reported in Table 5. We can perform a similar calculation for the volatility of growth. The results are shown in Table 8. Note that the median growth rate in the sample was 1.46%, so that for the median country a one standard deviation improvement in rule of law results in growth increasing to 2.38% (1.46 + 0.92). On the contrary, a one standard deviation increase in

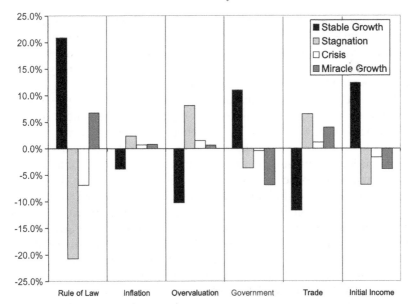

Fig. 13. *Effects of a one standard deviation change in the right-hand side variables on long run regime probabilities.* **Note:** *All right-hand side variables set to the sample median.*

Table 8. *Change in the average growth rate and volatility in response to one standard deviation change in the right hand side variables (in % points)*

Variable	Growth	Volatility
Rule of law	0.922	−1.270
Inflation	−0.037	0.149
Overvaluation	−0.188	0.388
Government	−0.200	−0.195
Trade	−0.004	0.294
Initial income	0.029	−0.387

government's size results in growth falling to 1.26%. This relatively small change is a net effect of the offsetting forces; larger government leads to less miracle growth but also less stagnation and more stable growth. Overall, we can conclude that at the median the effect of institutions on growth is much greater than that of any policy.[20] This reflects two findings. First, institutions do have a quantitatively large effect on growth, and

---

[20] Policies affect volatility more than average growth but again institutions are more important.

second, for some policies the effects on long run growth are off-setting across regimes. Similarly, note that despite evidence of convergence (richer countries are less likely to grow very fast) poor countries do not grow faster than rich ones. This is because at lower income levels they are also more susceptible to prolonged periods of stagnation.

Of course, the above calculations do not fully characterize the effects of policies as these are nonlinear and depend on the value of other explanatory variables. That is, the effect of inflation may be much different when it is close to the median level (as in the table above) than when it is in the hyperinflation range. Similarly, the effect on inflation may be different in countries with different quality of institutions. Finally, the distributions of the right hand side variables may be skewed so that a one standard deviation change (as in the table above) may be either large or small relative to realistic changes in these variables. To get a better understanding of these effects, we graph them for the entire distribution of the right hand side variables. We also look at whether the effects differ significantly across countries with different institutional environments.

Figure 14 shows plots of the probability of the stable growth regime as functions of the six explanatory variables. In each box the probabilities are

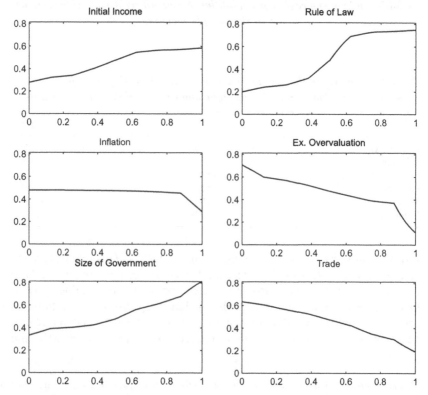

Fig. 14.   Probability of stable growth for the "median country."

calculated by setting the value of five variables to the sample median and varying the remaining variable over the percentiles of the sample distribution. The first box shows that for a median country the probability of stable growth is increasing with income. With low income the long run probability of growing at stable rates is one-third, while for the richest country it is 60%. The quality of institutions also improves the chances of stable growth (box two), however, the effect is small in the lower part of the institutions' distribution, it rises sharply around the median, and flattens out again around the 60th percentile. Inflation (box three) has very little effect except for values above the 88th percentile of the distribution where it significantly lowers the likelihood of stable growth. This corresponds to 0.287 log inflation or about 33% annual rate of inflation. Notice that while the effect of inflation on stable growth is consistent with the idea that only extreme values of inflation matter, the threshold is not exceedingly high. Real exchange rate overvaluation has a significant negative effect throughout the distribution but similarly to inflation the effect is much more pronounced beyond the 88th percentile, which is an overvaluation of 47%. The size of the government increases the chance of stable growth; the estimates imply that going from 10% of government consumption in GDP to 20% increases the long run probability of stable growth from 40% to 60%. Finally, trade lowers the probability of stable growth; quantitatively the estimates imply that increasing the trade to GDP ratio from 36% to 96% results in the long-run likelihood of stable growth falling from 60% to 20%.

Figure 15 shows the probabilities of the miracle growth regime for a median country. Income lowers the chance of fast growth reflecting convergence but the effect is not very large. As with stable growth, institutions have a positive effect which again is steepest in the middle of the distribution. Inflation matters only above the 88th percentile where it lowers the chances of miracle growth. Real exchange rate overvaluation does not appear to have a large effect. Government size significantly reduces the probability of a growth miracle; increasing the share of government consumption from 10% to 20% reduces the probability from 15% to only 5%. Finally, greater trade openness appears to increase the chances of a growth takeoff.

Note that in none of the boxes does the probability of miracle growth exceed 20%. In fact, a hypothetical country with all the right hand side variables set to the most miracle-growth conducive values is predicted to spend 55% of time in miracle growth regime - below actual values for countries like Hong Kong (72%) and Korea (86%). Of course, neither of these countries had the hypothetical perfect policy mix and consequently the model predicts they should spend even less than 55% of time in miracle growth. We conclude from this that while institutions and policy variables do affect the likelihood of miracle growth, there are other factors at work (including possibly pure chance). This result mirrors lack of success of Hausmann and co-authors in explaining growth accelerations.

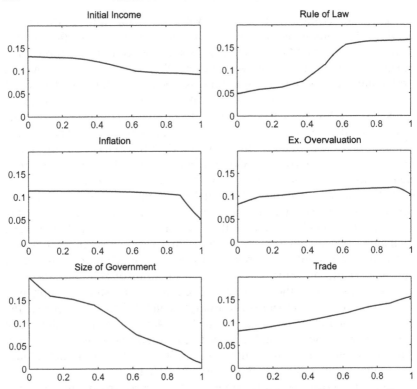

Fig. 15. Probability of miracle growth for the "median country."

Several authors have investigated the relationship between the quality of institutions and the effects of various other country characteristics on growth (e.g., Burnside & Dollar, 2000; Servén, Oviedo, & Loayza, 2005). Aghion, Bacchetta, and Banerjee (2004) show that the relationship between financial openness and volatility may depend on the degree of development of financial markets, which is presumably highly correlated with measures of institutions such as protection of property rights – a part of the rule of law index.[21] Here, because of the nonlinear nature of the probability model, the effects of one variable depend on the level of the remaining variables. Figure 15 shows plots of the miracle growth regime probabilities, calculated as above, for two hypothetical economies: one with the sample's highest value of quality of institutions (solid line) and another with the sample's lowest (dashed line). All other variables remain at the median level.

---

[21] Similarly, Aghion et al. (2007) provide a model and some evidence showing that the effects of fiscal policy on growth again depend on the development of financial markets.

Figure 16 compares the probabilities of the miracle growth state. The large gap between the two lines indicates how much higher the probability of the miracle regime is for countries with good institutions. With the exception of inflation, policies have very different effects depending on the quality of institutions. Exchange rate overvaluation, which appears to have no effect for countries with weak institutions, increases the chances of miracle growth for countries with good institutions. The opposite is true for the size of government; while it appears to have little effect when institutions are weak, it greatly reduces the likelihood of fast growth where institutions are strong. Finally, trade does not affect the probability of fast growth with weak institutions but greatly increases it with good institutions.[22]

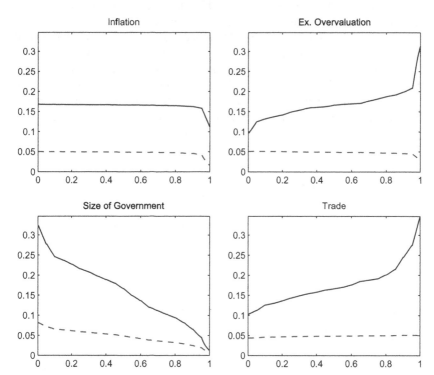

Fig. 16. Probability of miracle growth for good (solid line) and weak (dashed) institutions countries.

[22] The main findings for other regimes are that: (1) greater share of government consumption in GDP reduces the probability of stagnation for weak-institutions countries, while also increasing, albeit by much less, the chances of a crisis, (2) trade significantly increases the probability of a crisis but only for countries with weak institutions, and (3) extreme inflation increases the chance of a crisis everywhere, but the effect is much stronger with weak institutions.

We can take the approach used to construct Table 8 and translate the effects in Figures 14–16 into effects on long-run growth and volatility. First, consider again a country with all variables except that of interest set to the sample median (the "median country") without distinguishing between high- and low-quality institutions.

Figure 17 shows the effects of policies on long run growth for the median country. Inflation does not significantly affect growth as long as it remains below the 88th percentile or about 33%, however, instances of extreme inflation have a devastating effect on growth. Exchange rate overvaluation, especially when it is extremely high, lowers growth. The size of the government initially lowers growth and then raises it but the overall effect is small. This is a result of two offsetting forces affecting the median country. As government size increases the likelihood of miracle growth falls, however, so does the probability of stagnation, and the probability of stable growth rises significantly. This suggests that otherwise identical countries with different sizes of government may grow at similar rates but the nature of the growth process will be different. Countries with lower size of government will go through periods of stagnation but will also enjoy periods of fast growth. Countries with higher size of government are more likely to grow at moderate but uninterrupted rates.

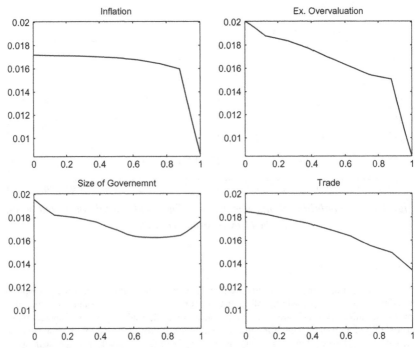

Fig. 17.   Effects of policies on growth in the "median country."

Figure 18 shows the effect of initial income and quality of institutions. As could be anticipated from the effects on regime probabilities, institutions have a stronger effect on long run growth than any of the policies examined in Figure 17. Note, however, that the effect is greatest around the median of the quality of institutions distribution. While the leveling off could well be expected at high levels of institutional quality, the relatively smaller effect for low quality of institutions is not obvious. It suggests the existence of a "threshold effect" with regards to institutions and casts doubt on the possibility of a sustained acceleration of growth in weak rule of law countries by gradual improvement of institutions. A qualitative summary is presented in Table 9.

Figure 19 contrasts the long run growth effects of policies for countries with good (solid line) and weak institutions (dashed line). The plots show growth relative to that of a country with all variables set to the sample median. Weak institutions appear to make economies more vulnerable to the damaging effect of real exchange rate overvaluation and high inflation. The size of government lowers growth for countries with good institutions in the entire range, while for countries with weak institutions it lowers growth, albeit less strongly, below median and raises it sharply above the

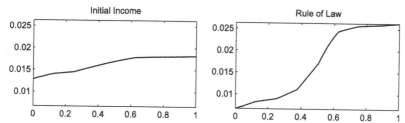

Fig. 18.   Effects of initial income and institutions on growth in the "median country."

Table 9.   Effect on long-run growth at the 10th percentile, the median, and the 90th percentile of variables' distribution

	10th percentile	Median	90th percentile
Inflation	0	0	− −
Real exchange overvaluation	−	−	− −
Government spending	−	−	+
Trade	−		−
Rule of law	+	++	0
Initial income	+	+	0

Note: Effects are categorized as strongly negative (− −), negative (−), negligible (0), positive (+), and strongly positive (++).

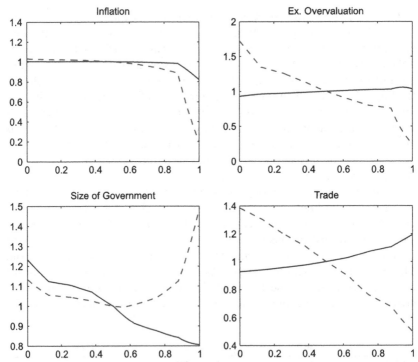

Fig. 19. *Effects of policies on growth for good (solid line) and weak (dashed) institutions countries.* **Notes:** *The vertical axis measures growth relative to an economy where all variables are equal to the median.*

median. As discussed above, this is a consequence of the differential effect of government on the likelihood of stable growth versus miracle growth – it increases the former while lowering the latter. For good-institutions countries, where stable growth is the most likely regime this lowers average growth. However, for weak-institutions countries, where stagnation dominates, stable growth is rare, and miracle growth is even rarer, this raises growth.

Trade's effect on growth also depends on institutions; it is positive when institutions are good but turns strongly negative when they are weak. The beneficial effect of trade is to increase the likelihood of miracle growth while the cost is the increase in the probability of a crisis. The former effect is very strong with good institutions but virtually nonexistent with weak ones (Figure 16). The latter on the other hand is insignificant for countries with good institutions and quite strong for weak institutions.

These results, summarized in Table 10, suggest that the relationship between policies and institutions is potentially quite complex and goes

Table 10. **Effect on long-run growth at the 10th percentile, the median, and the 90th percentile of variables' distribution; good institutions vs. weak institutions**

		10th percentile	Median	90th percentile
Inflation	Good inst.	0	0	−
	Weak inst.	0	0	− −
Real exchange overvaluation	Good inst.	0	0	0
	Weak inst.	−	−	− −
Government spending	Good inst.	−	−	−
	Weak inst.	−	0	++
Trade	Good inst.	+	+	+
	Weak inst.	−	−	−

Note: Effects are categorized as strongly negative (− −), negative (−), negligible (0) , positive (+), and strongly positive (++).

beyond the view that bad policies are merely a manifestation of weak institutions, which are the ultimate determinants of economic development as argued by Acemoglu et al. (2003). This is consistent with some other recent findings. Fatás and Mihov (2003) show that a country's degree of discretionary fiscal policy (measured by the unexplained variance from an estimated government spending rule) is related to lax political institutions and is associated with lower growth and higher GDP volatility. Cuberes and Mountford (2011) show that Fatás and Mihov's measure of fiscal discretion is, in part, explained by historical variables. In particular, they argue that a significant fraction of this "discretionary" policy is indeed better attributed to institutional quality. They then construct a tighter variable for fiscal discretion than the one explored in Fatás and Mihov (2003), that is, the part of the unexplained variance of government spending that is not accounted for by historical or geographical variables. Interestingly, they show that even this, much tighter, measure of discretionary fiscal policy is negatively associated with GDP growth. However, historical institutions also seem to have a direct impact. Thus as in the above analysis they conclude that while institutions are important for growth and volatility, fiscal policy has an independent effect on growth performance.

Before concluding we want to extent our analysis to include the effect of democracy on regime switching. We do so because the strong and robust effect on growth reversals reported above suggest the type of political institutions plays a role in growth transitions. Introducing democracy into the analysis decreases the sample size somewhat so we decide to treat this analysis in separation from the above main results.

The inclusion of democracy does not change the estimated effects of policies substantially so we omit their exposition and focus on the effects

358   *Michał Jerzmanowski and David Cuberes*

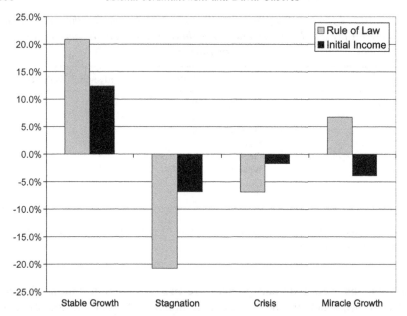

Fig. 20. *Effects of a one standard deviation change in initial income and rule of law index on long run regime probabilities.* Notes: *All right-hand side variables set to the sample median. Model without democracy.*

of the rule of law, level of income and democracy.[23] Figure 20 shows the estimated effects, evaluated at the median, of a one standard deviation change in initial income and the rule of law index from the model without democracy (these are the same estimates as in Figure 13 and Table 8).

As discussed above, rule of law increases the probability of good regimes (miracle and stable growth) while income increases the likelihood of stable growth and lowers that of stagnation but also decreases the frequency of miracle growth (convergence effect). Figure 21 shows the effects in a model with democracy included among the explanatory variables.

Democracy increases the likelihood of stable growth and the estimated effects of rule of law and income are now reduced. Democracy also slightly increases the probability of stagnation and has a negative effect on the chance of a crisis that is similar in magnitude to that of rule of law. Most importantly, however, democracy significantly lowers the likelihood of

---

[23] One interesting change is that the effect of the rule of law on growth does not flatten out at high levels, that is, it goes from being S-shaped (see Figures 14 and 15) to being J-shaped. It suggests that the flattening out was a consequence of the correlation between democracy and rule of law.

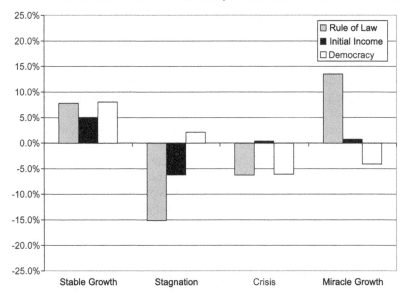

Fig. 21.   Effects of a one standard deviation change in initial income, rule of law index and democracy score on long-run regime probabilities. **Notes:** *All right-hand side variables set to the sample median.*

miracle growth episodes. Furthermore, once democracy is accounted for, income has a positive and small effect on the probability of miracle take-off. That is richer countries are less likely to grow rapidly because they are more democratic. This suggests that the convergence effect uncovered before works mainly through the political economy channel and not through standard channels such as diminishing marginal product of capital or technological catch-up.[24] This is consistent with the view of Olson (1982) who argued that democratic societies may stagnate in the long run due to the detrimental effect of special-interest groups that are able to organize and lobby for inefficient policies. Overall, the results imply that democracy favors the middle at the expense of extremes – either very fast growth or severe crises.

Overall the results of our investigation confirm some of the existing findings, namely that institutional quality is a key determinant of long-run growth, as well as Easterly's finding that only extreme values of the

---

[24] Note that to the extent that the Lipset hypothesis holds, that is, democracy increases with income, this effect will still lead to the standard convergence, whereby poor countries are catching up to the rich. However, see Acemoglu, Johnson, Robinson, and Yared (2009) for evidence against the Lipset hypothesis.

distortionary policies (inflation rate and real exchange rate overvaluation) have a significantly negative effect on growth. However, macro policies, especially trade openness and the size of government also matter for changes in growth patterns and thus influence the average growth and volatility in the long run. Crucially, policies also differ in the channel through which they affect long-run growth. For example, trade lowers the probability of stable growth and increases that of a crisis, while also making miracle growth more likely. The size of government, on the contrary, lowers the chances of miracle growth, while increasing the probability of stable growth at moderate rates. In addition, the effect of policies depend in an important way on the quality of institutions. In general, low quality of institutions makes economies more vulnerable to the harmful effects of inflation and real exchange rate overvaluation. In some cases the direction of the effect is actually reversed; trade appears to be conducive to growth for countries with good institutions and detrimental to growth for countries with bad ones. The size of government has the opposite effect – it lowers growth when combined with good institutions and increases it with weak institutions. Finally, when we extend the analysis to the effects of political institutions by including a measure of democracy among the explanatory variables, we find that, similarly to the rule of law, democracy increases the frequency of stable growth. Unlike rule of law, however, democracy significantly lowers the chances of miracle growth takeoffs. We also find that accounting for democracy removes the negative effect of initial income on the probability of miracle growth, that is, the convergence effect. This suggests that political economy, in addition to diminishing marginal product of capital or technological catch-up, is an important channel of convergence.

6. Conclusions

For most countries economic growth is not a smooth process. It consists of periods of rapid growth, stagnation, decline and crises. While this has been known for almost as long as the large cross-country data sets on output per capita have been available, only in the last seven years have researchers began exploring the within-country variation in growth. In this chapter we have summarized these recent contributions. Following earlier papers, which have documented growth variability and its lack of persistence, the latest papers try to identify distinct growth patterns in the data and use them to learn about the nature of the process of economic development. Most papers focus on detecting turning points in the growth process, instances when growth suddenly accelerates or falls for an extended period of time. Various papers, using different methods, have detected the existence of growth accelerations (and decelerations) – periods of sustained unusually high positive (negative) growth. The first key finding is that such episodes appear ubiquitous among both rich and poor countries. Unfortunately, in poor countries these episodes tend to last shorter or in many cases actually be undone by subsequent periods of decline. This leads to two critical set of questions: what triggers growth accelerations? and what makes them sustained? Unfortunately here the literature has been less successful. Some factors that help ignite growth have been identified: political transitions, economic reforms and external shocks all coincide with episodes of growth acceleration. Total factor productivity, rather than investment in physical capital, seems to be driving most accelerations. Finally, the degree of democracy appears to play an important role in growth reversals, that is, the episodes where a period of rapid growth is undone by an equally impressive decline. However, most episodes of growth acceleration remain unexplained. Similarly, we still know relatively little about what sustains growth at a high level once it accelerates. Several authors have come to the conclusions that the set of factors responsible for igniting growth may be quite different from that which is responsible for sustaining it but we still don't have convincing evidence of what they are. There is some indication that high quality of institutions, which has received enormous attention in the growth literature, may play is an important role in sustaining growth than in igniting it in the first place but much more work is needed.

We devote considerable space to discussing the idea of modeling growth as a sequence of transitions between different growth states. Originally proposed by Pritchett, this view suggests it is useful to think of the economy as obeying different growth regimes over time. Following a growth acceleration a country may look much like a Solow model economy growing rapidly due to the forces of convergence, however once a transition occurs it may resemble a poverty trapped economy. Obviously, the key question remains what triggers the transition between growth regimes. However, unlike in the growth acceleration approach, there is room for more diverse growth dynamics than just rapid growth or lack thereof. We discussed attempts to implement this idea empirically and provided an extension of one of them. Focusing on macroeconomic policies we have found that once we allow for different growth states, policies may have a very complex and subtle impact on growth. Some policies may leave the average long run growth unaffected by increasing the frequency of some growth regimes but decreasing that of others. For example, we found that the size of government spending reduces the frequency of both very rapid growth and large crises while increasing that of stable but slower growth. The net effect in the long run is small but clearly we would not want to conclude that the size of government spending is irrelevant for the process of growth.

We believe these results are interesting but much more work remains to be done. We see the research described above as only a beginning of a more ambitious research program. Understanding economic growth in a country is an extremely complex issue, since it necessarily implies dealing with not just the economics of the country, but also its political and institutional setup. Exploring within-country variation in growth gives us yet more information from which to try to uncover the laws governing the process of growth. Two key questions, from both an academic and a practical viewpoint: what causes growth accelerations and what makes them sustained still lack a satisfactory answer. All papers discussed above shared the very limited success in explaining what causes economic growth to suddenly accelerate. Jones and Olken (2008) finding that accelerations appear to be periods of rapid TFP growth isn't very comforting given our lack of understanding of what TFP is. Similarly, while some progress has been made on understanding what distinguishes sustained accelerations from unsustainable ones, we still know very little. Notice that our reduced form analysis of regime switching isn't very helpful here since we are not studying the direct effect of policies on regime changes but instead we ask what is their effect on the long run distribution of the frequency of visits to each regime. This means that if we find that a certain policy increases the fraction of time spent in a given regime, we will not be able to tell whether this is because the policy increases the persistence of this regime or because it makes the transition to that regime from other regimes more likely. Unbundling these effects an important next step for future research. We also believe that the link between political institutions (democracy) and growth transitions is one where important contributions can be made. The idea put forth by Rodrik (1999) that rapid growth may bring social conflict which in the absence of democratic institutions turns to turmoil and growth collapse is an intuitively appealing one but more work is needed to establish its validity. More broadly, the question of what policies outside the realm of the usual growth-promoting strategies are helpful in sustaining growth episodes seems worth exploring. Are there political or social arrangements which don't play a direct role in economic growth but help sustain it? Finally, we would like to emphasize the lack of a theory of growth transitions. Pritchett sketches out a model of growth regimes but despite a few interesting contributions we don't yet have a plausible theory of growth transitions.

In conclusion we would like to stress that after only several years, the research program focusing on the within-country growth patterns has delivered some interesting and promising results but remains yet largely unexplored. We see this as a potentially very fruitful avenue of empirical and theoretical research in economic growth.

References

Acemoglu, D. (2008). Oligarchic vs. Democratic Societies. *Journal of the European Economic Association, 6*, 1–44.

Acemoglu, D., Johnson, S., Robinson, J., & Thaichoren, Y. (2003). Institutional causes, macroeconomic symptoms: Volatility, crises and growth. *Journal of Monetary Economics, 50*(1), 49–123.

Acemoglu, D., Johnson, S., Robinson, J., & Yared, P. (2009). Reevaluating the modernization hypothesis. *Journal of Monetary Economics, 56,* 1043–1058.

Aghion, P., Alesina, A., & Trebbi, F. (2007). *Democracy, technology, and growth.* NBER Working Papers No. 13180. National Bureau of Economic Research, Inc. Boston, MA.

Aghion, P., Bacchetta, P., & Banerjee, A. (2004). Financial development and the instability of open economies. *Journal of Monetary Economics, 51*(6), 1077–1106.

Aghion, P., & Howitt, P. (1992). A model of growth through creative destruction. *Econometrica, Econometric Society, 60*(2), 323–351.

Aizenman, J., & Spiegel, M. (2010). Take-offs. *Review of Development Economics, 14*(2), 177–196.

Arellano, M., & Bond, S. (1991). Some tests of specification for panel data. *Review of Economic Studies, 58*(2), 277–297.

Bai, J., & Perron, P. (1998). Estimating and testing linear models with multiple structural changes. *Econometrica, 66,* 47–78.

Barro, R. J. (1991). Economic growth in a cross section of countries. *Quarterly Journal of Economics, 106*(2), 407–443.

Barro, R. J., & Sala-i-Martin, X. (1992). Convergence. *Journal of Political Economy, 100*(2), 223–251.

Barro, R. J., & Sala-i-Martin, X. (2003). *Economic growth* (2nd ed.). Cambridge, MA: MIT Press.

Ben-David, D., Lumsdaine, R., & Papell, D. H. (2003). Unit roots, postwar slowdowns and long-run growth: Evidence from two structural breaks. *Empirical Economics,* February, 303–319.

Berg, A., Ostry, J. D., & Zettelmeyer, J. (2008, July). *What makes growth sustained?* IMF Working Paper No. 08/59. IMF, Washington, DC.

Boucekkine, R., & Pintus, P.-A. (2011). Is history a blessing or a curse? International borrowing without commitment, leapfrogging and growth reversals. *Journal of Economic Growth* (Forthcoming).

Burnside, C., & Dollar, D. (2000). Aid, policies, and growth. *American Economic Review, 90*(4), 847–868.

Cuberes, D., & Jerzmanowski, M. (2009). Democracy, diversification, and growth reversals. *Economic Journal, 119*(October), 1270–1302.

Cuberes, D., & Mountford, A. (2011). *Fiscal policy institutions and history.* Working Paper. University of Alicante.

Dollar, D. (1992). Outward-oriented developing economies really do grow more rapidly: Evidence from 95 LDCs, 1976–1985. *Economic Development and Cultural change, 40*(3), 532–544.

Easterly, W. (2005). National policies and economic growth. In Aghion, P. & Durlauf, S. (Eds.), *Handbook of economic growth*. Amsterdam, Holland Elsevier.

Easterly, W. (2006). Reliving the 50s: The big push, poverty traps, and takeoffs in economic development. *Journal of Economic Growth, 11*(2), 289–318.

Easterly, W. (2011, May). *Benevolent Autocrats*. Mimeo, New York University.

Easterly, W., Kremer, M., Pritchett, L., & Summers, L. (1993). Good policy or good luck: Country growth performance and temporary shocks. *Journal of Monetary Economics, 32*(3), 459–483.

Easterly, W., & Levine, R. (2003). Tropics, germs, and crops: How endowments influence economic development. *Journal of Monetary Economics*, January, 3–39.

Fatás, A., & Mihov, I. (2003). The case for restricting fiscal policy discretion. *Quarterly Journal of Economics, 118*(4), 1419–1447.

Grossman, G. M., & Helpman, E. (1991). Quality ladders in the theory of growth. *Review of Economic Studies, 58*(1), 43–61.

de Haan, J., & Jong-A.-Pin, R. (2007). *Political regime change, economic reform and growth accelerations*. CESifo Working Paper Series 1905, CESifo Group Munich.

Hamilton, J. (1994). *Time series analysis*. Princeton, NJ: Princeton University Press.

Hausmann, R., Pritchett, L., & Rodrik, D. (2005). Growth accelerations. *Journal of Economic Growth, 10*(4), 303–329.

Heston, A., Summers, R., & Aten, B. (2006). *Penn world table version 6.2*, Center for International Comparison at the University of Pennsylvania (CICUP).

Imam, P. & Salinas, G. (2008). *Explaining episodes of growth accelerations, decelerations, and collapses in Western Africa*. IMF Working Paper. IMF, Washington, DC.

Jerzmanowski, M. (2006). Empirics of hills, plateaus, mountains and plains: A Markov-switching approach to growth. *Journal of Development Economics*, December, 357–385.

Johnson, S., Ostry, J., & Subramanian, A. (2007). *Africa's growth prospects: Benchmarking the constraints*. NBER Working Paper No. 13120. National Bureau of Economic Research, Inc. Boston, MA.

Jones, B. F., & Olken, B. A. (2008, August). The anatomy of start-stop growth. *Review of Economics and Statistics, 90*(3), 582–587.

Jones, B. F., & Olken, B. A. (2005). Do leaders matter? National leadership and growth since World War II. *Quarterly Journal of Economics, 120*(3), 835–864.

Kaufmann, D., Kraay, A., & Mastruzzi, M. (2003). *Governance matters III: Governance indicators for 1996–2002*. World Bank, World Bank Policy Research Working Paper No. 3106.

Kerekes, M. (2009) Growth miracles and failures in a Markov switching classification model of growth. *Journal of Development Economics* (Forthcoming).

Lucas, R. E., Jr. (1988). On the mechanics of economic development. *Journal of Monetary Economics*, *22*(1), 3–42.

Maddison, A. (1995). *Monitoring the world economy, 1820–1992*. Paris: Development Centre of the Organisation for Economic Co-operation and Development.

Maddison, A. (2001). *The world economy: A millennial perspective*. Paris: Development Centre of the Organisation for Economic Co-operation and Development.

Mankiw, N. G., Romer, D., & Weil, D. N. (1992). A contribution to the empirics of economic growth. *Quarterly Journal of Economics*, *107*(2), 407–437.

Marshall, M. G., & Jaggers, K. (2002). *Polity IV project. political regime characteristics and transitions, 1800–2002*. Integrated Network for Societal Conflict Research (INSCR), Program Center for International Development and Conflict Management (CIDCM), University of Maryland, retrieved from www.cidcm.umd.edu/inscr/polity

Olson, M. (1982). *The rise and decline of nations: Economic growth, stagnation, and social rigidities*. New Haven, CT: Yale University Press.

Pritchett, L. (2000). Understanding patterns of economic growth: Searching for hills among plateaus, mountains, and plains. *The World Bank Economic Review*, *14*(2), 221–250.

Pritchett, L. (2003). A toy collection, a socialist star and a democratic dud? (Growth theory, Vietnam and the Philippines). In Rodrik, D. (Ed.), *In search of prosperity Analytic narratives on economic growth*. Princeton, NJ: Princeton University Press.

Przeworski, A., & Limongi, F. (1993). Political regimes and economic growth. *Journal of Economic Perspectives* (7), 51–69.

Quinn, D., & Woolley, J. (2001). Democracy and national economic performance: The preference for stability. *American Journal of Political Science*, *45*(3), 634–657.

Rodrik, D. (1999). Where did all the growth go? *Journal of Economic Growth*, *4*(4), 385–412.

Rodrik, D. (2000). Participatory politics, social cooperation, and economic stability. *American Economic Review*, *90*(2), 140–144. Papers and Proceedings of the One Hundred Twelfth Annual Meeting of the American Economic Association.

Rodrik, D. (2003). *In search of prosperity: Analytic narratives on economic growth*. Princeton University Press.

Rodrik, D. (2005). Growth strategies. In Aghion, P. & Durlauf, S. (Eds.), *Handbook of economic growth* (Vol. 1A). North-Holland.

Romer, P. (1986). Increasing returns and long-run growth. *Journal of Political Economy*, *94*(5), 1002–1037.

Romer, P. (1990). Endogenous technological change. *Journal of Political Economy*, *98*(5).

Sachs, J. D., & Warner, A. M. (1995). Economic reform and the process of global integration. *Brookings Papers on Economic Activity*, *1*, 1–118.

Servén, L., Oviedo, A. M., & Loayza, N. V. (2005). *The impact of regulation on growth and informality - cross-country evidence*. World Bank Working Paper. Washington, DC.

Wang, J., & Zivot, E. (2000). A Bayesian time series model of multiple structural changes in level, trend, and variance. *Journal of Business & Economic Statistics*, *18*(3), 374–386.

CHAPTER 13

Modeling Parameter Heterogeneity in Cross-Country Regression Models

Andros Kourtellos

Department of Economics, University of Cyprus, P.O. Box 20537, CY 1678, Nicosia, CYPRUS
E-mail address: andros@ucy.ac.cy

Abstract
We employ various local generalizations of the Solow growth model that model parameter heterogeneity using adult literacy rates and life expectancy at birth. The model takes the form of a semiparametric varying coefficient model along the lines of Hastie and Tibshirani (1993). The empirical results show substantial parameter heterogeneity in the cross-country growth process, a finding that is consistent with the presence of multiple steady-state equilibria and the emergence of convergence clubs.

Keywords: Solow growth model, parameter heterogeneity, varying coefficient model, human development

JEL classifications: C14, C21, C50, N10

1. Introduction

Empirical growth research has become a dominant field in macroeconomics. However, despite the vast amount of research, there is remarkably little confidence in the results and the implications that have come from conventional empirical methods of growth analysis. A typical example is Pack (1994, pp. 68–69), who describes several problems with cross-country growth regression models:

> *The production function interpretation is further muddled by the assumption that all countries are on the same international production frontier ... regression equations that attempt to sort out the sources of growth also generally ignore interaction effects ... The recent spate of cross-country growth regressions also obscures some of the lessons that have been learned from the analysis of policy in individual countries.*

Frontiers of Economics and Globalization
Volume 11 ISSN: 1574-8715
DOI: 10.1108/S1574-8715(2011)0000011018

One of the major reasons for the general mistrust of the conventional approach is the assumption of parameter homogeneity in cross-country growth regression. Indeed, there is a growing number of recent empirical studies that question the assumption of a single linear model that can be applied to all countries. Instead, these studies find evidence that is consistent with multiple steady-state equilibria that classify the countries into different convergence clubs.

One approach to allowing for parameter heterogeneity in cross-country growth regressions is to use threshold regression models or classification algorithms such as a regression tree. In a pioneer paper, Durlauf and Johnson (1995) employ a regression tree approach to uncover multiple regimes in the data. This evidence is formally tested by Hansen (2000) who develops statistical theory for the threshold regression and applies procedures to formally test for the presence of threshold effects and to obtain a confidence set for the threshold parameter. More recently, using a generalized regression tree analysis, Tan (2010) investigates how fundamental determinants, such as institutions, interact to hinder or facilitate development outcomes for different groups of countries.

A conceptually different approach employs semiparametric models based on nonparametric smooth functions to identify general nonlinear growth patterns. Notable examples include Liu and Stengos (1999) and Kalaitzidakis, Mamuneas, Savvides, and Stengos (2001) who employ a partially linear model, Canova (2004) who uses a predictive density approach, Desdoigts (1999) who employs an exploratory projection pursuit (density estimation), and Kourtellos (2003) who uses a projection pursuit regression.

Durlauf, Kourtellos, and Minkin (2001) (DKM) extended this search for nonlinearities in cross-country growth regressions to one for parameter heterogeneity. In particular, DKM employ a varying coefficient approach to estimate a local Solow growth model that allows the parameters for each country to vary as smooth functions of initial income. They find evidence for substantial country-specific heterogeneity that is associated with differences in initial income in the Solow parameters. The varying coefficient approach is also employed in Mamuneas, Savvides, and Stengos (2006) who find nonlinearities in the estimates of the elasticity of human capital with respect to output using annual measures of Total Factor Productivity (TFP) for 51 countries.

There are several interpretations of parameter heterogeneity. First, modern economic growth models provide microfoundations for the presence of multiple steady states and the emergence of convergence clubs. Examples include models with human capital externalities (e.g., Azariadis & Drazen, 1990), imperfections in credit markets and indivisibilities of investment in human capital (e.g., Galor & Zeira, 1993), local technological spillovers (e.g., Durlauf, 1993), Schumpeterian patterns of innovation and technology (e.g., Howitt & Mayer-Foulkes, 2005), institutional barriers (e.g., Acemoglu, Aghion, & Zilibotti, 2006), and differential timing of take-offs (e.g., Galor & Weil, 1999, 2000). Each of these theories suggests that from the perspective of a local linear approximation of the growth process, different countries will be characterized by different parameters. Second, the assumption of Cobb–Douglas production function as the basis of the derivation of the Solow growth model has been challenged. Duffy and Papageorgiou (2000) and Masanjala and Papageorgiou (2004) find evidence in favor of a constant elasticity of substitution (CES) production function rather than the standard Cobb–Douglas specification. This finding is important given that a Cobb–Douglas production function is a necessary condition for the linearity of the Solow growth model. Third, parameter heterogeneity may be induced by omitted growth determinants. In fact, a range of new growth theories suggest additional covariates beyond those originally proposed by Solow. Durlauf, Johnson, and Temple (2005) identified more than 140 variables used by various researchers, including, but not limited to, market distortions, geographical regions, source endowments, climate, institutions, politics, and war.

In this chapter, we model parameter heterogeneity in the cross-country growth regression using two alternative human development variables that allow us to uncover their complex relationship to economic growth. Methodologically, we employ a local generalization of the Solow growth model along the lines of DKM in the sense that while the Solow model applies to all countries, the parameters of the aggregate production function vary across countries. More precisely, we allow these parameters to vary according to a country's initial human development level. We study local generalizations of Solow growth models with and without accounting for population growth and saving rates. That is, we study unconditional and conditional local Solow growth models.

The generalization of the Solow growth model takes the form of a semiparametric varying coefficient model along the lines of Hastie and Tibshirani (1993). This model is described as semiparametric because it is a conditional linear model that imposes no assumptions on the functional form of the coefficients, but the shape of the function is estimated by the data. While this restricts the form of parameter heterogeneity, it is an appealing way to generalize the traditional linear Solow model. That is, if we index the countries by an interesting variable, such as the initial conditions of human development, then, near steady state, the Solow model can provide a good approximation. Our approach also allows us to evaluate how the shares of human and physical capital vary with the initial levels of human development.

We measure human development using two key indicators of economic development beyond income: initial levels of adult literacy rates and life expectancy at birth. Literacy rates are a measure of the ability of a country to acquire human capital and may have a large impact on the ability of an economy to generate economic growth. Life expectancy at birth is the most commonly used measure of human capital health. High levels of longevity are critical for a country's economic and social well-being. Improving health outcomes can have large indirect payoffs because healthy citizens have a positive effect on economic growth. Better health stimulates learning ability, fosters education incentives, and encourages long-term savings (see, e.g., Bloom & Sachs, 1998).

Our findings suggest that there is substantial heterogeneity across countries. This heterogeneity is reflected in the estimated varying coefficients of the local Solow growth model. The findings also suggest that there is substantial evidence of a latent determinant of negative growth rates or poverty traps. The results suggest the presence of multiple steady-state equilibria in the growth process with respect to initial human capital. This evidence is consistent with the twin peaks found by Quah (1997) in the limit distribution of cross-country per capita income, the presence of multiple regimes found in Durlauf and Johnson (1995) and Masanjala and Papageorgiou (2004) and the global divergence found in Mayer-Foulkes (2006).

Section 2 revisits the standard approach to cross-country growth analysis and proposes a varying coefficient. Section 3 describes the data employed in this chapter. Section 4 presents estimates of the varying coefficients for Solow parameters in unconditional and conditional specifications using human development at the beginning of the period with adult literacy rates and life expectancy at birth as a proxy. Section 5 presents the summary and conclusion.

2. Econometric methodology

The standard approach to cross-country growth analysis as illustrated by Barro (1991, 1997), Barro and Sala-I-Martin (1995), and Mankiw, Romer, and Weil (1992) and extended by Evans (1998), Islam (1995), and Lee, Pesaran, and Smith (1997) to panel data has focused on the linear regression model. For each country, i, average per capita real GDP growth, g_i, is assumed to obey

$$g_i = X_i'\gamma + u_i, \tag{1}$$

where X_i is a p-dimensional vector of growth determinants and u_i is the regression error. In the standard Solow model, the determinants consist of the logarithm (log) of population growth rate plus 0.05, which corresponds to the sum of the constant rates of technical change and depreciation; the log of the savings rate for physical capital accumulation; and the log of the real per capita income of the country at the beginning of the period over which growth is measured.[1] The underlying assumption of this regression is that each country is associated with a common Cobb–Douglas aggregate production function.

---

[1] Mankiw et al. (1992) extended this model to include the savings rate for physical capital accumulation.

One way to model parameter heterogeneity in Equation (1) is to consider a local generalization, which effectively generalizes the constant coefficient γ to become a smooth function $\gamma(z_i)$ that maps the scalar index z_i into a set of country-specific Solow parameters using the human development index. By local, we refer to the idea that a Solow model applies to each country, but the parameters of the aggregate production function vary according to a slower moving variable, such as country's initial levels of human development. In other words, although the Solow model can be an inappropriate specification when applied to all countries, it can still be a good approximation locally for an individual country. This generalization yields the varying coefficient model:

$$g_i = X_i' \gamma(z_i) + u_i, \tag{2}$$

where $E(u_i|X_i) = 0$, $E(u_i^2|X_i) = \sigma^2(z_i)$, and $\gamma(z_i) = (\gamma_1(z_i), \gamma_2(z_i), \ldots, \gamma_p(z_i))'$.

Two important points need to be highlighted about the relationship of the varying coefficient model in Equation (2) with the linear regression and threshold regression or tree regression. First, the varying coefficient model encompasses not only the linear model in Equation (1) but also any regression model that augments the latter with z_i in a linear or nonlinear way. Notable examples of nonlinear models that can be viewed as nested models within the varying coefficient model are the semiparametric partially linear model and parametric models with higher-order polynomials or interactions. Second, one important difference of the varying coefficient model vis-a-vis the tree regression and threshold regression models is that the parameter heterogeneity is modeled through smooth functions as opposed to abrupt changes by using indicator functions. In effect, the human development index acts as a threshold variable but in a smooth way. One can argue that given the short span of time in cross-country growth data, smooth functions can be more efficient in identifying nonlinearities in the cross-country growth process.

Following Fan and Zhang (1999), we estimate the varying coefficient model in Equation (2) using simple local regression based on a two-stage estimation procedure. The major advantage of a two-stage estimation over a one-stage estimation is that it allows the functional coefficients to possess different degrees of smoothness, which ensures that the optimal rate of convergence for the asymptotic mean-squared error is achieved. The appendix describes the estimation procedure in detail.

3. Data

This chapter uses a balanced panel dataset for 88 countries (see Table 1). Data are averaged over four 10-year periods between 1960 and 1999.[2] The

---

[2] Similar results are obtained for a 20-year period panel data set.

Table 1. **List of countries and the logarithms of literacy rates and life expectancy in 1960**

Code	Country	lit_0	$lifee_0$	Code	Country	lit_0	$lifee_0$
ARG	Argentina	−0.09	4.18	JOR	Jordan	−1.14	3.85
AUS	Australia	−0.02	4.26	JPN	Japan	−0.02	4.22
AUT	Austria	−0.02	4.23	KEN	Kenya	−1.61	3.81
BDI	Burundi	−1.97	3.73	KOR	Korea, Rep.	−0.35	3.99
BEL	Belgium	−0.02	4.24	LKA	Sri Lanka	−0.29	4.13
BEN	Benin	−2.53	3.66	LUX	Luxembourg	−0.02	–
BFA	Burkina Faso	−4.20	3.59	LSO	Lesotho	–	3.86
BGD	Bangladesh	−1.53	3.78	MAR	Morocco	−1.97	3.85
BOL	Bolivia	−0.95	3.76	MDG	Madagascar	−1.02	3.71
BRA	Brazil	−0.49	4.01	MEX	Mexico	−0.43	4.05
BRB	Barbados	−0.06	–	MLI	Mali	−3.51	3.58
CAN	Canada	−0.07	4.26	MOZ	Mozambique	−2.53	3.56
CHE	Switzerland	−0.01	4.27	MUS	Mauritius	−0.50	4.08
CHL	Chile	−0.17	4.05	MWI	Malawi	−1.51	3.63
CHN	China	–	3.59	MYS	Malaysia	−0.63	3.99
CIV	Cote d'Ivoire	−3.00	3.68	NER	Niger	−4.61	3.57
CMR	Cameroon	−1.66	3.77	NGA	Nigeria	−1.90	3.68
COG	Congo, Rep.	−1.86	3.86	NIC	Nicaragua	−0.70	3.86
COL	Colombia	−0.46	3.97	NLD	Netherlands	−0.02	4.29
CRI	Costa Rica	−0.17	4.13	NOR	Norway	−0.01	4.30
DNK	Denmark	−0.01	4.28	NPL	Nepal	−2.41	3.65
DOM	Dominican Republic	−0.44	3.96	NZL	New Zealand	−0.02	4.26
DZA	Algeria	−2.30	3.86	PAK	Pakistan	−1.90	3.77
ECU	Ecuador	−0.39	3.98	PAN	Panama	−0.31	4.11
EGY	Egypt, Arab Rep.	−1.35	3.84	PER	Peru	−0.49	3.87
ESP	Spain	−0.14	4.23	PHL	Philippines	−0.33	3.97
ETH	Ethiopia	−2.81	3.74	PRT	Portugal	−0.48	4.15
FIN	Finland	−0.01	4.23	PRY	Paraguay	−0.29	4.16
FRA	France	−0.02	4.25	SEN	Senegal	−2.03	3.66
GAB	Gabon	−2.12	3.71	SLV	El Salvador	−2.66	3.45
GBR	United Kingdom	−0.04	4.26	SWE	Sweden	−0.01	4.29
GHA	Ghana	−1.31	3.81	SYR	Syrian Arab Republic	−1.20	3.91
GMB	Gambia, The	−2.81	3.48	TCD	Chad	–	3.55
GNB	Guinea−Bissau	−2.66	3.55	TGO	Togo	−2.30	3.68
GRC	Greece	−0.21	4.23	THA	Thailand	−0.39	3.96
GTM	Guatemala	−1.16	3.83	TTO	Trinidad and Tobago	−0.07	4.16
HKG	Hong Kong, China	−0.35	4.19	TUR	Turkey	−0.97	3.92
HND	Honduras	−0.80	3.85	TZA	Tanzania	−2.35	3.70
IDN	Indonesia	−0.94	3.73	UGA	Uganda	−1.05	3.77
IND	India	−1.27	3.75	URY	Uruguay	−0.10	4.21
IRL	Ireland	−0.04	4.24	USA	United States	−0.02	4.25
IRN	Iran, Islamic Rep.	−1.71	3.83	VEN	Venezuela	−0.46	4.09
ISL	Iceland	0.00	–	ZAF	South Africa	−0.56	3.90
ISR	Israel	−0.17	4.27	ZMB	Zambia	−1.26	3.73
ITA	Italy	−0.09	4.24	ZWE	Zimbabwe	−0.37	3.82
JAM	Jamaica	−0.20	4.14				

explanatory variables reflect the standard set variables suggested by the Solow growth theory (see Mankiw et al., 1992). They include the logarithm of average growth rate of the population plus 0.05 for depreciation, gpop; the logarithm of average proportion of real investments, including government, to real GDP, inv; and the logarithm of initial per capita income, y_0. The two human development indices that we use are as follows: (a) the logarithm of adult literacy rates defined as the fraction of the population over the age of 15 that is able to read and write in 1960, lit_0 and (b) the logarithm of life expectancy at birth in 1960, $lifee_0$. All explanatory variables, except schooling, were obtained from the Penn World Table 6.1. The two indices are from the *World Bank's World Report*. Table 1 presents the countries along with two human development indices, lit_0 and $lifee_0$.

4. Empirical results

4.1. Unconditional models

We start by investigating a simplified local generalization of growth regression that assumes that the steady-state value of per capita income is constant across countries. Then, using the human development index, z_i, the varying coefficient model takes the following form,

$$g_i = \gamma_1(z_i) + \gamma_2(z_i)y_{0i} + u_i. \tag{3}$$

Figures 1(a)–(d) and 2(a)–(d) present the results for $z = lit_0$ and $z = lifee_0$, respectively.[3] They present the point estimates and associated 95% pointwise confidence intervals for the varying coefficient functions, conditional variance, and implied convergence rates. Confidence intervals for the implied convergence rates and the implied shares of capital, estimated in the following sections, are computed using the delta method. The superimposed horizontal dashed lines refer to the corresponding least squares estimated (invariant) parameters of a linear Solow growth model.

The results are quite revealing. The varying coefficients are substantially different from the linear Solow growth model, as the least squares estimates cut the confidence intervals several times in all of the estimated models. The relationship between the log of adult literacy rates in 1960 and growth is increasing and nonlinear. The estimation reveals a

---

[3] Outliers were omitted from the graphs, as they render the graphs unreadable. For $z = lit_0$, Niger, Burkina Faso, Mali, and Cote d'Ivoire are omitted, and for $z = lifee_0$, El Salvador and Gambia are omitted. Despite these countries' omission from the graph, estimation is based on the full sample. Complete graphs are available upon request.

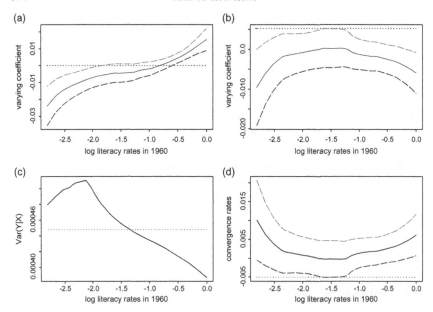

Fig. 1. (a) *Intercept.* (b) *Coefficient of log initial income.* (c) *Conditional variance.* (d) *Implied convergence rates.*

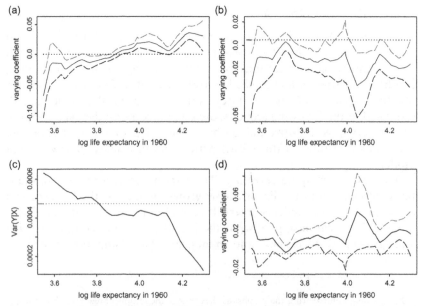

Fig. 2. (a) *Intercept.* (b) *Coefficient of log initial income.* (c) *Conditional variance.* (d) *Implied convergence rates.*

threshold at the level of the 45th percentile corresponding to Nicaragua, below which the relationship between literacy rates in 1960 and growth is negative and above which the relationship is positive. Figure 1(b) shows the estimates for the varying coefficient of the logarithm of initial income, y_0. Unlike the least squares estimate of the constant coefficient for the corresponding linear model, the estimates of $\gamma_2(z_i)$ are mostly negative with a quadratic shape, implying that high and low initial literacy countries have larger estimates than the countries with middle levels of initial literacy rates. These estimates suggest that the differences in per capita incomes are not temporary and that unconditional convergence to a common long-run level is not occurring. Figure 1(c) presents substantial evidence of parameter heterogeneity in the conditional variance, which takes the form of a hump-shaped function. Although the conditional variance initially appears to increase for the countries with the lowest levels of initial literacy rates, this variance monotonically decreases for countries with higher levels of initial literacy rates than Senegal.

We now turn to the case of life expectancy. While Figures 2(a)–(d) appear to be qualitatively similar to those obtained using literacy rates, the results based on the initial levels of life expectancy are more volatile. In particular, the estimates of the varying intercept reveal a threshold at the 42nd percentile, corresponding to Lesotho, below which the relationship between initial life expectancy rates and growth is negative, and above which the relationship is positive. The estimates of the varying coefficient of the log of initial income are mostly negative but with substantial variability. For example, the implied convergence rates vary from 0 to approximately 4%. Finally, the conditional variance appears to generally decrease with the levels of initial life expectancy.

In sum, we find that while the average relationship between growth and human development, as measured by the initial literacy rates or life expectancy at birth, appears to be generally increasing, the relationship is positive only for countries above the median index. We also find substantial parameter heterogeneity in the convergence rates when we index them by the initial levels of human development. Taking all of the evidence together, we conclude that initial levels of human development can determine long-run outcomes and that countries with similar initial conditions exhibit similar long-run outcomes. This finding suggests the presence of multiple steady-state equilibria and the emergence of convergence clubs in the growth process consistent with the twin peaks in the cross-country income distribution found by Quah (1997). Finally, we find that the conditional variance appears to be generally decreasing in the levels of initial human development index, which implies the beneficial effect of human development on growth volatility.

4.2. Conditional models on population growth and investments

This section estimates a local generalization of the basic Solow growth model which is based on a two-factor Cobb-Douglas production function with physical capital and labor as inputs. In this case, the varying coefficient model in Equation (3) is augmented by the variables of the population growth rates and the saving rate of physical capital and takes the form of Equation (4):

$$g_i = \gamma_1(z_i) + \gamma_2(z_i)\text{gpop}_i + \gamma_3(z_i)\text{inv}_i + \gamma_4(z_i)y_{0i} + u_i. \tag{4}$$

Figures 3(a)–(g) and 4(a)–(g) present the results for the two development indices lit_0 and lifee_0, respectively.

Let us first discuss the results based on adult literacy rates, $z = \text{lit}_0$. First, for the varying coefficients associated with the intercept, population growth, and physical capital, the estimates exhibit substantial parameter heterogeneity for countries with literacy rates in 1960 lower than the 18th percentile, corresponding to Senegal.

Second, the estimates of the varying intercept show that the relationship between literacy rates in 1960 and growth is negative for countries with literacy rates lower than the rate that corresponds to Senegal. Similar to unconditional models, this pattern suggests that negative growth rates may be the result of a latent determinant of countries with low literacy rates. However, this threshold appears to be lower than in the case of the unconditional models. It is estimated to be around the 18th percentile rather than around the 45th percentile.

Third, for countries with literacy rates lower than the 12th percentile, corresponding to Nepal, the estimates of the varying coefficient of population growth rates are positive. This finding suggests the presence of possible scale effects for the poorest countries.

Fourth, the estimates for the varying coefficients of physical capital and initial income do not exhibit any sort of monotonicity. The highest values of the varying coefficients of physical capital are associated with countries that have higher literacy rates. For the majority of countries with initial literacy rates higher than the 16th percentile, corresponding to Togo, the estimate for the varying coefficient of physical capital is larger than that predicted by the linear Solow model. For the varying coefficient of initial income, the estimates are negative and mostly significant. However, for countries with point estimates smaller than the 29th percentile, corresponding to Malawi, the estimates are insignificant. This finding may imply the absence of conditional convergence for this group. Alternatively, the non-monotonicity of the estimates may suggest the presence of multiple steady states. For instance, the majority of countries with lower initial literacy rates experience lower convergence rates, and countries with high initial literacy rates have higher convergence rates. It is worth noting that the estimates for the majority of countries are larger than the ones predicted by the linear Solow growth model.

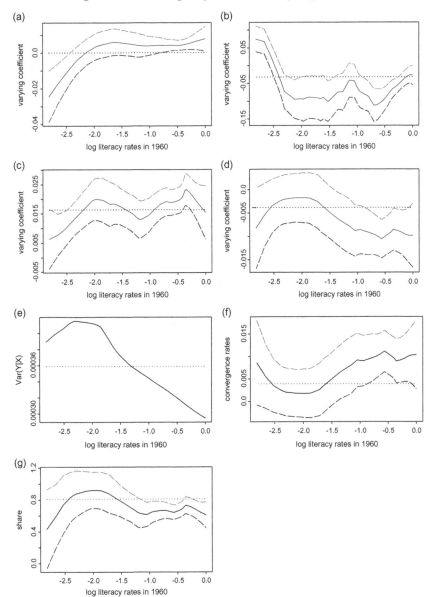

*Fig. 3. (a) Intercept. (b) Coefficient of log population growth rates
(c) Coefficient of log investments. (d) Coefficient of log initial income.
(e) Conditional variance. (f) Implied convergence rates. (g) Implied share
of physical capital.*

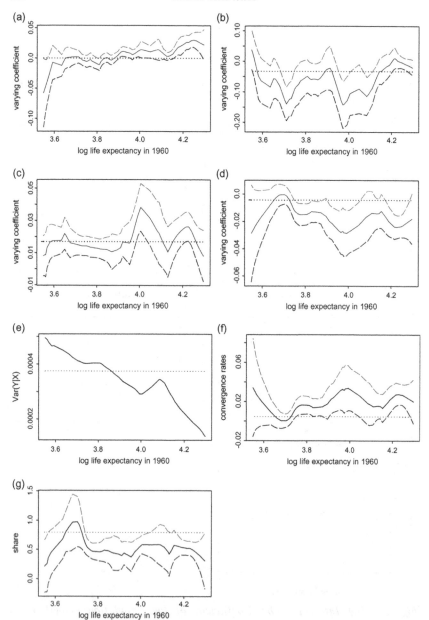

Fig. 4. *(a) Intercept. (b) Coefficient of log population growth rates.*
(c) Coefficient of log investments. (d) Coefficient of log initial income.
(e) Conditional variance. (f) Implied convergence rates. (g) Implied share
of physical capital.

Fifth, the implied shares of physical capital are generally quite large and display a hump for a range of countries with lower literacy rates, between the 9th percentile, corresponding to Benin, and the 32nd percentile, corresponding to Ghana. Countries within the above range exhibit higher shares of physical capital than countries with higher literacy rates. Notably, the estimate of the implied share of physical capital for Burundi is as high as 0.91. However, for countries with literacy rates higher than Ghana, the shares are much lower and rather stable, with an approximate value of about 0.65.

In the case of life expectancy at birth ($z = $ lifee$_0$), the results in Figure 4(a)–(g) show a stronger parameter heterogeneity. First, the estimates of the varying intercept exhibit an increasing pattern with negative estimates below the 49th percentile, corresponding to Peru. Second, although the evidence is weaker, there is also a group of countries with positive estimates for the varying coefficient of the population growth rates. More precisely, for countries with literacy rates lower than the 10th percentile, which corresponds to Benin, the estimates are positive. Third, for the majority of countries, the implied convergence rates are larger than the ones predicted by the linear Solow growth model. Interestingly, countries with the lowest rates of life expectancy enjoy convergence rates as high as countries with the highest rates of life expectancy. For instance, Mozambique has the same convergence rate as that of Switzerland. Fourth, the implied shares of physical capital is also hump shaped as that of lit$_0$. In particular, countries with rates of life expectancy between the 10th and 27th percentiles, corresponding to Nepal and India, respectively, have higher shares than the other countries in the sample. Interestingly, many countries in this interval enjoy shares very close to one. Morever, the only major difference between the two human development indices is that the evidence for parameter hetero-geneity in the varying coefficients of physical capital and initial income appears to be stronger for the estimates based on lifee$_0$ than those based on lit$_0$.

Furthermore, we impose the theoretical restriction that the coefficients on inv and gpop sum up to zero; see Mankiw et al. (1992). Under this restriction, we estimate the following varying coefficient model:

$$g_i = \gamma_1(z_i) + \gamma_2(z_i)(\text{inv}_i - \text{gpop}_i) + \gamma_3(z_i)y_{0i} + u_i. \tag{5}$$

Figures 5(a)–(f) and 6(a)–(f) present the results for adult literacy rate ($z = $ lit$_0$) and life expectancy at birth ($z = $ lifee$_0$), respectively. The results are similar to those obtained in the unrestricted models for both indices. The only notable exception is that many countries that have life expectancies between the 16th and 22nd percentiles, corresponding to Cote d'Ivoire and Madagascar, respectively, exhibit negative convergence rates and have shares of physical capital that are greater than one.

Andros Kourtellos

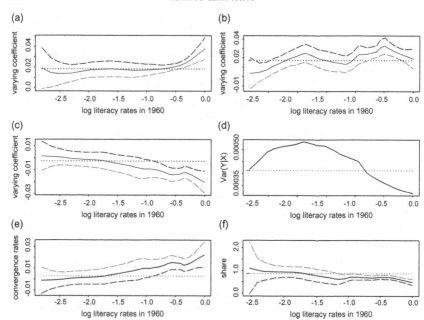

Fig. 5. (a) Coefficient of intercept. (b) Coefficient of log (investments/population growth rates). (c) Coefficient of log initial income. (d) Conditional variance. (e) Implied convergence rates. (f) Implied share of physical capital.

In sum, the empirical results show that the Solow growth model exhibits strong evidence of parameter heterogeneity. More precisely, the coefficients of the Solow regression and the corresponding implied parameters of the Solow model (convergence rates and shares of physical and human capital) vary substantially with initial levels of literacy rates and life expectancy. This evidence is consistent with the presence of multiple regimes found in Durlauf and Johnson (1995) and Masanjala and Papageorgiou (2004) that are associated with adult literacy rates and the global divergence found in Mayer-Foulkes (2006) that is associated with life expectancy. Furthermore, the average relationship between growth and human development appears to be nonlinear and generally increasing. This relationship suggests the presence of a latent determinant of negative growth rates or poverty trap that is omitted from the Solow model. Kourtellos (2003) provided evidence that this latent variable is not associated with the omitted variable of human capital accumulation. In particular, Kourtellos extended the basic local Solow growth model in Equation (4) to include human capital

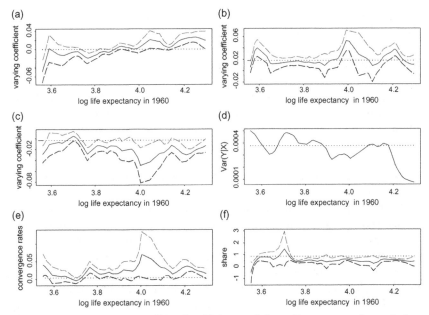

Fig. 6. (a) Intercept. (b) Coefficient of log (investments/population growth rates). (c) Coefficient of log initial income. (d) Conditional variance. (e) Implied convergence rates. (f) Implied share of physical capital.

accumulation along the lines of Mankiw et al. (1992) to find similar results.

5. Conclusion and directions for future research

This chapter studies local generalizations of the Solow model that take the form of varying coefficient models. In particular, using two measures of initial human development, initial literacy rates and initial life expectancy rates, we investigate parameter heterogeneity and study the complex relationship of human development and economic growth in the context of unconditional and conditional local Solow growth specifications.

We find that both development indices provide strong evidence of parameter heterogeneity. In particular, we find that the parameters of the local Solow growth model vary substantially with the initial levels of literacy rates and especially life expectancy in unconditional and conditional specifications. Furthermore, we find that there may be a latent determinant of negative growth rates or poverty trap that is omitted from the Solow model. Overall, our findings are suggestive of multiple steady states and richer growth dynamics than neoclassical theories, and hence, empirical studies that do not account for parameter heterogeneity are likely to produce a misleading inference.

Finally, we point out that this chapter does not purport to make strong structural claims per se; rather, it shows that structural claims in the literature are exaggerated due to the failure of the linear model to account for parameter heterogeneity. That being said, future research should attempt to unify the new set of statistical or reduced form findings with growth theories to provide testable econometric models that can be used for policy analysis.

A first step toward that direction is to deal with model uncertainty. As Brock and Durlauf (2001), among others, have argued, the inherent open-endedness of new growth theories presents unique challenges to researchers in exploring their quantitative consequences on growth. The statement that a particular theory of growth is empirically relevant does not logically preclude other theories of growth from also being relevant and therefore the inclusion or exclusion of growth variables may significantly alter previous conclusions.

One appealing approach to deal with the problem of model uncertainty is to employ a Bayesian model averaging (BMA) by constructing estimates conditional on a model space with elements that span an appropriate range of determinants suggested by a large body of work. A number of recent papers have documented the advantages of using BMA in constructing robust estimates primarily in the context of the linear model (see, e.g., Brock & Durlauf, 2001; Ciccone & Jarocinski, 2010; Doppelhofer, Miller, & Sala-i-Martin, 2004; Durlauf, Kourtellos, & Tan, 2008; Fernandez, Ley, & Steel, 2001; Masanjala & Papageorgiou, 2008). However, model averaging methods have yet to account for nonlinearities and parameter heterogeneity in a systematic way that deals with the problem of model uncertainty as a whole. Some initial attempts in this direction have been made by Brock and Durlauf (2001), Kourtellos, Tan, and Zhang (2007), and Cuaresma and Doppelhofer (2007). We expect this avenue of research to provide fruitful results.

Acknowledgments

I thank Steven Durlauf and William Brock for providing helpful and inspiring ideas on various drafts of this chapter. I also thank Chris Papageorgiou and Carl-Johan Dalgaard for their valuable comments.

Appendix

Following Fan and Zhang (1999), this chapter adopts a two-stage estimation procedure based on a simple local regression. The major advantage of a two-stage estimation over a one-stage estimation is that it allows the functional coefficients to possess different degrees of smoothness that ensure that the optimal rate of convergence for the asymptotic mean-squared error is achieved.

A one-stage estimation solves a simple weighted local least-squares problem. More precisely, for each given point z_0, the functions $\gamma_j(z)$, $j = 1, \ldots p$, are approximated by local linear polynomials

$$\gamma_j(z) \approx c_{j0} + c_{j1}(z - z_0) \tag{A.1}$$

for sample points z in a neighborhood of z_0. This approximation results in the following weighted local least-squares problem:

$$\min_{\{(c_{j0}, c_{j1})\}} \sum_{i=1}^{N} \left[g_i - \sum_{j=1}^{p} [c_{j0} + c_{j1}(z - z_0)] X_{ij} \right]^2 K_h(z_i - z_0) \tag{A.2}$$

where $K_h(\cdot) = (1/h)K(\cdot/h)$ and $K(\cdot)$ is the Epanechnikov kernel.

Let $\mathbf{g} = (g_1, \ldots, g_N)'$, $\mathbf{W} = \mathrm{diag}((1/h)K((z_1 - z_0)/h), \ldots, (1/h)K((z_N - z_0)/h))$, and

$$\mathbf{X} = \begin{pmatrix} X_{11} & (z_1 - z_0)X_{11} & \cdots & X_{1p} & (z_1 - z_0)X_{1p} \\ \vdots & \vdots & \ddots & \vdots & \vdots \\ X_{N1} & (z_N - z_0)X_{N1} & \cdots & X_{Np} & (z_N - z_0)X_{Np} \end{pmatrix} \tag{A.3}$$

The solution of the problem (A.2) is then given by

$$\hat{\gamma}_j(z) = e'_{2j-1,2p}(\mathbf{X}'\mathbf{W}\mathbf{X})^{-1}\mathbf{X}'\mathbf{W}\mathbf{g} \tag{A.4}$$

where $e_{k,m}$ denote the unit vector of length m with 1 at the kth position.

The conditional variance is estimated by a normalized weighted residual sum of squares

$$\hat{\sigma}^2(z) = \frac{\sum_{i=1}^{N}(g_i - \hat{g}_i)^2 K_h(z_i - z)}{\mathrm{tr}\{\mathbf{W} - \mathbf{W}\mathbf{X}(\mathbf{X}'\mathbf{W}\mathbf{X})^{-1}\mathbf{X}'\mathbf{W}\}} \tag{A.5}$$

where

$$\hat{\mathbf{g}} = (\hat{g}_1, \ldots, \hat{g}_N)' = \mathbf{X}(\mathbf{X}'\mathbf{W}\mathbf{X})^{-1}\mathbf{X}'\mathbf{W}\mathbf{g} \tag{A.6}$$

In the first stage of a two-stage procedure, we obtain initial estimates $\hat{\gamma}_{j,0}(z)$ using $h = h_0$, for $j = 1, 2, \ldots, p$; see Equation (A.4). In the second stage, a two-stage estimate $\hat{\gamma}_{j,2}(z)$ is obtained by replacing the unknown varying coefficient $\gamma_k(z)$, for $k \neq j$ into the local least squares (A.2) by their initial estimates $\hat{\gamma}_k(z)$, for $k{\neq}j$. Then, a local least-squares regression is fitted again by minimizing[4]

$$\sum_{i=1}^{N}\left[g_i - \sum_{k\neq j}^{p}\hat{\gamma}_{k,0}(z)X_{ik} - [c_{j0} + c_{j1}(z - z_0)]X_j\right]^2 K_{h_{j,2}}(z_i - z_0) \qquad (A.7)$$

This chapter employs the cross-validation to select both the initial and the two-step bandwidths. However, the initial bandwidth h_0 is chosen so that the estimate is undersmoothed. In particular, the optimal rates of convergence for estimating the two-stage coefficient is achieved when the optimal $h_{j,2}$ is of the order $O(N^{-1/9})$ and the initial bandwidth[5] is between $O(N^{-1/3})$ and $O(N^{-2/9})$. In practice, we choose the initial bandwidth to ensure that the bias of the initial estimator is small and that makes the two-step estimator not sensitive to the choice of the initial bandwidth (see Fan & Zhang, 1999).

By defining

$$\mathbf{A}_j = e'_{2j-1,2p}(\mathbf{X}'_j\mathbf{W}_j\mathbf{X}_j)^{-1}(\mathbf{X}'_j\mathbf{W}_j\mathbf{B}_j) \qquad (A.8)$$

the two-step estimator can be written in the familiar form of

$$\hat{\gamma}_{j,2} = \mathbf{A}_j\mathbf{g} \qquad (A.9)$$

where $\mathbf{X}_j$ denotes the matrix $\mathbf{X}$ with only those columns that refer to the variable j, $\mathbf{W}_j$ is the diagonal weight matrix $\mathbf{W}$ with $h = h_{j,2}$, and $\mathbf{B}_j$ is the $N \times N$ matrix of some complicated weights

$$\mathbf{B}_j = I_N - \sum_{k\neq j}^{p}\begin{pmatrix} X_{1k}e'_{2j-1,2p}(\mathbf{X}'_{(1)}\mathbf{W}_{(1)}\mathbf{X}_{(1)})^{-1}\mathbf{X}'_{(1)}\mathbf{W}_{(1)} \\ \vdots \\ X_{1k}e'_{2j-1,2p}(\mathbf{X}'_{(N)}\mathbf{W}_{(N)}\mathbf{X}_{(N)})^{-1}\mathbf{X}'_{(N)}\mathbf{W}_{(N)} \end{pmatrix}$$

where $\mathbf{X}_{(i)}$ and $\mathbf{W}_{(i)}$ are the matrices $\mathbf{X}$ and $\mathbf{W}$ with $z_0 = z_i$, respectively. The asymptotic confidence intervals for the two-stage estimator $\hat{\gamma}_{j,2}(z)$ are based on the asymptotic approximation of the variance given by

$$\mathbf{A}_j\mathbf{A}'_j\hat{\sigma}^2(z) \qquad (A.10)$$

where $\hat{\sigma}^2(z)$ is the estimate of the corresponding conditional variance.

---

[4] In theory, a local cubic fit should be used in the second step. In practice, however, it is not substantially different from the local linear fit to justify the extra computational burden.
[5] In practice, we use $h_0 = 0.5\hat{h}$ where $\hat{h}$ is the optimal h for one-stage estimation.

References

Acemoglu, D., Aghion, P., & Zilibotti, F. (2006). Distance to frontier, selection, and economic growth. *Journal of the European Economic Association, 4*(1), 37–74.

Azariadis, C., & Drazen, A. (1990). Threshold externalities in economic development. *Quarterly Journal of Economics, 105*(2), 501–526.

Barro, R. (1991). Economic growth in a cross-section of countries. *Quarterly Journal of Economics, 106*, 407–443.

Barro, R. (1997). *Determinants of economic growth*. Cambridge, MA: The MIT Press.

Barro, R., & Sala-I-Martin, X. (1995). *Economic Growth*. New York, NY: McGraw-Hill.

Bloom, D. E., & Sachs, J. D. (1998). Geography, demography, and economic growth in Africa. *Brookings Papers Economic Activity, 2*, 207–273.

Brock, W., & Durlauf, S. N. (2001). Growth economics and reality. *World Bank Economic Review, 15*, 229–272.

Canova, F. (2004). Testing for convergence clubs in income per capita: A predictive density approach. *International Economic Review, 45*(1), 49–77.

Ciccone, A., & Jarocinski, M. (2010). Determinants of economic growth: Will data tell? *American Economic Journal: Macroeconomics, 2*, 222–246.

Cuaresma, C. J., & Doppelhofer, G. (2007). Nonlinearities in cross-country growth regressions: A bayesian averaging of thresholds (BAT) approach. *Journal of Macroeconomics, 29*, 541–554.

Desdoigts, A. (1999). Patterns of economic development and the formation of clubs. *Journal of Economic Growth, 4*(3), 305–330.

Doppelhofer, G., Miller, R., & Sala-i-Martin, X. (2004). Determinants of long-term growth: A bayesian averaging of classical estimates (BACE) approach. *American Economic Review, 94*(4), 813–835.

Duffy, J., & Papageorgiou, C. (2000). A cross-country empirical investigation of the aggregate production function specification. *Journal of Economic Growth, 5*, 87–120.

Durlauf, N. S. (1993). Nonergodic economic growth. *Review of Economics Studies, 60*, 349–367.

Durlauf, S., & Johnson, P. (1995). Multiple regimes and cross-country growth behavior. *Journal of Applied Econometrics, 10*, 365–384.

Durlauf, S., Kourtellos, A., & Minkin, A. (2001). The local solow growth model. *European Economic Review, 15*, 928–940.

Durlauf, S. N., Johnson, P., & Temple, J. (2005). Growth econometrics. In P. Aghion & S. N. Durlauf (Eds.), *Handbook of economic growth*. Amsterdam: North Holland.

Durlauf, S. N., Kourtellos, A., & Tan, C. M. (2008). Are any growth theories robust? *Economic Journal, 118*, 329–346.

Evans, P. (1998). Using panel data to evaluate growth theories. *International Economic Review, 39*, 295–306.

Fan, J., & Zhang, W. (1999). Statistical estimation in varying-parameter models. *Annals of Statistics, 27*(5), 1491–1518.

Fernandez, C., Ley, E., & Steel, M. (2001). Model uncertainty in cross-country growth regressions. *Journal of Applied Econometrics, 16*(5), 563–576.

Galor, O., & Weil, D. N. (1999). From Malthusian stagnation to modern growth. *American Economic Review, 89*, 150–154.

Galor, O., & Weil, D. N. (2000). Population, technology and growth: From Malthusian stagnation to the demographic transition and beyond. *American Economic Review, 90*, 806–828.

Galor, O., & Zeira, J. (1993). Income distribution and macroeconomics. *Review of Economic Studies, 60*(1), 35–52.

Hansen, B. (2000). Sample splitting and threshold estimation. *Econometrica, 68*, 575–603.

Hastie, T., & Tibshirani, R. (1993). Varying parameter models (with discussion). *Journal of the Royal Statistical Society, Series B, 55*, 757–796.

Howitt, P., & Mayer-Foulkes, D. (2005). R&D, implementation and stagnation: A Schumpeterian theory of convergence clubs. *Journal of Money, Credit and Banking, 37*, 147–177.

Islam, N. (1995). Growth empirics: A panel data approach. *Quarterly Journal of Economics, 110*, 1127–1170.

Kalaitzidakis, P., Mamuneas, T. P., Savvides, A., & Stengos, T. (2001). Measures of human capital and nonlinearities in economic growth. *Journal of Economic Growth, 6*, 229–254.

Kourtellos, A. (2003). *Modeling parameter heterogeneity in cross-country growth regression models*. Mimeo, University of Cyprus.

Kourtellos, A., Tan, C. M., & Zhang, X. (2007). Is the relationship between aid and economic growth nonlinear? *Journal of Macroeconomics, 29*, 515–540.

Lee, K., Pesaran, M. H., & Smith, R. (1997). Growth and convergence in a multicountry stochastic solow model. *Journal of Applied Econometrics, 12*(4), 357–392.

Liu, C., & Stengos, T. (1999). Non-linearities in cross-country growth regressions: A semiparametric approach. *Journal of Applied Econometrics, 14*(5), 527–538.

Mamuneas, T., Savvides, A., & Stengos, T. (2006). Economic development and the return to human capital: A smooth coefficient semiparametric approach. *Journal of Applied Econometrics, 21*(1), 111–132.

Mankiw, N. G., Romer, D., & Weil, D. (1992). A contribution to the empirics of economic growth. *Quarterly Journal of Economics, CVII*, 407–437.

Masanjala, W., & Papageorgiou, C. (2008). Rough and lonely road to prosperity: A reexamination of the sources of growth in Africa using Bayesian model averaging. *Journal of Applied Econometrics, 23*, 671–682.

Masanjala, W. H., & Papageorgiou, C. (2004). The solow model with CES technology: Nonlinearities and parameter heterogeneity. *Journal of Applied Econometrics, 19*, 171–201.

Mayer-Foulkes, D. (2006). Global divergence. In G. Severov (Ed.), *International Finance and Monetary Policy*. New York: Nova Science Publishers.

Pack, H. (1994). Endogenous growth theory: Intellectual appeal and empirical shortcomings. *Journal of Economic Perspectives, 8*(1), 55–72.

Penn World Table Version 6.1, Center for International Comparisons at the University of Pennsylvania. Retrieved from http://pwt.econ. upenn.edu/

Quah, D. T. (1997). Empirics for growth and distribution: Stratification, polarization, and convergence clubs. *Journal of Economic Growth, 2*, 27–59.

Tan, C. M. (2010). No one true path: Uncovering the interplay between geography, institutions, and fractionalization in economic development. *Journal of Applied Econometrics, 25*, 1100–1127.

CHAPTER 14

How Much Should a Nation Save?
A New Answer

Olivier de La Grandville

*Department of Management Science and Engineering, Stanford University,
Stanford CA 94305, USA*
E-mail address: ola@stanford.edu

Thy letters have transported me beyond
This ignorant present, and I feel now
The future in the instant.

Lady MacBeth

Enrich the time to come with smooth-faced peace,
With smiling plenty and fair prosperous days!

Richmond (King Richard III)

Abstract
We introduce a formula for the optimal savings rate in an economy driven by
an investment policy reflecting competitive equilibrium. The reasonable
numbers generated by the formula should be of help not only to assess our
present situation but also to prepare our future. Moreover, this chapter
provides two theorems correcting a widely held belief in economic growth
theory, namely that a steady state defined by income per person growing at
the labor-augmenting rate can be asymptotically reached only if technical
progress is labor-augmenting. We finally show that the magnitudes of the
optimal savings rates are highly robust to very different, S-shaped evolutions
of population and technology. The chapter closes with a daring conjecture.

Keywords: dynamic optimisation, optimal economic growth, competitive
equilibrium, optimal savings rate

JEL classifications: 041, 010, 011

Throughout civilizations, our future has been an object of passionate
inquiry. In the past centuries, societies became increasingly aware that they
had not only the opportunity but also the responsibility to shape it. This is
perhaps why early classical treaties gave central importance to the subject

Frontiers of Economics and Globalization
Volume 11   ISSN: 1574-8715
DOI: 10.1108/S1574-8715(2011)0000011019

Olivier de La Grandville

of economic growth. We may then wonder why such a fundamental issue for our future as the determination of the optimal savings rate has not yet received a convincing, if not precise, answer.

Textbooks are highly discreet about the issue, as if they wanted to avoid some embarassment about the strange – and typically exceedingly high – savings profiles generated by traditional approaches. No debate about methodology or numbers takes place. Needless to say, no attempt has ever been made at evaluating the benefits generated for society by an optimal savings policy.

This dire situation, in our opinion, seems to owe as much to the way the problem has been tackled as to the results attained. Tradition would command that an optimality criterion for society be defined as follows: first, convert future consumption flows into utility units through a strictly concave function; choose a discounting factor for the future utility flows, and then sum up those discounted flows. Finally, maximize this sum by finding an optimal time path of capital, under the constraint that consumption plus investment equals the production potential of the economy. Two families of utility functions are declared fit for service – not necessarily because they showed any special merit, nor because they have been approved in some national referendum, but most probably because they had the good idea of being strictly concave: they are the affine transform of a power function $(C^\alpha - 1)/\alpha$ and the negative of a decreasing exponential, $-e^{-\beta C}/\beta$.

This is where serious difficulties are looming. A detailed analysis of the time paths resulting from the first of those families reveals that the initial savings rate necessary to set the economy on the lone, highly unstable path to equilibrium is inordinately high – sometimes in the order of 50%. To obtain acceptable initial savings rates, one must resort to assigning negative values to α, entailing a concavity of the utility function no one would ever suggest nor accept: after a sharp bend already at a very low consumption level, it becomes hardly distinguishable from a horizontal line. As to the negative exponential function, the situation is even worse since in that case an equilibrium point does not exist any more.[1] The model becomes completely unstable.

A first warning light could have been flashed already nearly half a century ago, thanks to Richard Goodwin's paper "The Optimal Growth Path for an Underdeveloped Economy" (1961), where at some point of time the optimal savings reached around 60% in both models he considered. And even Frank Ramsey, in his brilliant, path-breaking essay "A Mathematical Theory of Saving" (1928), trying to put some numbers on his own model, recognized that "the rate of saving which the rule requires is greatly in excess of that which anyone would suggest [...] the amount that should be saved out of a family income of £500 would be

---

[1] See La Grandville, *Economic Growth: A Unified Approach*, with two special contributions by Robert M. Solow, Cambridge University Press, Cambridge, 2009 (in particular pp. 224–229 and 240–256).

about £300." One can almost feel that Ramsey was not overwhelmingly happy with his result since he added that the concave utility function he used was "put forward merely as an illustration" (1928, p. 548).

We may venture to explain why, when optimal growth theory made a strong revival at the end of the 1950s and in the 1960s, no one analyzed in a systematic way the actual time paths generated by optimal growth theory. It may be due to the following, technical reason. The central model, as described above, incorporating strictly concave utility and production functions, almost invariably yields a Euler equation in the form of a second-order, nonlinear differential equation that does not possess an analytical solution. And in those days it would have taken not only a specialist in numerical analysis but also a good friend to do a complete, qualitative analysis of the results. Today we have very efficient programs – as well as excellent friends – that can help us in this task, so there are no more reasons not to recognize and deal with the problem at stake.

In this chapter we propose a competitive equilibrium model of optimal growth with a precise aim: to provide a convincing answer to the problem of a nation's optimal savings. By "convincing" we simply mean that it should yield reasonable, reachable numbers. The results – the optimal savings rate time path, as well as the ultimate benefits accrued to society – will then be the object of comparative dynamics. We certainly wish to know how these time paths and welfare indicator react to changes in parameters that may become the object of economic policy.

Our model will include labor as well as capital-augmenting technical progress. When deriving the optimal paths of the economy, we will then be led to correct a widely spread belief in economic growth theory, namely that a steady state, defined by an evolution of the economy such that income per person grows at the rate of labor-augmenting technical progress is asymptotically attainable only if technical progress is labor-augmenting (except in the well-known Cobb–Douglas case, considered until now as the only case contrary to the "rule"). With two theorems we demonstrate, precisely in the central cases that will be developed, that steady states will definitely be reached asymptotically with capital-augmenting progress.

The last section of this chapter extends the analysis to S-shaped evolutions of population and technology. In our conclusion we show how the results of the model enable us to assess the decrease in savings observed in most Western countries. Finally, we take the liberty of submitting a far-reaching – and certainly daring – conjecture.

1. A model of optimal growth

1.1. The production process

For many years optimal growth theory made the hypothesis that technological progress was purely labor-augmenting. There is of course no reason to assume that there are forms of technical progress equivalent to enhancing labor, and that none exist to do the same for the stock of capital. We thus examine the evolution of an economy where the production process is driven by a CES function, when technological progress increases capital by a factor $G_K(t)$ and labor by $G_L(t)$. Both $G_K(t)$ and $G_L(t)$ are increasing functions of time and are such that $G_K(0) = G_L(0) = 1$; their growth rates, which may be variable through time, are denoted $g_K(t)$ and $g_L(t)$. As to labor itself, it is supposed to grow exogenously at rate $n(t)$ and is also normalized to 1 at time 0.

The production function is then written

$$Y_t = F(K_t G_K(t), L_t G_L(t)) = \{[\delta K_t G_K(t)]^p + (1 - \delta)[L_t G_L(t)]^p\}^{1/p}, \quad p \neq 0$$
(1)

where Y stands for *net* real income (net of capital depreciation). Y_t is thus a general mean of order p of the augmented variables $K_t G_K(t)$ and $L_t G_L(t)$; p is linked to the elasticity of substitution σ by the increasing function $p = 1 - 1/\sigma$. The particular Wicksell–Cobb–Douglas case where $p = 0$ ($\sigma = 1$) corresponds to the geometric mean

$$Y_t = [K_t G_K(t)]^\delta [L_t G_L(t)]^{1-\delta}.$$
(2)

1.2. Choosing an optimality criterion

We are now to define an optimality criterion for society. Instead of trying to directly find a utility function that would suit our pressing need of reasonable results, we want to choose another tack. It is our hope that a consensus among society would be that we analyze the results entailed by the fundamental hypothesis of competitive equilibrium. Such an equilibrium is characterized by the equality between the marginal productivity of capital and society's rate of preference for the present, denoted $i(t)$:

$$\frac{\partial F}{\partial K}(K_t G_K(t), L_t G_L(t)) = i(t).$$
(3)

In a first step, let us examine what this criterion implies in terms of optimality for our future.

1.3. The surprises of competitive equilibrium

Innocuous as Equation (3) may seem, it conveys two pleasant surprises – and there will be more along the way. First, its implementation maximizes, from any initial time to infinity, the integral sum of all discounted consumption flows society may receive: indeed, if Leonhard Euler were peering over our shoulder, he would immediately recognize in (3) a necessary and sufficient condition for maximizing the integral

$$W = \int_0^\infty [F(K_t G_K(t), L_t G_L(t)) - \dot{K}_t] e^{-\int_0^t i(z)dz} dt. \tag{4}$$

For our benefit he would add that if (3) is not a second-order differential equation in K_t – as would generally be the case when maximizing a functional of the type $\int_a^b H(K, \dot{K}, t)dt$ – but simply an ordinary equation, the reason is that the integrand of the above functional is an affine function of $\dot{K}$.

There is even more to Equation (3). Remember the beautiful idea Robert Dorfman (1969) had when he introduced a "modified Hamiltonian" as follows – in order to honor Professor Dorfman's memory, we choose to call this new Hamiltonian a Dorfmanian, and designate it by D. Let λ_t denote the discounted valuation of one unit of capital received by society at time t, equal to $\partial W/\partial K_t = \partial/\partial K_t \{\int_t^\infty [F(K_\tau, \tau) - \dot{K}_\tau] e^{-\int_t^\tau i(z)dz} d\tau\}$. The Dorfmanian is equal to the traditional Hamiltonian H plus $\dot{\lambda}_t K_t$, or $D = [F(K_t, t) - \dot{K}_t] e^{-\int_0^t i(z)dz} + \lambda_t \dot{K}_t + \dot{\lambda}_t K_t$. In our case we have

$$D(K_t, \dot{K}_t, t) = C_t e^{-\int_0^t i(z)dz} + \frac{d}{dt}(\lambda_t K_t). \tag{5}$$

D thus represents the discounted valuation of society's activity at any point of time t, since it is equal to consumption plus the rate of increase in the value of capital at that time, in present value. Noting the concavity of D with respect to K_t and $\dot{K}_t$ and setting its gradient to zero, it can be verified that (3) maximizes D as well.

We therefore conclude that Equation (3) constitutes a necessary and sufficient condition for maximizing not only one, but *two* fundamental quantities: first, the sum over an infinite time horizon of all discounted consumption flows society may acquire; and second, at *any* point of time, the value of society's activity.

A final word is in order about the utility function implicit in this double optimization. Our friend Leonhard would point out that the infinity of affine transforms of C, namely $U(C) = aC + b$ such that, for instance, $a > 0$ and $b \geq 0$, would all lead to the same solution (Equation (3)). We feel that an affine, or even more simply a linear utility function is highly defensible in this aggregate evaluation of society's welfare for the following reasons.

First, the use of a strictly concave utility function would entail a contradiction between optimal growth and competitive equilibrium if utility flows are discounted with the rate of interest. Indeed, if we maximized

$$\int_0^\infty U(C_t) e^{-\int_0^t i(z)dz} dt = \int_0^\infty U[F(K_t G_K(t), L_t G_L(t)) - \dot{K}_t] e^{-\int_0^t i(z)dz} dt,$$

the Euler equation in that case would be

$$F'_K(K_t G_K(t), L_t G_L(t)) + \ddot{U}'(C)/U'(C) = i(t),$$

which contradicts (3). For this contradiction to be suppressed, one should explain to society that it must discount its utility flows at a rate equal to $i(t)$ plus $\ddot{U}'(C)/U'(C)$. Not only is that messsage hardly justifiable, but it would be probably undecipherable both by the speaker on any political platform and its polite, bewildered audience. It would be simply inapplicable, since this rate of preference for the present would depend on the optimal time path of capital – which is not known at the time of the discounting.

Second, we may well consider that technical progress as formalized here may well be directed toward the production of goods and services whose purpose is to increase the quality of our lives, and we do not see why such increases should bend to the rule of a concave utility function. Note finally that no international organization evaluating the welfare entailed by national income has ever transformed the former into utility flows.

2. Optimal growth paths for the economy

To derive the optimal time paths for the economy, we start by looking for a solution K_t^* to systems (1), (3) and (2), (3), respectively. Should such a solution exist, it will enable us to determine all optimal paths of interest, in particular income per person $y_t^* = F(K_t^*, t)/L_t$ and the optimal savings rate $s_t^* = \dot{K}_t^*/F(K_t^*, t)$; furthermore, it will permit us to perform comparative dynamics not only on those variables but also on the optimal benefits $W^* = \int_0^\infty C_t^* e^{-it} dt = \int_0^\infty (1 - s_t^*)F(K_t^*, t)e^{-it} dt$ accruing to society (for simplicity of the argument, we will assume that society's rate of preference for the present is a constant i, which of course can be set at different levels in comparative dynamics).

Solving first system (1), (3) we obtain

$$K_t^* = \left(\frac{1 - \delta}{\delta}\right)^{1/p} \frac{L_t G_L(t)/G_K(t)}{[\delta^{-\sigma} i^{\sigma-1} G_K(t)^{1-\sigma} - 1]^{1/p}}, \quad p \neq 0, \sigma \neq 1. \tag{6}$$

On the contrary, system (2), (3) yields

$$K_t^* = \left(\frac{\delta}{i}\right)^{1/(1-\delta)} G_K(t)^{\delta/(1-\delta)} L_t G_L(t), \quad p = 0, \sigma = 1. \tag{7}$$

While a unique, positive solution is defined by (7), examination of (6) reveals that such a solution exists if and only if the following condition on σ, i, δ, and $G_K(t)$ holds:

$$\sigma < \frac{\ln i - \ln G_K(t)}{\ln(i/\delta) - \ln G_K(t)}. \tag{8}$$

If σ is smaller than one, this condition is fulfilled because the right-hand side of the above inequality is always larger than one. However this condition does become binding if $\sigma > 1$. Even if we do not allow for capital-augmenting progress (if $G_K(t) = 1$), the condition is to be enforced for any value of $G_L(t)$ and t. For instance, at initial time $t = 0$, if $i = 0.04$ and $\delta = 0.3$, the inequality implies $\sigma < 1.59$. Observe also that, with $\sigma > 1$, the very existence of capital-augmenting progress implies that the condition becomes more restictive as time increases: there always exists a time $\bar{t}$ when competitive equilibrium as defined by (2) cannot be applied any more, since $\lim_{t \to \bar{t}} K_t = \infty$. For a concrete example, suppose that $G_K(t)$ is growing at constant rate g_K. This point in time is given by

$$\bar{t} = \frac{\sigma \ln \delta + (1 - \sigma) \ln i}{(1 - \sigma) g_K}, \quad \sigma > 1 \tag{9}$$

and is independent of $n(t)$ and $G_L(t)$. With $i = 0.04$, $\delta = 0.3$, $g_K = 0.007$, $\sigma = 1.4$, $\bar{t} \sim 142$ years. Those observations lead us to surmise that the optimal paths may well turn out to be of an entirely different nature in the case $\sigma \leq 1$ as opposed to $\sigma > 1$. Our task is now to make a crucial distinction between these two cases. They will lead to fundamentally different results.

2.1. Case $\sigma \leq 1$ ($p \leq 0$)

We first show that, contrary to well-entrenched beliefs, the economy may well tend toward a steady state[2] even if technical progress is capital-augmenting. Indeed, two families of cases will be shown to stand out and are expounded in the following theorems.

2.1.1. Two theorems on steady states

THEOREM 1. *Let an economy be driven by a CES production function with capital- and labor-augmenting technical progress, and by an investment process reflecting competitive equilibrium. Then a sufficient condition for the economy to reach a steady state asymptotically is that the elasticity of substitution is strictly between zero and one.*

PROOF. Denote the augmented variables $G_K(t) K(t) \equiv U(t)$ and $G_L(t) L(t) \equiv V(t)$. The production function is a mean of order p of U_t and V_t, written $M_p(U_t, V_t)$:

$$Y_t = F(K_t G_K(t), L_t G_L(t)) = M_p(U_t, V_t) = [\delta U_t^p + (1 - \delta) V_t^p]^{1/p}, \quad p \neq 0. \tag{10}$$

---

[2] A steady state is defined by an evolution of the economy such that income per person grows at the rate of labor-augmenting technical progress; this rate may be a function of time or a constant.

Its growth rate is

$$
\frac{\dot{Y}_t}{Y_t} = \frac{\dot{M}_t}{M_t} = \frac{\partial M}{\partial U}(t)\frac{U_t}{M_t}\left[\frac{\dot{U}_t}{U_t}\right] + \frac{\partial M}{\partial V}(t)\frac{V_t}{M_t}\left[\frac{\dot{V}_t}{V_t}\right]
$$

$$
= \frac{\partial M}{\partial U}(t)\frac{U_t}{M_t}\left[\frac{\dot{K}_t}{K_t} + g_K(t)\right] + \frac{\partial M}{\partial V}(t)\frac{V_t}{M_t}\left[\frac{\dot{L}_t}{L_t} + g_L(t)\right]. \tag{11}
$$

Without any loss in generality, suppose that $g_K(t)$ and $g_L(t)$ are bounded. As an intermediate result, the following property of a mean of order $p < 0$ of m positive functions of time $x_1(t), \ldots, x_m(t)$ will now be proved.

LEMMA. For $p < 0$, if $\lim_{t\to\infty} x_m(t)/x_j(t) = \infty, j = 1, \ldots, m-1$, the elasticity of $M_p(x_1(t), \ldots, x_m(t))$ with respect to x_m, denoted ε_{M,x_m}, tends toward zero, and $\lim_{t\to\infty}\sum_{j=1}^{m-1}\varepsilon_{M,x_j} = 1$.

PROOF. With $M_p(x_1(t), \ldots, x_m(t)) = [\sum_{j=1}^{m}(f_j x_j^p)]^{1/p}$, $\lim_{t\to\infty}\partial \ln M_p/\partial \ln x_m = \lim_{t\to\infty}[1 + \sum_{j=1}^{m-1}(f_j/f_m)(x_j/x_m)^p]^{-1} = 0$. Furthermore, M_p being homogeneous of degree 1 in $x_1, \ldots, x_m$, Euler's identity applies and $\lim_{t\to\infty}\sum_{j=1}^{m-1}\varepsilon_{M,x_j} = 1$.

We now show that U_t plays the role of $x_m(t)$ in the lemma. From (6) the growth rate of K_t is

$$
\frac{\dot{K}_t^*}{K_t^*} = g_L(t) + n(t) - g_K(t)\left[1 - \frac{\sigma}{1 - \delta^\sigma i^{1-\sigma}G_K(t)^{-(1-\sigma)}}\right]; \tag{12}
$$

using the fact that $\dot{V}_t/V_t = g_L(t) + n(t)$, this implies

$$
\frac{\dot{U}_t}{U_t} = \frac{\dot{K}_t^*}{K_t^*} + g_K(t) = \dot{V}_t/V_t + \sigma g_K(t)\left[\frac{1}{1 - \delta^\sigma i^{1-\sigma}G_K(t)^{-(1-\sigma)}}\right]. \tag{13}
$$

The difference between $\dot{U}_t/U_t$ and $\dot{V}_t/V_t$ is bounded away from zero; therefore $\lim_{t\to\infty}U_t/V_t = \infty$, and the lemma applies to U_t: $\lim_{t\to\infty}e_{M,U_t} = 0$, $\lim_{t\to\infty}e_{M,V_t} = 1$, from which we conclude that $\lim_{t\to\infty}\dot{Y}_t/Y_t = g_L(\infty) + n(\infty)$ and $\lim_{t\to\infty}\dot{y}_t/y_t = g(\infty)$. Theorem 1 is thus proved.

We can verify this theorem by determining the optimal time path of income per person $y_t^* = F(K_t^*, t)/L_t$, plugging (6) into (1), we get

$$
y_t^* = G_L(t)\left[\frac{1 - \delta}{1 - \delta^\sigma i^{1-\sigma}G_K(t)^{-(1-\sigma)}}\right]^{1/p}, \quad p \neq 0, \sigma \neq 1. \tag{14}
$$

Note that this formula can be further simplified by identifying the denominator of the bracketed term as the labor share. Indeed, in the standard model with labor-augmenting technical progress, the capital share, denoted $\pi(t)$, can be shown to be the geometric mean of δ and the marginal productivity of capital $F_K(K_t, t)$, σ acting as the weight of δ; $\pi(t) = \delta^\sigma F_K^{1-\sigma}(K_t, t)$.[3] In the present context, with $i = F_K(K_t, t)$ and capital-augmenting as well as labor-augmenting technical progress, the capital share keeps the same geometric mean structure, where i is now divided by $G_K(t)$. The formula becomes, using (6) and (14):

$$\pi(t) = \delta^\sigma [i/G_K(t)]^{1-\sigma}. \tag{15}$$

Observing that $\pi(t) = \varepsilon_{F,K} = \varepsilon_{M,U}$, we can immediately verify both the lemma and the fact that $\lim_{t\to\infty}\pi(t) = 0$. Denoting $\theta(t)$ the labor share ($\theta(t) = 1-\pi(t)$), the optimal time path of income per person can be written as

$$y_t^* = G_L(t)\left[\frac{1-\delta}{\theta(t)}\right]^{1/p}, \quad p \neq 0, \sigma \neq 1 \tag{16}$$

and its growth rate $\dot{y}_t/y_t$, denoted onwards r_t^*, shown to be equal to

$$r_t^* = g_L(t) + \frac{\sigma g_K(t)}{\delta^{-\sigma} i^{\sigma-1} G_K(t)^{1-\sigma} - 1} = g_L(t) + \sigma g_K(t)\frac{\pi(t)}{\theta(t)}, \tag{17}$$

which applies to $\sigma = 1$ as well. From (16), observe that in the limit, when $t \to \infty$, the optimal time path y_t^* becomes independent of $G_K(t)$, $n(t)$ and i. It tends toward $(1 - \delta)^{1/p}G_L(t)$, with its limiting growth rate being $g_L(t)$, a result confirmed by (17) as well.

Note also that r_t^* converges toward $g_L(t)$ for *one reason only*: the presence of capital-augmenting technical progress. If there was no such progress (if $G_K(t)$ was set to 1 in (14) or $g_K(t)$ to 0 in (17)), the growth rate r_t^* would be $g_L(t)$ at all times.

We now turn to our second result.

THEOREM 2. *If an economy is driven by a CES production function with capital- and labor-augmenting technical progress, and by an investment process reflecting competitive equilibrium, it will at all times be in a steady state if the elasticity of substitution is either equal to zero or to one.*

PROOF. If $\sigma \to 0$, then $p \to -\infty$, and from (6)

$$\lim_{\sigma \to 0} K_t^* = \lim_{\sigma \to 0} \left(\frac{1-\delta}{\delta}\right)^{1/p} \frac{L_t G_L(t)/G_K(t)}{[\delta^{-\sigma} i^{\sigma-1} G_K(t)^{1-\sigma} - 1]^{1/p}} = L_t G_L(t)/G_K(t). \tag{18}$$

In the limit, when $\sigma \to 0$, this implies that $K_t^* G_K(t) = L_t G_L(t)$ or $U_t = V_t$, and from (10) $Y_t = M_p(U_t, V_t) = V_t$. Therefore $\dot{Y}_t/Y_t = g_L(t) + n(t)$ and $\dot{y}_t/y_t = g_L(t)$ *at all times* t.

On the other hand, if $\sigma = 1$, Equations (2) and (7) lead to $\dot{y}_t/y_t = g_L(t) + (\delta/(1 - \delta))g_K(t)$. In this case the geometric mean structure of the production function implies that augmenting K_t by a factor $G_K(t)$ on the one hand and L_t by $G_L(t)$ on the other is tantamount to augmenting L_t

---

[3] See La Grandville (2009, p. 107).

by a factor $G_L(t)G_K(t)^{\delta/(1-\delta)}$, whose growth rate is $g_L(t) + (\delta/(1-\delta))g_K(t)$ at all times t as well. Theorem 2 is thus proved.

Until now we focused our attention on the properties of the optimal income per person time path. But optimal income per unit of capital is not less worthy of interest: while $\dot{y}_t^*/y_t^*$ was shown to *converge asymptotically* toward $g_L(t)$ for any value of σ in the *open* interval $(0,1)$, the growth rate of Y_t^*/K_t^* can be shown to be *equal at all times* to $(1-\sigma)g_K(t)$ for all σ in the *closed* interval $[0,1]$. Indeed, from (15) we can deduce that Y_t^*/K_t^* is equal *at all times* to the geometric mean $(i/\delta)^\sigma G_K(t)^{(1-\sigma)}$, for all values of σ from 0 to 1, from which the above property results.

2.1.2. The optimal time path income per person: examples

To quantify optimal time paths we should become specific about the possible magnitudes of i, $n(t)$, $g_L(t)$, and $g_K(t)$. In a first approach, we consider n, g_K and g_L as constants. It will be assumed that $n+g_L<i<\delta$; n and δ will be set at 0.01 and 1/3, respectively; i will be given values between 0.04 and 0.06. Regarding the elasticity of substitution σ, we will retain the range where it has been most frequently measured, that is, [0.5,1].

As to the parameters g_K and g_L, in a first step we want to choose them so as they square with a long series of real income per person, namely that for the United States from 1919 to 2008; for that purpose, we use the series established by Johnston and Williamson (2009) over the period 1790–2008. We look for values of g_K and g_L whose order of magnitude, once introduced into the formula for $\dot{y}_t^*/y_t^*$, yield a result close to the observed long-term growth rate of real GDP per person, namely 2.1% over that period.[4] If g_K and g_L are constants, Equation (14) becomes

$$y_t^* = e^{g_L t}\left[\frac{1-\delta}{1-\delta^\sigma i^{1-\sigma}e^{-(1-\sigma)g_K t}}\right]^{1/p}, \quad p\neq 0, \sigma\neq 1 \tag{19}$$

and its growth rate, denoted onwards r_t^*, is

$$r_t^* = g_L + \frac{\sigma g_K}{\delta^{-\sigma}i^{\sigma-1}e^{(1-\sigma)g_K t} - 1} = g_L + \sigma g_K \frac{\pi(t)}{\theta(t)} \tag{20}$$

which also applies if $\sigma = 1$, the rate becoming in that case the constant $g_L + g_K\delta/(1-\delta)$. Since most estimates of σ lie between 0.5 and 1,[5] we chose quite arbitrarily $\sigma = 0.7$, and, not less arbitrarily, a rate of preference for the

---

[4] As all growth rates in this chapter, this long-term rate, denoted $r_{0,T}$, is continuously compounded; if $r_{0,T}^{(m)}$ designates the yearly growth rate compounded m times per year over period T, the long-term continuously compounded rate is defined by the equality $y_T = y_0 \lim_{m\to\infty}(1 + r_{0,T}^{(m)}/m)^{mT}$. We thus have $r_{0,T}^{(\infty)} \equiv r_{0,T} = (1/T)\ln(y_T/y_0)$; as a consequence, it is equal to the average of the annual rates $\bar{r} = (1/T)\sum_{t=1}^{T}\ln(y_t/y_{t-1})$.

[5] See in particular Klump et al. (2007).

present equal to $i = 0.04$. We then set $g_K = 0.007$ and $g_L = 0.02$. When plugged into (17), these values lead to $r_t^* = 2.10\%, 2.10\%$ and 2.09% at times $t = 0$, 30 and 60 years, respectively. We feel that, for our purposes, these numbers for g_K and g_L seem reasonable because they are in the range of empirical estimates made by Ryuzo Sato (2006, p. 60) over the slightly different period 1909–1989. Sato obtained $g_K = .004$ and $g_L = 0.02$ with $\sigma = 0.8$, and it turns out that we would have obtained values for r_t^* extremely close to those above if we had used Sato's numbers; indeed, we would have gotten $r_0^* = 2.09\%$, $r_{30}^* = 2.09\%$, and $r_{60}^* = 2.08\%$. The differences of course are negligible if compared to the errors in measurement of y_t.

We may naturally ask ourselves what would have been the results for r_t^* if we had used, together with $g_K = 0.007$, $g_L = 0.02$ and $\sigma = 0.7$, values for i and δ different from 0.04 and 1/3. The outcome is the following: for i between 0.035 and 0.06, and δ between 0.25 and 0.35, the rounded value of r_t^* is 2.1% for the whole interval of time between 0 and 60 years. Obviously, the optimal growth rate is little affected by changes in i and δ – incidentally, this is good news. At this stage therefore, it seems fitting to use the values $g_K = 0.007$, $g_L = 0.02$ as preliminary benchmarks. But we want to stress that our aim is to provide a formula for the optimal savings rate for *any* economy, once we are able to estimate its fundamental coefficients. Later on in this chapter, we experiment with values of g_K and g_L quite different from those above.

Let us now look at the actual evolution through time of the optimal growth rate of income per person if the economy operates in competitive equilibrium and under the constraints of a CES function, with particular focus on its dependence up σ, g_L, and g_K. We have first represented this rate as a function of σ and t, for years $t = 0$, 30, and 60, respectively (Figure 1). The three curves bundle up at points $\sigma = 0$ and $\sigma = 1$,[6] where they become the constants $g_L = 0.02$ and $g_L + (\delta/(1 - \delta))g_K = 0.0235$, respectively; this is just a consequence of Theorem 2.

Theorem 1 is illustrated by the downward displacement of the curves in the open interval of σ (0,1) (in La Grandville, 2009, chapter 5). Note how very slowly the growth rates diminish: with $\sigma = 0.7$ for instance, r_0^* is 0.0212, and after 60 years it has become $r_{60}^* = 0.0210$, dropping by only two basis points, or 2% of a percent. We may thus consider the initial rate as a very useful indicator of the optimal rate that would be valid for medium to long horizons as well.

Figure 1 also gives a hint at answering – if only partially – the following question: why did some countries experience in the past two centuries a surge in the growth rate of real income per person? For instance, in the United States, between 1830 and 1919 this rate was 1.5% per year, and it increased to 2.1% during the period 1919–2008. For the United Kingdom,

---

[6] Increasing the length of the abscissa would make this apparent at point $\sigma = 0$.

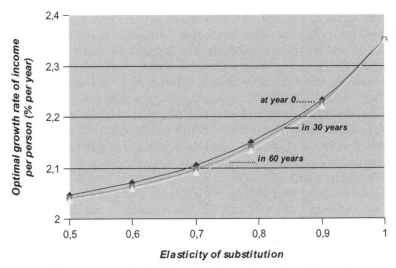

Fig. 1. The strong relationship between the optimal growth rate of income per person and the elasticity of substitution, and its slow downward displacement through time. ($\delta = 1/3$; $n = 0.01$; $g_L = 0.02$; $g_K = 0.007$)

the corresponding figures were 1.1% and 1.8% (data source: same as above, Johnston and Williamson, 2009). From Figure 1, we can immediately see that the natural decrease of the rate (solely due to the presece of capital-augmenting progress, as we noted earlier) may easily be compensated by a rise in the elasticity of substitution. In fact, σ may very well change through time – as early as 1932 John Hicks had discussed possible causes of this phenomenon. We have some indication that σ rose in the last half-century: for instance, by regressing the real wage rate on income per person, La Grandville (2009) showed that in a cross-section of 16 OECD countries the elasticity of substitution had markedly increased between 1966 and 1997.

But of course, changes in g_K and g_L may also be at play, and it is natural to examine their impact on the optimal growth rate $r_t^* \equiv \dot{y}_t^*/y_t^*$. The partial elasticities of r_t^* with respect to each of those variables are time-dependent as well, but the dependency is so weak that it is sufficient to consider these elasticities at time $t = 0$. They are equal to $\varepsilon_{r_0^*,g_K} = 0.34$, $\varepsilon_{r_0^*,g_L} = 0.87$ and $\varepsilon_{r_0^*,\sigma} = 0.96$ respectively. These numbers may already point out to the respective importance they might play in the growth process. However, a growth rate cannot constitute an aim in itself, and it is only when we evaluate the total benefits reaped by society in the form of the sum of the discounted consumption flows that we will discover the respective impacts of these parameters. We now turn to our variable of central importance.

2.1.3. The optimal savings rate

If the positive link between the efficiency parameters and the optimal growth rate makes good sense, the nature of the relationship between the same parameters and the optimal savings rate s^* is very hard to predict. For instance, one might well be tempted to imagine that an increase in the efficiency of production would lead to a reduction in s^*. To illustrate the extreme difficulty of predicting these effects, it seems appropriate to quote what Ramsey had to say on this issue.

> *It is worth pausing for a moment to consider how far our conclusions are affected by considerations which our simplifying assumptions have forced us to neglect. The probable increase of population constitutes a reason for saving even more, and so does the possibility that future inventions will put the bliss level higher than at present appears. On the other hand, the probability that future inventions and improvements in organisation are likely to make income obtainable with less sacrifice than at present is a reason for saving less. The influence of inventions thus works in two opposite ways: they give us new needs which we can better satisfy if we have saved up beforehand, but they also increase our productive capacity and make preliminary saving less urgent. (Ramsey, 1928, p. 549)*

We now examine how his intuition – which may well be ours – fits the above competitive equilibrium model. In particular, we will want to know whether any of the two forces identified by Ramsey dominates the other one.

The optimal savings rate $s_t^* = \dot{K}_t^*/Y_t^*$ can be determined from Equations (12), (6), and (1) as the following function of time:

$$
\begin{aligned}
s_t^*[i, \delta, \sigma, n(t), G_L(t), G_K(t)] &= (\delta/i)^\sigma G_K(t)^{-(1-\sigma)} \\
&\cdot \left[n(t) + g_L(t) + g_K(t) \left(\frac{\sigma}{1-\delta^\sigma i^{1-\sigma} G_K(t)^{-(1-\sigma)}} - 1 \right) \right],
\end{aligned} \tag{21}
$$

valid for all σ in $[0, 1]$. Complex as formula for s_t^* may look, it always yields very reasonable values, as we shall see. Before examining them, let us immediately note three properties:

a. If the growth rates n, g_L and g_K are constant, s_t^* is a decreasing function of time, tending ultimately to 0 (we will see that it does so very slowly) *except* for $\sigma = 1$; in this case, s_t^* is determined by $(\delta/i)[n(t) + g_L(t) + g_K(t)(\delta/(1 - \delta))]$.

b. The decrease of s_t^* through time is due to *one reason only*: the dependence of s_t^* on g_K. If there was no capital-augmenting technical progress – if g_L was acting alone – s_t^* would remain at the constant level $(\delta/i)^\sigma(n+g_L)$.

c. We can write s_t^* in terms of the shares $\pi(t)$ and $\theta(t)$; using (15) and (21), we have

$$s_t^* = \frac{\pi(t)}{i}\left[n + g_L(t) + g_K(t)\left(\frac{\sigma}{\theta(t)} - 1\right)\right] \tag{22}$$

from which the following property can be deduced: at the initial time the optimal savings rate s_t^* will be independent from g_K if the elasticity of substitution is equal to the labor share; and s_t^* will be an increasing or decreasing function of g_K if σ is larger or smaller than the labor share, respectively. Table 1 summarizes the expressions of s_t^* on the interval $0 \le \sigma \le 1$.

In a first step, for an order of magnitude of s_t^*, we have considered $n(t)$, $g_L(t)$, and $g_K(t)$ as constants. Given the initial conditions on $L(t)$, $G_L(t)$, and $G_K(t)$ defined earlier, Equation (22) becomes the 6-parameter function of time

$$s_t^*(i, \delta, \sigma, n, g_L, g_K) = (\delta/i)^\sigma e^{-(1-\sigma)g_K t}$$
$$\cdot \left[n + g_L + g_K\left(\frac{\sigma}{1 - \delta^\sigma i^{1-\sigma} e^{-(1-\sigma)g_K t}} - 1\right)\right]. \tag{23}$$

As an example we chose $g_K = .007$; $g_L = 0.02$; $n = .01$; $i = .04$; $\delta = 1/3$. Figure 2 depicts the optimal savings rate as a function of the elasticity of substitution and time, with $t = 0$, 30, and 60 years. Like the optimal growth rate of income per person, s_t^* is a strongly increasing function of σ, and its slow decrease through time is reflected in the following numbers: with $\sigma = 0.7$, from an initial value of 12.8% s_t^* diminishes to 11.2% only after 60 years.

We now address the issue of the influence of the coefficients g_L and g_K on s_t^*. For reasons just mentioned, we can concentrate on the initial value

$$s_0^* = (\delta/i)^\sigma\left[n + g_L + g_K\left(\frac{\sigma}{1 - \delta^\sigma i^{1-\sigma}} - 1\right)\right]. \tag{24}$$

The optimal savings rate $s_0^*(\sigma, g_L)$, where g_L plays the role of a parameter taking the percentage values 0.8, 1.2, 1.6, and 2 is given in Figure 3. The function $s_0^*(\sigma, g_L)$ is strongly increasing with g_L, and that positive dependence is itself an increasing function of σ. Contrary to what our intuition might suggest, although s_t^* will decrease – if ever so

Table 1. *The optimal savings rate $s_t^*(i, \delta, \sigma, n, g_L, g_K)$ for $\sigma = 0$, $0 < \sigma < 1$ and $\sigma = 1$*

$\sigma = 0$	$G_K(t)^{-1}[n(t) + g_L(t) - g_K(t)]$
$0 < \sigma < 1$	$(\delta/i)^\sigma G_K(t)^{-(1-\sigma)}\left[n(t) + g_L(t) + g_K(t)\left(\dfrac{\sigma}{1 - \delta^\sigma i^{1-\sigma} G_K(t)^{-(1-\sigma)}} - 1\right)\right]$
	$= [\pi(t)/i]\left[n(t) + g_L(t) + g_K(t)\left(\frac{\sigma}{\theta(t)} - 1\right)\right]$
$\sigma = 1$	$(\delta/i)\left[n(t) + g_L(t) + g_K(t)\frac{\delta}{1-\delta}\right]$

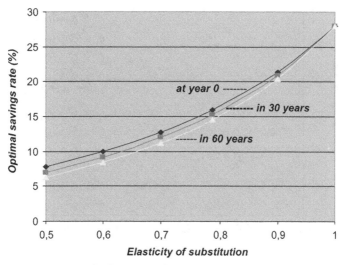

Fig. 2. *The optimal savings rate $s_t^*(\sigma, t)$; its slow decrease through time.*
$\delta = 1/3$; $n = 0.01$; $g_L = 0.02$; $g_K = 0.007$

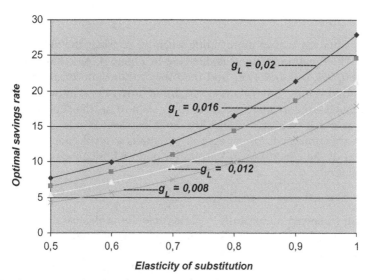

Fig. 3. *The optimal savings rate $s_0^*(\sigma, g_L)$: a strong dependence on g_L.*
$\delta = 1/3$; $n = 0.01$; $g_L = 0.02$; $g_K = 0.007$.

slowly – due to the mere existence of g_K, it is definitely in the interest of society to save *more* when it benefits from an advance in labor-augmenting technological progress or when the substitutability of labor with capital is enhanced.

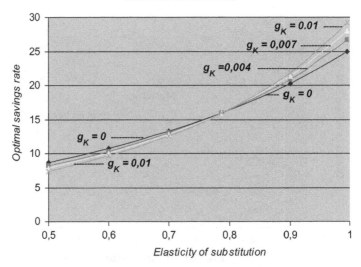

Fig. 4. **The optimal savings rate** $s_0^*(\sigma, g_K)$. **A weak dependence on** g_K**: an increase in** g_K **generates a small rotation of the** $s_0^*(\sigma, g_K)$ **curve around a fixed point whose abscissa is the solution of** $\sigma = 1 - \delta^\sigma i^{1-\sigma} = \theta_0$**;** $\delta = 1/3$**;** $n = 0.01$**;** $g_L = 0.02$**;** $g_K = 0.007$**.**

The situation is even more subtle when we consider the influence of g_K on s_t^*. The function $s_0^*(\sigma, g_K)$ is depicted in Figure 4, g_K taking the values (in %) 0, 0.4, 0.7, and 1, g_L and the other parameters remaining fixed at their initial values. Two observations are in order. First, although we have given much larger relative increases to g_K than to g_L, the dependance of s_t^* on g_K is much weaker. Second, the links between s_0^* and g_K mentioned earlier are confirmed: an increase in g_K entails a small counter-clockwise rotation of the curve $s_0^*(\sigma, g_K)$ around a point whose abscissa is given by the equality

$$\sigma = \theta_0(\sigma, i, \theta, \delta) = 1 - \delta^\sigma i^{1-\sigma}; \tag{25}$$

(25) can be solved numerically, yielding $\sigma = .79$ in this case.

We conclude that the only situation where the optimal savings rate will diminish because of an increase in the efficiency of the production process arises when g_K increases *and* when σ is relatively low. In all other cases it is in the interest of society to save more when either σ, g_L, or g_K increase, which tells us that in the present context the first force identified by Ramsey definitely dominates the second one.

2.1.4. Introducing uncertainty; its bearing on the optimal savings rate

Until now we confined our analysis of optimal paths of the economy and of the optimal savings rate in a deterministic approach. We now suppose that future consumption flows resut from predictions and that the initial interest rate used to discount those flows is augmented by a risk premium $\rho(t)$. Society will try then to maximize $W = \int_0^\infty [F(K_t G_K(t), L_t G_L(t)) - K_t] e^{-\int_0^t [i(z) + \rho(t)] dz} dt$, and the Euler Equation (3) would simply become $(\partial F/\partial K)(K_t G_K(t), L_t G_L(t)) = i(t) + \rho(t)$. Supposing that i and ρ are constants, we can see that a risk premium reduces the optimal savings rate, although not dramatically (Table 2). For all numbers in this table, the elasticity of s^* with respect to ρ is between -0.4 and -0.9. Observe also that this sentivity of s^* to ρ increases with the elasticity of substitution (Figure 5).

Table 2. The optimal savings rate as a function of the elasticity of substitution σ and the real interest rate augmented by a risk premium $(\delta = 1/3; \, n = 0.01; \, g_L = 0.02; \, g_K = 0.007)$

σ	0.5	0.6	0.7	0.8	0.9	1.0
$i+\rho$						
0.04	7.8	10.0	12.8	16.4	21.3	27.9
0.05	7.0	8.7	11.0	13.8	17.5	22.3
0.06	6.4	7.8	9.7	12.0	14.9	18.6
0.07	5.9	7.2	8.7	10.6	13.0	16.0

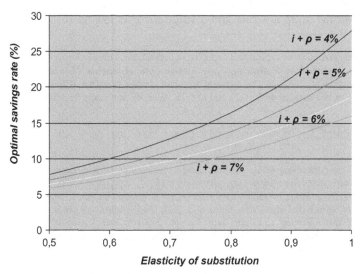

Fig. 5. Introducing a risk premium ρ lowers somewhat the optimal savings rate s_0^*; the sensitivity of s_0^* to ρ increases with the elasticity of substitution.

2.1.5. Evaluating the total benefits accruing to society

We are now able to measure the final outcome for society of an optimal savings policy. The optimal savings rate s_t^* determined in (23) will generate the sum of discounted consumption flows $W^* = \int_0^\infty C^*(t)e^{-it}dt = \int_0^\infty (1 - s_t^*)F(K_t^*, t)e^{-it}dt$; from (19) and (22), this optimal value is equal to

$$
W^*(i,\delta,\sigma,n,g_L,g_K) = \int_0^\infty e^{(n+g_L-i)t}\left\{\frac{1-\delta}{1-\delta^\sigma i^{1-\sigma}e^{-(1-\sigma)g_K t}}\right\}^{\sigma/(\sigma-1)} \cdot
$$

$$
\left\{1 - (\delta/i)^\sigma e^{-(1-\sigma)g_K t}\left[n + g_L - g_K\left(1 - \frac{\sigma}{1-\delta^\sigma i^{1-\sigma}e^{-(1-\sigma)g_K t}}\right)\right]\right\}dt, \quad \sigma < 1.
$$

(26)

Although the above integral does not possess an analytic solution,[7] it is easily calculated numerically; we briefly explain why it is so.

Two observations are in order. First, it can be shown that the integrand is strictly decreasing and convex over the whole integration interval. This implies that the exact value of W^* will always lie between a lower bound corresponding to the midpoint method and the higher trapeze bound; in addition, as is always the case when an integrand exihibits the above-mentioned properties, the exact result will be closer to the lower bound than to the higher one.

Second, over a one-year interval the evolution of the integrand, although strictly convex, is practically undistinguishable from that of a straight line. This implies that as we divide one year into n intervals, we can expect both methods to converge quickly toward the exact result as n increases, thus enabling to achieve more precision than ever needed simply by using the midpoint rule and a value for n as low as 10.[8]

---

[7] The only exception where a closed form for W is available is the particular $\sigma = 1$ case, which leads to a constant optimal savings rate, and an optimal time path for income which is a simple exponential. Using the constant optimal savings rate $(\delta = i)$ $(n+g_L+g_K(\delta/(1-\delta)))$ applying in this case, as well as (7) and (2), the value W^* can easily be determined as

$$
W^* = \frac{(\delta/i)^{\delta/(1-\delta)}\{(\delta/i)[(\delta/(1-\delta))g_K + n + g_L] - 1\}}{[\delta/(1-\delta)]g_K + n + g_L - i}.
$$

(27)

[8] For all the parameters within the usual range, it is possible to evaluate instantaneously W^* with 4-decimal precision by simply calculating $0.1\sum_{j=0}^{12800} C_{0.05+0.1j}^* e^{-i(0.05+0.1j)}$, i.e. the sum of all discounted consumption flows over a 1,280-year period, each of those being received in the middle of an interval equal to a tenth of a year. To illustrate the precision of the result, consider the following example: with $i = .04$, $\delta = 1/3$, $\sigma = .3$, $n = .01$, $g_L = .007$ and $g_K = .008$ the midpoint method gives 49.473 753; the trapeze method would yield 49.473 785 and the Simpson method 49.473 763 – in the latter approach, on each interval the integrand is approximated by a parabola going through the boundary and midpoint values; the resulting integral is equal to the average of the midpoint and trapeze integrals, with weights 2/3 and 1/3 to be exact within 6 decimals; we can confirm this thanks to our colleague Ernst Hairer who provided us with the result he obtained using an advanced, Gaussian-type method he had developed earlier, with 15-decimal precision.

Table 3. **Optimal value** $W^*(i, s; d, n, g_L, g_K) = \int_0^\infty C_t^* e^{-it} dt$ **as a function of the rate of preference for the present and the elasticity of substitution** ($\delta = 1/3$; $n = 0.01$; $g_L = 0.02$; $g_K = 0.007$)

σ	0.5	0.6	0.7	0.8	0.9	1.0
i						
0.04	129.3	142.0	160.0	186.8	230.9	320.1
0.05	62.8	68.1	75.1	84.8	99.0	121.5
0.06	41.2	44.3	48.3	53.7	61.3	72.4

Table 3 gives the results for the values of δ, n, g_L, and g_K and the intervals of σ and i used above. The sensitivity of W^* to σ is obvious, and so is the price paid by society in terms of its future welfare if its rate of preference for the present increases.

We now should explain why σ plays such an essential role in the size of W^*. The properties of the general mean $Y_t = M_p(U_t, V_t)$, considered either from a geometric or algebraic point of view, will prove of central importance. First, in (Y, U, V) space, $M_p(U_t, V_t)$ is a surface that opens up as p – or σ – increases at any given point of time. The opening up of the surface takes place around the ray from the origin $Y = U = V$. In turn this implies the opening up of the income per person curve $Y/L = G_L(t)\{\delta[U_t/V_t]^p + [1 - \delta]^p\}^{1/p}$ around point $U_t/V_t = 1$.[9] This feature of M_p is the geometrical interpretation of the fundamental property that the mean is an increasing function of its order,[10] except when $U = V$. It implies that, other things being equal, an economy with a higher elasticity of substitution will have a higher level of income; this property could be used for an alternate proof of Theorem 1 in Klump and La Grandville (2000).

Now two additional properties of M as a function of p come into play. First, numerical observations led La Grandville and Solow (2006) to conjecture that the increasing curve $M(p)$ had one and only one inflection point – a formal proof looked unassailable due to the extreme complexity of the second derivative $\partial^2 M/\partial p^2$. Thanh and Minh (2008) finally succeeded in demonstrating the conjecture in a 5-page, 3-step, highly skillful proof. The importance of this property is the following: if σ is between 0.5 and 1, optimal trajectories of the economy are such that income per person is precisely in the vicinity of this inflection point.

Furthermore, denoting $m \equiv M/V$ and $u \equiv U/V$, it can be shown numerically that when $\sigma > 0.4$ the positive slope of the curve $m(\sigma, \bar{u})$

---

[9] This observation led La Grandville (1989) to conjecture that the miracle growth in Japan and East Asia may be due to a higher elasticity of substitution in these countries. The conjecture was successfully tested by Yuhn (1991) in the case of South Korea.

[10] The original proof, due to Hardy, Littlewood, and Pólya (1952; Theorem 16, pp. 26–27) makes use of Hölder's inequality and is admittedly difficult. An easier, analytical proof relying on the convexity of $x\ln(x)$ can be found in La Grandville and Solow (2009, pp. 111–113).

in (m, σ) space, $\partial m(\sigma, u)/\partial \sigma$, becomes very sensitive to a change in u – in other words, $\partial^2 m(\sigma, u)/(\partial\sigma\partial u)$ becomes highly significant.

These are the two forces that combine to make σ an efficiency parameter that can compete with or even surpass g_L, as we will show. To that effect we will now compare the sensitivity of W^* – determined numerically – to a change in any of the three efficiency paremeters, σ, g_L, and g_K (Table 4).

It first appears that a change in g_K will have a much smaller impact on W^* than the same change in σ or in g_L. Also, the elasticity $\varepsilon(W^*, g_L)$ is

Table 4. Elasticities of the optimal value $W^* = \int_0^\infty C_t^* e^{-it} dt$ with respect to σ, g_L and g_K; $\delta = 1/3$; $n = 0.01$; $g_L = 0.02$; $g_K = 0.007$

σ	0.5	0.6	0.7	0.8	0.9	1.0
i						
			4a: $\partial\log W^*/\partial\log\sigma \equiv \varepsilon(W^*, \sigma)$			
0.04	0.42	0.63	0.94	1.43	2.28	4.16
0.05	0.36	0.53	0.76	1.09	1.59	2.38
0.06	0.33	0.48	0.67	0.94	1.32	1.89
			4b: $\partial\log W^*/\partial\log g_L \equiv \varepsilon(W^*, g_L)$			
0.04	2.03	2.06	2.10	2.18	2.34	2.75
0.05	0.98	0.98	0.98	0.99	1.00	1.04
0.06	0.64	0.63	0.63	0.62	0.62	0.62
			4c: $\partial\log W^*/\partial\log g_K \equiv \varepsilon(W^*, g_K)$			
0.04	0.05	0.07	0.10	0.15	0.24	0.48
0.05	0.04	0.05	0.07	0.09	0.12	0.18
0.06	0.03	0.04	0.05	0.06	0.08	0.11

Table 5. Ratio of elasticites $\varepsilon(W^*, \sigma)/\varepsilon(W^*, g_L)$ and $\varepsilon(W^*, \sigma)/\varepsilon(W^*, g_K)$ ($\delta = 1/3$; $n = 0.01$; $g_L = 0.02$; $g_K = 0.007$)

σ	0.5	0.6	0.7	0.8	0.9	1.0
i						
			5a: $\varepsilon(W^*, \sigma)/\varepsilon(W^*, g_L)$			
0.04	0.2	0.3	0.5	0.7	1.0	1.5
0.05	0.4	0.5	0.8	1.1	1.6	2.3
0.06	0.5	0.8	1.1	1.5	2.1	3.1
			5b: $\varepsilon(W^*, \sigma)/\varepsilon(W^*, g_K)$			
0.04	8.8	9.3	9.6	9.6	9.3	8.7
0.05	10.3	11.4	12.2	12.8	13.2	13.1
0.06	11.7	13.2	14.6	15.8	16.8	17.5

larger than $\varepsilon(W^*, \sigma)$ for small values of i and σ, the contrary being true in the opposite case. Table 5 gives the ratios of elasticities $\varepsilon(W^*, \sigma)/\varepsilon(W^*, g_L)$ and $\varepsilon(W^*, \sigma)/\varepsilon(W^*, g_K)$.

One might think that the weak role played by the rate g_K is due to its initial, relatively low value compared to that of g_L (0.07% against 2%). For that very reason we tested an entirely different production process, where g_K ($= 0.008$) is now slightly above g_L (0.007).

As could be expected, the W^* values (Table 6) are significantly lower than in the first scenario. What is surprising, on the contrary, is how the elasticity of W^* with respect to σ has remained practically the same as initially; note also how weak both elasticities of W^* with respect to g_L and g_K have become, and how σ now dominates both parameters (Tables 7 and 8).

Table 6. Optimal value $W^* \int_0^\infty C_t^* e^{-it} dt$ as a function of i and σ $(\delta = 1/3; n = 0.01; g_L = 0.007; g_K = 0.008)$

σ	0.5	0.6	0.7	0.8	0.9	1.0
i						
0.04	56.9	62.4	70.0	80.9	97.5	125.4
0.05	39.0	42.4	47.0	53.3	62.4	76.6
0.06	29.5	31.8	34.9	39.1	44.9	53.4

Table 7. Elasticities of the optimal value $W^* = \int_0^\infty C_t^* e^{-it} dt$ with respect to σ, g_L, and g_K $(\delta = 1/3; n(0) = 0.01; g_L = 0.007; g_K = 0.008)$

σ	0.5	0.6	0.7	0.8	0.9	1.0
i						
	7a: $\partial \log W^* / \partial \log \sigma \equiv \varepsilon(W^*, \sigma)$					
0.04	0.42	0.62	0.90	1.31	1.93	2.94
0.05	0.38	0.56	0.79	1.13	1.61	2.33
0.06	0.35	0.51	0.71	0.99	1.39	1.95
	7b: $\partial \log W^* / \partial \log_L \equiv \varepsilon(W^*, g_L)$					
0.04	0.29	0.29	0.29	0.29	0.29	0.30
0.05	0.20	0.20	0.20	0.19	0.19	0.19
0.06	0.15	0.15	0.14	0.14	0.14	0.14
	7c: $\partial \log W^* / \partial \log g_K \equiv \varepsilon(W^*, g_K)$					
0.04	0.03	0.04	0.06	0.08	0.11	0.17
0.05	0.03	0.03	0.04	0.06	0.08	0.11
0.06	0.02	0.03	0.04	0.05	0.06	0.08

Table 8. *Ratio of elasticites $\varepsilon(W^*, \sigma)/\varepsilon(W^*, g_L)$*
and $\varepsilon(W^*, \sigma)/\varepsilon(W^*, g_K)$; $g_L = 0.007$; $g_K = 0.008$

σ	0.5	0.6	0.7	0.8	0.9	1.0
i						
			8a: $\varepsilon(W^*,\sigma)/\varepsilon(W^*,g_L)$			
0.04	1.4	2.1	3.1	4.5	6.7	9.9
0.05	1.9	2.8	4.1	5.9	8.5	12.5
0.06	2.4	3.4	4.9	7.0	10.0	14.4
			8b: $\varepsilon(W^*,\sigma)/\varepsilon(W^*,g_K)$			
0.04	13.7	15.1	16.2	17.0	17.5	17.5
0.05	14.8	16.6	18.3	19.8	21.0	21.2
0.06	15.4	17.7	19.8	21.8	23.7	25.1

2.2. Case $\sigma > 1$, $p > 0$

What we surmised before regarding the entirely different behavior of the economy in the case $\sigma > 1$ (as opposed to $\sigma < 1$) can now be confirmed: not only K_t^* but y_t^* as well tend to infinity in *finite* time (when t approaches $\bar{t}$). There is an additional reason for which we think that this case is not sustainable in the long run: the capital share $\pi(t)$ would also tend to 1 in *finite* time. This can be seen as follows: if $\lim_{t\to\bar{t}} K_t^* = \infty$, $\lim_{t\to\bar{t}} L_t G_L(t)/(G_K(t)K_t^*) = 0$ since $L_{\bar{t}} G_L(\bar{t})/(G_K(\bar{t}))$ is finite. Therefore, from the properties of M_p, $\lim_{t\to\bar{t}} \pi(t) = \lim_{t\to\bar{t}} (\partial \ln M_p/\partial \ln K) = \lim_{t\to\bar{t}} (\partial \ln M_p/\partial \ln U) = \lim_{t\to\bar{t}} [1 + ((1-\delta)/\delta)(V_t/U_t)^p]^{-1} = 1$.

It is a good place to note that empirical measurements of σ in the past 50 years have in their vast majority yielded results in the range between 0.5 and 1 – very rarely above one – and that in the latter case estimates of σ were in the close vicinity of 1. At the time scale of an optimal growth model, if σ happens to be fluctuating above 1, it is not likely to do so during a long period.

3. Qualifications and extensions

Let us underline what the optimal savings formula (21) can and cannot do. It applies, first and foremost, to an economy that has been and is supposed to stay in competitive equilibrium. It does not pertain to a nation or a society that has been hit by a major catastrophy, natural or man-made. It is fair however to say that distressed times are no occasion to set policies suited for the long-term equilibrium of the economy. On the contrary, once reconstruction is on its way and a degree of confidence in the future production process is acquired, there is no reason why an optimal savings rate could not constitute a useful benchmark to aim for.

We should now examine what the optimal savings rate would be if, as was implicit in (21), the *growth rates* of $L(t)$, $G_K(t)$, and $G_L(t)$ were functions of time. One immediate, obvious candidate is the population growth rate, $n(t)$: indeed, since it is impossible that $n(t)$ could remain constant, an S-shaped curve for $L(t)$ is definitely called for. From the 19th century onward, many extensions of the logistic (Verhulst, 1845) and Gompertz (1825) curves have been proposed. We suggest here the following simple one, which will prove handy for our purposes. Let v designate the (negative) growth rate of $n(t)$; $v \equiv \dot{n}(t)/n(t)$ ($v < 0$). Suppose that the rate v is constant; if $n(0) = n_0$, $n(t) = n_0 e^{vt}$. It follows that $L(t)$ is now governed by $\dot{L}/L = n_0 e^{vt}$, whose solution is

$$L(L_0, n_0, t, v) = L_0 \exp[n_0(e^{vt} - 1)/v], \tag{28}$$

an S-shaped curve with an upper asymptote given by $L_\infty = L_0 e^{-n_0/v}$. Let k denote the ratio between this asymptote and L_0; $k \equiv L_\infty/L_0 = e^{-n_0/v}$. If we choose k, the corresponding growth rate of $n(t)$ is $v(k, n_0) = -n_0/\ln k$, $n_0 = -n_0/\ln k$, and $L(t)$ can equivalently be written as a function of k:

$$L(L_0, n_0, t, k) = L_0 k^{[1 - \exp(-n_0 t/\ln k)]}. \tag{27}$$

The inflection point of the curve $L(t)$ is given by $\hat{t} = (1/v)\ln(-v/n_0) = (1/n_0)\ln k \ln(\ln k)$. For such an inflection point to exist, it is necessary and sufficient that $v > -n_0$, or equivalently $k > e$.

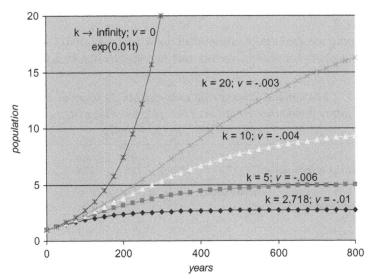

Fig. 6. *Exponential and S-shaped future population evolutions.*
$L_t = \exp[n_0(e^{vt} - 1)/v] = L_0 k^{[1 - \exp(-n_0 t/\ln k)]}$; $n_0 = 0.01$.

Supposing that the *initial* growth rate of our function $L(t)$ is equal to the mean value we used before ($n(0) = 0.01$), we have chosen four population scenarios by retaining for k: 20, 10, 5 and $e = 2.718...$, the corresponding values for v (in %, rounded) are -0.3, -0.43, -0.64 and -1. The time paths of L are depicted in Figure 6. For comparison, the exponential $e^{0.01t}$ has also been drawn (it would correspond to $k \to \infty$ and $v = 0$). Using (21) we have then tested the values of the optimal savings rate at horizon 30; results are in Table 9.

Note how fundamentally different population time paths will still lead to the same orders of magnitude for the optimal savings rates. Contrast for instance the exponential and the *S*-shaped population curve with a very low asymptote ($k = e$; $v = -0.01$); in the latter scenario one supposes that the maximum population would not exceed e times the present level – a voluntarily extreme hypothesis. Even in that case the optimal savings rate at horizon 30 years would diminish very little (for instance, if $\sigma = 0.7$, s_{30}^* would decrease from 12.0% to 10.9% only).

Consider now alternate evolutions of factor-enhancing functions $G_K(t)$ and $G_L(t)$ in the form of inverted *S*-curves; to simplify notation, let $G(t)$ and $g(t)$ designate the generic function and its growth rate, respectively. Suppose that $g(t)$ converges asymptotically toward a minimum value $\bar{g}$ ($0 < \bar{g} < g_0$), the difference between $g(t)$ and $\bar{g}$ decreasing exponentially at constant rate γ. Thus $g(t) = (g_0 - \bar{g})e^{\gamma t} + \bar{g}$. $G(t)$ now obeys $d \ln G(t)/dt = (g_0 - \bar{g})e^{\gamma t} + \bar{g}$, whose solution is

$$G(t) = G_0 \exp\{(g_0 - \bar{g})[(e^{\gamma t} - 1)/\gamma] + \bar{g}t\}. \tag{28}$$

Keeping the above population scenario ($k = e$; $v = -0.01$), we made the followings tests for tests of the optimal savings rate s_{30}^*. In a first step, we

Table 9. The optimal savings rate today and in 30 years as a function of future population evolutions ($\delta = 1/3$; $i = 4\%$; $n(0) = 0.01$; $g_K(0) = 0.007$; $g_L(0) = 0.02$)

σ	0.5	0.6	0.7	0.8	0.9	1.0
Initial optimal savings rate s_0^*	7.8	10.0	12.8	16.4	21.3	27.9
Optimal savings rate in 30 years, s_{30}^*						
Population evolution						
Exponential						
$k = \infty$; $v = 0$	7.0	9.1	12.0	15.7	20.8	27.9
S-shaped curves						
$k = 20$; $v = -.33$	6.7	8.8	11.6	15.2	20.2	27.1
$k = 10$; $v = -.43$	6.7	8.7	11.5	15.1	20.0	26.9
$k = 5$; $v = -.64$	6.6	8.6	11.3	14.8	19.7	26.5
$k = e$; $v = -.01$	6.3	8.3	10.9	14.4	19.1	25.8

Table 10. *The optimal savings rate today and in 30 years as a function of future population and technology evolutions ($\delta = 1/3$; $i = 4\%$; $n(0) = 0.01$; $g_K(0) = 0.007$; $g_L(0) = 0.02$)*

σ	0.5	0.6	0.7	0.8	0.9	1.0
Initial optimal savings rate s_0^*	7.8	10.0	12.8	16.4	21.3	27.9
Population and technology evolutions	Optimal savings rate in 30 years, s_{30}^*					
$L(t)$, $G_K(t)$, and $G_L(t)$ exponential	7.0	9.1	12.0	15.7	20.8	27.9
$L(t)$ S-shaped; $v = -.01$ $G_K(t)$, and $G_L(t)$ exponential	6.3	8.3	10.9	14.4	19.1	25.8
$L(t)$ and $G_K(t)$ S-shaped; $v = \gamma_K = -.01$; $\bar{g}_K = .003$; $-.01$; $\bar{g}_K = .003$; $G_L(t)$ exponential	6.5	8.4	11.0	14.4	19.0	25.3
$L(t)$, $G_K(t)$ and $G_L(t)$ S-shaped; $v = \gamma_K = \gamma_L = -.01$; $\bar{g}_K = .003$; $\bar{g}_L = .013$	6.0	7.8	10.3	13.5	17.8	23.8

set $g_K(0) = 0.007$, $\bar{g}_K = 0.003$ and $\gamma_K = -0.01$; g_L was kept at the constant level 0.02. Then we assumed that g_L would decrease as well, with $g_L(0) = 0.02$, $\bar{g}_L = 0.013$ and $\gamma_L = -0.01$. The results are in Table 10. In each case s_{30}^* remained very close to the values indicated in Table 9, and thus proved very robust to quite different evolutions of population and technology.

4. Conclusion

The first, inescapable conclusion is that we definitely save too little compared to what should be the case in a competitive economy if we were concerned about the welfare of future generations. Indeed, for the entire acceptable range of parameters or functions i, δ, n, g_L, g_K, our present savings rate should be between 8% and 16% for an elasticity of substitution σ between 0.5 and 0.8 (and it should be still higher for larger σ). Even if we allow for a very wide array of curves to describe the future evolution of population and technology advances, the rates in 30 years remain in the range of 6–16%. Those numbers are significantly above the current rates. Our conclusion is reinforced by the very fact that the *net* savings (net of any depreciation) presented here *do not* include provisions for the repair of any man-made harm to the capital bequeathed by nature.

A second conclusion is the relative importance of labor-enhancing technical progress and of the elasticity of substitution in our future welfare, compared to capital-augmenting technical progress. Also, from a policy point of view, it seems important to be able to measure not only the rewards but the costs of increasing g_L, g_K, or σ.

This brings us to a central hypothesis of our model, as well as to a conjecture. We have supposed that competitive equilibrium applied at all times, and have shown how it led to a double, intertemporal optimum for society. Now there might be a link between those cimcumstances and the determination of g_L, g_K and σ at any point of our history. We may then ask what could be the role – if any – of competitive equilibrium in the determination not only of the long-term factors $G_L(t)$ and $G_K(t)$, but also of $\sigma(t)$, which reflects one of our constant aims throughout the ages, that of resorting to capital to alleviate labor.

Acknowledgments

This essay was written in honor of Giancarlo Gandolfo, and will appear in *Studies in NonLinear Dynamics and Econometrics*. I thank Berkeley Electronic Press for their permission to reproduce it in this volume. I am also deeply grateful to Kenneth Arrow, Giuseppe De Archangelis, Robert Feicht, Jean-Marie Grether, Erich Gundlach, Bjarne Jensen, Rainer Klump, Ulrich Kohli, Peter McAdam, Bernardo Maggi, Martin Paldam, Enrico Saltari, Robert Solow, Wolfgang Stummer, Juerg Weber, Alpo Willman, and Milad Zarin-Nejadan, as well as to participants in seminars at Frankfurt, Nürnberg, Rome (La Sapienza), and Stanford for their highly helpful remarks. My heartfelt thanks also go to my colleague Ernst Hairer who checked the accuracy of the numerical calculation of the definite integral (27), using an advanced, Gaussian-type method he had developed earlier, with 15-decimal precision.

References

Dorfman, R. (1969). An economic interpretation of optimal control theory. *American Economic Review, 59*(5), 817–831.
Gompertz, B. (1825). On the nature of the function expressive of the law of human mortality, and on a new mode of determining the value of life contingencies. *Philosophical Transactions of the Royal Society of London, 115*, 513–585.
Goodwin, R. M. (1961). The optimal growth path for an underdeveloped economy. *The Economic Journal, 71*(284), 756–774.
Hardy, G. H., Littlewood, J. E., & Pólya, G. (1952). *Inequalities*. Cambridge: Cambridge University Press.
Johnston, L. D., Williamson, S. H. (2009, October). *The annual real and nominal GDP for the United States, 1790 – Present*. Economic History Services. Retrieved from www.eh.net/hmit/gdp/
Klump, R., & La Grandville, O. de (2000). Economic growth and the elasticity of substitution: Two theorems and some suggestions. *The American Economic Review, 90*(1), 282–291.

Klump, R., McAdam, P., & Willman, A. (2007). Factor substitution and factor augmenting technical progress in the US. *The Review of Economics and Statistics, 89*(1), 183–192.

La Grandville, O. de (1989). In quest of the Slutsky diamond. *The American Economic Review, 79*(3), 468–481.

La Grandville, O. de (2009). *Economic growth – A unified approach, with two special contributions by Robert M. Solow.* Cambridge: Cambridge University Press.

La Grandville, O. de, & Solow, R. M. (2006). A conjecture on general means. *Journal of Inequalities in Pure and Applied Mathematics, 7*(1), Article 3.

Ramsey, F. (1928). A mathematical theory of saving. *The Economic Journal, 38*(152), 543–559.

Sato, R. (2006). *Biased technical change and economic conservation laws.* New York, NY: Springer.

Thanh, N. P., & Minh, M. N. (2008). Proof of a conjecture on general means. *Journal of Inequalities in Pure and Applied Mathematics, 9*(3), Article 86.

Verhulst, P-F. (1845). Recherches mathématiques sur la loi d'accroissement de la population. *Nouveaux Mémoires de l'Académie Royale des Sciences et Belles-Lettres de Bruxelles.*

Yuhn, K. H. (1991). Economic growth, technical change biases, and the elasticity of substitution: A test of the de La Grandville hypothesis. *The Review of Economics and Statistics, LXIII*(2), 340–346.

CHAPTER 15

Aggregation, the Skill Premium, and the Two-Level Production Function

Miguel A. León-Ledesma[a], Peter McAdam[b] and Alpo Willman[c]

[a]School of Economics, University of Kent, Kent CT2 7NP, UK
E-mail address: m.a.leon-ledesma@kent.ac.uk
[b]Research Department, European Central Bank, Kaiserstr. 29, D-60311 Frankfurt am Main,
Germany; Department of Economics, University of Surrey, Guildford, UK
E-mail address: peter.mcadam@ecb.europa.eu
[c]Research Department, European Central Bank, Kaiserstr. 29, D-60311 Frankfurt am Main,
Germany
E-mail address: alpo.willman@ecb.europa.eu

Abstract
We examine the two-level nested constant elasticity of substitution production function where both capital and labor are disaggregated in two classes. We propose a normalized system estimation method to retrieve estimates of the inter- and intra-class elasticities of substitution and factor-augmenting technical progress coefficients. The system is estimated for US data for the 1963–2006 period. Our findings reveal that skilled and unskilled labor classes are gross substitutes, capital structures and equipment are gross complements, and aggregate capital and aggregate labor are gross complements with an elasticity of substitution close to 0.5. We discuss the implications of our findings and methodology for the analysis of the causes of the increase in the skill premium and, by implication, inequality in a growing economy.

Keywords: Two-level CES production function, factor-augmenting technical progress, factor substitution, aggregation, skill premium

JEL classifications: E25, J23, J24, O40

1. Introduction

The workhorse production function in almost all theoretical and empirical models in growth theory and, more generally, in microeconomics and macroeconomics has been the single-level production function – whether constant elasticity of substitution (CES) or Cobb–Douglas – starting from

Frontiers of Economics and Globalization
Volume 11   ISSN: 1574-8715
DOI: 10.1108/S1574-8715(2011)0000011020

Solow (1956, 1957) and Arrow, Chenery, Minhas, and Solow (1961). The single-level production function relates aggregate output to, commonly, two aggregate inputs: labor and capital (or land). That is to say, input types are aggregated into a single index.

One particular problem with this approach is that it obscures the interactions between and within different factor categories. Heterogeneity and aggregation problems have been a concern in economic theory for long. But implementation within a context amenable to empirical analysis implies that, in practical terms, researchers can only use a limited number of heterogeneous components in factor inputs. For example, there are high- and low-skill types of labor and different strata of capital such as equipments, software, and buildings and infrastructure. All of these within-factor categories may be expected to contain highly specific characteristics with important consequences for economic outcomes. They may display different depreciation rates, different rates of productivity growth, different cyclical co-movements, different cross elasticities of substitution, and so on. By aggregating them, we may thus miss these important aspects. One such aspect of interest is the effect of capital accumulation and technical progress on income distribution. Much of the recent changes in income distribution in the world can be associated with changes in the return to different labor input skills leading to wage inequality.

An important, and in practice implementable, departure from the aggregative framework was made in the seminal contributions of Kazuo Sato and Zvi Griliches. Sato (1967) generalized the CES production function by nesting the CES at two levels and augmenting the list of possible inputs. Abstracting from technical progress (although this will become important later), this typical two-level CES production function can be written as,

$$Y = [\beta\{\alpha_1 X_1^{\chi_1} + (1 - \alpha_1)X_1^{\chi_1}\}^{\chi/\chi_1} + (1 - \beta)\{\alpha_2 Z_1^{\chi_2} + (1 - \alpha_2)Z_2^{\chi_2}\}^{\chi/\chi_2}]^{1/\beta}$$

(1)

where X_i and Z_i, are different aggregate factor inputs (i.e., labor and capital), and $i = 1, 2$ are different factor categories. Defining $\gamma = 1/\chi$, this can be written more compactly as follows:

$$Y = [\beta CES_1^{1/\gamma} + (1 - \beta)CES_2^{1/\gamma}]^\gamma$$

(2)

This nested two-level CES specification allows for different substitution possibilities between factors of production and categories within them. Thus, for instance, CES_1 may be Leontief, while CES_2 may be of the Cobb–Douglas type. The impact of factor accumulation and technical progress will crucially depend on the relative values of the elasticities of substitution determined by χ, χ_1, and χ_2.

A popular focus for work on the two-level CES function is on explanations of the increase in the skill premium observed in western economies during the last three decades as reported in Acemoglu (2002b).[1] Such phenomena clearly has implications for inequality, long-run growth, and labor-market policies (e.g., Piva, Santarelli, & Vivarelli, 2005).

One approach, initiated by Griliches (1969), showed that – for US manufacturing – capital and skilled labor were more complementary than capital and unskilled labor. This spawned a considerable literature examining the so-called capital-skill complementarity hypothesis, for example, Greenwood, Hercowitz, and Krussel (1997), Krussel, Ohanian, Rios-Rull, and Violante (2000), and Duffy, Papageorgiou, and Perez-Sebastian (2004). The hypothesis gained particular currency given the sharp decline in the constant-quality relative price of equipment, for example, Gordon (1990), particularly for information and communication technologies. This decline naturally lead to an uptake in usage of such capital. Given complementarity between capital and skilled labor, the faster usage of such capital increased the relative demand for skilled labor and – despite the apparent increase in the supply of such labor – the skill or wage premium relative to unskilled labor increased in a dramatic and persistent manner (see Acemoglu, 2009, for a textbook discussion). On the other hand, authors such as Katz and Murphy (1992), Acemoglu (2002b), and Autor, Katz, and Kearney (2008) claimed that the skill premium can be attributed to technical change that was biased in favor of skilled workers. Given that skilled and unskilled workers are gross substitutes, an increase in skilled labor efficiency led to an increase in the relative wages (and factor shares) of skilled workers. Both approaches rely on particular nestings and estimated values for the elasticities of substitution between different categories of factors of production and their associated factor-biased technical progress parameters.

In this chapter, we make three contributions to the empirical literature on two-level CES production functions. First, we reexamine the Sato exercises using disaggregation in *both* capital and labor factors, rather than just in capital. Second, we estimate several specifications of the two-level CES function within a "normalized" system approach following Klump, McAdam, and Willman (2007) and León-Ledesma, McAdam, and Willman (2010a). This has several advantages over previous approaches to recover deep supply-side parameters as it estimates jointly the production function and first order conditions accounting for cross-equation restrictions. Finally, our specification pays particular attention to the role of factor-augmenting technical progress, also allowing us to be informative about the role of technical change in driving factor prices. We illustrate our results paying special attention to the evolution of the US skill premium.

The chapter is organized as follows. In Section 2, we describe the two-level production function form and the first-order conditions that constitute

---

[1] In our data section, we graph some of these trends.

the "normalized" supply system. In Section 3, we discuss the underlying US macro data, its properties, and transformations. In Section 4, we show empirical estimates of a variety of production-technology system estimates based on pairwise factor combinations. Finally, we conclude.

2. The normalized two-step four-factor CES production function

Assume that production Y is defined by the two-level CES production function with four separate inputs V_i $(i = 1, \ldots, 4)$ with factor-augmenting technical progress The inner part of the production function (in the normalized form) and the corresponding income identity are therefore defined as follows:[2]

$$X_{1,t} = \left[(1 - \beta) \left(e^{\gamma_1 \tilde{t}} \frac{V_{1,t}}{V_{1,0}} \right)^{(\eta-1)/\eta} + \beta \left(e^{\gamma_2 \tilde{t}} \frac{V_{2,t}}{V_{2,0}} \right)^{(\eta-1)/\eta} \right]^{\eta/(\eta-1)} \tag{3}$$

$$X_{2,t} = \left[(1 - \pi) \left(e^{\gamma_3 \tilde{t}} \frac{V_{3,t}}{V_{3,0}} \right)^{(\zeta-1)/\zeta} + \pi \left(e^{\gamma_3 \tilde{t}} \frac{V_{4,t}}{V_{4,0}} \right)^{(\zeta-1)/\zeta} \right]^{\zeta/(\zeta-1)} \tag{4}$$

where $\tilde{t} = (t - t_0)$, η is the elasticity of substitution between V_1 and V_2, and ζ is the elasticity of substitution between V_3 and V_4. The term $e^{\gamma_i \tilde{t}}$ denotes linear technical progress that increases the efficiency of factor i with constant growth rate γ_i (factor-augmenting technical progress). Subscripts zero indicate values at the point of normalization. It is straightforward to see that (3) and (4) imply that $X_{1,0} = X_{2,0} = 1$.

Denoting factor prices by w_i, the normalization implies that the distribution parameters β and π in (3) and (4) are defined by factor incomes at the normalization point as follows:

$$\beta = \frac{w_{2,0} \cdot V_{2,0}}{w_{1,0} \cdot V_{1,0} + w_{2,0} \cdot V_{3,0}} \tag{5}$$

$$\pi = \frac{w_{4,0} \cdot V_{4,0}}{w_{3,0} \cdot V_{3,0} + w_{4,0} \cdot V_{4,0}} \tag{6}$$

Now, the two step-CES function for production Y is as follows:

$$Y_t = Y_0 \left[\alpha X_{1,t}^{(\sigma-1)/\sigma} + (1 - \alpha) X_{2,t}^{(\sigma-1)/\sigma} \right]^{\sigma/(\sigma-1)}$$

---

[2] Normalization essentially implies representing the production and technology side of the model (i.e., production function and factor demands) in consistent indexed number form. Although a necessary expression of the CES function, it turns out also to be useful for econometric identification and for comparative static exercises. Appendix provides a refresher.

$$Y_t = Y_0 \left[\alpha X_{1,t}^{(\sigma-1)/\sigma} + (1-\alpha) X_{2,t}^{(\sigma-1)/\sigma} \right]^{\sigma/(\sigma-1)}$$

$$= Y_0 \left\{ \alpha \left[(1-\beta)\left(e^{\gamma_1 \tilde{t}} \frac{V_{1,t}}{V_{1,0}} \right)^{(\eta-1)/\eta} + \beta \left(e^{\gamma_2 \tilde{t}} \frac{V_{2,t}}{V_{2,0}} \right)^{(\eta-1)/\eta} \right]^{(\eta/(\eta-1))((\sigma-1)/\sigma)} \right.$$

$$+ (1-\alpha) \left[(1-\pi)\left(e^{\gamma_3 \tilde{t}} \frac{V_{3,t}}{V_{3,0}} \right)^{(\zeta-1)/\zeta} \right.$$

$$\left. \left. + \pi \left(e^{\gamma_4 \tilde{t}} \frac{V_{4,t}}{V_{4,0}} \right)^{(\zeta-1)/\zeta} \right]^{(\zeta/(\zeta-1))((\sigma-1)/\sigma)} \right\}^{\sigma/(\sigma-1)} \tag{7}$$

where σ is the elasticity of substitution between compound inputs X_1 and X_2, and the distribution parameter α is defined by factor incomes of the normalization point as follows:

$$\alpha = \frac{w_{1,0} \cdot V_{1,0} + w_{2,0} \cdot V_{2,0}}{w_{1,0} \cdot V_{1,0} + w_{2,0} \cdot V_{2,0} + w_{3,0} \cdot V_{3,0} + w_{4,0} \cdot V_{4,0}} \tag{8}$$

Assume a firm faces the demand function $Y_{it} = (P_{it}/P_t)^{-\varepsilon} Y_t$. Profit maximization results in four first-order conditions that, together with the (log) production function, results in the following five-equation normalized supply-side system:

$$\log w_{1,t} = \log\left[\frac{\alpha(1-\beta)}{(1+\mu)} \frac{Y_0}{V_{1,0}} \right] + \frac{(\eta-1)\gamma_1}{\eta}\tilde{t} + \frac{1}{\sigma}\log\left(\frac{Y_t}{Y_0}\right) - \frac{1}{\eta}\log\left(\frac{V_{1,t}}{V_{1,0}}\right)$$

$$+ \frac{\sigma-\eta}{\sigma(\eta-1)}\log\left[(1-\beta)\left(e^{\gamma_1 \tilde{t}} \frac{V_{1,t}}{V_{1,0}} \right)^{(\eta-1)/\eta} + \beta\left(e^{\gamma_2 \tilde{t}} \frac{V_{2,t}}{V_{2,0}} \right)^{(\eta-1)/\eta} \right] \tag{9}$$

$$\log w_{2,t} = \log\left[\frac{\alpha\beta}{(1+\mu)} \frac{Y_0}{V_{2,0}} \right] + \frac{(\eta-1)\gamma_2}{\eta}\tilde{t} + \frac{1}{\sigma}\log\left(\frac{Y_t}{Y_0}\right) - \frac{1}{\eta}\log\left(\frac{V_{2,t}}{V_{2,0}}\right)$$

$$+ \frac{\sigma-\eta}{\sigma(\eta-1)}\log\left[(1-\beta)\left(e^{\gamma_1 \tilde{t}} \frac{V_{1,t}}{V_{1,0}} \right)^{(\eta-1)/\eta} + \beta\left(e^{\gamma_2 \tilde{t}} \frac{V_{2,t}}{V_{2,0}} \right)^{(\eta-1)/\eta} \right] \tag{10}$$

$$\log w_{3,t} = \log\left[\frac{(1-\alpha)(1-\pi)}{(1+\mu)} \frac{Y_0}{V_{3,0}} \right] + \frac{(\zeta-1)\gamma_3}{\zeta}\tilde{t} + \frac{1}{\sigma}\log\left(\frac{Y_t}{Y_0}\right) - \frac{1}{\zeta}\log\left(\frac{V_{3,t}}{V_{3,0}}\right)$$

$$+ \frac{\sigma-\zeta}{\sigma(\zeta-1)}\log\left[(1-\pi)\left(e^{\gamma_3 \tilde{t}} \frac{V_{3,t}}{V_{3,0}} \right)^{(\zeta-1)/\zeta} + \pi\left(e^{\gamma_4 \tilde{t}} \frac{V_{4,t}}{V_{4,0}} \right)^{(\zeta-1)/\zeta} \right] \tag{11}$$

$$\log w_{4,t} = \log\left[\frac{(1-\alpha)\pi}{(1+\mu)} \frac{Y_0}{V_{4,0}} \right] + \frac{(\zeta-1)\gamma_4}{\zeta}\tilde{t} + \frac{1}{\sigma}\log\left(\frac{Y_t}{Y_0}\right) - \frac{1}{\zeta}\log\left(\frac{V_{4,t}}{V_{4,0}}\right)$$

$$+ \frac{\sigma-\zeta}{\sigma(\zeta-1)}\log\left[(1-\pi)\left(e^{\gamma_3 \tilde{t}} \frac{V_{3,t}}{V_{3,0}} \right)^{(\zeta-1)/\zeta} + \pi\left(e^{\gamma_4 \tilde{t}} \frac{V_{4,t}}{V_{4,0}} \right)^{(\zeta-1)/\zeta} \right] \tag{12}$$

$$\log\left(\frac{Y_t}{Y_0}\right) = \frac{\sigma}{\sigma-1}\log\left\{\alpha\left[(1-\beta)\left(e^{\gamma_1 \tilde{t}}\frac{V_{1,t}}{V_{1,0}}\right)^{(\eta-1)/\eta}\right.\right.$$

$$\left.+\beta\left(e^{\gamma_2 \tilde{t}}\frac{V_{2,t}}{V_{2,0}}\right)^{(\eta-1)/\eta}\right]^{(\eta/(\eta-1))((\sigma-1)/\sigma)}$$

$$+(1-\alpha)\left[(1-\pi)\left(e^{\gamma_3 \tilde{t}}\frac{V_{3,t}}{V_{3,0}}\right)^{(\zeta-1)/\zeta}\right.$$

$$\left.\left.+\pi\left(e^{\gamma_4 \tilde{t}}\frac{V_{4,t}}{V_{4,0}}\right)^{(\zeta-1)/\zeta}\right]^{(\zeta/(\zeta-1))((\sigma-1)/\sigma)}\right\} \tag{13}$$

where $1+\mu = \varepsilon/(\varepsilon-1)$ represents the equilibrium markup, and the income identity of the firm can be written as follows:

$$Y_t = (1+\mu)(w_{1,t} \cdot V_{1,t} + w_{2,t} \cdot V_{2,t} + w_{3,t} \cdot V_{3,t} + w_{4,t}V_{4,t}) \tag{14}$$

Estimation of Equations (9)–(13) yield the parameters: σ, ζ, η, and the various γ's. Parameters α, π, and β are imposed reflecting their values in the data. This is because using the normalized form, these parameters can be directly interpreted as income shares at the point of normalization. This is an added advantage of normalization, as it reduces the parameter space to estimate.

In the next sections, we estimate the system for the US economy distinguishing between skilled and unskilled workers on the one hand and structures and equipment capital on the other hand. We use a nesting such that both categories of capital and labor appear always within the same nested CES, implying the same substitution elasticity across different kinds of capital and different kinds of labor. These are, of course, not the only possible ways of nesting the two-level CES function. Our aim here is to show how the estimated system can track output and factor prices (notably the skill premium). We leave for future research an in-depth investigation into different kinds of CES nestings that could have consequences for the theoretical models of the skill premium discussed in Section 1. Here, we focus mostly on the consequences of aggregating categories of labor and capital for production function estimation under different assumptions about technical progress.

3. Data

Annual data were obtained from various sources for the US economy for the 1963–2006 period. The annual frequency is determined by the availability of skilled/unskilled hours and wages. Data for output, capital, total employment, and labor compensation are for the US private nonresidential sector. Most of the data come from NIPA series available from the Bureau of Economic Analysis. The output series are thus calculated as total output minus net indirect tax revenues, public sector, and residential output. After these adjustments, the output concept used is compatible with that of the capital stock series used, which is the quantity index of net stock of nonresidential private capital from NIPA tables. We also pay special attention to the construction of the hours and wage series by skill level, and the user cost of capital.

Data by skill levels were obtained from Autor et al. (2008).[3] Skilled workers are defined as those with (some) college education and above. Unskilled workers are defined as those with education levels up to (and including) high school. Autor et al. (2008) provide relative supply and relative wages (the skill premium) for both categories. Relative supply is defined in terms of hours worked.[4] Because the coverage of these data coming from the Current Population Survey is different from our coverage for the nonresidential private sector, we combined these data with Bureau of Labor Statistics (BLS) data. While preserving relative wages and relative labor supply, we correct both so as to be compatible with the evolution of total private employment and labor compensation. Hence, we proceed as follows. We define unskilled workers' wages (WU) as follows:

$$\text{WU} = \frac{W}{\text{NU}/N + (\text{NS}/N) \times \tilde{W}}$$

where W are wages of all workers, NU number of unskilled workers, N is total private sector workers, NS is number of skilled workers, and, finally, $\tilde{W}$ is the skilled/unskilled wage ratio. Then, WS, skilled wages, is simply defined as $W \times \tilde{W}$. We now need to define how some of these variables are obtained. We define W as labor income (NINC) over total private sector employment. A problem in calculating labor income is that it is unclear how the income of proprietors (self-employed) should be categorized in the labor-capital dichotomy. Some of the income earned by self-employed workers clearly represents labor income, while some represents a return on investment or economic profit. Following Klump et al. (2007), we use compensation per employee as a shadow price of labor of self-employed workers:

$$\text{NINC} = \left(1 + \frac{\text{self-employed}}{\text{total private employment}}\right) \cdot \text{Comp}$$

where Comp = private sector compensation of employees.

We then define $W = (\text{NINC}/\text{total private sector employment})$. Finally, we define NS as total private sector employment times relative skilled/

---

[3] We thank David Autor for providing the files for annual data by skill levels.
[4] See Autor et al. (2008) for further detail on data construction. We chose to use relative supply in terms of hours rather than the "efficiency units" measure also provided by the authors.

unskilled hours worked, and NU = N–NS. These transformations preserve relative quantities but correct the levels to comply with our previous definitions and the self-employment transformation. This assumes, of course, that relative wages and relative labor supply in the private sector evolve in a similar fashion to those in the (wider) definition provided by Autor et al. (2008).

Our capital stock concept is private nonhousing capital disaggregated into structures and equipment capital. As NIPA presents these data as the end-of-year levels, in our estimation, we use the two-year averages of these end of year stocks. The user cost of aggregate capital K was obtained using a residual method.[5] To do so, we first need to make an assumption about the share of income belonging to a pure markup. The markup share can be estimated directly within the normalized system. However, because of the relatively short sample and demands imposed by the system with three factors, we imposed an average markup of 10%, $\mu = 0.1$. This is consistent with estimates of the system using two factors (capital and aggregate labor). Under this assumption, the real user cost of capital, r, is defined as follows:

$$r = \frac{Y/(1 + \mu) - \text{NINC}}{K}$$

Similarly, in calculating the user cost measures also for the two disaggregates of the total capital stock, that is, nonresidential structures and equipment capital, we first decomposed the total capital income $Y/(1+\mu)$–NINC into components associated to structures and equipment capital and then proportioned them to the stocks. These capital income shares were based on capital income estimates obtained by multiplying – for scaling purposes – current dollar capital stocks by the relevant real user cost term of each type of capital.

To calculate the real user cost term, the real interest component was defined as the difference of the sample averages of the 10-year government bond rate and inflation in terms of the net investment deflators. As inflation of structures investment was higher than equipment investment, depreciation rates in turn were calculated on the basis of current dollar values of depreciations and current dollar value capital stocks and were markedly higher for structures than for equipment capital.

Figure 1 plots some relevant ratios related to capital and labor inputs. The top panel of 1 shows that the equipment capital (KQ) to output (Y) ratio displays a positive trend and the structures capital (KB) to output ratio has a negative trend over the sample and, hence, as the middle panel shows, the size of equipment capital relative to the structures capital rises

---

[5] Direct measures such as those used in León-Ledesma, McAdam, and Willman (2010b) did not change the results substantially.

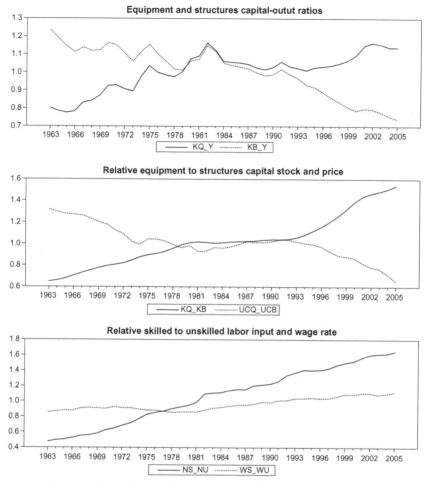

Fig. 1.   Some key ratios related to capital and labor inputs.

reflecting the downward trend in their relative user prices (UCQ and UCB). As these opposite trends largely compensate each other, their relative factor income shares remain relatively stable only marginally favoring equipment capital.

As regards skilled and unskilled labor inputs, corresponding trend developments look quite different. The bottom panel of Figure 1 shows that both relative input (NS/NU) and wage (WS/WU) developments favor skilled labor, that is, both of them have an upward trend implying an even steeper trend in the skilled labor income to unskilled labor income ratio. This provides indication against a unit substitution elasticity between these two labor inputs, since in the Cobb–Douglas case factor, shares are constant.

4. Estimation results

4.1. Overview

All the specifications were estimated using a nonlinear system estimator allowing for cross-equation parameter restrictions and correlated errors across equations as in the class of seemingly unrelated regression estimators (SURE). This estimator hence accounts for potential common shocks to the different factor markets and the production function. For estimation purposes, we used sample arithmetic averages for non-growing variables and geometric averages for growing variables as the point of normalization. Due to the nonlinearity of the CES function, the sample average of production need not exactly coincide with the level of production implied by the production function with sample averages of the right hand variables. Therefore, following Klump et al. (2007), we introduce an additional parameter ξ whose expected value is around unity (we call this the normalization constant).

Tables 1 to 4 show the estimation of Equations (9)–(13) and their restricted counterparts. In terms of those equations, our results set $w_1 = cb$ (i.e., cost of building capital), $w_2 = cq$ (i.e., cost of equipment capital), $w_3 = ws$ (i.e., wage of skilled labor), and $w_4 = wu$ (i.e., wage of unskilled labor), and $V_1 = KB$, $V_2 = KQ$, $V_3 = NS$, and $V_4 = NU$. The tables also display residual Augmented Dicky Fuller (ADF) tests for each of the equations in the system.

The conventional single-step production function where capital and labor are single indices are shown in Table 1. This yields what might be considered standard results: the overall elasticity of substitution at around 0.5. This is consistent with the 0.4–0.6 range that Chirinko (2008) finds in typical of US estimates. Technical progress is strongly net labor saving ($\gamma_N \gg \gamma_K$). Nevertheless, for the sample period considered, γ_K is still statistically significant at a rate of approximately 0.5% per year, which is not economically negligible.

Table 1. Single-level production technology system: $Y = F[K, N, \sigma]$

	Coefficient	Standard error
ξ	1.000	0.006
σ	0.512	0.002
γ^K	0.005	0.001
γ^N	0.017	0.001
Log determination	−26.914	
ADF_{FOC_K}	−3.422	
ADF_{FOC_N}	−2.435	
ADF_Y	−2.255	

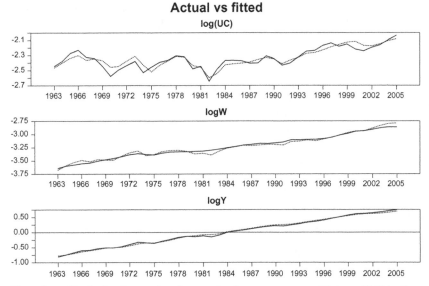

Fig. 2. Single-level production-technology system. Note: *Solid line represents data; dashed line represents model-generated values.*

To assess the fit of this system, in Figure 2, we graph the factor prices (in this case, merely the log real user cost and the log aggregate real wage) and that of potential output. The fit of all three series appears perfectly respectable, with that of the user cost noticeably good.[6] Wages are also fit reasonably well. It is important to stress that many production function specifications can yield a good fit for output, but, generally, they do a poor job at fitting factor prices, especially the user cost of capital.

The first two columns of Table 2 show the case where the production-technology system disaggregates into two capital types, but a single labor type. Again, we see the elasticity between the capital aggregate and the single labor input is around 0.5. The elasticity of substitution between different capital types is around 0.9 but still statistically significantly different from 1. The value of the labor-augmenting growth rate (at 1.7%) is the same as before. In terms of capital augmentation, we see different signs between buildings and equipment. We shall see this pattern repeated in subsequent results and we will rationalize it accordingly. When you impose the two capital augmentation growth terms to be equal, as reported in the next two columns of the table, the elasticity between capital types increases, but it insignificantly different from zero. The model fit also

---

[6] León-Ledesma et al. (2010b) discuss the typical fit of the first-order equation for capital.

Table 2. *Two-level production technology system:* $Y = F[(KB, KQ, \eta), N, \sigma]$, *that is,* $V_1 = KB$, $V_2 = KQ$, $V_3 = N$, $\pi = 0$

	Coefficient	Standard error	Coefficient	Standard error
ζ	1.001	0.006	1.002	0.006
σ	0.516	0.002	0.531	0.002
η	0.871	0.043	1.748	0.136
γ^{KB}	0.045	0.015	–	
γ^{KQ}	−0.023	0.005	–	
γ^N	0.017	0.001	0.017	0.001
Log determination	−34.008		−32.844	
$\text{ADF}_{\text{FOC}_{KB}}$	−2.695		−0.982	
$\text{ADF}_{\text{FOC}_{KQ}}$	−3.619		−2.773	
$\text{ADF}_{\text{FOC}_N}$	−2.424		−2.305	
ADF_Y	−2.316		−2.456	

Note: "–" indicates not applicable.

Table 3. *Two-level production technology system:* $Y = F[(KB, KQ, \eta), (NS, NU, \zeta), \sigma]$, $V_1 = KB$, $V_2 = KQ$, $V_3 = NS$, $V_4 = NU$

	Coefficient	Standard error	Coefficient	Standard error	Coefficient	Standard error
ζ	0.984	0.005	0.977	0.005	0.976	0.005
σ	0.535	0.002	0.665	0.003	0.652	0.004
η	0.819	0.077	1.631	0.116	1.647	0.110
ζ	3.640	0.680	3.156	0.475	2.841	0.067
γ^{KB}	0.032	0.013	–		–	
γ^{KQ}	−0.018	0.005	–			
γ^{NS}	0.024	0.002	0.025	0.002	0.026	0.001
γ^{NU}	0.004	0.002	0.002	0.002	–	
Log determination	−33.098		−39.634		−39.605	
$\text{ADF}_{\text{FOC}_{KB}}$	−3.012		−1.545		−1.480	
$\text{ADF}_{\text{FOC}_{KQ}}$	−3.667		−2.906		−2.910	
$\text{ADF}_{\text{FOC}_{NS}}$	−2.974		−2.658		−2.649	
$\text{ADF}_{\text{FOC}_{NU}}$	−2.967		−3.024		−3.231	
ADF_Y	−2.905		−3.171		−3.278	

tends to deteriorate when this equality (i.e., Hicks neutrality for the capital component) is imposed.

Table 3 represents the most general case whereby capital and labor types are disaggregated. The first two columns present the estimates with no restrictions imposed on technical progress. The elasticity of substitution between labor types is between 3 and 4, which, although marginally higher than some other estimates in the literature, nevertheless points to both gross substitutability between labor types.[7] The elasticity of substitution between capital types is, as before, around 0.8. Noticeably, the aggregate elasticity between capital and labor is again close to 0.5. As regards technical progress components, technical change augmenting equipment capital is high (3%) and higher than that of skilled labor (which in turn is six times as high as that associated with unskilled labor). As in Table 2, there is again negative technical change associated to equipment and a positive one to building/structures. The former can be rationalized as the natural outcome for a sustained decline in relative rental price (recall the middle panel of Figure 1) and an associated increase in usage. In short, equipment capital was not a scarce factor and – in the language of the "directed technical change" literature, for example, Acemoglu (2002a) – we would expect firms to bias technical improvements toward the scarce factor.

As in the conventional system, we can assess the fit (Figure 3). Again, to a visual approximation, the fit of the system is good. The fit of output is very good except for the early 1980s period. The fit of the user costs components is very impressive. It is worth recalling that previous studies using nested production functions such as Greenwood et al. (1997) and Krussel et al. (2000) focus on the fit of relative wages, whereas our system's performance depends on the fit of *all* factor prices and output simultaneously. Models that are able to fit relative wages well do not necessarily match other relevant data and can thus be only partially judged. In our case, while we fit well the trend of relative skilled to unskilled wages (the wage premium), we cannot capture completely the dip observed in the late 1970s.

The next four columns of Table 3 display the results restricting some technical progress parameters to zero. Although the elasticity between capital types increases, it becomes insignificant. However, the model fit deteriorates significantly judging by the log determinant and the ADF tests.

Finally, Table 4 presents results with disaggregated labor types and a single aggregate capital stock measure. The results are well in line with what we had before. A common inter-class elasticity of substitution of around 0.5 and an intra-class labor elasticity of around 3. However, this appears not to be statistically significant. Regarding technical progress, that of skilled labor dominates unskilled labor (which is around the same rate as that of capital). We then constrained technical progress for both labor classes to be the same, that is, intra-class Hicks neutral. The model,

---

[7] Katz and Murphy (1992), found point estimates for the elasticity of substitution between skilled and unskilled labor of 1.4 (a value echoed by other studies such as Krussel et al., 2000, and Heckman, Lochner, & Taber, 1998).

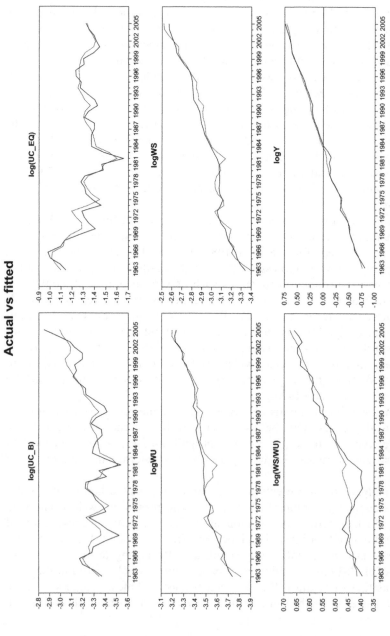

Fig. 3. Two-level production-technology system. Note: Solid line represents data; dashed line represents model-generated values.

Table 4. **Two-level production technology system:** $Y = F[K, (NU, NS, \zeta),$ $\sigma]$, $V_1 = K$, $\beta = 0$, $V_3 = NU$, $V_4 = NS$

	Coefficient	Standard error	Coefficient	Standard error
ζ	0.980	0.006	0.973	0.006
σ	0.457	0.001	0.464	0.010
ζ	3.525	0.641	100	–
γ^K	0.005	0.001	0.005	0.001
γ^{NS}	0.024	0.002	–	0.001
γ^{NU}	0.004	0.002	0.011	0.000
Log determination	−33.098		−27.1870	
$\text{ADF}_{\text{FOC}_K}$	−3.198		−3.2956	
$\text{ADF}_{\text{FOC}_{NU}}$	−3.067		−0.0222	
$\text{ADF}_{\text{FOC}_{NS}}$	−2.905		−2.0557	
ADF_Y	−2.829		−1.0459	

however, did not converge unless we imposed a large intra-class substitution elasticity (almost linear aggregation) as the value of 100 reported in the table. Even in that case, the model fit deteriorates dramatically, especially for both wages and output.

4.2. Discussion

We can now extract some conclusions about the evolution of relative intra-class factor prices from the results above.

Recall that Equations (9) and (10) imply,

$$\underbrace{\log\frac{cq_t}{cb_t} + \log\left(\frac{KQ_t}{KB_t}\right)}_{>0} = \left(\frac{\eta-1}{\eta}\right)\left[\log\left(\frac{KQ_t}{KB_t}\right) + (\gamma_q - \gamma_b)\tilde{t}\right] + C_1 \qquad (15)$$

where $C_1 = \log[(\beta/(1-\beta))(KB_0/KQ_0)]$.

Our previous data section made clear that the left hand price ratio cq_t/cb_t has a negative slope and the relative equipment capital to structures capital ratio KQ_t/KB_t has a positive one. In addition, since we know that the slope of the latter is steeper upwards than the downward slope of the former, then the slope of the left-hand side of (15) is positive (as indicated).

Now, in the special case of Hicks neutral technical change ($\gamma_q = \gamma_b$), it is straightforward to see that $\eta > 1$. However, with technical progress more structures saving than equipment saving, that is, $\gamma_q - \gamma_b < 0$, the right hand-side term in square brackets may turn negative if the trend in technical progress is stronger than that in KQ_t/KB_t. This would then be compatible with a below-unity substitution parameter $\eta < 1$. Our empirical results turn out to be fully in line with this case.

When we allow free factor-augmenting technical progress, we estimate negative equipment capital augmenting (i.e., equipment consuming) and positive structures capital augmenting (i.e., structures saving) technical progress and below unit substitution elasticity η. This result is in line with the fact the technical progress has continuously decreased the price of equipment capital increasing at the same time (especially the quality adjusted) volume of equipment capital. However, if we postulated a non-negativity constraint for technical change, our estimation results implied zero technical change for both capital components and above unit substitution elasticity η. However, this constraint decreased the fit of the system (see log determinant) and the stationarity properties of the residuals (ADF-test value).

Turning now to the skill-premium, Equations (11) and (12) imply that,

$$\underbrace{\log\frac{ws_t}{wu_t} + \log\left(\frac{NS_t}{NU_t}\right)}_{>0} = \left(\frac{\zeta - 1}{\zeta}\right)\left[\log\left(\frac{NS_t}{NU_t}\right) + (\gamma_S - \gamma_U)\tilde{i}\right] + C_2 \quad (16)$$

where $C_2 = \log[((1 - \pi)/\pi)(NS_0/NU_0)]$.

As both components of the left-hand side have a positive trend in our data, it is evident that, at least with $\gamma_S - \gamma_U \geq 0$, it must be that skilled and unskilled labor are gross substitutes and the intra-class substitution $\zeta > 1$. Only in the counterintuitive case of strongly net unskilled-saving technical change could gross complementarity be possible. Our estimation results are, in fact, in line with expectations. They suggest strong substitution between both types of labor inputs while technical progress is strongly skilled-labor augmenting. In fact, unskilled labor augmenting technical progress is only borderline statistically significant and around six times slower than skilled augmenting technical change.

It is also worth emphasizing that the inter class elasticity between capital and labor is close to 0.5 in most specifications, which is the value obtained also for the single-level CES production function. In the case in which a non-negativity constraint was imposed for all forms of factor-augmenting technical progress, the inter-class elasticity rose somewhat to around 0.65 but, simultaneously, the fit of the system decreased markedly.

5. Conclusions

We have empirically reexamined the two-level nested CES production function as in Sato (1967) but where we allow both capital and labor inputs to be disaggregated into two components: skilled and unskilled workers, and equipment and structures capital. We also paid particular attention to the role of factor-augmenting technical progress. Several specifications of the two-level CES function were examined within a "normalized" system approach to estimate deep supply-side parameters such as elasticities of substitution and factor-augmenting technical progress coefficients. The results were examined against the backdrop of observed trends in the skill premium and the relative price of equipment capital in the US economy. This can have important consequences for analyzing the impact of factor accumulation and technical progress on inequality.

Several findings from our estimates stand out:

- Skilled and unskilled labor display a high elasticity of substitution (well above 1) and are hence gross substitutes in production.
- Equipment and structures capital appear to display mild complementarity properties, with an elasticity of substitution around 0.8.
- The forms of technical progress that dominate are net skilled laborsaving and net structures-saving. In the first case, because of substitutability with unskilled labor, this tends to increase its relative wage and share in labor income.
- Importantly, the supply-side system formed by the production function and first-order conditions fits *simultaneously* all factor prices and output very well. The system also allows to analyze whether common restrictions in the literature may help fitting one part of the system such as the skill premium at the cost of a poor matching of other factor prices.
- Finally, the elasticity of substitution between aggregate capital and aggregate labor appears to be very robust to disaggregation. It takes a value of around 0.5, emphasizing the need to abandon the common usage of Cobb–Douglas functions in most growth and macroeconomic models.

This analysis, although exploratory, may open up interesting avenues for future research. One such avenue could be the use of the two-level CES system to test for different explanations of the rising relative wage of skilled workers observed in many countries for the last three decades such as the capital-skill complementarity or the skill-biased technical change hypotheses. The system provides natural a framework to test alternative production function nestings with different implications for intra- and inter-class factor substitution and their interaction with technical progress.

Acknowledgment

We are grateful to Olivier de La Grandville for helpful discussions.

Appendix. Normalization: A primer

Let us start with the general definition of a linear homogenous production function:

$$Y_t = F(\Gamma_t^K K_t, \Gamma_t^H H_t) = \Gamma_t^H H_t f(\kappa_t) \qquad (A.1)$$

where Y_t is output, K_t capital, and H_t the labor input. The terms Γ_t^K and Γ_t^H capture capital and labor-augmenting technical progress, respectively. To circumvent problems related to the "Diamond–McFadden impossibility theorem,"[8] researchers usually assume specific functional forms for these functions, for example, $\Gamma_t^j = \Gamma_0^j e^{z_t^j}$ where z_t^j can be a stochastic or deterministic technical progress function associated to factor i. The case where $z_t^K = z_t^H > 0$ denotes Hicks neutral technology; $z_t^K > 0$, $z_t^H = 0$ yields Solow neutrality; $z_t^K = 0$, $z_t^H > 0$ represents Harrod neutrality; and $z_t^K > 0 \neq z_t^H > 0$ indicates general factor augmentation. The term $\kappa_t = (\Gamma_t^K K_t)/(\Gamma_t^H H_t)$ is the capital-labor ratio in efficiency units. Likewise, define $\varphi_t = y_t/(\Gamma_t^H H_t)$ as per-capita production in efficiency units. The elasticity of substitution can then be expressed as follows:

$$\sigma = -\frac{f'(\kappa)\left[f(\kappa) - \kappa f'(\kappa)\right]}{\kappa f(\kappa) f''(\kappa)} \in [0, \infty]. \qquad (A.2)$$

This definition can be viewed as a second-order differential equation in κ having the following general CES production function as its solution:

$$\varphi_t = a\left[\kappa_t^{(\sigma-1)/\sigma} + b\right]^{\sigma/(\sigma-1)} \Rightarrow Y_t = a\left[(\Gamma_t^K K_t)^{(\sigma-1)/\sigma} + b(\Gamma_t^H H_t)^{(\sigma-1)/\sigma}\right]^{\sigma/(\sigma-1)} \qquad (A.3)$$

where a and b are two arbitrary constants of integration with the following correspondence with the original Arrow et al. (1961) non-normalized form, which, after some rearrangements, can be presented in conventional form:

$$Y_t = \mathbb{J}\left[\alpha(\Gamma_t^K K_t)^{(\sigma-1)/\sigma} + (1-\alpha)(\Gamma_t^H H_t)^{(\sigma-1)/\sigma}\right]^{\sigma/(\sigma-1)} \qquad (A.4)$$

where efficiency parameter $\mathbb{J} = a(1+b)^{\sigma/(\sigma-1)}$ and distribution parameter $\alpha = 1/(1+b) < 1$. An economically meaningful identification of these integration constants a and b (and further $\mathbb{J}$ and α) is given by the fact that σ is a *point* elasticity relying on three baseline (or "normalized", $t = 0$) values: a given capital intensity $\kappa_0 = \Gamma_0^K K_0/(\Gamma_0^H H_0)$, a given marginal rate of substitution, $\partial(Y_0/H_0)/\partial(Y_0/K_0)$, and a given level of per-capita production $\varphi_0 = Y_0/(\Gamma_0^H H_0)$. For simplicity, and without loss of generality, we scale the components of technical progress such that $\Gamma_0^K = \Gamma_0^H = 1$.

---

[8] See Diamond and McFadden (1965).

Accordingly, we can transform (A.4) into its key normalized form,

$$Y_t = Y_0 \left[\alpha_0 \left(\frac{K_t}{K_0} \Gamma_t^K \right)^{(\sigma-1)/\sigma} + (1-\alpha_0) \left(\frac{H_t}{H_0} \Gamma_t^H \right)^{(\sigma-1)/\sigma} \right]^{\sigma/(\sigma-1)} \tag{A.5}$$

where distribution parameter $\alpha_0 = r_0 K_0 / (r_0 K_0 + w_0 H_0)$ has a clear economic interpretation: the capital income share evaluated at the point of normalization. We see that all parameters of (A.5) are deep, demonstrated by the fact that at the point of normalization, the left-hand-side equals the right-hand side for all values of σ, α_0 and the parameterization of Γ_t^K and Γ_t^H. By contrast, as clearly shown in de La Grandville (2009, pp. 85–86), comparing (A.4) with (A.5) the parameters of the *non-normalized* function depend on the normalized value of the factors and factor returns as well as on σ itself:

$$\mathbb{J}(\sigma,\cdot) = Y_0 \left[\frac{r_0 K_0^{1/\sigma} + w_0 H_0^{1/\sigma}}{r_0 K_0 + w_0 H_0} \right]^{\sigma/(\sigma-1)} \tag{A.6}$$

$$\alpha(\sigma,\cdot) = \frac{r_0 K_0^{1/\sigma}}{r_0 K_0^{1/\sigma} + w_0 H_0^{1/\sigma}}. \tag{A.7}$$

Accordingly, in the non-normalized formulation, parameters $\mathbb{J}$ and α have no theoretical or empirical meaning. Hence, varying σ, while holding $\mathbb{J}$ and α constant, is inconsistent for comparative static purposes.

References

Acemoglu, D. (2002a). Directed technical change. *Review of Economic Studies, 69*(4), 781–809.

Acemoglu, D. (2002b). Technical change, inequality, and the labor market. *Journal of Economic Literature, 40*(1), 7–72.

Acemoglu, D. (2009). *Introduction to modern economic growth.* New Jersey, USA: Princeton University Press, Princeton.

Arrow, K. J., Chenery, H. B., Minhas, B. S., & Solow, R. M. (1961). Capital-labor substitution and economic efficiency. *Review of Economics and Statistics, 43*(3), 225–250.

Autor, D. H., Katz, L. F., & Kearney, M. S. (2008). Trends in U.S. wage inequality: Revising the revisionists. *Review of Economics and Statistics, 90*(2), 300–323.

Chirinko, R. S. (2008). σ: The long and short of it. *Journal of Macroeconomics, 30*(2), 671–686.

Diamond, P. A., & McFadden, D. (1965). Identification of the elasticity of substitution and the bias of technical change: An impossibility theorem. Working Paper No. 62, University of California Berkeley.

Duffy, J., Papageorgiou, C., & Perez-Sebastian, F. (2004). Capital-skill complementarity? Evidence from a panel of countries. *Review of Economics and Statistics, 86*(1), 327–344.

Gordon, R. (1990). *The measurement of durable goods prices.* Chicago, Illinois, USA: University of Chicago Press.

Greenwood, J., Hercowitz, Z., & Krussel, P. (1997). Long-run implications of investment-specific technical change. *American Economic Review, 87,* 342–362.

Griliches, Z. (1969). Capital-skill complementarity. *Review of Economics and Statistics, 51*(4), 465–468.

Heckman, J., Lochner, L., & Taber, C. (1998). Explaining rising wage inequality: Explorations with a dynamic general equilibrium model of labor earnings with heterogeneous agents. *Review of Economic Dynamics, 1*(3), 1–58.

Katz, L., & Murphy, K. (1992). Changes in relative wages, 1963–1987: Supply and demand factors. *Quarterly Journal of Economics, 107,* 35–78.

Klump, R., McAdam, P., & Willman, A. (2007). Factor substitution and factor augmenting technical progress in the US. *Review of Economics and Statistics, 89*(1), 183–192.

Krussel, P., Ohanian, L., Rios-Rull, J. V., & Violante, G. (2000). Capital-skill complementarity and inequality. *Econometrica, 68*(5), 1029–1053.

La Grandville, O. de. (2009). *Economic growth: A unified approach.* Cambridge, UK: Cambridge University Press.

León-Ledesma, M. A., McAdam, P., & Willman, A. (2010a). Identifying the elasticity of substitution with biased technical change. *American Economic Review, 100*(4), 1330–1357.

León-Ledesma, M. A., McAdam, P., & Willman, A. (2010b). In Dubio pro CES: Supply estimation with miss-specified technical change. Working Paper Series 1175, European Central Bank.

Piva, M., Santarelli, E., & Vivarelli, M. (2005). The skill bias effect of technological and organisational change: Evidence and policy implications. *Research Policy, 34*(2), 141–157.

Sato, K. (1967). A two-level constant-elasticity-of-substitution production function. *Review of Economic Studies, 34*(2), 201–218.

Solow, R. M. (1956). A contribution to the theory of economic growth. *Quarterly Journal of Economics, 70*(1), 65–94.

Solow, R. M. (1957). Technical change and the aggregate production function. *Review of Economics and Statistics, 39*(3), 312–320.

CHAPTER 16

Factor Substitution and Biased Technology with Balanced Growth

Miguel A. León-Ledesma and Mathan Satchi

School of Economics, University of Kent, Kent CT2 7NP, UK
E-mail addresses: m.a.leon-ledesma@kent.ac.uk; m.satchi@kent.ac.uk

Abstract
The famous Uzawa (1961) balanced growth theorem has exercised a tyranny of sorts over macroeconomics for decades. It is the prime reason why researchers use Cobb–Douglas production functions and abstract from considering movements in factor shares. Others have had to recourse to complex explanations for long-run labor augmentation in technical progress. In this chapter, we discuss the issues arising from this problem and propose a way of achieving balanced growth with a short-run production function where the elasticity of factor substitution is less than one, and capital augmenting technology shocks can be permanent. We do so by allowing firms to choose the relative reliance on capital in the production technology and introducing a suitable modification of the production function. We also provide some model simulations in the context of a simple deterministic neoclassical growth model.

Keywords: Balanced growth, distribution parameter, elasticity of substitution, factor augmentation

JEL classifications: E25, O33, O40

1. Introduction

The Uzawa (1961) balanced growth path (BGP) theorem states that, for a BGP to exist, technical progress must be labor augmenting or the production function must be Cobb–Douglas *in the long-run*. BGP refers to a dynamic equilibrium where the capital–output ratio, the real interest rate, and factor shares are all constant. Since the conventional wisdom is that these properties are observed over long periods of time in developed economies, it follows that the majority of macroeconomic models are built

Frontiers of Economics and Globalization
Volume 11   ISSN: 1574-8715
DOI: 10.1108/S1574-8715(2011)0000011021

in a way that deliver these outcomes. They either use a Cobb–Douglas production function, or assume all technical progress is labor augmenting in the long run.

In this chapter, we first discuss the approaches taken in the literature to justify that either technical progress is all labor augmenting, or that the production function is Cobb–Douglas in the long run. We then discuss the approach proposed by León-Ledesma and Satchi (2011) to tackle the question of whether we can obtain a BGP in the presence of (permanent) capital-augmenting technical progress through the imposition of a simple Constant Elasticity of Substitution (CES)-type production technology that allows an optimal choice of technique. Finally, we provide some simulation exercises in the context of an optimal growth model with technique choice. This approach can prove particularly attractive in cases where innovation itself is not the main question of interest. The main advantage in such cases is that it provides a simple production technology that gives the researcher the ability to include capital-augmenting technical progress and a less than unitary elasticity of substitution simply via a suitable specification of the production technology, without the usual consequent worry of the lack of a BGP.[1] This allows the researcher to depart from the standard Cobb–Douglas assumption, which sits at odds with the observed large (short- to medium-run) variations in factor shares, essentially just by introducing an extra first-order condition and some very straightforward modifications of existing ones.

The first requirement of such an approach is that it must be based on an optimizing choice of production technique where "choice of technique" is used here specifically to refer to the relative reliance on capital or labor in production, that is, the distribution parameter in a CES production function. The logic of the approach is as follows. In a standard CES specification, simply choosing the optimal technique as well as the optimal quantities of labor and capital leads to an asymmetric outcome and involves firms specializing only in capital or only in labor. We avoid this problem by multiplicatively augmenting the CES with a function that penalizes extreme choices of the distribution parameter, while leaving us with a production function that remains CES when the choice of technique is given. This captures the economically intuitive idea that while firms may alter their relative reliance on capital or labor, extreme choices such as relying *exclusively* on capital are likely to prove relatively unproductive. Furthermore, we can show that there is effectively only one specification for this multiplicative function that gives our problem of making an optimal choice of production technique a form that is satisfactorily invariant to an arbitrary change of measurement units for factors of

---

[1] We refer the reader to León-Ledesma and Satchi (2011) for a full exposition of the approach including mathematical proofs.

production. This "unit-invariance" provides the basic motivation for the production technology. An added benefit is that this production technology does not require further "normalization" as is the case with standard CES functions.

An important aspect in judging the appropriate context to use the approach taken here is that it is not based on a particular model of innovation. The early models of "induced innovation" used to justify the existence of long-run labor-augmenting technical progress relied on assumptions about firm behavior that were not well founded on microeconomic principles. As stressed by Acemoglu (2001), the usual assumption in these models is that firms maximized the rate of growth of output (the rate of cost reduction), simply because aggregate technology showed increasing returns. Hence, "to go beyond the heuristics of maximizing the instantaneous rate of cost reduction, we need a micro-founded model of innovation" (Acemoglu, 2001, p. 470). This approach presents a way to resolve these issues preserving the profit maximization behavior of firms without requiring explicit models of innovation. While modeling innovation is of course a fundamental issue, its complexity may represent an obstacle to its introduction in macroeconomic models preserving BGP when the research question does not concern innovation itself, making departures from a standard Cobb–Douglass framework difficult. In models that are focussed on innovation, this approach also liberates the researcher from the constraint that the innovation process itself should ensure balanced growth in the long run, since the choice of technique provides an alternative mechanism by which this occurs.

We proceed as follows. Section 2 briefly discusses some of the approaches taken in the literature to address the problem of achieving BGP. The production technology and the intuition behind it are presented briefly in Section 3. Section 4 introduces the production technology in the context of a very simple simulated dynamic macroeconomic model. Section 5 concludes.

2. Related literature

As mentioned above, the important drawback in assuming Cobb–Douglas is that it sits at odds with the observed large variations in factor shares, and the available empirical evidence on the elasticity of capital-labor substitution.[2] Clearly, if the elasticity of substitution is incorrectly assumed to be unity in the short-run, the implications for modeling short-run dynamics can be substantial (see Cantore, León-Ledesma, McAdam, & Willman, 2010). As a result, the steady-state growth theorem becomes

---

[2] Indeed, the weight of evidence reviewed in, for example, Chirinko (2008) and León-Ledesma et al. (2010), supports a value of this elasticity well below unity.

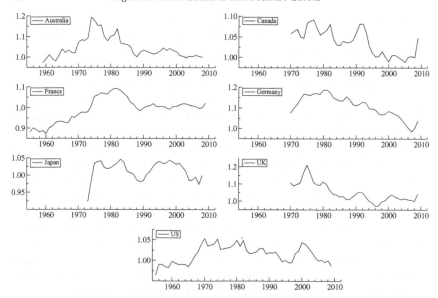

Fig. 1.   Evolution of the labor share (2008 = 1) for selected countries.

potentially restrictive if one wants to satisfy a BGP and still accurately model short-run dynamics. Figure 1 presents the evolution of the labor share for seven developed countries for about five decades.[3] What is striking, especially when talking about BGP, is that the labor share experiences important swings in the short and medium run. For most countries, especially in Europe, the labor share increases until the mid-1970s and then declines. A similar process occurs in the United States, although there is another inverted-U shaped movement centered around year 2000. Obviously, a Cobb–Douglas yields time-invariant factor shares and hence is not compatible with observed evidence.

In order to resolve this problem, it is worth stressing that the BGP theorem only restricts the shape of the production function or the form of technical progress *in the long run*. These two conditions can be easily violated in higher frequency models of fluctuations. Yet, these models still require a long-run steady-state compatible with BGP. Hence, the question that arises is precisely what economic mechanism ensures that either the production function is Cobb–Douglas or technical progress in the long run? Two main approaches have been developed to answer this question. On the one hand, models that focus on the nature of technical progress. On the other hand, models that focus on the shape of the production function.

---

[3] Data for Australia, Canada, France, Germany, Japan, and the United Kingdom come from the OECD, whereas data for the United States come from BLS.

The early literature on induced innovation was inspired by Hicks (1932), who stated that "a change in the relative prices of the factors of production is itself a spur to invention, and to invention of a particular kind – directed to economizing the use of a factor which has become relatively expensive (pp. 124–125)." This was followed by Kennedy (1964), Samuelson (1965), and Drandakis and Phelps (1966), who viewed this as the result of firms introducing innovations that save on expensive factors in the face of changes in relative factor prices. More recently, this line of thought has been revisited by Acemoglu (2002, 2003, 2007), Zeira (1998), and Zuleta (2008), amongst others, in what has been re-named as the theory of "directed" technical change. In these models, innovation is explicitly modeled in a profit maximizing framework and without relying on ad-hoc assumptions about the firms' objective function as in previous literature. In this stream, technical progress becomes labor augmenting because, in the long-run, labor is the only limit to growth as capital can be accumulated endogenously. Capital-intensive goods (or capital inputs) can be increased through both capital-augmenting technical change and capital accumulation. However, asymptotically, there is only one way to increase the production of labor-intensive (or labor input), through labor-augmenting technical change. Hence, the possibility of accumulating capital implies that technical change has to be labor augmenting in the long run. In the short-run, however, technical progress can be "directed." This will depend on two forces: the price effect and the market size effect. The price effect, in the spirit of Hicks (1932), directs innovations innovations towards scarce factors. The market size effect favors abundant factors. The elasticity of substitution between capital and labor is the key parameter which determines the relative strength of these effects.

The second stream, which is far smaller, focuses on the shape of the production function. It relies on exploiting the fact that all that is required for BGP is that the production function be Cobb–Douglas "in the long run." The aggregation approach is taken by Houthakker (1955/1956).[4] Jones (2005) and Lagos (2006) provide a very useful discussion of this classic chapter. In Houthakker (1955/1956), the aggregate production function is derived from the distribution of inputs across productive units. Lagos (2006), in the spirit of Houthakker, derives a Cobb–Douglas form for the aggregate production function by aggregating Leontief production technologies at the firm level using a model with search frictions.[5] Rosen (1978) uses a model of task assignment. The problem is to maximize aggregate output by assigning workers of different productive types to heterogenous tasks, from where the shape of the production function is

---

[4] See also Levhari (1968).

[5] The aims of that chapter, however, are very different to what is discussed here (for instance it assumes an exogenous rental on capital) and are primarily directed at accounting for the determinants of observed TFP.

442 Miguel A. León-Ledesma and Mathan Satchi

derived under certain distributional properties of tasks. Perhaps the best example here is Jones (2005) and chapters that follow such as Growiec (2008). Jones (2005), as we do here, provides a production function that is Cobb–Douglas in the long run but where the elasticity of substitution falls short of unity in the short run. Our approach is complementary to Jones (2005) as both approaches produce Cobb–Douglas at the firm level, rather than as a result of aggregation, and come from a choice of technology by firms. However, there are also some key differences. The most important one is the different approach used to rationalize the functions that justify the existence of a long-run Cobb–Douglas. In Jones (2005), it is based on the arrival process for ideas. The Cobb–Douglas case arises if this process is governed by Pareto distributions. Jones provides supportive evidence. In our case, we rely on a purely theoretical justification by seeking to generalize CES functions in a plausible way to provide *unit-invariance*. While the link between an arrival process for ideas and a long-run production function is clearly a very attractive one, perhaps a key advantage of the approach taken here is tractability. The stochastic processes involved in Jones (2005) and the extreme value nature of the problem are likely to make implementation in a standard dynamic framework extremely difficult, while the approach taken here is very straightforward. This is also likely to have a significant impact on the short-run dynamics of factor shares. In Jones (2005), due to the extreme value nature again, these factor shares can be quite volatile. Here, a standard adjustment cost mechanism results in smooth movements in factor shares. Finally, Jones (2005) produces the result that technical progress is labor augmenting, whereas here technical progress is exogenous.[6]

3. CES and the choice of production technique

We describe here the approach taken in León-Ledesma and Satchi (2011) that is based on allowing firms to choose the capital-labor distribution parameter in production. We refer the reader to the original chapter for the details of the derivation. Here we simply present the production technology itself and the intuition behind it. Allowing a choice of production technique results in an import modification of the CES production function. Using this modification then leads us to a production technology that both allows us to abstract from considerations of

---

[6] Note that Jones (2005) also concludes that "[...] Alternatively, it might be desirable to have microfoundations for a Cobb–Douglas production function that permits capital-augmenting technological change to occur in the steady state." This is in fact achieved by Growiec (2008) by allowing for dependence between the Pareto distributions of labor- and capital-augmenting developments.

normalization that often arise with the use of CES (see de La Grandville 1989, 2009; Klump & de La Grandville 2000; León-Ledesma et al., 2010) but, more importantly, ensures balanced growth in the long run even with capital-augmenting technical progress: the production function is essentially CES in the short run but Cobb–Douglass in the long run. That is, the simple approach we outline here is capable of generating the short-run versus long-run result in Jones (2005) by using a model of endogenous choice of technique. The approach is also very general, and can easily be implemented in a wide variety of models.

Take the CES production, omitting any time subscripts:

$$Y = \Gamma(\alpha(BK)^{\sigma-1/\sigma} + (1 - \alpha)(AL)^{\sigma-1/\sigma})^{\sigma/\sigma-1}, \tag{1}$$

where K is capital, L labor, B and A are capital- and labor-augmenting technical progress functions, Γ is a neutral efficiency parameter, σ is the elasticity of substitution between K and L, and α is the distribution parameter that determines the relative reliance on capital and labor in production. Suppose we allowed α to be a choice variable in (1) as well as K and L. We can clearly see that this does not give us a problem with an appropriately satisfied second-order condition in α. In fact, we straightforwardly show that allowing a choice of α in (1) results in an asymmetric problem where each firm only employs capital or only employs labor. This is because in a context where firms can choose the production technique, firms that employ both factors would make a negative profit.

Since this is not a satisfactory outcome, we propose in León-Ledesma and Satchi (2011) to modify the CES production function as follows:

$$Y = \Gamma f(\alpha)(\alpha(BK)^{\sigma-1/\sigma} + (1 - \alpha)(AL)^{\sigma-1/\sigma})^{\sigma/\sigma-1}. \tag{2}$$

The introduction of the term $f(\alpha)$ is the key step in this approach. Importantly, for any given α, the production function remains CES. We use it to essentially punish extreme choices of α, so while the firm can choose α, we are assuming that the firm cannot produce output with only labor or only capital. Therefore we impose $f(0) = f(1) = 0$ with $f(\alpha)$ strictly positive on $\alpha \in (0, 1)$. The choice of α is also a continuous one so $f(\alpha)$ is continuously differentiable and positive on $\alpha \in (0, 1)$. The addition of the $f(\alpha)$ term then introduces a time-invariant technological constraint on the choice of technique. The intuition behind this function, hence, is to capture the idea that extreme choices of α are likely to be costly since they imply all of the tasks being performed by capital or labor. If there is comparative advantage, a more balanced distribution of tasks between capital and labor could be more "efficiency enhancing."

Since we do not see in practice firms employing only one factor of production, we can argue that introducing $f(\alpha)$ in (2) is a necessary step in allowing the choice of the distribution parameter in a CES framework. However, it is also as yet clearly ad-hoc. It turns out that we can go a long way to resolving this issue by considering the problem of "unit invariance." As is well known, of the three parameters α,Γ, and σ in the CES production function, only σ is invariant to the choice of units. Because of this, in general if we start off with a particular functional form for $f(\alpha)$ in (2) we will end up with a different function form upon a change of units. This is clearly an unsatisfactory situation. However, we show in León-Ledesma and Satchi (2011) that up to a multiplicative constant, there is a unique functional form for $f(\alpha)$ that maintains this form upon a change of units. This is:

$$f(\alpha) = [\alpha^\gamma(1-\alpha)^{1-\gamma}]^{\sigma/1-\sigma} \tag{3}$$

for some $\gamma \in (0,1)$. Note that $f(\alpha)$ is maximized at $\alpha = \gamma$. We can then argue that since the change of units leaves $f(.)$ invariant, and since σ is invariant to a change of units, then so is γ. Thus we are excused from any of the normalization considerations that often surround CES; a change in units only produces a change in the efficiency parameter Γ.

Note that for the function form proposed in (3) to "work" we need to impose $\sigma < 1$: otherwise $f(\alpha)$ rewards extreme choices of α rather than punishing them. We can draw a link between this and the "strict essentiality" of the CES production function.[7] The CES production function does not satisfy strict essentiality when $\sigma > 1$. This does not normally matter since the marginal product of each factor tends to infinity at zero, but when α is a choice variable the possibility of one firm specializing in one factor and bidding up the price of that factor becomes a real one. Nonetheless, since the empirical evidence for departures from Cobb–Douglas lie very much on the side of a lower than unit elasticity of substitution, the restriction is not a significant one.

Writing $\theta = (1-\alpha)/\alpha$, the production function becomes:

$$Y = \Gamma(\theta^{\gamma-1}(BK)^{\sigma-1/\sigma} + \theta^\gamma(AL)^{\sigma-1/\sigma})^{\sigma/\sigma-1}, \tag{4}$$

With $r + \delta$ and w being respectively the rental rates for capital and labor, the first-order conditions with respect to K and L become:

$$\Gamma^{\sigma-1/\sigma}\left(\frac{Y}{BK}\right)^{1/\sigma} B\theta^{\gamma-1} = r + \delta, \tag{5}$$

$$\Gamma^{\sigma-1/\sigma}\left(\frac{Y}{AL}\right)^{1/\sigma} A\theta^\gamma = w. \tag{6}$$

If we hold θ constant, the elasticity of substitution is σ. However, θ is not constant and in fact we can straightforwardly see that the elasticity of

---

[7] Strict essentiality implies that some of each input is needed for a positive output, so that for production function $f(x_1, x_2,..., x_n)$, we have that $f(x_1, x_2,..., 0, ...,x_n) = 0$.

substitution between the two factors is unity. The first-order condition for θ, after some transformations yields

$$\theta = \frac{1 - \gamma}{\gamma} \left(\frac{BK}{AL} \right)^{\sigma - 1/\sigma}. \tag{7}$$

Substituting (7) in (5) and (6) immediately implies a unitary elasticity of substitution between the two factors. The second-order condition for (7) can be shown to be always satisfied for $\sigma < 1$. We can then rely on this second-order condition and the strict essentiality of the production function for a symmetric solution. These first-order conditions effectively yield a Cobb–Douglas production function with an exponent γ on capital. We can see this by substituting (5) and (6) into (7) to obtain the capital share: $((r + \delta)K/Y) = \gamma$.

The final step is to introduce some adjustment costs in θ. In the long-run θ adjusts to give us Cobb–Douglas, but incomplete adjustment in the short run produces a system where the short-run elasticity of substitution between factors falls short of one. As these adjustment costs become large, the short-run elasticity of substitution between capital and labor will approach σ. Hence, we can have short-run dynamics with a less than unitary elasticity of substitution but balanced growth in the long run regardless of whether productivity growth is labor augmenting or capital augmenting.[8] We now explore this in a simple dynamic model.

4. Dynamics and calibration

To give a flavor of the workings of our approach, we now present a dynamic model with short-run CES and long-run Cobb–Douglas technology. We do so by, as mentioned above, introducing adjustment costs in the choice of the distribution parameter. The model is very stylized. It is an optimal growth model with exogenous labor supply in a purely deterministic setting. In this context, we analyze the effect of a one-off productivity increase. Given CES technology in the short run, we distinguish between the effect of (expected) changes in labor- and capital-augmenting productivity and show the effect of these for the dynamics of output, consumption, factor prices, and the labor share. We carry out the exercise for both temporary changes in technology lasting for one period and permanent changes in technology.

Households choose lifetime consumption (c_t) subject to the standard intertemporal budget constraint. Firms choose capital, labor, and θ_t, the latter subject to an adjustment cost. Adjustment costs should be specified in terms of θ_t rather than α. This is important since the ratio θ_t/θ_{t-1} is

---

[8] Of course, both forms of technical progress are not distinguishable in the long run as we have Cobb–Douglas. But it is precisely the short- to medium-run dynamics that matter for the distinction between these two forms of technical progress.

invariant to the choice of units whereas α_t/α_{t-1} is not. We assume that the costs of adjusting θ, denoted by $\varphi(\cdot)$, are proportional to output. The problem can be solved from the point of view of the central planner:

$$\underset{c_t,k_t,\theta_t}{\text{Max}} \sum_t^{\infty} \beta^t \ln c_t$$

$$\text{s.t. } c_t + k_{t+1} - k_t + \delta k_t = y_t\left[1 - \varphi\left(\tfrac{\theta_t}{\theta_{t-1}}\right)\right],$$

(8)

where δ is the rate of capital depreciation. We assume adjustment costs to take the following form: $\varphi(x) = 1 - e^{-\frac{1}{2}\tau(x-1)^2}$. The functional form for adjustment costs can, of course, be different or more general. We choose this exponential function as it implies smooth and symmetric costs of adjustment.

Given that labor supply is exogenous, we can write the production function in intensive form, where all lower case letters are given in per capita terms:

$$y_t = \Gamma_t(\theta_t^{\gamma-1}(B_t k_t)^{\sigma-1/\sigma} + \theta_t^{\gamma}(A_t)^{\sigma-1/\sigma})^{\sigma/\sigma-1}.$$

(9)

The first-order conditions for k_t, labor, and θ_t are given by:

$$e^{-\frac{1}{2}\tau(\theta_t - \theta_{t-1}/\theta_{t-1})^2}\Gamma_t^{\sigma-1/\sigma}\left(\frac{y_t}{B_t k_t}\right)^{1/\sigma} B_t\theta_t^{\gamma-1} = r_t,$$

(10)

$$e^{-\frac{1}{2}\tau(\theta_t - \theta_{t-1}/\theta_{t-1})^2}\Gamma_t^{\sigma-1/\sigma}\left(\frac{y_t}{A_t}\right)^{1/\sigma} A_t\theta_t^{\gamma} = w_t,$$

(11)

$$\frac{\sigma}{\sigma-1}\left(\gamma - \frac{r_t k_t}{y_t}\right) - \tau\left\{\frac{\theta_t}{\theta_{t-1}}\left(\frac{\theta_t - \theta_{t-1}}{\theta_{t-1}}\right) - \frac{1}{1+r_t}\frac{\theta_{t+1}}{\theta_t}\left(\frac{\theta_{t+1} - \theta_t}{\theta_t}\right)\frac{y_{t+1}}{y_t}\right\} = 0.$$

(12)

The dynamic system is then completed by the consumption Euler equation and the budget constraint:

$$\frac{c_{t+1}}{c_t} = \beta(r_{t+1} + 1 - \delta),$$

(13)

$$c_t + k_{t+1} - k_t + \delta k_t = y_t\left[1 - \varphi\left(\frac{\theta_t}{\theta_{t-1}}\right)\right].$$

(14)

Note that the special case of pure Cobb–Douglas is achieved by setting adjustment costs $\tau = 0$ rather than setting $\sigma = 1$ in (9). In (12), as θ tends to a steady-state value, strictly positive and finite in the presence of purely labor-augmenting technical progress or zero otherwise, we can see that the capital share will tend towards γ ensuring balanced growth. If τ and so adjustment costs are large, then θ_t will have a sluggish response to short-run changes in factor prices, and so from (10) and (11) the elasticity of substitution will be close to σ.

Within this system, we then analyze the effect of a 5% increase in A and B. In the first set of simulations, we assume that the change in A and B is temporary, lasting for one period only and reverting back to their initial values thereafter. In the second set of simulations, we assume a permanent increase in the efficiency factors. This case is perhaps theoretically more relevant as, in standard models, BGP could not be achieved with permanent shocks to B. Since the model is deterministic, we are just interested on the transition from the initial to the final steady state. We leave for future research the analysis of the dynamics of the model with stochastic shocks and possibly endogenous labor supply, along the lines of modern business-cycle models.

Table 1 presents the parameter calibration values. We choose a value of γ such that the steady-state capital share is 33%. The elasticity of substitution (σ) takes a value of 0.5, similar to those obtained in estimates for the US economy (see Klump, McAdam, & Willman, 2007). The depreciation rate is 10% per year, and the discount factor is 0.95 (a discount *rate* of 5.2% per year). Finally, we set adjustment costs to 10. This is a relatively large value, so we assume that the adjustment towards Cobb–Douglas is very sluggish.

Figure 2 presents the effect of a temporary shock in the case of a Cobb–Douglas production function ($\tau = 0$) for comparison purposes. In this case, of course, there is no distinction between labor- and capital-augmenting shocks. We observe the standard dynamics with a temporary, short-lived increase in output and factor prices and a smoother reaction of consumption. The labor share remains constant. We then show, in Figures 3 and 4 the reaction to a temporary labor- and capital-augmenting shock respectively. For the labor-augmenting shock, the reaction of output and consumption mirrors that of the Cobb–Douglas. However, wages increase less and the rental price of capital experiences a larger increase on impact.[9]

Table 1. *Parameter calibration values*

γ	0.33
σ	0.5
δ	0.1
β	0.95
τ	10
$\Delta A, \Delta B$	5%

---

[9] The reaction of wages will depend on the value of σ relative to the equilibrium share γ. For $\gamma > \sigma$ the wage rate may decrease on impact. For an explanation, see Cantore et al. (2010).

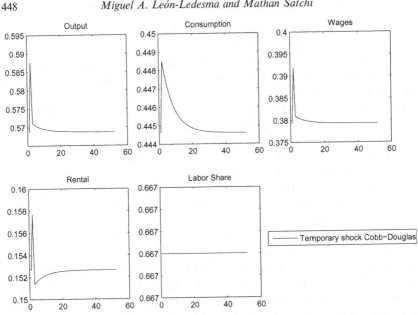

Fig. 2.   *Responses to a temporary labor-augmenting shock (5%): CD case.*

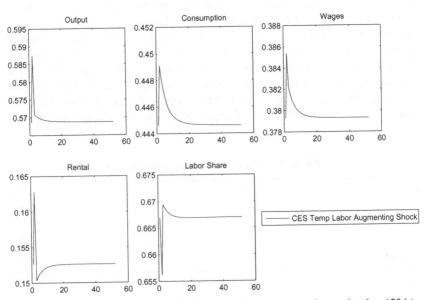

**Fig. 3.   *Responses to a temporary labor-augmenting shock (5%):
CES–CD case.***

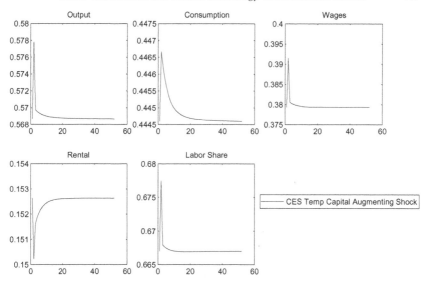

Fig. 4. *Responses to a temporary capital-augmenting shock (5%): CES–CD case.*

As a consequence, the labor share falls and then increases back to its equilibrium level. The increase is not monotonic, but suffers an overshooting and then drops back to equilibrium within around 12 periods. It is interesting, we note here, that this kind of overshooting has been reported in the empirical literature on the dynamics of factor shares (see Ríos-Rull & Santaeulàlia-Llopis, 2010). For the capital-augmenting shock, we observe the opposite pattern for the labor share. As the elasticity of substitution is below one, a capital-augmenting shock favors labor and increases its share. The rental price of capital falls. In this case we do not observe the overshooting effect present in the labor-augmenting shock.

For the case of a permanent shock, we also show first the transition towards the new steady state in the case of a Cobb–Douglas in Figure 5. After the initial shock, output and wages adjust slowly towards their new steady state. Consumption, as expected, takes longer to converge. The rental price of capital increases and then returns back to its initial steady state after the economy completes its capital accumulation adjustment. The labor share, of course, remains constant throughout.

Figures 6 and 7 present the dynamic responses of the variables to a labor-augmenting and a capital-augmenting permanent technology improvement respectively. In the case of the labor-augmenting shock, the reaction of output and consumption are similar to the Cobb–Douglas case. Wages, however, increase initially less whereas the rental price of capital increases by more just like in the temporary shock case. This results in a short-run fall in the labor share. The labor share then increases until

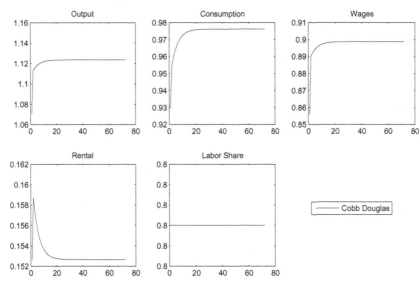

Fig. 5.   Responses to a permanent labor-augmenting shock (5%): CD case.

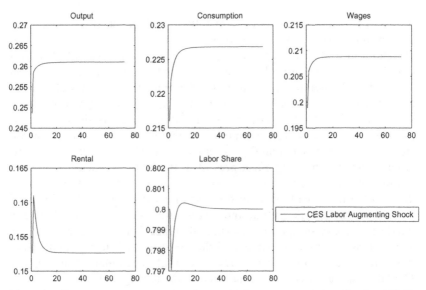

Fig. 6.   Responses to a permanent labor-augmenting shock (5%): CES–CD case.

around period 15 and, again, overshoots its equilibrium value. The adjustment is now slower than in the case of a temporary shock, but this will depend on the speed of adjustment of θ measured by τ. With a capital-

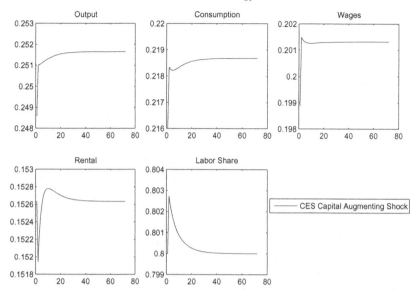

Fig. 7. Responses to a permanent capital-augmenting shock (5%): CES–CD case.

augmenting shock the labor share initially increases and then decreases. Wages increase faster and the rental price of capital initially falls[10] leading to an increase in the labor share. The increase in output and consumption is faster and both reflect the initial equilibrium overshooting of wages. What is important to note here, though, is that the endogenous choice of technique ensures that, after a permanent capital-augmenting shock, the labor share reverts back to equilibrium. We can clearly see that, with this mechanism, the two shocks are distinguishable in terms of their short to medium-run properties.

5. Conclusions

The BGP theorem states that for BGP to be achieved, either the production function must be Cobb–Douglas or technical progress must be all labor augmenting in the long run. Since BGP is approximately observed for developed economies, the majority of macroeconomic models face the constraint that these properties must be met in the long run. Hence, the use of Cobb–Douglas production functions, with their simplicity and tractability, has become common place. BGP, however, is not observed in the short to medium run. Substantial changes in factor shares occur at business-cycle frequencies (and even at longer horizons).

---

[10] The rental price falls as capital is predetermined at the time of the shock.

On the contrary, mounting evidence rejects the unitary elasticity of capital-labor substitution characteristic of Cobb–Douglas production functions.

In this chapter, we describe a simple way of modeling short-run departures from Cobb–Douglas that allows for permanent labor- *and* capital-augmenting technology changes based on León-Ledesma and Satchi (2011). In this approach, the short-run production function is CES with a less than unitary elasticity of substitution. The production function then becomes Cobb–Douglas in the long run. This is done by introducing two key elements. First, allowing firms to choose optimally not only factor inputs, but the distribution parameter determining the relative reliance on capital and labor (the production technique) responding to changes in factor prices. Second, the short-run CES is modified by introducing a function that penalizes extreme choices of the distribution parameter. The problem has a well-defined equilibrium. We then present a simple dynamic macro model in which the change in production technique is subject to adjustment costs. This allows us to have time-varying factor shares but long-run BGP even with permanent capital augmenting technology changes. Importantly, and as an advantage over other related approaches, this way of approaching the problem is simple and implementable within standard macroeconomic models.

Future work on this area may progress along both applied and theoretical lines. The method can be used to analyze factor shares dynamics in fully fledged dynamic general equilibrium models in stochastic settings with endogenous labor supply. The resulting dynamics can then be compared with empirical impulse response analysis arising from structural VARs. In fact, the introduction of short-run CES technologies in macroeconomic models is facilitated by our method. The elasticity of substitution is certainly a key parameter to understand the effect of policies for job creation. Along more theoretical lines, the introduction of this framework in two-sector growth models, and the analysis of transitional dynamics in growth models with endogenous choice of techniques both appear as natural extensions for future work.

Acknowledgment

We would like to thank, without implicating, Daron Acemoglu, Olivier de La Grandville, Paul Levine, and John Peirson for helpful discussions and suggestions.

References

Acemoglu, D. (2001). Factor prices and technical change: From induced innovations to recent debates. In Aghion, P., Frydman, R., Stiglitz, J. & Woodford, M. (Eds.), *Knowledge, information and expectations in modern macroeconomics: In honor of Edmund Phelps* (pp. 464–491). New Jersey: Princeton University Press.

Acemoglu, D. (2002). Directed technical change. *Review of Economic Studies, 69*(4), 781–809.

Acemoglu, D. (2003). Labor- and capital-augmenting technical change. *Journal of European Economic Association, 1,* 1–37.

Acemoglu, D. (2007). Equilibrium bias of technology. *Econometrica, 175,* 1371–1410.

Cantore, C., León-Ledesma, M. A., McAdam, P., & Willman, A. (2010). *Shocking stuff: Technology, hours, and factor substitution.* European Central Bank Working Paper No. 1278.

Chirinko, R. S. (2008). Sigma: The long and short of it. *Journal of Macroeconomics, 30,* 671–686.

de La Grandville, O. (1989). In quest of the Slutsky diamond. *American Economic Review, 79,* 468–481.

de La Grandville, O. (2009). *Economic growth: A unified approach.* Cambridge: Cambridge University Press.

Drandakis, E., & Phelps, E. S. (1966). A model of induced invention, growth, and distribution. *Economic Journal, 76,* 823–840.

Growiec, J. (2008). A new class of production functions and an argument against purely labor-augmenting technical change. *International Journal of Economic Theory, 4*(4), 483–502.

Hicks, J. (1932). *The theory of wages.* London: Macmillan.

Houthakker, H. S. (1955). The Pareto distribution and the Cobb–Douglas production function in activity analysis. *Review of Economic Studies, 23*(1), 27–31.

Jones, C. I. (2005). The shape of production functions and the direction of technical change. *Quarterly Journal of Economics, 120*(2), 517–549.

Kennedy, C. M. (1964). Induced bias in innovation and the theory of distribution. *Economic Journal, 74,* 541–547.

Klump, R., & de La Grandville, O. (2000). Economic growth and the elasticity of substitution: Two theorems and some suggestions. *American Economic Review, 90*(1), 282–291.

Klump, R., McAdam, P., & Willman, A. (2007). Factor substitution and factor augmenting technical process. *Review of Economics and Statistics, 89*(1), 183–192.

Lagos, R. (2006). A model of TFP. *Review of Economic Studies, 73,* 983–1007.

León-Ledesma, M. A., McAdam, P., & Willman, A. (2010). Identifying the elasticity of substitution with biased technical change. *American Economic Review, 100*(4), 1330–1357.

León-Ledesma, M. A., & Satchi, M. (2011). *The choice of CES production techniques and balanced growth.* University of Kent Economics Discussion Paper 11/12.

Levhari, D. (1968). A note on Houthakker's aggregate production function in a multifirm industry. *Econometrica, 36,* 151–154.

Rosen, S. (1978). Substitution and the division of labor. *Economica, 45,* 235–250.

Ríos-Rull, J-V., & Santaeulàlia-Llopis, R. (2010). Redistributive shocks and productivity shocks. *Journal of Monetary Economics, 57*(8), 931–948.

Samuelson, P. A. (1965). A theory of induced innovations along Kennedy–Weisacker lines. *Review of Economics and Statistics, 47,* 343–356.

Uzawa, H. (1961). Neutral inventions and the stability of growth equilibrium. *Review of Economic Studies, 28*(2), 117.

Zeira, J. (1998). Workers, machines and economic growth. *Quarterly Journal of Economics, 113*(4), 1091–1118.

Zuleta, H. (2008). Factor saving innovations and factor income shares. *Review of Economic Dynamics, 11,* 836–851.

CHAPTER 17

Illegal Immigration, Factor Substitution, and Economic Growth

Theodore Palivos[a], Jianpo Xue[b] and Chong K. Yip[c]

[a]Department of Economics, University of Macedonia, GR-540 06 Thessaloniki, Greece
E-mail address: tpalivos@uom.gr
[b]China Financial Policy Research Center, School of Finance, Renmin University of China,
Beijing, P.R. China
E-mail address: jpxue@ruc.edu.cn
[c]Department of Economics, The Chinese University of Hong Kong, Shatin, N.T., Hong Kong
E-mail address: chongkeeyip@cuhk.edu.hk

Abstract

This chapter develops a neoclassical growth model of illegal immigration with imperfect substitutability between native and immigrant workers in production. We investigate analytically and/or numerically the effects of illegal immigration on the average capital stock in the host economy as well as on the wage, income, and asset holdings of native workers. Our findings indicate that the effects of an increase in illegal immigration on the average levels of capital, consumption, and income are positive. Moreover, by employing the normalization technique (e.g., Klump & de La Grandville, 2000), we examine the effects of a change in the elasticity of substitution between immigrant workers and natives for any given immigration ratio. These effects are in general ambiguous, because of the presence of two opposing forces: the efficiency and the distribution effects. Finally, we extend the model by separating the domestic workers into skilled and unskilled and study the impact on distribution of income and wealth. We show that illegal immigration may not necessarily make the distribution of wealth more unequal and unskilled labor worse off. This is because the end results depend on the elasticities of substitution between different types of labor. Thus, assuming erroneously that immigrants and natives are perfect substitutes could lead to results that are not only overestimated but also of the wrong sign.

Keywords: Illegal immigration, income distribution, elasticity of substitution

JEL classifications: O41, E23, F22

Frontiers of Economics and Globalization
Volume 11   ISSN: 1574-8715
DOI: 10.1108/S1574-8715(2011)0000011022

1. Introduction

Illegal immigration is one of the most controversial and divisive issues in the developed world. This is evident even from the number of organizations and citizen groups that campaign either for or against it on the web. Moreover, every political party in developed countries seems to have included this issue in its agenda and proposes ways for the solution of the "problem."

On the other hand, an increasing number of scientific articles analyzes the economic consequences of illegal immigration. For example, Hazari and Sgro (2003), Moy and Yip (2006), and Palivos (2009) analyze the effects of illegal immigration in a one-sector optimal growth model and show that an increase in the number of immigrants can potentially increase the welfare of the representative household. Palivos and Yip (2010) analyze the same issue within a neoclassical growth model with two groups of workers, skilled and unskilled, under the assumption that domestic and immigrant workers are perfect substitutes. They show that although illegal immigration is a boon for the host country as a whole, there can be distributional effects. Liu (2010) concentrates on the welfare effects of illegal immigration within a dynamic general equilibrium model with search frictions. His basic model, where there is one type of domestic labor and immigrants and natives are imperfect substitutes, is calibrated to the US economy. He finds a U-shaped relationship between the population share of illegal immigrants and consumption per domestic resident in the long run. In an extended version of the model, where there are two types of domestic labor, namely skilled and unskilled, and illegal immigrants belong to the unskilled group, he finds distributional effects similar to those in Palivos and Yip (2010).

One of the crucial factors in the analysis of the effects of immigration is the degree of substitutability between natives and immigrants.[1] Illegal immigrants have usually acquired low levels of education. Moreover, they tend to have low language skills (see Peri & Sparber, 2009). Hence, they constitute an imperfect substitute for native workers of similar observable characteristics, for example, education level, and experience. In fact, the existing empirical literature has questioned the assumption of perfect substitutability between natives and immigrant workers (see, e.g., the discussion in Ottaviano & Peri, 2011), which is often employed in theoretical investigations. For example, when the substitutability between natives and immigrants is constrained to be the same across education and experience groups, Ottaviano and Peri (2011) estimate the elasticity of substitution to be about 20. When the substitutability is allowed to vary across education and experience groups, they find the elasticity of substitution between natives and immigrants to be 12.5 among low educated workers and 6.6 among young workers.

---

[1] This point is particularly emphasized in Ottaviano and Peri (2011), who, based on their estimates (see below), find that in the long run immigration has a small positive effect on US average native wages of about 0.6%.

In this article we construct a neoclassical growth model of illegal immigration, which allows explicitly for imperfect substitutability between native and immigrant workers. Based on such a model, we investigate analytically and/or numerically the effects of illegal immigration on the average capital stock in the host economy as well as on the wage, income, and assets holdings of native workers. Moreover, as time elapses, immigrant workers acquire language skills, adjust to the new culture and become assimilated into the new society. Thus, it is reasonable to assume that the elasticity of substitution between immigrant and domestic labor increases over time. Hence, we also analyze the effects of a change in the elasticity of substitution between immigrant workers and natives for any given immigration ratio. We do this by employing the normalization technique introduced by de La Grandville (1989) and advanced by Klump and de La Grandville (2000), Klump and Preissler (2000), and Papageorgiou and Saam (2008). We also analyze the impact of a change in the elasticity of substitution between skilled and unskilled labor.

The remainder of the article is organized as follows. Section 2 analyzes the effects of changes in the immigration ratio and in the elasticity of substitution between natives and immigrants in a basic model, where there is only one type of domestic labor. Section 3 examines similar issues in a model with two types of domestic labor. Section 4 summarizes the results and draws conclusions.

2. A model of illegal immigration with one type of domestic labor

The primary purpose of our chapter is to analyze the effects of illegal immigration on the distribution of income and wealth in the host economy, where natives and migrants are imperfect substitutes in production. Of course, the analysis of issues pertaining to the distribution of income presupposes the presence of heterogeneous agents. Nevertheless, to understand some of the mechanisms at work and to establish notation, it is useful to start with an economy that is inhabited by just one type of labor; a more elaborate version of this model is considered in the next section.

2.1. The model

Consider a Solow-type economy in which the production process is described by the function

$$Y = \Theta K^\alpha N^{1-\alpha}, \tag{1}$$

where Y denotes total output, K denotes aggregate capital, and N is an aggregate input of domestic (L) and immigrant labor (M).[2] Specifically,

---

[2] Since the elasticity of substitution between capital and aggregate labor is one, the model analyzed here cannot result in unbounded growth (see Palivos & Karagiannis, 2010; Solow, 1956).

$$N = B[\mu M^\beta + (1 - \mu)L^\beta]^{1/\beta}, \quad \beta \leq 1. \tag{2}$$

The elasticity of substitution between domestic and immigrant labor, denoted by σ, is defined as

$$\sigma = \frac{\partial(M/L)}{\partial(\text{MPM}/\text{MPL})} \frac{\text{MPM}/\text{MPL}}{M/L} = \frac{1}{1-\beta}, \tag{3}$$

where, throughout the chapter, MPX denotes the marginal product of factor X. Obviously, as β approaches one, the elasticity of substitution σ approaches infinity and L and M become perfect substitutes in production.

Substituting Equation (2) into Equation (1) yields the following two-level production function:

$$F(K, M, L) = AK^\alpha[\mu M^\beta + (1 - \mu)L^\beta]^{(1-\alpha)/\beta}, \tag{4}$$

which in intensive form can be written as

$$f(k, m) = F/L = Ak^\alpha[\mu m^\beta + (1 - \mu)]^{(1-\alpha)/\beta}, \tag{5}$$

where $A \equiv \Theta B^{1-\alpha}$, $k = K/L$ is capital per domestic worker and $m = M/L$ is the immigration ratio (number of immigrants per domestic citizen). For simplicity, we abstract from population growth.

All immigration $M \geq 0$ is assumed to be illegal (undocumented). Moreover, the following two assumptions are intended to characterize illegal immigration. First, there is a cost associated with the employment of an undocumented immigrant. If caught employing an illegal immigrant, an employer must pay a fine to the government. We denote the expected value of such a fine by γ (= the probability of being caught employing an illegal immigrant times the fine). Second, illegal immigrants do not save in terms of assets located in the host country. Instead, they send all their savings abroad.

This is a private ownership economy, where all resources (besides foreign labor of course) and firms are owned by households. Obviously, the constant returns to scale (CRS) property of the production function allows us to assume that there is only one firm, whose shares are held by domestic consumers. We also assume that all markets are competitive.

The income (y) of each domestic citizen consists of her capital income (rk), where r is the real interest rate, her labor income (w_L), and government transfers (τ).[3] Thus,

$$y = rk + w_L + \tau. \tag{6}$$

---

[3] Note that in general $y \neq Y/L$; the former denotes the income of each domestic citizen, while the latter is total output produced per domestic citizen. In other words, Y includes immigrant's income. The two variables are equal to each other only when there is no immigration ($M = 0$).

Furthermore, each domestic citizen saves a constant fraction $s \in (0,1)$ of her income (y).[4] Thus, savings per domestic citizen are sy.

The representative firm, which is assumed to be risk neutral, maximizes its expected profit

$$\Pi = F(K, L, M) - rK - w_L L - w_m M - \gamma M - \delta K, \tag{7}$$

where w_m is the wage paid to illegal immigrants and δ is the depreciation rate. The only source of uncertainty is with regard to the probability of being caught employing an illegal immigrant (recall that γ denotes the expected value of the fine). The first-order necessary conditions with respect to the three inputs are

$$F_K = r + \delta, \quad F_L = w_L, \quad F_M = w_m + \gamma, \tag{8}$$

where a subscript attached to a function symbol denotes the partial derivative with respect to that argument, for example, $F_K = \partial F/\partial K$. Differentiating Equation (5), we have

$$\alpha \frac{f}{k} = r + \delta, \quad (1 - \alpha - \pi)\frac{f}{m} = w_m + \gamma, \quad \pi f = w_L, \tag{9}$$

where π denotes the *income* share of domestic labor ($= w_L \times L/Y$).

The government raises revenue (R) by imposing fines on firms that employ undocumented immigrants. As mentioned above, the expected value of the fine, which equals the probability that the firm is caught employing an illegal immigrant times the value of the fine, is γ. Hence, the government raises total revenue equal to

$$R = \gamma M.$$

We assume that this revenue is distributed back to the households in a lump-sum manner so that, at the end of each period, the government budget is balanced.

As we are interested in studying the effects of immigration when the substitutability of labor varies, we need to normalize the constant elasticity of substitution (CES) production function (5).[5] To this end, we define the baseline point by choosing the marginal rate of substitution $\bar{\omega}$ (or, equivalently, the ratio of MPM to MPL), the level of income per capita $\bar{f}$, the capital–labor ratio $\bar{k}$, and the immigration ratio $\bar{m}$ to solve for:[6]

---

[4] For an analysis of the conditions that make the saving rate constant and render the Solow model isomorphic to the Ramsey model, see, among others, Litina and Palivos (2010).

[5] The CES function, when written in the traditional way, is inconsistent in units. This inconsistency disappears if one carefully identifies the two constants of integration involved in the original (Arrow, Chenery, Minhas, & Solow, 1961) derivation of the CES function, as implied from a particular concave power function between the wage rate and income per person (see de La Grandville, 2009). In that sense, normalization is necessary before proceeding to our analysis.

[6] Following common practice in the literature, we use the "over-bar" notation to denote normalized variables.

$$A(\beta) = \frac{\bar{f}}{\bar{k}^{\alpha}} \left[\frac{1 + \bar{m}^{1-\beta}\bar{\omega}}{1 + \bar{m}\bar{\omega}} \right]^{(1-\alpha)/\beta},$$

and

$$\mu(\beta) = \frac{\bar{m}^{1-\beta}\bar{\omega}}{1 + \bar{m}^{1-\beta}\bar{\omega}}.$$

After normalization, we have

$$f(k, m; \sigma) = A(\sigma)k^{\alpha}[\mu(\sigma)m^{\beta} + (1 - \mu(\sigma))]^{(1-\alpha)/\beta}. \tag{10}$$

Note that the labor share is independent of k:

$$\pi(\sigma, m) = \frac{\text{MPL} \times L}{F} = \frac{1 - \alpha}{1 + \bar{m}^{1-\beta}\bar{\omega}m^{\beta}} = \frac{(1 - \alpha)(1 - \mu)}{\mu m^{\beta} + 1 - \mu}, \tag{11}$$

and hence

$$\bar{\pi} = \frac{1 - \alpha}{1 + \bar{m}\bar{\omega}}.$$

Differentiating Equation (11), we have

$$\frac{\partial\pi}{\partial m} = -\frac{(1 - \alpha)(1 - \mu)\beta\mu m^{\beta-1}}{(\mu m^{\beta} + 1 - \mu)^2} < 0,$$

$$\frac{\partial\pi}{\partial\sigma} = \frac{\pi}{\sigma^2}\frac{1 - \alpha - \pi}{1 - \alpha}\ln\frac{\bar{m}}{m} \lessgtr 0 \quad \text{iff} \quad m \gtrless \bar{m}. \tag{12}$$

An increase in immigration reduces the income share of domestic workers. If we start the analysis from an initially no-migrant situation so that the normalized migrant-population ratio is taken to be zero, that is, $\bar{m} = 0$, then we always have $m > \bar{m}$.[7] Thus, we assume that $\partial\pi/\partial\sigma < 0$ in the remainder of the analysis, that is, an improvement in the substitutability between the two labor inputs raises the income share of the migrants starting from a lower migrant ratio. Next, assuming $m > \bar{m}$ and manipulating the production technology Equation (10) yields[8]

$$\frac{\partial f}{\partial\sigma} = -\frac{1 - \alpha}{\beta^2}\frac{f}{\sigma^2}\left[\frac{\pi}{1 - \alpha}\ln\left(\frac{\bar{\pi}}{\pi}\right) + \frac{1 - \alpha - \pi}{1 - \alpha}\ln\left(\frac{1 - \alpha - \bar{\pi}}{1 - \alpha - \pi}\right)\right] > 0. \tag{13}$$

This is a standard result in the literature. An improvement in the substitutability between the two labor inputs raises the aggregate labor input and leads to more output.

---

[7] Strictly speaking, in our calibrated exercises below, technically we cannot set $\bar{m} = 0$ as this would cause $\partial\pi/\partial\sigma$ to explode.

[8] Henceforth, whenever it does not cause any confusion and in order to simplify the notation, we simply denote with f the normalized CES function $f(k, m; \sigma)$ without specifying its arguments.

Finally, we examine the effect of immigration on wages. From Equation (9), we get

$$\frac{\partial w_m}{\partial m} = f_{mm} = -\frac{f}{m^2}\frac{1-\alpha-\pi}{(1-\alpha)\pi}[\alpha(1-\alpha-\pi)+(1-\beta)\pi] < 0,$$

$$\frac{\partial w_L}{\partial m} = f\frac{\partial \pi}{\partial m} + \pi f_m = (1-\alpha-\beta)\frac{\pi f}{m}\frac{\mu m^{\beta}}{\mu m^{\beta}+1-\mu}.$$

By diminishing returns, the wage of illegal migrants falls when more migrants come into the country; but the effect on the wage of native workers is ambiguous. This is because, on the one hand, diminishing factor returns due to the substitutability between workers raises the domestic wage when migrants come in. On the other hand, the increase in illegal migrants also reduces the native wage income share. In the special case where migrants and natives are perfect substitutes, both wages fall with illegal immigration since $w_L = w_m + \gamma$.

Next, we study the effect of a change in the substitutability between native and migrant workers on factor returns. According to Equation (13), an increase in σ raises the returns to all factors due to an improvement in production efficiency. We call this the *efficiency effect* of factor substitution. With the Cobb–Douglas specification of Equation (1), we know that the capital income share in output is constant and equals to α. Although the total share of income to all labor inputs $(L+M)$ remains unchanged, Equation (12) informs us that there is a distribution effect on individual labor returns when σ changes. In particular, an increase in σ raises (lowers) the share of labor income of illegal migrants (native workers). We call this the *distribution effect* of factor substitution. As a result, we can conclude that the returns to illegal migrants must go up when natives and migrants are more substitutable in production; the effect on the wage of domestic workers, however, is ambiguous:

$$\frac{\partial w_m}{\partial \sigma} = \frac{1-\alpha-\pi}{m}\frac{\partial f}{\partial \sigma} - \frac{f}{m}\frac{\partial \pi}{\partial \sigma} > 0,$$

$$\frac{\partial w_L}{\partial \sigma} = \pi\frac{\partial f}{\partial \sigma} + f\frac{\partial \pi}{\partial \sigma}.$$

2.2. Steady-state equilibrium

A balanced government budget requires that revenue equals transfers, which implies that the transfer received by each household is

$$\tau = \frac{R}{L} = \gamma \frac{M}{L} = \gamma m. \tag{14}$$

Furthermore, in equilibrium savings must equal investment. Measuring both variables per domestic citizen, we have

$$\dot{k} = s[f(k, m; \sigma) - \delta k - w_m m] - \delta k$$
$$= s[(\alpha + \pi)f(k, m; \sigma) - \delta k + \gamma m] - \delta k. \tag{15}$$

In steady state, we have $\dot{k} = 0$ so that

$$sy(k^*, m; \sigma) = \delta k^*, \tag{16}$$

where $y(k, m; \sigma) \equiv [(\alpha + \pi)f(k, m; \sigma) - \delta k + \gamma m]$. It is straightforward to show that $y(k, m; \sigma)$ is strictly concave in k, $y(0, m; \sigma) \geq 0$, $\lim_{k \to 0} \partial y/\partial k > \delta/s$ and $\lim_{k \to \infty} \partial y/\partial k < \delta/s$. To ensure existence, uniqueness and stability of a positive steady-state level of capital stock, we further assume that $y(k, m; \sigma)$ is strictly increasing in k so that $(\alpha + \pi)f_k - \delta > 0$.

2.3. Changes in wealth, income, and consumption

Totally differentiating Equation (16) yields

$$\frac{dk^*}{dm} = \frac{\partial y^*/\partial m}{(\delta/s) - (\partial y^*/\partial k^*)} > 0, \tag{17}$$

since

$$\frac{\partial y}{\partial m} = \gamma - m\frac{\partial w_m}{\partial m} = [(\alpha + \pi)(1 - \alpha) - \beta\pi]\frac{1 - \alpha - \pi}{1 - \alpha}\frac{f}{m} > 0 \tag{18}$$

and $(\delta/s) > \partial y^*/\partial k^* = (\alpha + \pi)f_k - \delta$ (from the conditions for existence, uniqueness, and stability). Since all steady-state variables remain in fixed proportion, that is, $y^* = (\delta/s)k^*$, $c^* = [(1-s)\delta/s]k^*$, the effects of immigration on income and consumption, y^* and c^*, are proportional to that on capital:

$$\frac{dy^*}{dm} = \frac{\delta}{s}\frac{dk^*}{dm} > 0, \quad \frac{dc^*}{dm} = \frac{(1-s)\delta}{s}\frac{dk^*}{dm} > 0.$$

Thus, we conclude:

PROPOSITION 1. *An increase in illegal immigration raises the steady-state per capita levels of capital, income, and consumption.*

This occurs for two reasons. First, an increase in immigration generates more revenue through the exploitation of new immigrants (this is captured by the term γ in $\partial y^*/\partial m$; see Equation (17)). Second, the increase in immigration lowers the domestic wage and, thus, the wage paid to the existing immigrants (this is captured by the term $-m(\partial w_m/\partial m) = mf_{mm} > 0$ in $\partial y^*/\partial m$). If $\gamma = 0$, then there is no exploitation and the first effect disappears. In addition, if initially there is no immigration (i.e., if we are examining an incremental change in immigration starting from $m = 0$), then the second effect disappears as well. These two special cases not withstanding, we can conclude that, in a framework where there is only one type of labor, illegal immigration is, in the long run, beneficial to domestic citizens, because it increases their steady-state level of consumption.

Regarding an increase in the substitutability between natives and migrants in production (σ), the effects on the steady-state levels of per capita capital and income are ambiguous:

$$\frac{dk^*}{d\sigma} = \frac{\partial y/\partial \sigma}{(\delta/s) - (\partial y/\partial k)} \Rightarrow sign\left(\frac{dk^*}{d\sigma}\right) = sign\left(\frac{\partial y}{\partial \sigma}\right).$$

The ambiguity is due to the presence of two opposing effects at work, the distribution versus the efficiency effect:

$$\frac{\partial y}{\partial \sigma} = (\pi + \alpha)\frac{\partial f}{\partial \sigma} + f\frac{\partial \pi}{\partial \sigma}. \tag{19}$$

On the one hand, according to the efficiency effect, the increased substitutability of workers expands the aggregate labor input so that more income is generated. On the other hand, the distribution effect reduces (raises) the share that goes to native workers (immigrants) and hence reduces y. If the efficiency effect dominates, then we have $dk^*/d\sigma > 0$ so that an increase in the substitutability between the two types of workers raises the steady-state levels of per capita capital and income. To understand the intuition behind the ambiguity, we note that the efficiency effect raises income and hence savings that can be channeled into capital accumulation. Nevertheless, the fact that migrants do not save (or more precisely their savings are invested abroad) generates a leakage in income. If the distribution effect dominates so that the income share of migrants increases enough, then it is possible to have a decline in aggregate savings and hence in capital accumulation. Of course, if migrants save, then we have $y(k, m; \sigma) \equiv f(k, m; \sigma) - \delta k$ so that

$$\frac{\partial y}{\partial \sigma} = \frac{\partial f}{\partial \sigma} > 0 \Rightarrow \frac{dk^*}{d\sigma} > 0.$$

We summarize our findings regarding the effects of factor substitution in the following proposition:

PROPOSITION 2. *If the efficiency effect dominates (is dominated by) the distribution effect of factor substitution, then an increase in the substitutability between immigrants and domestic workers raises (lowers) the steady-state levels of per capita capital, income, and consumption.*

We close this subsection by providing a numerical example regarding the steady-state effects. Based on Ottaviano and Peri (2011), we specify σ

to vary from 0.5 to 30. Moreover, based on calculations found in Palivos and Yip (2010), we set $\gamma = 0.25$. The value of $s = 0.15$ is based on Elwell (2010). The other parameter values are all common in the literature.

Baseline values for normalization	
$\bar{y} = 10$	$\bar{k} = 10$
$\bar{\pi} = 0.68$	$\bar{m} = 0.04$
Parameters for the benchmark model	
$\gamma = 0.25$	$\delta = 0.04$
$s = 0.15$	$\alpha = 0.3$
$m = 0.05, 0.1,$ and 0.15	$\sigma \in (0.5, 30)$

We report the steady-state values of the wage rates, capital, and income in Figure 1. In the upper panels, we see that, for any given σ, an increase in m always raises k^* and y^*. But given m, an increase in σ lowers both k^* and y^*. This implies that the distribution effect of factor substitution dominates the efficiency effect. The effects on the wage rates are shown in the lower panels of Figure 1. We see that the effects on w_m confirm our comparative static findings: w_m is increasing in σ, but decreasing in m. Also, the effect of σ on w_L is negative so that again the distribution effect dominates the efficiency effect of factor substitution. Finally, the effect of m on w_L depends on the size of the elasticity of substitution, as predicted by our comparative statics. If σ is large enough so that the two labor inputs are

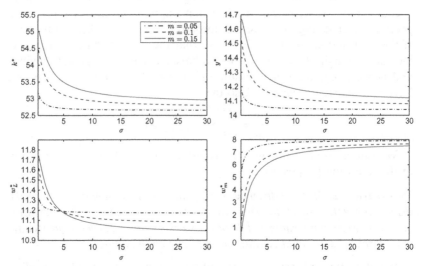

Fig. 1. *The effects of σ and m on the steady-state k^*, y^*, w_L^*, and w_m^*.*

good gross substitutes, then w_L is decreasing in m. Interestingly, however, if natives and immigrants are not very substitutable in production (i.e., σ is small enough), then w_L can increase with m.

2.4. Transitional dynamics

Next, we analyze the response of capital to an increase in m during the transition to the new steady-state equilibrium. The dynamic behavior of k is described by Equation (15). Given our assumptions on the function $y(k, m; \sigma)$, we have

$$\frac{\partial \dot{k}}{\partial k} = s\frac{\partial y}{\partial k} - \delta = s[(\alpha + \pi)f_k - \delta] - \delta,$$

$$\frac{\partial^2 \dot{k}}{\partial k^2} = s\frac{\partial^2 y}{\partial k^2} = s(\alpha + \pi)f_{kk} < 0.$$

The curve $\dot{k}(k, m; \sigma)$ is shown in Figure 2. According to Equation (18), an increase in m shifts up the $\dot{k}$ curve so that we have $dk^*/dm > 0$. Moreover,

$$\ddot{k} = \frac{d\dot{k}}{dt} = \frac{\partial \dot{k}}{\partial k}\frac{dk}{dt} = \left(s\frac{\partial y}{\partial k} - \delta\right)\dot{k} < 0,$$

since $s(\partial y/\partial k) - \delta < 0$ in the neighborhood of k^* and $\dot{k} > 0$ for $k < k^*$. Thus, we can deduce the dynamic adjustment of k (see Figure 3). The paths of consumption and income are similar. We conclude that in a society in

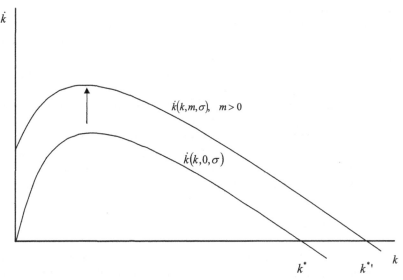

Fig. 2.   The effect of immigration on average capital accumulation.

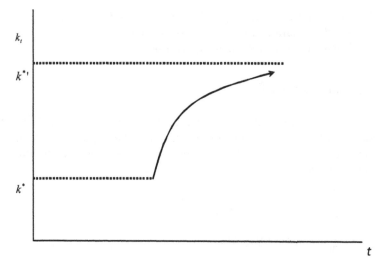

Fig. 3.   Capital adjustment after an increase in immigration.

which domestic and foreign labor are imperfect substitutes, illegal immigration is unambiguously beneficial to domestic citizens because it raises their consumption level both in the steady state and throughout the entire transition.

The effects of a change in σ are ambiguous due to the presence of the opposing efficiency and distribution effects. According to Equation (19) and in terms of Figure 2, the $\dot{k}$ locus can shift either up or down when σ changes so that k^* can go in either direction. Based on our numerical example above, it is likely that the distribution effect dominates the efficiency effect. As a result, for a given level of illegal immigration, an increase in the substitutability between natives and migrants is likely to reduce capital accumulation, income, and consumption in transition.

Figure 4 provides a numerical example for the effects during the transition of a change in m and σ on capital accumulation, using the same parameter values specified above. The upward-sloping path confirms the monotonic convergence of k over time. From the upper panel, illegal immigration raises the capital stock (and hence income and consumption) throughout the entire transition. On the contrary, an increase in the substitutability of workers lowers the capital stock (and hence income and consumption) over time in the transition toward the new steady state.

3. The general framework

In the general framework the *aggregate* labor input H consists of two types of workers, unskilled labor N and (domestic) skilled labor S. Immigrants, who are all illegal, are unskilled. The input H is another CES aggregate:

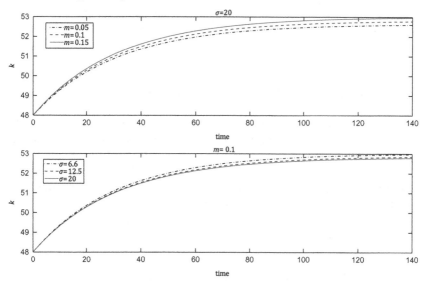

Fig. 4.   Transitional dynamics as σ or m change.

$$H = \Phi[\theta N^{\eta} + (1 - \theta)S^{\eta}]^{1/\eta}, \quad \eta \leq 1. \tag{20}$$

where N is given by Equation (2). Final output Y is then produced with two aggregate inputs, capital K and labor H, using a Cobb–Douglas technology:

$$Y = \Theta K^{\alpha} H^{1-\alpha}. \tag{21}$$

Substituting Equations (2) and (20) into Equation (21) yields the following aggregate production function:

$$F(K, M, L, S) = AK^{\alpha}\left\{\theta B^{\eta}[\mu M^{\beta} + (1 - \mu)L^{\beta}]^{\eta/\beta} + (1 - \theta)S^{\eta}\right\}^{(1-\alpha)/\eta},$$

where $A \equiv \Theta \Phi^{1-\alpha}$. Moreover, the aggregate production function can be written in intensive form as

$$y = f(k, m, l) = Ak^{\alpha}\left\{\theta B^{\eta}[\mu m^{\beta} + (1 - \mu)l^{\beta}]^{\eta/\beta} + (1 - \theta)(1 - l)^{\eta}\right\}^{(1-\alpha)/\eta},$$

where the lowercase variables k, m, and l are equal to the corresponding aggregate variable K, M, and L divided by the number of domestic citizens $L+S$. In particular, k and m denote the average capital stock and the immigration ratio, respectively.

Following the normalization concepts of Klump and de La Grandville (2000), as these were further elaborated by Papageorgiou and Saam (2008) for a two-level nested CES, we choose the baseline values in per capita term of $\bar{y}$, $\bar{k}$, $\bar{n}$, $\bar{h}$, $\bar{l}$, $\bar{m}$, $\bar{\pi}_M$, and $\bar{\pi}_N$, and calculate the normalized parameters of the CES production function (see Equations (A.3)–(A.6) in the Appendix).

3.1. The comparative static results of factor substitution

In this subsection we analyze the impact of a change in η and β on the nested inputs, aggregate output, factor shares and wages. First, define the nested inputs, namely, $n = N/(S+L)$ and $h = H/(S+L)$, and the *factor share*, $\hat{\pi}_i$ of factor i, as the ratio of the factor's value contribution (or its marginal value product) to its related nested quantity. For example, the factor share of M in N can be written as

$$\hat{\pi}_M = \frac{(\partial N/\partial M) \times M}{N} = \frac{\bar{\pi}_M (m/\bar{m})^\beta}{\bar{\pi}_M (m/\bar{m})^\beta + 1 - \bar{\pi}_M}.$$

Likewise, for the shares of L, N, and S, we have

$$\hat{\pi}_L = \frac{\partial N}{\partial L}\frac{L}{N} = 1 - \hat{\pi}_M,$$

$$\hat{\pi}_N = \frac{\partial H}{\partial N}\frac{N}{H} = \frac{\bar{\pi}_N (n/\bar{n})^\eta}{\bar{\pi}_N (n/\bar{n})^\eta + 1 - \bar{\pi}_N},$$

$$\hat{\pi}_S = \frac{\partial H}{\partial N}\frac{S}{H} = 1 - \hat{\pi}_N,$$

since both N and H exhibit CRS.

Next, we analyze the impact on the nested inputs n and h:

$$\frac{\partial n}{\partial \beta} = -\frac{n(1-\beta)^2}{\beta^2} \left[\hat{\pi}_M \ln \frac{\bar{\pi}_M}{\hat{\pi}_M} + (1 - \hat{\pi}_M) \ln \frac{1 - \bar{\pi}_M}{1 - \hat{\pi}_M} \right] > 0,$$

$$\frac{\partial h}{\partial \eta} = -\frac{h(1-\eta)^2}{\eta^2} \left[\hat{\pi}_N \ln \frac{\bar{\pi}_N}{\hat{\pi}_N} + (1 - \hat{\pi}_N) \ln \frac{1 - \bar{\pi}_N}{1 - \hat{\pi}_N} \right] > 0.$$

These results capture the standard efficiency effect of factor substitution, namely, better factor substitution is equivalent to an increase in factor inputs. This then yields a positive impact on the aggregate output per domestic citizen, $Y/(S+L)$:

$$\frac{\partial y}{\partial \eta} = \frac{\partial y}{\partial h}\frac{\partial h}{\partial \eta} > 0,$$

$$\frac{\partial y}{\partial \beta} = \frac{\partial y}{\partial h}\frac{\partial h}{\partial n}\frac{\partial n}{\partial \beta} > 0,$$

since $\partial y/\partial h > 0$ and $\partial h/\partial n > 0$.

Consider next the impact of η and β on factor shares. Simple differentiation yields

$$\frac{\partial \hat{\pi}_M}{\partial \beta} = -\frac{\partial \hat{\pi}_L}{\partial \beta} = (1 - \hat{\pi}_M)\hat{\pi}_M \ln \frac{m}{\bar{m}} > 0 \quad \text{iff} \quad m > \bar{m},$$

$$\frac{\partial \hat{\pi}_N}{\partial \eta} = -\frac{\partial \hat{\pi}_S}{\partial \eta} = (1 - \hat{\pi}_N)\hat{\pi}_N \ln \left[\frac{n/\bar{n}}{(1-l)/(1-\bar{l})} \right] \gtrless 0 \quad \text{iff} \quad \frac{n}{1-l} \gtrless \frac{\bar{n}}{1-\bar{l}}.$$

The effect of factor substitution on the factor shares depends on the relative abundance of the relevant factor. For instance, if migrants are relatively abundant (i.e., $m > \bar{m}$), then an improvement in factor substitution between native and immigrant unskilled labor leads to an increase in the employment of M. As a result, its factor share increases so that $\partial \hat{\pi}_M / \partial \beta > 0$. This is the distribution effect emphasized in Xue and Yip (2011). Next, there is no effect of η on $\hat{\pi}_M$ as the nesting structure does not allow for reversible impact of the upper-level substitutability on the lower-level factor shares, that is

$$\frac{\partial \hat{\pi}_M}{\partial \eta} = 0.$$

Finally, the effect of β on $\hat{\pi}_N$ is given by

$$\frac{\partial \hat{\pi}_N}{\partial \beta} = \frac{\partial \hat{\pi}_N}{\partial n}\frac{\partial n}{\partial \beta} = \frac{\eta}{n}\hat{\pi}_N(1 - \hat{\pi}_N)\frac{\partial n}{\partial \beta} \gtrless 0 \quad \text{iff} \quad \eta \gtrless 0.$$

The effect of factor substitution on the upper-level factor share depends on the substitutability of the factors in the upper nesting level. For instance, the effect of β on $\hat{\pi}_N$ depends on whether N and S are gross substitutes or gross complements in the formation of H (i.e., $\eta \gtrless 0$). If $\eta > 0$, then skilled and unskilled labor are gross substitutes in production. The efficiency effect of factor substitution expands the unskilled labor supply so that their share in aggregate labor increases.

Consider next the impact of η and β on the wage rates. We denote the marginal return of factor i by F_i. Moreover, profit maximization of the firm yields

$$F_K = r + \delta, F_M = w_m + \gamma, F_L = w_L, F_S = w_S,$$

where w_S is the real wage rate of skilled labor. Hence

$$w_S = F_S = \frac{\partial Y}{\partial H}\frac{\partial H}{\partial S} = (1 - \alpha)\hat{\pi}_S \frac{y}{1-l},$$

$$w_L = F_L = \frac{\partial Y}{\partial H}\frac{\partial H}{\partial N}\frac{\partial N}{\partial L} = (1 - \alpha)\hat{\pi}_N\hat{\pi}_L \frac{y}{l},$$

$$w_m = F_M - \gamma = \frac{\partial Y}{\partial H}\frac{\partial H}{\partial N}\frac{\partial N}{\partial M} - \gamma = (1 - \alpha)\hat{\pi}_N\hat{\pi}_M \frac{y}{m} - \gamma$$

$$r = F_K - \delta = \frac{\partial Y}{\partial K} - \delta = \alpha \frac{y}{k} - \delta.$$

If we define the *income* share of skilled labor in total output as π_S, we have

$$\pi_S = \frac{F_S S}{Y} = (1 - \alpha)\hat{\pi}_S.$$

Of course, for our results to have some meaning, the following restrictions on the parameter values must hold.

ASSUMPTION 1. The wage of a skilled worker should be higher than the wage of an unskilled, that is,

$$w_L < w_S \Rightarrow (1 + \hat{\pi}_L)\hat{\pi}_N < 1.$$

ASSUMPTION 2. The wage rate of an immigrant must be positive:

$$w_m > 0, \quad \text{or} \quad \gamma < (1 - \alpha)\hat{\pi}_N \hat{\pi}_M y / m.$$

Next, we define the wage premium $\tilde{w} \equiv w_S / w_L$ and study the impact of factor substitution on it. We note that

$$\tilde{w} \equiv \frac{w_S}{w_L} = \frac{1 - \hat{\pi}_N}{\hat{\pi}_N \hat{\pi}_L} \frac{l}{1 - l}.$$

Hence, the effects on the wage premium must work through the factor shares $\hat{\pi}_N$ and $\hat{\pi}_L(= 1 - \hat{\pi}_M)$. The wage premium increases with the relative factor share of migrants ($\hat{\pi}_M$) but decreases with the relative factor share of unskilled labor ($\hat{\pi}_N$). This is because a higher $\hat{\pi}_M$ leads to a lower wage for domestic workers, while a higher $\hat{\pi}_N$ yields both a lower w_S and a higher w_L. Formally, the effects of factor substitution on the wage premium are

$$\frac{\partial \tilde{w}}{\partial \beta} = \frac{l}{1 - l} \frac{1 - \hat{\pi}_N}{\hat{\pi}_N \hat{\pi}_L} \left(\hat{\pi}_M \ln \frac{m}{\overline{m}} - \frac{\eta}{n} \frac{\partial n}{\partial \beta} \right),$$

$$\frac{\partial \tilde{w}}{\partial \eta} = - \frac{l}{1 - l} \frac{(1 - \hat{\pi}_N)\hat{\pi}_L \hat{\pi}_N}{(\hat{\pi}_N \hat{\pi}_L)^2} \ln \left[\frac{n/\overline{n}}{(1 - l)/(1 - \overline{l})} \right] \gtreqless 0 \quad \text{iff} \quad \frac{n}{1 - l} \lessgtr \frac{\overline{n}}{1 - \overline{l}}$$

If $n/(1 - l) > \overline{n}/(1 - \overline{l})$, the wage premium decreases as η increases. Better factor substitution between skilled and unskilled labor results in a higher factor share of unskilled workers if they are relatively abundant. This lowers their relative wage and so the wage premium rises. If migrants are relative abundant ($m > \overline{m}$), then an increase in β raises the factor share of migrants ($\hat{\pi}_M$) so that real wage for domestic workers (w_L) falls. If unskilled labor is complementary to skilled labor in production ($\eta < 0$), this also leads to an increase of the relative factor of skilled workers ($\hat{\pi}_S$) and hence their real wage (w_S). Thus, the wage premium increases as β rises when $m > \overline{m}$ and $\eta < 0$. Thus, we have.

PROPOSITION 3. *If unskilled labor is relatively abundant, then better substitution between skilled and unskilled labor (higher η) results in a higher wage premium. If migrants are relative abundant and unskilled labor is complementary to skilled labor in production, then the wage premium increases as the substitutability between migrants and domestic unskilled workers goes up (higher β).*

3.2. Steady-state analysis

The total income of each domestic group i is

$$Y_i = rK_i + w_i L_i + T_i, \quad i = L, S,$$

where K_i is the total capital stock owned by group i and T_i denotes the total government transfers to the group. The asset accumulation function for each domestic citizen of type i is given by the net savings

$$\dot{k}_i = sy_i - \delta k_i,$$

where $y_i = rk_i + w_i + \gamma m$ and $k_i = K_i/i$, $y_i = Y_i/i$ are the per capita capital and output owned by members of group i, respectively. Using the CRS property of F, we can write

$$Y/(S+L) = F(k, l, 1-l, m)$$
$$= F_k k + F_L l + F_M m + F_H(1-l),$$

where $k = K/(S+L) = lk_L + (1-l)k_S$.

The equation that describes the accumulation of the (weighted) average capital stock, k, is given by

$$\dot{k} = sy(k, m) - \delta k,$$

where

$$y(k, m) = f(k, l, m) - mw_M - \delta k.$$

In steady state $\dot{k} = \dot{k}_i = 0$ and hence we have

$$sy(k^*, m) = \delta k^*, \tag{22}$$

or,

$$[1 - (1 - \alpha)\hat{\pi}_N \hat{\pi}_M] f(k^*, l, m) + \gamma m - \frac{(1+s)\delta}{s} k^* = 0.$$

Consider next the comparative statics results of a change on the immigration ratio m on the average level of the steady-state capital stock. Differentiating Equation (22) yields

$$\frac{dk^*}{dm} = \frac{\partial y^*/\partial m}{(\delta/s) - (\partial y^*/\partial k^*)} > 0,$$

because

$$\frac{\partial y^*}{\partial m} = F_M - w_M - mF_{MM} = \gamma - mF_{MM} > 0,$$

$$\frac{\partial y^*}{\partial k^*} = F_K - mF_{MK} - \delta < \frac{\delta}{s}.$$

The effect of m on the steady-state k^* remains qualitatively the same as in the case of perfect substitutes (see Palivos & Yip, 2010).[9] Moreover, an increase in m will also raise the average steady-state levels of income and consumption.

On the other hand, the impact of a change in β or η on the steady state k^* is ambiguous since

$$\frac{dk^*}{d\beta} = \frac{\partial y^*/\partial \beta}{(\delta/s) - (\partial y^*/\partial k^*)},$$

where

$$\frac{\partial y^*}{\partial \beta} = [1 - (1 - \alpha)\hat{\pi}_N\hat{\pi}_M]\frac{\partial f}{\partial \beta} - f(1 - \alpha)\left(\hat{\pi}_N\frac{\partial \hat{\pi}_M}{\partial \beta} + \hat{\pi}_M\frac{\partial \hat{\pi}_N}{\partial \beta}\right). \qquad (23)$$

Likewise, for the impact of η, we have

$$\frac{dk^*}{d\eta} = \frac{\partial y^*/\partial \eta}{(\delta/s) - (\partial y^*/\partial k^*)},$$

where

$$\frac{\partial y^*}{\partial \eta} = [1 - (1 - \alpha)\hat{\pi}_N\hat{\pi}_M]\frac{\partial f}{\partial \eta} - f(1 - \alpha)\hat{\pi}_M\frac{\partial \hat{\pi}_N}{\partial \eta}. \qquad (24)$$

Factor substitution affects the steady-state average variables via two channels: efficiency and distribution. The efficiency effect is always positive since better factor substitution is equivalent to an increase in factor inputs. The efficiency effect is given by the first term on the right-hand side of Equations (23) and (24). The distribution effect, however, is conditional on the relative abundance as well as the nature of substitutability between the two factors, that is, whether they are gross substitutes or gross complements in production. In general the distribution effect is ambiguous and this makes ambiguous the overall steady-state effects.

---

[9] The effect of m on the transition of k is also qualitatively unchanged.

PROPOSITION 4. *In the steady state, the effects of illegal immigration on the average levels of per capita capital and income are positive. The effects of factor substitution on the average levels of per capita capital and income are ambiguous due to the conflicting effects of efficiency and distribution.*

4. The distribution of wealth

In this section, we study the effects of illegal immigration on wealth distribution. In steady state, the holdings of assets by each member of group i are

$$k_i^* = \frac{w_i + \gamma m}{\delta/s - r}.$$

After substituting away the factor returns, we have

$$\alpha y \frac{k_i^*}{k^*} + F_i + \gamma m - \left(1 + \frac{\delta}{s}\right) k_i^* = 0. \tag{25}$$

Define the relative asset position of unskilled labor and skilled labor as κ_{Lt} and κ_{St} respectively, that is,

$$\kappa_{Lt} = \frac{l k_{Lt}}{k_t} \quad \text{and} \quad \kappa_{St} = \frac{(1-l)k_{St}}{k_t}.$$

For the transitional dynamics, we have

$$\dot{k} = sf[1 - (1-\alpha)\hat{\pi}_N\hat{\pi}_M] - (1+s)\delta k + s\gamma m,$$

$$\dot{k}_S = sf\left[\alpha\frac{k_S}{k} + (1-\alpha)\frac{\hat{\pi}_S}{1-l}\right] - (1+s)\delta k_S + s\gamma m,$$

$$\dot{k}_L = sf\left[\alpha\frac{k_L}{k} + (1-\alpha)\frac{\hat{\pi}_N\hat{\pi}_L}{l}\right] - (1+s)\delta k_L + s\gamma m.$$

From these three dynamic equations, we can solve for k, k_S, and k_L.

Since it is not possible to derive analytical results, we rely on reasonable parameters values and numerical methods. More specifically, following the literature mentioned in Section 2 and Ottaviano and Peri (2011) for the elasticities of substitution, we adopt the following parameter values:

Baseline values for normalization		
$\bar{y} = 10$	$\bar{n} = 0.5$	$\bar{h} = 0.5$
$\bar{k} = 10$	$\bar{l} = 0.5$	$\bar{m} = 0.04$
$\bar{\pi}_M = 0.08$	$\bar{\pi}_N = 0.3$	
Parameters for the benchmark model		
$\gamma = 0.25$	$\delta = 0.04$	$\alpha = 0.3$
$s = 0.15$	$l = 0.5$	$m = 0.05, 0.1,$ and 0.15
$\sigma_{NS} \in (0.5, 3)$ and $\sigma_{LM} = 20$	$\sigma_{LM} \in (0.5, 30)$	
	and $\sigma_{NS} = 2$	

where σ_{NS} is the elasticity of substitution between unskilled and skilled labor and σ_{LM} is the elasticity of substitution between domestic unskilled and illegal immigrant labor. Moreover,

$$\sigma_{NS} = \frac{1}{1-\eta}, \quad \sigma_{LM} = \frac{1}{1-\beta}.$$

The parameter values specified above have to satisfy the restrictions given in Assumptions 1 ($w_L < w_S$) and 2 ($w_m > 0$). We report the findings in Figures 5–11. Figures 5–8 present the steady-state effects while Figures 9–11 illustrate the outcomes during the transition.

Figure 5 shows the steady-state effect of illegal immigration on the average level of per capita capital in the presence of factor substitution. According to the comparative statics, a rise in illegal immigration always raises the average level of per capita capital and this is indicated by the upward shift of the curves in Figure 5. On the other hand, the effect of factor substitution is in general ambiguous; nevertheless, our numerical exercise in the right panel of Figure 5 yield a negative impact in the case of an increase in the substitutability between skilled and unskilled labor. In other words, the distributive effect of σ_{NS} seems to dominate the efficiency effect in most of our baseline parameterization. Figures 6 and 7 summarize the steady-state effects of illegal immigration on type-i workers's wage rate and capital accumulation when the elasticities of factor substitution (and hence the parameters β and η) vary. Figure 6 shows that an increase in the

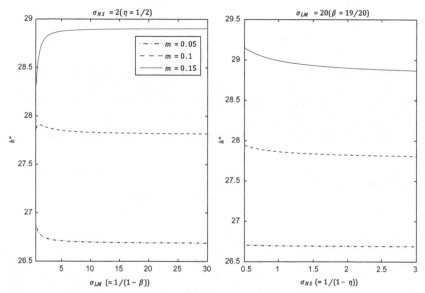

Fig. 5. The effects of σ_{LM}, σ_{NS}, and **m** *on the steady-state average capital* **k***.

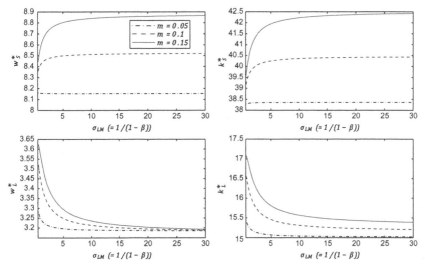

Fig. 6. The effects of σ_{LM} *and* m *on the steady-state values* w_S^*, w_L^*, k_S^*, *and* k_L^*.

elasticity of substitution between L and M (σ_{LM}) always reduces the unskilled wage but raises the wage of the skilled. This is because an increase in σ_{LM} works like an increase in aggregate unskilled labor N so that diminishing factor returns lead to a decrease (increase) in w_L (w_S). Figure 7 shows that an increase in the elasticity of substitution between N and S (σ_{NS}) instead reduces the skilled wage but raises the wage of the unskilled. This is because an increase in σ_{NS} allows for easier substitution between skilled and unskilled workers so that the returns between the two are converging. This in turn leads to a decrease in w_S and an increase in w_L. The intuition of the comparative static results on capital holdings, illustrated in Figures 6 and 7, follows the same reasoning. Finally, contrary to the findings of Palivos and Yip (2010), we have found that, given the elasticities of substitution, an increase in illegal migrants raises the wage rate and capital accumulation of both groups of domestic workers for most of the simulated cases in Figures 6 and 7 (shown by the shifts of the curves). In the presence of factor substitution, unskilled workers need not necessarily be worse off with illegal immigration. Only in the lower panel of Figure 7, we see that unskilled workers are worse off when the elasticity of substitution between skilled and unskilled labor (σ_{NS}) is relatively low. For instance, if $\sigma_{NS} < 1$, both the wage rate and capital holdings of the unskilled are decreasing with illegal immigration. Consequently, when skilled and unskilled workers are gross complements, illegal immigration worsens the income distribution between skilled and unskilled workers. This highlights the importance of factor substitution in understanding the effects of illegal immigration.

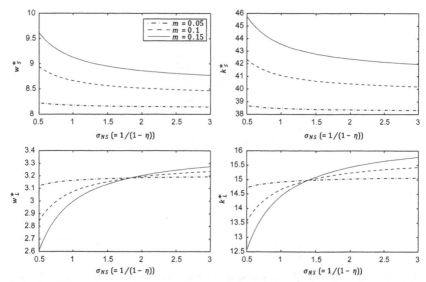

Fig. 7. *The effects of* σ_{NS} *and* m *on the steady-state values* w_S^*, w_L^*, k_S^*, *and* k_L^*.

In general, as illegal immigration raises the average and individual capital holdings in the economy, the interesting question is to examine the overall distributive effect in the presence of factor substitution. According to Figure 8 (the right panels), given the substitutability between migrants and domestic unskilled labor, the relative asset holdings between skilled and unskilled workers diverge with illegal immigration. Nevertheless, the uneven distribution of asset holdings becomes more egalitarian as σ_{NS} rises. The intuition is as follows. An increase in σ_{NS} allows firms to substitute the relative abundant unskilled labor for the skilled; this then leads to a rise (fall) in the unskilled (skilled) workers' wage rate, per capita capital, and relative capital share. Thus income distribution among the skilled and the unskilled is improved. From the left panels of Figure 8, we see that it is very likely that an increase in m and/or σ_{LM} worsens the domestic income distribution. The intuition is clear. As both an increase in σ_{LM} and m lead to an expansion of the unskilled labor supply N, their effects on income distribution are qualitatively equivalent. Only when σ_{LM} is low enough so that migrants and domestic unskilled workers are complementary in production, an increase in m may improve the domestic income distribution.

The transitional dynamic effects of a change in m, σ_{LM}, and σ_{NS} on wealth distribution are shown in Figures 9, 10, and 11 respectively. According to Figures 9 and 10, an increase in m or σ_{LM} worsens the wealth distribution in transition due to diminishing factor returns. This is because these changes of the parameters lead to an expansion of the total unskilled labor supply N in the economy. Finally, as shown in Figure 11, an increase in σ_{NS} allows firms to better substitute the relative abundant unskilled

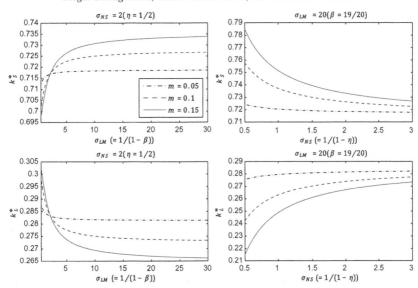

Fig. 8. The effects of σ_{LM}, σ_{NS} and m on the steady-state wealth share of the skilled and the unskilled, κ_S^* and κ_L^*.

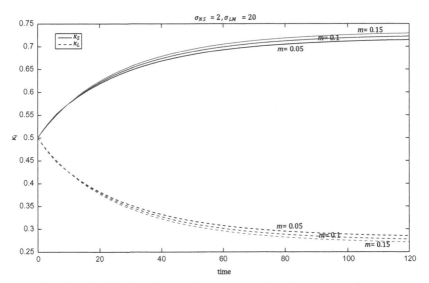

Fig. 9. Wealth distribution in transition for given σ_{NS} and σ_{LM}.

labor for the skilled so that the uneven wealth distribution among the two groups is reduced. In summary, the analysis of the effects of illegal immigration, both in the steady state and in transition, can be very misleading if one ignores factor substitution.

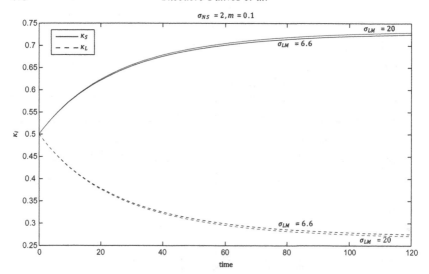

Fig. 10. *Wealth distribution in transition as* σ_{LM} *changes for given* σ_{NS} *and* **m.**

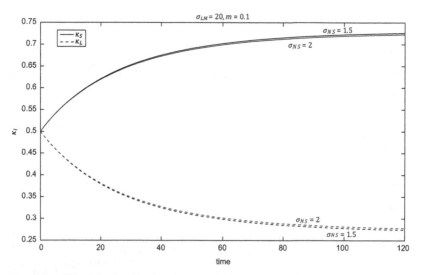

Fig. 11. *Wealth distribution in transition as* σ_{NS} *changes for given* σ_{LM} *and* **m.**

5. *Concluding remarks*

We have developed a Solow growth model with illegal immigration in which there exists either one or two types of domestic labor. We have also allowed for the possibility of imperfect substitution between unskilled and skilled labor as well as between natives and immigrants. Within such a framework we have analyzed the effects of an increase in immigration on the average capital stock, individual wages, asset holdings, and the distribution of wealth. Moreover, utilizing the normalization technique, we have investigated in a systematic and comparable way the effects of factor substitution in the aforementioned labor inputs.

Our findings indicate that the effect of an increase in illegal immigration on the average levels of capital, consumption, and income is positive. In other words, leaving distribution issues aside, an increase in illegal immigration makes a country as a whole better off. This result is in agreement with those found in previous studies. On the other hand, the effects of a change in the elasticities of substitution between different types of labor on the same variables are in general ambiguous, because of the presence of two often opposing effects: the efficiency and the distribution effects. Finally, contrary to previous results in the literature, we have shown that illegal immigration may not necessarily make the distribution of wealth more unequal and unskilled labor worse off. This is so because the end results depend on the elasticities of substitution between different types of labor. In fact, a lesson that has emerged throughout the article is that the distributional effects of illegal immigration depend crucially on the size of the aforementioned elasticities of factor substitution; assuming erroneously that immigrants and natives are perfect substitutes could lead to results that are not only overestimated but also of the wrong sign.

Finally, let us conclude the chapter with some interesting and relevant extensions of our analysis. One realistic extension is to allow for unemployment in the economy. In the model analyzed in this article, there is always full employment. Nevertheless, one of the arguments against illegal immigration is that it raises unemployment among native workers. Palivos (2009) studies the effects of illegal immigration in the presence of unemployment, when immigrants and natives are perfect substitutes. In this case, immigrants replace domestic unskilled workers on a one-to-one basis. There he finds that "immigration increases unemployment, leaves the capital stock unchanged, and decreases consumption and welfare" (p. 140). Nevertheless, if we allow for factor substitution so that natives and immigrants are imperfect substitutes (or even gross complements), then an increase in illegal immigration no longer exhibits a one-to-one negative effect on domestic employment. Consequently, the effects of illegal immigration can be very different from those in Palivos (2009). Also, within the Solow growth framework, where there is a fixed saving rate, savings is a fraction of total aggregate income. As pointed out in Xue and Yip (2011), in models with an optimizing saving behavior, savings may come either from capital or from labor income. Consequently, the distribution effects of factor substitution are different within these models. This then would affect the overall outcome of illegal immigration.

Acknowledgment

The authors would like to thank Olivier de La Grandville for useful comments and suggestions. Needless to say, we are solely responsible for any mistakes and shortcomings.

Appendix. *Normalization procedure of the two-level nested CES production function*

Following the normalization procedures of Klump and de La Grandville (2000) as well as Papageorgiou and Saam (2008), we define the baseline point of the CES functions by choosing the intensive (deflated by $L+S$) baseline values $\bar{y}$, $\bar{k}$, $\bar{n}$, $\bar{h}$, $\bar{l}$, and $\bar{m}$. Denoting $\hat{\pi}_M \equiv (\partial N/\partial M)(M/N)$ as the share of M in N and $\hat{\pi}_N \equiv (\partial H/\partial N)(N/H)$ as the share of N in H, the baseline values are given by

$$\bar{\pi}_M = \frac{\mu \bar{m}^\beta}{\mu \bar{m}^\beta + (1-\mu)\bar{l}^\beta},\tag{A.1}$$

and

$$\bar{\pi}_N = \frac{\theta \bar{n}^\eta}{\theta \bar{n}^\eta + (1-\theta)(1-\bar{l})^\eta}.\tag{A.2}$$

Next, we can use Equations (A.1) and (A.2) to solve for the parameters μ and θ:

$$\mu(\beta) = \frac{\bar{\pi}_M \bar{l}^\beta}{\bar{\pi}_M \bar{l}^\beta + (1-\bar{\pi}_M)\bar{m}^\beta},\tag{A.3}$$

$$\theta(\eta) = \frac{(1-\bar{\pi}_N)(1-\bar{l})^\eta}{\bar{\pi}_N \bar{n}^\eta + (1-\bar{\pi}_N)(1-\bar{l})^\eta}.\tag{A.4}$$

Also, from the aggregate unskilled labor function (2), we can solve for the parameter B:

$$B(\beta) = \left[\bar{\pi}_M \bar{m}^{-\beta} + (1-\bar{\pi}_M)\bar{l}^{-\beta}\right]^{1/\beta} \bar{n}.\tag{A.5}$$

Finally, combining these parameters with the normalized version of the CES production function, we can solve for A:

$$A(\eta) = \left[\bar{\pi}_N \bar{n}^{-\eta} + (1-\bar{\pi}_N)(1-\bar{l})^{-\eta}\right]^{(1-\alpha)/\eta} \bar{h}^{1-\alpha} \bar{k}^{-\alpha} \bar{y}.\tag{A.6}$$

References

Arrow, K. J., Chenery, H. B., Minhas, B. S., & Solow, R. M. (1961). Capital-labor substitution and economic efficiency. *Review of Economics and Statistics, 43,* 225–250.

Elwell, C. K. (2010). Saving rates in the United States: Calculation and comparison. CRS Report for Congress RS21480, Congressional Research Service, United States.

Hazari, B. R., & Sgro, P. M. (2003). The simple analytics of optimal growth with illegal migrants. *Journal of Economic Dynamics and Control, 28,* 141–151.

Klump, R., & de La Grandville, O. (2000). Economic growth and the elasticity of substitution: Two theorems and some suggestions. *American Economic Review, 90,* 282–291.

Klump, R., & Preissler, H. (2000). CES production functions and economic growth. *Scandinavian Journal of Economics, 102,* 41–56.

de La Grandville, O. (1989). In quest of the Slutsky diamond. *American Economic Review, 79,* 468–481.

de La Grandville, O. (2009). *Economic growth: A unified approach.* Cambridge: Cambridge University Press.

Litina, A., & Palivos, T. (2010). The behavior of the saving rate in the neoclassical optimal growth model. *Macroeconomic Dynamics, 14,* 482–500.

Liu, X. (2010). On the macroeconomic and welfare effects of illegal immigration. *Journal of Economic Dynamics and Control, 34,* 2547–2567.

Moy, H. M., & Yip, C. K. (2006). The simple analytics of optimal growth with illegal migrants: A clarification. *Journal of Economic Dynamics and Control, 30,* 2469–2475.

Ottaviano, G. I. P., & Peri, G. (2011). Rethinking the effects of immigration on wages. *Journal of the European Economic Association* (forthcoming).

Palivos, T. (2009). Welfare effects of illegal immigration. *Journal of Population Economics, 22,* 131–144.

Palivos, T., & Karagiannis, G. (2010). The elasticity of substitution as an engine of growth. *Macroeconomic Dynamics, 14,* 617–628.

Palivos, T., & Yip, C. K. (2010). Illegal immigration in a heterogeneous labor market. *Journal of Economics, 101,* 21–47.

Papageorgiou, C., & Saam, M. (2008). Two-level CES production technology in the Solow and diamond growth models. *Scandinavian Journal of Economics, 110,* 119–143.

Peri, G., & Sparber, C. (2009). Task specialization, immigration, and wages. *American Economic Journal: Applied Economics, 1,* 135–169.

Solow, R. M. (1956). A contribution to the theory of economic growth. *Quarterly Journal of Economics, 70,* 65–94.

Xue, J., & Yip, C. K. (2011). Factor substitution and economic growth. *Macroeconomic Dynamics* (forthcoming).

CHAPTER 18

Investment, Technical Progress, and the Consequences of the Global Economic Crisis

John Pawley and Ernst Juerg Weber

Business School, University of Western Australia, Crawley, WA 6009, Australia
E-mail address: john_pawley@hotmail.com; juerg.weber@uwa.edu.au

Abstract
The vintage model of capital accumulation predicts that technical progress depends on the installation of new capital equipment. In this chapter it is found that investment raises labor productivity in the G7 countries and Australia. This finding implies that the decline in investment during the global financial crisis will have a long lasting detrimental effect on labor productivity and hence wages.

Keywords: Vintage model of capital accumulation, technical change, labor productivity, global financial crisis

JEL classifications: O11, O30, O40, O47, E13, E22

Standard macroeconomic models imply that economic growth can be achieved either through capital accumulation or technical progress. Capital accumulation produces an ascending movement along the neoclassical production function and technical progress shifts the production function upwards. In growth accounting capital accumulation and technical progress are also viewed as independent sources of economic growth. Technical progress is the residual of output growth that cannot be explained by the growth in input factors, including among others capital. Yet, the widely accepted dichotomy between capital accumulation and technical progress as distinct sources of economic growth does not do justice to the diffusion of technology in the process of economic growth and development. Half a century ago, Johansen (1959), Salter (1955/1960), Solow (1960), and Kaldor and Mirrlees (1962) recognized that capital accumulation and technical progress are closely associated in the process of economic growth. Capital accumulation is a prerequisite for technical progress because, as Johansen put it, "new production techniques can be introduced

Frontiers of Economics and Globalization
Volume 11   ISSN: 1574-8715
DOI: 10.1108/S1574-8715(2011)0000011023

only by means of new capital equipment." The idea that technical progress requires investment in new capital equipment to become effective is the cornerstone of the vintage model of capital accumulation. Since the business cycle is driven by changes in investment expenditure, an important prediction of the vintage model is that technical progress is cyclical.

As the vintage model of capital accumulation plays only a peripheral role in contemporary macroeconomics thinking, it is worthwhile to consider its origin and elaborate briefly on it. Writing his Ph.D. thesis at the University of Cambridge, W. E. G. Salter was the first to work seriously on the vintage model of capital accumulation.[1] He submitted his Ph.D. thesis in 1955 and he published *Productivity and Technical Change*, which builds on his Ph.D. thesis, in 1960. Niehans (1993) opined that progress in economic theory follows a deterministic process because it is propelled by a drive for internal consistency. Each step is determined by the steps preceding it but creative minds can speed up the advance in economic theory along the largely preset path. Salter undoubtedly was a creative economist who advanced the understanding of the process of technical progress but the vintage model of capital accumulation would also have been discovered without him, albeit at a slower pace. Both Johansen (1959, 1961) and Solow (1960) appear to have discovered the vintage model independently of Salter – Solow refers to Johansen but neither of them mentions Salter – and also Kaldor (1957) and Kaldor and Mirrlees (1962) worked independently on it.

In the opening chapter of *Productivity and Technical Change*, Salter (1960) observes that actual labor productivity lags behind best-practice productivity in the manufacturing industry. There is a delay in the adoption of new technology because it is worthwhile to use old machines as long as they earn a surplus over operating costs. Old machines can compete with new machines because old machines need only to cover operating costs, whereas the decision to install a new machine depends on its operating costs and capital costs. The capital costs of old machines are no longer relevant in the production decision because "bygones are forever bygones." Salter's vintage model of capital accumulation explains why different vintages of capital coexist side-by-side in industrial countries and – even more so – in developing ones where it is often difficult to find finance for the capital cost of new equipment. For the purpose of this chapter, the essential insight is that gross investment determines the speed at which new technology is adopted in the production process.

Without gross investment, improving technology that requires new capital equipment simply represents a potential for higher productivity; to realize this potential requires gross investment. An economy with a low rate of

---

[1] Weber (2011) discusses Salter's contributions to production theory and international trade theory.

gross investment is restricted in the rate at which new techniques can be brought into use; an economy with a high rate of gross investment can quickly bring new methods into use, and thus realize the benefits of improving technology. In this way, the rate of gross investment is a vital determinant of the extent to which observed productivity lags behind best-practice productivity. (Salter, 1960, pp. 63–64)

To begin with, Solow (1960) considers a Cobb–Douglas production function with a technical shift factor:

$$Q(t) = A(t)L(t)^{\alpha}K(t)^{1-\alpha} \tag{1}$$

Here, $L(t)$ and $K(t)$ measure the inputs of labor and physical capital at time t, and $Q(t)$ the output. An increase in total factor productivity $A(t)$ shifts the production function upwards over time. Solow comments that in the Cobb–Douglas production function technical progress is "peculiarly disembodied." The technical dimension of capital goods is perfectly malleable because no distinction is made between old and new capital goods. Therefore, all capital goods participate equally in technical progress – even museum pieces! Solow then puts forward the opposite viewpoint that capital goods of a certain vintage embody a fixed level of technology that cannot be changed at a later date. In this situation, the diffusion of technical progress requires the installation of new machinery that replaces obsolete equipment.

The striking assumption is that old and new capital equipment participate equally in technical change. This conflicts with the casual observation that many if not most innovations need to be embodied in new kinds of durable equipment before they can be made effective. Improvements in technology affect output only to the extent that they are carried into practice either by net capital formation or by the replacement of old-fashioned equipment with the latest models, with a consequent shift in the distribution of equipment by date of birth. (Solow, 1960, p. 91)

The discovery of the vintage model of capital accumulation coincided with a shift from consumption to the production of armaments during World War II, which created favorable conditions for research in production theory. The activity analysis of Koopmans (1951a, 1951b, 1957) would have provided an excellent starting point for the analysis of technical progress. In fact, Salter (1960, pp. 13–16) employs activity analysis in an informal way. There is no reason to believe that technical progress affects economic activities evenly across the economy. However, it took almost two decades until Atkinson and Stiglitz (1969) pointed out that technical progress produces an uneven upward-shift of the neoclassical production function, possibly affecting only a single point or activity on it. This long delay proves Niehans right: it requires creativity to make the next predetermined step in the largely deterministic process of scientific discovery in economics. The evolution of economic theory also includes many instances in which theories fell into oblivion, only to be rediscovered at a later date. Ricardian equivalence provides a famous example – the vintage model of capital accumulation is another. In the 1970s and 1980s, the emphasis in macroeconomic research shifted back to consumption and the standard view on disembodied technical progress prevailed in growth theory. The vintage model of capital accumulation, which played no role in the development of endogenous growth models in the 1980s, did not live up to its potential until it was revived by Hulten (1992), Cooley, Greenwood, and Yorukogly (1997), and Greenwood, Hercowitz, and Krusell (1997) in the 1990s.

This chapter deals with the empirical side of the vintage model of capital accumulation. Since technical progress is embodied in new machinery and equipment, the vintage model predicts that an increase in gross investment will lead to a long lasting improvement in labor productivity. Both the replacement of worn out machinery and the expansion of production facilities create opportunities to install new technology. The empirical analysis focuses on labor productivity because the vintage model does not support the notion of total factor productivity, which presumes disembodied technical progress. Salter (1960, p. 36) reasons that technical progress "raises the productivity of labor in two stages: the first is the direct effect of technical advances in each industry; and the second is the substitution of capital for labor, following upon the cheapening of capital goods relative to wages." The price of capital goods falls relative to labor because technical progress makes it possible to produce commodities – including capital goods – with less labor and capital.

1. Decomposition of forecast-error-variances

The empirical analysis is based on VAR models that include gross investment, aggregate output (GDP), and output per worker. Eight models with three variables and two lags are estimated using annual data for the G7 countries and Australia from 1950 to 2009.[2] Following the original VAR methodology, which has never been abandoned by Sims (1980) and Doan (2007, p. 343), the logarithm of all variables is used because they grow exponentially but they are neither differenced nor de-trended. The point is that it is important to preserve long-term relationships between variables because it may take some time until the full effect of investment

---

[2] Germany 1970–2009. The data are from the Penn World Table 7.0. Real GDP was constructed by multiplying real GDP per capita with population and investment equals "investment share of real GDP per capita" times real GDP per capita.

on productivity is felt.[3] In VAR models the identification of variable specific innovations requires an assumption on the causal structure of the contemporaneous correlation matrix of innovations. Here, it is assumed that the contemporaneous correlation between variable-specific shocks represents a causal chain that runs from investment to GDP and to labor productivity. The effect of investment on GDP is suggested by the Keynesian multiplier, and the effect of GDP on labor productivity may reflect labor hoarding. The effect of investment on labor productivity, which arises in the vintage model of capital accumulation, is the main interest of this study. It should be noted that every VAR model is structural because the identification of variable specific shocks requires economic theory.

The moving-average representation of a VAR model can be written in two ways, as decompositions of forecast-error-variances and as impulse responses. In this section, the forecast-error-variances for labor productivity are decomposed into the innovations experienced by each variable during the forecasting period. Labor productivity moves independently if its k-step ahead forecast-error-variances are caused by its own innovations, while labor productivity depends on other variables if most of the forecast-error-variances arise from shocks to those variables. In Table 1 the decomposition of the forecast-error-variances is read along the rows, which add up to 100. For example, 49.3% of the 10-year ahead forecast-error-variance of Australian labor productivity is explained by shocks to investment, 43.3% by shocks to GDP and only 7.4% by shocks to labor productivity itself. Thus, Australian labor productivity is an endogenous variable that strongly depends on investment and GDP. The same pattern emerges in the other countries. At a forecasting horizon of 15–20 years, unforeseen investment shocks account for more than 80% of the forecast-error-variances in France and Japan; the share of investment lies between about 30% and 60% in Germany, the United Kingdom, Italy, and the USA; and it is less than 10% only in Canada. The large contributions of investment to the forecast-error-variances, which are found in Table 1, support the prediction of the vintage model of capital accumulation that investment is an important determinant of labor productivity.

In this section, it has been established that labor productivity depends strongly on investment in the G7 countries and Australia, except in Canada. The impulse response functions, which will be shown in the next

---

[3] The Johanson procedure indicates that variables are not co-integrated in most countries. All econometric work is included in an appendix of Economics Discussion Paper 11.10, Business School, University of Western Australia (available on SSRN, RePEc and the website of the UWA Business School). See Enders (2010, p. 303) for the continuing use of nonstationary VARs and Mills and Markellos (2008, pp. 375–378) for the impulse response asymptotics.

John Pawley and Ernst Juerg Weber

Table 1. Decomposition of forecast-error-variances for labor productivity

Year	Investment	GDP	Labor productivity
		Australia	
5	46.2	43.8	10.0
10	49.3	43.3	7.4
15	51.2	41.9	6.9
20	52.4	40.7	6.9
		Canada	
5	10.4	59.6	30.0
10	8.2	63.9	27.9
15	8.0	66.2	25.7
20	8.1	67.6	24.3
		France	
5	77.5	13.5	9.0
10	82.5	8.3	9.2
15	84.3	6.4	9.3
20	85.1	5.4	9.6
		Germany	
5	59.9	19.4	20.6
10	43.4	24.9	31.7
15	40.8	29.9	29.3
20	39.4	32.6	28.0
		Italy	
5	33.1	40.3	26.5
10	44.9	32.8	22.2
15	52.5	28.3	19.2
20	56.5	26.1	17.4
		Japan	
5	59.3	20.6	20.2
10	76.1	11.8	12.1
15	84.3	8.1	7.5
20	87.8	6.5	5.8
		United Kingdom	
5	30.1	47.0	22.9
10	30.6	51.5	17.9
15	30.4	55.1	14.5
20	29.8	57.6	12.6
		USA	
5	42.7	31.0	26.3
10	40.9	26.8	32.3
15	41.3	26.2	32.5
20	42.0	26.9	31.2

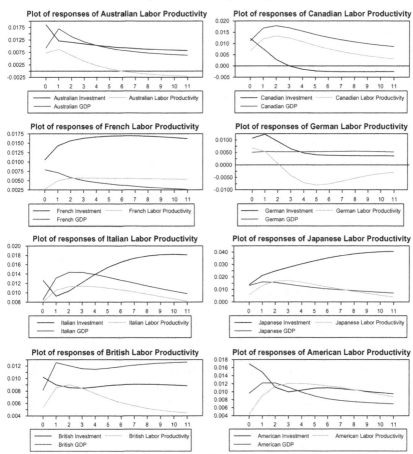

Fig. 1.   Responses of labor productivity in the G7 countries and Australia.

section, confirm that – as implied by the vintage model of capital accumulation – investment in new capital goods has a long lasting positive effect on labor productivity.

2. Impulse responses

Figure 1 displays the responses of labor productivity to investment shocks in the G7 countries and Australia. The investment shocks are temporary, lasting a single year, and their size equals one standard deviation of the residuals of the investment equation for each country. Accordingly, the investment shocks range from 4.9% in Germany to 10.2% in Australia, with the other countries lying between these limits.[4] The responses in labor productivity are plotted over 12 years along the lower axis and, since variables are logarithmic, the impulse responses are measured as percentage changes along the upper axis, using continuous growth compounding.

In Australia a temporary shock to investment immediately raises labor productivity by 1.8% and the productivity gain settles at 0.9% after about 10 years. The effect of investment on labor productivity is strongest in Japan and weakest in Canada. In Japan a shock to investment immediately raises productivity by 1.4% and the full effect of the investment shock is felt after about 10 years, when the productivity gain reaches 4%. In all countries productivity responds positively to investment, both in the short- and long-term, except for Canada where it rises only in the short-term. The positive impulse responses of labor productivity to investment shocks are meaningful because, as shown by the decompositions of forecast-error-variances in Table 1, investment accounts for a large share of the variation in labor productivity in all countries, except in Canada. As predicted by the vintage model of capital accumulation, a temporary increase in investment gives rise to a long lasting increase in labor productivity because investment creates opportunities to catch up with best practice productivity by installing new technology.

Besides the response of labor productivity to an investment shock, Figure 1 also displays the responses of productivity to GDP and to its own shocks. In all countries, a positive (negative) shock to GDP is followed by an increase (fall) in labor productivity, which may be explained by labor hoarding. Finally, the Keynesian multiplier prevails as an increase in investment raises GDP in all countries and there is evidence for an accelerator effect of GDP on investment in some countries (impulse responses not shown).[5]

3. Conclusion

One goal of this chapter was to unearth the origins of the vintage model of capital accumulation, which are not well known. The vintage model was independently discovered by Johansen (1959, 1961), Salter (1955/1960), Solow (1960), Kaldor (1957), and Kaldor and Mirrlees (1962), and it was rediscovered by Hulten (1992), Cooley et al. (1997), and Greenwood

---

[4] The standard errors of the estimated investment equations are: Australia (10.2%), Canada (7.9%), France (6.5%), Germany (4.9%), Italy (7.2%), Japan (7.7%), the United Kingdom (7.4%), and the United States (7.3%).
[5] A VAR model with three variables produces nine impulse response functions, which gives 72 impulse response functions for 8 countries.

et al. (1997). The second goal was to demonstrate the empirical relevance of the vintage model. It was found that the dynamic interaction between investment, aggregate output and labor productivity supports the prediction of the vintage model that an increase in investment produces a long lasting improvement in labor productivity.

The vintage model of capital accumulation is still awaiting widespread application in macroeconomic analysis that would be commensurate with its significance. Indeed, the vintage model is of particular relevance in the current economic situation. Since investment is required for technical progress, the decline in investment during the global economic crisis will have a long lasting detrimental effect on labor productivity and hence wages in many countries.

Acknowledgments

This chapter extends the research that John Pawley (2010) conducted for his Honours thesis at the University of Western Australia. The financial support of the C.A. Vargovic Memorial Fund and the UWA Business School is gratefully acknowledged. We are indebted to Rod Tyers and the participants in an economics workshop at the University of Western Australia.

References

Atkinson, A. B., & Stiglitz, J. (1969). A new view of technical change. *Economic Journal, 79*(315), 573–578.

Cooley, T. F., Greenwood, J., & Yorukogly, M. (1997). The replacement problem. *Journal of Monetary Economics, 40,* 457–499.

Doan, T. A. (2007). *RATS user's guide*, Version 7. Evanston, IL: Estima.

Enders, W. (2010). *Applied econometric time series*. New York: Wiley.

Greenwood, J., Hercowitz, Z., & Krusell, P. (1997). Long-run implications of investment-specific technological change. *American Economic Review, 87*(3), 342–362.

Hulten, C. R. (1992). Growth accounting when technical change is embodied in capital. *American Economic Review, 82*(4), 964–980.

Johansen, L. (1959). Substitution versus fixed production coefficients in the theory of economic growth: A synthesis. *Econometrica, 27*(2), 157–176.

Johansen, L. (1961). A method of separating the effects of capital accumulation and shifts in production functions upon growth in labour productivity. *Economic Journal, 71,* 775–782.

Kaldor, N. (1957). A model of economic growth. *Economic Journal, 67*(268), 591–624.

Kaldor, N., & Mirrlees, J. A. (1962). A new model of economic growth. *Review of Economic Studies, 29*(3), 174–192.

Koopmans, T. C. (1951). Analysis of production as an efficient combination of activities. In Koopmans, T. C. (Ed.), *Activity analysis of production and allocation*, Cowles Commission Monograph 13, Chapter III. New York: Wiley.

Koopmans, T. C. (1951). Efficient allocation of resources. *Econometrica, 19*(4), 455–465.

Koopmans, T. C. (1957). *Three essays on the state of economic science.* New York: McGraw-Hill.

Mills, T. C., & Markellos, R. N. (2008). *The econometric modelling of financial time series* (3rd ed.). Cambridge: Cambridge University Press.

Niehans, J. (1993). Revolution and evolution in economic theory, Bateman lecture, University of Western Australia. *Australian Quarterly, 65*(1), 498–515.

Pawley, J. (2010). *Investment and productivity in Australia, 1965–2007.* Honours thesis, Business School, University of Western Australia.

Salter, W. E. G. (1960). *Productivity and technical change.* Cambridge: Cambridge University Press.

Sims, C. A. (1980). Macroeconomics and reality. *Econometrica, 48,* 1–49.

Solow, R. M. (1960). Investment and technical progress. In Arrow, K.J., Karlin, S. & Suppes, P. (Eds.), *Mathematical methods in the social sciences.* Stanford: Stanford University Press.

Weber, E. J. (2011). Wilfred E.G. Salter: The merits of a classical economic education. *History of Economics Review, 54* (summer, in press).

CHAPTER 19

Market Power, Growth, and Unemployment

Pietro F. Peretto

Department of Economics, Duke University, Durham, NC 27708, USA
E-mail address: peretto@econ.duke.edu

Abstract
I present a model where firms and workers set wages above the market-clearing level. Unemployment is thus generated by their exercise of market power. Because both the labor and product markets are imperfectly competitive, market power in the labor market interacts with market power in the product market. This interaction sheds new light on the effects of policy interventions on unemployment and growth. For example, labor market reforms that reduce labor costs reduce unemployment *and* boost growth because they expand the scale of the economy and generate more competition in the product market.

Keywords: Market power, market structure, endogenous growth, unemployment

JEL classification: E10, L16, O31, O40

1. Introduction

Traditional explanations of unemployment focus on labor market rigidities and ignore the characteristics of the product market. This leaves out important factors that should be included in the analysis of the effects of institutions and policies. In this chapter, I exploit this argument, and recent developments in endogenous growth theory, to argue that unemployment and productivity growth are related because they both depend on the structure of the product market.

The source of the relation is the pricing behavior of agents with market power. Workers and firms have control over wages and prices; the exercise of market power in the product market interacts with its exercise in the labor market. Analysis of this interaction sheds new light on the effects on unemployment and growth of policy interventions in the two markets.

Frontiers of Economics and Globalization
Volume 11   ISSN: 1574-8715
DOI: 10.1108/S1574-8715(2011)0000011024

In order to focus on market power, I deviate from the existing literature on growth and unemployment that follows the "creative destruction" tradition.[1] I consider a model where growth is driven by the activities of firms that are not put out of business by outside innovators but are long-lived profit centers that innovate repeatedly in-house.[2] The main difference between the two approaches is that "creative destruction" models exhibit a *negative* relation between product market competition and growth, while the "creative accumulation" model that I consider exhibits a *positive* relation. This relation, supported empirically by the work of, among others, Nickell (1996) and Pagano and Schivardi (2003), has the important implication that a more competitive product market generates both faster growth and lower unemployment. Moreover, in "creative destruction" models the degree of competition is an exogenous parameter whereas in my "creative accumulation" model it depends on the mass of firms, which is endogenous.

Another important feature of the chapter is that I consider an environment with endogenous labor supply: agents choose whether to participate to the labor market in the presence of unemployment risk. Specifically, unemployment is *involuntary*: households control the mass of members that supply labor but not their probability of employment. Thus, some of the participating members do not find employment even if at the going wage they wish to work. This approach allows me to identify separately supply-side and demand-side determinants of employment and unemployment and, more importantly, allows me to derive from the model's primitives a reservation wage that is decreasing in the unemployment rate.

This structure yields interesting results concerning institutions, tax policy and other factors that affect the labor market. Specifically:

- policies that reduce labor costs raise employment and growth and reduce unemployment;
- the benefits of these policies are larger when one considers their (indirect) effects on the structure of the product market.

To illustrate, consider labor income taxes (unemployment benefits have similar effects). Given the structure of the product market, higher labor income taxes generate lower employment and higher unemployment via their traditional effect on the cost of labor. The economy then operates at a smaller scale. This results in lower returns to entry and less competition in the product market. Growth is lower because firms operate in a less competitive market. Moreover, employment and unemployment are, respectively, lower and higher than they would if the structure of the product market remained constant. This is consistent with the evidence

---

[1] See Aghion and Howitt (1992 and 1998, chapter 4) and Mortensen (2005) for a review of recent results.
[2] See Peretto (1996, 1998, 1999) and Smulders and van de Klundert (1995) for a sample of early papers that developed this approach.

discussed in Nickell and Layard (1999), who find that the total tax burden on labor has a negative effect on growth. It is also consistent with the evidence discussed in Daveri and Tabellini (2000), who show that the increase in unemployment and reduction in growth that occurred in the recent decades in the OECD is driven by the increase in labor income taxes. Finally, it is consistent with the evidence provided by Wu and Zhang (2000), who show that in the OECD countries there is a positive correlation between taxation and the mark-ups that firms charge over marginal cost.

It is also interesting to consider factors that raise the cost of innovation, reduce product substitution and thus price competition, or raise entry costs for entrants but do not affect incumbents. The analysis provides three results:

• lower costs of innovation raise employment and growth and reduce unemployment;
• tougher price competition raises growth and has ambiguous effects on employment and unemployment;
• lower barriers to entry reduce growth while do not necessarily raise employment and reduce unemployment.

These results emphasize the importance of the details of the pro-growth policy that a country adopts. Reducing barriers to innovation is the most effective policy because it reduces at the same time barriers to the creation of new firms and barriers to innovation within the firm. As a result, it fosters investment on both the intensive and the extensive margin and, more importantly, it exploits the positive relation between competition and growth. In contrast, promoting growth by protecting incumbents – which is fairly common in Europe where governments protect "national champions" – might reduce employment and raise unemployment by restricting competition.

I organize the chapter as follows. In Section 2, I set up the model. In Section 3, I study bargaining over wages and employment at the firm level, the associated R&D policy, and characterize the relation between wages and R&D. In Section 4, I study the labor market and show how the exercise of market power over prices and wages generates unemployment. In Section 5, I study the general equilibrium of the model and determine unemployment, market structure, and growth. In Section 6, I discuss the effects of structural parameters and policy instruments. I conclude in Section 7.

2. The model

I consider a closed economy. A representative competitive firm assembles intermediate differentiated goods to produce a homogeneous final good that can be consumed or invested. The assembly technology is

$$Y = N^{-1/e(N)-1} \left[\int_0^N X_i^{e(N)-1/e(N)} \mathrm{d}i \right]^{e(N)/e(N)-1}, \quad e'(N) > 0, \tag{1}$$

where $e(N)$ is the elasticity of product substitution, X_i the final producer's use of each differentiated good, and N the mass of intermediate goods (the mass of intermediate firms). The elasticity of substitution is an increasing function of the mass of firms, bounded from above and from below, $\infty > e(\infty) > e(0) \geq 1$. This allows me to capture the role of endogenous market power while retaining the desirable features of a monopolistic competition model defined over a continuum of goods.

The final good is the *numeraire*. The final producer thus maximizes profits subject to the budget constraint $Y = \int_0^N P_i X_i \, \mathrm{d}i$, where P_i is the price of intermediate good i. This yields the demand schedule for good i,

$$X_i = \frac{Y}{N} \left(\frac{P_i}{P} \right)^{-e(N)}. \tag{2}$$

Notice that the price index of intermediate goods,

$$P = \left[\frac{1}{N} \int_0^N P_j^{1-\varepsilon} \mathrm{d}j \right]^{1/1-\varepsilon},$$

which the atomistic intermediate firms take as given, must be equal to the price of the final good and thus is equal to one and can be omitted from (2) without loss of generality.

The typical intermediate firm produces with the technology

$$X_i = Z_i L_i^\theta, \quad 0 < \theta < 1, \tag{3}$$

where X_i is the output, L_i the labor, and Z_i the firm's cumulated stock of cost-reducing innovations. The firm also runs in-house R&D facilities to produce a continuous flow of innovations according to

$$\dot{Z}_i = \alpha R_i, \quad \alpha > 0, \tag{4}$$

where $\dot{Z}_i$ is the flow of innovations generated by an R&D project employing R_i units of the final good for an interval of time $\mathrm{d}t$.

Firms are created by entrepreneurs that develop new products and their manufacturing processes. The cost of entry is proportional to the entry level of productivity. Specifically, setting up a firm with initial productivity Z_i requires $(\beta/\alpha)Z_i$ units of final output. This captures two types of entry costs. First, the entrant needs to create the initial product-specific knowledge, and according to Equation (4) creating a stock of knowledge Z_i requires $(1/\alpha)Z_i$ units of final output. Second, the entrant needs to pay additional costs, not related to R&D, that allow operations to begin. The parameter β captures this non-R&D component of the entry cost by reducing the overall productivity of resources devoted to entry. The important feature of this parameter is that it does not affect incumbents. Hence, it captures exogenous barriers to entry.

The economy is populated by a representative household with a continuum of mass λ of members. Each member is endowed with one unit of labor. The household maximizes

$$U(0) = \int_0^\infty e^{-\rho t} \lambda \left[\log\left(\frac{C}{\lambda}\right) + \psi \log\left(\frac{\lambda - L^s}{\lambda}\right) \right] dt, \quad \rho > 0, \psi > 0,$$

subject to the flow budget constraint

$$\dot{A} = rA + L^s[W(1 - \tau)(1 - u) + Bu] + T - C, \quad 0 < \tau < 1,$$

where ρ is the individual discount rate, C the consumption, L^s the mass of household members that offer their labor for a wage (participate in the labor market), A the assets holding, and T a lump-sum transfer from the government. The assets available to the household are ownership shares of firms. Hence, r is the rate of return on stocks.

Three features of this setup are important. First, the household controls the mass of members that supply labor but not their probability of employment. This is where the assumption that there is a continuum of agents within the household becomes very useful. By the law of large numbers I can equate the individual probability of unemployment to the economy's unemployment rate

$$u \equiv 1 - \frac{L}{L^s},$$

where $L = \int_0^N L_i \, di$ is aggregate employment. Similarly, with a continuum of firms the law of large numbers allows me to equate an employed worker's probability of being assigned to firm i with the firm's share of aggregate employment L_i/L. It follows that the pre-tax wage that the employed member earns is the weighted average

$$W = \int_0^N W_i \frac{L_i}{L} di,$$

where W_i is the wage paid by firm i. This approach implies a job rationing mechanism that takes the form of assigning job seekers at random to the unemployment pool and to the employment pool; those assigned to the employment pool are then assigned at random across the N existing firms and negotiate the terms of employment (see below).[3] Its main advantage is that it allows me to think of the term $1 - u$ in the budget constraint as the fraction of the household members that participate to the labor market

---

[3] One could think of this as a particular type of matching mechanism. With respect to the traditional approach in search theory (e.g., Pissarides 2002), it has two advantages. First, it does not imply unfilled vacancies and thus allows me to focus only on the supply side of the labor market as subject to rationing. Second, it does not require time and thus does not force me to model unemployment as a state variable, thereby reducing the dimensionality of the general equilibrium system (see below).

and earn the after-tax wage $W(1-\tau)$, while u is the fraction that earn the after-tax unemployment benefit B.

The second feature captures the basic trade-off that governs labor supply and thus determines workers' wage demands. The household's instantaneous utility contains a term that captures the role of household members that do not participate in the labor market; one can think of home production or other related activities the output of which is shared by all household members. This determines the opportunity cost of labor market participation, and thus contributes to determine the wage demands of employed workers. Participation takes 100% of the household's member time.

The third feature is that the household insures its members participating in the labor market against individual unemployment risk. This simplifies the analysis because all household members get the same flow of utility regardless of the outcome of the job rationing mechanism.[4] More importantly, it implies that each individual worker is indifferent between employment and unemployment in the bargaining process (see below).

The maximization problem outlined above yields well-known results with some novel features. The household follows the usual saving rule

$$\frac{\dot{C}}{C} = r - \rho \tag{5}$$

and equates the benefit from the marginal household member's participation to the cost. Formally,

$$W(1-\tau)(1-u) + Bu = \frac{\psi C}{\lambda - L^s}.$$

On the left-hand-side of this expression there is the expected income from participation, on the right-hand-side there is the expected cost – the foregone contribution of the marginal individual to household production. Participation therefore can be written

$$L^s = \lambda - \frac{\psi C}{W(1-\tau) - [W(1-\tau) - B]u}. \tag{6}$$

This is the economy's upward sloping labor supply curve. Consumption, C, enters negatively because it raises the opportunity cost of participation; the unemployment insurance benefit, B, enters positively because it raises the expected income from participation.

Labor supply depends on the unemployment rate via two effects. First, higher unemployment means that the participating individual is less likely to be employed and thus to earn the after-tax wage. This lowers the expected benefit of participation. Second, higher unemployment means that the individual is more likely to be unemployed and thus to draw the insurance benefit B. This raises the expected benefit of participation. The

---

[4] Examples of previous work using this approach are Merz (1995) and Pissarides (2002).

model's equilibrium conditions imply that the after-tax wage is higher than the unemployment benefit so that labor supply is *decreasing* in the unemployment rate (see below). This captures a "discouraged worker effect" whereby worse employment prospects in the labor market lower a worker's expected income and thus reduce participation.

3. Wages, prices, and R&D at the firm level

The typical intermediate firm maximizes the present discounted value of net cash flow,

$$V_i(0) = \int_0^\infty e^{-\int_0^t r(v)\mathrm{d}v} \Pi_i(t)\mathrm{d}t$$

subject to the demand schedule (2), the production function (3), the R&D function (4), $Z_i(0) > 0$ (the initial knowledge stock is given), $Z_j(t)$ for $t > 0$ and $j \neq i$ (the firm takes as given the rivals' innovation paths), and $\dot{Z}_j(t) \geq 0$ for $t > 0$ (innovation is irreversible).

Instantaneous profit is $\Pi_i = P_i X_i - W_i L_i - R_i$. The firm bargains with its workers over the wage and employment – this is equivalent to bargaining over the wage and the product's price since employment (the scale of activity of the firm) and the price are related through the demand curve. The firm then sets its R&D policy taking as given the instantaneous outcome of the bargaining process.

I model bargaining as

$$\max_{W_i, L_i} \quad [(1 - \gamma)\log\Pi_i + \gamma\log(W_i(1 - \tau) - W_a)L_i], \quad 0 < \gamma < 1$$

subject to the production function (3) and the demand curve (2). The parameter γ is the relative bargaining power of the workers. The firm and its workers maximize jointly the log-geometric average of profits and employees surplus. The firm and the workers take the alternative,

$$W_a = W(1 - \tau)(1 - u) + Bu = \frac{\psi C}{\lambda - L}$$

as given since it depends on aggregate variables. If negotiations break down, the worker can quit the firm and reenter the labor market, in which case he gets the expected labor income. Alternatively, he can allocate all of his time to household production, in which case he gets the value of his marginal contribution. These two options are equivalent because in deciding labor supply the household sets them equal (see above).

The solution of the bargaining problem yields (see the appendix for details on the derivation):

$$W_i = \frac{W_a}{1 - \tau} + \frac{\gamma}{1 - \gamma}\frac{\Pi_i}{L_i};$$

$$L_i = \frac{1 - \tau}{W_a}\frac{\theta(e - 1)}{e}P_i X_i. \tag{7}$$

The first expression is very important and quite general. It follows solely from the first-order condition for the wage and says that the workers get the reservation wage (adjusted for labor income taxation) plus a fraction of the firm's profit. The latter term establishes a connection between the wage and the firm's R&D policy. This is one of the most important features of the model and is worth exploring in detail.

The expression for firm employment (7) and the definition of profit allow me to write

$$W_i = \frac{W_a}{1-\tau} + \gamma \frac{P_i X_i}{L_i} \left[\frac{e - \theta(e-1)}{e} - \frac{R_i}{P_i X_i} \right]$$

$$= \frac{W_a}{1-\tau}(1 + m_i), \tag{8}$$

where

$$m_i \equiv \gamma \frac{e}{\theta(e-1)} \left[\frac{e - \theta(e-1)}{e} - \frac{R_i}{P_i X_i} \right]. \tag{9}$$

This is the markup of the after-tax wage over the reservation wage that the firm and its workers agree on. It says that on top of the reservation wage, each worker gets a fraction of revenues given by the product of the bargaining power of workers, γ, times a term that results from subtracting R&D intensity from the margin of revenues over the reservation wage bill. This is important: the firm's R&D activity *reduces* the markup because R&D expenditure – which is a recurrent fixed cost – reduces the firm's cash flow and thus reduces what is available to distribute as extra wages to workers and as dividends to stockholders.[5]

The expressions for firm wage and employment yield the reduced-form profit function (see the appendix for details on the derivation)

$$\Pi_i = (1 - \gamma) \left[P_i X_i \frac{e - \theta(e-1)}{e} - R_i \right], \tag{10}$$

where

$$P_i X_i = \left(\frac{Y}{N} \right)^{1/e - \theta(e-1)} \left[\frac{(W_a/1-\tau)e}{\theta(e-1)} \right]^{-\theta(e-1)/e-\theta(e-1)} Z_i^{e-1/e-\theta(e-1)}.$$

If the firm has no bargaining power, if $\gamma = 1$, reduced-form profit is zero because workers extract all rents in the form of higher wages. If the firm has all the bargaining power, if $\gamma = 0$, the firm captures all rents and the wage is set at the competitive level. The firm chooses R_i in order to maximize V_i evaluated using this reduced-form profit function.

---

[5] The markup is positive because of the nonnegativity constraint on profits, which follows from the fact that firms can always choose to set R&D equal to zero.

The R&D strategy can be characterized in an intuitive way. Suppose that the firm finances R&D by issuing ownership claims on the flow of profits generated by cost-reducing innovations. Let the market value of such financial assets be q_i. The firm is willing to undertake R&D if the value of the innovation is equal to its cost, if $q_i = 1/\alpha$. If conditions are such that $q_i < 1/\alpha$, the firm does zero R&D (see below). Situations with $q_i > 1/\alpha$ cannot be equilibria because they entail infinite investment in R&D, which violates the economy's resources constraint. Since the innovation is implemented in-house, its benefits are determined by the marginal profit it generates. Thus, the value of the innovation must satisfy the arbitrage condition

$$r = \frac{\partial \Pi_i}{\partial Z_i} \frac{1}{q_i} + \frac{\dot{q}_i}{q_i}.$$

The marginal profit reads:

$$\frac{\partial \Pi_i}{\partial Z_i} = (1 - \gamma) \left(\frac{Y}{N}\right)^{1/e - \theta(e-1)} \left[\frac{(W_a/1 - \tau)e}{\theta(e-1)}\right]^{-\theta(e-1)/e - \theta(e-1)}$$

$$Z_i^{(e-1/e-\theta(e-1))-1} \frac{e-1}{e} = \frac{(1-\gamma)(e-1)P_i X_i}{eZ_i}.$$

Taking logs and time-derivatives of $q_i = 1/\alpha$, substituting into the arbitrage condition and rearranging terms yields

$$r = \frac{\alpha(1 - \gamma)(e - 1)P_i X_i}{eZ_i}, \tag{11}$$

which defines the rate of return to in-house innovation.

To justify my focus on symmetric equilibria, I need to argue that the "economic" returns to the firm's R&D are diminishing. Otherwise, one firm could take over the whole market by exploiting "physical" increasing returns to knowledge and labor – the fact that cost falls linearly with Z_i. Intuitively, this involves a restriction on the price elasticity of demand such that marginal profit is monotonically decreasing in Z_i. A sufficient condition for this to happen is

$$\frac{e-1}{e - \theta(e-1)} < 1 \Leftrightarrow e < \frac{1 + \theta}{\theta},$$

which says that the marginal profit approaches infinity as the firm's knowledge stock approaches zero while it approaches zero as the firms' knowledge stock approaches infinity.[6]

---

[6] The reader familiar with this class of endogenous growth models might be interested to notice that this condition for symmetry does not require diminishing returns to knowledge or spillovers across firms. It solely follows from diminishing returns to labor, which yield that the marginal cost is a convex function of output. The reason why this implies symmetry, if the price elasticity of demand is sufficiently low, is that expanding output too rapidly raises

Entrants anticipate that once in the market they set wage, price, and R&D spending according to the above characterization. The associated value of the firm must satisfy the arbitrage condition

$$r = \frac{\Pi_i}{V_i} + \frac{\dot{V}_i}{V_i}.$$

Entrants are active if the value of entry is equal to its cost, if $V_i = (\beta/\alpha)Z_i$. Taking logs and time derivatives and substituting into the arbitrage condition, I obtain

$$r = \frac{\alpha\Pi_i}{\beta Z_i} + \frac{\dot{Z}_i}{Z_i}.$$

Using the reduced-form expression for profits (10) and the R&D technology (4), I obtain

$$r = \frac{\alpha(1-\gamma)e - \theta(e-1)}{\beta} \frac{P_i X_i}{e} + \frac{\alpha R_i}{Z_i}\left(1 - \frac{1-\gamma}{\beta}\right). \tag{12}$$

This equation holds as long as there is entry. If conditions are such that $V_i < (\beta/\alpha)Z_i$, there is no entry and the model works like one with an exogenous mass of firms (see below). Situations with $V_i > (\beta/\alpha)Z_i$ cannot be equilibria because they entail infinite investment in entry, which violates the economy's resources constraint.

Equations (11) and (12) define the returns to two types of investment. A standard arbitrage argument for the assets market requires that they yield equal rates of return. Hence,

$$\frac{R_i}{P_i X_i} = \begin{cases} 0 & 0 \le N \le N_0 \\ \left[\frac{e-1}{e}(\beta + \theta) - 1\right]\frac{1-\gamma}{\beta+\gamma-1} & N > N_0 \end{cases}. \tag{13}$$

This equation determines the firm's R&D intensity as a function of product market competition, the entry cost and the firm's bargaining power.

To understand the properties of this equilibrium, one can represent the interaction of incumbents and entrants in a diagram with the rate of return, r, on the vertical axis and R&D, R_i, on the horizontal axis. The equilibrium with positive R&D is at the intersection of the horizontal line (11) with the upward sloping line (12).[7] It exists if (11) is higher than the intercept of (12), otherwise (11) and (12) cross for a negative value of R_i,

---

production costs and offsets the cost advantage stemming from knowledge accumulation. One can visualize this in a simple diagram with an increasing and convex marginal cost curve. Innovation shifts the curve down; the resulting output expansion involves a movement up along the new curve.

[7] This equilibrium is stable in the following sense: to its right the rate of return to R&D is lower than the rate of return to entry and investors wish to reduce growth since this reduces

the nonnegativity constraint on R&D is binding, and $R_i = 0$. Hence, there exists a threshold N_0, determined by $e(N) = 1 + 1/\beta + \theta$, such that $R_i > 0$ for $N > N_0$ and $R_i = 0$ for $0 \leq N \leq N_0$.

According to Equation (13), R&D is proportional to the firm's revenues, $P_i X_i$. To see why, note that the rate of return to R&D increases with the scale of production over which cost-reducing innovations apply. Similarly, the rate of return to entry increases with the anticipated scale of production of the firm. In both cases, the intuition is that R&D and entry costs are fixed costs that larger firms spread over larger volumes of production. Recent work by Cohen and Klepper (1996a, 1996b) and Adams and Jaffe (1996) shows that this cost-spreading mechanism is important in explaining the role of firm size emphasized in many empirical studies.

To characterize the labor market more sharply, it is useful to assume that the government cannot borrow and satisfies the budget constraint $T = \tau W L^d - B(L^s - L^d)$, which determines the lump-sum transfer, T, as the difference between tax revenues and expenditure on benefits.[8] It is also useful to assume that the unemployment benefit is a constant fraction of the wage. I thus posit $B = \sigma W$.

I now make use of the fact that symmetry implies that all firms pay the same wage so that $W_i = W$. The wage Equation (8) yields

$$1 = \frac{(1 - \tau)(1 - u) + \sigma u}{1 - \tau}(1 + m).$$

This can be solved for

$$u = \frac{1 - \tau}{1 - \tau - \sigma}\frac{m}{1 + m}. \qquad (14)$$

Notice that $u > 0$ because $m > 0$, while $u < 1$ if

$$1 + m < \frac{1 - \tau}{\sigma}.$$

This says that, given the markup m, if the replacement ratio is too high unemployment is 100%. To see what this means, use the wage Equation (8) to rewrite the condition as

$$\sigma < \frac{W_a}{W} \Leftrightarrow B < (1 - \tau)W.$$

---

the rate of return to entry; to its left the rate of return to R&D is higher than the rate of return to entry and investors wish to raise growth since this raises the rate of return to entry.

[8] This setup keeps to a minimum the effect of the government on economic activity. Only two distortions matter: taxation, which lowers labor supply and raises the pre-tax wage that unions demand, and the unemployment benefit, which raises both labor supply and the pre-tax wage that unions demand.

This is intuitive: a replacement ratio that is "too high" is one that makes unemployment a better outcome than employment.[9] To rule out situations like this it is sufficient to impose $\sigma < 1 - \tau$.

It is clear from the wage Equation (8) that unemployment is decreasing in R&D intensity because the firm's R&D activity reduces the markup over the reservation wage. More importantly, the relation between unemployment and R&D activity is *invariant to the specifics of the determination of R&D intensity*. Hence, the implied negative relation between growth and unemployment is *causal* and *general*: however R&D intensity is determined, the higher is R&D intensity, the lower is the markup and the lower is unemployment. The specifics of the relation, however, depend on whether entrants are active or not. When entrants are active, Equation (12) applies and R&D spending is determined by the arbitrage condition (13); when entrants are not active, Equation (12) does not apply and R&D spending is determined by the economy's resources constraint. Thus, spelling out the details of the relation between unemployment and growth requires analysis of the economy's general equilibrium.

The expression for firm employment (7), the wage Equation (8) and aggregation across firms yield

$$L = \int_0^N L_i \, di = \frac{1 + m}{W} \frac{\theta(e-1)}{e} Y.$$

The assembly technology (1), the production technology (3), and symmetry yield the reduced-form production function

$$Y = ZN\left(\frac{L}{N}\right)^{\theta} = ZN^{1-\theta}L^{\theta}. \tag{15}$$

Hence,

$$W = (1 + m)\frac{\theta(e-1)}{e} Z\left(\frac{L}{N}\right)^{-(1-\theta)}.$$

The wage is increasing in product market competition e and the markup m, and is proportional to productivity Z. Employment per firm L/N enters negatively because of diminishing returns to labor.

---

[9] This raises the question of how the government can pay for unemployment benefits if nobody works. In this chapter's setup this is not necessarily a problem because the government pays (net) lump-sum transfers that can be converted to lump-sum taxes. The question, however, is really about how one can justify as an equilibrium a situation with 100% unemployment. One should also notice that the condition for $u < 1$ is surely satisfied if unemployment benefits are taxed at the same rate as wages. More generally, the condition should be that the replacement ratio be lower than the ratio $(1-\tau_W/1-\tau_B)$, where τ_W and τ_B are, respectively, the tax rate on wages and benefits.

To calculate employment now observe that

$$L = (1 - u)L^s$$

$$= \lambda \frac{1 - \tau - \sigma(1 + m)}{(1 - \tau - \sigma)(1 + m)} \left[1 - \frac{\psi e (L/N)^{1-\theta}}{(1 - \tau)\theta(e - 1)} c \right], \tag{16}$$

where $c \equiv C/\lambda Z$ denotes consumption per effective person (*not* worker). It is straightforward to show that L is increasing in N and decreasing in c. This is intuitive: higher consumption lowers labor supply and thus employment (holding constant the unemployment rate u which does not depend directly on c). The reason why employment rises with the mass of firms is twofold. First, a larger mass of firms disperses employment and reduces firm size. As a result, the marginal product of labor rises, the wage rises and labor supply rises. Second, a larger mass of firms raises the price elasticity of demand. This in turn has two effects: it raises the wage and thus labor supply, and it lowers the markup and thus unemployment.

4. General equilibrium

To characterize the general equilibrium of this economy I impose output and capital market clearing. The partial equilibrium of the labor market affects the path of the economy through the reduced-form production function (15) which determines the resources constraint. (Notice that the mass of firms plays the role of capital in an otherwise standard reduced-form production function.) The saving schedule (5) determines the rate of return to saving that the household demands. The construction of the general equilibrium of this economy is then straightforward. There is an Euler equation characterizing the equilibrium of the assets market, whereby all rates of return are equalized, and an equation characterizing the equilibrium of the goods market, whereby output is allocated to consumption and investment. The latter equation is where this model deviates from the standard setup because the state variable of this economy is the mass of firms.

The phase diagram in Figure 1 and the following Proposition characterize dynamics in (N, c) space.

PROPOSITION 1. *There is a unique perfect-foresight general equilibrium. If the initial mass of firms is smaller than N^*, the economy jumps on the saddle path and converges to the steady state (N^*, c^*). If the initial mass of firms is larger than N^*, the economy enters immediately a steady state with no entry.*

PROOF. See the appendix. j

This proposition implies that there is a continuum of steady states to the right of N^* where the mass of firms is exogenous. This is the region of

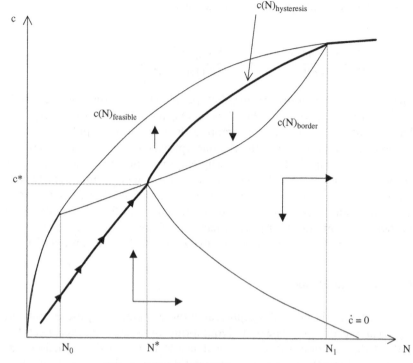

Fig. 1.   General equilibrium dynamics.

hysteresis where entry is not profitable and the mass of firms does not respond to parameter changes. To fully appreciate the model's implications, these must be taken into account.

Let $g \equiv \dot{Z}/Z$ be the rate of innovation, the rate of growth of labor productivity. To characterize the triple (g^*, u^*, L^*) associated to the steady state (N^*, c^*) it is useful to proceed as follows. The R&D intensity Equation (13) and the R&D technology (4) yield

$$
g = \begin{cases} 0 & 0 \leq N \leq N_0 \\ \frac{PX}{Z}\alpha\left[\frac{e-1}{e}(\beta + \theta) - 1\right]\frac{1-\gamma}{\beta+\gamma-1} & N > N_0 \end{cases} .
\tag{17}
$$

Equation (11) yields the rate of return to investment (*both* in-house R&D and entry since arbitrage equalizes returns). Now notice that working with consumption per effective person implies that asset market equilibrium requires that the rate of return be equal to the discount rate plus the growth rate, $r = \rho + g$. Hence,

$$
\rho + g = \frac{PX}{Z}\frac{\alpha(1 - \gamma)(e - 1)}{e}.
\tag{18}
$$

Solving this equation for PX/Z and substituting into (17) yields an equation that describes growth as an increasing function of market competition,

$$g = \begin{cases} 0 & 0 \leq N \leq N_0 \\ \rho \dfrac{(\beta + \theta)(e - 1/e) - 1}{1 - (1 - \gamma + \theta)(e - 1/e)} & N > N_0 \end{cases} \qquad \text{(GG)}$$

An important property of this equation is that the parameter α is missing. This is because its effects on the intensive and extensive margins are identical and thus cancel out in the arbitrage condition that equalizes the returns to R&D by incumbents and R&D by entrants.[10]

A similar equation characterizing equilibria with entry in (N, u) space obtains by evaluating the unemployment Equation (14) at the relevant values of the markup. Substituting the R&D intensity Equation (13) into the markup Equation (9) yields

$$m = \begin{cases} \gamma \dfrac{e - \theta(e - 1)}{\theta(e - 1)} & 0 \leq N \leq N_0 \\ \gamma \dfrac{e - (1 - \gamma + \theta)(e - 1)}{\theta(e - 1)(1 - (1 - \gamma/\beta))} & N > N_0 \end{cases}$$

Accordingly,

$$u = \frac{1 - \tau}{1 - \tau - \sigma} \frac{m}{1 + m} \qquad \text{(UU)}$$

defines a kinked curve that is monotonically decreasing in N.

The economy's resources constraint and the reduced-form production function (15) yield a relation between R&D intensity and consumption,

$$\frac{R}{PX} = 1 - \frac{\lambda c}{N} \left(\frac{L}{N} \right)^{-\theta}.$$

Solving the markup Equation (9) for R&D intensity and substituting into this expression allows one to eliminate consumption from the employment Equation (16) and write

$$L = \lambda \left[\frac{(1 - \tau - \sigma)(1 + m)}{1 - \tau - \sigma(1 + m)} + \frac{\psi}{1 - \tau} \left(\frac{m}{\gamma} + 1 \right) \right]^{-1}. \qquad \text{(LL)}$$

---

[10] The reader should also note that the equation does not contain terms that measure the size of the economy. Hence, the economy's labor endowment affects growth only through its (positive) effect on the number of firms. As a result, the model exhibits a nonlinear scale effect, bounded from above. Since I have already discussed this property of this class of models in Peretto (1998, 1999), I do not examine this effect here and refer the reader to those papers for details.

Evaluating this at the markup given above yields a kinked employment curve in (N, L) space that is monotonically increasing.

When entrants are not active, the rate of return to investment is given by the rate of return to R&D (11). Asset market equilibrium requires $r = \rho + g$. Hence,

$$
g = \begin{cases} \dfrac{\alpha(1 - \gamma)(e - 1)}{e} \left(\dfrac{L}{N}\right)^{\theta} - \rho & 0 \le N < N_1 \\[2mm] 0 & N \ge N_1 \end{cases}.
\tag{HHg}
$$

One can characterize firm size L/N as a function of the mass of firms N so that this equation describes a locus in (N, g) space.

To see this, observe that the procedure followed above yields

$$
L = \lambda \left[\frac{(1 - \tau - \sigma)(1 + \tilde{m})}{1 - \tau - \sigma(1 + \tilde{m})} + \frac{\psi}{1 - \tau} \left(\frac{\tilde{m}}{\gamma} + 1 \right) \right]^{-1}
\tag{HHL}
$$

and

$$
u = \frac{1 - \tau}{1 - \tau - \sigma} \frac{\tilde{m}}{1 + \tilde{m}},
\tag{HHu}
$$

where the assets market equilibrium condition yields

$$
\tilde{m} = \begin{cases} \gamma \left[\dfrac{e - (1 - \gamma + \theta)(e - 1)}{\theta(e - 1)} + \dfrac{e}{\theta(e - 1)} \dfrac{\rho}{\alpha} \left(\dfrac{L}{N}\right)^{-\theta} \right] & 0 \le N < N_1 \\[3mm] \gamma \dfrac{e - \theta(e - 1)}{\theta(e - 1)} & N \ge N_1 \end{cases}.
$$

These two equations determine employment L and the markup $\tilde{m}$ as functions of N. (The detailed analysis is available on request.) Accordingly, they determine the unemployment and employment equations, (HH_u), and (HH_L), that apply in the hysteresis region.

There are two effects of the mass of firms. The first is the standard one of tougher competition that reduces market power. The second is specific to equilibria with no entry wherein R&D is determined by the resources constraint and – contrary to equilibria with entry – is *decreasing* in N. As a consequence, a larger mass of firms *can* result in a higher markup. The appendix discusses a sufficient condition for the former effect to dominate and thus have the plausible property that the (HH_L) curve is upward sloping while the markup $\tilde{m}$ is decreasing in N. In this case, equation (HH_g) describes a monotonically decreasing curve in (N, g) space. It intersects the horizontal axis at point N_1, which means that R&D is zero whenever the mass of firms is too large. This is intuitive: when there are too many firms, each firm is small and the returns to innovation are low. As a result, firms set R&D to zero. Similarly, equation (HH_u) is downward sloping.

The values g^*, L^*, u^* associated to (N^*, c^*) are at the intersection of (GG) with (HH_g), (LL) with (HH_L), and (UU) with (HH_u). All points on the

(HH_g), (HH_L), and (HH_u) curves to the right of N^* are steady states. These are situations where entry is not profitable and the mass of firms does not respond to shocks and changes in policy variables. Figure 2 illustrates. Comparative statics are as follows.

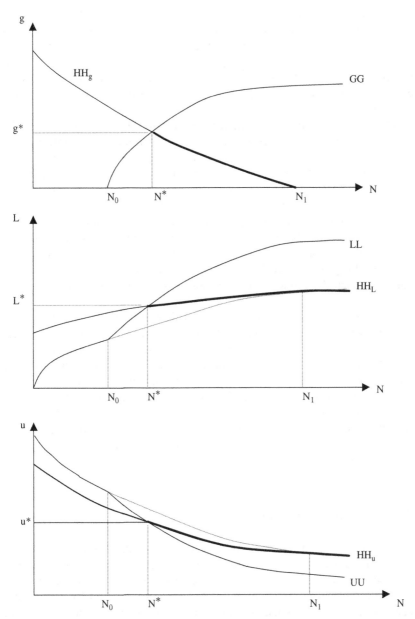

Fig. 2.   The set of steady-state equilibria.

PROPOSITION 2. *Growth* g^* *is increasing in* α, β, ε, *and decreasing in* γ, τ, σ. *The mass of firms* N^* *is increasing in* α, *decreasing in* γ, τ, σ, β *while the effect of* ε *is ambiguous. Employment* L^* *is increasing in* α, *decreasing in* γ, τ, σ, *while the effects of* β *and* ε *are ambiguous. Unemployment* u^* *is decreasing in* α, *increasing in* γ, τ, σ, *while the effects of* β *and* ε *are ambiguous.*

In the region $N_0 < N < N_1$, the figure emphasizes the underlying employment and unemployment curves for the case with zero R&D because comparing these curves to the other two highlights that there is more employment and less unemployment when there is growth – this is illustrated by the fact that the employment and unemployment curves for equilibria with R&D are, respectively, above and below the curves for the case without.

The positive relation between competition and growth captured by the (GG) locus determines the growth effects of policy interventions and exogenous shocks that affect the labor market. Specifically, changes in labor market equilibrium are transmitted to the product market through shifts of the (HH_g) locus that produce a movement along the (GG) locus. This happens, for example, in the case of reductions of the labor tax τ or the replacement ratio σ. Thus, policy interventions in the labor market that raise employment – because they lower unemployment, raise labor supply or do both – attract entry and, as a result of tougher competition, raise growth. This growth effect is larger the less competitive is the economy and vanishes when the economy approaches the upper bound for the elasticity of substitution.

The slopes of the (LL) and (UU) loci determine the employment and unemployment effects of policy interventions and exogenous shocks that affect the product market. Specifically, changes in product market equilibrium are transmitted to the labor market through shifts of the (HH_L) and (HH_u) loci that produce movements along the (LL) and (UU) curves. One can see that policy interventions in the product market that attract entry raise employment and reduce unemployment purely because they increase competition and thus reduce the wage premium. I discuss in detail the effects of interventions in the labor and product markets in the next section.

5. Implications for the analysis of reforms

The dynamic response of the economy to a change in parameters is subject to hysteresis since increases in the mass of firms are irreversible. It is thus necessary to distinguish between (a) results that characterize economies with different parameters (comparative statics results) and (b) results that characterize the response of one economy to a parameter change (comparative dynamics results).

5.1. Labor market reforms

Three parameters capture institutional features of the labor market that affect labor costs for firms: the tax on wages, τ, the replacement ratio, σ, and the bargaining power of workers, γ. This subsection makes three related points:

- policies that reduce labor costs raise employment – by raising labor market participation – and reduce unemployment;
- the rise in employment and the reduction in unemployment are larger when one considers the endogenous mass of firms;
- because these improvements in labor market conditions are associated to more competition, these policies raise growth.

To illustrate, I consider the effects of labor income taxes.

PROPOSITION 3. *Effects of the labor income tax rate, τ. (a) An economy with higher τ converges to a steady state with lower growth, a smaller mass of firms, lower employment and higher unemployment than economies with lower τ. (b) In response to an increase in τ, the economy jumps to a steady state with lower growth, the same mass of firms, lower employment and higher unemployment. In response to a reduction in τ, the economy converges to a steady state with higher growth, a larger mass of firms, higher employment, and lower unemployment.*

Consider Figure 3. Point *A* is the steady state reached by an economy with a high tax rate; point *B* is the steady state reached by an economy with a low tax rate. The arrows describe the shifts due to a reduction of the tax rate. Consider the economy at point *B*. If τ increases, the economy is in the hysteresis region and employment and growth fall immediately while unemployment raises. This is the jump from point *B* to point *C* on the hysteresis curves corresponding to the high tax rate. If τ returns to the original value, employment, output, growth, and unemployment return to the original values. Consider now the economy at point *A*. If τ decreases, the economy jumps on the saddle path that converges to point *B*.

The economics behind these results is as follows. The lower labor tax yields a higher after-tax wage for workers and a lower pre-tax wage for firms. Hence, it raises labor supply (participation) and lowers the wage premium. As a result, given the mass of firms, it is associated to higher employment and lower unemployment. This is captured by the shift up of the (HH_L) curve and the shift down of the (HH_u) curve. These are just the traditional effects of lower labor income taxation on participation and unemployment. On top of these, there are the indirect effects due to the mass of firms. The higher level of activity due to higher employment means that firm size is larger. To keep the net rate of return equal to the discount rate, the mass of firms must be larger so that there is a compensating market share effect. The effect of the change in the mass of firms is

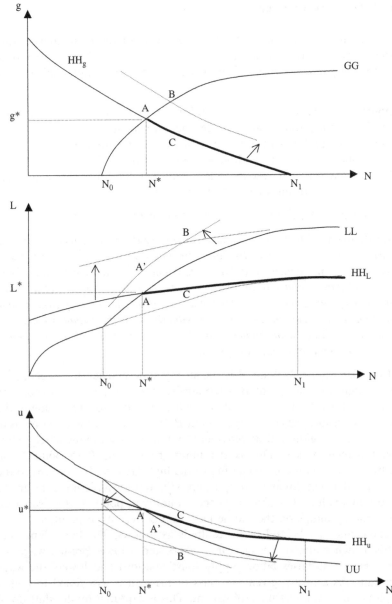

Fig. 3.   Effects of the labor income tax.

captured by the movements along the (GG), (LL) and (UU) loci which
incorporate entry. Since the (GG) locus does not shift, because it does not
depend directly on the tax, growth is higher purely because the lower tax
yields more competition. The (LL) and (UU) loci shift, respectively, up and

down. As one can see, the lower tax is associated to higher employment and lower unemployment.

Consider now the dynamics. When the tax increases, the mass of firms does not change while unemployment rises. Holding constant labor supply, this reduces the firms' scale of activity and thereby reduces growth. Labor supply however is endogenous. The higher tax rate causes labor supply, and thus employment, to fall. These effects are in line with traditional intuition built on models that ignore the effects of the endogenous structure of the product market. Things are quite different when the mass of firms adjusts endogenously, as it happens when taxes are reduced. A lower tax generates a positive feedback through the product market that reinforces the benefits of lower taxation. These benefits are reaped over time as the mass of firms raises. Figure 3 illustrates this point by separating the *pro-competitive* or *product market effect* of the lower tax rate from its traditional *labor market effect*. Given the mass of firms, the lower tax rate yields a lower (HH_u) locus and a higher (HH_L) locus, and thus reduces unemployment and raises employment. These effects are captured in the figure by the movement from point A to point A'. The larger mass of firms then reduces unemployment further. This is captured by the movement from point A' to point B along the new (LL) and (UU) curves.

The asymmetric response of the economy to decreases and increases in the labor income tax rate requires one to distinguish the time-series implications of the model from its cross-section implications. The model predicts that countries with higher labor income taxes exhibit higher unemployment and lower growth. This is consistent with intuition. This correlation, however, is very hard to detect in studies that cover several countries at a moment in time because it is dominated by country-specific fixed effects in cross-sectional regressions. One then needs to check how variations of tax rates over time affect unemployment within a country (Daveri & Tabellini, 2000). If labor taxation keeps increasing over a period of time, the time-paths of unemployment and growth track the time-path of the tax rate. More precisely, the model predicts that each time the tax rate rises, unemployment rises and growth falls. This is consistent with the empirical evidence provided by Daveri and Tabellini (2000) for the OECD countries. They show that the upward trend in labor income tax rates drives the upward trend in unemployment and the downward trend in growth.[11] On the other hand, the model predicts that the effects of tax

---

[11] The model understates the negative effect of rising taxes because it does not allow for exit, and thus rules out the possibility that the upward trend in taxation lead to fewer firms and less competition. Including exit, for example by positing that firms incur instantaneous fixed costs, complicates the algebra but does not change the results discussed in the text. In particular, allowing for exit reduces the size of the region of hysteresis but does not eliminate it. The size of this region depends on how large is the entry sunk cost relative to the instantaneous fixed

breaks are spread over time and generate a protracted expansion of output accompanied by a falling rate of unemployment.

The replacement ratio has effects similar to those of the tax with the difference that the labor income tax reduces labor supply (because it reduces expected income) while the replacement ratio raises it. Hence, the tax is associated to less employment than the replacement ratio.

The parameter capturing the bargaining power of workers has intuitive effects that are similar to the ones outlined above. Because it raises the wage premium, it reduces employment and the mass of firms – two measures of the scale of economic activity – and through the associated anti-competitive effect rises unemployment and reduces growth.

5.2. Product market reforms

Several factors determine competition in the product market. The model allows me to consider the following:

- regulations/frictions that raise the cost of innovation can be modeled as a lower α;
- regulations/frictions that reduce product substitution and thus price competition can be modeled as a lower ε, where ε is a parameter that shifts up the function $e(N; \varepsilon)$;
- regulations/frictions that raise entry costs for entrants but do not affect incumbents can be modeled as a higher β.

This subsection makes the following points, which illustrate the interactions between the labor and product markets:

- lower costs of innovation raise growth and employment and reduce unemployment;
- tougher price competition raises growth and has an ambiguous effect on employment and unemployment;
- lower barriers to entry reduce growth and ambiguous effects on employment and unemployment.

These results suggest that the details of the pro-competitive policy that a country adopts matter. In particular, reducing barriers to innovation is the best policy because it reduces at the same time barriers to entry and barriers to innovation within the firm. As a result, it fosters investment on both the intensive and the extensive margin and, more importantly, it

---

cost. If the latter is zero, as in this model, firms never exit and the region of hysteresis extends from the interior steady state to infinity; if it is positive, the region of hysteresis is a finite interval. In the latter case, the negative effect of taxation on firms' cash flow could be large enough to push them against the exit margin thereby triggering a feedback through the product market that reinforces the negative effects of taxation of labor by reducing competition.

exploits the positive relation between competition and growth and the negative relation between competition and unemployment. I now illustrate these results in some detail.

PROPOSITION 4. *Effects of the R&D productivity parameter, α. (a) An economy with higher α converges to a steady state with higher growth, a larger mass of firms, higher employment, and lower unemployment. (b) In response to an increase in α, the economy converges to a steady state with higher growth, a larger mass of firms, higher employment, and lower unemployment. In response to a decrease in α, the economy jumps to a steady state with lower growth, the same mass of firms, and the same levels of employment and unemployment.*

It is simple to see what drives these results. The direct effect of the higher α is to shift up the (HH_g) and (HH_L) loci and to shift down the (HH_u) locus. Growth and employment rise while unemployment falls. The higher α also implies that to keep the net rate of return equal to the discount rate the mass of firms must be larger. The rise in the mass of firms feeds back positively on employment and growth and negatively on unemployment. The key intuition behind these results is that the higher α boosts productivity of investment on *both* the extensive and the intensive margin. Hence, the economy supports faster growth *and* a large mass of firms, with all the benefits that follow for the labor market.

PROPOSITION 5. *Effects of the elasticity of product substitution, ε. (a) An economy with higher ε converges to a steady state with a smaller mass of firms. If the direct effect of ε dominates over the indirect effect, growth and employment are higher and unemployment is lower in the economy with higher ε. (b) In response to an increase in ε, the economy jumps to a steady state with the same mass of firms, higher growth and employment and lower unemployment. In response to a decrease in ε, the economy converges to a steady state with a larger mass of firms. If the direct effect of ε dominates over the indirect effect, growth and employment are lower and unemployment is higher in the new steady state.*

These results are relatively straightforward. Holding constant the mass of firms, in the product market the direct effect of tougher price competition is to raise growth while in the labor market it is to raise employment and lower unemployment. There are two conflicting effects on the mass of firms. The increase in the firms' scale of activity associated to higher employment implies that to keep the net rate of return equal to the discount rate the mass of firms must be higher. However, tougher price competition leads firms to spend more on R&D, which is a fixed cost that makes incumbency more costly. Firms, moreover, are less profitable because price-cost margins are lower. Both these forces tend to reduce the mass of firms. As a result of this conflict, the effect of ε on the mass of firms in ambiguous. If it is positive – if the mass of firms rises because the employment effect dominates over the incumbency cost and the profit margin effects – the overall effect of ε is to rise growth and employment and reduce unemployment because the pro-competitive indirect effects associated to the larger mass of firms work in the same direction as the direct effects associated to the lower price and wage markups.

PROPOSITION 6. *Effects of the entry cost parameter, β. (a) An economy with higher β converges to a steady state a smaller mass of firms, lower employment and higher unemployment. If growth is very responsive to product market competition, it is lower in the economy with the smaller mass of firms. (b) In response to a reduction in β, the economy converges to a steady state with a larger mass of firms, higher employment, and lower unemployment. If growth is very responsive to product market competition, it is higher in the new steady state. An increase in β has no effects.*

This case provides a surprise of sort in that lower barriers to entry are not necessarily associated to higher employment and lower unemployment. Here is why. The higher cost of entry yields *higher* growth. This is due to the *protection effect*: incumbent firms protected by high barriers to entry are larger and do more R&D. Quite important is the fact that faster growth is due to higher R&D intensity, which – as argued in detail in Section 4 – reduces the wage markup and thus is associated to higher employment and lower unemployment. Opposite these direct effects, there is the fact that higher barriers to entry are associated to fewer firms, which means weaker competition and a higher wage markup, a force that tends to lower employment and raise unemployment. The tension between the direct and indirect effects of barriers to entry gives rise to ambiguous results.

This ambiguity can be resolved if one can show that the (HH_L) is upward sloping and the (HH_u) locus is downward sloping, which is the case if there is a *sufficiently strong response of the elasticity of substitution to the mass of firms*. The appendix provides a formal analysis of the conditions under which this happens. Figures 2 and 3 illustrate this case.

An important point that emerges from this discussion is that preferential treatment of incumbents in order to boost growth – a policy that can be modeled as a high β – is potentially self-defeating because faster growth might come at the cost of worse conditions in the labor market. Given the importance that recent studies attach to the role of barriers to entry for labor market outcomes, two additional remarks concerning these results are in order.

First, the result that higher barriers to entry reduce the wage markup because they promote growth depends crucially on the assumption of efficient bargaining between firms and workers. If the wage setting process takes the form of a standard right to manage model with monopolistic unions, the wage follows

$$W_i = \frac{e_W}{e_W - 1}\frac{W_a}{1 - \tau}, \quad e_W \equiv \frac{1}{1 - \theta(e - 1/e)},$$

which produces a markup that does not depend on R&D intensity. Breaking the link between the wage markup and R&D intensity has the crucial implication that the wage markup does not decrease directly with barriers to entry – like in Equation (9) – and therefore the only effect of barriers to entry is through the mass of firms. It is then immediate to show that barriers to entry reduce employment and raise unemployment simply because they reduce product market competition. More generally, one should observe that the result that higher barriers to entry do not necessarily worsen labor market outcomes is predicated on (a) a strong response of the wage markup to R&D intensity and (b) a weak response of the wage markup to product market competition. Let me stress that the comparative statics results discussed above concerning the other parameters are robust to this change in the description of the bargaining process and thus do not depend on these two conditions. Barriers to entry, in contrast, appear to play a special role in this environment where firms undertake R&D investment, and their effects depend on the strength of the relationship between R&D intensity and the wage markup.

The second remark concerns the general implications of this line of analysis for the recent literature on the role of labor and product market reforms as different means to the same end of improving labor market performance. Since the effect of price competition and barriers to entry are potentially ambiguous, reforms of the product market do not substitute for reforms of the labor market. One could see in the recent literature on the labor market effects of product market deregulation an argument that the same desirable outcomes – higher employment, lower unemployment – could be accomplished by reforming the product market *instead of* the labor market. The analysis in this section suggests that the mechanisms involved are quite different. Reforming the labor market triggers indirect effects through the product market that work in the same direction as the direct effects because the transmission channel runs through larger market size (higher employment) that attracts entry and thus raises competition. This mechanism, moreover, applies to all the three dimensions of labor market reform considered here: taxation, unemployment benefits, bargaining power of workers. It follows that reforming the labor market is unambiguously good for employment and unemployment, with the additional bonus that it fosters growth. Reforming the product market instead triggers indirect effects that potentially offset the direct effects. More importantly, the overall effects are specific to the particular dimension that one wishes to pursue – lower costs of innovation for both incumbents and entrants, tougher price competition, lower barriers to entry – and to the particular form of the wage bargaining process. The robust result that emerges is that product market deregulation that reduces innovation costs for *both* incumbents and entrants boosts growth and produces better labor market performance.

6. Conclusion

The view that unemployment is high in economies where the welfare state provides long-lasting unemployment benefits that are unrelated to the individual's effort to find work, the labor force is organized in sectoral or firm-level unions that do not coordinate their activities, and taxation raises the cost of labor, is generally correct and supported by much of the available empirical evidence. It is, however, incomplete because it ignores the characteristics of the product market. There are good reasons, theoretical and empirical, to think that in addition to labor market frictions, unemployment depends on a broad class of factors that characterize the structure of the product market. An interesting implication of this argument is that there exists a relation between unemployment and growth. The reason is that growth is driven by firms' R&D investments, which are affected by the structure of the product market.

In this chapter, I discussed a model where firms and workers set wages above the market-clearing level. Unemployment is thus generated by their exercise of market power. Because both the labor and product markets are imperfectly competitive, market power in the labor market interacts with market power in the product market. This interaction sheds new light on the effects of policy interventions on unemployment and growth. For example, labor market reforms that reduce labor costs reduce unemployment *and* boost growth because they expand the scale of the economy and generate more competition in the product market. Moreover, the reduction in unemployment is larger than one would expect if the reforms' effects in the product market were ignored. If such reforms are implemented jointly with a reduction of barriers to innovation an even larger reduction in unemployment is achieved.

The approach developed here lends itself easily to extensions and further analysis of important issues that are part of the current policy debate. First and foremost, it would be worthwhile to explore how different bargaining environments, or surplus sharing arrangements different from bargaining, might affect the results. For example, if the surplus sharing process is construed as bargaining between the firm and its unionized workforce, then it is possible to obtain different solutions according to whether one takes a right to manage approach or an approach where bargaining covers both employment and the wage. Even more interesting would be to investigate how the solution changes if the firm bargains with the workforce over the R&D strategy as well. Although rarely observed, such arrangements might yield surprises: in preliminary work, for example, I found that it would lead to higher R&D intensity and faster growth, suggesting a novel benefit of letting the workforce have a stake in the growth of the firm.

Acknowledgments

I thank Peter Arcidiacono, Michelle Connolly, Enrique Mendoza, Rob, Reed, Jonathan Temple and John Seater for useful comments.

Appendix

A.1. The bargaining problem

The firm and its workers solve

$$\max_{W_i, L_i} \quad [(1 - \gamma) \log \Pi_i + \gamma \log (W_i(1 - \tau) - W_a)L_i].$$

Using the production function (3) and the demand curve (2) profit becomes

$$\Pi_i = \left(\frac{Y}{N}\right)^{1/e} Z_i^{1-(1/e)} L_i^{\theta(e-1)/e} - W_i L_i - R_i.$$

At this stage, R&D spending R_i is taken as given – the assumption being that the firm's management sets R&D policy independently of its workers. Taking derivatives with respect to W_i and L_i:

$$(1 - \gamma)\frac{L_i}{\Pi_i} = \gamma \frac{(1 - \tau)L_i}{(W_i(1 - \tau) - W_a)L_i};$$

$$(1 - \gamma) \frac{-(\theta(e - 1)/e)(Y/N)^{1/e} Z_i^{1-(1/e)} L_i^{(\theta(e-1)/e)-1} + W_i}{\Pi_i}$$

$$= \gamma \frac{W_i(1 - \tau) - W_a}{(W_i(1 - \tau) - W_a)L_i}.$$

The first equation can be rearranged to obtain

$$W_i = \frac{W_a}{1 - \tau} + \frac{\gamma}{1 - \gamma}\frac{\Pi_i}{L_i}.$$

The ratio of the two first-order conditions yields

$$L_i = \frac{\theta(e - 1)}{e}\frac{1 - \tau}{W_a}\left(\frac{Y}{N}\right)^{1/e} Z_i^{1-(1/e)} L_i^{\theta(e-1)/e}$$

$$= \frac{1 - \tau}{W_a}\frac{\theta(e - 1)}{e} P_i X_i.$$

A.2. The reduced-form revenue function

The production technology (3) and the expression for firm employment yield the price

$$P_i = \frac{W_a}{1 - \tau} \frac{e}{\theta(e-1)} \frac{L_i^{1-\theta}}{Z_i}.$$

Using the demand curve (2) I can write

$$P_i X_i = \frac{Y}{N} P_i^{1-e}$$

$$= \frac{Y}{N} \left[\frac{W_a}{1 - \tau} \frac{e}{\theta(e-1)} \frac{L_i^{1-\theta}}{Z_i} \right]^{1-e}.$$

The expression for firm employment then yields

$$L_i = \frac{1 - \tau}{W_a} \frac{\theta(e-1)}{e} \frac{Y}{N} \left[\frac{W_a}{1 - \tau} \frac{e}{\theta(e-1)} \frac{L_i^{1-\theta}}{Z_i} \right]^{1-e}.$$

Solving for L_i yields

$$L_i = \left[\frac{Y}{N} \left[\frac{W_a}{1 - \tau} \frac{e}{\theta(e-1)} \right]^{-e} Z_i^{e-1} \right]^{1/e - \theta(e-1)}.$$

The reduced-form revenue function then is

$$P_i X_i = \left(\frac{Y}{N} \right)^{1/e - \theta(e-1)} \left[\frac{(W_a/1 - \tau)e}{\theta(e-1)} \right]^{-\theta(e-1)/e - \theta(e-1)} Z_i^{(e-1)/e - \theta(e-1)}.$$

A.3. Proof of Proposition 1

The output market clearing condition is

$$Y = C + NR + \frac{\beta Z}{\alpha} \dot{N}.$$

Since entry is nonnegative, one has $\dot{N} > 0$ for $Y > C + NR$ and $\dot{N} = 0$ otherwise. This condition identifies two regions in (N,c) space: the entry region, where entry is profitable, and the hysteresis region, where entry is not profitable and the mass of firms is fixed.

Consider the entry region. Dividing through by Z, and using the R&D Equation (13) and the reduced-form production function (15), I can write the resources constraint as

$$\dot{N} = \begin{cases} \frac{\alpha}{\beta}[N^{1-\theta}L^{\theta} - \lambda c] & 0 \le N \le N_0 \\ \frac{\alpha}{\beta}\left[N^{1-\theta}L^{\theta}\left(1 - \left[\frac{e-1}{e}(\beta + \theta) - 1\right]\frac{1-\gamma}{\beta+\gamma-1} \right) - \lambda c \right] & N > N_0 \end{cases}.$$

Taking logs and time derivatives of $c \equiv C/\lambda Z$ and using the saving schedule (5), the rate of return to investment (18), the R&D Equation (13), and the reduced-form production function (15) I obtain

$$\frac{\dot{c}}{c} = \begin{cases} \left(\frac{L}{N}\right)^{\theta} \dfrac{1 - (e - 1/e)(\theta - \gamma + 1)}{\beta + \gamma - 1} \alpha(1 - \gamma) - \rho & 0 \leq N \leq N_0 \\[2ex] \left(\frac{L}{N}\right)^{\theta} \dfrac{1 - (e - 1/e)\theta}{\beta} \alpha(1 - \gamma) - \rho & N > N_0 \end{cases}.$$

Recall the employment Equation (16)

$$L = \lambda \frac{1 - \tau - \sigma(1 + m)}{(1 - \tau - \sigma)(1 + m)} \left[1 - \frac{\psi e(L/N)^{1-\theta}}{(1 - \tau)\theta(e - 1)} c \right],$$

where

$$m = \begin{cases} \gamma \dfrac{e - \theta(e - 1)}{\theta(e - 1)} & 0 \leq N \leq N_0 \\[2ex] \gamma \dfrac{e - (1 - \gamma + \theta)(e - 1)}{\theta(e - 1)(1 - (1 - \gamma/\beta))} & N > N_0 \end{cases}.$$

These two equations jointly determine L as increasing in N and decreasing in c. It is useful to use the employment equation to analyze the effects of consumption and the mass of firms on employment per firm, L/N. One simply writes

$$\frac{L}{N} = \frac{\lambda}{N} \frac{1 - \tau - \sigma(1 + m)}{(1 - \tau - \sigma)(1 + m)} \left[1 - \frac{\psi e(L/N)^{1-\theta}}{(1 - \tau)\theta(e - 1)} c \right].$$

This implicit equation in L/N captures two effects of the mass of firms. First, there is the straightforward effect that more firms disperse *potential* labor supply; this is the term λ/N reflecting the basic fact that – whatever the conditions of the labor market, i.e., whatever the fraction of the labor endowment that is actually employed – a larger mass of firms means smaller firm size. Second, a larger mass of firms raises the price elasticity of demand, e, and reduces the markup m. As discussed in the text, these effects tend to raise labor supply. One can show analytically, however, that the dispersion effect dominates so that the right-hand side of the equation is decreasing in N. The implicit function theorem then says that firm size L/N is decreasing in both N and c.[12] With these results in hand, one can see that the two differential equations derived above fully describe dynamics in (N,c) space. The $\dot{c} = 0$ locus is

---

[12] The key step in the proof is to show that employment rises less than linearly with the number of firms so that the ratio L/N approaches infinity as N approaches zero. This analysis is available on request.

$$\begin{cases} \left(\frac{L}{N}\right)^\theta \dfrac{1 - (e - 1/e)(\theta - \gamma + 1)}{\beta + \gamma - 1}\alpha(1 - \gamma) = \rho & 0 \le N \le N_0 \\[3mm] \left(\frac{L}{N}\right)^\theta \dfrac{1 - (e - 1/e)\theta}{\beta}\alpha(1 - \gamma) = \rho & N > N_0 \end{cases}$$

Since L is increasing in N and decreasing in c, this equation defines a downward sloping locus $c(N)_{\text{entry}}$ such that $\dot{c} \ge 0$ whenever $c \le c(N)_{\text{entry}}$. Notice that the locus intersects the horizontal axis.

The hysteresis region is identified by the weak inequality

$$c \ge \begin{cases} \dfrac{N^{1-\theta}L^\theta}{\lambda} & 0 \le N \le N_0 \\[3mm] \dfrac{N^{1-\theta}L^\theta}{\lambda}\left(1 - \left[\frac{e-1}{e}(\beta + \theta) - 1\right]\frac{1-\gamma}{\beta+\gamma-1}\right) & N > N_0 \end{cases}.$$

Since L is increasing in N and decreasing in c, this says that $\dot{N} = 0$ whenever $c \ge c(N)_{\text{border}}$, where $c(N)_{\text{border}}$ is increasing in N.

Inside this region Equation (13) does not hold and one must determine R&D effort through the resources constraint. Hence,

$$\frac{Y}{ZN} = \frac{\lambda}{N}c + \frac{R}{Z} \Rightarrow g = \alpha\left[\left(\frac{L}{N}\right)^\theta - \frac{\lambda}{N}c\right].$$

Equation (11) determines the rate of return to investment. The resulting asset market equilibrium condition reads:

$$\frac{\dot{c}}{c} = \frac{\alpha\lambda c}{N} - \left(\frac{L}{N}\right)^\theta \alpha\left[1 - \frac{(1 - \gamma)(e - 1)}{e}\right] - \rho.$$

Recall that L is determined by

$$L = \lambda\frac{1 - \tau - \sigma(1 + \tilde{m})}{(1 - \tau - \sigma)(1 + \tilde{m})}\left[1 - \left(\frac{L}{N}\right)^{1-\theta}\frac{\psi e}{(1 - \tau)\theta(e - 1)}c\right],$$

where

$$\tilde{m} = \begin{cases} \gamma\left[\frac{e}{\theta(e-1)}\left(\frac{N}{L}\right)^\theta \frac{\lambda}{N}c - 1\right] & 0 \le N < N_1 \\[3mm] \gamma\frac{e}{\theta(e-1)} & N > N_1 \end{cases}.$$

These two equations determine L as increasing in N and decreasing in c. Therefore, the asset market equilibrium condition reduces to an unstable differential equation in c. Specifically, $\dot{c} = 0$ whenever

$$\frac{\alpha}{N}\left(\lambda c - N^{1-\theta}L^\theta\left[1 - \frac{(1 - \gamma)(e - 1)}{e}\right]\right) = \rho.$$

Hence, $\dot{c} \ge 0$ whenever $c \ge c(N)_{\text{hysteresis}}$ where $c(N)_{\text{hysteresis}}$ is increasing in N and eventually intersects the feasibility constraint. This is the point N_1 where R&D becomes unprofitable because there are too many firms.

Observe now that the output market implies the feasibility constraint $Y \geq C$. In other words, the region of the state-space $C > Y$ must be ruled out because there the resources constraint is violated. This region can be specified as

$$\frac{N^{1-\theta}L^{\theta}}{\lambda} < c.$$

Since on this locus R&D is zero, L is determined by the employment equation as increasing in N and decreasing in c. It follows that the unfeasible region is $c > c(N)_{\text{unfeasible}}$ where $c(N)_{\text{unfeasible}}$ is increasing in N. This information allows me to construct the phase diagram in Figure 1. The intersection of $c(N)_{\text{entry}}$ and $c(N)_{\text{border}}$ determines the steady state (N^*, c^*). The $\dot{c} = 0$ locus is the kinked curve formed by the portion of $c(N)_{\text{entry}}$ in the entry region to the left of N^*, the portion of $c(N)_{\text{hysteresis}}$ in the hysteresis region that lies to the right of N^* and to the left of N_1, and the portion of the feasibility constraint to the right of N_1. In the entry region to the left of (N^*, c^*) there is a saddle path leading to that point. All points on $c(N)_{\text{hysteresis}}$ to the right of (N^*, c^*) are steady states. The stable manifold of the system is the union of the saddle path in the entry region and the portion of $c(N)_{\text{hysteresis}}$ inside the hysteresis region. Paths above the stable manifold eventually violate the feasibility constraint and cannot be equilibria. Similarly, paths below the stable manifold cannot be equilibria because they eventually cross the horizontal axis and yield zero or negative c. Hence, whenever $N < N^*$ the economy jumps on the saddle path and converges to the steady state; whenever $N \geq N^*$ the economy jumps on the $c(N)_{\text{hysteresis}}$ locus and enters a steady state with no entry.

A.4. A condition for $\tilde{m}$ decreasing in N

Recall that L and $\tilde{m}$ obey

$$L = \frac{1 - \tau - \sigma(1 + \tilde{m})}{(1 - \tau - \sigma)(1 + \tilde{m})} \left[\lambda - L \frac{\psi}{1 - \tau} \left(\frac{\tilde{m}}{\gamma} + 1 \right) \right]$$

and

$$\tilde{m} = \gamma \left[\frac{e - (1 - \gamma + \theta)(e - 1)}{\theta(e - 1)} + \frac{e}{\theta(e - 1)} \left(\frac{L}{N} \right)^{-\theta} \frac{\rho}{\alpha} \right].$$

(I consider only situations with positive R&D since those with zero R&D do not give rise to ambiguities.) These describe two downward sloping markup curves in $(\tilde{m}, L)$ space. The markup curve intersects the employment curve from below. Changes in N shift the markup curve and produce movements along the employment curve. A sufficient condition for $\tilde{m}$ decreasing in N, therefore, is that the markup curve shift down; that is, that holding constant L the effect of an increase in the mass of firms be negative. Formally,

$$\left[\theta(e-1)-\frac{e'N}{e}\right]\left(\frac{L}{N}\right)^{-\theta}\frac{\rho}{\alpha}<\frac{e'N}{e}.$$

Recall now that positive R&D obtains if

$$\left(\frac{L}{N}\right)^{\theta}>\frac{\lambda c}{N}\Rightarrow\left(\frac{L}{N}\right)^{-\theta}\frac{\rho}{\alpha}<\frac{(1-\gamma)(e-1)}{e}.$$

The desired sufficient condition therefore is

$$\frac{(1-\gamma)(e-1)}{e}<\frac{e'N/e}{\theta(e-1)-e'N/e}\Rightarrow\frac{e'N}{e}>\frac{\theta(e-1)}{1+(e/(1-\gamma)(e-1))}.$$

This requires that the function $e(N)$ be sufficiently elastic over the range $0\le N<N_1$.

References

Adams, J., & Jaffe, A. (1996). Bounding the effects of R&D: An investigation using matched establishment-firm data. *Rand Journal of Economics, 27*, 700–721.

Aghion, P., & Howitt, P. (1994). Growth and unemployment. *Review of Economic Studies, 61*, 477–494.

Cohen, W., & Klepper, S. (1996a). A reprise of size and R&D. *Economic Journal, 106*, 925–951.

Cohen, W., & Klepper, S. (1996b). Firm size and the nature of innovation within industries: The case of process and product R&D. *Review of Economics and Statistics, 78*(2), 232–243.

Daveri, F., & Tabellini, G. (2000). Unemployment, growth and taxation in industrial countries. *Economic Policy, 30*, 49–88.

Merz, M. (1995). Search in the labor market and the real business cycle. *Journal of Monetary Economics, 36*, 269–300.

Mortensen, D. (2005). Growth, unemployment and labor market policy. *Journal of the European Association, 3*, 236–258.

Nickell, S. (1996). Competition and corporate performance. *Journal of Political Economy, 104*, 724–746.

Nickell, S., & Layard, R. (1999). Labor market institutions and economic performance. In O. Ashenfelter & D. Card (Eds.), *Handbook of Labor Economics* (1st ed., Vol. 3, chapter 46, pp. 3029–3084). Elsevier.

Pagano, P., & Schivardi, F. (2003). Firm size distribution and growth. *Scandinavian Journal of Economics, 105*, 255–274.

Peretto, P. (1996). Sunk costs, market structure and growth. *International Economic Review, 37*, 895–923.

Peretto, P. (1998). Market rivalry, technological change and the evolution of the capitalist engine of growth. *Journal of Economic Growth, 3,* 53–80.

Peretto, P. (1999). Cost reduction, entry, and the interdependence of market structure and economic growth. *Journal of Monetary Economics, 43,* 173–195.

Pissarides, C. (2002). *Equilibrium Unemployment Theory* (2nd ed.). Cambridge MA: MIT University Press.

Smulders, S., & van de Klundert, T. (1995). *European Economic Review, 39*(1), 139–160

Wu, Y., & Zhang, J. (2000). Endogenous markups and the effects of income taxation: Theory and evidence from OECD countries. *Journal of Public Economics, 77,* 383–406.

CHAPTER 20

Optimal Abatement Investment and Environmental Policies Under Pollution Uncertainty

Enrico Saltari[a] and Giuseppe Travaglini[b]

[a]Dipartimento di Economia e Diritto, Facoltà di Economia, Università "La Sapienza" di Roma, Via del Castro Laurenziano 9, Roma, Italy
E-mail address: Enrico.Saltari@uniroma1.it
[b]Dipartimento di Economia, Società e Politica, Facoltà di Economia, Università "Carlo Bo" di Urbino, Via Saffi 42, 61029, Urbino (PU), Italy
E-mail address: Giuseppe.Travaglini@uniurb.it

Abstract
In this chapter we present a continuous time model with reversible abatement capital in order to analyze the effects of environmental policies on the value of the firm and investment decisions. We show that the effects depend on what sort of future policy are implemented. We focus on investment effects of changes in corrective taxes to control the use of polluting inputs, and subsidies to promote abatement investment. We show that (1) while taxes have a depressive effect on capital accumulation, subsidies boost investment; (2) the impact of these policies on the value of the firm is ambiguous. This latter result has important empirical implications insofar as investment are based on the average value of the firm rather than the (unobservable) marginal value.

Keywords: Pollution uncertainty, externality, capital reversibility, environmental policy

JEL classifications: E22, L51, H23, Q28

1. Introduction

This chapter examines the effect of environmental policies on the abatement investment decisions of a competitive firm, facing pollution uncertainty. The relationship between economic decisions and pollution dynamics has been extensively studied over the past decade (Bretschger &

Frontiers of Economics and Globalization
Volume 11   ISSN: 1574-8715
DOI: 10.1108/S1574-8715(2011)0000011025

Smulders, 2007; Egli & Steger 2007; Soretz, 2007). The standard problem concerns the optimal timing of a discrete policy that a society or a government should adopt to reduce emissions of environmental pollutant. Some common features characterize this class of models. Smulders and Gradus (1996), and Soretz (2007) model pollution as an externality which affects the productivity of inputs and/or utility of consumption. Fisher (2000) and Pindyck (2000) remark that irreversibility is a feature that frequently comes into play together with pollution, shaping the optimal abatement investment strategies. Pindyck (2000) emphasizes that abatement investment and pollution have to do with the effects of uncertainty, and that when irreversibility and uncertainty come together, delaying policy adoption may be optimal for an investor.

These models captured a growing attention and many theorists investigated the consequences of environmental policies on abatement investment strategies using the real option value approach (Ansar & Spark, 2009; Fisher, 2000; Lin & Huang, 2010; Lin, Ko, & Yeh, 2007; Pindyck, 2002).

Recently, Lin and Huang (2011) and Saltari and Travaglini (2011) (hereafter LH and ST) extended the basic model of option value, shifting the attention from the net social benefits of a policy, to the net private benefits of a firm investing in clean capital goods. As they argue, an efficient energy-saving or abatement investment program need to take account of the trajectory of costs and profits over time associated to the project, rather than just at a single point in time. Both these papers are related to the literature on optimal stopping time, but they start from different assumptions and reach different results.

Specifically, LH study the entry and exit strategy in energy industry, using an option value approach which allows to manage the flexibility of environmental real assets (Dixit & Pindyck, 1994). They combine the concept of Tobin's q – the viewpoint of firm value – and the concept of real option to determine the optimal stopping time of adopting a new energy-saving project. In their setup, the firm has the monopoly right to invest in a single, discrete project, and future discounted profits and costs are assumed to follow a geometric Brownian motion. As they show, the greater uncertainty makes waiting more valuable relative to investing at once, reducing the present value of the active "green" firm relative to the one of the idle.

However, ST argue that in many situations investments are made sequentially by the firm choosing the time path of its capital stock. Therefore, they sustain, it must be specified in more detail how abatement investment decisions are affected by adjustment costs of investment, and how alternative environmental policies impinge upon the optimal investment strategy chosen by the green firm. Following this idea, ST examine the effects of environmental policies aimed at stimulating private investment in pollution abatement capital. In their framework, firm operates in a competitive market, capital is irreversible, and pollution follows a geometric Brownian motion. Basically, aggregate pollution is seen as an externality which affects the investment decisions of any single firm. They show that, with irreversibility *and* uncertainty, environmental policies promoted to enforce abatement capital may generate the unexpected result of reducing the firm value and the abatement investment rate. Interestingly, ST underline that their results generalize LH's results because their model not only provides the optimal stopping time of the investment strategy, as it is in LH, but also how much to invest in a new abatement project at each instant of time.

The model developed herein is a version of the ST model. We study the effects of environmental policies under the assumption of pollution uncertainty but reversible capital. The questions at the heart of the present chapter are: is the blend between irreversibility and uncertainty a necessary condition to determine the counterintuitive effects of environmental policies on investment decisions of a firm? Are taxes and subsidies equivalent instruments to stimulate abatement investments?

To scrutinize these questions, we investigate the properties of an investment model where aggregate pollution is an externality which affects negatively the productivity of inputs. We assume however that abatement investment is reversible with an adjustment cost of investing given by a quadratic convex function. In this setup, incentive-based policy instruments work by altering incentives for firm investment decisions. We focus on taxes on the level of particular inputs (such as oil), and subsidies on abatement capital. We get two main results. First, we show that corrective taxes on the polluting input will reduce investment while subsidies will stimulate them. Second, environmental policies can have a positive or negative impact on the value of the firm, depending on the magnitudes of parameters affecting the operating profit and the rents accruing to the firm.

The organization of the chapter is as follows. In the next section we introduce the pollution process and the Bellman equation for the value of the firm. We then relate the abatement investment to the form of the investment cost function. Next we study the effects of environmental policies on both the value of the firm and the optimal abatement investment decision. The last section concludes.

2. The model

Let p_t be a variable that represents the stock of aggregate pollution, say the concentration of CO_2 in the atmosphere. The flow of pollution p_t evolves according to the geometric Brownian motion:

$$\frac{dp_t}{p_t} = (v - \varphi)dt + \sigma dz_t \tag{1}$$

where v is the instantaneous drift, σ is the instantaneous standard deviation, and dz is the increment to a Wiener process with mean of zero and standard deviation of $\sqrt{dt}$. Note that in Equation (1) pollution growth is reduced by a factor φ which measures the environmental benefits associated to the aggregate abatement investments. In other words, the advantage in adding new units of abatement capital is given by the growth rate φ which quantifies the slowdown of pollution growth induced by the abatement activities of the whole economy. It is helpful to rewrite Equation (1) as

$$\frac{dp_t}{p_t} = \mu dt + \sigma dz_t \tag{2}$$

where $\mu \equiv v - \varphi$ is the net instantaneous growth rate of pollution.

The firm undertakes gross abatement investment A_t and incurs depreciation at a constant rate $\delta \geq 0$. Thus, the change in the abatement capital stock M_t is:

$$dM_t = (A_t - \delta M_t)dt \tag{3}$$

and in steady state $A_t/M_t = \delta$.

Pollution enters as a negative externality in the production function of any single firm, decreasing the productivity of inputs (Bretschger & Smulders, 2007; Smulders & Gradus, 1996). Conceptually, we treat aggregate pollution as a negative technical change. The production function has the Cobb-Douglas form:

$$Y_t = U_t^\alpha (p_t^{-\beta} M_t)^{1-\alpha} \tag{4}$$

where α is the income share of the polluting input and satisfies the inequality $0 < \alpha < 1$. The Cobb-Douglas specification is, perhaps, restrictive (due to the unit elasticity of substitution), but it is adopted here for its analytical tractability (Bretschger & Smulders, 2007; Mulder & De Groot, 2007; Shadbegiana & Gray, 2005).

The firm produces at each instant of time an output Y_t using M_t units of abatement capital and U_t units of polluting input. Because of the pollution externality, the effective units of capital are reduced by a factor p_t^β, so that in efficiency units capital is M_t/p_t^β. In this formulation β is a measure of the strength of the effects of aggregate pollution on abatement capital: the higher is β, the lower is the capital in effective units (Smulders & Gradus, 1996). Equation (4) can be rewritten as

$$Y_t = p_t^{-\varepsilon}(U_t^\alpha M_t^{1-\alpha}) \tag{5}$$

with $\varepsilon = \beta(1 - \alpha)$ to emphasize that pollution is a global externality affecting negatively the level of output.

The firm pays a fixed unit cost ω to use the polluting input U_t and an exogenously environmental tax rate τ to employ the input, so that total cost of U_t is $(\omega + \tau)U_t$. The tax τ internalizes the externality by inducing the firm to behave as if pollution costs enter its private cost function. In addition, tax τ alters the payoffs that firm faces because the operating profit at time t equals instantaneous revenue minus total cost,

$$\pi_t = p_t^{-\varepsilon}(U_t^\alpha M_t^{1-\alpha}) - (\omega + \tau)U_t$$

The firm chooses U_t to maximize the instantaneous operating profit π_t. It is easily shown that

$$\max_{U_t} p_t^{-\varepsilon}(U_t^\alpha M_t^{1-\alpha}) - (\omega + \tau)U_t = hp_t^\theta M_t \tag{6}$$

where $h = (1 - \alpha)(\alpha/(\omega + \tau))^{\alpha/(1-\alpha)} > 0$ and $\theta = -\beta < 0$. Note that hp_t^θ is the marginal revenue of abatement capital at time t, and the pollution effect on operating profit is negative.

2.1. The value of the firm

The value of the firm is

$$V(M_t, p_t) = \max_{A_s} E \int_t^\infty [hp_s^\theta M_s - c(A_s) + \eta A_s]e^{-rs}\mathrm{d}s \tag{7}$$

where $r > 0$ is the (assumed) constant interest rate. In Equation (7) the cost for increasing the stock of abatement capital by A_s is $c(A_s) - \eta A_s$, where $c(A_s)$ denotes the cost of investing at the rate A_s, and $0 \leq \eta \leq 1$ is a subsidy potentially given by the government to cover some of the expenses for expanding the abatement capital by A_s. Note that taxes and subsidies are different in their effects on profits. A firm gains an additional income from an abatement subsidy η only when it decides to invest; whereas, a tax τ results in a loss to the firms since it pays tax on all polluting inputs employed in production. As we will see, in detail, below, the asymmetric effect on profit of taxes and subsidies will shape the firm's investment abatement decisions, and the impact of a specific environmental policy.

The value of the firm satisfies the following Bellman equation

$$rV(M,p)\mathrm{d}t = \max_A[(hp^\theta M - c(A) + \eta A)\mathrm{d}t + E(\mathrm{d}V)] \tag{8}$$

(we suppress time subscripts unless they are needed for clarity). Applying Ito's lemma to $E(\mathrm{d}V)$ we get the expected change in the value of the firm over the time interval $\mathrm{d}t$

$$E(\mathrm{d}V) = \left[(A - \delta M)V_M + \mu V_p p + \frac{1}{2}\sigma^2 V_{pp}p^2\right]\mathrm{d}t \tag{9}$$

Since $V_M \equiv q$ is the marginal valuation of a unit of installed capital, substituting q for V_M in (9), and then substituting (9) in (8) yields

$$rV(M,p) = \max_{A}\left[hp^{\theta}M - c(A) + \eta A + (A - \delta M)q + \mu V_p p + \frac{1}{2}\sigma^2 V_{pp}p^2\right]$$

$$(10)$$

This expression can be simplified by "maximizing out" the rate of investment to obtain:

$$rV(M,p) = hp^{\theta}M + \psi - \delta Mq + \mu V_p p + \frac{1}{2}\sigma^2 V_{pp}p^2 \qquad (11)$$

where

$$\psi \equiv \max_{A}[Aq + \eta A - c(A)] \qquad (12)$$

In expression (12) ψ is the value of the *rents* obtained from undertaking investment at the rate A. When the green firm invests, it acquires $A dt$ units of capital, whose value is $(qA + \eta A)dt$, but it pays $c(A)dt$ to increase the abatement capital. Hence, $Aq + \eta A - c(A)$ is the net value the firm gains per unit of time to invest at the rate A.

2.2. Investment, rents, and the value of firm

Let us explore Equation (12) a little further. We assume that abatement capital is reversible. We use a specialized version of the framework of Abel and Eberly (1997), under the assumption of reversible abatement capital stock. The case of irreversibility is studied in ST (2011).

We here assume that the cost of investing at time t is given by the following convex function:

$$c(A_t) = bA_t + \frac{\gamma}{2}A_t^2 \qquad (13)$$

where bA_t is the fixed cost for purchasing abatement capital at the rate A_t; and $\frac{\gamma}{2}A_t^2$ is a quadratic cost of adjustment. Using (13), Equation (12) becomes

$$\psi \equiv \max_{A}\left[Aq - (b - \eta)A - \frac{\gamma}{2}A^2\right] \qquad (14)$$

Because the investment cost function is convex, the firm earns rents on inframarginal units of investment when investment is non zero, that is, when $q \neq b - \eta$ that is when $q + \eta \neq b$.

The rents ψ are illustrated in Figure 1. The convex curve represents the net cost function $(b - \eta)A_t + \frac{\gamma}{2}A_t^2$. It is strictly convex, passes through the origin, and has a slope equal to $b-\eta$ at the origin. When $q > b - \eta$ the marginal value of capital is greater than the net cost of capital, so the straight line representing qA is steeper than $(b - \eta)A_t + \frac{\gamma}{2}A_t^2$ at the origin. In this case, q exceeds the net cost for some positive values of $A > 0$, and the optimal value of investment A is the value that maximizes

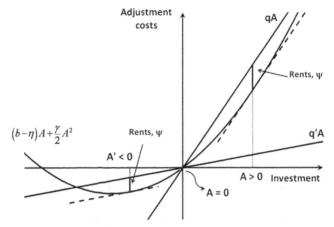

Fig. 1.   *Reversible investment when* q>b−η *and* q′<b−η.

$Aq - (b - \eta)A - \frac{\gamma}{2}A^2$. In Figure 1 the rents ψ, for positive value of the investment, are shown as the vertical distance between the straight line and the curve at A.

Note, however, that when $q' < b - \eta$ the straight line representing $q'A$ is less steep than $(b - \eta)A_t + \frac{\gamma}{2}A_t^2$, at the origin. In this case, $q'A$ exceeds $(b - \eta)A_t + \frac{\gamma}{2}A_t^2$ for some negative values of investment. In this scenario, the optimal value of investment A' is negative, and the value of the rents ψ is again shown as the vertical distance between $q'A$ and $(b - \eta)A_t + \frac{\gamma}{2}A_t^2$ at A'. Since the optimal gross investment can be negative or positive when the cost function is given by Equation (13), we consider this case as one in which abatement investment is *reversible*.

To sum up, the optimal investment solution takes the form

$$A^* = \frac{1}{\gamma}[q - (b - \eta)] \tag{15}$$

and the optimal rents are given by the expression

$$\psi^* = [q - (b - \eta)]^2 \frac{1}{2\gamma} \tag{16}$$

Equations (11) and (16) together generate a nonlinear second order partial differential equation. However, we imposed enough structure on our intertemporal problem to obtain an explicit solution. Appendix shows that the solutions below satisfy Equations (11) and (16)

$$V(M,p) = q(p)M + G(p) \tag{17}$$

where

$$q(p) = \frac{hp^\theta}{r + \delta - \mu\theta - \frac{\theta}{2}(\theta - 1)\sigma^2} \equiv Bp^\theta \tag{18}$$

and

$$G(p) = \frac{1}{2\gamma} \left(\frac{(Bp^{\theta})^2}{r - 2\mu\theta - \theta(2\theta - 1)\sigma^2} - 2\frac{Bp^{\theta}(b - \eta)}{r - \mu\theta - \frac{\theta}{2}(\theta - 1)\sigma^2} + \frac{(b - \eta)^2}{r} \right)$$

(19)

where $B = h/(r + \delta - \mu\theta - \frac{\theta}{2}(\theta - 1)\sigma^2)$ Further, recall that $G(p) = 0$ when $q = b - n$, since at this point the slope of the adjustment cost function is equal to the marginal q, and the rents are equal to zero by definition (see Figure 1).

To complete the analysis of Equation (19), notice that the denominators in the formula are the growth-adjusted discount rates, assumed positive to assure convergence. In detail, since $b-\eta$ is a constant, there is no adjustment for the discount rate r. The adjustment factor is instead needed for the middle term in parenthesis since $q = Bp^{\theta}$. In fact, p^{θ} has the lognormal distribution whose expected growth rate is $\theta\mu + \frac{\theta}{2}(\theta - 1)\sigma^2$, so that r is adjusted by this factor. Finally, since $q^2 = (Bp^{\theta})^2$, the corresponding expected growth rate is $2\theta\mu + \theta(2\theta - 1)\sigma^2$, and the discount rate must be adjusted in consequence.

Several results follow immediately from these conditions. First, we observe that the value of the firm is a linear function of the abatement capital stock M, since the slope of q is independent of M. For a competitive firm with constant returns to scale of production, the marginal operating profit depends only on the direct cost $(\omega + \tau)$ of the polluting input, and, thus, it is independent on the capital stock M. Second, the rents $G(p)$ and the value $V(M,p)$ depend on both q and η, given the interest rate r and the other parameters. Finally, investment A is an increasing function of q. But q depends on pollution p and taxes τ, whereas it is not affected by subsidies η.

Obviously, these features affect the value of the firm when the environmental policy changes. This focal matter is examined in the next section.

3. Environmental policy

In this section we address two policy issues: first, we investigate if, in the model described above, taxes and subsidies are equivalent instruments to stimulate abatement investments and second, we wonder, what are the effects of those policies on the value of the firm?

3.1. Taxes

To see what are the effects of an increase in tax on investment, recall that investment depends positively on q. Thus, it is straightforward to realize that an increase in τ reduces investment. In fact, taxes directly affects the cost of the polluting input U. We know that the marginal revenue of capital is hp^θ with $h = (1 - \alpha)(\alpha/(w + \tau))^{\alpha/(1-\alpha)} > 0$. Hence:

$$\frac{\mathrm{d}h}{\mathrm{d}\tau} < 0 \tag{20}$$

Expression (20) says that as τ increases h decreases, and, therefore, so does hp^θ. Hence, an increase of τ reduces the marginal q value of the firm and thus investment. Notice that this is a distorsive effect. The aim was to reduce pollution but the result is a reduction in abatement investment.

Let us now scrutinize the effect of a tax τ increase on the value of the firm. Although the effects on q are clear, the same cannot be said for the rents. The change in τ also alters the present value of rents but in an indefinite direction since

$$\frac{\partial G(p)}{\partial h} \frac{\partial h}{\partial \tau} \lessgtr 0 \tag{21}$$

This is because the the sign of the first derivative is indeterminate:

$$\frac{\partial G(p)}{\partial h} = \frac{p^\theta}{\gamma(r + \delta - \mu\theta - \frac{\theta}{2}(\theta - 1)\sigma^2)} \times$$
$$\left(\frac{q}{r - 2\mu\theta - \theta(2\theta - 1)\sigma^2} - \frac{b - \eta}{r - \mu\theta - \frac{\theta}{2}(\theta - 1)\sigma^2} \right) \tag{22}$$

The above derivative is just an algebraic illustration of the relationship depicted in Figure 1. Looking at this graph, it is evident that rents ψ are positive both when $q < b - \eta$ and when $q > b - \eta$, and equal to zero when $q = b - \eta$. Recall, however, that the present value of rents $G(p)$ depends directly on tax τ. Hence, ψ has a nonlinear pattern: it is positive but decreasing until $q = b - \eta$ where it becomes equal to zero, and it is positive and rising afterwards. This nonlinearity shapes the function $G(p)$ and its relation with τ. This in turn means that a tax increase may reduce or increase the value of the firm.

3.2. Subsidies

Let us now focus on the subsidy η. An increase in subsidy directly impacts on investment by decreasing the cost of purchasing capital goods. Differently from a tax increase on the polluting input, a subsidy increase stimulates investment in abatement capital by directly reducing its purchasing cost.

To see the effects on the value of the firm, we have to look at the rents created by the adjustment costs. In fact, the incentive deriving from a subsidy increase directly affects the present value of rents $G(p)$

without affecting the q value. Looking at the effect of a change in subsidy, we get:

$$\frac{\partial G(p)}{\partial \eta} = \frac{1}{\gamma} \left(\frac{q}{r - \theta\mu - \frac{\theta}{2}(\theta - 1)\sigma^2} - \frac{b - \eta}{r} \right) \gtreqless 0 \qquad (23)$$

As in the case of a tax increase, the effect of an increase in subsidy on the value of the firm is indeterminate. At first sight, this result may appear counterintuitive. The ambiguity of the relationship depends on two features: firstly, subsidies directly affect the cost of the investment rate; secondly, the adjustment cost function is convex, and this nonlinearity affects the optimal investment decision.

The above Equation (23) can also be clearly seen by looking again at Figure 1. Begin in the region where the marginal cost of investment $(b - \eta + \gamma A)$ is grater than the marginal q value of the firm so that $A < 0$. If we now increase the subsidy, disinvestment will decrease, thus reducing the rents accruing to the firm. This result implies that in this region $\partial G(p)/\partial \eta < 0$. However, once past the value of $q = b - \eta$, where $A = 0$, investment becomes positive, $A > 0$. In this region an increase in subsidy will increase investment and thus the rents, implying that $\partial G(p)/\partial \eta > 0$. To sum up, in this case too the effect of environmental policy on the value of the firm is ambiguous.

4. Conclusion

Lin and Huang (2011) demonstrated that the theory of Tobin's q and real options can be usefully employed to evaluate the feasibility of investing in energy-saving equipment. Saltari and Travaglini (2011) emphasized that, with irreversible capital and pollution uncertainty, the value of a firm captures the option value of the costly technology for disinvesting. Both these papers provide a new flexible thinking for decision making criteria in environmental issues. Nonetheless, these papers do not provide an analysis of the effect of environmental policies when abatement capital is reversible.

In this chapter we presented a continuous time model with reversible abatement capital in which the effect of environmental policies on the value of the firm and investments depends on what policies are implemented, focusing in particular on effects of changes in corrective taxes, to control the use of polluting inputs, and subsidies, to promote abatement investment. We have shown that taxes and subsidies have opposite effects on investment and that the impact of these policies on the value of the firm is ambiguous.

In our framework, pollution is an externality which affects negatively the productivity of the firm. Abatement investment is affected by pollution and quadratic adjustment costs. Both pollution and adjustment costs influence the impact of policies aimed at promoting abatement investment. An increase in tax rate reduces the marginal revenue of capital, inducing a lower investment rate for any given pollution level. Therefore, if corrective taxes have the indirect effect of reducing the after-tax return of private capital, the firm can find optimal to lower investment rather than raise it. Conversely, subsidies will stimulate abatement investment.

Nonetheless, the effect of these policies on the value of the firm is indeterminate. The main reason is that when taxes or subsidies change the (present value of) rents change in a non-monotonic way because of the form of adjustment cost function. Thus, environmental policies have an ambiguous effect on the value of the firm, depending on the magnitudes of parameters affecting the operating profit and the rents. This ambiguity has important empirical implications since it implies that the average $\hat{q}$ value of the firm changes in an unpredictable way.

This result has important implications for the relationship between the marginal and average value of the firm and the rate of investment. At each instant of time the firm chooses the rate of investment. In theory, as we saw earlier, investment depends on the marginal value of the firm. However, the average value of the firm, namely the ratio of the market value of the existing capital to its replacement cost

$$\hat{q} = \frac{V(p)}{(b - \eta)M} = \frac{qM + G(p)}{(b - \eta)M}$$

is the only operational index that the firm can observe and use during investment process. Comparing average $\hat{q}$ with marginal q, we notice that the change in $\hat{q}$, in response of a change in either taxes or subsidy, is ambiguous, while that of marginal q is determinate. Thus, since environmental policies have ambiguous effects on $G(p)$, they will have indefinite effects on $\hat{q}$ as well. Thus, as far as investment decisions are based on the average value of the firm rather than its marginal value, the effects of changes in taxes or subsidies on investment are unpredictable.

Two main suggestions for economic policy can be gathered from our analysis. First, when the policy maker defines an emissions abatement objective, subsidies should be preferred to corrective taxes. Some project of interest such as the introduction of a carbon tax can, indeed, have some long-term unexpected consequences on pollution dynamics, as it is in the case presented in our chapter. A carbon tax is an environmental tax that is levied on the carbon content of fossil fuels. From an economic perspective, it is a Pigovian tax. Since it reduces the marginal value of the firm, this kind of pollution charge will have the distorsive effect of decreasing the spending in abatement investment. Over time, this phenomenon will contribute to rise pollution rather than to reduce it. Second, as we noted above, the firm observes only the average value. In this context even for a regulator (government) there may be difficulties in identifying economically efficient targets. As we have shown, the firm average value is affected by both taxes and subsidies in indeterminate ways. Therefore, the difficulties in designing environmental packages to defend environment and welfare are immense. However, a reasonable conclusion is that, at least in our setup, environmental policy instruments such as subsidies will have superior long-run properties to control pollution emission, enhancing the quality of environment and welfare. Therefore, the present framework does deliver scenarios that appear to be innovative when environmental and economic consideration suggest significant nonlinearities in behavior.

Appendix

In this appendix we determine the value of the firm as a function of the aggregate pollution p. We assume that $V(M,p)$ is a linear function of M so that

$$V(M,p) = q(p)M + G(p) \tag{A1}$$

To determine the functions $q(p)$ and $G(p)$, substitute Equation (A1) in (11) and use the expression for ψ in (16) to obtain:

$$rq(p)M + rG(p) = hp^\theta M + [q - (b - \eta)]^2 \frac{1}{2\gamma} - \delta Mq +$$

$$+ \mu p q_p M + \mu p G_p + \frac{1}{2}\sigma^2 p^2 q_{pp} M + \frac{1}{2}\sigma^2 p^2 G_{pp} \tag{A2}$$

This differential equation must hold for all M. Therefore, the term multiplying M on the left-hand side must equal the sum of the terms multiplying M on the right-hand side. In addition, the term not involving M on the left-hand side must equal the sum of the terms not involving M on the right-hand side. This feature implies that

$$rq(p) = hp^\theta - \delta q + \mu p q_p + \frac{1}{2}\sigma^2 p^2 q_{pp} \tag{A3}$$

and

$$rG(p) = [q - (b - h)]^2 \frac{1}{2\gamma} + \mu p G_p + \frac{1}{2}\sigma^2 p^2 G_{pp} \tag{A4}$$

These equations have a recursive structure. The differential equation for $q(p)$ in (A3) does not depend on $G(p)$, but the differential equation for $G(p)$ in (A4) depends on $q(p)$. Hence, we employ a two steps procedure: we will solve Equation (A3) for $q(p)$, and then proceed to solve Equation (A4) for $G(p)$.

Equation (A3) provides the marginal q value of installed abatement capital. It can be rewritten as

$$\frac{1}{2}\sigma^2 p^2 q_{pp}^{(i)} + \mu p q_p^{(i)} - (r + \delta)q^{(i)}(p) + hp^\theta = 0 \tag{A5}$$

Simple substitution shows that the homogeneous part of the equation has solution of the form $q(p) = Cp^\lambda$, whereas the particular solution has the form

$$\frac{hp^\theta}{r + \delta - \mu\theta - \frac{1}{2}\sigma^2\theta(\theta - 1)} \tag{A6}$$

Intuitively, the particular solution is the present value of the marginal revenue hp^θ, and the denominator is the growth-adjusted discount rate, assumed that strictly positive to assure that the firm has a finite value. Thus, the general solution of Equation (A5) is:

$$q(p) = C_1 p^{\lambda_1} + C_2 p^{\lambda_2} + \frac{hp^\theta}{r + \delta - \mu\theta - \frac{\sigma^2}{2}\theta(\theta - 1)} \tag{A7}$$

The two terms in Equation (A7) $C_1 p^{\lambda_1}$ and $C_2 p^{\lambda_2}$ are the speculative components of value. We can rule them out by invoking economic considerations. Since $\lambda_2 < 0$, that power of p goes to infinity as pollution p goes to zero. To prevent the value from diverging, we must set the corresponding coefficient $C_2 = 0$. The other root is $\lambda_1 > 1$ and this implies that the marginal value of the green firm rises as the value of aggregate pollution increases. Restricting our attention to the fundamental value of $q(p)$ implies that $C_1 = C_2 = 0$. Hence:

$$q(p) = Bp^\theta, \text{where} \quad B \equiv \frac{h}{r + \delta - \mu\theta - \frac{\sigma^2}{2}\theta(\theta - 1)} \tag{A8}$$

We will employ this solution to compute the value of the intercept term $G(p)$ which represents the present value of rents associated to the adjustment cost function. It is determined by the differential Equation (A4). Since the rents are $\frac{1}{2\gamma}[q - (b - \eta)]^2$, the second order differential equation is:

$$rG(p) = \frac{1}{2\gamma}[q - (b - h)]^2 + \mu p G_p + \frac{1}{2}\sigma^2 p^2 G_{pp} \tag{A9}$$

The solution of the homogenous part is:

$$G(p) = D_1 p^{z_1} + D_2 p^{z_2} \tag{A10}$$

where $z_1 > 1$ and $z_2 < 0$, and D_1 and D_2 are constants to be determined. Again, the solution of the homogenous part represents bubbles unrelated to the fundamentals and can thus can be eliminated. Hence, the solution of (A9) is given by the particular solution:

$$G(p) = \frac{1}{2\gamma}\left[\frac{q^2}{r - 2\theta\mu - \theta(2\theta - 1)\sigma^2} - \frac{2q(b - \eta)}{r - \theta\mu - \frac{\theta}{2}(\theta - 1)\sigma^2} + \frac{(b - \eta)^2}{r}\right] \tag{A11}$$

where $G(p)$ is the present value of the rents accruing to the firm because of the presence of adjustment costs. It can be verified, by direct substitution, that this expression satisfies Equation (A9). Further, $G(p) = 0$ when $q = b - n$, because at this point the rents are equal to zero.

Adding the two components of the value of the firm, we get the solution:

$$V(M,p) = q(p)M + G(p) \qquad (A12)$$

which is the sum of two parts: the present value of profits associated to the assets in place, $q(p)M$, and the present value $G(p)$ of the rents accruing to the firm because of the presence of adjustment costs.

References

Abel, A. B., & Eberly, J. C. (1997). An exact solution for the investment and value of a firm facing uncertainty, adjustment costs, and irreversibility. *Journal of Economic Dynamics and Control, 21*, 831–852.

Ansar, J., & Spark, R. (2009). The experience curve, option value and the energy paradox. *Energy Policy, 37*, 1012–1020.

Bretschger, L., & Smulders, S. (2007). Introduction to sustainable resource use and economic dynamics. In L. Bretschger & S. Smulders (Eds.), *Sustainable resource use and economic dynamics* (pp. 1–16). Berlin: Springer.

Dixit, A., & Pindyck, R. S. (1994). *Investment under uncertainty*. Princeton, NJ: Princeton University Press.

Egli, H., & Steger, T. M. (2007). A dynamic model of the environmental Kuznets curve: Turning point and public policy. In L. Bretschger & S. Smulders (Eds.), *Sustainable resource use and economic dynamics* (pp. 17–34). Berlin: Springer.

Fisher, A. (2000). Investment under uncertainty and option value on environmental economics. *Resource and Energy Economics, 22*, 197–204.

Lin, T. T., & Huang, S. (2010). An entry and exit model on the energy-saving investment strategy with real options. *Energy Policy, 38*, 794–802.

Lin, T. T., & Huang, S. (2011). Application of the modified Tobin's q to an uncertain energy-saving project with the real options concept. *Energy Policy, 39*, 408–420.

Lin, T. T., Ko, C., & Yeh, H. (2007). Applying real options in investment decisions relating to environmental pollution. *Energy Policy, 35*, 2426–2432.

Mulder, P., & De Groot, H. L. F. (2007). Sectoral energy and labor productivity convergence. In L. Bretschger & S. Smulders (Eds.), *Sustainable resource use and economic dynamics* (pp. 165–190). Berlin: Springer.

Pindyck, R. S. (2000). Irreversibilities and the timing of environmental policy. *Resource and Energy Economics, 22,* 233–259.

Pindyck, R. S. (2002). Optimal timing problems in environmental economics. *Journal of Economic Dynamics & Control, 26,* 1677–1697.

Saltari, E., & Travaglini, G. (2011). The effects of environmental policies on the abatement investment decisions of a green firm. *Resource and Energy Economics, 33,* 666–685.

Shadbegiana, R. J., & Gray, W. B. (2005). Pollution abatement expenditures and plant-level productivity: A production function approach. *Ecological Economics, 54,* 196–208.

Smulders, S., & Gradus, R. (1996). Pollution abatement and long-term growth. *European Journal of Political Economy, 12,* 505–532.

Soretz, S. (2007). Efficient dynamic pollution taxation in an uncertain environment. In L. Bretschger & S. Smulders (Eds.), *Sustainable resource use and economic dynamics* (pp. 101–125). Berlin: Springer.

CHAPTER 21

Robotics and Growth

Erling Steigum

Department of Economics, BI Norwegian School of Management, 0442 Oslo, Norway
E-mail address: Erling.steigum@bi.no

Abstract
This chapter examines the implications of introducing "robot capital goods" in a one-sector optimal growth model, assuming a high elasticity of substitution between workers and robots. The growth path will either converge to a steady state, or involve endogenous growth without scale effects. In the latter case, the optimal growth rate of output per worker will converge to a positive number that depends on both technological and preference parameter. Moreover, the rate of growth could be increased permanently by subsidizing saving.

Keywords: robotics, capital accumulation, endogenous growth

JEL classifications: O11, O41

1. Introduction

According to the definition by Robotics Institute of America (RIA), "a robot is a reprogrammable multifunctional manipulator designed to move material, parts, tools, or specialized devices through variable programmed motions for the performance of a variety of tasks." The first modern industrial robots were the Unimates in the early 1960s, and are due to the work of J. Engelberger (the "father of modern robots"). In his engineering textbook, Jazar (2010) mentions that the first modern robots combined the two technologies, teleoperators and computer numerical control (CNC) of milling machines." He refers to a modern robot simply as "a multidisciplinary engineering device." From an economic perspective, the crucial feature of robots is that they perform valuable tasks in the physical world on behalf of human beings. In other words, robots are close substitutes to labor. Since the 1980s, economic applications of robotics have increased enormously.

This chapter examines the implications of introducing "robot capital goods" in a one-sector optimal growth model, in addition to ordinary physical capital. We assume a high elasticity of substitution between

Frontiers of Economics and Globalization
Volume 11   ISSN: 1574-8715
DOI: 10.1108/S1574-8715(2011)0000011026

robots and workers. The optimal growth path will either converge to a steady state, or involve endogenous growth without scale effects. In the latter case, the optimal growth rate converges to a positive number that depends on both technological and preference parameters.

It is well known that the Solow model does not converge to a steady state if the elasticity of substitution between labor and capital inputs is sufficiently large.[1] Solow (1956) discussed an example (the "third case") in which the elasticity of substitution was equal to 2, such that the marginal product of capital converged to a positive number when the capital/labor ratio approached infinity. Growth models involving an elasticity of substitution greater than one have also been analyzed by Klump and Preissler (2000) and Klump and de La Grandville (2000). The present chapter offers a new interpretation of why Solow's "third case" deserves to be taken seriously when thinking about future economic growth. We show that the emergence of robot capital would have similar effects as an elasticity of substitution greater than one in an aggregate production function with only labor and aggregate capital.

In the literature of endogenous economic growth, most of the attention has been paid to models with increasing returns to scale. Following Arrow (1962), Romer (1986), and Lucas (1988), the subsequent models introduced endogenous technological change (Aghion & Howitt, 1992, 1998; Grossman & Helpman, 1991a, 1991b; Romer, 1990).[2] This generation of endogenous growth models featured "scale effects," however, effects that are inconsistent with the time-series evidence from industrialized countries (Jones, 1995a, 1995b). Jones (1995b) showed that a more realistic calibration of the crucial parameters in R&D-based models of economic growth that eliminated the scale effects, would also generate a long-run growth rate that is a function of parameters usually taken to be invariant to government policy (so-called semi-endogenous growth). In the present model, however, there are no scale effects, but still tax policy that strengthens private incentives to save and invest can raise the endogenous growth rate permanently.

The rest of the chapter is organized as follows. In the next section a parameterized optimal growth model is set up. Section 3 analyzes the special case of full substitutability between labor and robot capital, including tax policy, and the simpler case of an exogenous share of gross investment in total output. Section 4 examines the optimal solution in the case of imperfect substitutability between robots and workers. Section 5 concludes.

2. The model

We consider a one-sector growth model of a closed economy, where the technology is represented by a neoclassical aggregate production

---

[1] The Inada conditions are not satisfied for any elasticity of substitution greater than 1.
[2] An early contribution to this literature is Frankel (1962).

function, $Y = F(K, G(K_R, L))$. Here Y is aggregate output, L the labor input (growing exponentially with the rate n), and there are two forms of fixed capital: $K =$ ordinary fixed capital and $K_R =$ robots, both measured in output units. We assume that the two functions F and G both exhibit constant returns to scale in their respective arguments. Output per worker ($y = Y/L$) can therefore be expressed as $y = F(k, G(k_R,1)) \equiv f(k, k_R)$, where $k = K/L$ and $k_R = K_R/L$. Using subscripts to denote partial derivatives, all the following partial derivatives must be positive:

$$F_1 \equiv f_1 > 0, \quad F_2 > 0, \quad G_1 > 0, \quad G_2 > 0, \quad F_{12} > 0, \quad G_{12} > 0,$$

$$f_2 \equiv F_2 G_1 > 0, \quad f_{12} \equiv F_{12} G_1 > 0.$$

What distinguishes robots from other capital goods is a high substitutability between labor and robots. The following inequality is a necessary and sufficient condition for labor and robot capital to be technical substitutes:

$$\frac{\partial^2 Y}{\partial K_R \partial L} = F_2 G_{12} + F_{22} G_1 G_2 < 0.$$

However, it turns out that endogenous growth is possible even if this condition is not fulfilled.

We assume for simplicity that the two forms of capital share a common rate of depreciation (δ). Then it is natural to assume that the marginal products of K and K_R are equal in equilibrium ($f_1 = f_2$). It follows that k can be written as an increasing function of k_R: $k = h(k_R)$, ($h' > 0$). Therefore, output per worker can also be expressed as a function of k_R alone:

$$y = f(h(k_R), k_R) \quad \left(\frac{dy}{dk_R} = (1 + h')f_1 \right). \tag{1}$$

We denote by X the total stock of capital goods: $X = K + K_R$, and correspondingly: $x = k + k_R$, where $x = X/L$ and $k_R = K_R/L$. Clearly, x can be expressed as a function of k_R: $x = h(k_R) + k_R$, with a positive derivative $h' + 1$. Inverting this function yields $k_R = p(x)$, with derivative $p' = 1/(1 + h')$. Using the latter function, output per worker can be expressed as a function of aggregate capital per worker:

$$y = f(h(p(x)), p(x)) \equiv \varphi(x), \quad (\varphi' \equiv f_1). \tag{2}$$

We assume that the marginal productivities of labor and capital are equal to the factor prices $w(x)$ and $f_1 = f_2 = r(x) + \delta$, respectively, where the real wage is

$$w(x) = \frac{\partial Y}{\partial L} = \varphi(x) - (r(x) + \delta)x. \tag{3}$$

Y is shared between consumption (C) and aggregate gross investment (I), the latter being the sum of gross investment in physical capital and robots. Adopting the standard notation ($\dot{X}$) for time derivatives, $I = \dot{X} + \delta X$ and

$\dot{x} = \varphi(x) - c - (n + \delta)x$. Using (3), we can therefore express the time derivative of capital per worker as

$$\dot{x}(t) = (r(x(t)) - n)x(t) - c(t) + w(x(t)), \quad \left(c(t) = \frac{C(t)}{L(t)} \right). \tag{4}$$

The welfare function is a CRRA function:

$$U_0 = \int_0^\infty \frac{c^{1-\theta} - 1}{1 - \theta} e^{-(\rho-n)t} \mathrm{d}t. \tag{5}$$

The subjective rate of time preference (ρ) is positive and $\rho > n$. The optimal investment and consumption plan follows from maximization of (5), subject to (4), $x(0) = x_0 > 0$, as well as convergence and transversality conditions to be spelled out later.

In what follows we adopt a parametric representation of the technology to highlight the role of the elasticity of substitution between robots and labor:

$$Y = F(K, G) = AK^\alpha G^{1-\alpha} (0 < \alpha < 1). \tag{6a}$$

Letting $G(K_R, L)$ be a CES composite input good, the production function becomes

$$Y = AK^\alpha (v(\varepsilon K_R)^\mu + (1-v)L^\mu)^{(1-\alpha)/\mu} \left(\mu \leq 1, v = \frac{\beta}{1-\alpha}, 0 < \beta < 1-\alpha \right). \tag{6b}$$

Here, $\mu = 1 - 1/\sigma$ where $\sigma > 0$ is the constant elasticity of substitution between labor and robots. It is straightforward to show that the condition $\mu > 1 - \alpha$ (or equivalently, $\sigma > 1/\alpha$) makes sure that labor and robots are technical substitutes. To rule out exogenous growth, the efficiency parameters $A > 0$ and $\varepsilon > 0$ do not depend on time. Note that we have defined the parameter β such that the positive weights v and $(1-v)$ in (6b) can be expressed as $v = \beta/(1-\alpha)$ and $1 - v = (1-\alpha-\beta)/(1-\alpha)$. We first look at the simple ideal type model in which labor and robots are perfect substitutes $(\mu = 1)$. Then, in Section 4, we consider the more general case of imperfect substitutes, when $1 > \mu > 1-\alpha$.

3. The special case of perfect substitutes

The assumption of perfect substitutability between labor and robots is admittedly unrealistic, not only because there are many types of skilled tasks and personal services that cannot be performed by robots in the foreseeable future, but also because robots perform a lot of operations better than humans do, both in terms of accuracy and repeatability.[3]

---

[3] Robots are superior to workers when it comes to 4A performance (automation, augmentation, assistance, and autonomous) in 4D environments (dangerous, dirty, dull, and difficult), (Jazar, 2010).

In the special case when labor and robots are perfect substitutes ($\mu = 1$), labor productivity is a linear function of capital per worker (x):

$$y(t) = (r + \delta)x(t) + w. \tag{7}$$

The factor prices are constants, independent of x:

$$r + \delta = A\alpha^{\alpha}(\varepsilon\beta)^{1-\alpha} \tag{8a}$$

$$w = A(1 - \alpha - \beta)\alpha^{\alpha}(\varepsilon\beta)^{-\alpha}. \tag{8b}$$

Observe that – due to constant returns to scale – there are no scale effects in this model. Both factor prices are positively affected by increased total factor productivity. The real rate of return is an increasing function of both the efficiency of robots and the weight of robots in the CES composite input good. The two latter parameters both reduce the real wage. Note that the return to capital only depends on technology, but neither on preference parameters nor on the population growth rate (n).

Now (4) simplifies to:

$$\dot{x}(t) = (r - n)x(t) - c(t) + w. \tag{9}$$

We define permanent income per worker ($c_p(t)$) as the consumption that corresponds to a constant aggregate capital stock per worker (such that $\dot{x} = 0$):

$$c_p(t) = (r - n)x(t) + w. \tag{10a}$$

Permanent income per worker can also be expressed as

$$c_p(t) = (r - n)\left(x(t) + \frac{w}{r - n}\right), \tag{10b}$$

where $x(t)+w/(r-n)$ is total national wealth per worker, including the adjusted present value of all future labor income. In this model, it turns out that as long as $r > \rho$, it is always optimal to consume less than c_p. Therefore, the optimal plan involves increasing permanent income and total wealth per worker over time.

3.1. Optimal growth

To obtain positive optimal growth, we assume that $r > \rho$. Since $\rho > n$ by assumption, $r > n$, excluding the possibility of dynamic inefficiency. For the utility integral to converge, we must assume in addition that

$$\frac{r - \rho}{\theta} < r - n. \tag{11}$$

Maximizing (5) subject to (9) and $x(0) = x_0 > 0$, yields the familiar necessary condition for optimal growth:

$$\frac{\dot{c}}{c} = \frac{r - \rho}{\theta} \equiv g > 0. \tag{12}$$

It implies a constant growth rate of consumption per worker ($g < r - n$), see (11). Therefore, optimal consumption per worker grows exponentially:

$$c(t) = c(0)e^{gt}. \tag{13}$$

The initial consumption level ($c(0)$) can be found by exploiting the intertemporal resource constraint. Assuming that the transversality condition,

$$\lim_{t \to \infty} x(t)e^{-(r-n)t} = 0, \tag{14}$$

is fulfilled, the present value of consumption must be equal to the initial total wealth. On a per worker basis, this condition can be expressed as:

$$\int_0^\infty c(t)e^{-(r-n)t}\mathrm{d}t = x_0 + \frac{w}{r - n}. \tag{15}$$

Substituting for $c(t)$ from (13), we can use (15) to solve for $c(0)$:

$$c(0) = (r - n - g)\left(x_0 + \frac{w}{r - n}\right). \tag{16}$$

Substituting (16) into (13) and (9), the following nonhomogenous, linear differential equation is obtained:

$$\dot{x}(t) = (r - n)x(t) - (r - n - g)\left(x_0 + \frac{w}{r - n}\right)e^{gt} + w. \tag{17}$$

This equation has the following general solution:

$$x(t) = Be^{(r-n)t} + \left(x_0 + \frac{w}{r - n}\right)e^{gt} - \frac{w}{r - n}. \tag{18}$$

Setting $t = 0$, it follows that the integration constant B must be zero. Hence:

$$x(t) = \left(x_0 + \frac{w}{r - n}\right)e^{gt} - \frac{w}{r - n}. \tag{19}$$

Since the growth rate of labor income is n, and the capital income growth rate is always greater than $g + n$, the capital income share approaches 1 as time goes to infinity.

It follows from (19) that the rates of growth of capital and output per worker are

$$\frac{\dot{x}}{x} = \frac{g}{1 - (we^{-gt}/c_p(0))} \tag{20a}$$

$$\frac{\dot{y}}{y} = \frac{g}{1 - ((n + \delta)we^{-gt}/(r + \delta)(r - n)c_p(0))} .$$ (20b)

We see from (20) that both growth rates slow down gradually, approaching the per capita consumption growth rate (g) asymptotically. Moreover, the growth rate of output is smaller than the growth rate of aggregate capital, but still greater than g. We note that when $t = 0$, the initial growth rate of aggregate capital per worker is equal to

$$\frac{\dot{x}_0}{x_0} = \frac{g}{s_k(0)} \quad \left(s_k(0) = \frac{(r - n)x_0}{c_p(0)} \right).$$ (21)

The denominator in (21) $(s_k(0))$ is the initial share of capital income in permanent income. The initial growth rate is therefore equal to the long-run growth rate divided by the initial share of capital income in permanent income.

3.2. The optimal saving rate is increasing when $n > 0$

We now look at the net saving rate $s(t)$:

$$s(t) = \frac{rx(t) + w - c(t)}{rx(t) + w} .$$ (22a)

Substituting from (10b), (13), (16) and (19), the net saving rate can be expressed as:

$$s(t) = 1 - \frac{(r - n - g)c_p(0)}{rc_p(0) - nwe^{-gt}} .$$ (22b)

It is straightforward to see from (22b) that the optimal rate of saving is increasing over time (when $n > 0$), approaching the asymptotic value $s(\infty) = (n+g)/r$. This is a reflection of the positive difference between the growth rates in capital and output per worker and consumption per worker. The increasing time profile of the optimal net saving rate is mirrored by a falling share of consumption in net income $(1-s)$. This share is approaching $(r-n-g)/r$ as time goes to infinity.

3.3. Tax and subsidy policy

Let τ be a constant tax (which may be negative) on the net real return from saving. Since $\tau = 0$ is a first-best optimum, this tax policy must reduce welfare. The capital income tax is returned as a lump-sum transfer to households. It is straightforward to show that the first-order condition for the dynamic plan of the representative (infinitely living) household is

$$\frac{\dot{c}}{c} = \frac{(1 - \tau)r - \rho}{\theta} .$$

The rate of growth of optimal consumption is clearly greater than g in the case of a capital income subsidy ($\tau < 0$). It follows that the initial consumption level is lower than previously and that capital accumulation is faster. Therefore, if capital income is subsidized, the growth increases both in the short and in the long run. Consumers postpone consumption and capital accumulation is faster than in the case of no subsidy.

3.4. How fast does the rate of growth approach the asymptotic growth rate?

In the absence of a steady state, it is not meaningful to study the speed by which total capital per worker approaches a long-run level, but we can examine the speed of the slowdown of the growth rate of $x(t)$ to its asymptotic level g. We now derive the time it takes for the initial growth rate ($\dot{x}_0/x_0$) to go half the way toward g. This involves solving the following equation with respect to time t:

$$\frac{\dot{x}}{x}(t) = \frac{1}{2}\left(\frac{\dot{x}_0}{x_0} + g\right). \tag{23}$$

Substituting from (20a) and (21), and rearranging, yields:

$$e^{gt} = 1 + s_k(0). \tag{24}$$

As explained in Section 3.1, $s_k(0) = (r - n)x_0/c_p(0)$ is the share of capital income in permanent income. Taking logs in (24), and using the approximation $\ln(1+s_k(0)) \approx s_k(0)$, we obtain:

$$t^* \approx \frac{s_k(0)}{g}. \tag{25}$$

Suppose, for example, $g = 0.02$ and $s_k(0) = 0.2$. Then the growth rate will be half the way toward g in 10 years. The half-time will however increase proportionally with the capital share of permanent income. As this share approaches its asymptotic value of 1, the half-time approaches $1/g$. This corresponds to 50 years if $g = 0.02$.

Let us compare this result with the Solow model (an exogenous gross investment share of output), assuming an aggregate production function $Y = K(t)^{\alpha}(L(0)E(0))^{(1-\alpha)(n+g)t}$, where g is now the exogenous growth rate. Now it can be shown that under a linear approximation close to the steady state, the half-time of the growth rate of $k(t)$ increases when approaching steady state, and it converges to

$$t_{\max} \approx \frac{1}{(1-\alpha)(n+\delta+g)}. \tag{26}$$

Adopting the conventional parameterization $\alpha = 1/3$, $n+\delta+g = 0.06$ this implies an approximate half-time of 25 years for the rate of growth.

3.5. An exogenous gross investment share

Let us briefly consider the simpler case in which the gross investment share of output ($i = I/Y$) is a positive constant, corresponding to the Solow model. We assume again that $\mu = 1$ (robots and labor are perfect substitutes). Now $c = (1-i)y$, where y follows from (7), and the factor prices are given by (8). Substituting $c = (1-i)y$ into (9), the rate of change of aggregate capital per worker becomes:

$$\dot{x}(t) = -((r + \delta)i - (n + \delta))x(t) + iw. \tag{27}$$

Assuming that $(r+\delta)i-(n+\delta) \neq 0$, this differential equation has the following solution:

$$x(t) = \left(x(0) + \frac{iw}{(r + \delta)i - (n + \delta)}\right)e^{((r+\delta)i-(n+\delta))t} - \frac{iw}{(r + \delta)i - (n + \delta)}. \tag{28}$$

If $(r+\delta)i < n+\delta$, we see that a steady state exists, with total capital per worker equal to

$$x^* = \frac{iw}{n + \delta - (r + \delta)i}. \tag{29}$$

Now an increase in i will increase the steady state capital intensity.

If the investment share is sufficiently large such that $(r+\delta)i > n+\delta$, it follows from (29) that no steady state will exist, and the endogenous growth rate of aggregate capital per worker becomes:

$$\frac{\dot{x}}{x} = (r + \delta)i - (n + \delta) + \frac{iw}{x}. \tag{30}$$

The asymptotic growth rate of aggregate capital per worker (g_∞) is therefore

$$g_\infty = (r + \delta)i - (n + \delta). \tag{31}$$

This is also the asymptotic growth rate of output and consumption per worker. It follows that an increase in the investment share will increase the growth rate permanently. Another possibility is that the initial equilibrium is a steady state, and that an increase in the investment share of output triggers a take-off into permanent endogenous growth.

Note that a constant i and steady state involve a constant rate of saving (s) equal to

$$s = \frac{ni}{n + (1 - i)\delta}. \tag{32}$$

As explained in Section 3, a positive constant rate of saving cannot be an optimum, given the welfare function (5). It is therefore not surprising that a golden rule equilibrium does not exist.[4]

4. The case of imperfect substitution between robots and labor

We now assume that $1 > \mu > 1 - \alpha$, or equivalently, that the elasticity of substitution is $\sigma > 1/\alpha$. We denote by r_μ the asymptotic rate of interest when t approaches infinity. In the appendix, we show that this interest rate only depends on technology parameters:

$$r_\mu = A\alpha^\alpha \varepsilon^{1-\alpha}(1 - \alpha)^{-(1-\alpha)(1-\mu)/\mu}\beta^{(1-\alpha)/\mu} - \delta. \tag{33}$$

The asymptotic interest rate is increasing in A, μ (and the elasticity of substitution) and ε, and declining in δ. Three possibilities arise:

(1) $r_\mu < \rho$. A steady state (x^*, y^*, c^*) exists
(2) $r_\mu > \rho$. Endogenous growth. No steady state exists
(3) $r_\mu = \rho$. No steady state exists. The long run growth rates of x, y, and c all approach zero as t (and $x(t)$) goes to infinity.

4.1. A steady state exists $(r_\mu < \rho)$

Maximizing (5) subject to (4) and the other conditions spelled out in Section 3, yields the familiar first-order condition

$$\frac{\dot{c}}{c} = \frac{r(x^*) - \rho}{\theta}. \tag{34}$$

In steady state, $r(x^*) = \rho$. The analysis of this case is well known. Now a capital income subsidy will increase the steady state capital stock, but not the long-run growth rate. Like in the case of perfect substitutability, it is possible that the economy takes off into endogenous growth from a steady state if a one-time increase in the efficiency of robots (or an increase in total factor productivity A) shifts the asymptotic interest rate (r_μ) to a higher level than the rate of time preference (ρ). We now will take a closer look at this case.

---

[4] It is easy to see that consumption per worker is an increasing function of i (and x^*) as long as $(r+\delta)i < n+\delta$.

4.2. Endogenous growth $(r_\mu > \rho)$

From (34), it follows that optimal growth rate of consumption becomes

$$\frac{\dot{c}}{c} = \frac{r(x(t)) - \rho}{\theta} > 0. \tag{35}$$

It is not possible to express the $r(x)$ as an explicit function of the parameters, except in the special case when $\mu = 0.5$ (Solow's third case). Due to the space constraint, we will not investigate this special case further in this chapter.

When time approaches infinity, this growth rate of $c(t)$ converges to

$$g_\mu = \frac{r_\mu - \rho}{\theta} > 0. \tag{36}$$

Also the asymptotic growth rates of y and x will converge to g_μ. The growth rate of the real wage will however approach $(1-\mu)g_\mu$, see the appendix. Therefore, not unexpectedly, the capital share will approach 1 when time goes to infinity.

The analysis of an income tax subsidy leads to a similar conclusion as in the case of Section 3.4. This policy will increase the economic growth rate both in the short and the long run, i.e. the asymptotic growth rate will increase as well.

4.3. The special case $r_\mu = \rho$

For all $x(t)$, consumption, capital, and output per worker grow faster than n. The long run growth rates of x, y, and c will all approach zero, however, as t approaches infinity. This case is similar to the previous case, except that the asymptotic growth rate (g_μ) is zero. A capital income subsidy will therefore increase the growth rate permanently in this case too.

5. Discussion

This chapter has investigated the implications of assuming the existence of a type of capital goods – referred to as robots – in a Cass-Ramsey model of optimal growth. Given that robots are sufficiently efficient, and that the elasticity of substitution between labor and robots is sufficiently high, endogenous growth without scale effects will take place. Whether these conditions are present today is questionable, but over time the development and improvements of robots may increase the probability that robots will become a source of endogenous growth some time in the future.

Up until now, the increasing use of robots in production of goods and services (as well as outsourcing of tasks to low-wage countries) has

changed patterns of employment and earnings. Acemoglu and Autor
(2010) lists several empirical developments of the past three decades, for
example "significant declines in real wages of low skill workers,
particularly low-skilled males," "broad-based increases in employment
in high- and low-skill occupations relative to middle skilled occupations
(i.e., job "polarization")," and "rapid diffusion of new technologies that
directly substitute capital for labor in tasks previously performed by
moderately skilled workers."

It remains to see if the rapid growth of robotics in the economy will also
increase the capital share in national income in the future, as the growth
model in the present chapter predicts.

Acknowledgment

Thanks are due to Tron Foss and Espen R. Moen for useful comments on
an earlier draft.

Appendix

We first derive the marginal products of K and K_R from (6b):

$$\frac{\partial Y}{\partial K} = \alpha A k^{\alpha-1}(v(\varepsilon k_R)^\mu + 1 - v)^{(1-\alpha)/\mu} \tag{A.1a}$$

$$\frac{\partial Y}{\partial K_R} = A(1-\alpha)v\varepsilon k^\alpha(v(\varepsilon k_R)^\mu + 1 - v)^{\frac{(1-\alpha-\mu)}{\mu}}(\varepsilon k_R)^{\mu-1}. \tag{A.1b}$$

Equalizing the two marginal products, $k(t)$ becomes the following
function of $k_R(t)$:

$$k(t) = \frac{\alpha}{(1-\alpha)v\varepsilon(v\varepsilon k_R(t) + (1-v)(\varepsilon k_R(t)^{1-\mu})}. \tag{A.2}$$

Substituting (A.2) into (A.1a), and using that $v = \beta/(1-\alpha)$, we obtain
$(r(t)+\delta)$ as a function of $k_R(t)$ alone:

$$r(t) + \delta = A\alpha^\alpha(\beta\varepsilon)^{1-\alpha}\left(\frac{\beta}{1-\alpha} + \frac{1-\alpha-\beta}{1-\alpha}(\varepsilon k_R(t))^{-\mu}\right)^{(1-\alpha)(1-\mu)/\mu}. \tag{A.3}$$

Since $x = k_R + k$, we can substitute from (A.2), and express $x(t)$ as a
function of robots per worker:

$$x(t) = \frac{1}{1-\alpha}k_R(t) + \frac{\alpha}{\beta}\varepsilon^{-\mu}k_R(t)^{1-\mu}. \tag{A.4}$$

Since x must go to infinity when k_R does, we can find the asymptotic
value of the interest rate (r_μ) when k_R approaches infinity:

$$r_\mu = A\alpha^\alpha\varepsilon^{1-\alpha}(1-\alpha)^{-(1-\alpha)(1-\mu)/\mu}\beta^{(1-\alpha)/\mu} - \delta. \tag{A.5}$$

It is straightforward to show that r_μ is an increasing function of μ and that it corresponds to (8a) when $\mu = 1$. Let From (6a), we derive the real wage as the following function of k_R:

$$w(t) = A(1 - \alpha - \beta)\alpha^\alpha(\beta\varepsilon)^{-\alpha}(\varepsilon k_R(t))^{1-\mu}(v + (1 - v)(\varepsilon k_R(t))^{-\mu})^{(1-\alpha)(1-\mu)/\mu}.$$

(A.6)

Is not difficult to verify that the asymptotic growth rate of the real wage is $(1-\mu)g_\mu$.

References

Acemoglu, D., & Autor, D. H. (2010). Skills, tasks and technologies: Implications for employment and earnings. In O. Ashenfelter & D. E. Card (Eds.), *Handbook of labor economics* (Vol. 4). Amsterdam: Elsevier.

Aghion, P., & Howitt, P. (1992). A model of growth through creative destruction. *Econometrica, 60*, 323–351.

Aghion, P., & Howitt, P. (1998). *Endogenous growth theory*. Cambridge, MA: The MIT Press.

Arrow, K. J. (1962). The economic implications of learning-by-doing. *Review of Economic Studies, 29*(1), 155–173.

Frankel, M. (1962). The production function in allocation and growth: A synthesis. *American Economic Review, 52*, 995–1022.

Grossman, G., & Helpman, E. (1991a). *Innovation and growth in the global economy*. Cambridge: MIT Press.

Grossman, G., & Helpman, E. (1991b). Quality ladders in the theory of economic growth. *Review of Economic Studies, 58*, 43–61.

Jazar, R. N. (2010). *Theory of applied robotics. Kinematics, dynamics, and control* (2nd ed.). New York, Dordrecht Heidelberg, London: Springer.

Jones, C. I. (1995a). Time series tests of endogenous growth models. *Quarterly Journal of Economics, 110*, 495–525.

Jones, C. I. (1995b). R&D-based models of economic growth. *Journal of Political Economy, 103*, 759–784.

Klump, R., & de La Grandville, O. (2000). Economic growth and the elasticity of substitution: Two theorems and some suggestions. *American Economic Review, 90*, 282–291.

Klump, R., & Preissler, H. (2000). CES production functions and economic growth. *Scandinavian Journal of Economics, 102*, 41–56.

Lucas, R. E., Jr. (1988). On the mechanics of economic development. *Journal of Monetary Economics, 22*(1), 3–42.

Romer, P. M. (1986). Increasing returns and long-run growth. *Journal of Political Economy, 94*(5), 1002–1037.

Romer, P. M. (1990). Endogenous technological change. *Journal of Political Economy, 98*(5), S71–S103, (part 2).

Solow, R. M. (1956). A contribution to the theory of economic growth. *Quarterly Journal of Economics, 70*(1), 65–94.

CHAPTER 22

Government and Growth: Friend or Foe?

Milad Zarin-Nejadan

Institute of Economic Research, University of Neuchâtel, 7 Pierre-à-Mazel, 2000 Neuchâtel, Switzerland
E-mail address: milad.zarin@unine.ch

> *Government is not the solution to our problem; government is* the
> *problem* (Ronald Reagan, 1981)
>
> *Increased taxation is the price of growth* (James Tobin, 1966)

Abstract
The relative size of the State in industrialized economies has increased dramatically during the past century giving rise to legitimate fears that such a trend might end up having an adverse impact on growth. This chapter explores the relationship between the development of government activities and economic growth. It starts by evoking problems related to the measurement of the public sector before reviewing statistical evidence on the long-term growth of the share of the State in the economy. It then provides a number of explanations for this phenomenon including those pertaining to the functioning of the political system itself thereby pointing toward inefficiencies. The next step is to explore the principal avenues along which government interventions can positively or negatively interfere with the growth potential of the economy. It turns out that while public expenditures – especially those responding to market failures – tend to be favorable to growth, most taxes are growth-hindering. The final part of the chapter singles out some pitfalls in the empirical investigation of this relationship. The conjecture is that the nonlinear and possibly endogenous nature of the hypothesized nexus can explain the lack of consensus in empirical studies conducted so far.

Keywords: Government growth, public expenditure, taxes, economic growth, endogenous growth

JEL classifications: E62, H11, H21, H50, O40

Frontiers of Economics and Globalization
Volume 11   ISSN: 1574-8715
DOI: 10.1108/S1574-8715(2011)0000011027

1. Introduction

The nature of the relationship between the extent of government activities
and real economic growth is not only a challenging research topic but also
a passionately debated political issue.[1] Despite the recent financial and
economic crisis and the ensuing widely acclaimed Keynesian-type State
interventions not only in the United States but also in other industrialized
countries, the controversy regarding the government's ever-growing role in
the economy remains as lively as ever. The debate goes beyond the
business cycle time frame and concentrates on the question of the impact
of long-term government expansion on the economy's growth potential.
Those who press for less government intervention in the economy presume
a negative impact on growth. Others who call for a more prominent and
extensive economic role for the State see a positive – or at least no negative –
relationship. As in many other cases, the reality is less one-sided and the
truth lies somewhere in between. At the theoretical level, the relationship
can go either way, depending on the nature of the welfare society, the prior
share of the government in the economy, the structure of expenditures and
revenues, the performance and efficiency of the public sector, etc.
Therefore, the question can only be settled on empirical grounds. But as
we see below, there are also caveats in the empirical investigation of the
presumed link between government activities and growth, which might
explain the wide spectrum of results obtained so far.

This chapter is an attempt to clarify the nature of the relationship
between the development of government activities and economic growth.
It is organized in six sections. After this brief introduction, Section 2
evokes some pitfalls in the measurement of the size of the public sector and
reviews statistical evidence on the long-term growth of the share of the
State in the economy throughout the 20th century and beyond. Section 3
provides a number of explanations for this phenomenon including those
related to the (mal-)functioning of the political system itself pointing
toward inefficiencies. Section 4 explores the principal avenues along which
government interventions can positively or negatively impact the growth
potential of the economy. Section 5 singles out the hurdles in the empirical
investigation of this relationship. Finally, Section 6 concludes by
summarizing the main findings and sketching a path for future action.

2. Long-term public sector growth

This section discusses briefly the main issues related to the definition of the
public sector and the determination of its size before presenting stylized
facts on public sector growth.

---

[1] See Yergin and Stanislaw (2002) for the evolution of this debate.

2.1. Measuring the size of the public sector

There is no unique way of measuring the relative size of the State in the economy. The most widely used indicators are the ratio of public spending or taxes (each one more or less broadly defined) to GDP or to resident population. Another popular measure of government size is the share of government employees (converted into full-time equivalent) in total employment. Of course, these indicators do not convey the same information regarding the evolution of the State's role in the economy. Besides, none of them can be defined without any ambiguity and independently from institutional features. Obviously, this complicates international comparisons, but even within the same country a wide variation of the estimation of government's share in the economy often nourishes politically motivated arguments in favor and against State's role in the economy.

The reasons for the difficulty of measuring government's share in the economy are manifold. For instance, the evolution of public sector's share in total employment can falsely reflect that of government activities in the economy if structural changes take place in parallel, say, regarding labor productivity or subcontracting practices. However, difficulties of interpretation are mostly due to uncertainties related to the scope of the definition of taxes and public expenditure used, especially with respect to social security contributions and benefits. In some countries, specific components of social security are regulated by the State but privately organized (e.g., pension funds, health insurance) so that these elements tend to be excluded from the numerator of the government's share. In others, they clearly belong to the State as they are entirely managed by and within the public sector and therefore arguably appear in the numerator of the ratios. Another problem concerns government-subsidized private entities which do not formally belong to the public sector while performing public tasks (e.g., hospitals, transport enterprises, educational institutions). As a general rule, national accounting considers such entities as being part of the public sector if the proportion of State subsidies in total receipts exceeds 50%.

Another major difficulty of measurement is the insufficient reflection of the extent of government regulations through the aforementioned indicators. Given that regulatory activity can replace taxes or expenditure, resulting in an unchanged – if not greater – degree of public intervention in the economy, one can easily notice why conventional measures of government's share in the economy can be misleading. Some 1,000 pages of federal regulations were added each year under the George W. Bush administration. The activity of a quarter of a million Americans consists of just devising and implementing federal rules.[2] Although useful indices

---

[2] *The Economist*, March 19, 2011.

measuring the degree of regulation have been developed during the past years (e.g., OECD's product market regulation index), these can only complement and not replace traditional measures such as the expenditure to GDP ratio.

A less-known but equally serious problem is related to the fact that expenditure or tax to GDP ratios are calculated by dividing data from government financial statistics by GDP (including its public component) estimated within the National Accounting framework. Not only this raises an incompatibility problem, but it also suffers from a methodological peculiarity. Given the non-market-oriented character of most government activities, public sector's output (which is part of GDP) is derived from its costs (inputs) rather than its value-added (sales minus intermediate consumption). This might lead to under or overestimation problems in case of major productivity changes (Stiglitz, Senn, & Fitoussi, 2009).

Note also that, in the case of the public sector, even a correct measure of output would not be totally satisfactory as ideally one should try to get a grasp of "outcome." Expenditures on health or education are perfect examples of cases where what really counts is the outcome of public interventions (e.g., life expectancy, literacy) rather than output (e.g., number of patients treated, number of pupils taught). The latter is however preferred to input indicators (e.g., number of hospital beds, number of teachers).

Finally, note that problems arise also when disaggregate measures of public sector activity are used. For example, one might split public spending into consumption and investment, the latter being particularly relevant for the growth process. However, difficulties exist in defining public investment outlays as government statistics do not refer to investment in the economic sense.

2.2. Long-term growth of the State: stylized facts

Irrespective of the statistical measure used, there is no doubt that the relative size of the public sector in the economy has continuously risen throughout the past century and well into the beginning of the current one. As shown in Table 1, the increasing trend has been common among industrialized countries albeit with different intensities. This is one of the most interesting and intriguing economic phenomena of modern times that, oddly enough, also happens to be one of the most widely ignored by the general public.

Around 1870, the average share of government spending in GDP was about 10%. Just before World War I, it had slightly risen close to levels considered in those years as being the sustainable limit.[3] Since then, the

---

[3] Pierre-Paul Leroy-Beaulieu, a French economist, wrote in 1888 that 12%–13% of GDP was the sustainable limit for government's share in the economy (Tanzi & Schuknecht, 2000).

Table 1. **Public spending in selected OECD countries 1870–2009**
(% of GDP) a (insert footnote a here)

	1870	1913	1920	1937	1960	1980	1990	2000	2005	2009
Austria	10.5	17.0	14.7	20.6	35.7	48.1	38.6	52.1	50.2	52.3
Belgium	NA	13.8	22.1	21.8	30.3	58.6	54.8	49.1	52.0	54.0
Britain	9.4	12.7	26.2	30.0	32.2	43.0	39.9	36.6	40.6	47.2
Canada	NA	NA	16.7	25.0	28.6	38.8	46.0	40.6	39.2	43.8
France	12.6	17.0	27.6	29.0	34.6	46.1	49.8	51.6	53.4	56.0
Germany	10.0	14.8	25.0	34.1	32.4	47.9	45.1	45.1	46.8	47.6
Italy	13.7	17.1	30.1	31.1	30.1	42.1	53.4	46.2	48.2	51.9
Japan	8.8	8.3	14.8	25.4	17.5	32.0	31.3	37.3	34.2	39.7
Netherlands	9.1	9.0	13.5	19.0	33.7	55.8	54.1	44.2	44.8	50.0
Spain	NA	11.0	8.3	13.2	18.8	32.2	42.0	39.1	38.4	45.8
Sweden	5.7	10.4	10.9	16.5	31.0	60.1	59.1	52.7	51.8	52.7
Switzerland	16.5	14.0	17.0	24.1	17.2	32.8	33.5	33.7	37.3	36.7
United States	7.3	7.5	12.1	19.7	27.0	31.4	33.3	32.8	36.1	42.2
Average	10.4	12.7	18.4	23.8	28.4	43.8	44.7	43.2	44.1	47.7

Source: *The Economist* (March 19, 2011) based on Tanzi and Schuknecht (2000), IMF, and OECD.
[a]1870–1937 central government, 1960–2009 general government.

public sector has grown at a faster pace than GDP. The upward movement was of course facilitated by the two world wars and the Great Depression in between.

The growth was particularly dynamic during the 1960s and 1970s, mainly due to the fundamental change in the general attitude toward the role of the State, more precisely regarding its capacity to solve various economic and social problems and to reduce risks for the citizens (Tanzi & Schuknecht, 2000). During those two decades – called "golden age" of the public sector growth – most social security systems that characterize today's welfare states were put in place. As a result, transfer expenditure soared, also in comparison to outlays on consumption (goods and services, wages) and investment, especially in European economies.

After euphoria came disillusionment and the ensuing slowdown in government growth during the 1980s and 1990s. While many observers then predicted the definite end of the growth of the State and even its reversal, so far there has been no flattening out of the trend. The relative size of the public sector even hit record levels in the aftermath of the recent financial and economic crisis. During the past century, on average, the share of public expenditure in GDP was multiplied by a factor of approximately 4. Demographic patterns – mainly population ageing that will aggravate public finances through rising expenditures on health and pensions – at least until the 2030s do not leave much hope for any major change in the trend in near future.

3. Factors behind public sector growth[4]

Numerous explanations for government growth can be found in the vast and expanding scientific literature on the subject. Undoubtedly, the growth of government cannot be attributed to a single factor. One should rather look for a combination of different factors including country- or region-specific ones. The main explanatory factors can be divided into two categories: economic and public-choice (political economy). The economic factors intervene either on the demand or the supply side, whereas the public-choice approach looks at the interactions.

3.1. Economic explanations

Generally speaking, economic explanations of the growth of the public sector can all be somehow related to the median-voter theorem (Downs, 1957, 1961). The median voter's demand for publicly provided commodities is supposed to be a function of the individual's income and tastes as well as relative prices.

3.1.1. Demand-based explanations

The oldest attempt to explain the growth of the public sector pertains to the first category and is known as Wagner's (1876) "Law of Increasing State Activity." According to this explanation – expressed in today's terms – the increase in demand for a greater scope of public sector interventions in the economy is a natural consequence of higher living standards and increasing complexity which accompany economic growth. In other words, the income elasticity of demand for publicly provided goods and services tends to exceed unity (luxury goods).

The evolution of tastes in favor of publicly provided goods and services can explain the rise in their demand. Rodrik (1998) shows that the more open the economy is, the larger its government tends to be. The basic idea is the following: citizens faced with a larger volatility of income and employment resulting from an increasing degree of openness of the economy might call on government to act as the ultimate insurer of risks through social security, unemployment insurance, etc.

Finally, the role of demand (and supply) was also put forward in an application of Baumol's (1967) law of unbalanced productivity growth, sometimes referred to as Baumol's "disease." According to this explanation, lagging productivity gains in the public sector relative to the private sector – while both sectors are basically faced with the same wage rate – lead to an increase in the former's relative costs and prices. Because

---

[4] See OECD (1985) and Garret and Rhine (2006) for a thorough discussion of these factors.

relative demand does not contract accordingly as a result of low-price elasticity and high-income elasticity (Wagner's law) of public services, government's nominal share of the economy increases automatically through time.[5] The validity of Baumol's law is even reinforced by the fact that wages in the (more-unionized) public sector tend to increase faster than in the private sector (Ferris & West, 1999).

3.1.2. Supply-based explanations

The importance of supply-side factors was first highlighted by Peacock and Wiseman (1961). The authors stressed the role of large-scale social upheavals such as wars and other economic and social emergencies that modify taxpayers' perception of the "tolerable tax burden," allowing the government to maintain a higher level of expenditure once the emergency is over ("displacement effect").

Other authors have dealt with supply-side factors by focusing on the role of government as a redistributor of income and wealth. Kristov, Lindert, and McClelland (1992) reinforce the displacement effect phenomenon by arguing that the closer the middle-class voters feel to the poor, or the slower incomes grow in the economy, the greater the amount of redistribution the government is asked to operate, resulting in the growth of the public sector during such periods. Following a totally different line of argument, Peltzman (1980) explains how, paradoxically, the trend toward a more equal distribution of income can result in higher amounts of redistributive measures. According to his explanation, because candidates promise redistributive policies in favor of various socioeconomic groups to win their votes, the more equally income gets to be distributed through time, the greater will be the magnitude of redistribution needed to gain the same degree of political support and get elected. Meltzer and Richard (1978, 1981, 1983) argue that individuals with lower productivities and incomes tend to vote mostly in favor of high taxes and transfers as they pay relatively less taxes and receive relatively more transfers. The growth in government size is then explained by the fact that over time the voting population has grown with new entrants coming mostly from the lower income population. Finally, the existence of electoral cycles responding to citizen demands can explain the relative size of the government and its growth (Coughlin, 1992; Downs, 1957).

---

[5] Beck (1979) argues that real government expenditure as a percentage of real GDP (i.e., each one deflated by the appropriate price index) is significantly lower than the same ratio in nominal terms.

3.2. Explanations from the public-choice literature

There have also been attempts – in the framework of the public-choice literature – to explain the growth of government in terms of the political decision-making process. The idea is that modern democracies are characterized by an inherent bias towards excessive government size, resulting in inefficiencies and subsequently lower aggregate economic growth.

One of the early explanations draws on the role of interest groups and coalitions. The benefits of public goods tend to be concentrated on a subset of voters while the costs are more widely spread. The outcome is the formation of voter coalitions by individuals for whom benefits exceed costs and who therefore naturally press for additional provisions (Buchanan & Tullock, 1962). Weingast, Shepsle, and Johnsen (1981) base their argument on the fact that the benefits of redistributive measures tend to be concentrated within one interest group while its costs are borne by a much larger population. This results in an undue growth of the public sector given that each organized political pressure group has a stronger motivation for claiming an increase in public expenditure in its favor that others have for opposing such moves. Becker (1983) stresses the role of competition among interacting interest groups that increases the power of the special interest lobby and leads to greater special interest spending.

A famous argument from the public-choice school focuses on the role of bureaucracy in government expansion (Niskanen, 1971, 2001). Bureaucrats have a natural tendency to maximize the size of their budgets. As monopolists they confront legislators who act as monopsonists trying to sanction budgetary demands exceeding citizens' preferences. Like any other bilateral monopoly situation, the equilibrium solution is a negotiated one. However, in this specific case, the bureaucrats have a decisive advantage over legislators given that the former determine their own costs while the latter suffer from informational asymmetries. Other difficulties preventing the legislators from exercising effective monitoring include problems related to the less palpable nature of services as compared to manufacturing, the monopoly provision of services involved which render price comparisons difficult, and the bureaucrats' reluctance to present alternatives. Also the ability to extend the budget beyond the demands made by the legislator depends on the bureaucracy's capacity to misrepresent the true prices and quantities, especially when the budget is large and complex (Mueller, 2003).

The role of bureaucracy is strengthened by the influence of public employee voting behavior on democratic decisions about government expansion. As direct beneficiaries of government expenditures, public employees not only tend to support expansions but they also have a higher propensity to vote in elections. This allows them to exert a disproportionate influence on voting outcomes – especially in direct democracies – and possibly leads to government expansion beyond average citizen preferences.

Other features of decision-making processes can be shown to contribute to the growth of government expenditure. Taxpayers suffer from various forms of fiscal illusion. In other words, they may not be necessarily aware of the full cost of government expansion due to their ignorance of the underlying financing system given the complexity of the tax structure which masks the extent of revenues transferred from taxpayers to government. A well-known mechanism is related to the lack of fiscal discipline. Frequent recourse to debt in order to finance expenditure may give today's taxpayers the false impression that they can benefit from a "free lunch" (unless Ricardian equivalence type of behavior prevails). Another source of illusion might be the "flypaper effect" according to which grants received by one level of government from another are not (totally) offset by a decrease in taxes, thereby resulting in further expenditure growth (Hines & Thaler, 1995). Sometimes, government gets more resources as a result of built-in mechanisms. The fiscal drag mechanism resulting from progressive tax schedules and inflation is a well-known case. Note that even in the absence of inflation tax revenues rise automatically (and more than proportionally) as a result of real growth, providing the government with the opportunity to finance additional expenditure without increasing tax rates.

Finally, the monopoly power exercised by the government provides additional explanations for public-sector growth. As a monopolist, the executive branch can practice "bundling" of projects which results in higher levels of government output (Tullock, 1959). Bundling and legislator vote trading can ensure the legislative approval of projects that otherwise would not have secured the majority needed. Brennan and Buchanan (1977, 1980) also adopt the monopolist view of government. Their "leviathan" government maximizes its revenues with citizens exerting no control on the size of the State.

4. Government's impact on growth

In addition to the inefficiencies of the government itself, its interventions and size may affect economic growth through both sides of the budget, that is, expenditures and revenues. This section gives an overview of these effects in the framework of the theory of economic growth.

4.1. Growth-theoretical underpinnings

Although the relationship between State interventions and economic growth has been the subject of a great number of studies in the economic literature, up until recently it lacked a solid theoretical basis in the sense that it was not possible to establish a formal growth-theoretic-based linkage between the two variables. The problem was related to the shortcomings of the neoclassical growth theory (Solow, 1956). According to these models, government policies can impact the rate of growth of the economy during the transitional period to the steady state, but this equilibrium growth rate is determined by the rates of technical progress and population growth, both assumed exogenous.

The development of the endogenous (or new) growth theory (e.g., Lucas, 1988; Romer, 1986) has provided a sound theoretical basis for the study of the impact of government activities on economic growth. According to this theory, public expenditure and taxes can influence the long-term rate of growth of output per capita (Barro & Sala-i-Martin, 1995). This can take place via various mechanisms that help counter the diminishing returns to capital accumulation "fatality" that cripples the neoclassical growth theory and makes the growth of output per capita contingent upon the occurrence of exogenous technical progress. In the new growth theory, a sustainable growth of output per capita can result from endogenous variables within the model. Then, various state interventions (through regulation, expenditure, or taxation), to the extent that they influence these variables, can have an impact on the equilibrium growth rate of the economy.

Several endogenous growth mechanisms have been explored in the literature. Some of them act through improvements in labor productivity. Investment in new fixed capital can increase labor productivity. Also, labor's skills and therefore productivity tend to be improved through time as a result of learning by doing. Another important factor is the accumulation of human capital that can enhance productivity directly and indirectly through spillover effects (positive externalities). Other contributions to the endogenous growth theory concentrate on R&D expenditure, typically modeled within monopsonistic competition type of frameworks (Romer, 1990). Innovations embodied in new capital goods help improve productivity, providing an additional channel through which the diminishing returns to capital fatality can be overcome. The growth-promoting effect of human capital accumulation and R&D tends to be compounded by agglomeration economies (clustering).

Permanent changes in variables such as savings and investment (in fixed and human capital) as a result of government policies lead to a permanent shift in the steady-state growth rate. Therefore, government interventions can have an impact on the long-run growth rate of the economy. Besides, endogenous growth models allow for an analysis of possibly differentiated effects of various types of public expenditure on growth.

4.2. Impact of public expenditure on growth

Here we review the impact of various types of government expenditure on growth, concentrating on changes in terms of allocation of resources.[6] Of

---

[6] See Colombier (2004) for an extensive theoretical review of the impact of public expenditure on growth.

particular interest are expenditures that enhance the performance of labor, those that can be considered as free additional inputs used by firms fostering their capital and labor productivity, and those that improve efficiency indirectly through framework conditions like social stability and security.

Note that in addition to the volume of government expenditure, one should ideally also take into account the quality of publicly provided services. This dimension is even more important for the State as compared to the private sector given that public production is predominantly composed of services. However, the quality is notoriously hard to measure and even harder to compare from one country or jurisdiction to another.

Government spending on education can be growth promoting by increasing labor productivity because of related positive externalities that are not captured by market prices. Social benefits – compared to privately captured returns – tend to be higher the lower is the level of education concerned, implying varying degrees of public sector involvement. Financial assistance for education helps overcome credit-market imperfections due to informational asymmetries and lack of collateral.

In this context, one should also mention active labor market policies that help improve or preserve the capabilities of the unemployed, thereby facilitating their reintegration into the labor market. Family policy and fight against gender-based discrimination can boost female participation rates, providing the economy with much-needed untapped human resources. Such policies have additional positive effects on growth by encouraging women to invest more in the acquisition of human capital (Schubert, 1997).

Government's expenditure on health care mainly responds not only to the existence of positive externalities but also to informational asymmetries. It exerts a positive impact on productivity by improving performance in the workplace and reducing absenteeism and workdays lost as a result of illness or poor health. A further growth-enhancing effect is through the improvement in the capacity to acquire human capital as a result of better health conditions. One can also include indirect positive effects through the acquisition and preservation of social capital. State's involvement in the field of sports also responds to the same type of preoccupation.

Note that the impact of government's educational and health spending on growth can well be ambiguous. First, the potential productivity-enhancing effects of such expenditure could finally end up being lower than expected in case of a large-scale emigration of workers. Second, this type of expenditure reduces the incentive for households to save privately to face such expenses in the future. If total savings diminish as a result of such policies, this will have a negative impact on long-term growth. Third, government expenditure includes transfers through welfare programs. To the extent that these payments lower the price of goods and services, overconsumption might result.

Publicly conducted or subsidized R&D activities can positively impact innovation and thereby growth. Like human capital, R&D activities generate important spillover effects, legitimizing some degree of public intervention without which investment in R&D, especially in fundamental research, would be insufficient. Public support of R&D can take several forms: protection of intellectual property (IP), research conducted within the public sector, and subsidies or tax incentives for private R&D activities. Note that there exists a trade-off and therefore an optimal degree of IP protection as too heavy protection by means of patenting can become counter-productive, hindering researcher access to (fundamental) knowledge and consequently harming innovation and growth.

Private factor productivity can benefit from core infrastructure investment realized by the government. These are, for instance, transport grid, telecommunication networks, payment systems, infrastructure for utilities (energy, water, sewer, etc.), technological parks, etc. All these services are characterized by indivisibilities of supply due to huge upfront fixed (and largely sunk) costs. The resulting natural monopoly type of market organization – mainly related to economies of scale but also to otherwise exorbitant costs of exclusion – justifies some form of State intervention either by direct public provision of the service or regulation of the activities of private firms. During the past two decades, the trend in the OECD countries has been towards less direct implication of the government in such activities and a thorough reform of regulatory frameworks to introduce more competition and help boost growth through innovation (see, e.g., OECD, 2007).

More generally, governments can also enhance growth by improving the legal and institutional framework of the country via spending on law and order as well as on (internal and external) security. This effort is essential for ensuring that private economic activity is not hampered and can be conducted within a harmonious, stable, and predictable environment. To these spending items one should definitely add social expenditure that is usually considered in the context of the redistributive function of the State. This type of expenditure can have significant albeit indirect implications for the allocation of resources and growth as it helps secure a minimal degree of social cohesion, thus contributing to political stability and a more favorable environment for private sector activities. Failure to act against inequalities and poverty can adversely affect factor productivities and exert destabilizing effects on the society. Note that the impact of these factors is compounded by the fact that too much inequality or poverty tends to discourage low-income individuals from educating themselves and leading healthy lifestyles (Gerson, 1998).

In the same vein, one should mention Keynesian-type government interventions that can play a role in the long-run growth process beyond the well-known and controversial short-run business-cycle stabilization aspects. A standard case is the possible induced growth effect of infrastructure investment undertaken during periods of recession to help stabilize the economy. Another example concerns government policies against cyclical unemployment. If unemployment is characterized by some degree of hysteresis, then the failure to intervene during business-cycle downturns creates long-term unemployment that tends to persist even when the economy reverts to its long-term growth path. The multiple causes of hysteresis are now well-documented and fit many European economies. The most convincing explanation refers to human capital depreciation that takes place during long unemployment spells, carrying the risk of transforming the jobless into unemployables (Pissarides, 1992).[7]

To summarize, one can say that, in general, public expenditure tends to have a positive – or at least no negative – impact on growth. There are of course limits to this assertion which brings us to believe that there is an optimal volume of public spending. Beyond a certain threshold, additional spending in many areas becomes excessive and unduly diverts resources away from the private sector, hampering growth. For example, in many countries defense spending considered as growth-promoting during the cold-war era may have become wasteful and growth-stifling since. Also, government spending can have adverse effects on private savings and investment. Debt-financed public expenditure crowds out private investment by increasing the cost of capital for firms. Total savings by private households may be reduced because of social security transfers, thereby negatively affecting private investment. Finally, as discussed above, the size of the State in the economy may well have overgrown as a result of built-in mechanisms within the political system. In that case, a reduction rather than an increase of public spending would be growth promoting.

The most important limit to the positive impact of government expenditure is however set by its financing pattern, mainly through taxation, that almost always creates distortions and hinders growth. This is the problem to which we now turn.

4.3. Impact of public revenues on growth

The impact of taxes on growth is intimately connected to the concept of distortion. Generally speaking, tax distortion refers to any reaction by economic agents to changes in relative prices induced by taxation

---

[7] Among the explanations of this phenomenon, one can mention the "insider-outsider" model that stresses the conflict of interest between employed and unemployed and the fact that wage negotiations take into account mainly the interest of the former. Another possible cause is the insufficiency of investment during recessions that delays job creation and prevents the absorption of cyclical unemployment during recoveries. A powerful argument refers to the perverse effect of labor protection policies and legislation – especially those regarding hire-and-fire and wages – as a result of which firms might have become unwilling to recruit during recoveries.

(Hagemann, Jones, & Montador, 1988). Taxes introduce a "wedge" between before- and after-tax prices of products or factors of production. When the amount of this gap is different from one good or factor of production to another, relative prices change. This modifies the behavior of economic agents in a way that transforms the respective shares of taxed products or factors, resulting in a new allocation of resources in the economy. In a large number of cases, distortions cause economic inefficiencies, the exceptions being restricted to cases where taxes help internalize externalities (e.g., "green" taxes). Differences in the tax burden affecting factors of production can lead to economic inefficiencies and a lower level of output, whereas applying different tax rates on final goods modifies the structure of consumption and reduces aggregate well-being. In many cases, these tax-induced changes negatively affect the growth potential of the economy.

4.3.1. Taxation and factors of production

The most distortive tax is the income tax levied on labor and capital income, usually at progressive rates (see Atkinson & Stiglitz, 1980). It distorts the allocation of time between labor and leisure. As a result of the introduction of an income tax, the after-tax return to labor (after-tax wage rate) falls, provoking a possibly large substitution effect in favor of leisure that might ultimately lead to a decrease in the number of hours worked. This outcome is reinforced by the degree of the progressivity of the tax schedule. But given that the wage rate of the worker depends on the productivity of labor and that the latter is raised by investment in human capital, the labor income tax can exert an additional negative impact on growth by discouraging investment in human capital (Myles, 2000). Moreover, taxes can affect the labor supply decision via other mechanisms such as the consumption tax to the extent that it is (partially) shifted on to consumers, thereby reducing the real wage rate.

In addition to the intra-temporal work-leisure choice, the income tax also distorts the inter-temporal consumption-savings decision of the individual. In a standard two-period new-growth-theory type of model, the introduction of an income tax diminishes the after-tax return to savings, causing an increase in consumption of period t and therefore a reduction in savings (which allow consumption of period $t+1$). Given that total disposable income is adversely affected by the tax, private consumption tends to fall in both periods. The reduction of savings restricts physical investment and exerts a depressing effect on capital accumulation and steady-state growth of the economy. In the absence of restrictions on international capital movements, the outcome could even be worse as a result of capital flight. The negative impact on growth can be further strengthened if physical capital is essential for the production and acquisition of human capital.

Capital income taxation also includes taxes levied on profits that affect the investment decision of firms (see, e.g., Jorgenson & Yun, 2001). Profit taxes tend to increase the user cost of capital, thus exerting a negative impact on private-sector capital outlays. This can cause an insufficient level of capital stock and hamper growth. Other features of the tax system such as tax credits, deductions allowed for depreciation, rules admitted for the evaluation of goods sold from inventory and provisions regarding loss carry forward also affect the user cost of capital.

A less-prominent distortion caused by taxation of income is related to the differentiated taxation of factors of production in general and of capital income in particular. In many countries there exist significant differences between marginal effective tax rates on capital income depending on the type of investment involved, the source of financing and the location of the firm. Convergence of after-tax real rates of return on substitutable assets results in a misallocation of productive resources and a lower productivity of the capital stock compared to the case where capital income receives the same tax treatment irrespective of its form and origin. Differential tax treatment can have negative implications for growth at the regional level but also in cases where investment in key productive assets (such as IT equipment) or sources of financing used by highly innovative firms (equity financing) receive a less favorable tax treatment.

Note that many tax distortions tend to be aggravated by inflation. Inflation increases the user cost of capital for firms because of depreciation at historical – rather than replacement – cost. It also raises the tax burden if firms use the first-in, first-out (FIFO) method for evaluating their inventories. Finally, inflation favors consumption over savings under regimes that tax nominal interest receipts while exonerating nominal interest payments.

4.3.2. Other tax distortions

One can also identify some less-known tax distortions that can cause inefficiencies and hurt growth. From the growth-theory perspective, one important effect is the impact of taxation on risk taking (Denison, 1979). Taxation favors less risky investments and R&D projects. As long as government shares gains, but not losses, with the investor, relatively risky projects tend to have lower expected net values. Certain promising avenues for growth will therefore remain unexplored. Although the literature on the impact of taxes on risk taking does not allow to conclude unambiguously on this issue, one can assert that the more asymmetric a tax system is regarding its treatment of gains and losses, the higher is the probability of an adverse effect of taxation on the propensity to engage in risky ventures (Boadway, 1979).

Milad Zarin-Nejadan

Uncertainty related to future taxes is another factor to be mentioned that can interfere with the allocation of resources and the growth path of the economy. Although investment is essentially a forward-looking process and involves many uncertain parameters, the mere possibility of changes in tax rates and other related provisions during a project's lifetime introduces yet another source of uncertainty that has to be dealt with. Tax changes can *ex post* render suboptimal investment projects selected on the basis of prevailing tax laws. Probably more than any other policy domain, tax policy changes are hard to forecast as a function of past observations.

Taxation of capital gains upon realization – rather than accrual – constitutes another way taxes create inefficiencies and harm growth. Under a regime where capital gains are taxed only when assets are sold, the holders of such assets have an incentive to postpone the realization of their gains ("locked-in" effect). There are at least three reasons why the locked-in effect can lead to inefficiencies and impact negatively the growth potential of the economy (Stiglitz, 1983). First, it increases the volatility of the assets involved in comparison to other forms of investment and therefore reduces their attractiveness. Second, in cases where financial assets confer to their owners a certain degree of influence on corporate decisions, it prevents the passage of assets to those who would be most capable of managing them. Third, when the return on an investment project takes the form of capital gains, its termination date might be artificially delayed to reduce the present value of tax liabilities. Under a progressive income tax system, inflation strengthens this phenomenon as capital gains are usually taxed in nominal terms.

Note that taxation, through the establishment and management of a tax system but also the tax-compliance mechanism, generates administrative costs which by themselves constitute a waste of productive resources.[8] Compliance costs intervene on different levels (Sandford, 1981). First, understanding the features and the requirements of the tax system implies additional costs when a new tax law is introduced or when the existing framework is revised. Second, the obligation to pay taxes imposes on firms largely unavoidable costs related to the necessity to maintain an adequate accounting system. Compliance costs are even higher under systems requiring the employers to levy withholding taxes on behalf on tax authorities. Note that because of the largely fixed nature of compliance costs, these tend to weigh heavily on smaller firms. Given that a large number of highly innovative firms are relatively small (and financially fragile) entities, these costs can exert a negative impact on innovation and growth.

---

[8] Many studies have shown that these costs can be considerable. In the United Kingdom, for instance, tax-related costs are estimated at 1.5% of GDP. Compliance costs of all regulations are believed to be much larger, between 10% and 20% of GDP (*The Economist*, March 19, 2011).

To summarize, income taxes including personal income taxes on labor and capital income, business taxes, payroll taxes, and social security contributions are the most distortive. In contrast, consumption taxes and various property taxes such as those on wealth, real-estate, bequest, and gift are the least distortive. Therefore, in order to judge the degree of harmfulness of taxes with respect to growth, one should consider not only the total tax burden (e.g., percentage of taxes in GDP) but also the structure of the tax system as well as the compliance costs imposed on taxpayers.

4.4. Government's own inefficiencies

Given that the government sector accounts for a large chunk of GDP, inefficiencies within the State itself affect automatically and significantly the growth performance of the economy as a whole. In Section 3 we reviewed several political mechanisms that lead to an inflated, and therefore inefficient, public sector and bureaucracy. Another problem is the lack, or at least insufficiency, of incentives for public servants and managers compared to their private sector counterparts. Here we briefly mention two factors that can mitigate State inefficiencies: decentralization and outsourcing.

One can identify at least two mechanisms through which fiscal decentralization is expected to affect positively government efficiency. First, a higher degree of control reduces the incentives for incumbents to pursue their own interests by increasing the risk of not being reelected (Salmon, 1987). Second, yardstick competition among sub-national and local entities allows citizens to better evaluate the performance of their officials by providing them with relevant benchmarks for comparison (Besley & Case, 1995). Henceforth, fiscal decentralization tends to enhance public sector performance and efficiency by enabling the citizens to either vote officials out of office or just vote "by their feet."[9]

As for recourse to outsourcing, it has the advantage of exposing the production of services in the government sector to competitive pressure. Unless public production is as efficient as private production, the task is subcontracted to the private sector. The activities best suited for outsourcing are those for which transactions costs of contracting are relatively low. This is the case for standardized – or at least easily definable – outputs (e.g., garbage collection).

---

[9] Note that, theoretically, one cannot exclude a negative effect of decentralization on growth as a result of diseconomies of scale but also the lower quality – in terms of human capital – of civil servants at the local/regional level in comparison to the central government and their higher risk of being subject to pressure from special interest groups.

5. Evidence from empirical studies

Government interventions can impact economic growth basically through three channels: the quantity as well as quality of the factors of production, the combination of factors used in the production function, and the production process itself. Given the theoretical arguments reviewed above, the answer to the question of whether government activities serve or hinder growth can therefore only be empirical.[10]

Starting with the path-breaking study by Barro (1990), the impact of government interventions on economic growth has been subject to a great number of empirical investigations. However, based on a large array of evidence gathered so far on this issue, it is difficult to detect a clear-cut relationship between aggregate public spending/revenues and growth, both at the international and the individual country levels.[11] This can be explained *inter alia* by the fact that until now empirical studies have paid little attention the direction of causality between the relative size of the public sector and economic growth as well as to the non-linearity of the relationship.

A major difficulty is that it is hard to ascertain the direction of causality between the two variables. An expanding public sector can just as well be a cause or a consequence of weak growth. The latter is the type of causality underlying Wagner's law. To take a recent example, the exceptionally low growth rates of the Swiss economy during the 1990s (lowest among all OECD countries) are often associated to the increase in the relative size of the public sector. However, this increase has largely been the result – rather than the cause – of anemic growth. In particular, the spectacular and unprecedented surge in Swiss unemployment in the early 1990s brought about the need for new public programs and heavier government involvement in this field.

Another serious problem is related to the fact that most studies ignore the possible nonlinearity of the hypothesized nexus. It is therefore not surprising to observe contradictory and mostly nonrobust results (Fölster & Henrekson, 1999, 2001). Intuitively, there can be no harmonious relationship between the relative size of the State and economic growth. A zero share of the public sector means chaos and would be hardly compatible with economic development. The same is true when the government accounts for 100% or more of GDP. This suggests an inverted U-shape type of relationship between government's size and economic growth, rather than a monotonous locus. Therefore, one can speculate on the existence of an "optimal" size of the State that maximizes growth (Mittnik & Neumann, 2003). Below that threshold, development of

---

[10] See Kirchgässner (2006) for an excellent critical review of the empirical literature.

[11] See, for example, Sala-i-Martin (1997), Tanzi and Zee (1997), Agell, Lindh, and Ohlson (1997), and Bassanini and Scarpetta (2001). More recently, a meta-analysis conducted by Nijkamp and Poot (2004) did not allow to establish clearer results.

governmental activities is favorable to economic growth while beyond that point any further expansion of the State becomes detrimental to growth. Note that if the relationship is Laffer-shaped and characterized by a flat intermediate portion instead of a single peak, then a statistically nonsignificant result might mean that the government size falls within the optimal range.

It would be illusory to think that there is a unique optimal level of government size in the economy. This optimal size crucially depends on the society's conception of the welfare state. As in Scandinavian countries, a relatively high level of government involvement in the economy can be compatible with decent rates of economic growth provided that the State produces goods and services efficiently in response to market failures. For instance, free or highly subsidized child-care services allow more women to enter the workforce and can help increase birth rates. A safe conjecture is that there exists a specific optimal size of the government corresponding to a given model of welfare state. Besides, one should take into account the quality of government in determining the optimal size of the State (La Porta, Lopez-de-Silanes, Shleifer, & Vishny, 1999).

To avoid problems related to institutional differences, especially those regarding the contours of the welfare state, a solution would be to test the link between government and growth at the sub-national level within a federalist country. But this type of investigation remains marred by the reversal of causality problem. To the extent that sub-national entities provide more or less the same volume of public services, higher-income entities will have lower shares of government expenditure and taxes than lower-income ones.

A possible source of bias might be that in most cases either public expenditure or taxes – rarely both – are considered as explanatory variables in growth equations. In other words, the interactions between the two sides of the ledger (i.e., budget constraint) are not correctly reflected in many empirical studies. One should keep in mind that more than the magnitude of State activity, what really matters for the citizen is the balance between the price paid in form of various levies and the public services received in return.

Despite the frustratingly inconclusive nature of the empirical evidence on the impact of aggregate spending on growth, a few certainties remain. One is the fact that independently of the size of public expenditure and taxes in the economy, frequent and large changes in government policy is detrimental to growth. Brunetti (1998) shows a negative and significant impact of the volatility of fiscal and monetary policies on growth in a cross-country perspective.

Also, a much more coherent pattern is observed at the disaggregate level. This strand of research has investigated the specific effect of certain categories of expenditure (Temple, 1999). For example, Kneller, Bleaney, and Gemmel (1999) and Bleaney, Gemmel, and Kneller (2001) find positive effects on growth of expenditure on infrastructure such as transports and communications. More recently, the existence of a positive but slight correlation between growth and spending on education, research or transport infrastructure for the OECD countries was established by Colombier (2004).

6. Conclusion

In this chapter we reviewed both theoretical and empirical evidence on the relative growth of the State and its possible implications for economic growth. We first stressed that measuring the size of the public sector is a risky business. In particular, the existence of "gray zones" might explain to a certain extent the controversies around government's role in the economy. We then went on to argue that, no matter which definition or indicator is used to gauge the relative size of the public sector, the latter has risen inexorably, if not always smoothly, in relative terms in almost all industrialized countries during the past century. Although one can guess that such a trend cannot go on forever in market-based economies, the fact that it has not slowed down toward the end of the past century despite growing skepticism regarding the economic role of government should be a legitimate matter of concern for citizens.

The investigation of the causes of the relative growth of the State allowed us to identify some purely economic factors stressing the role of demand and supply, but also a series of other convincing arguments suggested by the public-choice literature. The latter pinpoint a certain number of built-in democratic political processes that tend to inflate the size of the public sector and create inefficiencies. The idea is that the government has grown beyond what the desires expressed by the citizens and the characteristics of publicly provided goods and services could possibly justify.

After a brief reminder of the appropriate growth-theoretic framework of reference provided by the endogenous growth models, we reviewed the possible impacts of government spending and revenues on the economy's growth potential. While most government expenditures tend to be favorable to growth as long as they respond to market failures, many taxes, especially those on personal income and business profits, create distortions in individual decisions regarding labor supply, savings and investment (in physical and human capital as well as in R&D) and therefore might constitute serious obstacles to growth. The empirical evidence is however largely inconclusive, except for the impact of specific categories of spending on growth. While expenditure items such as education and core infrastructure tend to favor growth, those on defense often turn out to be growth-hindering. Finally, one should also bear in mind that inefficiencies of the public sector itself can negatively affect growth. These inefficiencies can be partly overcome by fiscal decentralization and outsourcing.

What do these findings suggest regarding the future of the State's role in the economy? One major conclusion is that there is no such thing as a "one-size-fits-all" State. As long as citizens get enough "bang for the buck" in terms of government services, basically any size could fit. However, admitting that the relationship between government activities and growth is Laffer-shaped, a continuously growing share of the State will inevitably end up becoming harmful to growth. There are signs that in most cases the public sector has swelled beyond necessity and become inefficient. But this should not be taken as a fatality. The government can be scaled down without reneging on its commitments. In fact, studies show that small governments generally fare better in terms of efficiency and even performance.[12]

How can this downsizing be realized? One can distinguish three stages in the reform process leading to a "leaner but not meaner" State. The first stage – probably the less difficult to implement because it encounters relatively little opposition from citizens – consists of improving public management practices. Inter- as well as intra-national benchmarking can help governments at various levels become more efficient. Whenever possible, decentralization and outsourcing should be used to improve the quality of government services and gain in terms of efficiency. E-government solutions can also help, subject to limits imposed by the nature of publicly provided services.

The second stage involves a much-needed drastic simplification of the regulatory framework. Although, technically speaking, this movement – sometimes improperly qualified as deregulatory rather than *re*-regulatory – has been under way in the OECD countries during the past two decades, it has been rather sluggish due to fierce opposition by vested interests. While some progress has been achieved on various fronts, other areas have witnessed a densification of regulation (e.g., environmental policy). Also, within the European Union, the effort realized at the national level has been offset by a thick layer of regulation imposed at the supra-national level. A solution would be to use sunset clauses so that all regulations expire automatically after a time limit unless they are explicitly extended.

The third and final stage of reform, which is going to be politically the most difficult to realize, consists of a thorough review and downscaling of government expenditure and taxes. On the expenditure side, the challenge is to limit the scope of government services, especially entitlements. This will require a lot of political will and courage, but unless fundamental reforms are undertaken soon, unfavorable demographic headwinds will ruin all other efforts towards a more efficient and growth-friendly State. To take the area of pensions as an example, the list of required reforms is clear: lifting the retirement age rather than increasing employee and employer

---

[12] For example, see Afonso, Schuknecht, and Tanzi (2003).

contributions, replacing pay-as-you-go systems by those based on capitalization, using the defined-contribution rather than defined-benefit principle, etc. Realization of these reforms is however another story.

On the tax side, the recipes are well-known: more simplicity and less distortion. The tax system can be considerably simplified and rendered more transparent if its use is primarily limited to raising revenue for the State to finance expenditure and not for other (laudable) purposes such as redistribution.[13] Furthermore, the tax revenue necessary for the State to carry out its duties should be levied by causing the least distortion possible and minimizing administrative as well as compliance costs. This will require a restructuring of the tax system mainly by shifting the burden from income to consumption taxes. Moreover, the level of taxes can be reduced at the same time as cuts in public spending by eliminating fiscal churning wherever possible. Fiscal churning is best illustrated by the case where the same individual pays taxes and receives an equivalent amount of benefits through transfers. While canceling out these flows leaves the financial situation of the individual unchanged, it reduces the distortions caused by taxes (and transfers) and saves the economy valuable resources used by the administration for enforcing both tax and transfer schemes.

Acknowledgments

Precious comments from Olivier de La Grandville and Alain Schoenenberger are gratefully acknowledged. The usual disclaimer applies.

References

Afonso, A., Schuknecht, L., & Tanzi, V. (2003, July). *Public sector efficiency: An international comparison.* European Central Bank Working Papers, No. 242.

Agell, J., Lindh, T., & Ohlson, H. (1997). Growth and the public sector: A critical review essay. *European Journal of Political Economy, 13*(1), 33–52.

Atkinson, A. B., & Stiglitz, J. E. (1980). *Lectures on public economics.* London: McGraw-Hill.

Barro, R. (1990). Government spending in a simple model of exogenous growth. *Journal of Political Economy, 98*(5), 103–126.

Barro, R., & Sala-i-Martin, X. (1995). *Economic growth.* New York, NY: McGraw Hill.

---

[13] The U.S. tax code has grown from 1.4m words in 2001 to 3.8m in 2010 (*The Economist*, March 19, 2011).

Bassanini, A., & Scarpetta, S. (2001). The driving forces of economic growth: Panel-data evidence for the OECD countries. *OECD Economic Studies, 33*(2), 9–56.

Baumol, W. J. (1967). Macroeconomics of unbalanced growth: The anatomy of urban crisis. *American Economic Review, 57*(3), 415–426.

Beck, M. (1979). Inflation, government spending and the real size of the public sector. *Atlantic Economic Journal, 7*(3), 25–34.

Becker, G. (1983). A theory of competition among pressure groups for political influence. *Quarterly Journal of Economics, 98*(3), 371–400.

Besley, T., & Case, A. (1995). Incumbent behavior, vote-seeking, tax-setting and yardstick competition. *American Economic Review, 85*(1), 25–45.

Bleaney, M. F., Gemmel, N., & Kneller, R. (2001). Testing the endogenous growth model: Public expenditure, taxation and growth over the long run. *Canadian Journal of Economics, 34*(1), 36–57.

Boadway, R. (1979). *Public sector economics*. Cambridge: Winthrop.

Brennan, G., & Buchanan, J. M. (1977). Towards a tax constitution for leviathan. *Journal of Public Economics, 8*(3), 255–273.

Brennan, G., & Buchanan, J. M. (1980). *The power to tax: Analytical foundations of a fiscal constitution*. Cambridge: Cambridge University Press.

Brunetti, A. (1998). Policy volatility and economic growth: A comparative empirical analysis. *European Journal of Political Economy, 14*(1), 35–52.

Buchanan, J. M., & Tullock, G. (1962). *Calculus of consent: Logical foundations of constitutional democracy*. Ann Arbor, MI: University of Michigan Press.

Colombier, C. (2004). *Government and growth*. Working Paper, No. 4, Federal Finance Administration, Bern.

Coughlin, P. (1992). *Probabilistic voting theory*. Cambridge: Cambridge University Press.

Denison, E. F. (1979). *Accounting for slower economic growth: The United States in the 1970s*. Washington, DC: The Brookings Institution.

Downs, A. (1957). *An economic theory of democracy*. New York, NY: Harper and Row.

Downs, A. (1961). Problems of majority voting: In defense of majority voting. *Journal of Political Economy, 69*(2), 192–199.

Ferris, J. S., & West, E. G. (1999). Cost disease versus leviathan explanations of rising government costs: An empirical investigation. *Public Choice, 98*(3–4), 307–316.

Fölster, S., & Henrekson, M. (1999). Growth and the public sector: A critique of the critics. *European Journal of Political Economy, 15*(2), 337–358.

Fölster, S., & Henrekson, M. (2001). Growth effects of government expenditure and taxation in rich countries. *European Economic Review, 45*(8), 1501–1520.

Garret, T. A., & Rhine, R. M. (2006). On the size and growth of government. *Federal Reserve Bank of Saint Louis Review*, 88(1), 13–30.

Gerson, P. (1998). *The impact of public policy variables on output growth.* IMF Working Paper, No. 98/1.

Hagemann, R. P., Jones, B., & Montador, R. B. (1988). Tax reform in OECD countries: Motives, constraints and practice. *OECD Economic Studies*, 10, 185–226.

Hines, J. R., Jr.., & Thaler, R. H. (1995). The flypaper effect. *Journal of Economic Perspectives*, 9(4), 217–226.

Jorgenson, D. W., & Yun, K.-Y. (2001). *Investment – Volume 3: Lifting the burden.* Cambridge, MA: MIT Press.

Kirchgässner, G. (2006). On the relation between government size and economic development: Some methodological and econometric remarks. Paper presented at the Annual Meeting of the Public Choice Society, New Orleans, March 30 to April 2.

Kneller, R., Bleaney, M. F., & Gemmel, N. (1999). Fiscal policy and growth: Evidence from OECD countries. *Journal of Public Economics*, 74(2), 171–190.

Kristov, L., Lindert, P., & McClelland, R. (1992). Pressure groups and redistribution. *Journal of Public Economics*, 48(2), 135–163.

La Porta, R., Lopez-de-Silanes, F., Shleifer, A., & Vishny, R. (1999). The quality of government. *Journal of Law, Economics and Organizations*, 15(1), 222–279.

Lucas, R. (1988). On the mechanics of economic development. *Journal of Monetary Economics*, 22(1), 3–42.

Meltzer, A. H., & Richard, S. F. (1978). Why government grows (and grows) in a democracy. *Public Interest*, 52(Summer), 111–118.

Meltzer, A. H., & Richard, S. F. (1981). A rational theory of the size of government. *Journal of Political Economy*, 89(5), 914–927.

Meltzer, A. H., & Richard, S. F. (1983). Tests of a rational theory of the size of government. *Public Choice*, 41(3), 403–418.

Mittnik, S., & Neumann, T. (2003). Time-series evidence on the nonlinearity hypothesis for public spending. *Economic Inquiry*, 41(4), 565–573.

Mueller, D. C. (2003). *Public choice III.* Cambridge: Cambridge University Press.

Myles, G. (2000). Taxation and economic growth. *Fiscal Studies*, 21(1), 141–168.

Nijkamp, P., & Poot, J. (2004). Meta-analysis of the effect of fiscal policies on long-run growth. *European Journal of Political Economy*, 20(1), 91–124.

Niskanen, W. (1971). *Bureaucracy and representative government.* Chicago, IL: Aldine-Atherton.

Niskanen, W. (2001). Bureaucracy. In Shughart, W. & Razzolini, L. (Eds.), *The Elgar companion to public choice*. Northampton: Edward Elgar.

OECD (1985). The role of the public sector: Causes and consequences of the growth of government. *OECD Economic Review*, Special issue, No. 4 (Spring).

OECD. (2007). *Economic policy reforms – Going for growth: Structural policy indicators and priorities in OECD countries.* Paris: OECD.

Peacock, A. T., & Wiseman, J. (1961). *The growth of public expenditure in the United Kingdom* ((2nd ed., 1967)). Princeton, NJ; London: Princeton University Press and Oxford University Press.

Peltzman, S. (1980). The growth of government. *Journal of Law and Economics, 23*(2), 209–287.

Pissarides, C. (1992). Loss of skill during unemployment and the persistence of unemployment shocks. *Quarterly Journal of Economics, 107*(4), 1371–1392.

Rodrik, D. (1998). Why do more open economies have bigger governments?. *Journal of Political Economy, 106*(5), 997–1032.

Romer, P. (1986). Increasing returns and long-run growth. *Journal of Political Economy, 94*(5), 1002–1037.

Romer, P. (1990). Endogenous technological change. *Journal of Political Economy, 98*(5 Pt 2), S71–S102.

Sala-i-Martin, X. (1997). I just ran two millions regressions. *American Economic Review, 87*(2), 178–183Papers and Proceedings.

Salmon, P. (1987). Decentralization as an incentive scheme. *Oxford Review of Economic Policy, 3*(2), 24–43.

Sandford, C. (1981). Economic aspects of compliance costs. In Peacock, A. & Forte, F. (Eds.), *The political economy of taxation.* Oxford: Basil Blackwell.

Schubert, R. (1997). Discrimination in the labor market: A gender perspective. In Bacchetta, P. & Wasserfallen, W. (Eds.), *Economic policy in Switzerland.* London: Macmillan.

Solow, R. M. (1956). A contribution to the theory of economic growth. *Quarterly Journal of Economics, 70*(1), 65–94.

Stiglitz, J. E. (1983). Some aspects of the taxation of capital gains. *Journal of Public Economics, 21*(2), 257–293.

Stiglitz, J. E., Senn, A., & Fitoussi, J.-P. (2009). *Report by the commission on the measurement of economic performance and social progress.* Retrieved from http://stiglitz-sen-fitoussi.fr/documents/rapport_anglais.pdf.

Tanzi, V., & Schuknecht, L. (2000). *Public spending in the 20th century: A global perspective.* Cambridge: Cambridge University Press.

Tanzi, V., & Zee, H. H. (1997). Fiscal policy and long-run growth. *IMF Staff Papers, 44*(2), 179–209.

Temple, J. (1999). The new growth evidence. *Journal of Economic Literature, 37*(1), 112–156.

Tobin, J. (1966). *National economic policy: Essays.* New Haven, CT: Yale University Press.

Tullock, G. (1959). Problems of majority voting. *Journal of Political Economy, 67*(6), 571–579.